MW01148718

CIVIL WAR
SAINTS

CIVIL WAR SAINTS

Kenneth L. Alford

EDITOR

Published by the Religious Studies Center, Brigham Young University, Provo, Utah, in cooperation with Deseret Book Company, Salt Lake City
http://rsc.byu.edu

Printed in the United States by Sheridan Books, Inc.

DESERET BOOK is a registered trademark of Deseret Book Company.
Visit us at DeseretBook.com.

ISBN: 978-0-8425-2816-0
U.S. Retail: $31.99

Front cover image: "Plan of the Gettysburg Battle Ground," by Charles Wellington Reed, 1864. (Library of Congress)

Front cover image (inset): "Gallant Charge of the Sixty-Ninth Regiment, New York, State Militia, upon a rebel battery at the Battle of Bull Run," *Harper's Weekly*, August 10, 1861.

Back cover image: "Preliminary map of routes reconnoitred [sic] and opened in the Territory of Utah / by Captain J. H. Simpson . . . under the orders of Brigadier General, A. D. [sic] Johnston, commanding the Department of Utah," U.S. Army Corps of Engineers. (L. Tom Perry Special Collections, Brigham Young University)

Library of Congress Cataloging-in-Publication Data

Civil War Saints / Kenneth L. Alford.
pages cm

Summary: Collection of essays and articles about the US Civil War, with a focus on, but not limited to, people who were either members or later became members of The Church of Jesus Christ of Latter-day Saints. Topics include historical facts about actual events, people, landmarks, and stories; most of which are connected to the US Civil War.
Includes bibliographical references and index.

ISBN 978-0-8425-2816-0 (hard cover : alk. paper)

1. Mormons—United States—History—19th century. 2. United States—History—Civil War, 1861–1865. 3. Utah—History—19th century. I. Alford, Kenneth L., 1955–, editor.

BX8611.C59 2012
289.3'7309034—dc23

2012014397

CONTENTS

This woodcut from the January 26, 1861, issue of Harper's Weekly *shows Confederate artillery firing on the* Star of the West *at Charleston, South Carolina, on January 9, 1861.* (Harper's Weekly)

As illustrated in this April 27, 1861, woodcut, the bombardment of Fort Sumter in Charleston Harbor during April 1861 is considered by many as the formal beginning of the Civil War. (Library of Congress)

INTRODUCTION

Kenneth L. Alford

LATTER-DAY SAINTS AND THE CIVIL WAR

The Civil War had a deep and lasting effect on the United States. In many ways it shaped the nation that Americans live in today. Although Utah Territory was physically removed from the war's battlefields and the resulting devastation, the Civil War also had a deep impact on the territory and its inhabitants. To a large extent, though, Utah Territory watched the war from the sidelines—providing only one active-duty military unit for ninety days of federal service guarding a portion of the Overland Trail. Latter-day Saints who lived outside of Utah were often more directly and deeply influenced by the course of the war.

The genesis of this volume was the sesquicentennial of the Civil War, especially the 150th anniversary of the active federal service of Captain Lot Smith's Utah Cavalry company. Previous histories, especially Margaret Fisher's 1929 book *Utah and the Civil War* and E. B. Long's *The Saints and the Union* in 1981, have addressed Utah Territory and the Civil War. The purpose of this book is to take a fresh look at several aspects of the intersection between Latter-day Saints, Utah Territory, and the Civil War.

In December 1860, a few months before Abraham Lincoln was inaugurated as the sixteenth president of the United States, delegates from the state of South Carolina met in Charleston to draft an Ordinance of Secession. They appealed "to the Supreme Judge of the world for the rectitude of our intentions" and "declared that the Union heretofore existing between this State and the other States of North America, is dissolved, and that the State of South Carolina has resumed her position among the nations of the world, as a separate and independent State." The primary reason they gave to justify secession was the "increasing hostility on the part of the non-slaveholding States to the Institution of Slavery."[1]

It is generally accepted that Civil War hostilities began on April 12, 1861, when Confederate forces fired upon Fort Sumter in Charleston Harbor. The opening artillery rounds of the Civil War were actually fired, though, on January 9, 1861, when a

Confederate artillery battery in Charleston Harbor opened fire on the USS *Star of the West*, a ship sent to resupply the Union garrison stationed at Fort Sumter.[2]

As an example of the many personal and family dramas that would play out during the next four years, the commander of the Confederate artillery battery that shelled Fort Sumter was P. G. T. Beauregard, a West Point graduate who served as superintendent at the United States Military Academy for just five days in 1861 before being asked to resign because of his well-known Southern sympathies. Beauregard's antagonist commanding Fort Sumter was Major Robert Anderson. Ironically, Anderson had been Beauregard's artillery instructor when Beauregard was a

Major Robert Anderson commanded Union forces garrisoned on Fort Sumter. He had been P. G. T. Beauregard's artillery instructor at West Point. (Library of Congress)

West Point cadet, and the two officers knew each other well.[3]

Two months after Fort Sumter was attacked, on July 22, 1861, the U.S. House of Representatives adopted the following resolution that officially recognized that a civil war existed between the Northern and Southern states:

> Resolved by the House of Representatives of the Congress of the United States, That the present deplorable civil war has been forced upon the country by the dis-unionists of the Southern States now in revolt against the constitutional Government and in arms around the capital; that in this national emergency Congress, banishing all feelings of mere passion or resentment, will recollect only its duty

Confederate General P. G. T. Beauregard commanded the Confederate artillery battery that fired upon Fort Sumter in April 1861. (Library of Congress)

to the whole country that this war is not waged upon our part in any spirit of oppression[,] nor for any purpose of conquest or subjugation, nor purpose of overthrowing or interfering with the rights or established institutions of those States, but to defend and maintain the supremacy of the Constitution and to preserve the Union, with all the dignity, equality, and rights of the several States unimpaired; and that as soon as these objects are accomplished the war ought to cease.[4]

Three days later, on July 25, 1861, the Senate adopted a similar resolution.[5]

It is likewise generally accepted that the Civil War ended on April 9, 1865, when General Robert E. Lee surrendered to General Ulysses S. Grant at Appomattox, Virginia. Lee's surrender was a major turning point in the war, and it clearly marked the beginning of the war's end, but General Lee actually only surrendered the Army of Northern Virginia. It took over two months for the remaining Confederate armies to surrender to Union forces. The Cherokee general Stand Watie surrendered the final Confederate forces at Fort Towson in the Indian Territory (today Oklahoma) on June 23, 1865.[6]

It may come as a surprise to many readers to learn that the Civil War did not come to a complete end until almost fourteen months after the last Confederate soldiers laid down their arms. On June 13, 1865, as a preliminary step toward formally ending the war, President Andrew Johnson issued a proclamation that declared "that the insurrection which heretofore existed in the several States before named, except in Texas, was at an

Stand Watie, a Confederate brigadier who served as a chief of the Cherokee nation (1862–66), was the last Confederate general to surrender (on June 23, 1865, at Fort Towson in the Indian Territory). (Courtesy of Wilson's Creek National Battlefield; WICR 31445)

end and was henceforth to be so regarded." Likewise, it was not until April 2, 1866, that the president proclaimed, "The insurrection in the State of Texas has been completely and everywhere suppressed and ended and the authority of the United States has been successfully and completely established in the said State of Texas and now remains therein unresisted and undisputed." And it was not until August 20, 1866, that President Johnson signed Proclamation 157, which declared that "the insurrection is at an end and that peace, order, tranquility, and civil authority now exist in and throughout the whole of the United States of America."[7]

The time line provides a summary of events for both the United States and the Latter-day Saints (with an emphasis on events within Utah Territory). The time line begins prior to the Civil War and continues past 1865, listing events that both influenced and were influenced by the Civil

War. The years 1861 to 1865 are outlined in greater detail.

In chapter 1, William P. MacKinnon sets the stage for the opening of the Civil

The Star of the West, *a civilian steamship hired by the U.S. government to carry supplies and soldiers to Fort Sumter, was fired upon by cadets from the Citadel and was struck three times before abandoning its mission and returning to New York City.*
(Harper's Weekly, *January 19, 1861*)

War by demonstrating numerous ways that the Utah War—the U.S. Army's last major deployment prior to the Civil War—had a pervasive impact on the leadership skills of its veterans who served across the country in both the Union and Confederate armies while unleashing a variety of political, economic, religious, geographical, and societal forces that affected Utah during the Civil War and thereafter. Sherman L. Fleek provides an overview of the Civil War in chapter 2 to give readers an overview of the wartime events that transpired beyond Utah's borders.

Latter-day Saints believe that on Christmas Day in 1832, Joseph Smith received a revelation from the Lord prophesying in some detail the sources and causes of the American Civil War. In chapter 3, Scott C.

Esplin discusses the history and varied uses of this revelation from 1832 to the present—with an emphasis on the period surrounding the Civil War.

It is difficult to mention the Civil War without considering the towering presence of Abraham Lincoln. In chapter 4, Mary Jane Woodger provides insight into the relationship between Abraham Lincoln and the Mormons that stretched over several decades.

Throughout the Civil War, rumors swirled across the nation that Utah Territory was going to secede. Craig K. Manscill observes in chapter 5 that suspicion of Mormon secession began decades prior to the war—even before Latter-day Saints established themselves in the Rocky Mountains.

In chapter 6, Richard E. Bennett, in an article reprinted from *Mormon Historical Studies*, has assembled some of the wartime public pronouncements made by Brigham Young, Wilford Woodruff, Heber C. Kimball, and other Latter-day Saint leaders.

Brett Dowdle, who read and researched the 1860–65 correspondence, both public and private, of Brigham Young, Wilford Woodruff, and other Latter-day Saint Church leaders, presents his findings in chapter 7. The views those leaders expressed in letters reveal a more complete understanding of their feelings regarding the war than can be obtained from examining only the public record.

In chapter 8, "The Lot Smith Cavalry Company: Utah Goes to War," Joseph R. Stuart and Kenneth L. Alford take a close look at the cavalry unit that was called to military service on April 28, 1862, at President Lincoln's request. Their ninety-day period of service was the only unit-level active duty military contribution Utah Territory made during the Civil War.

In addition to Latter-day Saints who served on active duty in Union and Confederate armies and navies during the Civil War, Mormons also served in non-federalized state and territorial militias. In chapter 9, Ephriam Dickson examines the service of the Nauvoo Legion, Utah's territorial militia. While not considered pension-eligible Civil War veterans, those men provided valuable service throughout the period of the Civil War.

In the following chapter, Kenneth L. Alford and William P. MacKinnon investigate the wartime establishment of Camp Douglas in the foothills overlooking Salt Lake City—which served as a continuing source of friction between the army and the Latter-day Saints throughout the remainder of the Civil War.

In chapter 11, Brant W. Ellsworth and Kenneth L. Alford introduce us to several Latter-day Saint Civil War veterans, both Union and Confederate, as they seek to uncover the motivation for their military service. The wartime experiences of Joseph Barlow Forbes (Union), David Crockett Stuart (Confederate), David Harold Peery (Confederate), Lorenzo Dow Watson (Union), Lewis Albert Huffaker (Union), Reuben Parley Miller (Union), Edwin Brown (Union), Saul Norman (Union), Hans N. Chlarson (Union), and John Rozsa (Union) are shared. They also share the unique story of a "galvanized Yankee" who served during the Civil War as a soldier in both the Confederate army and the Union army.

Edmund Ruffin, a strong secessionist, is often credited with firing the first shot of the Civil War. Ruffin committed suicide near the end of the war. (National Archives)

Utah and the other federal territories also had to contend with various challenges from Native Americans throughout the Civil War. Chapter 12 provides an overview of the relationship between settlers and Native Americans in Utah Territory during the war. In January 1863, Union forces under the command of Colonel Patrick Edward Connor killed approximately three hundred Indians—men, women, and children—during what was known at the time as the Battle of Bear River; it is most frequently referenced today as the Bear River Massacre. Chapter 13 is a reprint of Harold Schindler's 1999 article from *Utah Historical Quarterly* entitled "The Bear River Massacre: New

A view of an overland coach in front of the tithing storehouse in Great Salt Lake City in 1865. Throughout the Civil War, residents of Utah Territory generally found their day-to-day lives removed from the war that raged "in the States."
(Church History Library and Archives)

Historical Evidence." An addendum by Ephriam Dickson shares recently discovered information regarding William Leake Beach, a California Volunteer soldier who sketched the contemporary battle map included in that chapter—information not available to the late Harold Schindler when he researched and wrote his article.

Throughout the nineteenth century, members of The Church of Jesus Christ of Latter-day Saints were expected to "gather to Zion" to join the main body of the Church. Emigration to Utah, primarily of converts from the British Isles and Scandinavia, faced new sail, rail, and trail challenges because of Civil War conditions. In chapter 14, William G. Hartley examines the war's impact on LDS emigration from 1861 through 1865.

During the Utah War, 1857–58, Utah and Mormonism were among the most frequent topics of reports in American newspapers. Mormons, polygamy, Utah Territory, and Brigham Young also continued to be a source of frequent news reported during the Civil War. In chapter 15, Kenneth L. Alford shares numerous Civil War newspaper stories about Latter-day Saints and Mormonism from both Northern and Southern newspapers.

Robert C. Freeman shares additional information regarding Latter-day Saint Civil War veterans in chapter 16. Readers will learn about Union soldiers Henry Wells Jackson, William Rex, John Davis Evans, and John Rozsa, as well as Confederate soldiers David Harold Peery and Simon Shelby Higginbotham.

As Andrew C. Skinner points out in chapter 17, the end of hostilities did not bring with it an immediate healing of the war's wounds. During Reconstruction, the nation turned from defeating slavery to eliminating polygamy—with Utah Territory as the focal point of that continuing campaign.

Civil War veterans, like most military veterans, enjoyed continued association following the war. The Grand Army of the Republic (GAR) veterans' organization was established in 1866 and grew to be a large and politically powerful organization. Chapter 18 by Kenneth L. Alford provides an overview of the GAR's history in Utah with an emphasis on relations between Latter-day Saints and the GAR. The final chapter, by Ardis E. Parshall, shares the delightful story of the GAR's 1909 National Encampment in Salt Lake City. The city and The Church of Jesus Christ of Latter-day Saints went to great lengths to ensure that the Civil War veterans who attended had a wonderful and memorable experience.

A bibliography and eight appendices follow. In Appendix A, William P. MacKinnon supplements chapter 1 with three letters and a 1907 reminiscence from a solider who remembered meeting the infamous William Quantrill who served as a civilian teamster in Utah Territory during the Utah War. The three letters were written during the Utah War, by West Point–trained officers who served as generals during the Civil War. Appendix B by Ephriam Dickson shares the Camp Douglas photographs and story of Private Charles D. Beckwith, who opened a studio and photographed Camp Douglas in 1864.

How many Latter-day Saints served in the Union and Confederate military forces during the American Civil War, and who were they? Surprisingly, the answers have remained elusive. In the one hundred and fifty years that have passed since the beginning of the Civil War, no thorough search for Latter-day Saint Civil War veterans has apparently been undertaken and published—until now. Appendix C is an explanation of the methodology used to document Latter-day Saints who served in both Union and Confederate military forces during the Civil War. Appendix D contains two tables that explain the Latter-day Saint Civil War veteran records found in the next two appendices. The first table discusses each field within individual veteran records; the second table explains the various codes and acronyms that are included in Appendices E and F for the databases, books, and resources used to document Latter-day Saint membership and Civil War veteran status for the veterans included. Appendix E is an alphabetic listing of Latter-day Saint Civil War veterans. Each entry includes personal details regarding their life, Civil War service, and LDS Church membership. Source information and general interest notes are also included. Appendix F is a smaller list of soldiers who are also noteworthy. The appendix includes records for soldiers, such as teamsters for the Lot Smith Utah Cavalry, who served during the war but were not considered veterans, soldiers whose LDS baptism is uncertain, and soldiers who were not baptized as members of The Church of Jesus Christ of Latter-day Saints or whose Latter-day Saint baptisms could not be verified but who are interesting in their own right and deserve recognition. The final two appendixes provide summary information for the Latter-day Saint Civil War veterans who are listed in Appendix E. Baptismal date summary information and the corresponding veteran lists are found in Appendix G;

In this room in Wilmer McLean's home at Appomattox Court House, Virginia, General Robert E. Lee surrendered to General Ulysses S. Grant on April 9, 1865. McLean, who formerly lived at Manassas, Virginia, moved his family to Appomattox in an effort to avoid the war after the Battle of Manassas (Bull Run) was fought on his farm in July 1861. (Library of Congress)

Appendix H provides a summary of military service (Union or Confederate and branch of service) and associated lists of the individuals in each category.

The Civil War had little direct effect on Utah Territory. No Union versus Confederate battles took place within her borders. Few Utahns served on active duty for either the United States of America or the Confederate States of America. But it would be folly to believe that the Civil War did not deeply affect Utah Territory, Utahns, and Latter-day Saints throughout the world. This volume is an effort to consider and understand some of the many ways that Latter-day Saints were affected by the American Civil War. It is hoped that readers will gain a deeper appreciation for the experiences and sacrifices that made the Civil War and its effect upon the United States and Latter-day Saints such a watershed event.

Kenneth L. Alford is an associate professor of Church history and doctrine at Brigham Young University.

NOTES

1. Declaration of the Immediate Causes Which Induce and Justify the Secession of South Carolina from the Federal Union; and the Ordinance of Secession (Charleston, SC: Evans and Cogswell, Printers to the Convention, 1860), 7–10.

2. "The Firing on the 'Star of the West,'" *Harper's Weekly*, January 26, 1861, 54.

3. "Anderson, Robert," *The New American Cyclopedia: A Popular Dictionary of General Knowledge* (New York: D. Appleton, 1863), 16:668.

4. Proclamation No. 157 (August 20, 1866), "Declaring that Peace, Order, Tranquillity, and Civil Authority Now Exists in and Throughout the Whole of the United States of America." The American Presidency Project, http://www.presidency.ucsb.edu/ws/index.php?pid=71992.

5. Proclamation No. 157.

6. W. P. Adair and James M. Bell to Brig. Gen. J. C. Veatch, 19 July 1865, in *The War of the Rebellion: A Compilation of the Official Records of the Union and Confederate Armies*, series 1, vol. 58, pt. 2 (Washington, DC: Government Printing Office, 1897), 1099–1101. In the surrender document, Watie is referred to as "Brigadier-General Stand Watie, governor and principal chief of that part of the Cherokee Nation lately allied with the Confederate States in acts of hostility against the Government of the United States."

7. Proclamation No. 157.

A Union soldier from the Thirty-seventh
Pennsylvania Infantry holds a torn flag that had
been carried into battle. (Library of Congress)

Printed on April 6, 1861, this Harper's Weekly woodcut includes crests
representing much of the United States at the beginning of the Civil War.
(Note that Utah is the only territory included.)

TIMELINES OF
THE UNITED STATES AND
LDS / UTAH TERRITORY

*This woodcut, entitled "Reading the War News in Broadway, New York," appeared
in the* Illustrated London News *near the beginning of the Civil War. (Library of Congress)*

The accompanying illustrations and photographs are courtesy of the Utah State Historical Society,
the Library of Congress, Intellectual Reserve, *Harper's Weekly*, the National Archives, Utah Digital
Newspapers, Frank Thomas, David Safranski, and public domain sources.

★ UNITED STATES

NOV
South Carolina
threatens to secede

FEB
Congress passes a tariff
satisfactory to South Carolina

MAR
Martin Van Buren
inaugurated

21 AUG
Nat Turner starts
slave rebellion in
Virginia

MAR
South Carolina
repeals the Nullification
ordinance

1830	1831	1832	1833	1837	1838	1839

6 APR
Joseph Smith organizes
the Church of Christ
(Fayette, New York)

25 DEC
Joseph Smith receives a
revelation and prophecy
on war (D&C 87)

29 NOV
Van Buren tells Joseph
Smith that nothing
can be done to help
persecuted Saints

28 NOV
Joseph Smith and others
imprisoned in Liberty Jail

 LDS / UTAH TERRITORY

5 JUN
President Polk asks for 500 Mormon volunteer soldiers

13 MAY
Mexican-American War begins

2 FEB
Treaty of Guadalupe Hidalgo is signed; Mexico gives up land rights north of the Rio Grande (including Utah)

SEP
Compromise of 1850 passes after heated debate

1841 1844 1846 1847 1848 1849 1850

4 FEB
Nauvoo Legion organized (Illinois)

13 JUL
First volunteer companies of Mormon Battalion enlisted

MAY
"Miracle of the seagulls" saves pioneer crops

5 MAR
Provisional state of Deseret proposed

29 JAN
Joseph Smith nominated as a presidential candidate (Nauvoo, Illinois)

22 JUL
Pioneer advance party enters the Salt Lake Valley

24 JUL
Brigham Young and main body of pioneers enter the Salt Lake Valley

30 DEC
First Mormon-Ute treaty signed

9 SEP
Utah Territory established

27 JUN
Joseph and Hyrum Smith killed by mob at Carthage Jail (Illinois)

UNITED STATES

4 MAR
Pres. James Buchanan inaugurated

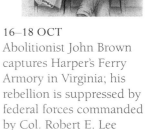

6 MAR
U.S. Supreme Court decides Dred Scott case

21 APR–15 OCT
Lincoln-Douglas debates

20 MAR
Harriet Beecher Stowe's *Uncle Tom's Cabin* is published

28 MAY
Pres. Buchanan sends army to put down reported rebellion in Utah, starting the Utah War

16–18 OCT
Abolitionist John Brown captures Harper's Ferry Armory in Virginia; his rebellion is suppressed by federal forces commanded by Col. Robert E. Lee

30 MAY
Kansas-Nebraska Act becomes law

11 JUL
President Buchanan appoints Alfred Cumming governor of Utah

1851	1852	1854	1857	1858	1859

3 FEB
Brigham Young becomes governor of Utah Territory and superintendent of Indian affairs

11 SEP
Mountain Meadows Massacre

15 SEP
Utah militia sent to prevent federal soldiers from entering Salt Lake Valley

28–29 AUG
The Church of Jesus Christ of Latter-day Saints publicly announces its doctrine of plural marriage

24 FEB
Thomas L. Kane arrives in Salt Lake City to help negotiate an end to the Utah War

26 JUN
U.S. Army marches through Salt Lake City essentially ending the Utah War

 LDS / UTAH TERRITORY

9 JAN 1861
Mississippi secedes;
Star of the West fired
upon

10 JAN 1861
Florida secedes

11 JAN 1861
Alabama secedes

19 JAN 1861
Georgia secedes

21 JAN 1861
Five Southern U.S.
senators leave the senate

26 JAN 1861
Louisiana secedes

29 JAN 1861
Kansas gains statehood
and prohibits slavery

2 MAR
Nevada Territory formed

4 MAR
Abraham Lincoln
inaugurated

4–8 FEB
Confederate States of
America organized in
Montgomery, Alabama,
with Jefferson Davis as
provisional president

18 FEB
Davis inaugurated as
president of Confederacy
at Montgomery, Alabama

23 FEB
Texas voters approve
secession

12 APR
South Carolina fires on
Fort Sumter in Charleston
Harbor, South Carolina

13 APR
Fort Sumter surrenders

15 APR
Pres. Lincoln calls
for militia

17 APR
Virginia secedes

3 APR
Pony Express begins

6 NOV
Abraham Lincoln elected

20 DEC
South Carolina secedes
in response to Lincoln's
election

1860   1861

FEB
Joseph Morris,
prophet and leader
of the Morrisites, is
excommunicated

6 FEB
Camp Floyd renamed
Fort Crittenden after
Secretary of War John B.
Floyd aligns with the
Confederacy

6 APR
Joseph Morris organizes
a new church in South
Weber (Utah Territory)

UNITED STATES

1 JUN
Skirmish at Fairfax Courthouse, Virginia

3 JUN
Battle of Philippi (in western Virginia)

8 JUN
Tennessee secedes

6 MAY
Arkansas secedes

20 MAY
North Carolina secedes

20 MAY
Baltimore occupied by Union soldiers

24 MAY
Union troops capture and occupy Alexandria, Virginia

28 NOV
Missouri admitted to the Confederacy (even though it did not formally secede)

6 FEB
Union captures Fort Henry, Tennessee

16 FEB
Union captures Fort Donelson, Tennessee

8–9 MARCH
Battle of Hampton Roads, first battle between ironclads (USS Monitor and CSS Virginia) fought inconclusively in Virginia

1861   1862

17 MAY
Gov. Cumming leaves Salt Lake City

JUL
U.S. Army stationed at Fort Crittenden recalled east for Civil War service

3 OCT
John W. Dawson appointed governor of Utah

18 OCT
Telegraph reaches Salt Lake City from the east

24 OCT
Overland Telegraph Line reaches Salt Lake City from California, making the Pony Express obsolete

4 DEC
Pioneers called to found St. George

7 DEC
Gov. Dawson arrives in Salt Lake City

31 DEC
Gov. Dawson flees Salt Lake City, Secretary Frank Fuller becomes acting governor

20 JAN
Utah statehood convention convenes in Salt Lake City

6 MAR
Salt Lake Theatre dedicated

LDS / UTAH TERRITORY

6 APR
Battle of Shiloh (Tennessee);
Confederate General Albert
Sidney Johnston killed

7 APR
After heavy casualties,
Union victory at
Battle of Shiloh

8 APR
Morrill Anti-Bigamy Act
introduced in House of
Representatives

25 APR
Union captures New
Orleans, Louisiana

8 MAY
Confederate victory
at Battle of McDowell
(Virginia)

3 JUN
Morrill Act passed in the
Senate, the House accepts
its revisions

9 JUN
Constitution of State of
Deseret introduced in the
U.S. House of Representatives
and the following day in the
U.S. Senate

25 JUN – 1 JUL
Confederacy repels Union
troops from Richmond,
Virginia following Seven
Days Battles

1862

26 APR
Nauvoo Legion militia
troops, under command of
Colonel Robert T. Burton,
depart Salt Lake City to
protect mail routes

28 APR
Brigham Young receives
request for a U.S. cavalry
company to protect the
Overland Trail

30 APR
Lot Smith Utah Cavalry
volunteers enlisted to protect
the Overland Trail

MAY
Col. Patrick Edward
Connor and California
Volunteers ordered to Utah

1 MAY
Lot Smith Utah Cavalry
leave Salt Lake Valley

24 MAY
Utah Territory Chief Justice
Kinney issues a writ of habeas
corpus commanding Morrisites
to release any prisoners

12 JUN
Robert T. Burton, deputy
marshal, leads a posse of
several hundred men to
capture Joseph Morris

13 JUN
Two Morrisites and one
posse member killed

15 JUN
Joseph Morris and
other Morrisites killed
in a skirmish; ninety
Morrisites arrested

16 JUN
Morrisites brought
to Salt Lake City to
stand trial

7 JUL
Stephen G. Harding,
Utah's new governor,
arrives in Salt Lake City

8 JUL
Pres. Lincoln signs
Morrill Anti-Bigamy Act

25 JUL
Private McNichols, a
member of Capt. Smith's
expedition, drowns in
the Snake River

✪ UNITED STATES

17 SEP
Battle of Antietam (Maryland) ends following the bloodiest day in U.S. history with nearly 23,000 casualties

17–23 AUG
Sioux uprising in Minnesota

22 SEP
Pres. Lincoln issues the Emancipation Proclamation

13 DEC
Confederate victory at Battle of Fredericksburg (Virginia)

28–30 AUG
Confederate victory at Second Battle of Manassas (Virginia)

8 OCT
Battle of Perryville (Kentucky) fought inconclusively

1 JAN
Emancipation Proclamation takes effect

1862   1863

14 AUG
Lot Smith Utah Cavalry released from active duty

17 OCT
Col. Connor's troops arrive at Fort Crittenden

29 JAN
Bear River Massacre

20 OCT
Col. Connor's troops arrive at Salt Lake City and establish Camp Douglas nearby

MAR
Tensions rise between federal troops and Utahns; Seven Morrisites convicted of second degree murder, 62 convicted of resistance

3 MAR
Utahns petition removal of Gov. Harding; Idaho Territory created

4 MAR
Utah delegates ask Gov. Harding to resign; he refuses

22 MAR
Native Americans attack mail coach near Eight Mile Creek Station

10 MAR
Brigham Young arrested for bigamy but not brought to trial

31 MAR
Gov. Harding pardons Morrisites

 # LDS / UTAH TERRITORY

JUN
Confederate victory at Battle of Brandy Station (Virginia)

20 JUN
West Virginia separates from Virginia and joins the Union as the 35th state

17 AUG
Fort Sumter bombarded by Union artillery

10 MAY
Confederate Gen. "Stonewall" Jackson dies of pneumonia

1–3 JUL
Battle of Gettysburg (Pennsylvania)

19–20 SEP
Confederate victory at Battle of Chickamauga (Georgia)

19 NOV
Lincoln delivers Gettysburg Address

23–25 NOV
Union captures Chattanooga, Tennessee

18 MAY
Siege of Vicksburg, Mississippi begins

4 JUL
Union captures Vicksburg, Mississippi, securing control of the Mississippi River

7 APR
Confederate victory at Charleston, South Carolina

13–15 JUL
Draft riots in New York City

3 DEC
Pres. Lincoln issues his Ten-Percent Plan, beginning Reconstruction

1863

12–15 APR
Fights occur between federal troops and Native Americans

10 JUN
Native American band attacks stagecoach in Utah County, killing two people

20 NOV
First issue of the *Union Vedette*, an Army newspaper, issued at Camp Douglas

5 APR
Troops defeat Native American band near Spanish Fork

11 JUN
Gov. Harding leaves Salt Lake City

3 JUL
Native American band attacks Canyon Station, killing five people

30 JUL
Peace treaty signed with Shoshone tribe at Brigham City

1 OCT
Peace treaty signed with Native Americans at Ruby Valley

22 JUN
James D. Doty becomes governor of Utah

8 MAY
Native American band raids Box Elder Valley

UNITED STATES

5–6 MAY
Battle of the
Wilderness (Virginia)
fought inconclusively

1–3 JUN
Confederate victory at
Battle of Cold Harbor
(Virginia)

5 AUG
Union victory at Battle of
Mobile Bay (Alabama)

16 DEC
Union victory at Battle of
Nashville (Tennessee)

7 MAY
General Sherman's Atlanta
Campaign begins (in Tennessee)

2 SEP
Union captures
Atlanta, Georgia

8–21 MAY
Battle of Spotsylvania
Court House (Virginia)
fought inconclusively

18 JUN
Union siege
of Petersburg,
Virginia begun

31 OCT
Nevada gains statehood
as the 36th state

11 MAY
Union victory at Battle of
Yellow Tavern (Virginia)

28 JUN
Fugitive slave
laws repealed

8 NOV
Abraham Lincoln
reelected

15 MAY
Battle of New Market (Virginia)

16 NOV
Union Gen. William T.
Sherman begins "march to
the sea" campaign

7 MAR
Five Utah Territory Indian
treaties ratified by U.S. Senate

30 JUL
Battle of the Crater
(Petersburg, Virginia)

21 DEC
Union captures
Savannah, Georgia

1864

5 JAN
The *Daily Vedette*
replaces the *Union
Vedette* as the Camp
Douglas newspaper.

4 JUL
First issue of the *Daily
Telegraph* newspaper
issued in Salt Lake

12 DEC
The 14th annual
session of the Utah
legislature convenes in
Great Salt Lake City

28 APR
The ship Monarch
of the Sea, sails from
Liverpool, England,
with 973 Saints.

 LDS / UTAH TERRITORY

3 MAR
Freedmen's Bureau created

4 MAR
Abraham Lincoln inaugurated for second term

29 MAR
Union begins Appomattox campaign

17 FEB
Columbia, South Carolina destroyed by fire

31 JAN
Thirteenth Amendment passed

3 APR
Union forces capture Richmond, Virginia

9 APR
General Robert E. Lee surrenders the Army of Northern Virginia at Appomattox (Virginia)

12 APR
Mobile, Alabama surrenders to Union forces

14 APR
John Wilkes Booth assassinates Pres. Lincoln, co-conspirator Lewis Powell attempts assassination of Secretary of State William H. Seward

15 APR
Abraham Lincoln dies; Andrew Johnson inaugurated president

21 APR
Mosby's Rangers disbanded

26 APR
John Wilkes Booth killed by Union soldiers in Virginia; Confederate Gen. Joseph E. Johnston surrenders at Durham Station, NC

4 MAY
Confederate Lt. Gen. Richard Taylor surrenders Confederate departments of Alabama, Mississippi, and East Louisiana at Citronelle, Alabama

5 MAY
Maj. Gen. Dabney Maury surrenders the Confederate District of the Gulf at Citronelle, Alabama

9 MAY
Lt. Gen.Nathan Bedford Forrest surrenders at Gainesville, Alabama

1865

4 MAR
Celebration of Pres. Lincoln's Inauguration

9 APR
Utah's Black Hawk War begins (and continues until October 1872)

10 APR
LDS Church agrees to build telegraph line between Utah settlements (completed in 1867); Native Americans attack men near Twelve Mile Creek

12 APR
Troops pursue Native American band, killing several

15 APR
Utah mourns Pres. Lincoln's assassination

UNITED STATES

10 MAY
Confederate President
Jefferson Davis captured; Maj.
Gen. Samuel Jones surrenders
Confederate departments of
Florida and South Georgia

12 MAY
Brig. Gen. William T.
Wofford surrenders the
Confederate forces of
North Georgia

22 JUN
CSS Shenandoah fires
upon Union whaling
ships (the last shots of
the Civil War)

12–13 MAY
Battle of Palmito Ranch,
Texas (last battle of the
Civil War)

23 JUN
Confederate Brig. Gen. Stand
Watie (a Cherokee Indian)
surrenders at Doaksville,
Indian Territory

6 NOV
CSS Shenandoah
surrenders

26 MAY
Confederate Lt. Gen.
Simon B. Bucker surrenders
at New Orleans, Louisiana

7 JUL
Lincoln conspirators
hanged in
Washington, DC

18 DEC
Thirteenth Amendment
adopted, abolishes slavery
in all states

1865

26 MAY
Native American
band kills family
of six

11 JUN
Speaker of the U.S. House
of Representatives Schuyler
Colfax visits Salt Lake City

14 JUL
Native American
band kills two people
near Salina

21 SEP
Militia engages
Native American
band near Fish Lake
killing seven people

29 MAY
Native American
band kill a man
near Fairview

13 JUN
Gov. Doty dies in
Salt Lake City

15 JUL
Charles Durkee
appointed governor
of Utah

22 SEP
Native American band
attacks immigrating
Mormons near Ft. Laramie

18 JUL
Militia attacks Native
American band, killing
twelve people

30 SEP
Gov. Durkee
arrives in
Salt Lake City

26 JUL
Native American band
attacks Glenwood,
Sevier County

LDS / UTAH TERRITORY

6 APR
Grand Army of the Republic
(G.A.R.) organized at
Decatur, Illinois

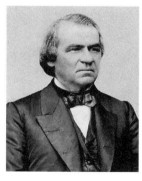

26 MAY
President Johnson
acquitted by one vote

20 AUG
U.S. President Andrew Johnson signs
Proclamation 157 (Declaring that
Peace, Order, Tranquillity [sic], and
Civil Authority Now Exists in and
Throughout the Whole of the United
States of America) proclaiming the
official end of the Civil War

24 FEB
President Andrew
Johnson impeached
by U.S. House of
Representatives

9 JUL
Fourteenth Amendment
adopted, defines citizenship
(overturns the Dred Scott case)

NOV
Republicans win
overwhelming control
of Congress and begin
a period of Radical
Reconstruction

20 NOV
First G.A.R. National
Encampment held in
Indianapolis, Indiana

MAR–MAY
President Johnson tried
by the U.S. Senate

1866   1867   1868

8 DEC
Brigham Young asks
bishops to reorganize
Relief Societies (which
were disbanded during
the Utah War)

29 JAN
Great Salt Lake City is
renamed Salt Lake City

UNITED STATES

3 FEB
Fifteenth Amendment ratified, defines voting rights for all American citizens

4 MAR
Ulysses S. Grant inaugurated President; Schuyler Colfax Vice President

1-2 MAR
Democratic and Republican Congressmen unofficially agree to the Compromise of 1877, allowing Rutherford B. Hayes to win the presidency while removing federal troops from Southern states, ending Reconstruction

1869 1870 1877 1878 1879 1887 1890

10 MAY
Transcontinental railroad completed at Promontory Summit, Utah Territory

29 AUG
Brigham Young dies

5 MAY
U.S. Supreme Court announces decision in Reynolds v U.S. polygamy case

6 OCT
LDS Church accepts "The Manifesto" (Official Declaration #1)

12 FEB
Utah Territorial legislature passes women's suffrage law

FEB
Robert T. Burton tried and acquitted for the murder of Isabella Bowman, one of two Morrisite women killed in 1862 at South Weber

3 MAR
Edmunds-Tucker Act becomes law, disincorporating the LDS Church and excluding polygamists from politics

18 SEP
First documented Utah G.A.R. post organized in Salt Lake City

LDS / UTAH TERRITORY

2 AUG
Albert Henry Woolson—last
surviving Union Army veteran,
G.A.R. member, and undisputed
Civil War veteran—dies

28 AUG–1 SEP
Last National Encampment
of the G.A.R. held in
Indianapolis, Indiana

1896 1909 1911 1926 1949 1956 1969

4 JAN
Utah becomes
the 45th state

7 JUL
Lot Smith Utah Cavalry
Civil War veterans declared
eligible to join the G.A.R.

The Church of Jesus of Saints of
the Most High (an offshoot of the
Morrisites) officially disbanded

9–14 AUG
Grand Army of the Republic
(G.A.R.) National Encampment
held in Salt Lake City

9 OCT
John Quincy Knowlton
G.A.R. post organized in Salt
Lake City for veterans of the
Lot Smith Utah Cavalry

29 JAN
Harvey Coe Hullinger
(reported as the oldest LDS
Civil War veteran and oldest
practicing physician in
the U.S.) dies in Vernal, Utah

Albert Sidney Johnston, the principal commander of the Utah Expedition, appears here uniformed as a brevet brigadier general, the rank to which he was promoted in the winter of 1858 in recognition of his leadership during the expedition's perilous march of the previous November. He was respected by Brigham Young for his ability to bring discipline and control to his command. Johnston left Camp Floyd in March 1860 and two years later was the Confederacy's leading field general, a role in which he died at the Battle of Shiloh on April 6, 1862. (Utah State Historical Society)

CHAPTER 1

William P. MacKinnon

PRELUDE TO CIVIL WAR

THE UTAH WAR'S IMPACT AND LEGACY

While you were with us in our Mountain home [during the late 1850s], little did many imagine the signal reversion that has taken place in so brief a period. . . . The threatened war of 1857–8 has thickly canopied its lurid clouds over those who would have destroyed us, while the serene light of Heaven smiles upon our valleys and mountains, and crowns their peaks with its halos.

—Brigham Young to Thomas L. Kane, April 29, 1864

It was a rough winter we spent at Chattanooga [Tennessee]. I had served in the expedition to Utah in 1857–58 and participated in the hardships, privations and starvations of that luckless march, but taking all I saw or felt in the expedition to Utah into consideration I must say that I never beheld so much suffering and misery from want of food and clothing as I saw in the camps of the Federal troops at Chattanooga from the date of my joining [on December 31, 1863] until the opening of February, 1864.

—Major Albert Tracy, commander of First Battalion,
Fifteenth U.S. Infantry, ca. 1890

The Utah War of 1857–58 was the armed struggle for power and authority in Utah Territory between the newly inaugurated administration of President James Buchanan and the leadership of The Church of Jesus Christ of Latter-day Saints, principally President Brigham Young, who also held federal office as Utah's governor, superintendent of Indian affairs, and militia commander. It was a struggle ten years in the making that eventually pitted the nation's most experienced and active militia (although not technically the largest) against nearly one-third of the U.S. Army. The campaign was the nation's most extensive and expensive military undertaking during the period between the Mexican and Civil Wars. When Abraham Lincoln assumed the presidency, the army's largest garrison was in Utah, and the U.S. Treasury had been drained to an extent that precluded Lincoln from paying the federal establishment for his first several months in office.[1]

There is a notion among some commentators that the Utah War was essentially an expensive but bloodless, almost cartoon-ish David-versus-Goliath affair featuring a strategically and tactically brilliant Brigham Young and a bumbling, blundering James Buchanan. The campaign was not bloodless, for like most civil wars or guerrilla conflicts, the Utah War degenerated into a series of sordid atrocities marked for their ferocity. In addition to the fatalities from accidental gun-shot wounds on both sides as well as deaths in the federal camps from drunken duels, heart attacks, and a case of lockjaw, there was the September 11, 1857, execution by Mormon militiamen and Indian auxiliaries at Mountain Meadows of 120 emigrant infants, women, and unarmed men—the greatest incident of organized mass murder of civil-ians in the nation's history until the Okla-homa City bombing of 1995. Also, in Octo-ber of 1857 there was the lynching at Smiths Fork of the Green River of Private George W. Clark, a deserter from the Utah Expedition's Tenth U.S. Infantry, by unknown parties, and the fatal bludgeoning of Richard E. Yates, a civilian mountaineer and ammunition trader, by Nauvoo Legion officers in Echo Canyon near the legion's Cache Cave headquarters. In November 1857 the six-member Aiken party, a group of well-heeled, non-Mormon Cali-fornia adventurers of ambiguous intent, were detained by the legion in Salt Lake City while trying to reach the army at Fort Bridger. Five of the Aikens were subsequently assassinated while being compelled to return to California on the southern route. In February 1858, there was further loss of life and injury when Bannock warriors—allegedly accompanied by civilian scouts from the army's Utah Expe-dition—raided the Mormon Fort Limhi mis-sion on Oregon Territory's Salmon River. In total the fatalities on both sides during the

Utah War approximated the bloodshed that in the 1850s earned Utah's eastern neighbor the enduring label "Bleeding Kansas."[2]

Notwithstanding a recent renewal of interest in the conflict, it would be a mistake to assume that the Utah War is well known either in Utah or elsewhere. Yet obscure as it has been—and quite apart from the mes-merizing, sensational Mountain Meadows Massacre story—the Utah War spawned an exotic military and civilian legacy that remains with us, though largely unrecognized. It is a legacy comprised of rich, colorful, and fas-cinating personal stories and societal forces that helped to shape not only post-1858 Mormonism but the subsequent history of Utah, the American West, and most imme-diately the Civil War. For this reason alone the Utah War is a conflict with an impact and aftermath worth understanding.

THE PLAYERS

At the time, the Utah War was the Ameri-can West's biggest show. As such, it was a magnet for the adventuresome and an ordeal for the innocent—a cauldron in which the mettle of all involved was tested.

What happened to all of these people—Latter-day Saints, non-Mormons, Indians, Hispanics, Anglos, women, mountaineers, dandies, illiterates, PhDs, rogues, soldiers, and civilians—after the Utah Expedition marched into and through Salt Lake City on June 26, 1858? For most of the participants, involvement in the Utah War was the most colorful experience of their life. Thereafter they receded into historical anonymity filled with the workaday responsibilities, accom-plishments, and disappointments of ordinary life but flavored with a lifetime of personal stories about the Mormon move south, riding with Lot Smith's Nauvoo Legion raiders, or the Utah Expedition's brutal march to the charred remains of Fort Bridger and a frustrating winter on short rations at nearby Camp Scott.

But for the members of a smaller group on both sides, the Utah War was a foundational experience, if not an epiphany, from which they sprang into a panoply of even more colorful adventures of both heroic and tragic stripe. At the extremes one finds that among the Nauvoo Legion's leaders and private soldiers were men destined to be the second through sixth presidents of the LDS Church, while among the Utah Expedition's officers a captain of artillery and an infantry lieutenant did their duty, oblivious to their presidential candidacies to come.[3] Most cases of post-1858 prominence or notoriety for such people are well known somewhere in Utah, the American West, or Europe. But what has been largely lost is an awareness of the linkage of such adventures to the earlier Utah War and vice versa. Therein lies the definition of a real but unfortunately forgotten legacy.

James Buchanan was the fifteenth U.S. president (1857–61). This Pennsylvanian's first exposure to armed confrontation and bloodshed was the Utah War. His handling of "the Mormon problem" began a reputational slide accelerated by his fecklessness during the secession crisis three years later. No monument was erected to his memory in Washington until 1930, and today he continues to be ranked at the bottom in terms of presidential effectiveness. (Wikimedia Commons)

THE CIVILIAN LEADERS

For President James Buchanan and his cabinet, the Utah War—together with the simultaneous uproar over "Bleeding Kansas"—was a first confrontation with the unnerving specter of civil disobedience, armed conflict, bloodshed, and the firestorm of public criticism that they spawned. So anxious was Buchanan to extricate himself from the massive expenses and political costs of the Utah War that he, in effect, declared victory and, starting in 1858, permitted himself to be co-opted by both Brigham Young and Thomas L. Kane as well as by their alcoholic, four-hundred-pound pawn, Governor Alfred Cumming.

This failure of nerve foreshadowed Buchanan's lawyerly but disastrous handling of the secession crisis of 1860–61, an ineffective performance that with the onset of the Civil War brought widespread criticism of the president which persists today.[4] During the Civil War, it was necessary for Buchanan's Masonic lodge brothers to stand guard over his Lancaster, Pennsylvania, retirement mansion. Townspeople stopped speaking to him. Dr. Jonathan M. Foltz—the Lancaster physician who nursed Buchanan through the nearly fatal "National Hotel Disease" during the spring of 1857 while he decided Utah's fate—came to feel so negatively about the president and his handling of secession that he legally changed his firstborn son's middle name from Buchanan to Steinman.[5] Even decades after the Civil War, hostility to Buchanan was such that it was not until 1930 that Congress was willing to provide and dedicate land for an obscure park in Washington to erect a statue in his honor, although his niece had provided funds to defray the cost of the monument nearly a half century earlier.[6]

Just months before his death in 1868 at age seventy-eight, Buchanan resolved his ambivalent dithering about formal religion—especially the necessity for kneeling in some rites—and joined Lancaster's Presbyterian church.[7] In 1932 Latter-day Saint temple work on his behalf was performed in the Salt Lake Temple.[8] Today the simple but handsome marble sarcophagus marking President Buchanan's grave stands neglected in the midst of a seedy Pennsylvania cemetery, adorned only by a floral wreath sent annually by his incumbent successor. As Buchanan so presciently phrased it at the beginning of the Utah War, while politely deflecting the ludicrous but serious proffer of a Brooklyn cemetery plot and monument by a former Nauvoo Legion general: "Whether I shall be worthy of the distinguished honor . . . is a question which cannot be wisely determined until after I shall have finished my course."[9]

Among Buchanan's cabinet officers, Secretary of War John B. Floyd—the prime hawk in the Utah War—clearly proved to be the least capable and most hapless. In December 1860, Floyd resigned under pressure in the midst of a scandal over his financing of the Utah War, a performance for which he was subsequently indicted for malfeasance in office. With Floyd's departure and rumors of his disloyalty, the name of the army's principal garrison in Utah—the nation's largest—was changed from Camp Floyd to Fort Crittenden to honor a senator then engaged in trying to broker a sectional compromise. During the Civil War, his predecessor as secretary, Jefferson Davis, appointed Floyd a Confederate brigadier and then relieved him of command after his disgraceful abandonment of

Fort Donelson, Tennessee, to General U. S. Grant. Floyd, who experienced poor health throughout Buchanan's administration, died in Virginia of natural causes in 1863.[10]

So many of Buchanan's cabinet officers either became Confederate generals or were perceived as Southern sympathizers that the historiography of the Utah War's origins came to be shrouded in a misguided conspiracy theory in which a Southern cabinet cabal supposedly plotted to isolate the army and bankrupt the federal treasury as early as 1857. Compounding the early enthusiasm for this theory was the obvious (but irrelevant) fact that for the first year of the Civil War, Albert Sidney Johnston was the Confederacy's leading field general. Nowhere has this fanciful—but typically American—conspiracy notion been more vigorously embraced than in Utah.[11]

After returning to Salt Lake City from the move south on July 1, 1858, President Young—no longer Utah's governor but under federal indictment for treason—went into a months-long period of seclusion and perhaps even depression.[12] Soon, however, the prophet's resilience returned, the treason indictment was quashed, and President Young resumed the active rule if not the governance of Utah. This was a distinction well understood by Governor Alfred Cumming, although Utah's new chief executive was unaware that as early as April 1858 Thomas L. Kane had cynically described (if not arranged) these dynamics in telling Brigham Young, "[I have] caught the fish, now you can cook it as you have a mind to."[13] And so Brigham Young did so—poaching Cumming in a daily broth of civility seasoned with a barely masked flavoring of intimidation and manipulation.

With the outbreak of the Civil War, Governor Cumming returned to the Atlantic coast and unsuccessfully sought President Lincoln's sanction for passage through Union lines to his native Georgia, where his namesake and nephew, a former captain in the Utah Expedition's Tenth U.S. Infantry, had become a Confederate brigadier. It would be the end of the war before the senior Alfred Cumming arrived in Augusta, where he died in 1873 at age seventy-two.[14]

If Alfred Cumming literally sat out the Civil War, so, figuratively, did Utah and Brigham Young, who, with lingering bitterness over the Utah War and contempt for President Lincoln, viewed it as a non-Mormon fight. Consequently, the territory's support for the Union Army was confined to compliance with President Lincoln's request early in the war for a single mounted company to protect the telegraph line and trail east of Fort Bridger for ninety days until regulars or other volunteers could be assigned to the area. As discussed elsewhere in this volume, private citizen Young used his substantial influence to block reenlistment of this unit, thus concluding Utah's contribution to the Union Army and confining it to a token demonstration of patriotism. From this ambivalence would come decades of debate within the LDS Church's hierarchy, if not its membership, about the wisdom of supporting the U.S. government's foreign military ventures.[15]

In the wake of Cumming's departure, President Young endured during the 1860s and 1870s a series of federally appointed governors of uneven quality and tenure as well as sensational legal difficulties flowing from the passage of multiple federal antipolygamy laws. There was also his long-delayed indictment in 1871 for an 1857 Utah War murder involving, among other defendants, Nauvoo Legion lieutenant William Adams

Alfred Cumming was successor to Brigham Young as Utah's governor until the Civil War. This corpulent, alcoholic Georgian was sympathetic to the territory's Mormon population as a virtual pawn of Young in his continuing effort to rule Utah on a de facto basis by splitting her federal appointees into warring factions. Forbidden by Lincoln to cross into the South, Cumming sat out the Civil War in the North while his namesake, a former infantry captain in the U.S. Army's Utah Expedition, served as a distinguished Confederate brigadier. (Utah State Historical Society)

(Bill) Hickman, a legal complexity later quashed by the U.S. Supreme Court on a technicality. Brigham Young died of appendicitis in 1877 at age seventy-six, soon after the execution by firing squad of his religiously adopted and embittered son, Nauvoo Legion major John D. Lee, for his responsibility in the Mountain Meadows Massacre.[16]

Given the fact that during 1857–58 Brigham Young had pitted himself against a large expeditionary force of U.S. Army regulars led by West Pointers, one of the more surprising facts of President Young's legacies is that he sent one of his sons, Willard Young, and a grandson, Richard Whitehead Young, to the United States Military Academy. Both cadets graduated and eventually became highly respected general officers in the Utah National Guard and U.S. Army during the Spanish-American and First World wars. Through

Willard Young's line, four consecutive generations of Brigham Young's direct descendants served in the U.S. Army, three generations of them through officers' commissions earned at West Point.[17]

THE SOLDIERS

The initial commander of the Utah Expedition was Brevet Brigadier General William S. Harney, an officer whose reputation for severity was such that news of his appointment had the unintended consequence of stiffening Mormon resolve to deny the army access to Utah during the summer of 1857. Harney was so feared during the 1850s that one Sioux band had dubbed him "Mad Bear." It was an apt name, but probably one coined independent of any Indian (or for that matter Mormon) awareness that on four occasions an exasperated army had court-martialed Harney while a civil court had tried (and acquitted) him a fifth time for a non-military offense—bludgeoning a female slave to death. Notwithstanding his formal Utah assignment, Harney spent the entire campaign in Kansas Territory. During the late summer of 1858—with Kansas temporarily pacified and the Utah Expedition entering a presumably quieter phase—Harney was ordered to the Pacific Northwest to command the department of Oregon. This disastrous assignment nearly brought the United States into armed conflict with Great Britain during a sensitive border dispute due to Harney's unauthorized, heavy-handed occupation of San Juan Island—the so-called "Pig War" of 1859. Because of his lack of political skills, Harney spent most of the Civil War vainly awaiting orders for a command that never materialized. Eventually he was breveted a major general for long and faithful service

and retired, although in 1868 he was brought back to active duty briefly for treaty negotiations with the Plains tribes. Harney died in 1889 at age 88.[18]

Harney's successor as field commander of the Utah Expedition in September 1857 was a quite different officer with a far more stellar destiny—Colonel (later Brevet Brigadier General) Albert Sidney Johnston, theretofore commander of the Second Regiment of Cavalry and before that secretary of war for the Republic of Texas. With the Utah Expedition ensconced at Camp Floyd, Mormon leaders scrupulously avoided vilifying Johnston on a personal basis in public. Nonetheless, by 1859 Johnston found himself in the middle of corrosive policy and civil affairs disputes through which he became increasingly marginalized in a deadly dull role. Thus Johnston was enveloped not only in political ambiguity but in the maddening local sandstorms and whirlwinds that the troops at Camp Floyd sarcastically dubbed "Johnsoons." After repeated denial of his requests for furlough or reassignment, Johnston finally cantered out of Camp Floyd on March 1, 1860, headed for the desert, San Bernardino, and the Pacific steamer home. It was a journey that produced one of the eeriest documents of the Utah War—the account by Johnston's adjutant of their final westward passage across the rim of the Great Basin near the killing field of Mountain Meadows. At that grim location a startled Major Fitz John Porter realized that General Johnston, he, and their fifty-dragoon escort had been quietly shadowed for miles by a lone and distant horseman—one heavily bearded and with a dog slung over his saddle in signature fashion. The outrider was almost certainly Orrin Porter Rockwell, Brigham Young's bodyguard, whose solitary vigil three hundred miles from home sent an unmistakable message to the departing general about power and authority in Utah Territory.[19]

After furlough in Kentucky, the War Department sent Johnston back to California to command the Department of the Pacific from San Francisco. Speculation persisted that he was to be General Scott's successor as general in chief, if not a presidential candidate. With the secession crisis, though, Johnston resigned his commission, offered his services to the Confederacy, and soon became her leading general in the field. On April 6, 1862, in the midst of the battle of Shiloh, the fifty-nine-year-old Johnston bled to death from an untended leg wound received while astride the horse he had ridden throughout the Utah War. Today the effectiveness of Albert Sidney Johnston's Civil War generalship continues to undergo critical reappraisal.[20]

Among the officers, enlisted men, and even civilians who served under Johnston during the Utah War, more than thirty-five of them would become Union or Confederate generals soon thereafter. In a sense, the Utah War was as much a proving ground for military talent in a later war as the Spanish Civil War would be eighty years later for World War II. Several among Johnston's troops—enlistees as well as officers and even a few civilians—were destined to receive the Medal of Honor during the Civil War or the Indian campaigns that followed. Perhaps least known and most enigmatic among Johnston's troops was First Lieutenant Robert L. Browning, the U.S. Marine Corps' one-man contribution to the Utah Expedition subsequently lost at sea in 1861 with the entire ship's company of USS *Levant*, the naval vessel aboard which Edward Everett Hale was to exile a fictive army officer, Philip Nolan, in his Civil War era novella, *The Man without a Country*.[21]

One quick and graphic way to illustrate the vastness of the Utah Expedition's experiential contribution to the Civil War's talent pool is through the command structure of just the Union Army at a single but crucial 1863 battle—Gettysburg. It is a list that reads like a who's who of Utah War veterans. Of course, it was a Confederate brigadier, Henry Heth, formerly a captain in the Utah Expedition's Tenth Infantry, whom folklore credits with touching off the battle. Soon arrayed against Heth and his Confederate comrades—some of them Utah War veterans like General J. E. B. Stuart—were Union generals such as John F. Reynolds (who had served in Utah during 1854–55 and later with Johnston), Elon John Farnsworth (of whom more will be discussed later), and John Cleveland Robinson (the former Fifth Infantry captain in whose tent civilian Thomas L. Kane, a Union brigadier at Gettysburg, first found shelter upon his exhausted 1858 arrival at Camp Scott). Generals Reynolds and Farnsworth died famously at Gettysburg; General Robinson survived, later lost a leg, received the Medal of Honor, and went on to command the Grand Army of the Republic and serve as lieutenant governor of New York.[22] Also rendering extraordinary service to the Union at Gettysburg were General Stephen H. Weed, a former first lieutenant in Phelps's battery who died while defending Little Round Top, as well as Generals John Buford and Alfred Pleasonton, both formerly of the Utah Expedition's Second Dragoons. Among the tragic deaths at Gettysburg was that of Confederate brigadier Lewis A. Armistead, killed while fighting his friend and brother officer from the Utah Expedition's Sixth U.S. Infantry, Major General Winfield Scott Hancock, a subsequent candidate for president.[23]

Lower in the Union Army's leadership cadre at Gettysburg, this partial list includes First Lieutenant James ("Jock") Stewart, Scottish-born commander of the battle's most decimated unit—Light Battery "B" of the Fourth U.S. Artillery, the unit in which Stewart served as first sergeant throughout the Utah War. Like Albert Sidney Johnston, Jock Stewart campaigned in the Civil War astride his Utah War horse—in this case a twice-wounded animal dubbed Tartar, which had spent the winter of 1857–58 near Fort Bridger recuperating with the Shoshones.[24]

The Utah War was also a federal proving ground for not only generals-in-waiting but for materiel, weapons, rations, tactics, communications arrangements, and transportation schemes involving field tests for the rifled .58 caliber Springfield, the Sharps breech loader, the tepee-like Sibley tent, the telegraph, railroads, and dried vegetables.

On the Mormon side of the Utah War, the military talent was as colorful as that of the federals but not as well known because of the Nauvoo Legion's almost total absence from the Civil War. The military leader of the legion was, of course, Lieutenant General Daniel H. Wells, known irreverently to some non-Mormons and later the *Salt Lake Tribune* as "the one-eyed pirate of the Wasatch"—a man indicted for treason and murder, as had been Brigham Young. Uniformed as resplendently as Winfield Scott, Wells commanded the legion during the fall of 1857 from a smokey cave in Echo Canyon. He had been called to the religious role of Brigham Young's second counselor following the 1856 death of Jedediah M. Grant, and he remained a part of the First Presidency as well as mayor of Salt Lake City for decades thereafter. In 1870 Utah's non-Mormon governor removed Wells

from his legion command, and seventeen years later Congress abolished the Nauvoo Legion itself through the Edmunds-Tucker Act. During the 1880s, Wells wrote his unpublished military memoirs for H. H. Bancroft without a single reference to the Utah War, a not unusual omission by senior Mormon leaders in legal jeopardy but a vexing gap for historians. In 1891, at age 77, Daniel H. Wells died in Salt Lake, leaving behind, among other family members, Emmeline B. Wells, an incredibly accomplished wife, and sons Junius F. Wells, the long-time editor of the *Contributor*, and Heber Manning Wells, Utah's first state governor.[25]

Actively aiding General Wells in the mountains during the legion's crucial fall 1857 campaign was an extraordinary apostolic delegation involving such lions as Heber C. Kimball, John Taylor, Wilford Woodruff, and George A. Smith. Of these leaders, none bore formal military rank, although Smith had once been a militia colonel and John Taylor carried the moral authority of multiple wounds from Illinois militia bullets sustained during his unsuccessful attempt to shield Joseph Smith at Carthage Jail in 1844. After Brigham Young's death in 1877, Apostles Taylor and Woodruff, of course, went on to serve sequentially as Brigham Young's successors, while Heber C. Kimball and George A. Smith provided long service during the last half of the nineteenth century as counselors in the First Presidency. During the Utah War, Lorenzo Snow and Joseph F. Smith, men subsequently called as the LDS Church's fifth and sixth presidents, respectively, served in such disparate Nauvoo Legion roles as brigadier general and private. As President Joseph F. Smith later told it, he arrived home from a two-year Hawaiian mission in February 1858, stopped to mold a few bullets from lead mined at the Church's Las Vegas diggings, and galloped off to serve as a teenaged cavalryman in Echo Canyon.[26]

Among the legion's other brigadiers during the Utah War, Charles C. Rich, cofounder of San Bernardino, went on after the campaign to lead the settlement of Idaho's Bear Lake area. The town of St. Charles was named after Rich, much as in 1861 George A. Smith became the namesake for St. George, Utah.[27] Brigadier General Hiram B. Clawson, husband to two of Brigham Young's daughters (among other wives), returned to civilian life to become President Young's principal business manager, leader of ZCMI, and a pillar of the Salt Lake Theater.[28] Brigadier Aaron Johnson spent the winter of 1858–59 bivouacked in the mountains to avoid Judge John Cradlebaugh's investigation of the March 1857 Parrish-Potter murders, following which he resumed his principal responsibilities as the longtime bishop of Springville and commander of the legion's Peteetneet Military District.[29] Adjutant General James Ferguson, a man of enormous talent and personal appeal who had once been sergeant major of the Mexican War's Mormon Battalion, went on to take part in some of Utah's most bruising legal disputes of the late 1850s. In 1859 he was a cofounder of the *Mountaineer*, a newspaper established in Salt Lake to counteract the anti-LDS *Valley Tan*. Tragically, Ferguson died of acute alcoholism in 1863 at the age of thirty-five.[30]

In the ranks of legion colonels, one finds men like Chauncey West and Lorin Farr, Utah War veterans who in the late 1860s played key roles in constructing the last segments of the Transcontinental Railroad after jointly giving their names to the town of Farr West, Utah.

Among the most colorful of the legion's veterans were four men who during the campaign carried relatively modest military and church rank but were among the West's most accomplished horsemen: Major Lot Smith, Captain Orrin Porter Rockwell, Lieutenant William Adams Hickman, and Colonel Robert Taylor Burton—all of whom were dogged throughout the rest of their lives by violence and controversy.[31] Best known of these, of course, was Lot Smith, a veteran of the Mormon Battalion, from whom came the Utah War's most famous utterance during his spectacular, fiery raid on the army's supply trains near Green River during the night of October 4–5, 1857. When an excited federal wagonmaster reportedly shouted, "For God's sake, don't burn the trains," Smith's reaction was, "I said it was for His sake that I was going to burn them."[32] As discussed elsewhere in this volume, it fell to Smith to command the single mounted company constituting Utah Territory's contribution to the Union Army, a role that he carried out efficiently as a federal captain. In 1892, living in self-imposed exile in the slick rock canyons of northern Arizona and somewhat estranged from his church, Lot Smith died of wounds sustained in a close-range exchange of gunfire with a Navajo shepherd in a grazing dispute. A decade later, Smith's body was exhumed and transported north to his former home at Farmington, Utah, for an extraordinary recommital service attended by virtually the entire hierarchy of the LDS Church. This was a direct reflection of his standing as the Utah War's best-known veteran on either side. For years thereafter, Lot Smith's comrades-in-arms from the Utah and

Lot Smith was one of the few Mormon settlers of Utah whose military service spanned both the Utah War's Nauvoo Legion and the Civil War's Union Army as well as the Mexican War's Mormon Battalion in the rank of major, captain, and private, respectively. For these exploits, Smith became Utah's most famous soldier of the nineteenth century, if not beyond. (Utah State Historical Society)

by Brigham Young) but probably an inactive one, although he continued to style himself as a major general of the Nauvoo Legion. Incredibly, two of these legion generals—James Arlington Bennet and John Cook Bennett, a former assistant president of the LDS Church who was excommunicated in 1842—offered their services to the federal government against the Mormons during 1857–58, while the third, James Gordon Bennett of the New York *Herald*, wrote anti-Mormon newspaper editorials during the campaign and assigned at least three reporters to the Utah Expedition—one of whom, Captain Randolph B. Marcy of the Fifth Infantry, became a general officer during the Civil War as well as chief of staff for his more famous son-in-law, Major General George B. McClellan. The ultimate destinies of the legion's three Generals Bennet(t) were as a Brooklyn cemetery developer, an Iowa poultry breeder, and a Manhattan press baron, respectively.[34] During the Civil War an increasingly erratic James Arlington Bennet wrote President Lincoln from Brooklyn to offer him up to ten thousand Mormon troops for the Union Army, a ludicrous gesture unknown in Utah and unacknowledged by the president.[35]

Civil Wars met for annual reunions at his grave. Even during the twenty-first century uniformed reenactments of these gatherings continue periodically in Farmington as a gesture of respect for Lot Smith and pride in Mormon military service.[33]

Perhaps the most bizarre of the many stories of Nauvoo Legionnaires and their fates is that involving three former legion generals who shared a surname, while two of the three also had the same given name. At the time of the Utah War, John C. Bennett was an excommunicated Mormon; James Gordon Bennett never had been a member; and James Arlington Bennet was a member (baptized

Space limitations do not permit discussion of all the other soldiers—federal troops as well as legionnaires—who later entered the history books but did so largely unconnected to the Utah War in which they served. And so this essay passes by the stories of men like Private William Gentles of the Tenth U.S. Infantry, a veteran of Marcy's epic winter march from Fort Bridger to New Mexico for remounts. It was Gentles, with an ironic last name, who allegedly delivered the mortal bayonet thrust to Chief Crazy Horse at the Fort Robinson, Nebraska, guardhouse in 1877 and who was subsequently buried at Fort Douglas.[36] Then there are Private Robert Foote of the Second Dragoons, who became a prominent civilian player in Wyoming's Johnson County War of 1892; Corporal Myles Moylan of the same regiment, who during the Civil War was commissioned and then cashiered, reenlisted as a private under an alias, was commissioned in the Seventh U.S. Cavalry, and retired as a major in 1893 after surviving the Battle of the Little Bighorn in 1876 and receiving the Medal of Honor; Lieutenant Colonel Barnard E. Bee, the Volunteer Battalion's commander, who died heroically as a Confederate brigadier at First Bull Run after giving General Thomas J. Jackson the nickname "Stonewall"; Bee's Volunteer Battalion subordinate, Private Benjamin Harrison Clark, who became extraordinarily proficient in Cheyenne and served as chief scout and interpreter for Generals Custer, Sheridan, Sherman, and Miles during the post–Civil War plains campaigns; Second Lieutenant Samuel Wragg Ferguson of the Second U.S. Dragoons, the Confederate brigadier who at the opening of the war accepted the surrender of Fort Sumter and who at the end escorted Jefferson Davis in his last futile dash south from Richmond; Captain Jesse Lee Reno, commander of the Utah Expedition's siege battery, who died a federal major general at South Mountain with defiant old Barbara Fritchie's famous American flag in his saddle bags and later draped across his coffin; and William H. F. (Rooney) Lee, Robert E. Lee's son, who wangled a lieutenant's commission in the Utah Expedition's Sixth Infantry against his father's wishes by having his Harvard roommate, the talented Henry Adams, ghostwrite an eloquent, irresistible plea to General Winfield Scott. Rooney Lee was to become the Confederacy's youngest major general.[37]

James Grodon Bennett was commissioned a brigadier general in the Nauvoo Legion by Joseph Smith in the early 1840s. This New York newspaper publisher-editor never took this Illinois militia role as seriously as two other legion generals of similar name, John Cook Bennett and James Arlington Bennet. During the Utah War, James Gordon Bennett had multiple field correspondents (some army officers) sending dispatches to his Herald, *the nation's highest-circulation newspaper.* (Harper's Weekly, July 10, 1858)

Of all the postwar exploits of the Utah War's soldiers, it would be most intriguing to probe the experiences of Private Charles H. Wilcken, a Prussian Army veteran with an iron cross to his credit, who deserted the U.S. Army's Fourth Artillery during the fall of 1857. Wilcken was probably unique in having served both the federal and Mormon sides. After the Utah War, he took part in so many of late-nineteenth-century Utah's seminal events that his story takes on a Forrest Gump–like quality. As a coachman, bodyguard, nurse, and eventually pallbearer for Presidents Taylor and Woodruff, Wilcken was everywhere and saw everything. Two of Wilcken's Romney descendants would even become presidential candidates in the elections of 1968, 2008, and 2012.[38]

If Private Wilcken had a rival for most intriguing post-1858 life, it might well be his comrade-in-arms in the Fourth U.S. Artillery with a wonderful last name, Sergeant Thomas Moonlight. With the Civil War, Moonlight rose to brevet brigadier general, was forced out in 1865, was appointed Kansas's adjutant general, became governor of Wyoming Territory, and was appointed U.S. Ambassador to Bolivia before dying in 1899. It was as Wyoming's governor that former sergeant Moonlight granted a pardon to that famous Utahn, the Sundance Kid, who also ended his career in Bolivia.[39]

THE CAMP FOLLOWERS

Among the Utah War's most colorful dramatis personae were the civilian employees and hangers-on who accompanied Albert Sidney Johnston's troops. In a sense, they had no real counterparts on the Mormon side. I refer, of course, to people like William Clarke Quantrill, who found work as a monte dealer at Fort Bridger in 1858 and later as a mess cook at Camp Floyd before becoming the most notorious guerrilla of the Civil War. Quantrill was shot down by a federal patrol in Kentucky in 1865, and until relatively recently his skull occupied a refrigerator in an Ohio household. Young David Poole and George Sheppard, who toiled as Utah War teamsters, subsequently joined Quantrill's Confederate band. Sheppard then rode with the Jesse James–Cole Younger gang to execute a variety of bank robberies that took him to further government service in a Kentucky penitentiary.[40]

Charlie Morehead, a youthful employee of the massive freighting firm of Russell, Majors and Waddell, left the Utah campaign for a rendezvous with destiny as mayor of such tough frontier towns as Leavenworth, Kansas, and El Paso, Texas, during the salad days of the notorious gunman John Wesley Hardin.[41] Then there were the Michigan college boys, who included the son of Kalamazoo College's president as well as three lads who signed on as assistant foragemasters in Utah after being expelled from the University of Michigan following their involvement in a fatal drinking bout. The most famous of these former students, Elon John Farnsworth, later entered the Civil War with an Illinois cavalry regiment commanded by his congressman-uncle. Four days after vaulting from the grade of captain to brigadier general with Custer and Wesley Merritt, Farnsworth was shot down at Gettysburg leading a futile cavalry charge against Alabama troops likened to that of the Crimean War's Light Brigade.[42]

Among the army's civilian guides was the legendary Jim Bridger, who returned to the charred remains of his trading post in November 1857 as an army employee with the equivalent grade of a major. Among the illiterate Bridger's mess mates was Albert G. Browne Jr., a young newspaper reporter with two Harvard degrees, a PhD from Heidelberg University, and a murder indictment from a Boston grand jury to his credit. During the Civil War Browne became a lieutenant colonel and military secretary to the governor of Massachusetts. Postwar efforts by Jim Bridger and his heirs to obtain compensation for first the Mormons' and then the army's occupation of Fort Bridger went on in Congress well into the 1880s.

Accompanying Jim Bridger as Utah War guides were other veterans of the wild old fur-trapping days—Jim Baker, Tim Goodale, and Mariano Medina (a founder of what is now Loveland, Colorado)—as well as such

Camp Floyd, Utah Territory, sketched here in 1860 by the Utah Expedition's talented Captain Albert Tracy. Until the Civil War, this enormous post—named after Buchanan's secretary of war—was the nation's largest military garrison, the cost of which virtually drained the U.S. Treasury. Decommissioned with the outbreak of the Civil War, it was bypassed by Colonel Connor in 1862 in favor of building a new post, Camp Douglas, on the east bench overlooking Salt Lake City. (Utah State Historical Society)

newcomers as Benjamin Franklin Ficklin, a tough, practical-joking alumnus of Virginia Military Institute who subsequently was one of the founders of the Pony Express as well as the owner of Thomas Jefferson's Monticello. One of the young express riders who worked for Ben Ficklin after the Utah War was Charles W. Becker, a lad who had accompanied the army to Camp Scott as a teamster and then been captured by the Nauvoo Legion. After his Utah War and Pony Express days, Charlie Becker moved to Malheur County, Oregon, and amassed a huge cattle spread which by the early twenty-first century had grown to 180,000 acres.[43]

So colorful were the Utah War adventures of even the conflict's civilian participants that dozens of uninvolved people later embellished their life's story to "join" them. For example, in the 1870s Frederick William

"Buffalo Bill" Cody shamelessly fabricated a story that he had been along on the campaign as an eleven-year-old assistant teamster protected at Fort Bridger during the winter of 1857–58 by James Butler "Wild Bill" Hickok, a bravo who himself never claimed to be part of the Utah War.[44]

THE SOCIETAL FORCES

Aside from spawning a legacy of fascinating personal outcomes, many of which had Civil War implications, the Utah War also set in motion a series of societal forces with economic, geographic, political, and even literary impact on the post-1858 development of Mormonism, Utah, and the American West. Some of these forces ran their course during the last half of the nineteenth century, while others remain actively at work today, although the latter are rarely thought of as by-products of a territorial-federal confrontation that took place more than 150 years ago.

Economic impact. With respect to economics, the impact of what most Mormons today call the move south was devastating, and the cost of the Utah Expedition on the federal side drained the U.S. Treasury. The strains of the Utah War were such that they drove Russell, Majors and Waddell—the nation's largest freighting firm—into bankruptcy, while perhaps stimulating the subsequent rise of one of Utah's creative design and manufacturing marvels, what later became the Browning Arms Company. Finally, it should be mentioned that the Utah War had a positive impact on the territory's economy through its stimulus for the 1861 completion of the transcontinental telegraph line in Salt Lake City and the exploration and development of multiple road systems in Utah. Albert Sidney Johnston should be remembered today as much as the commander of explorers and road builders in Utah as leader of the Utah Expedition. There was also the economic impact of the April 1858 discovery of gold by Colonel W. W. Loring's Mounted Rifles as they marched north from New Mexico to reinforce the Utah Expedition through what is now Denver's Cherry Creek, thereby helping to trigger the Pike's Peak rush. Likewise for the impact of U.S. Army lieutenant Joseph C. Ives's ascent of the Colorado River during early 1858, a journey that led not only to Ives's rediscovery of the Grand Canyon (and a subsequent tourism bonanza) but to Brigham Young's subsequent decision to exploit trade on the Colorado River through Call's Landing.[45]

Political legacy and geographical consequences. Even more important than its economic legacy was the fact that the Utah War marked the beginning of a process by which not only the arithmetic ratio of the Mormon-Gentile relationship in Utah changed irretrievably but with it the governmental balance of power as well. With the simultaneous influx during 1858 of thousands of U.S. troops, their civilian camp followers, a new slate of federal appointees, and the establishment of the *Valley Tan* newspaper, Utah's physical and psychological sense of isolation from national influence began to fade. No longer was the U.S. government or the non-Mormon world to be without substantial influence in Utah as they were during the period 1847–57.

A companion legacy of the Utah War was the fact that these changes took decades to unfold for a variety of reasons, including James Buchanan's fecklessness during 1858–61, the enormous national distraction of the Civil War, Thomas L. Kane's dedicated lobbying, and most importantly Brigham Young's iron resolve. And just as the active (or 1857–58) phase of the Utah War was ten years in the making rather than the result of a single critical incident, the assertion of federal authority which Buchanan had sought so ineptly by intervening in Utah came not entirely in 1858 but rather through another four decades of conflict and confrontation. In the interim, statehood for Utah was, in effect, held hostage politically until 1896.

Notwithstanding what appeared to be Brigham Young's successes in this exhausting, decades-long process, there were some forces that not even he could control, with prices to be paid by Utah. Consequently, Mormon Utah—highly unpopular as well as relatively defenseless in Congress—suffered the punishing indignity during the 1860s of losing roughly 60 percent of its territory in multiple "bites" to form Nevada Territory, the state of Nevada, and the territories of Colorado and Wyoming, while also enlarging Nebraska

Territory. Utah's current boundaries emerged from this process by 1868. And so, postwar consequences or legacies could be geographical as well as economic and political. This was a lesson that Russian tsar Alexander II contemplated during the Utah War as he faced the possibility of a wholesale, armed Mormon exodus from Utah to the Pacific Coast, a prospect that strengthened the tsar's resolve in 1857 to sell Russian America to the United States government rather than to see it seized without compensation by Brigham Young.[46] The sale was completed in 1867 after a delay attributable to the Civil War.

If one doubts that the Utah War has had long-term political impact, consider the spectacle during the summer of 1996 in which President Clinton had to announce his unpopular creation of Grand Staircase–Escalante National Monument not at its Utah location but rather from the safe distance of northern Arizona because of the depth of feelings in Utah's three southernmost counties. Ironically, in the Utah county named after Thomas L. Kane, residents muttered about Grand Staircase–Escalante in terms of "Johnston's Army" and "1858 all over again." Utah Congressman Chris Cannon capitalized on the furor by creating a 1996 campaign video that pointedly linked President Clinton's unilateral political-environmental action to President Buchanan's earlier decision to intervene militarily in Utah. The so-called Sagebrush rebellion against federal authority in the West was not created by the Utah War, but the depth of its roots in this region should be considered a special legacy of that conflict's anticolonialism.[47]

Literary legacy. To date, no attempt has been made to construct a comprehensive bibliography of the Utah War's contribution to literature, although even while being prosecuted the campaign inspired works of fiction and drama published in various formats on both the Mormon and federal sides. This is not the place to attempt such a review. Suffice it to say that what followed the war was a rich legacy of fictive works ranging between the fascinating and the absurd, some published in Europe. Few of these literary works bridge the Utah War and the Civil War, although with the rise of "alternate history" in the late twentieth century, a small group of novelists have created fictive scenarios in which the operations of the Utah War morph into those of the massive conflict soon to follow.[48]

CONCLUSION

If the origins and prosecution of the Utah War have too often been neglected, this essay has sought to provide a few glimpses of the conflict's post-1858 impact in hopes of nurturing a growing awareness of its colorful legacy. It is a need which comes to mind when reading the prelude to Jay Winik's 2001 book, *April 1865: The Month That Saved America.* Here Winik presents Thomas Jefferson's neglected mansion, Monticello, as emblematic of a divided nation teetering at war's end on the brink of an uncertain destiny. To drive home his opening point about the mansion and the nation, Winik describes Monticello as the property of two competing owners: "one Northern—the estate of naval officer Uriah Levy—one Southern—the Confederate entrepreneur Benjamin Finklin." There it is—an unintended but nevertheless real mangling of Benjamin Franklin Ficklin, the Utah War veteran discussed earlier, into "Benjamin Finklin." Lost in the process is not only Ficklin's name but his extraordinary Mexican War and VMI record, Utah War adventures, Pony Express role, experiences as a leading

Confederate blockade runner, and postwar success as a Texas mail contractor after whom an entire county was named. Small wonder that Ben Ficklin choked to death. If he had not done so on a fish bone in Georgetown in 1871, he surely would have gagged over Jay Winik's presentation of his career and its significance 130 years later.[49]

When in 1866 Major General Randolph B. Marcy published an account of his incredible winter journey from Fort Bridger to New Mexico to remount the Utah Expedition, he concluded his narrative with a brief, throw-away comment that virtually passed over the entire balance of the Utah War: "The sequel of the Mormon expedition is well known to the public."[50] Perhaps Marcy's statement was accurate just after the Civil War, but not now. And we are all the poorer for our collective loss of such a story.

William P. MacKinnon is an independent historian in Montecito, California.

NOTES

This chapter is a distillation and revision of two earlier works by the author: "The Utah War's Impact: A Military Campaign's Legacy for Both Utah and the Nation," unpublished paper presented on October 26, 2002, for the symposium commemorating the 140th anniversary of Fort Douglas's founding, and "Epilogue to the Utah War: Impact and Legacy," *Journal of Mormon History* 29 (Fall 2003): 186–248.

1. The most recent comprehensive narrative and documentary accounts of the Utah War, its origins, and prosecution are David L. Bigler and Will Bagley, *The Mormon Rebellion: America's First Civil War, 1857–1858* (Norman: University of Oklahoma Press, 2011); Norman F. Furniss, *The Mormon Conflict, 1850–1859* (New Haven, CT: Yale University Press, 1960, rept. 1966); William P. MacKinnon, ed., *At Sword's Point, Part 1: A Documentary History of the Utah War to 1858* (Norman, OK: Arthur H. Clark, 2008); LeRoy R. Hafen and Ann W. Hafen, eds., *The Utah Expedition, 1857–1858: A Documentary Account of the United States Military Movement under Colonel Albert Sidney Johnston and the Resistance by Brigham Young and the Mormon Nauvoo Legion* (Glendale, CA: Arthur H. Clark, 1958, repr. 1982). The Hafens' book was more recently reprinted as *Mormon Resistance: A Documentary Account of the Utah Expedition, 1857–1858* (Lincoln: University of Nebraska Press, 2005). The most recent summary account of the conflict is MacKinnon, "The Utah War, 1857–1858," in W. Paul Reeve and Ardis E. Parshall, eds., *Mormonism: A Historical Encyclopedia* (Santa Barbara, CA: ABC-Clio, 2010), 120–22.

2. For a summary of this carnage, see MacKinnon, "'Lonely Bones': Leadership and Utah War Violence," *Journal of Mormon History* 33 (Spring 2007): 121–78; *At Sword's Point, Part 1*, 295–328. For the best analysis of the Aiken party atrocity, see David L. Bigler, "The Aiken Party Executions and the Utah War, 1857–1858," *Western Historical Quarterly* 38, no. 4 (Winter 2007): 457–76.

3. The Church presidents involved were Brigham Young, John Taylor, Wilford Woodruff, Lorenzo Snow, and Joseph F. Smith. In 1880 former Utah Expedition comrades-in-arms John W. Phelps and Winfield Scott Hancock ran unsuccessfully for the U.S. presidency, as did two descendants of Charles H. Wilcken, one of Phelps's privates—George W. Romney and Mitt Romney—in 1968, 2008, and 2012.

4. An assessment of Buchanan's handling of the Utah War early in his administration and the implications of this performance for the onset of the Civil War appears in MacKinnon, "Prelude to Armageddon: James Buchanan, Brigham Young and a President's Initiation to Bloodshed," in Michael J. Birkner and John W. Quist, eds., *Disrupted Democracy: James*

Buchanan and the Coming of the Civil War (Gainesville: University of Florida Press, forthcoming).

5. Charles S. Foltz, *Surgeon of the Seas: The Adventurous Life of Jonathan M. Foltz in the Days of Wooden Ships* (Indianapolis: Bobbs-Merrill, 1931), 339.

6. Homer T. Rosenberger, "Two Monuments for the Fifteenth President of the United States," *Journal of the Lancaster County Historical Society* 78 (1974): 29–48.

7. Theodore Appel, *The Life and Work of John Williamson Nevin, D.D., L.L.D.* (Philadelphia: Reformed Church Publication House, 1889), 601–4.

8. Brian H. Stuy, "Wilford Woodruff's Vision of the Signers of the Declaration of Independence," *Journal of Mormon History* 26 (Spring 2000): 64–90.

9. James Buchanan to James Arlington Bennet, July 1, 1857, James Buchanan Papers, Historical Society of Pennsylvania, Philadelphia. James Arlington Bennet was Joseph Smith's first choice to serve as his vice presidential running mate in the 1844 U.S. presidential election; Bennet declined Joseph's offer, and Sidney Rigdon was subsequently selected. Baptized in 1843, Bennet became disassociated with the Mormon Church in 1845 after Brigham Young failed to select him as head of the Nauvoo Legion, but he continued to use his Nauvoo Legion military title— at least in correspondence with Presidents Buchanan and Lincoln. See Lyndon W. Cook, "James Arlington Bennet and the Mormons," *BYU Studies* 19 (Winter 1979): 247–49.

10. Charles Pinnegar, *Brand of Infamy: A Biography of John Buchanan Floyd* (Westport, CT: Greenwood, 2002); Philip G. Auchampaugh, "John B. Floyd and James Buchanan," *Tyler's Quarterly Historical and Genealogical Magazine* 4 (April 1923): 381–88; John M. Belohlavek, "The Politics of Scandal: A Reassessment of John B. Floyd as Secretary of War," *West Virginia History* 31 (April 1970): 145–60.

11. The conspiracy literature is summarized in MacKinnon, "125 Years of Conspiracy Theories: Origins of the Utah Expedition of 1857–58," *Utah Historical Quarterly* 52 (Summer 1984): 212–30; Richard D. Poll and MacKinnon, "Causes of the Utah War Reconsidered," *Journal of Mormon History* 20 (Fall 1994): 28–33; Benjamin F. Gilbert, "The Mythical Johnston Conspiracy," *California Historical Society Quarterly* 28 (June 1949): 165–73.

12. In December 1857, a less-than-impartial federal grand jury, empaneled at Ecklesville near Fort Bridger under the protection of the Utah Expedition, returned an indictment of treason against Brigham Young and hundreds of others (probably all Mormons). In 1859, Utah's non-Mormon U.S. attorney quashed this indictment shortly after Young instructed the Nauvoo Legion's judge advocate that most of the Church's legal business was to be steered to the private practice of the U.S. attorney (Alexander Wilson), a juxtaposition of events as suspect as were the composition and biases of the grand jury that had started this chain of events two years earlier. For the circumstances and text of this indictment and its dismissal, see MacKinnon, *At Sword's Point, Part 1*, 468–74, and "Epilogue to the Utah War," 245n134.

13. Kane quoted by Mormon Apostle George A. Smith, Historian's Office Journal, April 13, 1858, CR 100/1, vol. 20, LDS Church History Library.

14. Ray R. Canning and Beverly Beeton, eds., "Epilogue," *The Genteel Gentile: Letters of Elizabeth Cumming, 1857–1858* (Salt Lake City: University of Utah Library Tanner Trust Series, 1977), 101.

15. See the chapter on Lot Smith's Civil War cavalry company elsewhere in this volume as well as E. B. Long, *The Saints and the Union: Utah Territory during the Civil War* (Urbana: University of Illinois Press, 1981); Margaret M. Fisher, comp. and ed., *Utah and the Civil War. Being the Story of the Part Played by the People of Utah in That Great Conflict with Special Reference to the Lot Smith Expedition and the Robert T. Burton Expedition* (Salt Lake City: Deseret Book, 1929); Ronald W. Walker, "Sheaves, Bucklers and the State: Mormon Leaders Respond to the Dilemmas of War," *Sunstone Review* 7 (July/August 1982): 43–56.

16. Leonard J. Arrington, *Brigham Young: American Moses* (New York: Knopf, 1985), 250–401; Newell G. Bringhurst, *Brigham Young and the Expanding American Frontier* (Boston: Little, Brown, 1986), 133–219; Lester E. Bush Jr., "Brigham Young in Life and Death: A Medical Overview," *Journal of Mormon History* 5 (1978): 79–103.

17. Sidney Hooper Young Jr., San Francisco, late grandson of Willard Young and an alumnus of West Point, Class of 1942, correspondence with MacKinnon, 1998–2002; Arrington, "Willard Young: The Prophet's Son at West Point," *Dialogue: A Journal of Mormon Thought* 4 (Winter 1969): 37–46.

18. George Rollie Adams, *General William S. Harney: Prince of Dragoons* (Lincoln: University of Nebraska

Press, 2001); MacKinnon, "Review Essay," *New Mexico Historical Review* 76 (October 2001): 431–37.

19. For the complexities of Johnston's command of the Utah Expedition, especially vis-à-vis Harney, see MacKinnon, "'Who's in Charge Here?': Utah Expedition Command Ambiguity," *Dialogue: A Journal of Mormon Thought* 42 (Spring 2009): 30–64. Johnston's departure from Utah is described in Fitz John Porter, "A Characteristic (Mormon) Conspiracy. (From Incidents of the Utah Expedition of 1859 to 1860, under Genl. A. S. Johnston)," unpublished holograph, 9–11, box 53 (microfilm 25), Fitz John Porter Papers, Manuscript Division, Library of Congress, Washington, DC.

20. Stanley Zamonski, "Border Ruffian and the Gold Nugget Race," *Wild West* 12 (April 2000): 28–34; Jerry Thompson, "When Albert Sidney Johnston Came Home to Texas: Reconstruction Politics and the Reburial of a Hero," *Southwestern Historical Quarterly* 103 (April 2000): 453–78. Differing assessments of Johnston's Civil War performance appear in William Preston Johnston, *The Life of Gen. Albert Sidney Johnston, Embracing His Services in the Armies of the United States, the Republic of Texas, and the Confederate States* (1878; repr., Austin: State House Press, 1997); Charles P. Roland, *Albert Sidney Johnston: Soldier of Three Republics*, rev. ed. (Lexington: University Press of Kentucky, 2001); Roland, *Jefferson Davis's Greatest General: Albert Sidney Johnston* (College Station: Texas A&M Press Consortium, 2000); Larry J. Daniel, *Shiloh: The Battle That Decided the Civil War* (New York: Simon & Schuster, 1997).

21. Browning's service records and his reports from the Utah Expedition are in the National Archives, Washington; a glimpse of him crossing the plains with the expedition's reinforcements in 1858 may be found in Dale F. Giese, ed., *My Life with the Army in the West: The Memoirs of James E. Farmer, 1858–1898* (Santa Fe, NM: Stagecoach Press, 1967), 18, 21–22.

22. Thomas L. Kane, draft letter to President James Buchanan, March 15, 1858, Kane Collection, L. Tom Perry Special Collections, Harold B. Lee Library, Brigham Young University, Provo, UT. Robinson later wrote "The Utah Expedition," *Magazine of American History* 11 (January–June 1884): 325–41, which criticized the Mormons and repeated virtually all of the conspiracy theories associated with the Utah War's origins. General Reynolds's first tour of duty in Utah was with the expedition led by Brevet

Lieutenant Colonel Edward J. Steptoe, which wintered over in Utah during 1854–55 on its way to the Pacific Coast with a detachment of recruits and herd of animals for posts in California and Oregon.

23. Most studies of Gettysburg provide information about the earlier service of these generals as company grade officers in Utah.

24. Augustus Buell, *"The Cannoneer": Recollections of Service in the Army of the Potomac* (Washington, DC: National Tribune, 1890), 389–98; James Stewart, "Battery B Fourth United States Artillery at Gettysburg," *Sketches of War History* (Columbus, OH: Military Order of the Loyal Legion of the United States, 1893), 4:180–93; Harold Schindler, "Tartar the War Horse," *Salt Lake Tribune*, September 4, 1994.

25. Wells, "Narrative of Daniel H. Wells," unpublished holograph, Bancroft Library, University of California–Berkeley. His most extensive published comment about the Utah War was a brief interview with George A. Townsend in connection with his indictment, along with Brigham Young and Bill Hickman, for the Yates murder. Townsend, *The Mormon Trials at Salt Lake City* (New York: American News, 1871), 25–26.

26. Joseph F. Smith, "Reminiscences of the First Presidency," *Deseret News*, December 21, 1901; Joseph Fielding Smith, comp., *Life of Joseph F. Smith, Sixth President of the Church of Jesus Christ of Latter-day Saints* (Salt Lake City: Deseret News, 1938), 194–96.

27. For a disappointingly brief account of Rich's Utah War involvement, see Arrington, *Charles C. Rich: Mormon General and Western Frontiersman* (Provo, UT: Brigham Young University Press, 1974), 215–23.

28. Hiram Clawson earned almost half of the funds used to build the Salt Lake Theater by reselling material purchased on discount when the U.S. Army abandoned Fort Crittenden at the beginning of the Civil War. Here is the way Clawson explained it during a 1907 talk to the Daughters of Utah Pioneers: "I found building material, glass, nails, tents, sugar and other groceries, and many necessities. I was cordially received and favored by the officers. . . . I made my purchase as instructed. Tents with cook stoves that sold in New York City for $12 or $15, I bought for $1, nails worth $40 a box for $6, and other things in proportion. From the sale of a part of the things that I purchased, which realized $40,000.00, and with nails, glass and other building

material, so conveniently provided, the building of the Salt Lake Theatre was made possible." Clawson was also selected by Brigham Young to become the theater's first manager. See George D. Pyper, *The Romance of an Old Playhouse* (Salt Lake City: Seagull, 1928), 75–76; S. George Ellsworth, *Dear Ellen: Two Mormon Women and Their Letters* (Salt Lake City: University of Utah Tanner Trust Series, 1974), 14, 50–51, 72–75; Orson F. Whitney, *History of Utah* (Salt Lake City: George Q. Cannon, 1892–1904), 4:201–3; "Hiram B. Clawson," *Tullidge's Quarterly Magazine* 1 (July 1881): 678–84.

29. Lyndon W. Cook, ed., *Aaron Johnson Correspondence* (Orem, UT: Center for Research of Mormon Origins, 1990); Alan P. Johnson, *Aaron Johnson: Faithful Steward* (Salt Lake City: Publishers Press, 1991).

30. Will Bagley, ed., *"A Bright, Rising Star": A Brief Life of James Ferguson, Sergeant Major, Mormon Battalion; Adjutant General, Nauvoo Legion* (Salt Lake City: Prairie Dog, 2000).

31. Harold Schindler, *Orrin Porter Rockwell: Man of God, Son of Thunder*, rev. ed. (Salt Lake City: University of Utah Press, 1983); Hope A. Hilton, *"Wild Bill" Hickman and the Mormon Frontier* (Salt Lake City: Signature Books, 1988); Janet Burton Seegmiller, *"Be Kind to the Poor": The Life Story of Robert Taylor Burton* (n.p.: Burton Family Organization, 1988). Robert Taylor Burton served as a member of the LDS Church's Presiding Bishopric from 1874 until his death in 1907.

32. MacKinnon, *At Sword's Point, Part 1*, 355–58.

33. Charles S. Peterson, "A Portrait of Lot Smith, Mormon Frontiersman," *Western Historical Quarterly* 1 (October 1970): 393–414; "After Lapse of Ten Years, Remains of Captain Smith Interred at Farmington. A Most Notable Occasion," *Deseret News*, April 9, 1902, 5.

34. James Arlington Bennet's proposals for Utah War service are discussed in Bennet to President James Buchanan, April 8, 1858, James Buchanan Papers, Historical Society of Pennsylvania, and Bennet to Brigham Young, November 20, 1858, Church History Library, while those of John Cook Bennett are in Bennett to Stephen A. Douglas, January 20, 1858, Stephen A. Douglas Papers, Special Collections, University of Chicago. James Gordon Bennett (as well as some historians) did not take his commission as legion brigadier seriously, and he is not even mentioned in such a role in Richard E. Bennett,

Susan Easton Black, and Donald Q. Cannon, *The Nauvoo Legion in Illinois: A History of the Mormon Militia, 1841–1846* (Norman, OK: Arthur H. Clark, 2010). A summary of the military roles of all three Bennet(t)s appears in Andrew F. Smith, *The Saintly Scoundrel: The Life and Times of Dr. John Cook Bennett* (Urbana: University of Illinois Press, 1997), 65, 68–72, 108–9, 115, 126.

35. James Arlington Bennet to President Abraham Lincoln, October 22, 1861, Abraham Lincoln Papers, Manuscript Division, Library of Congress, microfilm reel 28.

36. "People of Ft. Douglas," accessed June 29, 2003, http://www.fortdouglas.org/fdpeopleGentile.htm; Richard G. Hardoff, comp., *The Death of Crazy Horse: A Tragic Episode in Lakota History* (Lincoln: University of Nebraska Press, 2001); Jerome A. Greene, ed. and comp., *Lakota and Cheyenne: Indian Views of the Great Sioux War, 1876–1877* (Norman: University of Oklahoma Press, 1994), 150–52. The most focused study of this incident, which casts serious doubt on the traditional accounts of Gentles's responsibility, is Ephriam D. Dickson III, "Crazy Horse: Who Really Wielded the Bayonet that Killed the Oglala Leader?," *Greasy Grass* 12 (May 1996): 2–10.

37. Murray L. Carroll, "Robert Foote: A Forgotten Wyoming Pioneer," *Annals of Wyoming* 74 (Winter 2002): 9–23; Mrs. Charles Ellis, "Robert Foote," *Annals of Wyoming* 15:1:50–62; Curtis R. Allen, "Myles Moylan," Moylan family website, http://www.freespace.com/moylan/MylesMoylan.html; James B. Agnew, "General Barnard Bee," *Civil War Times Illustrated* 14 (December 1975): 4–9, 45–47; Agnew, "'A Day of Sorrow and a Day of Glory': A Brief Chronicle of the Career of Brigadier General Barnard E. Bee, CSA," 1974, unpublished paper, collections of U.S. Army Military History Institute, Carlisle Barracks, Pennsylvania; Bob Rea, "Ben Clark: Chief of Scouts" (paper delivered at the symposium "Through the Eyes of History," Washita, OK, November 2002); James Marvin Lowrey, *Samuel Wragg Ferguson: Brig. General, CSA, and Wife Catherine Lee, Featuring Selections from Their Writings* (Sulphur, LA: n.p., 1994); Heyward and Ferguson Family Papers, Southern History Collection, Wilson Library, University of North Carolina–Chapel Hill; Samuel Wragg Ferguson Papers, Special Collections, Hill Memorial Library, Louisiana State University, Baton Rouge; Samuel W. Ferguson, "With Albert

Sidney Johnston's Expedition to Utah, 1857," *Collections of the Kansas State History Society* 12 (1912): 303–12; Conrad Reno, "General Jesse Lee Reno at Frederick [Maryland], Barbara Fritchie, and Her Flag," *Civil War Papers Read before the Commandery of the State of Massachusetts, Military Order of the Loyal Legion of the United States* (Wilmington, NC: Broadfoot, 1993), 2:553–69; Henry Adams, *The Education of Henry Adams: An Autobiography* (Boston: Houghton Mifflin, 1918), 59.

38. William C. Seifrit, "Charles Henry Wilcken: An Undervalued Saint," *Utah Historical Quarterly* 55 (Fall 1987), 308–21.

39. W. Turrentine Jackson, "Administration of Governor Thomas Moonlight," *Annals of Wyoming* 18 (1946): 139–62.

40. Henry S. Clarke, "W. C. Quantrill in 1858," *Kansas Historical Collections* 7 (1901–2): 218–23; William Elsey Connelley, *Quantrill and the Border Wars* (Lawrence: Kansas Heritage Press, 1992), 1–7, 66, 75–81, 87, 94–96, 99–100, 103–4, 109–10; Barry A. Crouch, "A 'Fiend in Human Shape'? William Clarke Quantrill and His Biographers," *Kansas History* 22 (Summer 1999): 143–56; Edward E. Leslie, *The Devil Knows How to Ride: The True Story of William Clarke Quantrill and His Confederate Raiders* (New York: Random House, 1996), 52–63; Martin E. Ismert, "Quantrill-Charley Hart?" (paper presented at the Posse of the Westerners of Kansas City, October 13, 1959), William Clarke Quantrill Research Collection, McCain Library, University of Southern Mississippi, Hattiesburg; Charles Becker, "With Johnston's Army, 1857," 4, typescript, Merrill-Cazier Library, Utah State University, Logan; Joanne Chiles Eakin and Donald R. Hale, comps., *Branded as Rebels: A List of Bushwhackers, Guerrillas, Partisan Rangers, Confederates and Southern Sympathizers from Missouri during the War Years* (Independence, MO: Wee Print, 1993), 391; Gilbert Cuthbertson, "Shepherd Was Name to Fear in Border War Era," *Kansas City (Missouri) Times*, September 9, 1965, 140.

41. "Charles R. Morehead, Pioneer Banker, City Builder, Farmer, Mayor of El Paso, Dead at 86," *El Paso Times*, December 16, 1921, 1, 3; Owen P. White, *Out of the Desert: A Historical Romance of El Paso* (El Paso, TX: McMath Co., 1923), 339–45; William Elsey Connelley, *War with Mexico, 1846–1847: Doniphan's Expedition and the Conquest of New Mexico and California* (Topeka, KS: n.p., 1907), 600–622.

42. Larry Massie, "Local Officer Made Daring Escape from Confederate Prison," *Kalamazoo Gazette*, March 19, 1989, F2; James M. Wells, *"With Touch of Elbow," or, Death Before Dishonor. A Thrilling Narrative of Adventure on Land and Sea* (Philadelphia: John C. Winston, 1909); D. L. Jaehnig, "The Brigadier," *Livingston County (Michigan) Press*, May 11, 1977, A1, 5, 9; Eric Wittenberg, "A Bold and Fearless Rider: Brig. Gen. Elon J. Farnsworth," accessed February 25, 2002, http://www.gdg.org/efarnswo.html; Francis F. McKinney, "The Last Act at Gettysburg, The Death of Farnsworth," *Quarterly Review of the Michigan Alumnus* 65 (Autumn 1959): 75–79.

43. J. Cecil Alter, *Jim Bridger* (Norman: University of Oklahoma Press, 1979), 273–82, 337–41; Fred R. Gowans and Eugene E. Campbell, *Fort Bridger: Island in the Wilderness* (Provo, UT: Brigham Young University Press, 1975), 159–62; MacKinnon, "Vita: Albert Gallatin Browne Jr., Brief Life of an Early War Correspondent: 1832–1891," *Harvard Magazine* 111 (November/December 2008); 48–49; Nolie Mumey, *The Life of Jim Baker, 1818–1898: Trapper, Scout, Guide and Indian Fighter* (Denver, CO: World Press, 1931); James W. McGill, *Rediscovered Frontiersman: Timothy Goodale* (Independence, MO: OCTA, 2009); Harvey L. Carter, "Tim Goodale," in *The Mountain Men and the Fur Trade of the Far West*, ed. LeRoy R. Hafen (Glendale, CA: Arthur H. Clark, 1969), 7:147–53; Zethyl Gates, *Mariano Medina: Colorado Mountain Man* (Boulder, CO: Johnson, 1981); B. M. Read, "Ben Ficklin, 1849, and the Pony Express," *Virginia Military Institute Alumni Review* 50 (Summer 1973): 13–14; Marie Pinney, "Charles Becker, Pony Express Rider and Oregon Pioneer," *Oregon Historical Quarterly* 67 (September 1966): 213–56; Wanda Morgan, "The Pony Express Rider and the President," *Signal Mountain* 1 (Fall 1998): 4–9.

44. John S. Gray, "Fact Versus Fiction in the Kansas Boyhood of Buffalo Bill," *Kansas History* 8 (Spring 1985): 2–20.

45. MacKinnon, "Epilogue to the Utah War," 238–43; and Jesse G. Petersen, *A Route for the Overland Stage: James H. Simpson's 1859 Trail across the Great Basin* (Logan: Utah State University Press, 2008).

46. MacKinnon, *At Sword's Point, Part 1*, 441–44.

47. MacKinnon, "Epilogue to the Utah War," 243–48.

48. See, for example, Lee Allred, *For the Strength of the Hills* (n.p.: Bridge Publications, 1997). Much of this genre is rooted in the allied Mormon love of science

fiction. While many of the novels devising alternate scenarios for the conduct of the Utah War after 1858 find a way to insert Robert E. Lee into the fighting, few, if any, seem aware that for a brief period during the spring of 1858, Lee and his Second U.S. Cavalry, then in Texas, were actually under orders to join the Utah Expedition, in which Lee's second son, Rooney, was already serving.

49. Jay Winik, *April 1865, The Month That Saved America* (New York: HarperCollins, 2001), 25.
50. Randolph B. Marcy, *Thirty Years of Army Life on the Border* (New York: Harper & Brothers, 1866), 275.

This lithograph of the Battle of Fort Donelson, Tennessee (fought on February 16, 1862), represents the close-quarters fighting that marked much of the tactics used throughout the Civil War. (Library of Congress)

CHAPTER 2

Sherman L. Fleek

OVERVIEW OF
THE CIVIL WAR

The greatest danger to American survival at mid-century, however, was neither class tension nor ethnic division. Rather it was sectional conflict between North and South over the future of slavery.
—James M. McPherson[1]

The American Civil War, fought between 1861 and 1865, has been the subject of some of the great literary giants in America, such as Shelby Foote, Robert Penn Warren, Bruce Catton, and Stephen Crane. Filmmakers such as Ken Burns have tried to describe it in sweeping prose and narrative language that capture both the grandeur and the brutality of this awful but critical episode in our history. Great historical minds of recent generations, such as James McPherson, Alan Nevins, Kenneth Stampp, and T. Harry Williams have tried to analyze, define, and interpret the war in accurate and reasonable terms. Even the venerable Winston Churchill provided his opinion on the scope and meaning of this great conflict.[2] All these individuals have shed a little more light on a complex historical problem.

For many in America, the Civil War was, at the crossroads of American democracy and progress, the defining moment that brutally ushered in a new way of life for most and fresh opportunities for many. Others perceive it as a major military conflict, introducing a new era of war with a viciousness that was unprecedented. Still others view it as a dramatic course correction that has not only destroyed a culture and a wicked form of economic labor but also put in jeopardy a fundamental political right—states' rights. Yet for most Americans it is a colossal event that we learned about in school, reading, listening, and just as quickly dismissing because, like so much else in history, the Civil War was so long ago, and what does it mean for us today?

Perhaps President Abraham Lincoln's clarity and centrality from his Gettysburg Address provides guidance in at least one line: "The world will little note nor long remember what we say here, but it can never forget what they did here." This statement is true regarding any attempt to understand, write, and analyze this incredible war and conflict, this monstrous tragedy set upon the path of American history that our grandparents and their grandparents had to face and grapple with. As with any major war, entire cultures, peoples, and nations changed and had to reconcile themselves with this momentous episode.

After the founding of the United States in the eighteenth century, the Civil War was the second greatest historical event in the American experience as well as the most revolutionary in the way of change and evolution. This great landmark event was also catastrophic, with some 620,000 dead Americans. This war was America's deadliest, but for some four million people, it also marked the escape from the bonds of a miserable and immoral institution; both of these aspects still haunt us today.[3]

Militarily, the war introduced or expanded two great evolutions in warfare. The Civil War was "modern," with its technological improvements and vast new methods of not only death and destruction in advanced weaponry but also breakthroughs in transportation, communication, industrial output, and logistical methods. The war was also a foreshadowing of "total" war—when a nation attempts to harness all its resources, all facets of society, and its entire populace into a coherent, coordinated, marshaled effort and machine to fulfill its war aims and achieve victory. The American Civil War may be one of the first conflicts to harness both these types of warfare; at the very least, it was certainly a harbinger of wars to come.

CAUSES OF THE WAR

The causes and results of the Civil War are just as nebulous to define and describe, but simply put, at the center of all the political jousting, compromising, state and federal disputing, and economic and legal wrangling was the ugly moral dilemma of slavery. And the overriding question was what to do with it. Perhaps the best explanation remains that the Civil War came as a result of the secession of Southern states after forty years of sectional feuds and the national crisis of politics, economics, and social morality that was the expansion and status of slavery into the ever-growing republic. By 1860 the two sections could no longer compromise and avoid war as they had in the past. What may have been a seemingly inevitable conflict germinated in the colonial period and was not resolved in the succeeding eighty years since the founding of the republic. In the words of perhaps the most eloquent writer on the Civil War, Bruce Catton, "Without slavery, the problems between the sections could probably have been worked out by the ordinary give-and-take of politics; with slavery, they became insoluble. So, in 1861 the North and South went to war, destroying one America and beginning the building of another which is not even yet complete."[4]

Undoubtedly, the issue of states' rights was a huge catalyst behind all the gesturing, posturing, and politicking of the 1820s through the 1850s. But what was the one right the South was willing to defend and fight over, and what was the one right the North was unwilling to allow? Slavery. The expansion of slavery into the new territories gained from Mexico was the real cause of the regional conflict. From 1820 with the Missouri Compromise to 1854 with the Kansas-Nebraska Act, slavery and its future were always the critical sectional issue that divided the country and came to divide the parties. This issue destroyed the Whig Party and gave birth to the Republican Party in the early 1850s.[5] Abraham Lincoln's election to the presidency in 1860, with the Republican

At the center of all the political jousting, compromising, state and federal disputing, and economic and legal wrangling
was the ugly moral dilemma of slavery. And the overriding question was what to do with it. This July 1861
Harper's Weekly *image shows a slave auction in the South.* (Harper's Weekly)

free soil, free labor, and free man notions, was too much for the Southern Democrats—they decided to secede. This secession was a not a mass exit: state by state seceded over a period of several months once the first hostilities began. Eleven states eventually formed the Confederacy, but only after a concerted and organized campaign involving newspaper editorializing and dedicated speakers and lobbyists who flocked to the undecided states encouraging them to join with the seceding states. There these "firebrands" stoked the flames of secession, worshiped the common culture of racism, and created a vitriolic campaign against the "Black" Republicans in the symbol of Lincoln. A Mississippi judge led a delegation to address Georgia legislators and offered these fiery words: "Sink or swim, live or die, survive or perish, the part of Mississippi is chosen, she will never submit to the principles and policy of this Black Republic administration," adding this threat, that the South would avoid "submission to negro equality. . . . Secession is inevitable." Ironically, as each Southern state clamored for its individual sovereignty and the right to separate from the Union, the first thing the South did was form another union of states.[6]

Most people today find it difficult to grasp and understand the causes and outcomes of this complicated and complex national crisis. The fact that fathers and brothers opposed members of their own family, that people and region were at odds with each other, was a terrible prospect. Fortunately, the military campaigns, national politics, and final resolution are more easily narrated than are the causes and consequences of the war.

HISTORICAL BACKGROUND

The American Civil War began at Fort Sumter, South Carolina, in April 1861. Yet, in some regards, if one really considers the facts, relationships, issues, and causes, one could argue that the war actually began in the Territory of Kansas in the spring of 1856. At that time, Americans were killing each other for the same reason they would five years later: the future of slavery. Yet since there was no secessionist government intact and no clean break of states rebelling against the mother country in 1856, the attack on Fort Sumter remains the distinct starting point.[7]

The election of Abraham Lincoln (1809–65) set in motion events that culminated in the American Civil War (1861–65). Lincoln was very involved as commander in chief and often wrote personal letters to the families of fallen soldiers. (Mathew Brady Collection, National Archives)

On a dark morning in Charleston Harbor on April 12, 1861, heavy Confederate siege guns opened fire, and the war started. Four years and a few months later, the last field armies surrendered, and resistance crumbled as the Federal Union was holding a grand review in Washington, DC. Some historians have argued for decades that the South did not have a chance to win their independence. Many feel the Confederacy was doomed because of the North's overwhelming resources, industrial base, and population. Then the obvious question is, why go to war if the outcome was inevitable? If there is one event in the course of human history that is not inevitable, it has to be war.[8]

Jefferson Davis (1808–89) served as the only president of the Confederacy. Davis was a West Point graduate, veteran of the Mexican War, U.S. senator, and former secretary of war. (Mathew Brady Collection, National Archives)

Perhaps the South had some chances to negotiate peace, but it did not have enough military might to win the war. The Confederacy never envisioned and developed the war aims necessary to achieve victory, and thus its national strategy was inadequate to coordinate, employ, and conduct the full spectrum of total warfare, though the Southern nation bled itself white in the attempt. On the other hand, toward the end of the war, the Federal union, its president, and the principal commanders learned and understood how to use modern war, with its powerful new technologies and tactics, to achieve a total war strategy to defeat the Confederacy and end America's deadliest war.[9]

Except for the small professional army of eighteen thousand authorized officers and men, the war was fought by volunteers—many of whom were amateurs who learned their skills well through war's terribly bloody apprenticeship program. The ranks of enlistments, state regiments, and casualty lists swelled during the four years of conflict.

As the smoke cleared at Fort Sumter, there was no calculable equality between the North and the South regarding the resources in each area. The Northern states carried the advantage in population, finances, resources, railroads, industry, shipping, foundries, business, and even the strength of education and institutions of learning. Perhaps the only area where the Confederate states held an advantage was a reckoning of animals, livestock, some agricultural produce, and, of course, cotton. Yet as soon as the U.S. Navy entrapped the Southern ports with its tightening blockade, which took some time to perfect, European buyers began to search elsewhere for cotton, namely, Egypt, or turned to other substitutes, such as wool in England's case.[10]

This 1861 lithograph was "a biting vilification of the Confederacy, representing it as a government in league with Satan. From left to right are: 'Mr. Mob Law Chief Justice,' a well-armed ruffian carrying a pot of tar; Secretary of State Robert Toombs raising a staff with a 'Letter of Marque' (a governmental authorization to seize subjects or property of foreign state, here a reference to Georgia's January seizure of federal Fort Pulaski and the Augusta arsenal); CSA President Jefferson Davis, wearing saber and spurs. Vice President Alexander Stephens holds forward a list of 'The Fundamental Principles of our Government,' including treason, rebellion, murder, robbery, incendiarism, and theft. Behind the group, on horseback, is Confederate general Pierre Gustave Toutant Beauregard, commander of forces at the bombardment of Fort Sumter. The delegation is received by Satan and two demonic attendants, who sit in a large cave at right. One attendant has over his shoulder a gallows from which hangs a corpse; the other holds a pitchfork. Satan holds a crown and scepter for Davis in his right hand, while in his left hand he hides a noose behind his back. He greets the Confederates, 'Truly! Fit representatives of our Realm.' Over his head flies a banner with the palmetto of South Carolina and six stars. A large snake curls round its staff." (Library of Congress)

Historians have argued for more than a hundred years about whether the Confederacy actually had a chance or not to win the war, to accomplish the political goal of separation and independence from the United States. Of course, these arguments are speculative, as interesting as they may seem. After Fort Sumter and due to President Abraham Lincoln's call for volunteers, other Southern states—especially Virginia—defected from the Union. The secession of states was not a general mass exodus; states departed one at a time, sometimes in clusters, but it was an individual process.

Men joined both sides in droves. The armies marched forth and clashed for the next

On August 17, 1861, Harper's Weekly *printed this summary of Confederate military uniforms.* (Harper's Weekly)

Two weeks later, on August 31, 1861, Harper's Weekly *printed these samples of Union military uniforms.*
(Harper's Weekly)

four years while women and children waited, worried, and in most ways took over the roles of father and provider. At home they dreaded the casualty lists posted at the courthouse or town square.

The war developed into two major efforts or areas of operation. (Some historians use an older and less accurate World War II distinction: theaters of war.) Divided by the Appalachian Mountains, the front lines were mostly east and west. Field armies bore down on one another in killing fields that soon matched the butcher's bills at Waterloo or Austerlitz. Such major battles in previous European wars usually decided the war, and peace ensued. But in this new era of total war, Americans would fight several dozen Waterloo-type battles, and the outcome would continue to be undecided for years. Virginia especially became the nexus of a dozen Napoleonic War–sized battles that just plowed more ground for graves.

Here it may be appropriate to state that the Civil War represents portions of both modern war, technological advancements on a vast scale, and total war, where a nation's complete resources, population, and efforts are unleashed to bring about the "unconditional surrender" or total defeat of the enemy. A major factor in the Union grand strategy was to blockade Southern ports. The naval war was important and sometimes romantic with ironclads, and the blockade was a

Confederate General Robert Edward Lee (1807–70) in 1863. Interestingly, it was Lee, a graduate and former superintendent of the United States Military Academy at West Point, who commanded the military detachment that captured the abolitionist John Brown at Harpers Ferry, Virginia, in 1859. (Mathew Brady Collection, National Archives)

significant war aim that squeezed the life out of the South's once-vital maritime commerce. However, the true battlefield of victory or defeat was accomplished on land—warfare of maneuver and technology as never seen before.[11]

In 1861 the first major contest was along Bull Run, a creek near the railroad junction at Manassas, Virginia. Most people, especially the politicians and journalists on both sides, wrongly thought the war would be decided by one major, bloody contest. On July 21, along Bull Run, the Federals had the upper hand most of the day until Confederate reinforcements arrived, and through lack of command and control, uncoordinated piecemeal attacks caused the Union effort to unravel. Confederate defense of the high ground, especially on the key terrain of Henry House Hill, won the day. The long, defeated, and straggling columns of discouraged Federal soldiers fled back to Washington as a rabble and not an army. Hundreds of civilians who came out to picnic and observe the exciting day were among the exhausted throng. From this time forth, both sides knew they had serious conflict before them.[12]

After the Rebel victory, the Federals regrouped, and soon thereafter the administration appointed forty-year-old George McClellan to command all the Union forces in the field. Soon the slogan "On to Richmond" echoed in a thousand camp sites, especially in the East. This new army, called the Army of the Potomac, nearly became McClellan's private army, a well-organized and disciplined but inert specimen. This early concept of victory, taking the Confederate capital, cost the North dearly for nearly three years until President Lincoln, after trial and error, battle after battle, general after general, and tens of thousands of corpses, finally found a few commanders who devised the relentless strategy and had the guts to execute total war.[13]

The Confederacy, on the other hand, adopted flawed war aims and strategy that would eventually spell their doom. Every Yankee incursion and invasion was to be met and defeated; every square inch of Dixie was to be defended and, if lost, then later redeemed. No leaders with the vision of modern warfare came to the forefront. None understood how to achieve victory using a total war strategy—though the South employed the ingredients of total war without knowing it, in the sense that they sacrificed nearly everything to win. Even a limited war of attrition, fighting only when absolutely necessary and conserving resources and men, such as George Washington conducted against the British, may have, over time, proved more successful.[14]

STRATEGY AND TACTICS

The true nature and perhaps even the outcome of the conflict manifested itself in the pivotal year of 1862. The western area of operations along the Mississippi River was the effort that eventually gave the North victory. The now-glamorous and bloody war along

General Ulysses S. Grant (1822–85) at Cold Harbor, Virginia, in 1864. Born Hiram Ulysses Grant, he was elected in 1868 as the eighteenth president the United States. (Mathew Brady Collection, National Archives)

the East Coast, especially in Virginia, was nothing more than a mobile Western Front. These campaigns became a foreshadowing of the stalemate of World War I, a deadly war of attrition with no clear victory until the last months of the war.

President Lincoln became increasingly doubtful about General McClellan's leadership and enthusiasm for victory when the general failed to move and strike the heart of the Confederacy at Richmond. In fact, at one point he asked McClellan if he could "borrow the Army" for a time.[15] Finally, McClellan executed his grandiose plan to move some one hundred thousand men by boats and barges down the Potomac River into the Chesapeake Bay, farther down to the James River, then up the river to Harrison Landing, only twenty miles from Richmond. It was a masterful logistical exercise and daring operation, but within three months, the Peninsula Campaign was an ignominious failure for the United States. After nearly entering Richmond, the two opponents fought a series of battles, the "Seven Days Battles," where the Confederacy rose triumphant and McClellan had to withdraw his still-mammoth army to save it. During this period, the rise of one of the most spectacular field commanders in history was established in the likes of gentlemanly but aggressive leader

Robert E. Lee of Virginia. A West Point graduate and career army officer, he turned his back on oath and country and declared that his loyalty to Virginia was a higher, more sacred duty than that which he owed to the United States. The Confederacy now had its foremost warrior and his army, soon to be named the Army of Northern Virginia. Lee and his lean, aggressive men were a formidable force that defeated Federal efforts in the East again and again. Yet Lee's entire operational theory was based in the past—he searched vainly for the great, final victory or battle of annihilation, such as Waterloo or Yorktown, that would end the war. He was fighting a modern war with sixteenth- and seventeenth-century tactics and assumptions that cost the South dearly in the end.[16]

There were other contests—smaller campaigns that later became the stuff of romance and legends rather than substantive military value—such as the Confederate victories by General Thomas Jackson and his defense of the Shenandoah Valley in the spring of 1862.[17] The amazing introduction of modern war at sea by the clash of ironclads at Hampton Roads between the USS *Monitor* and the CSS *Virginia* changed forever naval warfare and spelled the end of the military age of sail.[18]

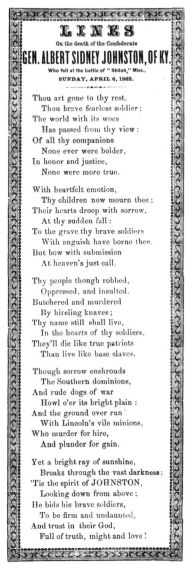

This broadsheet was published shortly after the death of Confederate general Albert Sidney Johnston, of Kentucky. (American Song Sheets, David M. Rubenstein Rare Book & Manuscript Library, Duke University)

There were also battles in distant New Mexico and modern-day Arizona where small armies fought among canyons, cactus, and high mountain passes; these small engagements had little effect on the overall war.[19]

In the West, a rather common and insignificant commander of Federal forces now rose to the forefront. General Ulysses S. Grant, also a West Pointer, was a man who had failed at most civilian pursuits since leaving the army in early 1850s. He had a small force based in Illinois; employed river boats to ferry his troops south into Tennessee in bitter cold February 1862; and in a daring and brilliant campaign, captured two of the South's major fortifications, Forts Henry and Donelson, along river fronts, forcing the evacuation of Rebel forces from Nashville.[20]

With the tenacity of a bulldog, Grant won an incredible victory at Shiloh in April 1862—a battle where he was initially surprised by a major Confederate attack. The Southern army, under General Albert Sidney Johnston, who died at Shiloh, led the Federal troops during the Utah War of 1857–58. Losing

A Confederate artillery battery at Pensacola, Florida (circa 1861). (National Archives)

most of the advantages of terrain and with heavy casualties and the remainder his army in chaos, Grant had already decided to attack the next morning as reinforcements arrived from another army. Grant's cold and bold determination soon overwhelmed the Southerners. This stubborn willpower was one of the great measures that led him to final victory three years later.[21]

By the end of 1862, General Lee had won more victories in Virginia but made no progress against the North other than piling up many more thousands of corpses. In the summer, his victories were at Second Bull Run and Chantilly, and then he invaded Maryland only to fight an indecisive contest near Sharpsburg on Antietam Creek in September. The battle of Antietam remains the bloodiest day in American history, with 4,808 killed in action.[22] The operational defeat dashed the Confederacy's misplaced hope to have foreign powers recognize the South as a legitimate government and also to gain thousands of recruits from neutral Maryland, a border state.[23]

One of the unanticipated reasons for the bloodiness and gruesomeness of the war was the advancement of technology beyond the evolution of tactical art. The new rifle-musket was lethal to four hundred and five hundred yards, three and four times the range during the Napoleonic era and even the Mexican War, which meant volley fire at longer ranges and with greater accuracy. During the first year or two, all the generals fought the Civil War as they had against the Mexicans, at close ranges, in closed ranks, and by firing in successive orders of volley fire. With the advanced lethality and velocity of the Minié ball, a conical-shaped projectile, the results were devastating. Soon, the generals learned and adapted their tactics and deployments, but not until thousands were killed because tactics had not advanced as technology had—a sad reality in almost all wars.[24]

A much larger result from victory at Antietam was a brilliant political and moral move. Lincoln announced the Emancipation Proclamation, which changed the very purpose of the war by freeing the slaves who were not under Federal control in those portions of the South that were still in rebellion. The North was now fighting not only to defeat the rebellion and reunite the nation but also to destroy slavery. Announced on September 22, 1862, the proclamation went into effect on January 1, 1863. The proclamation underwent several drafts and revisions, but perhaps one of the dramatic passages reflected Lincoln's reliance upon a higher religious power and his faith that all would come to pass. He wrote the concluding paragraph later, adding the phrase "upon military necessity" after the word "constitution," based on his belief that as commander in chief, his exclusive war powers were not enumerated in the Constitution. It was a wise revision with this final passage: "And upon this act, sincerely believing it to be an act of justice, warranted by the *Constitution*, upon military necessity, I invoke the considerate judgment of mankind, and the gracious favor of Almighty God."[25]

Then with a final victory by the North, the institution of slavery would end, and all those held in bondage would be "then, thenceforth and forever free."[26]

With Federal forces gaining the upper hand in the West by late 1862, Grant's slow but determined advance south to divide the Confederacy, and Lee's stubborn wins in the East, the war was far from over. Lee's great success at Fredericksburg in December 1862 was a gory day indeed. Union General Ambrose Burnside (legend has it that he was the father of sideburns because of his thick, lamb-chop whiskers) ordered thirteen frightful, bloody charges uphill against stone walls and earthworks bristling with rifle-muskets and twelve-pound field pieces. Thousands of blue-uniformed bodies lay scattered across a landscape shrouded by snow. Along with other Union commanding officers, Burnside was sacked directly but resigned his post as commander of the Army of the Potomac. Next came Joseph "Fighting Joe" Hooker, a bold, vulgar, and egotistical officer who took command of the Army of Potomac. He then led the army to perhaps its most terrible defeat: against General Lee, who orchestrated his tactical masterpiece of maneuver warfare at Chancellorsville in early May 1863, which move confirmed his legacy then and now.[27]

Lee's great victory at Chancellorsville led to his illogical proposal to once again, with limited resources dwindling every day, invade the North and take the war to the Federal hearthstone. His reasons were to destroy the Union army, pillage the land of provisions and goods, and then, while at the gates of "Festung Washington," he hoped that the Northern willpower would dissipate like a cloud. Then, with foreign recognition, the Confederacy would triumph with their independence established. Lee's great pride in his rough and tattered army could not possibly penetrate some sixty-eight separate Union forts and thousands of men and heavy artillery that guarded the nearly impregnable Federal capital. This plan was the Southern

This lithograph, created after the war, shows "full-length portraits of Stonewall Jackson, P. G.T. Beauregard, and Robert E. Lee with four versions of the Confederate flag surrounded by bust portraits of Jefferson Davis and Confederate Army officers." (Library of Congress)

operational scheme in the East during the summer of 1863.[28]

Lee advanced north without proper reconnaissance to assist him and found himself in a battle not of his choosing at a small crossroads town named Gettysburg. After three days of incredible slaughter and a final disastrous charge losing some seven thousand men, Lee retired on July 4, and this offensive campaign was his last of the war. Some fifty-eight thousand men from both sides fell or were casualties in this, the bloodiest of all Civil War battles.[29]

Many have stated and believed that Gettysburg was the decisive engagement of the Civil War, but on the very day that Lee retreated in ignominious defeat, the true turning point occurred about one thousand miles to the west at a Mississippi River town called Vicksburg.[30] The eventual victor of the war was General U. S. Grant. After three major failed attempts to outmaneuver or dig a canal past Vicksburg, Grant finally transported his army south by gunboats and riverboats under the heavily entrenched and armed batteries built on a high river bluff, a natural fortress. Grant then defeated three separate Confederate armies in five battles while completely cut off from his logistical base. He then approached, besieged, and starved the city and Confederate army into submission. By taking Vicksburg, the Mississippi River soon fell to complete Union control, and Lincoln in guarded exultation said that the mighty "father of waters" could now continue to flow. Other Federal forces, namely, General William Sherman's march through Georgia, would eventually divide the South again and cause the loss or disruption of great resources, especially livestock, that the Confederacy desperately needed.

Vicksburg, we have learned after nearly 150 years, was the true turning point in the war. The nation and army that controlled the Mississippi River would eventually win the war.[31]

GUERRILLA WARFARE

Perhaps one of the most interesting untold stories of the Civil War is that some of the vicious and terrible fighting did not occur in the great battles in Virginia or Tennessee or even Georgia but in hundreds of gruesome firefights in Missouri. As one of several border states that did not join the Confederacy but had a strong pro-slavery sentiment, Missouri was the focal point of another awful condition of modern warfare—guerrilla war. For nearly four years, towns, farms, homes, and barns were burned and people dragged from their homes at night. Even captured soldiers were dragged from trains or camps and murdered. Guerrilla war in any form and intensity is appalling, but in Missouri it was worse than most.

It was Missouri "border ruffians" who caused the uproar and violence in "bleeding Kansas" in the late 1850s. Because there were few conventional armies and outposts in Missouri, the rich land of pastures, farms, and riverboat commerce became a killing ground for wicked desperadoes on both sides, but the Southern cause especially attracted some of the most notorious villains in American history. William Quantrill, who served on the Utah expedition in 1857–58 as a teamster and cook, gathered a group of mean and nasty killers that had a field day for several years murdering anyone who stood for the Union or was anti-slavery. Romantic figures—brutal killers really—such as Jesse and Frank James, the Younger brothers, "Bloody" Bill Anderson, and other equally wanton killers and thieves learned their trade in the Civil War. The land of Missouri ran with partisan blood, and it is now impossible to quantify just how many hundreds, perhaps even thousands, of soldiers, citizens, men, women, and children perished through this ferocious guerrilla war.[32]

THE END OF THE WAR

The crucial year of 1864 was the last great year of battles and political anxiety in the North. In April, Lincoln finally found his general who would bring final victory: U. S. Grant. Promoted to lieutenant general and commander of all Federal armies, Grant designed what would become his famous "overland" maneuver that would finally force the tough and seasoned Confederate army under General Lee to its knees. In coming east to command, Grant chose to command from the field. He left the western area of operations to his faithful and competent friend, William Tecumseh Sherman. After several minor engagements along the Tennessee and Georgia border, Sherman pressed forward with some eighty thousand men toward the great commercial and transportation hub of Atlanta, perhaps the most important city in the Confederacy with its railroad links and manufacturing power. Eastward in Virginia, after several major and bloody fights at the Wilderness, Spotsylvania, and then Cold Harbor, was Grant's huge and poorly conceived frontal attack. Finally, Grant

General William Tecumseh Sherman (1820–91) is probably best known for his "scorched earth" march to the sea through Georgia. Sherman succeeded Grant as commanding general of the army following the Civil War. (Pictured here in 1864–65.) (Mathew Brady Collection, National Archives)

forced Lee into a box south of Richmond at Petersburg, where the war entered into a new phase of warfare, foreshadowing the Western Front of 1915–16: trenches and stalemate. The summer maneuvers cost the Federals some forty-four thousand men, but those lost were soon replaced with new faces. Ironically, the Confederates lost less than half that number, but they could not replace their losses.[33]

The gruesome war slugged along as both populaces on the home front grew weary of the casualty lists. The politics of 1864 grew intense as the "peace" Democrats pilloried Lincoln and his advisors as warmongers who were no more than butchers. The nomination for president of former General George McClellan, who hoped to arrange a "negotiated peace" with the recalcitrant Southerners, hoped to end the bloodletting by putting "ole Abe" out to pasture.[34]

The war had evolved since the issue of the Emancipation Proclamation; it was now a crusade against slavery. Tens of thousands of African Americans flocked to the colors and fought in United States Colored Troops, "USCT" regiments led by white officers. Dozens were awarded the Medal of Honor, established during the war as the highest award in America for valor. Meanwhile in the Confederacy, there was a great debate about whether to use slaves in the ranks or at least free the slaves to finally gain international recognition. These measures were never adopted, however; a more sinister policy was enacted. The Confederate government did decree that white officers, along with their black soldiers who were captured, were to be executed as rebels in sedition.[35]

The Southern diplomatic campaign failed—only one small German monarchy recognized the Confederacy as a sovereign nation. The great nations of Europe, France, Spain, Great Britain, and Russia wanted Southern cotton but would not lift a finger to help the Confederacy beyond selling war material and building Confederate ships for commerce raiding and blockade running.[36] Slowly but surely, the South was starving and dying, and its only hope was to stop Grant and his hordes in blue and continue to make the war an awful burden for the North. Little did they know or understand the will and determination of Americans in the Northern states.

The military victory that sealed Lincoln's reelection and the Confederacy's fate was Sherman's capture of Atlanta on September 2, 1864. Then followed Sherman's legendary march to Savannah and to the sea. In this campaign, Sherman introduced total war to Georgia and then to the Carolinas. The great campaign that divided the South also broke the will of the Southern people. The Federals cut a swath sixty miles wide that destroyed war resources and commodities. Rumors and myths evolved later that Union troops burned all homes and destroyed all private property in their way. Of course, war causes destruction, but Sherman issued stern orders to maintain control, which unfortunately were not always followed.[37]

Life slowly ebbed away from Lee's once-invincible Army of Northern Virginia; his men were starving, provisions were meager, and the once-battle-hardened core of veterans was mostly gone. There were battles in the trenches at Petersburg; the most spectacular was the "Crater," when former miners in the Union forces dug a tunnel under the Rebel earthworks and detonated tons of explosives, only losing the great opportunity by poor planning and poor leadership. So, as the winter came, the trenches stretched farther and farther, encircling Petersburg.

Just before the presidential election in November 1864, General Phil Sheridan, a diminutive infantryman turned cavalryman, won a string of decisive victories in Virginia's once-bountiful Shenandoah Valley. Here also, the inhabitants faced the flames of "total" war. Lincoln won a landslide victory at the polls, carrying most of the North against McClellan and peace Democrats. Victory was now assured both politically and militarily.

The spring thaw of 1865 brought bleakness for the Southern rebellion. In one last, risky attempt, General Lee cleverly withdrew from his trench lines and marched west for freedom and stores of goods near Charlottesville and Lynchburg. The Federals quickly pursued and surrounded his meager army after several meaningless and wasteful battles that finally ended in the parlor of a house at Appomattox. Lee surrendered his field army, but there were still several armies afield and more battles to fight and win for the North.[38]

After Richmond fell to the Federals, Mr. Lincoln visited the capital of the Confederacy but saw a gleam of hope for the once again united nation. Just days later, a coward's bullet killed the great statesman and father of freedom.

The results of the bloody Civil War are still with us. Historian Eric Foner labeled the events after the war, especially Reconstruction, as "the unfinished revolution." The nation's failure to establish and safeguard full citizenship and civil rights for former slaves and to redeem the South remains a tragic chapter in American history. Books are still being written on every major and minute subject possible; it remains the most published and popular American war. More than 620,000 Americans perished. The nation was once again united, but the cost and memory of this war is still with us today. Beyond the great sacrifice, as President Lincoln declared, "a new nation" was born. The slaves were free, Constitutional amendments were added to define their freedom, the states were united, and a strong feeling of reconciliation later grew from the ashes of war. There was still much to do; the new freedmen had decades of prejudice to overcome, and the economic and political transformation of the South would occur for a century.

Sherman L. Fleek is command historian for the United States Military Academy at West Point, New York.

NOTES

1. James M. McPherson, *Battle Cry of Freedom: The Civil War Era* (New York: Oxford University Press, 1988), 7.

2. Henry Steele Commager, ed., *Churchill's History of the English-Speaking Peoples* (New York: Barnes & Noble Books, 1995), 380–440.

3. The Civil War was the deadliest war but not the bloodiest war; there is a difference. Some two-thirds, roughly 417,000 soldiers, in the Civil War died of natural causes, diseases, and accidents; some 206,000 or less died in battle or later from the results of wounds. In World War II some 290,000 died in action; thus it is our bloodiest war. See Alan R. Millet and Peter Maslowski, *For the Common Defense: A Military History of the United States of America* (New York: Free Press, 1994), 653.

4. Bruce Catton, *The Civil War* (1960; repr., New York: Fairfax, 1980), 3.

5. The Whig Party was developed in the mid-1830s by those opposed to President Andrew Jackson's campaign to end the Second United States Bank, which was a combination of both public and private assets and funds. There were other issues that caused the aligning of a new political party, many of whom were former Federalists, but the opposition to Jackson's Democratic issues and platform were major incentives. William Henry Harrison was the first Whig president, elected in 1840.

6. Charles B. Dew, *Apostles of Disunion: Southern Secession Commissioners and the Causes of the Civil War* (Charlottesville: University of Virginia Press, 2001), 29.

7. See Nicole Etcheson, *Bleeding Kansas: Contested Liberty in the Civil War Era* (Lawrence: University of Kansas Press, 2004).

8. Millett and Maslowski, *For the Common Defense*, 172.

9. Millett and Maslowski, *For the Common Defense*, 171–72.

10. McPherson, *Battle Cry of Freedom*, 370–71.

11. Russell F. Weigley, *The American Way of War: A History of the United States Strategy and Policy* (Bloomington: University of Indiana Press, 1973), 151–52.

12. Millett and Maslowski, *For the Common Defense*, 172–73.

13. See T. Harry Williams, *Lincoln and the Generals* (New York: Knopf, 1952), 300–302.

14. McPherson, *Battle Cry of Freedom*, 856–57.

15. Jeffrey D. Wert, *The Sword of Lincoln: The Army of the Potomac* (New York: Simon and Schuster, 200), 55.

16. Peter S. Carmichael, ed., *Audacity Personified: The Generalship of Robert E. Lee* (Baton Rouge: University of Louisiana Press, 2004), xvii, 6–7, 12–13.

17. Peter Cozzens, *Shenandoah 1862: Stonewall Jackson's Valley Campaign* (Chapel Hill: University of North Carolina Press, 2008).

18. Millet and Maslowski, *For the Common Defense*, 221.

19. McPherson, *Battle Cry of Freedom*, 376–77.

20. Benjamin Franklin Cooling, *Forts Henry and Donelson: The Key to the Confederate Heartland* (Knoxville: University of Tennessee Press, 1987).

21. See Charles Bracelen Flood, *Grant and Sherman: The Friendship That Won the Civil War* (New York: Farrar, Straus and Giroux, 2005).

22. Mark M. Boatner III, *The Civil War Dictionary* (New York: David McKay, 1987), 21.

23. Wert, *Sword of Lincoln*, 172–73.

24. Gregory J. W. Urwin, *The United States Infantry: An Illustrated History, 1775–1918* (New York: Sterling, 1991), 85.

25. Geoffrey Perret, *Lincoln's War: The Untold Story of America's Greatest President and Commander in Chief* (New York: Random House, 2004), 294.

26. Catton, *The Civil War*, 109.

27. Edwin B. Coddington, *The Gettysburg Campaign: A Study in Command* (New York: Scribner's Sons, 1968), 6.

28. Patricia L. Faust, ed., *Historical Times Illustrated Encyclopedia of the Civil War* (New York: Harper & Row, 1986), 804–5.

29. Faust, *Historical Times Illustrated Encyclopedia*, 307.

30. McPherson, *Battle Cry of Freedom*, 664–65.

31. Flood, *Grant and Sherman*, 188–89.

32. See Michael Fellman, *Inside War: The Guerrilla Conflict in Missouri during the American Civil War* (New York: Oxford University Press, 1989).

33. McPherson, *Battle Cry of Freedom*, 733.

34. McPherson, *Battle Cry of Freedom*, 771–72.

35. McPherson, *Battle Cry of Freedom*, 565–66.

36. McPherson, *Battle Cry of Freedom*, 837–38.

37. See Burke Davis, *Sherman's March* (New York: Vintage Books, 1988).

38. McPherson, *Battle Cry of Freedom*, 848–52.

Prophecy or **Commandments** given Decem. 25. 1832

157

Verily thus saith the Lord concerning the wars that will shortly come to pass begining at the rebellion of south Carolina which will eventually terminate in the death & misery of many Souls & the days will come that war will be poured out upon all nations begining at this place for behold the southern states shall be divided against the northern states and the Southern States will call an other nations begining at this place for behold the south ern states even the nation of great Brittan as it is called & they shall also call upon other nations in order to defend themselves against other nations & then war shall be poured out upon all nations & it shall come to pass after many days slaves shall rise up against their masters who shall be marshaled & disciplined for war & it shall come to pass after many days also that the remnant who are left of the Land will marshal themselves & shall become exceed -ing angry & shall vex the gentiles with a sore vexation & then with the sword & by bloodshed the inhabitants of the Earth shall mourn. and with famine & pestilence plague & earthquakes & the thunder of heaven & the fierce vivid lightning also shall the inhabitants of the earth be made to feel the wrath & in -dignation & chastning hand of an Almighty God. untill the consumption decreed hath made a full end of all nations that the cry of the Saints of the bloodshed of the saints shall cease to come into the ears of the Lord of Sabaoth from the earth to be avenged of their enemies; wherefore stand ye in holy places & be not moved untill the day of the Lord come for Behold it cometh quickly saith the Lord. Amen.

Manuscript copy of D&C 87, copied by John Whitmer in Revelation Book 1. The volume concludes with a second copy of the text in the hand of Oliver Cowdery. A third version, in the hand of Frederick G. Williams, is in Revelation Book 2. (Church History Library, The Church of Jesus Christ of Latter-day Saints)

CHAPTER 3

Scott C. Esplin

"HAVE WE NOT HAD A PROPHET AMONG US?"

JOSEPH SMITH'S CIVIL WAR PROPHECY

A month following the artillery rounds fired at Fort Sumter, South Carolina, signaling the start to the Civil War, the *Philadelphia Sunday Mercury* remarked, "We have in our possession a pamphlet, published at Liverpool, in 1851, containing a selection from the 'revelations, translations and narrations' of Joseph Smith, the founder of Mormonism." Citing what is now Doctrine and Covenants 87, the paper continued, "The following prophecy is here said to have been made by Smith, on the 25th of December, 1832. In view of our present troubles, this prediction seems to be in progress of fulfilment, whether Joe Smith was a humbug or not." Though early in the war's advancement, the paper nevertheless speculated about the prophecy, concluding: "The war began in South Carolina. Insurrections of slaves are already dreaded. Famine will certainly afflict some Southern communities. The interference of Great Britain, on account of the want of cotton, is not improbable, if the war is protracted. In the meantime, a general war in

Europe appears to be imminent. *Have we not had a prophet among us?*"[1]

Using Doctrine and Covenants 87 as proof of Joseph Smith's prophetic nature, however, is only part of the section's history. The prophecy's use has changed over time, reflecting prophetic reinterpretation, geopolitical developments, and shifts in Church relations with the world. The receipt, recording, and publishing of section 87 reveals much about the Church, including how it uses Joseph Smith's prophecies, how that use changes over time, and how it interacts with society. At the same time, society's reporting of section 87 reflects reaction to the message of Mormonism and its central tenet, modern revelation.

RECEIVING, RECORDING, AND PUBLISHING THE REVELATION

Most analysis of Doctrine and Covenants 87 focuses on the historical context that led to its receipt.[2] Like so many other revelations of the Prophet, the section, received on

December 25, 1832, is rooted in the history of his day. Unfortunately, Joseph Smith's only surviving journal from the period reveals nothing of the event. Its daily entries, which began on November 28, 1832, inexplicably end after little more than a week, only to resume again ten months later on October 4, 1833.[3] However, working on the *History of the Church* a decade later in Nauvoo, Willard Richards penned, on behalf of the Prophet, an introduction to the section:

> Appearances of troubles among the nations became more visible this season than they had previously been since the Church began her journey out of the wilderness. The ravages of the cholera were frightful in almost all the large cities on the globe. The plague broke out in India, while the United States, amid all her pomp and greatness, was threatened with immediate dissolution. The people of South Carolina, in convention assembled (in November), passed ordinances, declaring their state a free and independent nation; and appointed Thursday, the 31st day of January, 1833, as a day of humiliation and prayer, to implore Almighty God to vouchsafe His blessings, and restore liberty and happiness within their borders. President Jackson issued his proclamation against this rebellion, called out a force sufficient to quell it, and implored the blessings of God to assist the nation to extricate itself from the horrors of the approaching and solemn crisis.

Prefacing the text of the revelation itself, Richards concluded on behalf of the Prophet, "On Christmas day [1832], I received the following revelation and prophecy on war."[4]

While world events, including cholera and plague, clearly contribute to the context, the revelation is most connected to the Nullification Crisis of 1832–33. Latter-day Saint historian Donald Q. Cannon summarized the conflict as follows:

> This crisis grew out of the tensions existing between various geographic sections of the pre–Civil War United States. Specifically, the South felt itself threatened by the North. The state of South Carolina was the center of the unrest generated by this controversy. Southerners, and particularly South Carolinians, felt oppressed and disadvantaged by the high protective tariff of 1828, the so-called "Tariff of Abominations." This tariff imposed heavy duties on foreign manufactured goods, which favored the industrial North, while at the same time it worked against the interest of the agrarian South. In addition to the economic problems, the South was becoming increasingly wary of the nascent antislavery movement in the North. In order to protect itself from these threats, South Carolina passed an Ordinance of Nullification.[5]

That ordinance, founded on a philosophy of states' rights, argued that because the states had created the federal government, an individual state could declare a federal law unconstitutional, something the state of South Carolina did on November 24, 1832, to the Tariff Act of 1828, together with its companion, the Tariff Act of 1832. Prohibiting the collecting of duties in the state after February 1, 1833, the stage was set for conflict. Clearly influenced by this issue, Joseph Smith received the revelation.

Though compromise was achieved and conflict averted in February 1833, the word of the Lord reached beyond the Nullification Crisis that precipitated it. An early reference to the revelation came little more than two weeks after its receipt when the Prophet referred to it in a January 4, 1833, letter to N. E. Seaton, editor of a Rochester, New York, newspaper. "I am prepared to say by the authority of Jesus Christ," the Prophet declared, "that not many years shall pass away before the United States shall present such a scene of *bloodshed* as has not a parallel in the history of our nation; pestilence, hail, famine, and earthquake will sweep the wicked of this generation from off the face of the land."[6]

Joseph Smith received his "revelation and prophecy on war" on December 25, 1832. (Community of Christ Library-Archives)

Beyond referring to the warnings contained in the revelation, the recording of the text itself is unique. The revelation appears multiple times in what is known today as "Revelation Book 1" (also known as the "Book of Commandments and Revelations"), a collection containing revelations received between 1828 and 1834, and once in "Revelation Book 2" (formerly known as the "Book of Revelations" or the "Kirtland Revelation Book"), a volume containing revelatory text generally received by the Prophet between 1832 and 1834.[7] However, recording text in a scriptory book and disseminating it are two different matters. Importantly, the revelation, as recorded in Revelation Book 2, lacks the crosshatched symbol found at the beginning of the section that preceded it (D&C 86),

together with the phrase "to go into th[e] covenants," an indication that D&C 86 was approved for publication in the 1835 edition of the Doctrine and Covenants while section 87 was not. In fact, though recorded in multiple places, the revelation remained unpublished for nearly two decades and noncanonized for nearly forty-eight years.

While it was unpublished, the full text of section 87 was not unknown. In addition to his 1833 letter, the Prophet also publicly confirmed the revelation more than ten years later in a meeting in Ramus, Illinois, on April 2, 1843 (see D&C 130:12–13). Furthermore, he allowed the entire revelation to be copied by multiple individuals. A year into the Civil War, Wilford Woodruff affirmed, "I copied a revelation more than twenty-five years ago, in which it is stated that war should be in the south and in the north, and that nation after nation would become embroiled in the tumult and excitement, until war should be poured out upon the whole earth, and that this war would commence at the rebellion of South Carolina, and that times should be such that every man who did not flee to Zion would have to take up the sword against his neighbor or against his brother."[8] A decade later, Woodruff added, "I wrote this revelation twenty-five years before the rebellion took place; others also wrote it."[9]

In addition to Woodruff's personal copy, historian Robert Woodford identified eight other manuscript copies of the prophecy on war, including reproductions in the handwriting of William W. Phelps, Thomas Bullock, Willard Richards, and Edward Partridge.[10] The most prominent individual regularly using a prepublication copy of this revelation was Orson Pratt, who later recalled, "When I was a boy, I traveled extensively in the United States and the Canadas, preaching this restored Gospel. I had a manuscript copy of this revelation, which I carried in my pocket, and I was in the habit of reading it to the people among whom I traveled and preached." Continuing, Pratt detailed the response he received to this message: "As a general thing the people regarded it as the height of nonsense, saying the Union was too strong to be broken; and I, they said, was led away, the victim of an impostor. I knew the prophecy was true, for the Lord had spoken to me and had given me revelation. I knew also concerning the divinity of this work. Year after year passed away, while every little while some of the acquaintances I had formerly made would say, 'Well, what is going to become of that prediction? It's never going to be fulfilled.' Said I, 'Wait, the Lord has his set time.'" Concluding his experience, Pratt summarized, "By and by it came along, and the first battle was fought at Charleston, South Carolina. This is another testimony that Joseph Smith was a Prophet of the Most High God; he not only foretold the coming of a great civil war at a time when statesman even never dreamed of such a thing, but he named the very place where it should commence."[11]

In spite of its prominence, the revelation itself was never formally published in Joseph Smith's lifetime. As noted, the Prophet and the rest of the scripture committee did not mark it for publication in the 1835 edition of the Doctrine and Covenants, nor was it included in the 1844 Nauvoo edition. In

1860, Brigham Young explained, "That revelation was reserved at the time the compilation for that book was made by Oliver Cowdery and others, in Kirtland. It was not wisdom to publish it to the world, and it remained in the private *escritoire*."[12] Nine years later, Orson Pratt further explained the omission of this section from early editions of the Doctrine and Covenants: "Why did not the revelations in the Book of Doctrine and Covenants come to us in print years before they did? Why were they shut up in Joseph's cupboard years and years without being suffered to be printed and sent broadcast throughout the land? Because the Lord had His own time again to accomplish His purposes, and He suffered the revelations to be printed just when He saw proper. He did not suffer the revelation on the great American war to be published until some time after it was given."[13]

Joseph's revelation was originally excluded not only from published scripture but also from other public records. For example, though the manuscript version of the history of Joseph Smith, authored in Nauvoo in the 1840s, includes both the entire text of the revelation and the background that led up to it, the published accounts of the same history that appeared in Nauvoo's *Times and Seasons* and later in Britain in the *Latter-day Saints' Millennial Star* both printed the background of the section but omitted the revelation itself.[14]

While missionaries relied on manuscript copies of the text for decades, Church leaders finally moved to formally publish the revelation prior to its fulfillment, a development later stressed by Wilford Woodruff: "It was published to the world before there was any prospect of the fearful events it predicted coming to pass."[15] Ironically, the first publication of the revelation occurred outside the continent where the Civil War began. In 1850, Church membership worldwide numbered more than fifty-seven thousand, nearly thirty-one thousand of whom lived in Great Britain.[16] Orson Pratt, the individual who seemingly used the prophecy on war most emphatically, presided over the British Mission from August 1848 to February 1851. The day Pratt left for America, his successor, fellow Apostle Franklin D. Richards, wrote his plan "of issueing a collection of revelations, prophecies &c., in a tract form of a character not designed to pioneer our doctrines to the world, so much as for the use of the Elders and Saints to arm and better qualify them for their service in our great *war*." Included in the proposed publication later named the Pearl of Great Price was "the destiny of the American Union . . . Joseph's prophecy of the Union," a copy of which Richards indicated he received from Orson Pratt while in Liverpool.[17] The Pearl of Great Price, containing the first published account of the prophecy on war, rolled off the Church's Liverpool presses on July 11, 1851. Noting that "a smaller portion of this work has never before appeared in print," the book's preface stressed that the contents, including what it called "A Revelation and Prophecy by the Prophet, Seer, and Revelator, Joseph Smith. Given December 25th, 1832," were

Apostle and prominent missionary Orson Pratt was instrumental in disseminating the revelation. In addition to frequently citing it, Pratt gave a copy to Franklin D. Richards for publication in the Pearl of Great Price, published it himself in his newspaper, the Seer, *in 1854, arranged for it to appear in the* New York Times *in 1861, and served as editor when it was first included in the 1876 edition of the* Doctrine and Covenants. *(Wikimedia Commons)*

designed primarily for members. "Although not adapted, not designed, as a pioneer of the faith among unbelievers," editors acknowledged, "still it will commend itself to all careful students of the scriptures, as detailing many important facts which are therein only alluded to."[18]

As British converts and returning missionaries immigrated to America, the Pearl of Great Price, together with its published account of the prophecy on war, became more familiar to the American Church membership. Ultimately, Orson Pratt again affected the history of the revelation when, as editor of the 1876 edition of the Doctrine and Covenants, he added it to that text for the first time. Two years later, he edited the first American edition of the Pearl of Great Price, keeping the revelation on war in both texts.[19] In the Church's general conference on October 10, 1880, revised editions of both the Doctrine and Covenants and the Pearl of Great Price, each containing this revelation, were formally canonized. President George Q. Cannon, who as a youth anticipated the section's fulfillment, declared at the time: "I hold in my hand the Book of Doctrine and Covenants and also the book The Pearl of Great Price, which books contain revelations of God. In Kirtland, the Doctrine and Covenants in its original form, as first printed, was submitted to the officers of the Church and the members of the Church to vote upon. As there have been additions made to it by the publishing of revelations which were not contained in the original edition, it has been deemed wise to submit these books with their contents to the Conference, to see whether the Conference will vote to accept the books and their contents as from God, and binding upon us as a people and as a Church."[20] With that action, Joseph Smith's prophecy on war became scripture.

CONFIRMATION AND CONDEMNATION—THE PROPHECY DURING THE CIVIL WAR

While the prophecy on war was working its way to publication and ultimately canonization from 1851 through 1880, the section experienced its most emphatic use as the conflict it prophesied erupted in South Carolina in 1861. The use of Joseph Smith's prophecy prior to as well as during the Civil War reflects the Church's feelings about the conflict, its relationship toward the government of the United States, its millennial fervor, and, most importantly, its feelings for the prophetic ministry of Joseph Smith.

References to this revelation increased as war clouds loomed on the national horizon in 1860. Referring to the role South Carolina played in leading the insurrection, Orson Hyde noted in October 1860:

> On the 25th day of December, 1832, the Lord spoke to Joseph Smith, and said—"Verily, thus saith the Lord, concerning the wars that will shortly come to pass, beginning at the rebellion of South Carolina, which will eventually terminate in the death and misery of many souls. The days will come that war will be poured out upon

all nations, beginning at that place." The Democratic party found it necessary to call a convention of delegates to nominate a successor to President Buchanan. No place but Charleston, South Carolina, could be agreed upon as the place for that body to assemble in. A most unlikely place, indeed!— entirely out of the political centre—a small town of about twenty or twenty-five thousand white inhabitants, accomodations very limited for such a body of men, and at a half-dozen prices. But to South Carolina they must go; for the prophecy, twenty-seven years before, said that the serious troubles of the land should begin at that place. The Democratic party of administration fell upon that stone of present revelation, and, according to our Saviour's words, they must be broken. They had to go to Charleston to break. They did go there, and there they did break into several pieces—split asunder.[21]

For others, like Orson Pratt, the role South Carolina would play in secession seemed to be key. A decade after the war began, Pratt recalled, "When they were talking about a war commencing down here in Kansas, I told them that was not the place; I also told them that the revelation had designated South Carolina, 'and,' said I, 'you have no need to think that the Kansas war is going to be the war that is to be so terribly destructive in its character and nature. No, it must commence at the place the Lord has designated by revelation.'" Pratt told their response: "What did they have to say to me? They thought it was a Mormon humbug, and laughed me to scorn, and they looked upon that revelation as they do upon all others that God has given in these latter days—as without divine authority. But behold and lo! in process of time it came to pass, again establishing the divinity of this work, and giving another proof that God is in this work."[22]

Still others continued to use the prophecy in missionary opportunities, seeking to warn eastern inhabitants while proving that Joseph Smith was a prophet. George Q. Cannon recalled his experience just months before the outbreak of the war:

> In 1860, Brothers Orson Pratt, Erastus Snow, myself, and others, were going on missions, and we arrived at Omaha in the month of November of that year. A deputation of the leading citizens of that city came to our camp and tendered to us the use of the Court House, as they wished to hear our principles. The invitation was accepted, and Elder Pratt preached to them. During the service, there was read the revelation to which I have referred—the revelation concerning the division between the South and the North. The reason probably, for reading it was that when we reached Omaha, the news came that trouble was alreading [sic] brewing, and several States were threatening to secede from the Union. Its reading made considerable impression upon the people. A good many had never heard of it before, and quite a number were struck with the remarkable character of the prophecy. It might have been expected, naturally speaking and looking at it as men naturally do, that the reading of such a revelation, at such a time, when the crisis was approaching, would have had the effect to direct men's attention to it, and they would be led to investigate its truth and the doctrines of the Church and the foundation we had for our belief. But if there were any converted in that audience I am not aware of it. Good seed was sown, but we did not remain to see what effect it produced. The revelation being so remarkable, and the events then transpiring being so corroborative of its truth, one might naturally think, as there were present on that occasion the leading and thinking portion of that community, that a great number would have been impressed with the probability of its truth, and would have investigated and joined the Church.[23]

Missionary use of the revelation may have been the motivation for Orson Pratt's arranging to have it published in the *New York Times*. During the war's infancy, the newspaper reproduced the prophecy in its entirety on June 2, 1861, with a brief introductory commentary: "Elder Orson Pratt desires us to publish the following extract."[24]

Though the Church certainly emphasized the prophecy the most, not all Civil War era references came from Latter-day Saint sources. As the war approached, an increase in its use from Latter-day Saint pulpits led observers to report the prediction. In 1858, San Francisco's *Daily Evening Bulletin* published an account from its "Special Correspondent" in Utah, detailing talk of a "prophecy, the fulfillment of which [is] near at hand, . . . in which Joseph declared that the time should come when this nation should divide—when the South should rise up against the North, and the North against the South." Calling

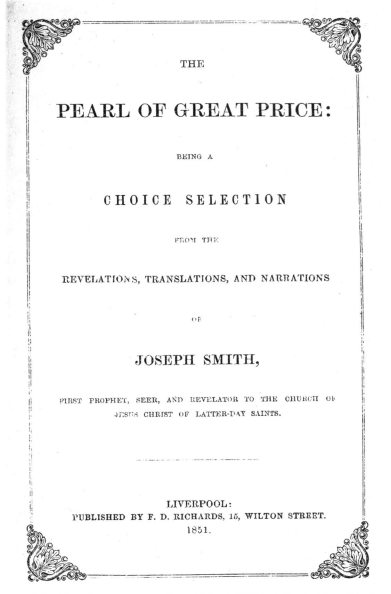

THE

PEARL OF GREAT PRICE:

BEING A

CHOICE SELECTION

FROM THE

REVELATIONS, TRANSLATIONS, AND NARRATIONS

OF

JOSEPH SMITH,

FIRST PROPHET, SEER, AND REVELATOR TO THE CHURCH OF
JESUS CHRIST OF LATTER-DAY SAINTS.

LIVERPOOL:
PUBLISHED BY F. D. RICHARDS, 15, WILTON STREET.
1851.

Joseph Smith's revelation on war was first published in 1851 in the Pearl of Great Price by the Church's Liverpool, England, press. (L. Tom Perry Special Collections, Harold B. Lee Library, Brigham Young University)

Pratt, the reporter cynically noted, "I saw upon every countenance a deep settled smile of malignity and savage delight, as the traitorous fiends glutted their imaginations upon the blood of my countrymen."[26] As war approached, the *New York Herald* recorded another of Pratt's talks involving the prophecy, causing the reporter to go "hunting for it for two days" and calling his interpretation of South Carolina's pending actions "a very facetous turn and interpretation."[27] Apparently those with faith in Joseph Smith's ministry saw one thing in the prophecy, while those who doubted his calling found something very different.

For the Saints, the escalation of conflict between North and South was vindication of Joseph Smith's words. "The revelation upon this subject had been written; it had been published. It was well known to the great bulk of the Latter-day Saints years previous to this," George Q. Cannon later recalled. "I, when quite a child heard it, and looked for its fulfillment until it came to pass. And this was the case with the body of the people who were familiar with the predictions which had been uttered by the Prophet Joseph Smith."[28] Later, he further

the address "disjointed and incoherent," the reporter downplayed the prediction as "full of holes as is a broken net."[25] In a similarly negative tone, a correspondent reported in the *New York Times* Orson Pratt's 1860 use of the prophecy. "At this fearful picture" painted by speculated, "I suppose there is not a boy who has been brought up in this community who did not know of the revelation years before it was published, and, still longer, before it was fulfilled."[29]

Latter-day Saint newspapers may have contributed most to Cannon's conjecture that all were familiar with the prophecy. Orson Pratt's short-lived Washington, DC, periodical, the *Seer*, produced the first newspaper account of the text in April 1854. Under the heading, "War," Pratt cited the Pearl of Great Price account of the revelation, adding personal and scriptural commentary regarding its fulfillment.[30] In addition, Great Britain's *Latter-day Saints' Millennial Star* influenced interpretation of Joseph Smith's prophecy as the United States raced to war. The paper made repeated reference to the revelation as war clouds gathered. In January 1860, the British periodical published the text, noting, "We have not quoted this revelation with the view to attempt to do justice to its many points and wonderful predictions; for, though but short in its wording, it is so full of matter, that a series of articles would not be too much to bring out its points and predictions, glancing at events since it was given in 1832, and looking into the dark future directly before us. The time is coming, and seems near at hand, when not only this revelation, but many others of Joseph's revelations and prophecies must be brought before the world, and their truth forced upon nations by the course of events and the fulfilment of those prophecies."[31]

Indeed, the tenor of Civil War references to Joseph Smith's prophecy highlights the conflict as a condemnation upon the nation for having rejected the Lord. An ocean away from the fray, the most pointed attacks came from the British Church press. "That nation *was* once under 'the special protection of Divine Providence,' and God sent to them a 'special' message and a 'special' day of opportunities by one of the greatest of Prophets," the *Millennial Star* opined in 1860. "But they rejected him, and the special message, and their special day of opportunities; and the cry of Saints, with their wrongs and their repeated drivings, and the cries of the blood of Saints and the blood of Prophets and Apostles, and finally, the injustice of the intended exterminating Utah Expedition, and the pleadings of the last exodus of the Church have gone up into the ears of the Lord of Sabaoth. . . . Because of their many 'demerits' and special sins, they have lost 'the special protection of Divine Providence.' The dark day of the United States has indeed come."[32] As Southern states formally seceded throughout the winter of 1860–61, the paper reprinted the entire prophecy once more, laying the blame again at the feet of a nation who had rejected God's word. Noting that "slavery on the one side and fanatical hostility on the other were some of the means" which led to war, the paper concluded: "But it was not the operation of these evils alone that brought so speedily the fulfillment of this prophecy. . . . It was crime the most gross and terrible in its consequences of any that man can commit. It was the shedding of the blood of innocence—it was the murdering of Prophets and Apostles and Saints. Whenever a man or nation was guilty of this crime in ancient times, the retributive justice of the Almighty speedily followed them, and their downfall was sure." Emphasizing its distance from the conflict, the paper concluded, "Who can behold what is now taking place in that land

and not feel that the Lord's hand is in the events that have transpired? What power but His could so signally have brought to pass his word spoken by his Prophets?"[33]

Still smarting from the 1858 invasion by federal troops, Church leaders in Salt Lake likewise connected the Prophet's revelation to national condemnation. "The 'harmonious democracy' that undertook to destroy this people," Brigham Young blasted on the eve of war in October 1860,

> broke in pieces in the State where the Lord, twenty-eight years ago, on the 25th of next December, revealed to the Prophet Joseph that the nation would begin to break. But I do not wish to make a political speech, nor to have anything to do with the politics and parties in our Government. They love sin, and roll it as a sweet morsel under their tongues. Had they the power, they would dethrone Jehovah; had they the power, they would to-day crucify every Saint there is upon the earth; they would not leave upon the earth one alive in whose veins runs the blood of the Priesthood. . . . They are broken in pieces. Do I wish to predict this? No, for it was predicted long ago.[34]

Interpreting the nation's woes as condemnation for persecuting the Saints was so pervasive that even non-Mormon sources repeated the accusation. Mormons believe "the United States Government is being chastened for its sin of persecuting the Latter Day Saints," a Colorado newspaper reported in 1862. "The nation, totally regardless of law and order, ran wild, and the natural result of such a state of things, was the Southern rebellion," it continued. "The only means of cure," the newspaper claimed, "is for the nation to go right back to where it commenced—to repair the wrongs from the beginning—that is, to reinstate the Mormons in their possessions in Missouri."[35]

As the conflict continued, however, leaders eventually downplayed this rhetoric, emphasizing the revelation as a sign of Joseph Smith's prophetic mission while trying to maintain loyalty to the Union. In 1864, Brigham Young stressed the Prophet's prophecy as well as the consequences of sin:

> The war now raging in our nation is in the providence of God, and was told us years and years ago by the Prophet Joseph; and what we are now coming to was foreseen by him, and no power can hinder. Can the inhabitants of our once beautiful, delightful and happy country avert the horrors and evils that are now upon them? Only by turning from their wickedness, and calling upon the Lord. If they will turn unto the Lord and seek after Him, they will avert this terrible calamity, otherwise it cannot be averted. There is no power on the earth, nor under it, but the power of God, that can avert the evils that are now upon and are coming upon the nation.

However, Young also expressed concern for the suffering:

> It is distressing to see the condition our nation is in, but I cannot help it. Who can? The people *en masse*, by turning to God, and ceasing to do wickedly, ceasing to persecute the honest and the truth-lover. If they had done that thirty years ago, it would have been better for them to-day. When we appealed

to the government of our nation for justice, the answer was:—"Your cause is just, but we have no power." Did not Joseph Smith tell them in Washington and Philadelphia, that the time would come when their State rights would be trampled upon?

Joseph said, many and many a time, to us,—"Never be anxious for the Lord to pour out his judgments upon the nation; many of you will see the distress and evils poured out upon this nation till you will weep like children." Many of us have felt to do so already, and it seems to be coming upon us more and more; it seems as though the fangs of destruction were piercing the very vitals of the nation.[36]

As the war neared its end in 1865, Church leaders emphasized that talk of the prophecy did not demonstrate disloyalty to the union. "We frequently hear, 'You are not loyal,'" John Taylor observed. "Who is it that talks of loyalty?" he countered. "Those who are stabbing the country to its very vitals. Are they the men that are loyal? . . . We will stand by that constitution and uphold the flag of our country when everybody else forsakes it. We cannot shut our eyes to things transpiring around us. . . . But did not Joseph Smith prophecy [sic] that there would be a rebellion in the United States? He did, and so have I scores and hundreds of times; and what of that? Could I help that?" Taylor concluded. "Could Joseph Smith help knowing that a rebellion would take place in the United States? Could he help knowing it would commence in South Carolina? You could not blame him for that."[37]

Joseph Smith's revelation on war was also presented as proof of the Prophet's divine calling. "These things ought to be a warning to us. We comfort our souls sometimes on the fulfillment of the prophesies of God," John Taylor noted in October 1863. "We say 'Mormonism' must be true because Joseph Smith prophesied thus and so concerning a division of this nation, and that the calamities which are now causing it to mourn should commence in South Carolina. That is true, he did prophecy [sic] that, and did foretell the events that have since transpired, and did tell where the commencement of those difficulties should originate. Well if this is true, are not other things true."[38] Brigham Young similarly observed, "There is no man can see, unless he sees by the gift and power of revelation, that every move that has been made by the Government has been made to fulfil the sayings of Joseph Smith the Prophet, and all earth and hell cannot help it. The wedge to divide the Union was entered in South Carolina, and all the power of the Government could not prevent it."[39] Of course, not everyone reached the same conclusion. Colorado's *Tri-Weekly Miner Register* countered, "[Mormons] regard it as proof positive that Joseph Smith was a true prophet of the Lord, because that his prophecy is now being fulfilled to the letter. The old Abolition party might, perhaps, have the same reason for believing their leaders to be divinely inspired, for who does not remember . . . to have listened to prophecies in substance exactly the same as this one, from the lips of the earnest apostles of emancipation."[40]

In spite of a skeptical nation's response, Church leaders continued to turn to this section as evidence even after the war ended. A generation later, George Q. Cannon declared:

"God has sent a mighty Prophet who predicted, among other things, the civil war that took place in 1861. It is on record in this book (the Book of Doctrine and Covenants). Joseph Smith warned this nation of it—twenty-eight years before it occurred. He told them the cause of it, and the consequences that would follow. This great Prophet has been in their midst, and they have slain him, and have destroyed as far as possible those who believe in his doctrine. God will hold this generation to a strict accountability for these acts."[41]

A CHANGING EMPHASIS— POST–CIVIL WAR USE OF THE PROPHECY

With the conclusion of the Civil War in April 1865, Joseph Smith's prophecy entered a new phase. While Church leadership continued to reference the revelation, using its fulfillment as proof of the Prophet's divine calling, they also began noting that the section went much further. Nearly twenty years after the war's final shots, B. H. Roberts characterized the changing use of the prophecy. "Thus you see this prophecy, so far as we have read it, has been minutely fulfilled—fulfilled in every particular," Roberts declared. Turning to future fulfillment, he continued, "And the rest of it will be, so fast as the wheels of time shall bring the events due; and the fulfillment of these prophecies prove beyond *controversy*, that Joseph Smith was a Prophet of God, and 'spake as he was moved upon by the Holy Ghost.'"[42] The same year, Joseph F. Smith noted that only "a portion of that revelation has been literally fulfilled."[43] Increasingly, attention turned to future conflicts in the last days. "This great war," said Orson Pratt following the conclusion of the Civil War, "is only a small degree of chastisement, just the beginning; nothing compared to that which God has spoken concerning this nation, if they will not repent."[44]

Following the conclusion of the Civil War, Church leaders increasingly looked beyond the first part of the section to the latter half, which prophesies conflicts that will culminate in "a full end of all nations" (D&C 87:6). Reflecting the apocalyptic fervor of the day, Orson Pratt answered the question "Do you really believe that such judgments are coming upon our nation?" by declaring, "I do not merely believe, but I *know* it, just as well as I knew, twenty-eight years before it commenced, that there would be war between the North and the South. . . . We know that these judgments are coming with the same certainty that we knew concerning the war of the rebellion."[45] John Taylor made a similar interpretation: "Were we surprised when the last terrible war took place here in the United States?" Taylor queried. "No; good Latter-day Saints were not, for they had been told about it. Joseph Smith had told them where it would start, that it should be a terrible time of bloodshed and that it should start in South Carolina. But I tell you today the end is not yet. You will see worse things than that, for God will lay his hand upon this nation, and they will feel it more terribly than ever they have done before; there will be more bloodshed, more ruin, more devastation than ever they have seen before. Write it down! You will see it come to pass."[46] Indeed, in the decades following the war, Church leaders seemed to echo Orson Pratt's interpretation:

> That war that destroyed the lives of some fifteen or sixteen hundred thousand people was nothing, compared to that which will eventually devastate that country. The time is not very far distant

in the future, when the Lord God will lay his hand heavily upon that nation. "How do you know this? inquires one." I know from the revelations which God has given upon this subject. I read these revelations, when they were first given. I waited over twenty-eight years and saw their fulfillment to the very letter. Should I not, then, expect that the balance of them should be fulfilled? That same God who gave the revelations to his servant Joseph Smith in regard to these matters, will fulfill every jot and every tittle that has been spoken, concerning that nation.[47]

In addition to looking for future fulfillment, Church leaders also connected the revelation to other Joseph Smith prophecies, warning that they too would be fulfilled. "Just as sure as the Lord lives," Brigham Young declared in 1868, "we are going to see times when our neighbors around us will be in want. But some may say, here have ten years, twenty years, thirty years gone, and the sayings of Joseph and the Apostles have not all come to pass. If they have not all been fulfilled, they all will be fulfilled. When we saw the flaming sword unsheathed in the terrible war between the north and the south, we could see in it the fulfillment in part of the prophecies of Joseph. But when peace comes for a short time we forget all about it, like a person who comes into the Church because of seeing a miracle."[48] Wilford Woodruff reached a similar conclusion,

Wilford Woodruff, fourth President of the Church, preserved an early copy of Joseph Smith's prophecy on war and used it frequently in his teachings. (Utah State Historical Society)

citing the prophecy in 1881 while declaring, "Joseph Smith was a true Prophet of God. . . . That revelation was published to the world broadcast, and I merely refer to it because it is a thing that is clear to the minds of all men. All the revelations in the Book of Doctrine and Covenants, the Bible, and the Book of Mormon, will have their fulfilment in the earth."[49]

While Church leaders discussed the future, others skeptically challenged the prophecy's past. Aware of its acceptance among the Mormon faithful, the *Salt Lake Tribune* attacked the prophecy in 1874, claiming that Joseph merely used the succession crisis of 1833 as "a splendid show to build up a cheap reputation as a Prophet." When war failed to immediately follow, the "unfortunate turn in affairs sent the inspired document to its tomb in the archives of the Church, there to await resurrection should circumstances ever favor," something the paper claimed the "half crazed fanatic" Orson Pratt did beginning in 1854.[50] Brigham Young's estranged wife Ann Eliza Young used the revelation to rile up an audience in San Francisco, claiming the "memorable prophecy of Joseph Smith that civil war would work the destruction of the United States" was "promulgated" by the Church so that "when the rebellion finally broke out the Mormons exulted greatly, and held a jubilee to congratulate over the expected destruction of the Government and total slaughter of the male population, when the Church would at once assume supreme control of the country."[51]

Others, like Chicago's *Daily Inter Ocean* newspaper, refused to directly confront the revelation. When asked, "Is it true that Joseph Smith predicted about the war of rebellion, and where it would commence?" the paper dodged an answer by tersely responding, "Some of our readers may be able to contribute to this . . . query."[52] In the South, the *News and Observer* in Raleigh, North Carolina, warned inhabitants of "two 'unrighteous pastors' spreading their doctrines in Wake County." These Mormon elders were circulating a pamphlet containing what "purports to be a prophecy made by Smith in 1832," but which, after republishing the revelation in its entirety, the paper concluded, "No proof whatever of the authenticity of this prophecy is given. It is certainly an imposition on the credulity of intelligent people."[53] Most viciously, Maine's *Bangor Daily Whig & Courier* called for the extermination of the Church over its Civil War stance. "The Mormon leaders have discovered and published the 'singular fact,' that they have among them a prophetic account, written thirty-three years ago, of the great war between the North and South," the paper sarcastically announced. "This is a fair specimen of the teachings of the Mormon Church," it continued. "The audacious blasphemy of the leaders, and the wicked social practices of the people, should condemn them, were miracles wrought now a days, to the fate of Sodom and Gomorrah. The next best thing that can befall them is the vengeance of Congress, which, by the way, is no trifle. Measures should be taken for the thorough eradication of this monstrous and growing evil."[54]

Though the nation followed through, in some measure, with "vengeance" against the Church, the two parties eventually reconciled themselves. The way the section has been used, therefore, reflects the changing relationship between the Church and society. Over time, the insinuation that the American Civil War was a chastisement for the nation's rejecting the Latter-day Saint message has been downplayed. In 1981, Ezra Taft Benson characterized the softened tone. "The desire of the Prophet Joseph Smith was to save the Union from that bloody conflict," Benson declared.[55]

The change in church and state relationships coincided with a decline in millennialism within the Church at the end of the nineteenth and beginning of the twentieth centuries.[56] The de-emphasis on the imminence of the Millennium seems to have lessened the influence of this prophecy. In fact, whereas it was featured prominently throughout much of the nineteenth century, the prophecy was not cited in general conference in the first decade of the twentieth century and used only once in the second. Eventually, apocalyptic references to the "chastening hand of an Almighty God" making "a full end of all nations" (D&C 87:6) dropped off significantly, replaced by messages of salvation present in the revelation.

Furthermore, as subsequent conflicts have occurred, section 87 has been reinterpreted to reflect geopolitical tensions. "It received its widest coverage at the time of the Civil War," Robert Woodford noted, "but it was revived again when the First World War began and seems to receive some mention with just about every war since then."[57] Former Presiding Bishop Joseph L. Wirthlin exemplified the expanded interpretation section 87 has received. "In many cases," Wirthlin declared, "I am quite sure we all think this has to do particularly with the slaves in the Southern States, but I believe, brethren and sisters, that it was intended that this referred to slaves all over the world, and I think of those, particularly in the land of Russia and other countries wherein they have been taken over by that great nation and where the people are actually the slaves of those individuals who guide and direct the affairs of Russia and China, and where the rights and the privilege to worship God and to come to a knowledge that Jesus Christ is his Son is denied them." Connecting to post–Civil War conflicts, Wirthlin continued:

> In the matter of famine and plague and earthquakes, we can go back to World War I, where 40,000,000 individuals lost their lives either through the war or through famine or plague. And in the world war just passed wherein our own nation was involved, we lost 408,789 of our men. In Korea, we lost 33,629.
>
> The Prophet Joseph gave us this marvelous revelation in 1832. The Civil War came in 1861; the war between Denmark and Prussia in 1864; Italy and Austria in 1865 and 1866; Austria and Prussia in 1866; Russia and Turkey in 1877; China and Japan in 1894 and 1895; Spanish-American in 1898; Japan and Russia in 1904 and 1905; World War I in 1914–1918; then the next war was a comparatively small one, Ethiopia and Italy, when the people in that land of Ethiopia were taken over and controlled by Italy. I am grateful to the Lord that they now have their freedom. Then, the World War just passed and, of course, the Korean War.[58]

A generation later, Elder Neal A. Maxwell reached a similar interpretation: "War has been the almost continuing experience of modern man. There have been 141 wars, large and small, just since the end of World War II in 1945. As the American Civil War was about to begin, the Lord declared there would be a succession of wars poured out upon all nations, resulting in the 'death and misery of many souls' (D&C 87:1). Moreover, that continuum of conflict will culminate in 'a full end of all nations' (D&C 87:6)."[59]

The section's references to additional wars led to one of the most interesting conflicts over the use of Joseph Smith's prophecy. During debate regarding the League of Nations following the end of World War I, Utah senator and Apostle Reed Smoot apparently used the prophecy to lobby against the treaty's passage. Fellow Apostle James E. Talmage recorded in his journal, "There is much agitation throughout the land over the question of the adoption of the Covenant of the League of Nations, and the ratification of the Treaty of Peace. Through an unwise and unwarranted misapplication of Scripture, many sensational newspapers are claiming that the 'Mormon' Church is opposed to the adoption of the Covenant of the League of Nations. Senator Reed Smoot tried to apply certain passages from the Book of Mormon and the Doctrine & Covenants to show that war is yet to come, and therefore that the League of Nations cannot be regarded as a preventative of war. We regret this misrepresentation, upon which the sensational press has seized." In a newspaper account that had apparently reached four million readers, Smoot claimed: "You evidently think that when this covenant is ratified we will have no more wars. Do not be deceived, for such will not be the case. If so, the revelations of Prophet Joseph Smith as recorded in the Doctrine and Covenants are not true. I ask you to read the many passages of the Book of Mormon referring to this nation, as well as the many revelations given to the Prophet Joseph Smith, as to the destiny of the same." A supporter of the League, Talmage retorted, "In this connection it is proper to say that the First Presidency and all members of the Quorum of the Twelve now at home hold unanimously that there is nothing to be found in the standard works of the Church that can in any reasonable way be construed as in opposition to the proposed League of Nations."[60] Though the United States ultimately failed to join the League, the view that section 87 ought not to be used to lobby against it carried the day when, in the subsequent general conference, Talmage observed that "a point emphasized by all [speakers] was that none of the Scriptures accepted by the Church are in any way opposed to the adoption of the proposed League of Nations, but that on the contrary it is the duty of the Church to raise an ensign of peace and to proclaim peace among the nations."[61]

The controversy over Smoot's application of the prophecy to international politics highlights a final shift in the section's use. Indeed, as the Church has become more international, the message of section 87 has broadened. Importantly, focus has turned to the gospel as the means of salvation from calamity. Even as the Civil War began, the *Millennial Star* declared, "What the length of the period may be before all these things be fulfilled, we cannot say; but this we can say, and verily know, that the rebellion of South Carolina is the beginning of wars which will surely 'terminate in the death and misery of many souls' and in the 'consumption decreed,' which is to make 'a full end of all nations.' These events convey this warning—one more powerful to the people of God

and to all the world than any mortal voice is capable of giving—'Stand ye in holy places, and be not moved, until the day of the Lord come; for behold it cometh quickly, saith the Lord. Amen.'"[62] Apostle Marion G. Romney summarized this emphasis, noting that "the Lord's purpose in revealing these unhappy impending calamities was not to condemn but to save mankind is evidenced by the fact that with the warning he identified the cause and revealed the means by which the calamities may be turned aside."[63]

Indeed, the greatest focus in recent decades has been on the phrase in the prophecy encouraging Church members to "stand ye in holy places, and be not moved" (D&C 87:8). Harold B. Lee, Marvin J. Ashton, Neal A. Maxwell, Dallin H. Oaks, Gordon B. Hinckley, Thomas S. Monson, and scores of other General Authorities have all cited D&C 87:8 in the past four decades.[64] Each emphasized that, in spite of difficulties ahead, safety can be found in righteousness. In many ways, Spencer W. Kimball's 1979 plea typifies current use of Joseph Smith's prophecy on war. "Our constant prayer and our major efforts," Kimball announced, "are to see that the members are sanctified through their righteousness. We urge our people to 'stand in holy places' (D&C 87:8)."[65]

CONCLUSION

The use of Joseph Smith's "revelation and prophecy on war" has changed alongside the Church that continues to revere it. Unbounded by time, it reaches beyond the Nullification Crisis that precipitated it, the division between Southern and Northern States it most famously predicted, and even periods when war has been "poured out upon all nations" (D&C 87:3). The history of its receipt, recording, and publication demonstrates how the Church and its leaders have used it as a proof of Joseph's prophetic mantle, a condemnation for a disobedient nation, a warning of future calamity, and even a reason to question international peace efforts. At the same time, the world has reacted with varying levels of wonder, skepticism, cynicism, or ridicule to the notion that a New York farm boy could know the future.

However, though the revelation points to a time when the "chastening hand of an Almighty God" will make "a full end of all nations" (D&C 87:6), it also provides a singular solution for escaping the Lord's wrath (see D&C 87:8). Standing in holy places, Saints have continually benefited from a prophecy on war, delivered to a prophet of God on Christmas Day, 1832, by the Prince of Peace.

Scott C. Esplin is an associate professor of Church history and doctrine at Brigham Young University.

NOTES

1. "A Mormon Prophecy," *Philadelphia Sunday Mercury*, May 5, 1861, cited in Robert J. Woodford, "Historical Development of the Doctrine and Covenants" (PhD diss., Brigham Young University, 1974), 2:1110; emphasis added.

2. Nearly every Doctrine and Covenants commentary discusses the Nullification Crisis of 1832. For examples, see Hyrum M. Smith and Janne M. Sjodahl, *Doctrine and Covenants Commentary* (Salt Lake City: Deseret Book, 1967), 533–34; Lyndon W. Cook, *The Revelations of the Prophet Joseph Smith* (Salt Lake City: Deseret Book, 1985), 180; Stephen E. Robinson and H. Dean Garrett, *A Commentary on the Doctrine and Covenants* (Salt Lake City: Deseret Book, 2004), 3:84–85; Steven C. Harper, *Making Sense of the Doctrine and Covenants: A Guided Tour through Modern Revelations* (Salt Lake City: Deseret Book, 2008), 310.

3. Dean C. Jessee, Mark Ashurst-McGee, and Richard L. Jensen, eds., *Journals, Volume 1: 1832–1839*, vol. 1 of the Journals series of *The Joseph Smith Papers*, ed. Dean C. Jessee, Ronald K. Esplin, and Richard Lyman Bushman (Salt Lake City: Church Historian's Press, 2008), 11.

4. *History of the Church of Jesus Christ of Latter-day Saints*, ed. B. H. Roberts, 2nd ed. rev. (Salt Lake City: Deseret Book, 1980), 1:301. This citation uses Roberts's published edition of *History of the Church*. Interestingly, the manuscript version in Willard Richards's hand is nearly identical, except in one

significant instance. The original states, "The people of North Carolina, in convention assembled," over the top of which someone clearly corrected, "The people of South Carolina, in convention assembled." This error appeared in its original printing in the *Times and Seasons* on November 1, 1844 and the subsequent British reprinting in the *Latter-day Saints' Millennial Star* on July 3, 1852.

5. Donald Q. Cannon, "A Prophecy of War (D&C 87)," in *Studies in Scripture*, vol. 1: *The Doctrine and Covenants*, ed. Robert L. Millet and Kent P. Jackson (Sandy, UT: Randall Book, 1984), 335; for an extended analysis, see William W. Freehling, *Prelude to Civil War: The Nullification Controversy in South Carolina, 1816–1836* (New York: Harper & Row, 1965).

6. *History of the Church*, 1:315. In addition to section 87, this statement by the Prophet may have been influenced by earlier revelations referring to destruction upon the American continent, including D&C 38:28–29, 42:64, and 45:63–64. Seaton apparently only published a portion of Joseph's message in his newspaper, which drew the ire of the Prophet (see *History of the Church*, 1:326).

7. Determining which copy is the earliest is problematic because the records were kept simultaneously. Revelation Book 1, kept by John Whitmer and used in Missouri during the publication of the Book of Commandments, generally appears to be the more complete record because it contains some revelations missing from Revelation Book 2. However, this

particular revelation would have been delivered to Whitmer, as he was in Missouri while the Prophet was in Ohio in December 1832. Revelation Book 2, on the other hand, was kept in Kirtland by Joseph Smith and his scribes during the time this revelation was received. Interestingly, for some reason Oliver Cowdery made a second copy of the revelation, including it as the last item in Revelation Book 1, dated July 3, 1835. Also, though dated December 25, 1832, in Revelation Book 2, the text itself was likely copied into that collection by the Prophet's scribe, Frederick G. Williams, sometime later because Williams referred to himself as "counceller" to Joseph Smith in the line immediately preceding this section. He was not appointed to that position until January 22, 1833. Robin Scott Jensen, Robert J. Woodford, and Steven C. Harper, eds., *Revelations and Translations, Volume 1: Manuscript Revelation Books*, vol. 1 of the Revelations and Translations series of *The Joseph Smith Papers*, ed. Dean C. Jessee, Ronald K. Esplin, and Richard Lyman Bushman (Salt Lake City: Church Historian's Press, 2009), "Revelation Book 2," 5–6, 290–91, 380–83, 409, and 476–79.

8. Wilford Woodruff, in *Journal of Discourses* (London: Latter-day Saints' Book Depot, 1854–86), 10:13. Woodruff's writing down of the revelation was an idea he frequently repeated (see *Journal of Discourses*, 10:219, 14:2, 22:175, and 24:242).

9. Woodruff, in *Journal of Discourses*, 14:2.

10. Woodford, "Historical Development of the Doctrine and Covenants," 2:1112–14. Of the eight copies, two are identified in Phelps's hand (with a third also possibly his), two in the hand of Thomas Bullock, one each by Willard Richards and Edward Partridge, and a final one that is unidentified.

11. Orson Pratt, in *Journal of Discourses*, 18:224–25. Like Woodruff, Pratt frequently referred to his use of this section (see *Journal of Discourses*, 13:135, 18:340–41).

12. Brigham Young, in *Journal of Discourses*, 8:58. An *escritoire* is a writing desk.

13. Orson Pratt, in *Journal of Discourses*, 13:193–94.

14. See "History of Joseph Smith," *Times and Seasons*, November 1, 1844, 688; "History of Joseph Smith," *Millennial Star*, July 3, 1852, 296.

15. Woodruff, in *Journal of Discourses*, 14:2.

16. H. Donl Peterson, *The Pearl of Great Price: A History and Commentary* (Salt Lake City: Deseret Book, 1987), 9.

17. Franklin D. Richards to Levi Richards, February 1, 1851, cited in Peterson, *Pearl of Great Price*, 11; emphasis in original. See also Journal History of The Church of Jesus Christ of Latter-day Saint, April 10, 1896, 6, Church History Library, http://ldsarch.lib.byu.edu/CD%20Volume%202/Disc19/v322-323/seg8.htm.

18. Preface to the Pearl of Great Price (Liverpool, 1851), cited in Peterson, *Pearl of Great Price*, 13–15.

19. To eliminate duplication, the revelation on war was finally removed from the 1902 Pearl of Great Price edition (see Peterson, *Pearl of Great Price*, 23).

20. Journal History, October 10, 1880, 4, http://ldsarch.lib.byu.edu/CD%20Volume%202/Disc8/v135-137/seg25.htm.

21. Orson Hyde, in *Journal of Discourses*, 8:236.

22. Orson Pratt, in *Journal of Discourses*, 13:135.

23. George Q. Cannon, in *Journal of Discourses*, 21:265–66. Like Woodruff and Pratt, Cannon made frequent reference both to this revelation and to his experience with it (see *Journal of Discourses* 12:41, 22:135, and 23:104–5).

24. "A Mormon Prophecy," *New York Times*, June 2, 1861, 3.

25. "Continuation of Letter from Great Salt Lake," *Daily Evening Bulletin*, July 23, 1858.

26. "Affairs in Utah," *New York Times*, June 7, 1860, 1.

27. "Interesting News from Utah," *New York Herald*, November 18, 1860, 2.

28. George Q. Cannon, in *Journal of Discourses*, 22:135.

29. George Q. Cannon, in *Journal of Discourses*, 23:104.

30. "War," *Seer*, April 1854, 241–47.

31. "The Dark Day of the United States," *Millennial Star*, January 28, 1860, 51.

32. "The Dark Day of the United States," *Millennial Star*, January 28, 1860, 52–53.

33. "Division of the United States—Causes Which Have Hastened It," *Millennial Star*, February 16, 1861, 100–101.

34. Brigham Young, in *Journal of Discourses*, 8:195.

35. "Mormonism and the War," *Tri-Weekly Miner Register*, October 15, 1862.

36. Brigham Young, in *Journal of Discourses*, 10:294–95.

37. John Taylor, in *Journal of Discourses*, 11:92–93.

38. John Taylor, in *Journal of Discourses*, 10:278.

39. Brigham Young, in *Journal of Discourses*, 9:367.

40. "Mormonism and the War," *Tri-Weekly Miner Register*, October 15, 1862.

41. George Q. Cannon, in *Journal of Discourses*, 24:140. See also George Q. Cannon, in *Journal of Discourses*, 25:176.

42. B. H. Roberts, in *Journal of Discourses*, 25:143. Interestingly, not only did B. H. Roberts characterize the changing use of D&C 87; he had a hand in changing slightly the wording of the text itself. Early print versions of D&C 87 concluded verse 3 with the phrase "and *thus* war shall be poured out upon all nations" (emphasis added). During the height of World War I, Roberts remarked in the October 1916 general conference, "It reads in the current print of the Doctrine and Covenants 'and "thus" war shall be poured out upon all nations.' But when revising the *History of the Church* some years ago, we found that in the manuscript, it read 'then,' that is, when Great Britain shall call upon other nations to defend herself against other nations, 'then war shall be poured out upon all nations,'" thereby applying the verse to the present conflict. B. H. Roberts, in Conference Report, October 1916, 141. The Church changed the wording from *thus* to *then* beginning with the 1921 edition of the Doctrine and Covenants. See B. H. Roberts, *A Comprehensive History of the Church of Jesus Christ of Latter-day Saints* (Salt Lake City: Deseret News, 1948–57), 1:300–301. *Then* is, indeed, in the manuscript version of the *History of the Church*, as penned by Willard Richards in Nauvoo. However, earlier manuscript copies preserve both options. "Then" is used in John Whitmer's version of the revelation, found in Revelation Book 1, but "thus" is used in Oliver Cowdery's later copy in the same book and in Frederick G. Williams's version recorded in Revelation Book 2. See note 7 and Jensen, Woodford, and Harper, *Revelations and Translations, Volume 1: Manuscript Revelation Books*, 5–6, 290–91, 380–81, and 478–79.

43. Joseph F. Smith, in *Journal of Discourses*, 25:97.

44. Orson Pratt, in *Journal of Discourses*, 12:344.

45. Orson Pratt, in *Journal of Discourses*, 17:319.

46. John Taylor, in *Journal of Discourses*, 20:318.

47. Orson Pratt, in *Journal of Discourses*, 20:151.

48. Brigham Young, in *Journal of Discourses*, 12:242.

49. Wilford Woodruff, in *Journal of Discourses*, 22:175; see also Wilford Woodruff, in *Journal of Discourses*, 24:242; and George Q. Cannon, in *Journal of Discourses*, 22:178.

50. "The Prophet Joe Smith," *Salt Lake Tribune*, April 8, 1874, 2.

51. "The Mormon Faith," *Daily Evening Bulletin*, October 12, 1874.

52. "Author of the Book of Mormon," *Daily Inter Ocean*, June 11, 1881.

53. "Mormon Priests," *News and Observer*, March 27, 1895, 5.

54. "Mormon Prophecies," *Bangor Daily Whig & Courier*, March 2, 1867.

55. Ezra Taft Benson, in Conference Report, October 1981, 83.

56. See Thomas G. Alexander, *Mormonism in Transition: A History of the Latter-day Saints, 1890–1930* (Urbana: University of Illinois Press, 1986), 288–90. See also Grant Underwood, *The Millenarian World of Early Mormonism* (Urbana: University of Illinois Press, 1993).

57. Woodford, "Historical Development of the Doctrine and Covenants," 2:1109.

58. Joseph L. Wirthlin, in Conference Report, October 1958, 32–33.

59. Neal A. Maxwell, in Conference Report, October 1982, 96.

60. James E. Talmage, September 17, 1919, James E. Talmage Diary, in James Edward Talmage Collection; L. Tom Perry Special Collections, Harold B. Lee Library, Brigham Young University, Provo, UT.

61. James E. Talmage, October 3, 1919, James E. Talmage Diary, in James Edward Talmage Collection; L. Tom Perry Special Collections.

62. "Division of the United States—Causes Which Have Hastened It," *Millennial Star*, February 16, 1861, 102.

63. Marion G. Romney, in Conference Report, April 1965, 104.

64. See Harold B. Lee, in Conference Report, October 1971, 62; Marvin J. Ashton, in Conference Report, April 1974, 52; Thomas S. Monson, "Pathways to Perfection," *Ensign*, May 2002, 99; Neal A. Maxwell, in Conference Report, October 2002, 17; Dallin H. Oaks, in Conference Report, April 2004, 8; Gordon B. Hinckley, in Conference Report, October 2005, 65–66.

65. Spencer W. Kimball, in Conference Report, April 1979, 115.

Abraham Lincoln and his son Tad are shown looking at a photographic album in this studio portrait taken by Mathew Brady on February 4, 1864. This is the only known close-up photograph showing Lincoln wearing spectacles. (Library of Congress)

CHAPTER 4

Mary Jane Woodger

ABRAHAM LINCOLN AND THE MORMONS

In early June of 1863, Brigham Young sent Mormon convert and journalist Thomas B. H. Stenhouse to transact Church business in Washington, DC, and to ascertain what policy President Abraham Lincoln would pursue in regard to the Mormons. At this time, Stenhouse was an active Church member and an assistant editor of the *Deseret News*. Stenhouse "had a wide reputation throughout America and [had] journalistic contact with hundreds of editors east and west with whom he was personally acquainted."[1] When Stenhouse asked Lincoln about his intentions in regard to the Mormon situation, Lincoln reportedly responded: "Stenhouse, when I was a boy on the farm in Illinois there was a great deal of timber on the farm which we had to clear away. Occasionally we would come to a log which had fallen down. It was too hard to split, too wet to burn, and too heavy to move, so we plowed around it. You go back and tell Brigham Young that if he will let me alone I will let him alone."[2]

George A. Hubbard, who has done extensive research on this subject, sees this incident as "the real turning point in the Mormon attitude toward President Lincoln." Hubbard suggests, "This was precisely the kind of governmental policy which the Mormons had sought in vain" since The Church of Jesus Christ of Latter-day Saints was organized thirty-three years earlier.[3] During his tenure as president of the United States, Lincoln influenced the history of the Church when his path intersected with the Mormons. Hubbard added, "It was the political activities of both Lincoln and the Mormons that brought them into contact with each other."[4] Lincoln's political career from 1834 to 1860 centered in the area of Springfield, Illinois, about 120 miles southeast of Nauvoo. As a lawyer, a member of the Illinois State Legislature, and finally the chief executive of the nation, Lincoln filled key positions which inherently involved interaction with LDS Church leaders. Lincoln's attitude of restraint and even unconcern toward the Mormons became important in the history of the Church during the Civil War when he was president. Such an attitude may have been in part because of his associations with Latter-day Saints during his early political career.

As Brigham Young was establishing communities in the West, Lincoln made several executive decisions that affected their lives and history. Lincoln is known for his ability to value people despite individual differences, a characteristic that led to generous decisions in his assessment of the Latter-day Saints. He could have demanded that a moral high ground be maintained in his positions; instead, he consistently took a stance of toleration.

A February 1857 photograph of Abraham Lincoln taken prior to his nomination as a U.S. senator. (Brady National Photographic Art Gallery)

NAUVOO

As the Saints moved into Hancock County, Illinois, beginning in the spring of 1839, Hancock County leaned toward the Whig Party. In both the 1836 and 1838 elections, Hancock County voted overwhelmingly Whig.[5] However, both political parties welcomed the Mormons and energetically tried to secure their support.[6] Although Stephen A. Douglas was in his twenties during the late 1830s and early 1840s, he was seen as the foremost Democrat in the area.[7] In December 1839, Lincoln and Douglas had first debated each other and repeatedly faced one another across Illinois in the spring and summer of 1840 as they campaigned for each party's presidential nominee: Lincoln for Whig William Henry Harrison, and Douglas for Democrat Martin Van Buren. Political historian and Douglas biographer Robert W. Johansen observed that Douglas immediately befriended the Church

leaders when the Mormons emigrated from Missouri in 1838. At the time, he lived in nearby Quincy and served as the circuit court judge in the Fifth Judicial Circuit, which included Hancock County.[8]

According to Johannsen, Douglas also emphasized that the Mormons had their "right to worship God as [they pleased]," while Lincoln was seen as somewhat irreligious.[9] Lincoln once observed, "It was every where contended that no ch[r]istian ought to go for me, because I belonged to no church, was suspected of being a deist, and had talked about fighting a duel."[10] Though the 1840s saw the tail end of the Second Great Awakening, launched about fifty years earlier, the general climate created social pressure to join a church. Remaining religiously unattached created a political disadvantage for Lincoln, who distanced himself from organized religion and generally refused to discuss his beliefs.[11]

As Hubbard observes, "The Mormon vote at this time virtually assured the outcome of any election in Hancock County; and as a result of this unique position, the Mormons frequently, and sometimes unexpectedly, shifted their support from one party to the other in order to bargain for political favors."[12] In the presidential election in November 1840, Hancock County (mostly a Mormon constituency) voted for William Henry Harrison, the Whig candidate, with 752 votes. But to recognize both parties, two hundred Mormons voted as a block, scratching off the last name on the Whig electoral ticket and substituting that of a Democrat, James H. Ralston. The name they marked off was that of Abraham Lincoln, who was then running for presidential elector but lost.[13] This direct snub did not seem to influence Lincoln's later decisions regarding Mormons. According to historian Daniel Walker Howe, Lincoln was still one of the Illinois politicians most sympathetic to Mormons.[14]

In December of 1840, John C. Bennett, seeking a charter for their city, led a Mormon delegation representing fifteen thousand votes to the state legislature.[15] They succeeded in obtaining an expansive charter that included provisions for a military legion, a city council, and a university. Bennett reported to the LDS *Times and Seasons*:

> Many members in this house, likewise, were warmly in our favor, and with only one or two dissenting voices, *every* representative appeared inclined to extend to us all such powers as they considered us justly entitled to, and voted for the law: and here I should not forget to mention that Lincoln, whose name we erased from the electoral ticket in November, (not, however, on account of any dislike to him as a man, but simply because his was the last name on the ticket, and we desired to show our friendship to the Democratic party by substituting the name of Ralston for some one of the Whigs,) had the magnanimity to vote for our act, and came forward, after the final vote, to the bar of the house, and cordially congratulated me on its passage.[16]

Though Lincoln had voted affirmatively for the Nauvoo Charter, Church leaders apparently preferred Douglas to Lincoln. On New Year's Day in 1842, Joseph Smith himself expressed gratitude for Douglas in the *Times and Seasons*: "Douglass is a *Master Spirit*, and *his friends are our friends*—we are willing to cast our banners on the air, and fight by his side in the cause of humanity, and equal rights—the cause of liberty and the law."[17]

However, at one time Joseph Smith made a statement about Lincoln's future presidential opponent that could be viewed as either a curse or a warning. William Clayton, Joseph Smith's private secretary who was present at the time, reported a conversation that took place on May 18, 1843. Stephen Douglas was dining with Joseph Smith at Backenstos's in Carthage. After the meal, Douglas asked the Prophet to describe the Saints' experiences in Missouri. For three hours the Prophet gave a history of the persecution the Saints had endured. He also shared his experience with President Van Buren. Judge Douglas listened attentively and was empathetic. In conclusion, Joseph Smith then said, "Judge, you will aspire to the presidency of the United States; and if ever you turn your hand against me or the Latter-day Saints, you will feel the weight of the hand of Almighty upon you; and you will live to see and know that I have testified the truth to you; for the conversation of this day will stick to you through life."[18]

This prophecy was first published in Utah in the *Deseret News* of September 24, 1856, and then published in England in the *Millennial Star* in February 1859 in the "History of Joseph Smith" section. The publication of this prophecy added to the folk belief that would be with Latter-day Saints for generations that Douglas and Smith had a close personal relationship.

JOSEPH SMITH AND ABRAHAM LINCOLN

Lincoln and Joseph Smith were in the Illinois State Capital at the same time from November 4 to 8, 1839, and from December 31, 1842, to January 6, 1843.[19] Although there is no evidence that the two men had any personal contact, they were probably aware of each other's presence in the city and had the opportunity to meet in person if either desired to do so.

Joseph Smith Jr., founder of The Church of Jesus Christ of Latter-day Saints. While there has been much research on the topic, there is no direct evidence that Joseph Smith and Abraham Lincoln met face-to-face. (Del Parson, American Prophet, *© 2001 IRI)*

With the murder of Joseph Smith in June 1844 at Carthage, Illinois, "Douglas and his fellow Democrats demanded that the Prophet's murderers be brought to justice, while the Whigs [Lincoln's party] slipped into an increasingly anti-Mormon stance," summarized Bruce A. Van Orden. The next fall saw a "continued deterioration [of] relationships

between the Mormons and their Illinois neighbors." Governor Thomas Ford commissioned four politicians, including Douglas, to raise an armed volunteer force to "negotiate the removal of the Mormons from Illinois."[20] The commission convinced Brigham Young and other Church leaders to leave the state by the

Photograph of Abraham Lincoln taken at Pittsfield, Illinois, October 1, 1858, two weeks before the final Lincoln–Douglas debate in Lincoln's unsuccessful bid for the Senate. (Photo by Calvin Jackson, Library of Congress)

next spring.[21] During the Mormons' early years in the West, "Douglas continued to serve as a contact" in Congress for the Church.[22] Lincoln served his only term in Congress during the Mormon exodus (1847–49).

THE PRESIDENCY AND THE TERRITORY, 1848–60

During the 1840s, according to Douglas's biographer, Lincoln wanted to be seen as the leader who would "provide [the] governmental organization to the west."[23] Lincoln aides and memoirists John Hay and John G. Nicolay observed that, by 1852, "the control of legislation for the territories was for the moment completely in the hands of Douglas. He was himself chairman of the Committee of the Senate; and his special personal friend and political lieutenant in his own State, William A. Richardson, of Illinois, was chairman of the Territorial Committee of the House."[24]

During the stormy political controversy over the Compromise of 1850, "Douglas and other Northern Democrats contended that slavery was subject to local law, and that the people of a Territory, like those of a State, could establish or prohibit it."[25] "After months of wrangling and compromising," writes Van Orden, "Congress barely succeeded in September 1850 in passing the several laws, including the Organic Act establishing Utah Territory, which made up the Compromise of 1850."[26] "By these provisions, . . . California was admitted to the Union as a free state; the territories of Utah and New Mexico were organized . . . , later to be 'received into the Union, with or without slavery, as their constitutions . . . [might] prescribe at the time of their admission.'"[27]

While Douglas was engineering the Compromise of 1850, Lincoln had no national presence but had resumed his law practice in Illinois. Six years later, Lincoln became one of the founders of the Republican Party in Illinois. At their first national convention in February 1856 in Philadelphia, Republicans adopted a plank in their platform that it was "the duty of Congress to prohibit in the Territories those twin relics of barbarism, polygamy and slavery."[28]

This 1860 photograph of Abraham Lincoln was taken during his presidential campaign. (Library of Congress)

Douglas, running a strong Democratic campaign, committed a strategic error in making the Mormons and Utah a campaign issue, according to Van Orden. Douglas had "engineered" the Kansas–Nebraska Act, maneuvering it "through Congress to promote his 'popular sovereignty' doctrine," in 1854.[29] The 1854 Kansas–Nebraska Act dogged Douglas in his presidential campaign of 1856, his senatorial contest against Lincoln in 1858, and his presidential campaign in 1860. Douglas's opponents attacked his role in the Kansas–Nebraska Act as a way to "bring Utah in[to the Union] as a polygamous state."[30] The Republican Party immediately hopped on the bandwagon, hoping to make political hay out of Mormon polygamy. On June 12, 1857, with Lincoln present, the grand jury of Springfield's district court "asked Douglas to express his views on three of the most important topics 'now agitating the minds of the American people'—Kansas, the Dred Scott decision, and conditions in Utah Territory."[31] Douglas tried to position himself as a super-patriot by being extremely critical of the Mormons, accusing them of being "bound by horrid oaths and terrible penalties to recognize and maintain the authority of Brigham Young." He also said the Mormons were attempting "to subvert the Government of the United States, and resist its authority." Among his charges were the following: (1) nine-tenths of Utah's citizens were aliens who refused to become naturalized, (2) Brigham Young was guilty of inciting the

Indians to rob and murder American citizens, (3) the Mormons were a "loathsome, disgusting ulcer," (4) Utah's territorial government and the Organic Act should be repealed, and (5) Brigham Young should be brought back east to stand trial—in Missouri. The "Little Giant" closed his speech by inviting anyone with a better proposition to bring it forward.[32] Lincoln, who was present in the audience, promised a rebuttal in two weeks.[33]

Although Lincoln's main thrust in his rebuttal was to contend that popular sovereignty was ineffective, he also refuted Douglas's plans for Utah.[34] Without Douglas being present, he began his half-hour speech with this:

> I am here to-night, partly by the invitation of some of you, and partly by my own inclination. Two weeks ago Judge Douglas spoke here on the several subjects of Kansas, the Dred Scott decision and Utah. I listened to the speech at the time, and have read the report of it since. It was intended to controvert opinions which I think just, and to assail (politically not personally,) those men who, in common with me, entertain those opinions. For this reason I wished then, and still wish, to make some answer to it, which I now take the opportunity of doing. I begin with Utah.[35]

Civil War scholar E. B. Long tells us that Lincoln's reference to the Mormons was "mainly in the context of his arguments with Senator Douglas over state sovereignty. He was critical of Douglas's suggestion to divide up Utah, as that would not be in line with the senator's view of popular sovereignty."[36] Lincoln's response included the following:

> If it prove to be true, as is probable, that the people of Utah are in open rebellion to the United States, . . . I say too, if they are in rebellion, they ought to be somehow coerced to obedience. . . .[37]

But in all this, it is very plain the Judge evades the only question the Republicans have ever pressed upon the Democracy in regard to Utah. That question the Judge well knew to be this: "If the people of Utah shall peacefully form a State Constitution tolerating polygamy, will the Democracy admit them into the Union?" There is nothing in the United States constitution or Law against polygamy; and why is it not a part of the Judge's "sacred right of self-government" for the people to have it, or rather to keep it, if they choose?[38]

Lincoln took this stance not because he supported polygamy but because Douglas opposed it, even in a territory where the people wanted it. Polygamy thus became evidence of the glaring inconsistency of popular sovereignty. Lincoln saw the Mormons as a political problem to be managed, and he used the issue to embarrass Douglas by pushing his thinking to a logical conclusion. That polygamy is not forbidden by the Constitution was an argumentative point, not a defense of it. For the most part, Mormons in Utah completely ignored Lincoln's rebuttal but were vehement about Douglas's speech. A *Deseret News* editorial provided a lengthy review of Douglas's speech condemning polygamy, followed by the account of the interview between Joseph Smith and Douglas as recorded in the Journal of William Clayton.[39]

In the *Virginia Law Review*, Attorney Kelly Elizabeth Phipps argues that, while the reasons for criticizing polygamy have changed over time, Lincoln's tough question remains the same: "How do you draw the line between rescuing victims and oppressing communities?" Before the Civil War, Northern politicians, including Lincoln, portrayed polygamy as another Southern slave power waiting to rebel. In these politicians' view, polygamists were holding their wives hostage as slaves.

In the mid-nineteenth century, opposition to polygamy was always linked to slavery. Lincoln Republicans portrayed Mormon plural wives as innocent victims held in subjugation akin to enslaved blacks in the South. They wanted to purge the nation of licentious power, including such tyrants as "slave-masters and polygamous husbands."[40] As a Republican, Lincoln was committed to ending slavery in the territories and argued that the federal government, not popular sovereignty, should govern territories, including Utah. Utah became vital to his vision of expanded power for the federal government, and he continued to use Utah "to illustrate the flaw in Stephen A. Douglas' 'Popular Sovereignty' argument."[41]

Although Lincoln was willing to invoke polygamy to validate federal power to govern the territories, he was not committed to any particular plan for using federal power to eradicate the practice. This stance worked to the advantage of Mormons who were committed to continuing plural marriage. By 1860, with Lincoln as the leader of the Republican

Abraham Lincoln in a reflective pose (May 16, 1861). (Library of Congress)

Party, the platform dropped all references to polygamy; and in Lincoln's presidential race, antipolygamy was seen as a derivative of the antislavery movement.[42]

In a speech given on April 10, 1860, at Bloomington, Illinois, six weeks before he would accept the Republican nomination, Lincoln reminded his listeners that only that week the U.S. House of Representatives had passed HR7, which was designed to punish the practice of polygamy. "While the Senate would ultimately let the bill languish and die in committee," the issue of polygamy was still on Lincoln's mind.[43] A newspaper account of his speech summarized, "Mr. Lincoln said he *supposed* that the friends of popular sovereignty would say—if they dared speak out—that *polygamy* was wrong and slavery right; and therefore one might thus be put down and the other not."[44] Thus, prior to his presidency, Lincoln did not seem concerned with polygamy except as an illustration of political principles. Lincoln's attitude was instrumental in allowing the Saints to get a foothold in the West. If he had been adamant about eradicating polygamy during the 1860s, conditions would have been much different for the LDS Church.

Many Mormons believed that, because Douglas turned against the Mormons, he failed politically as Joseph Smith had prophesied and that despite Douglas's popularity, Lincoln had ascended to the presidency. Van Orden tells us that "according to Mormon

Major Allan Pinkerton, President Lincoln, and General John A. McClelland at Antietam, Maryland, in October 1862. (National Archives)

tradition, Douglas had every reason to believe that he would win the presidency, but would lose according to Joseph Smith's prophecy."[45]

The people of Utah learned of Lincoln's election in the weekly *Deseret News* on November 14, 1860. On November 28, it editorialized:

There will be jolly times at the seat of Government during the session, and the members of Congress will have enough business to attend to, in all probability, in which they will be more particularly interested and concerned than in the annihilation of the Saints; and may be expected to be otherwise engaged, than in providing for . . . the overthrow and destruction of those, who by the spirit of inspiration, have long been advised of the calamities that were coming upon the nations, and upon the United States in particular, in consequence of the iniquities and abominations, of the people and their rejection of the gospel which has been proclaimed unto them.[46]

This editorial is only one of many forecasts of doom that had been uttered since the days of Joseph Smith and would continue to be repeated in the years to come. Nor were Mormons the only religion to make dire predictions. Although Mormons were glad that Lincoln had triumphed over Douglas, they were still not in Lincoln's corner. On November 19, 1860, Brigham Young wrote territorial delegate William H. Hooper that Mormons "from outside the borders of Utah were very much chopfallen at Lincoln's election."[47] When Douglas died in June 1861, Brigham Young told his office intimates that Douglas "should be president in the lower world."[48] Two months later, however, Young remarked to the same group that "Stephen A. Douglas was a far better man than President Abel [sic] Lincoln for he [Young] knew his [Lincoln's] feelings were hostile to this people."[49]

Previously, on December 20, 1860, Young had written to Hooper, By your letters and papers I perceive that the secession question was being violently agitated, but without much definite action. Latest accounts seem to indicate that the South will so far back down as to give "Old Abe" a trial as to what course he will pursue. . . . But while the waves of commotion are whelming nearly the whole country, Utah in her rock fortresses is biding

her time to step in and rescue the constitution and aid all lovers of freedom in sustaining such laws as will secure justice and rights to all irrespective of creed or party.[50]

Although Young did not know it, South Carolina had seceded on the same day, December 20, and the South, of course, did not back down. On January 25, 1861, after receiving news by Pony Express, Young commented to his office intimates, "If Abraham Lincoln when inaugurated would coerce the South there would be a pretty fight and if he did not he would be no President at all. . . . [W]hen Anarchy and confusion reigned the Devil's poor prospered."[51]

Prior to Lincoln's presidency, the Mormons had petitioned Congress for statehood twice, in 1850 and 1856. Still hoping for statehood, Mormons were angered when Nevada Territory was created on March 2, 1861, just two days before Lincoln's inauguration, and was assigned some of the land that had previously belonged to Utah Territory.[52]

Brigham Young's records provide a veritable litany of negativity about the government in general and Abraham Lincoln in particular. On March 15, Young criticized, "Abe Lincoln was no friend to Christ, particularly, he had never raised his voice in our favor when he was aware that we were being persecuted."[53] At the April conference in 1861, Young declared that Lincoln was a very weak executive: "Like a rope of sand, or like a rope made of water. He is as weak as water."[54] By July 9, 1861, Young confided to those in his office: "Old 'Abe' the President of the U. S. has it in his mind to pitch into us when he had got through with the South. . . . Pres. Young was of opinion the sympathy of the people for the South was in case they should be whipped, and the northern party remain in power, he thought they wanted the war to go [so] that both parties might be used up." Two days later, on July 11, he suggested, "It would not do for the northern and southern party to fight too much at once." On July 24, Young accused the government as having "in them a spirit to destroy everything."[55]

In the Bowery on July 28, Young declared:

President Lincoln called out soldiers for three months, and was going to wipe the blot of secession from the escutcheon of the American Republic. The three months are gone, and the labor is scarcely begun. Now they are beginning to enlist men for three years; soon they will want to enlist during the war; and then, I was going to say, they will want them to enlist during the duration of hell. Do they know what they are doing? No; but they have begun to empty the earth, to cleanse the land, and prepare the way for the return of the Latter-day Saints to the centre Stake of Zion.[56]

With this attitude of suspicion, Young entered into a turbulent relationship with the nation's chief executive as a "nongovernor" and Church leader.

UTAH TERRITORY DURING THE CIVIL WAR

Though Utah is seldom seen as being part of the Civil War, Long argues that its role was "central to the American West during the Civil War, . . . though it receives scant mention in Civil War histories and only a little more in volumes on the American West. Utah

Territory would have been important because of its geographical position astride transportation and communications arteries even if it had not been an anomaly. And it was also unprecedented in this country, being both a civil and a religious entity of considerable size and influence."[57]

During the war, many Americans found Utah's support for the Union inadequate. Although most Mormons were from the North and Midwest and therefore favored the North, Church leadership took a neutral position. On July 4, 1861, Apostle John Taylor announced, "We know no North, no South, no East, no West; we abide strictly and positively by the Constitution, and cannot, by the intrigues or sophism of either party, be cajoled into any other attitude."[58]

Edward Tullidge, Brigham Young's contemporary biographer, believed that if the Southern states had done precisely what Utah did and placed themselves on the defensive ground of their rights and institutions and under the political leadership of Brigham Young, they might have triumphed. Tullidge stated:

With the exception of the slavery question and the policy of seccession, the South stood upon the same ground that Utah had stood upon just previously. True, she had no intention to follow any example set by Utah, for old and powerful States, which had ranked first in the Union from the very foundation of the nation, would not have taken Utah as their example. Yet this very fact, coupled with the stupendous view of North and South engaged in deadly conflict, shows how fundamental was the cause which Utah maintained, and how pregnant were the times with a common national issue. . . . Brigham Young stands not only justified, but his conduct claims extraordinary admiration, for he led his people safely through that controversy without seccession.[59]

On October 22, 1861, General James Arlington Bennett of New York, who had left the Mormon Church in 1844, asked Lincoln if one thousand to ten thousand Mormon volunteers could be accepted for military service.[60] No existing record shows whether Bennett had spontaneously floated this possibility or one of Brigham's agents had asked him to do it. Lincoln could have drafted Mormons into the Union cause, since they were citizens in a territory. For unknown reasons, Lincoln denied the request, thus preserving Mormon isolation. Except for Lot Smith's Company,[61] Utah basically opted out of the Civil War—a fray that claimed more casualties than all other wars in American history from the Revolution to Vietnam combined.[62]

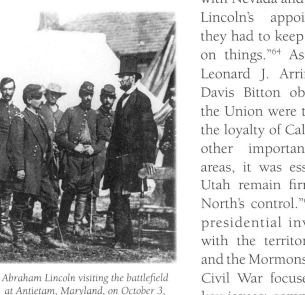

Abraham Lincoln visiting the battlefield at Antietam, Maryland, on October 3, 1862. (Photo by Alexander Gardner, Library of Congress)

After Lincoln nominee John Titus, chief justice of the Utah Territorial Court, was appointed May 6, 1863, his actions showed him to be in harmony with the policy for the Saints in Utah to "let them alone." Titus allegedly observed that the only desire of the Utah populace, since being admitted as a territory, was such: "To be left alone."[63] According to

Lincoln historian Calvin N. Smith, "While Lincoln would have been happy to ignore the Mormons during those turbulent years of his presidency, he was unable to do so. The Utah Territory, in general, and Salt Lake City, in particular, comprised vital links in the Union's communication and transportation system with Nevada and California; Lincoln's appointees felt they had to keep a keen eye on things."[64] As historians Leonard J. Arrington and Davis Bitton observed, "If the Union were to maintain the loyalty of California and other important western areas, it was essential that Utah remain firmly in the North's control."[65] Lincoln's presidential involvement with the territory of Utah and the Mormons during the Civil War focused on four key issues: communication, transportation, polygamy, and federal appointees.

Communication and transportation. One act of Lincoln's presidency that had a direct impact on Utah was shifting the stage lines north, away from Confederate troops with a new route passing directly through Salt Lake City. A key segment of the transcontinental telegraph also ran through Utah. According to Edward Tullidge, Utah pioneers were among the "first projectors and first proposers to the American nation of a trans-continental railroad" and telegraph.[66] The Enabling Act, which provided "aid in the construction of a railroad and telegraph line from The Missouri river to the Pacific ocean, and to secure to the government the use of the same for postal, military, and other purposes" was signed by Lincoln on July 1, 1862.[67] The telegraph was a tremendous improvement in communication speed over the short-lived Pony Express.[68] The telegraph also provided communicational support for the North. Brigham Young sent his first telegram on October 18, 1861, to J. H. Wade, president of the Pacific Telegraph Company, in Cleveland, Ohio. It does not reflect his earlier negative comments about Lincoln but instead affirms, "Utah has not seceded, but is firm for the Constitution and laws of our once happy country." President Lincoln sent a return message two days later, on October 20: "The completion of the Telegraph to Great Salt Lake City, is auspicious of the stability and union of the Republic. The Government reciprocates your congratulations."[69]

An 1862 portrait of Brigham Young, whose views of Abraham Lincoln were often less than favorable. (Charles R. Savage Photograph Collection, L. Tom Perry Special Collections, Harold B. Lee Library, Brigham Young University)

To deal with concerns that Indians might attempt to destroy or disable the telegraph, Young wired Washington, DC, on April 14, 1862, asserting that "the militia of Utah are ready and able . . . to take care of all the Indians within [Utah's] borders."[70] On April 26, 1862, Milton S. Latham, a U.S. representative from California, sent a wire to Lincoln about the "depredations which Indians were committing on the line of the Overland Mail and Telegraph near Independence Rock" and suggested that a troop of one hundred Mormons be raised and equipped to protect the telegraph.[71] Acting on this advice, Lincoln bypassed federal appointees and authorized

Young to raise, arm, and equip one company of cavalry for ninety days of service.

Despite the quick Mormon response, Colonel Patrick Edward Connor and a force of seven hundred California volunteers were ordered into Salt Lake City, arriving on October 22, 1862. Connor eventually built a camp on the eastern bench overlooking the city and named it Camp Douglas, to honor Stephen A. Douglas, who had turned against the Mormon people.[72] Historically, this situation is baffling and remains without satisfactory explanation.[73]

The Union Pacific broke ground in Omaha on December 2, 1863. On that day, Young sent Lincoln a telegram that read, "Let the hands of the honest be united to aid the great national improvement."[74] Young lost no time in showing his own support and, on July 1, 1862, "subscribed for $5,000 worth of stock in the newly organized Union Pacific Railroad Company, and became a director in 1865."[75] From that day on, Young contracted with both the Union Pacific and Central Pacific railroads to furnish supplies and "grade all of the transcontinental line in Utah, thus bringing cash revenue to Mormons and inhibiting the influx of non-Mormon laborers."[76] Union Pacific historian L. O. Leonard asserts that "no statesman that ever lived had a keener interest in the Union Pacific than Abraham Lincoln."[77] However, most of the construction in or near Utah occurred after Lincoln's assassination. The railroad itself was completed with a ceremonial uniting of both

Located on a picturesque hilltop in Washington, D.C., President Lincoln's cottage is the most significant historic site directly associated with Lincoln's presidency aside from the White House. During the Civil War, President Lincoln and his family resided here from June to November of 1862, 1863, and 1864. (Carol M. Highsmith's America, Library of Congress, Prints and Photographs Division)

railway lines on May 10, 1869, at Promontory Point, Utah.

Polygamy. On November 18, 1861, the Executive Mansion borrowed the following books from the Library of Congress: *The Works of Victor Hugo*, John Gunnison's *The Mormons or Latter Day Saints*, John Hyde's *Mormonism: Its Leaders and Designs*, and the Book of Mormon. Four days later, the White House requested, among other items, *Mormonism in All Ages* by Julian M. Sturtevant and *Memoirs of the Life and Death of Joseph Smith* by Henry Maheur. Lincoln kept the Book of Mormon for eight months before returning it.[78] His reasons (or those of his staff) for requesting these items are not explained in the documentary record; however, the president was considering the appointment of a new territorial governor for Utah and Utah's most recent petition for statehood.[79]

On July 2, 1862, Lincoln signed into law the Morrill Anti-Polygamy Act, aimed specifically at punishing Utah's polygamy by declaring bigamy a crime in U.S. territories. However, it seems unlikely that anyone, including Lincoln, thought the bill would end polygamy.[80]

If Lincoln as an attorney carefully read the bill, he may have recognized its flaws. First, the law gave prosecutors an insurmountable burden in proving marriages. Mormon plural marriages were performed in secret, and Church officiators were not likely to turn evidence over to prosecutors. Second, Phipps and Steven E. Cresswell, professor of history at West Virginia Wesleyan College, suggest jury nullification could block prosecutions. Lincoln appointed federal district court judges, but the all-Mormon territorial legislature appointed probate judges, some of whom were Mormon bishops or other Church leaders. During the 1850s, the Utah legislature required federal district courts to select jurors from lists prepared by the probate judges; therefore, most juries were comprised of Mormons who would nullify any polygamy prosecutions.[81]

Thus Phipps sees the Morrill Act as primarily "a symbolic assertion of federal power, not a realistic piece of anti-polygamy legislation." It meant that "the Republican Party entered the post-war era with a catchy phrase about polygamy and a useless law on the books."[82] Looking back, we can see that Lincoln and his administration took no steps whatsoever to enforce this law in Utah.

It is interesting to speculate on Lincoln's motives for signing this bill, whether he would have enforced it had he lived into his second term and whether, had he vetoed it, the progressively harsher legislation such as the Edmunds-Tucker Act (1887) would have passed under his successors. We hypothesize that Lincoln signed the Morrill Act to fulfill the antipolygamy plank in his presidential platform, but not because he had serious concerns about polygamy. When Brigham Young sent one of his sons (unnamed in the article) to Washington as a member of a delegation to lobby for the "political and polygmatic interests of Utah," Lincoln dismissed polygamy with a joke: "It was absurd to talk about polygamy, as 'he never yet heard of a man having a wife who wanted two.'"[83] Utahns likewise ignored the Morrill Act. Two days after its passage, the territory celebrated 1862's Independence Day in grand style, with Salt Lake's mayor proposing toasts to Lincoln's health and the Union's success.[84] The Saints also celebrated Lincoln's Emancipation Proclamation and several Union victories.[85] Mormon support for Lincoln increased during his first term despite his signing the Morrill Act.[86] The Mormons ignored the law; and for a decade and a half, they declared that it was unconstitutional.[87]

Federal appointees. On April 1, 1861, William H. Hooper, Utah's delegate to Congress, presented to the Senate a list of Utahns for territorial government offices, including Brigham Young for governor.[88] On April 11, Young wrote to Hooper:

> It was quite proper and correct to suggest to Mr. Lincoln that our appointments belong to us, by every just construction of the spirit of the Constitution. But should he be unwilling or unable to make our appointments from names you may present . . . it will doubtless still be the best policy to patiently bide our time, for plausible pretext against us would tend more than aught else to heal the present breach and unite them in a crusade to Utah, like the Irishman and his wife, who both pitched into the man who parted them when fighting.[89]

Brigham Young was not appointed governor. During the Civil War, a strange dichotomy continued in Utah that greatly affected the territory's relationship with the executive branch of the federal government: there was an amazingly effective leadership, on one hand, with Brigham Young and his theocracy and an equal but frustrating lack of leadership, on the other hand, with U.S. federal appointees.

On October 3, 1861, Lincoln made his first appointments for Utah Territory: "John W. Dawson as governor, John F. Kinney as chief justice, R. P. Flenniken and J. R. Crosby [as] associate judges, Frank Fuller [as] secretary, and James Duane Doty [as] superintendent of Indian Affairs."[90] The Dawson appointment was not popular. According to Norman Furniss, historian of the Utah War,

Mormons knew Dawson as "a man of loose morals whom the Republican chieftains of Fort Wayne had nominated in order to rid themselves of an objectionable person."[91] He did not arrive in Utah until December 7, 1861. Ten days later, the territorial legislature passed a bill calling for a convention of delegates to create a constitution and organize a state government. Territorial secretary Frank Fuller, acting governor at the time, was in support of the bill. However, when Dawson arrived, he vetoed it. This action did not win him any support with the Mormons.[92] Dawson also made improper advances toward his Mormon housekeeper,[93] which resulted in such hostility that he "took his enforced flight on December 31, 1861."[94] Ironically, when Dawson arrived in Washington, DC, he found that the Senate had refused to confirm his appointment and he would have had to leave Utah anyway.[95] Flenniken and Crosby left the territory a month later, with news of their departure being telegraphed to Lincoln.[96] Fuller replaced Dawson until Lincoln could appoint another governor.[97]

Lincoln's next choice, Stephen S. Harding, along with Justices Charles B. Waite and Thomas J. Drake, did not fare much better in Utah than their predecessors. Harding had had "some previous positive associations with the Mormons" and therefore was expected to be a popular choice.[98] Harding had visited Palmyra, New York, and had met Joseph Smith during the summer of 1829, an encounter that he wrote about in 1890.[99] Harding told

This February 9, 1864, photograph of Abraham Lincoln is used for the image that appears on the American five-dollar bill. (Library of Congress)

Utahns, after he was appointed in March 1862, that he was "a messenger of peace and good will" with "no religious prejudices to overcome."[100] However, when Mormon leaders explained their view that the Morrill Act was unconstitutional and their desire for a ruling by the U.S. Supreme Court, Harding attacked this perspective as "dangerous and disloyal."[101]

Meanwhile, Harding, Drake, and Waite were writing letters to Washington discrediting the Mormons and asking Lincoln to put down Indian uprisings by using "paroled [federal]" troops.[102] These letters claimed that the people of Utah were trying to "stir up strife between the people of the Territory of Utah and the troops . . . in Douglas."[103] In the spring of 1863, mass meetings were held in Salt Lake City, the outcome of which was a petition asking Lincoln to remove the three from office.[104] It referred to Harding as "an unsafe bridge over a dangerous stream—jeopardizing the lives of all who pass over it—or as . . . a pestiferous cesspool in our district breeding disease and death."[105]

As soon as the action of the Mormon mass-meeting became known at Camp Douglas, all the commissioned officers signed a counter-petition to President Lincoln, which stated that, "as an act of duty we owe our government," they felt compelled to state that the Mormon petition "was a base and unqualified falsehood . . . and that there was no good reason for [the three officers'] removal."[106] Waite and Drake also assured Lincoln a force

Abraham Lincoln delivering his second inaugural address as president of the United States in Washington, DC. This photo shows President Lincoln standing in the center (below the flag and to the left), on the east front of the U.S. Capitol. (Library of Congress)

of five thousand troops would be required to allow federal courts in Utah to function effectively.[107] Judge Waite resigned in 1864 after a complete court term in which he suffered the mortification of not having a single case on the docket. Judge Drake remained but simply went through a futile form of holding court.[108]

Interestingly, instead of siding with Harding's support of the Morrill law or the petition sent by the federal officers, Lincoln acted on the Mormon petition. On June 11, 1863, he replaced Harding with James Duane Doty, a man "of high capabilities" who had served as superintendent of Indian Affairs.[109] According to historian Hubert Howe Bancroft, Lincoln himself made the appointment and "endeavored to restore peace by making concessions

on both sides." As governor, Doty arose "above petty smallness" and "made many friends and scarcely a single enemy," earning the respect of Utahns. This appointment must have increased Lincoln's popularity among the Mormons. After Lincoln's reelection in 1864, the citizens of Salt Lake celebrated with a mile-long parade, patriotic speeches, and toasts to the president's health. Then, in mourning for his assassination, on April 19, 1865, businesses closed and flags were hung at half-mast.[110] The theater postponed its Saturday performance, buildings were draped in crepe, and in a special memorial service, Apostles Wilford W. Woodruff, Franklin D. Richards, and George Q. Cannon eulogized the fallen president.[111]

CONCLUSION

Lincoln had ties to the Mormons when they came to Illinois and continued to interact with them until he died after being shot in Ford's Theatre on April 14, 1865. In Illinois, Mormons were the clients, friends, and neighbors of his associates. It may never be known if his relationships with individual Mormons affected Lincoln personally or changed him or his views over time. If the Church headquarters had remained in Illinois, Lincoln's political career, attitudes, and subsequent presidential decisions might have taken a different turn; but this hypothesis requires the double speculation that the Mormons themselves would have altered their behavior and approach to local politics in such a way that staying remained a possibility.

There is little evidence that the Mormons were ever more than a political object for Lincoln. We are aware of no documentation that Mormons, as individuals or as a group, affected his personal life. It seems likely that the explosive reaction to his "Rebecca" articles made him cautious about constructing public statements. Hence, it is difficult, if not impossible, to speculate on his personal reaction to the Church's activities.

Mormons had a more direct relationship with Stephen A. Douglas, Lincoln's chief opponent. Clearly documented, however, is Douglas's later outspoken opposition to Mormonism while, in contrast, Lincoln as president maintained a "hands-off" stance— not enforcing the Morrill Act or imposing the draft—that gave the Church the time to establish strong communities in the Mountain West. This policy may owe less to Lincoln's views on Mormonism, however, than the constant attention demanded by the Civil War.

Abraham Lincoln with his son Tad (Thomas) at the White House in 1865. (Library of Congress)

Lincoln did not grant Utah's petition for statehood, but numerous reasons seem more likely than dislike for Mormons. He did succeed in establishing a cooperative and respectful relationship between Utah and the federal government, an achievement predecessor James Buchanan had signally failed to do. Although there is no documentation on this point, Lincoln as an attorney may have been aware that statehood might make it difficult to repress polygamy, an action to which his party was politically committed.

For their part, Utahns during Lincoln's presidency, except for some markedly acerbic private comments by Brigham Young early on, were appreciative and respectful. They recognized him as the nation's chief executive, affiliated with the Union which he represented during the civil strife, and were grateful that he had defeated Douglas. Over the course of his presidency, their affection and admiration grew steadily. They celebrated his second inauguration and mourned his assassination.

Lincoln's attitudes may have been formed by his dealings with Latter-day Saints on a personal level, but he was generally tolerant of all human beings. Holland observes:

All through his life Lincoln saw people as the same. He saw that human nature was relatively consistent wherever you were. If you saw significant differences in behavior, you should chalk things up primarily to the environment people were in and thus be quite generous in your assessments of others. All through his life he effectively said to the North: "Don't get on your moral high horse. If you lived in the South, you would probably be proslavery too.

There are such strong incentives financially; there is such a strong culture and tradition of it; be a little bit careful about being morally self-righteous."[112]

In like manner, Lincoln may have felt that the culture and environment of Mormons rather than some moral degeneration in their character influenced them to live polygamy. Lincoln's ability and predisposition to accept people not as "others" but as the "same" was extremely advantageous to the Mormon community. Lincoln seems to have accepted Mormons as part of the American whole, and his toleration had a distinctly positive influence on Mormon society during the Civil War period.

Mary Jane Woodger is a professor of Church history and doctrine at Brigham Young University.

NOTES

Parts of this chapter were previously published in the *Journal of Mormon History* and are used by permission.

1. Edward W. Tullidge, *Tullidge's Histories*, 2 vols. (Salt Lake City: Juvenile Instructor, 1889), 2:167.

2. T. B. H. Stenhouse to Brigham Young, June 7, 1863, Brigham Young Correspondence, Church Archives, as cited in Leonard J. Arrington and Davis Bitton, *The Mormon Experience: A History of the Latter-day Saints* (New York: Alfred A. Knopf, 1979), 170; also found in Gustive O. Larson, *The "Americanization" of Utah for Statehood* (San Marino, CA: Huntington Library, 1971), 60n61. Also see Preston Nibley, *Brigham Young: The Man and His Work* (Salt Lake City: Deseret Book, 1936), 369. Nibley told the writer that his account was based on Orson F. Whitney, *Popular History of Utah* (Salt Lake City: Deseret News, 1916), 180, 2:24–25, and verbal statements from Whitney. Young to G. Q. Cannon, Great Salt Lake City, June 25, 1863, credits the statement "I will leave them alone, if they will let me alone" to Lincoln's conversation with Stenhouse on the 6th inst. Journal History of The Church of Jesus Christ of Latter-day Saints (chronological scrapbook of typed entries and newspaper clippings, 1830–present), June 25, 1863, Church History Library, Salt Lake City. An AP dispatch from Washington, June 7, mentions the presence in the capital of "a prominent Mormon." *New York Times*, June 8, 1863, 5. In a sermon on June 4, 1864, Young told the plowing anecdote but identified it as "what was told the President . . . said to a gentleman who is a preacher and a member of Congress." *Deseret News*, June 22, 1864, 303. At an anti-Cullom bill meeting in Salt Lake in 1870, Stenhouse, who had left the Church, stated that he had heard Lincoln make the "let them alone" pledge. *Tullidge's Quarterly Magazine*, October 1880, 60. For

Brigham Young's version of Lincoln's statement in a letter to George Q. Cannon, see B. H. Roberts, *A Comprehensive History of the Church of Jesus Christ of Latter-day Saints*, 6 vols. (Provo, UT: Brigham Young University Press, 1965), 5:70. Yet another version appears in Whitney, *Popular History of Utah*, 180.

3. George U. Hubbard, "Abraham Lincoln as Seen by the Mormons," *Utah Historical Quarterly* 31, no. 2 (Spring 1963): 103.

4. Hubbard, "Abraham Lincoln as Seen by the Mormons," 91.

5. Howard W. Allen and Vincent A. Lacey, eds., *Illinois Elections, 1818–1992* (Carbondale, IL: Southern Illinois University Press, 1992), 5–7.

6. George R. Gayler, "The Mormons and Politics in Illinois: 1839–1844," *Journal of the Illinois State Historical Society* 59 (Spring 1956): 48–49; and Robert W. Johannsen, *Stephen A. Douglas* (New York: Oxford University Press, 1973), 104.

7. Bruce A. Van Orden, "Stephen A. Douglas and the Mormons," in *Regional Studies in Latter-day Saint Church History: Illinois* (Provo, UT: BYU Department of Church History and Doctrine, 1995), 361, 367.

8. Johannsen, *Stephen A. Douglas*, 104–11.

9. Johannsen, *Stephen A. Douglas*, 108–9.

10. The Abraham Lincoln Association, *The Collected Works of Abraham Lincoln*, ed. Roy P. Basler (New Brunswick, NJ: Rutgers University Press, 1953), 1:320.

11. David Herbert Donald, *Lincoln's Herndon* (Cambridge, MA: Da Capo Press, 1989), 214; and Allen C. Guelzo, *Abraham Lincoln, Redeemer President* (Grand Rapids: William B. Eerdmans, 1999), 152–54.

12. Hubbard, "Abraham Lincoln as Seen by the Mormons," 93.

13. "Whig Veracity," *Illinois State Register*, Springfield, IL, November 13, 1840.

14. Daniel Walker Howe, *The Transformation of America, 1815–1848* (New York: Oxford University Press, 2007), 724.

15. John C. Bennett, *History of the Saints; or, an Exposé of Joe Smith and Mormonism* (Boston: Leland & Whiting, 1842), 139.

16. JOAB, General in Israel (John C. Bennett), *Times and Seasons*, January 1, 1841, 267; emphasis in original.

17. Joseph Smith, "State Gubernatorial Convention," *Times and Seasons*, January 1, 1842, 651; emphasis in original.

18. William Clayton, Daily Journal, as quoted in *History of the Church of Jesus Christ of Latter-day Saints*, ed. B. H. Roberts, 2nd ed. rev. (Salt Lake City: Deseret Book, 1978), 5:393–94.

19. Earl Schenck Miers, ed., *Lincoln Day by Day: A Chronology*, 3 vols. (Washington, DC: Lincoln Sesquicentennial Commission, 1960), 1:119–20, 175; Roberts, *Comprehensive History of the Church*, 5:212–33; and *Personal Writings of Joseph Smith*, comp. Dean C. Jessee (Salt Lake City: Deseret Book, 2002), 483–88.

20. Van Orden, "Stephen A. Douglas and the Mormons," 365.

21. Roberts, *Comprehensive History of the Church*, 2:482–83, 504–20.

22. Johannsen, *Stephen A. Douglas*, 161; Journal History, December 17, 1845, 1; February 3, 1847, 2.

23. Johannsen, *Stephen A. Douglas*, 268.

24. John G. Nicolay and John Hay, *Abraham Lincoln: A History* (New York: Century, 1914), 337.

25. Nicolay and Hay, *Abraham Lincoln: A History*, 343–44.

26. "An Act to Establish a Territorial Government for Utah" (9 Stat. 453); Van Orden, "Stephen A. Douglas and the Mormons," 367.

27. J. G. Randall and David Donald, *The Civil War and Reconstruction* (Boston: D. C. Heath, 1961), 88–89.

28. Edward Stanwood, *A History of the Presidency*, 2 vols. (Boston and New York: Houghton Mifflin, 1904), 1:272.

29. Van Orden, "Stephen A. Douglas and the Mormons," 368.

30. Vern L. Bullough, "Polygamy: An Issue in the Election of 1860?," *Utah Historical Quarterly* 29 (April 1961): 119–23.

31. Johannsen, *Stephen A. Douglas*, 545–67.

32. "Speech of Senator Douglas," *Daily National Intelligencer*, June 30, 1857.

33. "Speech at Springfield, Illinois," in Basler, *Collected Works of Abraham Lincoln*, 2:398–99.

34. Johannsen, *Stephen A. Douglas*, 573–74.

35. "Speech of the Hon. Abram Lincoln, in Reply to Judge Douglas, Delivered in Representatives' Hall," Springfield, IL, June 26, 1857, 1; Albert J. Beveridge, *Abraham Lincoln* (New York: Houghton Mifflin, 1928), 7.

36. E. B. Long, *The Saints and the Union: Utah Territory during the Civil War* (Chicago: University of Illinois Press, 1981), 9.

37. Long, *Saints and the Union*, 9.

38. "Speech of the Hon. Abram Lincoln" and Beveridge, *Abraham Lincoln*, 7.

39. "Comments upon The Remarks of Hon. Stephen Arnold Douglas," *Deseret News*, September 2, 1857, 204.

40. Kelly Elizabeth Phipps, "Marriage and Redemption: Mormon Polygamy in the Congressional Imagination, 1862–1887," *Virginia Law Review* 95, no. 2 (April 2009): 441, 445, 448, 451.

41. Ralph Y. McGinnis and Calvin N. Smith, eds., *Abraham Lincoln and the Western Territories* (Chicago: Nelson-Hall, 1994), 100; Gary C. Vitale, "Abraham Lincoln and the Mormons: Another Legacy of Limited Freedom," *Journal of the Illinois State Historical Society* 101 (Fall–Winter 2008): 3–4.

42. Phipps, "Marriage and Redemption," 447.

43. McGinnis and Smith, *Abraham Lincoln and the Western Territories*, 100.

44. Basler, *Collected Works of Abraham Lincoln*, 4:42; emphasis in original.

45. Van Orden, "Stephen A. Douglas and the Mormons," 374.

46. "Prospective Dissolution," *Deseret News*, November 28, 1860, 4.

47. Brigham Young to William H. Hooper, November 19, 1860, Brigham Young Letters, Bienecke Rare Book and Manuscript Library, Yale University, New Haven, Connecticut (hereafter Bienecke Library).

48. Brigham Young, office journal, June 12 and March 2, 1861, Church History Library, as cited in Long, *Saints and the Union*, 8.

49. Brigham Young, office journal, August 5, 1861, as cited in Long, *Saints and the Union*, 9. The identification of "he" in this quotation from Brigham Young's office journal is open to interpretation. Many scholars have interpreted "he" to refer to either Douglas or Lincoln. If "he" had referred to Young, you would usually expect it to read "I" (Young the writer) instead of "he." If Young's Journal was written by someone other than Young, it could be that a scribe wrote in third person rather than first person. The interpretation of this sentence is open to question. Long states, "It is not quite clear whether Young meant Douglas or Lincoln was hostile."

50. Brigham Young to William H. Hooper, December 20, 1860, Brigham Young Letters, Bienecke Library.

51. Brigham Young, office journal, January 25, 1861, Church History Library, as cited in Long, *Saints and the Union*, 24.

52. Long, *Saints and the Union*, 26.

53. Brigham Young, office journal, March 2. 1861, LDS Church History Library, as cited in E. B. Long, *Saints and the Union*, 27.

54. Brigham Young, April 6, 1851, in *Journal of Discourses* (London: Latter-day Saints' Book Depot, 1855–86), 9:4.

55. Brigham Young, office journal, March 15, July 9, and July 24, 1861, Church History Library, as cited in E. B. Long, *Saints and the Union*, 36.

56. Brigham Young, July 24, 1861, in *Journal of Discourses*, 9:142.

57. Long, *Saints and the Union*, xi.

58. John Taylor, "Ceremonies at the Bowery," *Deseret News*, July 10, 1861, 152; spelling standardized.

59. Edward W. Tullidge, *Life of Brigham Young; or, Utah and Her Founders* (New York: n.p., 1877), 346.

60. Miers, *Lincoln Day by Day*, 3:73. "When Joseph asked him to be his vice presidential running mate, Bennett declined. After the martyrdom of the Prophet in 1844, he left the Church. A year later, however, he visited Nauvoo and declared his intentions to go west with the Saints. He aspired to be leader of the Nauvoo Legion, but when Brigham Young turned him down, Bennett disassociated himself from the Saints and spent the rest of his life in the eastern United States." Arnold K. Garr, Donald Q. Cannon, and Richard O. Cowan, eds., *Encyclopedia of Latter-day Saint History* (Salt Lake City: Deseret Book, 2000), 86–87.

61. See Joseph Stuart and Kenneth L. Alford's chapter on the Lot Smith Utah Cavalry herein.

62. See Maris A. Vinovskis, "Have Social Historians Lost the Civil War? Some Preliminary Demographic Speculations," in *Toward a Social History of the American Civil War: Exploratory Essays* (New York: Cambridge University Press, 1990), 3–7.

63. Roberts, *Comprehensive History of the Church*, 5:25.

64. Smith, "Utah Territory," in *Abraham Lincoln and the Western Territories*, 97, 103.

65. Arrington and Bitton, *The Mormon Experience*, 170.

66. Edward W. Tullidge, *History of Salt Lake City* (Salt Lake City: Star Printing, 1886), 708.

67. Pacific Railroad Act of July 1, 1862, 12 Stat. 489, (1862), http://cprr.org/Museum/Pacific_Railroad_Acts.html.

68. Andrew Jenson, *Church Chronology: A Record of Important Events* (Salt Lake City: Deseret News, 1914), 63.

69. "The Completion of the Telegraph," *Deseret News*, October 23, 1861, 5.

70. Brigham Young, telegram, April 14, 1862, as quoted in Long, *Saints and the Union*, 82.

71. *New Letters and Papers of Lincoln*, comp. Paul M. Angle (New York: Houghton Mifflin, 1930), 292.

72. Leonard J. Arrington, *Brigham Young: American Moses* (New York: Alfred A. Knopf, 1985), 296.

73. See Kenneth L. Alford and William P. MacKinnon's chapter on Camp Douglas herein.

74. *History of the Union Pacific Railroad* (Ogden, UT: Union Pacific Railroad, 1919), 11.

75. Arrington, *Brigham Young*, 348.

76. Arrington, *Brigham Young*, 349.

77. John William Starr Jr. and others, *Lincoln & the Railroads* (New York: Ayer Printing, 1981), 200.

78. Library of Congress Archives, *Borrower's Ledger, 1861–1863*, 114, as quoted in Miers, *Lincoln Day by Day*, 77–78.

79. Robert Bray, "What Abraham Lincoln Read: An Evaluative and Annotated List," *Journal of the Abraham Lincoln Association* 28, no. 2 (Summer 2007): 39n24: "'It is probable . . . that the half dozen volumes dealing with Mormonism, called for in August and November, 1861, and retained for periods varying from two to eight months, were sought by Lincoln as throwing desired light on one of the minor problems of his administration.' But while Lincoln may have needed to know about the Mormons in Utah, it does not follow that he would have been interested in the *Book of Mormon*, though he would have known *of it* from his earliest Illinois years" (emphasis in original).

80. Phipps, "Marriage and Redemption," 451; and Stephen E. Cresswell, *Mormons, Cowboys, Moonshiners & Klansman: Federal Law Enforcement in the South and West* (Tuscaloosa: University of Alabama Press, 1991), 81–82.

81. Phipps, "Marriage and Redemption," 448–49.

82. Phipps, "Marriage and Redemption," 451.

83. *Liberty Weekly Tribune*, October 3, 1862, no. 29.

84. "The Reunion at the City Hall," *Daily Union Vedette*, March 6, 1865.

85. "The Inaugural Celebration," *Daily Union Vedette*, March 6, 1865.

86. McGinnis and Smith, *Abraham Lincoln and the Western Territories*, 109.

87. Hubert Howe Bancroft, *History of Utah, 1540–1886*, 26 vols. (San Francisco: History, 1889), 26:604.

88. Long, *Saints and the Union*, 28.

89. Brigham Young to William H. Hooper, April 11, 1861, Brigham Young Letters, Bienecke Library.

90. Bancroft, *History of Utah*, 26:604.

91. Norman F. Furniss, *The Mormon Conflict: 1850–1859* (New Haven: Yale University Press, 1960), 232.

92. Long, *Saints and the Union*, 49.

93. Furniss, *Mormon Conflict*, 232.

94. McGinnis and Smith, *Abraham Lincoln and the Western Territories*, 104.

95. McGinnis and Smith, *Abraham Lincoln and the Western Territories*, 104.

96. McGinnis and Smith, *Abraham Lincoln and the Western Territories*, 104–5.

97. Whitney, *Popular History of Utah*, 183.

98. McGinnis and Smith, *Abraham Lincoln and the Western Territories*, 105.

99. Stephen S. Harding as cited in Thomas Gregg, *The Prophet of Palmyra* (New York: John B. Alden, 1890), 34–44.

100. "Speech of Governor Harding," in Tullidge, *History of Salt Lake City*, 269–70.

101. R. N. Baskin, *Reminiscences of Early Utah* (n.p.: R. N. Baskin), 8.

102. Basler, *Collected Works of Abraham Lincoln*, 5:432.

103. C. V. Waite, *The Mormon Prophet and His Harem; or, an Authentic History of Brigham Young, His Numerous Wives and Children* (Chicago: J. S. Goodman, 1868), 104.

104. McGinnis and Smith, *Abraham Lincoln and the Western Territories*, 107.

105. Bancroft, *History of Utah*, 26:620–21.

106. Quoted in William Alexander Linn, *The Story of the Mormons from the Date of Their Origin to the Year 1901* (New York: Macmillan, 1902), 548–49.

107. Linn, *Story of the Mormons*, 550.

108. Bancroft, *History of Utah*, 26:620–21.

109. News Department, "Journal of Indian Treaty Days," *Washington Historical Quarterly* 11, no. 1 (January 1920): 75.

110. Bancroft, *History of Utah*, 26:621–22, 625; and Long, *Saints and the Union*, 262.

111. Matthias F. Cowley, *Wilford Woodruff* (Salt Lake City: Bookcraft, 1964), 441.

112. Matthew S. Holland, "With Charity for All," *Clark Memorandum* (Fall 2008): 24.

South Carolina became the first state to secede when the state legislature voted 169–0 on December 16, 1860, to leave the Union. Other Southern states seceded in rapid order. Various rumors indicated the possible secession of Utah Territory, but Brigham Young did not seriously consider such an action. (Library of Congress)

CHAPTER 5

Craig K. Manscill

RUMORS OF SECESSION IN THE UTAH TERRITORY, 1847–61

Even before vital national questions climaxed in Southern secession, there was a history of distrust between Mormons and non-Mormons. Events over several years had created a widespread belief in the disloyalty of Brigham Young and his Great Basin Kingdom. Any group which did not wholeheartedly support one side in the war was distrusted by both the North and the South. Anti-Mormon sentiment accused the people in Utah Territory of having secessionist views. Francis Wootton, Utah's acting governor, replied to those charges:

> At this time [1861] because of rumors which I observe to be in general circulation through the various presses of the country to the effect that Brigham Young had declared Utah independent and that the property of the government at Fort Crittenden . . . and other military stations of the Department of Utah have been violently seized and appropriated by the Mormons. Such

reports based on the idle and mendacious representations of the irresponsible parties, if unnoticed, may produce a false impression at Washington and lead to unnecessary troubles; therefore, I have deemed it my duty to give them an official contradiction.[1]

This was not the first time rumors accused Brigham Young and Mormons of secessionist tendencies. The 1846 exodus from Nauvoo, Illinois, to the frontier territories was the beginning of those rumors, and many dynamics in the 1850s led to further secession accusations. These dynamics included Young's theocratic government, opposition to the Utah War, and rhetorical outbursts as well as poor communication between the Mormons and Washington, anti-Mormon political pundits and Territorial appointees, Connor's California Volunteers, the Mormons' relationship with the Indians, and the Mountain Meadow Massacre. This essay will not address all of these forces (some of which are reviewed elsewhere in this book), but it will look at the exodus, Young's theocracy and outbursts, and the Confederacy's attempts to woo the Mormons at the beginning of the Civil War.

Secession rumors began with the hurried 1846 Mormon exodus from Nauvoo, Illinois. Mormons had always been a hounded and harried people. From the April 1830 organization of the Church in Fayette, New York, its members had faced misunderstanding, persecution, and expulsion. Mormons surely expected America to suffer consequences for the persecution of the Saints and the murder of their prophet Joseph Smith. Brigham Young acknowledged: "The whisperings of the Spirit to us have invariably been of the same import, to depart, to go hence, to flee into the mountains, to retire to our strongholds that we may be secure in the visitations of the Judgments that must pass upon this land, that is crimsoned with the blood of Martyrs; and that we may be hid, as it were, in the clefts of the rocks, and in the hollows of the land of the Great Jehovah, while the guilty land of our fathers is purifying by the overwhelming scourge."[2] This feeling of collective hurt—an almost Old Testament–style wrath for their enemies—was a carryover from the Latter-day Saints' earlier sufferings from persecutions and murders in Missouri and Illinois. Coming to the forefront shortly after the martyrdom of their prophet, these expectations reached a crescendo by the time they left Nauvoo.

Illinois Governor Thomas Ford, who had known for nearly a year of Joseph Smith's

Thomas Ford (1800–1850) was Illinois's eighth governor (1842–46). As a ploy to lure the Mormons to evacuate Illinois early, Ford warned Brigham Young that the federal government would oppose colonizing plans on foreign soil in the West. (Wikimedia Commons)

plans to colonize in the West, warned Mormon leaders that the federal government would oppose any such invasion of foreign soil.[3] The Mormon leadership, particularly the council of fifty, considered all western territories to be potential destinations but confidentially favored a central location somewhere in the middle of the Rockies or along the eastern rim of the Great Basin. Rather than risk government interference, Brigham Young and the Twelve Apostles decided on February 2, 1846, to depart immediately—three months earlier than scheduled. They sought a place where neither the laws of the United States nor the sanctions of other religions could prevent them from freely living their religion. Their destination was viewed as a place of refuge that would ensure protection, isolation, good health, and ample provision for a self-sustaining people of a rapidly growing, young American religion desperately trying to find its way. Brigham Young wrote to his followers at Mount Pisgah, Iowa, in the winter of 1847 regarding the plans to travel west: "This is a subject that has long attracted our attention and concerning which we have thought and felt deeply and well we might; for situated as the Church of Jesus Christ is, and has been, for a considerable length of time, the only human hope or prospect of her salvation, has appeared to rest on the removal of the Saints from a land of oppression and violence to some more congenial clime."[4]

Their Rocky Mountain plan owed much to Joseph Smith, a fact Brigham Young knew well. Speaking from the Salt Lake Valley in 1848, Young reminisced, "We are here! Thank the Almighty God of Israel! Some have marveled when the Saints agreed to leave the States, but it was no sacrifice. From the days of Oliver Cowdery and Parley Pratt on the borders of the Lamanites [1831] Joseph Smith had longed to be here. . . . They would not let us come and at last we have accomplished it."[5] While some have argued otherwise, evidence indicates that, late in his life, Joseph Smith began to look to the Rocky Mountains as a probable place of refuge. In an 1845 letter, Governor Ford wrote, "I was informed by General Joseph Smith last summer that he contemplated a removal west; and from what I learned from him and others at that time, I think if he had lived, he would have begun to move in the matter before this time."[6]

Nevertheless, the Mormons had no intention of broadcasting their destination—and for good reason. There was fear that their Missouri enemies might disrupt their march. Prudence dictated that they speak about the subject in a general, even oblique, manner. There was also concern that powerful senators, like Mormon-hating Thomas Benton, might influence Washington to send an army to obstruct their way. Washington was then settling the Oregon question with England and preparing for war with Mexico over California. Thus, the government might wonder at the intentions of a wounded and persecuted people moving en masse amidst an Indian population to some ill-defined homeland "beyond the states." By keeping all their enemies guessing, the Latter-day Saints walked a fine line between defending themselves and giving the impression that they were seceding.

From the Omaha plains, Young looked into the frontier land of the Mexican-owned

James K. Polk (November 2, 1795–June 15, 1849), the eleventh president of the United States (1845–49), was known for his foreign policy. He met with Jesse C. Little on June 5, 1846, and offered to enlist five hundred volunteers in the Mexican War in order to placate the Mormons and retain their loyalty as U.S. citizens. (Library of Congress)

Great Basin, desperately hoping the future would ease the tragedies of Ohio, Missouri, and Illinois. Looking over his shoulder, Young may have wondered how American civil leaders perceived the Saints' exit. Declaring his allegiance to the American Constitution, Young wrote U.S. President James K. Polk and explained that, although the Saints respected the American Constitution, his people would "rather retreat to the deserts, island or mountain caves than consent to be ruled by governors & judges . . . who delight in injustice and oppression."[7]

However, not all Mormons were as concerned with showing their allegiance. In an editorial comparing the wickedness of the United States to the biblical Sodom and Gomorrah, John Taylor wrote: "We owe the United States nothing: we go out by force as exiles from freedom. The Government and people owe us millions for the destruction of life and property in Missouri and Illinois. The blood of our best men stains the land, and the ashes of our property will preserve it till God comes out of his hiding place, and gives this nation a hotter portion than he did Sodom and Gomorrah. 'When they cease to spoil they shall be spoiled,' for the Lord hath spoken it."[8]

Threats of secession were also used as leverage in favor of the Mormon cause. Jesse C. Little, the presiding Church officer in the East and official Church agent in Washington, met Thomas S. Kane in Philadelphia during May 1846 while Elder Little was seeking means to transport eastern Saints to upper California by ship. Kane, a young adventurer who became an articulate, self-appointed guardian for the interests of the Saints, suggested the political tactic that Elder Little later used to persuade President Polk to aid the Mormons. Armed with letters of introduction from Kane and others, Elder Little sought an audience with Polk. Little had been told by Brigham Young to seek government contracts to build blockhouses and forts along the Oregon Trail. Failing that, he was authorized to embrace any offer

Tokens such as these were minted throughout the Civil War, primarily in the North, by businesses and individuals to promote national union and decry secession. (Courtesy of Kenneth L. Alford)

that would aid the emigration. Elder Little's first hope was for a shipping contract, which would provide money as well as inexpensive transportation. His request was timely, for the government needed to send supplies around Cape Horn for its forces in California. Former postmaster general Amos Kendall told Elder Little that he would urge the cabinet to authorize one thousand Mormons to travel by sea and another thousand overland to California.[9]

When five days passed without a response, Elder Little addressed a personal letter to Polk. He threatened, as Kane had suggested, that lack of federal aid to help the Mormons migrate "under the outstretched wings of the American Eagle" might "compel us to be foreigners."[10] This was indeed a clever ploy, for the Mormons had no intention of becoming disloyal, but the government had heard rumors of British interest in the Pacific Coast. It was not impossible that an independent Mormon state might gain the support of England, which would certainly complicate American interests in the West.

As an alternative, Polk asked Little in a meeting on June 5 if the Mormons would offer five hundred volunteers to enlist after the Mormon exiles reached California. That request, the president confided in his diary, was a move to placate the Mormons and retain their loyalty. "The main object of taking them into service would be to conciliate them," admitted Polk in his diary.[11] Kane's strategy worked. Little pressed for an immediate enlistment, but the request was turned down. Two days prior to the June 5 meeting, orders had been sent by Secretary of War William L. Marcy to Colonel Stephen W. Kearny (later brigadier general) authorizing the Mormon enlistment in vague terms. Even though President Polk apparently intended the enlistment to take place in California, Kearny interpreted his instructions differently and, on June 19, ordered the enlistment to take place immediately as the Mormon exodus was crossing Iowa. Thus the way was paved for an important episode in Mormon history—the march of the Mormon Battalion.

Stephen W. Kearny (1794–1846) was one of the foremost antebellum frontier officers of the United States Army. At President James Polk's request, Kearny ordered the immediate formation of a battalion of volunteers from the Mormons who were in Iowa traveling west during the Mormon exodus. (General Land Office Research website, Department of Landscape Architecture, Iowa State University)

Polk intended to win the Mormons' loyalty by enlisting a Mormon military, appeasing Little and Young's request for federal aid, and sympathizing with the plight of the Mormon suffering and history, thereby ensuring that the Mormons did not turn against the United States and establish their own independent country. Leverage or not, Little's tactic not only opened the way for the mustering in of the Mormon Battalion but also left the impression with President Polk that the Mormons may secede.

Brigham Young's establishment of a theocracy—or theo-democratic society—in Utah led to further rumors of secession. Most Americans in the mid-nineteenth century considered theocracy an already-turned page from

John Winthrop's Massachusetts Bay Colony two hundred years before. The Mormons, however, were still determined to create a religious commonwealth. During the first days of their settlement, they spoke of a land of promise held in reserve by the hand of God that fulfilled the promises of Isaiah 2:2–4; 11:10–12. Other sermons insisted on the need for a strict Christian piety—Sabbath-keeping, honesty, and order and righteousness. Outsiders willing to obey this new standard would be accepted, but those who would not obey it were expected to go elsewhere. As a symbol of the new society, members of the first pioneer party in the Salt Lake Valley were rebaptized and reconfirmed as members of the Church. "We had as it were entered a new world and wished to renew our covenants and commence in newness of life," explained one of the men.[12]

Young had come west, hoping to establish his society under a favored constitutional theory of the time: popular sovereignty. Presidential candidates Lewis Cass, in 1848, and Stephen A. Douglas, in 1860, took the idea of neighborhood majority rule and applied it to the western territories. They hoped to quiet the rising storm in Washington over expanding slavery in the territories. Cass and Douglas argued that a community was ready for self-government from the moment it was settled; majorities in the territories should be allowed self-government—and should not be required to live by federal administration.

The flag of the kingdom of God was first suggested by Joseph Smith as early as June 22, 1844. The flag was a symbol of the political kingdom of God established in the Great Basin by Brigham Young in 1847. (No photographs of original flags exist; this artistic representation, courtesy of Julie M. Ogborn, is based on contemporary reports.)

Extending this thinking, if power lay with the people in a territory, then Utah Mormons had a right to establish their theocracy and maintain their practice of polygamy.

The pioneers called their new community *Deseret*, a name that was meant to set it apart as the kingdom of God—a religious and political government which, when fully established, might prepare for Christ's coming reign. "All other governments are illegal and unauthorized," said a Mormon theoretical tract. "Any people attempting to govern themselves by laws of their own making, and by officers of their own appointment, are in direct rebellion against the kingdom of God."[13]

Associated with Young's theocracy was the "flag of the kingdom of God," furthering the

perception of secession.[14] A flag is designed to proclaim intentions and represent a cause, and it almost has a voice of its own. The Mormon flag was designed under Joseph Smith's direction as early as 1844.[15] By the time Brigham Young led the first pioneer company toward the Great Basin in the spring of 1847, the Saints viewed this flag for the mountain haven of the Saints as the flag of the political kingdom of God. While it is debatable how early the flag was posted, there is evidence that the flag was given public display in 1859 when William Henry Knight attended the Fourth of July celebration in the Salt Lake Valley.[16] In a letter to his mother on July 7, 1859, Knight wrote, "The Mormons were celebrating the day with a flag of their own, firing cannon and marching about to Yankee music."[17] The stripes of the Mormon flag were blue and white, and in the upper left corner was a circle of twelve stars with one large star in the center.[18] Other versions of the flag had three stars in the center of a circle of twelve stars.[19]

When the Mormons migrated into the Great Basin, they had no charter from any existing government. The job of civil government and good order in the community was left entirely to them for a few years; however, their hopes for a quiet society in Utah were dashed with the coming of a federal territorial government. The American territorial system enacted in 1787, known as the Northwest Ordinance, required settlers to gain self-government and statehood through a step-by-step process. Territories were virtual colonies—not unlike colonies under British rule before the American Revolution. Citizens in the territories were denied the right to self-government that most white males elsewhere took for granted. Federal officials often focused on their personal careers and not on the welfare of the citizens. Territorial government placed the Mormon community and their theocracy on a collision course and led to new rumors of secession. During 1850, as many as sixteen federal officials left their positions in the territory in "frustration, fright, or both."[20] Neither appointed federal officials nor outside observers understood the Mormons. One such observer, W. M. F. Magraw, who lived briefly in Utah, wrote President Franklin Pierce in October 1856, claiming that there was "no vestige of law and order" in the territory and that the "so-styled ecclesiastical organization" was "despotic, dangerous and damnable."[21]

The Mormons saw two rival kingdoms or cultures that opposed each other: a worldly kingdom that supported territorial government and oppressive appointees, and the kingdom of God, which established a theocracy to purify the saints in preparation for the return of their Savior. One was religious and local; the other was civil and national. The issue was not just law and religion but *whose* law and religion. As troops marched toward Deseret, Brigham Young took to the pulpit. His rhetorical outbursts, printed in Mormon publications, found their way to Washington—leading to fresh rumors of secession and contributing to the dispatch of federal troops to Utah in 1857. "The Lord is . . . bringing to pass the sayings of the Prophets faster than the people are prepared to receive them," Young said. "The time must come when there will be a separation between this kingdom and the kingdoms of this world. . . . The time must come when this kingdom must be free and independent from all other kingdoms." Young asked the congregation, "Are you prepared to have the thread cut to-day?"[22] During the 1857 Silver Lake celebration,[23] Heber C. Kimball, Young's First Counselor, framed the dilemma that faced the Mormons. "If we will not yield to [the government's] meanness," he said, "they will say we have mutinized [sic] against the President of the United States and then they will put us under martial law and massacre this people."[24]

Rumors of secession reached a crescendo when Brigham Young became the target of remarks by territorial officials (such as the associate supreme court justice W. W. Drummond, Utah chief justice John F. Kinney, and Utah surveyor general David H. Burr). These officials reported that Young was "more traitorous than ever" and was responsible for the killing of Lieutenant John W. Gunnison in 1853 and the death of Territorial Secretary Almon W. Babbitt in 1856.[25] Newspaper campaigns across the nation mounted against the Mormons. The April 29 issue of the *American Journal*, published in 1859, "made the outlandish claim that one hundred thousand Mormons were poised to fight the U.S. government, aided by two hundred thousand 'spies and emissaries' and three hundred thousand 'savage' Indian allies."[26]

Once the Confederate states became a reality, Confederate leaders had high hopes that the western territories would be relatively easy to enlist in their cause. Secession strategists projected that the Mormons in Utah Territory had good reason to join their cause. Richard Vetterli, in *Mormonism, Americanism and Politics*, argued that the position of the Mormons in Utah Territory presented a more promising ally than any other of the six territories.[27] Southern strategists assumed that the Mormons would favorably lean toward the South. It was assumed that Mormons were bitter over their treatment by the United States and were "on the eve of revolution." Vetterli listed the following reasons for favoring Utah's secession to join the Confederacy: (1) the federal government had refused to grant the Saints redress for indignities suffered at the hands of the mobocrats in Missouri and Illinois; (2) Congress had refused multiple petitions for Utah statehood and instead had granted territorial status, thereby giving Congress the right to appoint unacceptable federal officers; (3) unfounded reports of rebellion and secession drove the President of the United States to send an army to Utah; (4) Governor Cumming had been sent by the President to relieve Brigham Young as governor of the Utah Territory—Young was respected, loved, and accepted by the Mormons, but Cumming was an outsider from Georgia; and (5) both Mormons and Southerners were advocates of popular sovereignty, which protected the institutions of slavery and polygamy as domestic issues that should be decided by the people, not by the federal government.[28] While these reasons seem applicable to the Mormon situation, there is no evidence that the Mormons had any significant negotiations with the Confederacy. E. B. Long's research concluded, "The myths and rumors of emissaries coming to Utah from the South, which have persisted over the years, have little substance."[29]

Despite compelling reasons for Utah's secession, Southern strategists underestimated the allegiance Mormons had to the Union and the divinely inspired Constitution of the United States. "We have had our difficulties with the government," Church leaders declared, "but we calculate they will be righted in the government or we will endure them!"[30] Utah chose to stand by the Union. In one of the first telegraphic messages sent east from Salt Lake City, Brigham Young proclaimed, "Utah has not seceded, but is firm for the Constitution and laws of our once happy country."[31]

The multiple dynamic forces at work during the 1850s and early 1860s led to a widespread image of Mormon disloyalty. The Mormon passion for self-government, both religious and secular, sometimes made them appear like secessionists, but it was an inaccurate portrayal. The Mormons were loyal to the United States and the Constitution, but also to Brigham Young, their Church, and their God.

Craig K. Manscill is an associate professor of Church history and doctrine at Brigham Young University.

NOTES

Thanks to Julie M. Ogborn and John Weist for their research and editing assistance.

1. E. B. Long, *The Saints and the Union: Utah Territory during the Civil War* (Urbana, Chicago, and London: University of Illinois Press, 1981), 40.

2. "Brigham Young to the Saints at Mount Pisgah and Garden Grove, Iowa Territory, January 27, 1847," *Selected Collections: From the Archives of The Church of Jesus Christ of Latter-day Saints*, vol. 1, disc 2, vols. 17 and 18, 30–31.

3. Leonard J. Arrington, *Brigham Young: American Moses* (New York: Alfred A. Knopf, 1985), 126–27.

4. "Brigham Young to the Saints at Mount Pisgah and Garden Grove, Iowa Territory, January 27, 1847," 30–31.

5. Ronald K. Esplin, "'A Place Prepared': Joseph, Brigham, and the Quest for Promised Refuge in the West," *Journal of Mormon History* 9 (1982): 85.

6. Hyrum L. Andrus, "Joseph Smith and the West," *BYU Studies* 1–2 (1959–60): 135; see also Helen Mar Whitney, "Scenes in Nauvoo," *Woman's Exponent* 11, no. 8 (September 15, 1882): 161.

7. B. H. Roberts, *A Comprehensive History of The Church of Jesus Christ of Latter-day Saints*, vol. 3 (Provo, UT: Brigham Young University Press, 1965), 414.

8. "To Our Patrons," *Nauvoo Neighbor*, October 29, 1845.

9. Sergeant Daniel Tyler, *A Concise History of the Mormon Battalion in the Mexican War, 1846–1847* (n.p.: 1881), 112.

10. Edward W. Tullidge, *Life of Brigham Young; or, Utah and Her Founders* (New York: Tullidge and Crandall, 1877), 50.

11. "The Diary of James K. Polk," *Chicago Historical Society's Collection*, vol. 1 (Chicago: A. C. McClurg, 1910), 446.

12. Dean L. May, *Utah: A People's History* (Salt Lake City: University of Utah Press, 1987), 60.

13. Orson Pratt, *The Kingdom of God* (Liverpool: R. James, 1848), 48.

14. D. Michael Quinn, "The Flag of the Kingdom of God," *BYU Studies* 14 (1973): 109; see also William P. MacKinnon, *At Sword's Point, Part 1* (Norman, OK: University of Oklahoma Press, 2008), 230. MacKinnon associated secession with a flag unfurled on July 24, 1857, at the Silver Lake celebration.

15. Ronald W. Walker, "'A Banner Is Unfurled': Mormonism's Ensign Peak," *Dialogue* 26 (1993): 73; *History of the Church of Jesus Christ of Latter-day Saints*, ed. B. H. Roberts, 2nd ed. rev. (Salt Lake City: Deseret Book, 1967), 6:528.

16. William Henry Knight was born in Harmony, Chautauqua County, New York, on April 19, 1835. He was an immigrant bound for California who attended the July 4, 1859, celebration at Silver Lake up Little Cottonwood Canyon.

17. Quinn, "Flag of the Kingdom of God," 111.

18. Quinn, "Flag of the Kingdom of God," 111–12.

19. Quinn, "Flag of the Kingdom of God," 114.

20. David L. Bigler, *Forgotten Kingdom: The Mormon Theocracy in the American West, 1847–1896* (Logan, UT: Utah State University Press, 1998), 59.

21. W. M. F. Magraw to Mr. President, October 3, 1856, *Executive Documents Printed by Order of the House of Representatives during the First Session of the Thirty-Fifth Congress* (Washington, DC: James B. Steedman, 1858), 2.

22. Brigham Young, in *Journal of Discourses* (London: Latter-day Saints' Book Depot, 1854–86), 5:98.

23. The celebration commemorates the arrival of the Mormons into the Salt Lake Valley on July 24, 1847. Silver Lake, today called Brighton, Utah, is at the top of Little Cottonwood Canyon in the Wasatch Mountains.

24. Heber C. Kimball, in *Journal of Discourses*, 5:88.

25. "Dreadful State of Affairs in Utah," *New York Herald*, March 20, 1857.

26. Ronald W. Walker, Richard E. Turley Jr., Glen M. Leonard, *Massacre at Mountain Meadows* (New York: Oxford University Press, 2008), 28.

27. Richard Vetterli, *Mormonism, Americanism, and Politics* (Salt Lake City: Ensign, 1961), 515–17.

28. Vetterli, *Mormonism, Americanism, and Politics*, 516.

29. E. B. Long, *Saints and the Union*, 274.

30. Vetterli, *Mormonism, Americanism, and Politics*, 517.

31. Edward W. Tullidge, *The History of Salt Lake City and Its Founders* (Salt Lake City: published by author, 1886), 250. See also Orson F. Whitney, *History of Utah* (Salt Lake City: George Q. Cannon, 1892–98), 2:30.

This full portrait photograph of Brigham Young (1801–77) by Charles R. Savage was possibly taken during the Civil War. (C. R. Savage Photograph Collection, L. Tom Perry Special Collections, Brigham Young University)

CHAPTER 6

Richard E. Bennett

"WE KNOW NO NORTH, NO SOUTH, NO EAST, NO WEST"

MORMON INTERPRETATIONS OF THE CIVIL WAR, 1861–65

While peace reigns in Utah, civil war, with all its horrors, prevails among those who earnestly desired to see the soil of these valleys crimsoned with the blood of the Saints, and, if we are not mistaken in the signs of the times, before the conflict between the North and the South shall have ended, all they unitedly desired to see meted out to the Mormons, will be poured out without measure upon those who have initiated the war of extermination, and are now carrying it on with all the energy they severally possess.[1]

—*Deseret News*, May 18, 1861

So read the lead editorial in the Salt Lake *Deseret News* shortly after Confederate gun boats and shore batteries blasted Fort Sumter into submission and surrender at the April 1861 outbreak of the war between the North and the South.

The history of that great American conflict continues to attract discussion and debate. Books and articles continue to be written, battles and skirmishes are every year reenacted, and new views and interpretations abound in a field of study that remains riveted deeply in our history. Yet Mormon scholars have tended to leave it alone and far away, as if it were the other guys' war—that conflict beyond the mountains to the east that America had brought upon itself.[2]

This short study attempts to somewhat redress that imbalance, not by reexamining what minor role Utah and the Mormons played militarily in the conflict in the territories but by proffering a preliminary analysis of public statements made by the leading authorities of The Church of Jesus Christ of Latter-day Saints during the Civil War years of 1861 to 1865, comments that reveal their interpretations of the conflict and the causes of the nation's discomfiture.

Let me emphasize at the outset the words *public* and *preliminary*. I have deliberately restricted my research to those statements made in public and also recorded in newspapers, magazines, and various compilations of sermons and discourses. A thorough

A few weeks before Fort Sumter was fired upon, Brigham Young (1801–77), second President of the LDS Church, said that "God has come out of his hiding place and has commenced to vex the nation that has rejected us." (Utah State Historical Society)

manuscript study into letters, diaries, and the like will have to wait for another time. Furthermore, this is a preliminary probe into a very complicated field of study. Although hundreds of discourses and comments made by numerous Church leaders have been examined, any seasoned researcher knows that so much, even of that which is recorded, is hard to find. Likewise, what has been recorded is often incomplete, if not incorrect.

It is never easy to capture faithfully the tenor of a past time, the mood in the air, and in this case, the more rarified air of a Rocky Mountain Zion. The times seemed so black and white, North and South, a Mormon political kingdom and a nation apart. America, when it took the time, regarded Utah as an evil miscreant, a religion out of time and out of tune, harboring that other "relic of barbarism"—polygamy. On the other hand, from most Mormon pulpits and papers spilled forth a tirade of wrathful indignation

against those who had so badly treated them in the past. Somewhere in between, perhaps this side of moderation, lay the truth.

Whatever the case, the purpose of this paper is to try to answer the following four questions: (1) How did prominent Mormon leaders interpret the underlying cause of the American Civil War? (2) Did their feelings and attitudes change as the conflict deepened and degenerated into the worst spectacle of human suffering the country had ever experienced? (3) Were there recognizable differences in opinion and viewpoint among the most prominent leaders? (4) What effect, if any, did the war have on the leaders' views of returning to their Missouri Zion?

"A DESOLATING SCOURGE"— PROPHECY FULFILLED

The cup of Mormon indignation was brimful long before 1861. Ever since the government sanctioned the expulsion of Mormons from their homes in Missouri in the 1830s, followed by the awful persecutions of Illinois, the martyrdom of their prophet-leaders, and later, President James Buchanan's dispatching of an entire U.S. Army to Utah to put down and destroy an alleged religious dictatorship, Mormons had been hurt, hated, and hunted by an America bent on their religion's reformation, if not its destruction.

There is ample evidence in Mormon scripture that the Saints themselves were responsible for many of their greatest troubles. "For shall the children of the kingdom pollute my holy land? Verily, I say unto you, Nay" (D&C 84:59). Yet as the years passed, different interpretations came to predominate. In one of his earliest revelations, in 1829, Joseph Smith prophesied of "a desolating scourge [that] shall go forth among the inhabitants of the earth, and shall continue to be poured out from time to time, if they repent not, until the earth is empty, and the inhabitants thereof are consumed away and utterly destroyed by the brightness of my coming" (D&C 5:19). By the time the Latter-day Saints were driven from Illinois seventeen years later, diary and sermon were replete with condemnations, warnings, and expectations of imminent premillennial judgment and wrath. To deny such is to deny their sense of history, justice, and prophecy. Prior to leaving Winter Quarters for the West in 1847, Brigham Young said, "The whisperings of the Spirit to us have invariably been of the same import, to depart, to go hence, to flee into the mountains, to retire to our strongholds that we may be secure in the visitation of the judgments that must pass upon this land, that is crimsoned with the blood of Martyrs; and that we may be hid, as it were, in the clefts of the rocks, and in the hollows of the land of the Great Jehova[h], while the guilty land of our fathers is purifying by the overwhelming scourge."[3] There simply had to be a price to pay, an inevitable meting out of justice, a balancing of the equation for the several injustices inflicted upon the Saints.

On the first point—that of prophecy—the evidence is overwhelming that to the Latter-day Saints, the Civil War was a fulfillment of prophecy. Said Brigham Young, just weeks before the outbreak of war, "I have heard Joseph say, 'You will see the sorrows and misery that will be upon this land, until you will turn away and pray that your eyes may not be obliged to look upon it. . . . There are men in this Council that will live to see the affliction that will come upon this nation, until their hearts sink within them.'"[4] Orson Hyde, on a later occasion, referred to the same prophecy when he said, "Joseph Smith once said, on

the stand in Nauvoo, Illinois, that if the Government of the United States did not redress the wrongs of the Mormon people inflicted upon them in the State of Missouri, the whole nation should be distracted by mobs from one end to the other; and that they should have mobs to the full and to their 'hearts' content.' I heard the foregoing statement myself, as it fell from the lips of the Prophet in the presence of thousands of witnesses."[5]

Besides his 1829 revelation already cited, Joseph Smith was best remembered for his 1832 prophecy about "the wars that will shortly come to pass, beginning at the rebellion of South Carolina, which will eventually terminate in the death and misery of many souls" (D&C 87:1). Given twelve years before his own death and twenty-nine years before the war itself broke out, Joseph Smith's revelation gave several more details, ending with a statement of cause not overlooked by his followers and successors: "that the cry of the saints, and of the blood of the saints, shall cease to come up . . . to be avenged of their enemies" (D&C 87:7).

Wilford Woodruff, speaking in 1862, was but one of many who repeated the prophecy, arguing, "It is a hard dealing of the Almighty and we cannot help it." He continued, "Every Elder in this Church who lives his religion knows that this which is now transpiring is according to the mind and foreshadowings of the Holy Spirit. . . . It is out of the power of man, excepting by the repentance of the whole nation, for they have shed the blood of the Prophets, driven this church and people from their midst, . . . [and] have turned those keys that will seal their condemnation."[6] And Brigham Young said on an earlier occasion, "I heard Joseph Smith say, nearly thirty years ago, 'They shall have mobbing to their hearts'

Referring to the Civil War, John Taylor (1808–87), third Church President (from 1880 to 1887), made the statement on July 4, 1861, "They [the North and the South] have both . . . brought it upon themselves, and we have no hand in the matter." (Private Collection of Norma Dawn Livingston Worthington)

those who believed the Latter-day Saints had lost faith in America because of such prophecies. "But did not Joseph Smith prophesy that there would be rebellion in the United States?" he countered. Continuing, he remarked:

He did, and so have I scores and hundreds of times; And what of that? Could I help that? Could Joseph Smith help knowing that a rebellion would take place in the United States? Could he help knowing it would commence in South Carolina? You could not blame him for that. He was in his grave at that time it commenced. . . . If the Lord, we all talk about the Lord you know, Christians as well as "Mormons," and about the providence of God, and the interposition of the Almighty, if the Lord has a design to accomplish, if there is a fate, if you like the word any better, and some infidels as well as Christians believe strongly in the doctrine of fate, if there is a fate in these things who ordered it? Who can change its course? Who can stop it? Who can alter it?⁹

"A REQUISITION UPON THE NATION"—RETRIBUTIVE JUSTICE

No less earnest to the Latter-day Saints than the fulfillment of prophecy was the urgent expectation, at least among most leaders, of retributive justice. "God has come out of his hiding place," said Brigham Young, "and has commenced to vex the nation that has rejected us, and he will vex it with a sore vexation. It will not be patched up—it never can come together again—but it will be sifted with a sieve of vanity, and in a short time it will be like water spilled on the ground."¹⁰

content, if they do not redress the wrongs of the Latter-day Saints.' Mobs will not decrease, but will increase until the whole Government becomes a mob, and eventually it will be State against State, city against city, neighbourhood against neighbourhood, Methodists against Methodists, and so on."⁷ Brigham Young returned to this theme of prophecy fulfilled in 1864, nearer the war's end, when he said, "Joseph said many and many a time to us— 'Never be anxious for the Lord to pour out his judgments upon the nation; many of you will see the distress and evils poured out upon this nation till you will weep like children.'"⁸

One last reference to the prophetic element is worth mentioning. John Taylor, just one week before the end of the war, argued against

"I have never prayed for the destruction of this Government," said Heber C. Kimball in April 1861, "but I know that dissolution, sorrow, weeping and distress are in store for the inhabitants of the United States, because of their conduct towards the people of God."[11]

More of a "hard liner," perhaps, than most of his colleagues, Heber C. Kimball often expressed such strong feelings. Speaking just a few months later, he reminded his listeners, several of whom were recent convert-emigrants from England, of their paths of persecution. "Many of you are strangers to these things, both members and Elders because you were not baptized into the Church until afterwards," he said. "But still you can see what the world has done to us; and everything in the shape of persecution or affliction which the world have brought upon us, will come back upon their heads ten-fold and this nation in particular will reap what they have sown and their troubles have already commenced; but I shall live to see them broken to pieces a great deal worse than they are now . . . the blood of retributive justice is on them . . . [and] the destruction of this nation is sealed, except they will repent, which is not very probable."[12] In May of 1862, Kimball returned to the same theme. "The South and the North are at war with each other," he said, and they "are slaying each other, and if they were not doing that they would be trying to slay us; this they do already in their hearts, and the sin is the same upon the nation as though they did it in reality; I am a martyr of God, and so is Brother Brigham and other men of God whose lives they have hunted. God will chastise them and all those who had a hand in seeking our destruction. . . . Let the Saints acknowledge the hand of God in it all."[13] Orson Hyde echoed Kimball's

Heber C. Kimball (1801–68), a prominent and influential early Mormon leader, was a counselor to Brigham Young, missionary, polygamist with dozens of wives, and a successful land owner. Upon learning about the battle of Gettysburg, he announced that "When the trouble will be at an end, is not for me to say." (Utah State Historical Society)

sentiments, at least early on in the war, when he said of the atrocities committed earlier against the Saints, "What can we expect other than that a righteous God, a faithful Sovereign would make just such a requisition upon the nation as he is now making. . . . Justice, though sometimes slow in its operations, is, nevertheless, sure to obtain its demands."[14]

The specifics are not hard to find. The expulsion of the Mormons from Missouri, the extermination order of Governor Lilburn W. Boggs, the Haun's Mill Massacre, and Martin Van Buren's weakness and unwillingness to intervene federally, especially in light of President Buchanan's 1857 decision to send an army of intervention to Utah—these were deep and long-festering wounds the Saints would not be allowed to forget. Brigham Young stated, "If Van Buren had said, 'Be still, or I will chasten you and keep sacred the oath of my office,' we should not have been mobbed, and the nation would not have been as it is to-day."[15] And as to Johnston's Army, the following response portrays the overriding sentiment: "Who frustrated that army in their design?" asked Wilford Woodruff. "The Lord our God, and now the judgments that have come upon the nation in consequence of their treatment to this people are a sore vexation to them but it is the hard dealing of the Almighty and we cannot help it."[16]

Though these and other grievances received their space, it was Carthage Jail and June of 1844 that most galvanized Mormon attitudes. As per the lyrics "Wake up the world for the conflict of justice" in William W. Phelps's enduring poem, and later a hymn of praise, it was the martyrdom of Joseph Smith and his brother Hyrum that forever remained. Writer after writer, speaker after speaker, returned to Carthage, choosing to see it as the watershed of God's wrath. Brigham Young said of the persecutors of Jospeh Smith, "They spurned from their presence the man who would acknowledge that God should reign King of Nations. . . . He was [like] a God to us, and is to the nations of the earth and will continue to be. . . . He was the Prophet of the Lord. . . . Were they aware of it at the seat of Government? I have no doubt they as well knew of the plans for destroying the Prophet as did those in Carthage or in Warsaw, Illinois. It was planned by some of the leading men of the nation."[17] "In killing him, they killed their best earthly friend," wrote another, "the man who of all others was best able to save them from themselves—from that anarchy, misery, and destruction they would bring upon themselves."[18]

Perhaps this 1864 *Millennial Star* editorial, likely penned by George Q. Cannon while yet

president of the British Mission, expressed the sentiment best: "War! Dreadful and continued war! War and its concomitants, famine and pestilence, will purge and purify the earth of the ungodly. Already our boasted land of liberty, the asylum for the oppressed in the new world, is deluged with blood, and will continue to be so until it has atoned for rejecting the Gospel and refusing to avenge the wrongs of our people, and for passively sanctioning the murder of God's servants."[19]

The rock-bed sentiment is not always synonymous with the public rhetoric. To the contemporary ear, such Mormon statements may be as hard to accommodate as are the columns and cartoons in the same time period's eastern press of hate and prejudice against the Latter-day Saints. There can be no mistaking the division and the hard feelings. Yet the Latter-day Saints were expressing convictions, not seeking vengeance. Their belief that America would suffer was motivated less out of a desire to see that suffering and more out of their conviction in the Restoration and in the mission of the Prophet Joseph Smith. "For do ye suppose that ye can get rid of the justice of an offended God, who hath been trampled under feet of men?" (3 Nephi 28:35). As surely as ancient empires were destroyed for neglecting the prophets of old, so history must repeat itself, or, as George A. Smith put it in 1861, "By-and-by it will be like it was with the Jaredites and the Nephites."[20]

Some other comments, particularly those made at the outset of the war, deserve attention. If some in the East were expecting a short conflict with a quick and glorious Union victory, no such interpretation came out of Utah. Even before the first shot was fired, the Mormon expectation was that the war would be long and horrible. "Do any of you think this war is going to be over in a few days?" asked Heber C. Kimball in May 1861. "If you do, you are greatly mistaken."[21] "Will it be over in six months or three years?" followed Brigham Young just a few months later. "No, it will take years and years, and will never cease until the work is accomplished. There may be seasons that the fire will appear to be extinguished, and the first you know it will break out in another portion, and all is on fire again, and it will spread and continue until the land is emptied."[22]

As late as September 1864, some were predicting an almost never-ending conflict, or at least a season of many wars. "A very large proportion of the people . . . imagine that the nation is on the eve of peace and an entire settlement of the difficulties," said George Q. Cannon. "But you and I, and all believers in God's revelations know how cruelly they deceive themselves, or, rather, suffer the great enemy of their souls to deceive them upon this point."[23]

Running parallel to these dire predictions of an extended conflict were the repeated expressions of gratitude and appreciation that the Saints were now far removed from the arena of war. "If we were in Missouri, we should be obliged to take sides in the present lamentable strife of brother against brother," said George A. Smith in March 1861. "If we were there, we should be in constant trouble."[24] Later, on July 4 of that same year, he said, "Now, brethren, are we not thankful that, at least, we can see the providence of the Almighty in suffering us to be driven into these valleys, where we can enjoy the sweets of true liberty—where none dare molest or make afraid?"[25] Brigham Young followed suit: "Do we appreciate the blessings of this our

An Apostle and member of the Church's First Presidency, George A. Smith (1817–75) asked in 1861, "Now, brethren, are we not thankful that, at least, we can see the providence of the Almighty in suffering us to be driven into these valleys, where we can enjoy the sweets of true liberty—where none dare molest or make afraid?" (Utah State Historical Society)

mountain home, far removed from the war, blood, carnage and death that are laying low in the dust thousands of our fellow creatures in the very streets we have walked, and in the cities and towns where we have lived?"[26]

Indeed, the Latter-day Saints as a people were not drawn into taking sides in the war. While it was true that Utah remained loyal to the Union and when called upon even equipped small regiments to defend government property during the war, the Mormon view was essentially one of neutrality. John Taylor's famous comments given on July 4, 1861, early in the war are worth repeating in this regard:

It may now be proper to inquire what part shall we take in the present difficulties. . . . In regard to the present strife, it is a warfare among brothers. We have neither inaugurated it, nor assisted in its inauguration. . . . We have been hunted like the deer on the mountains, our men have been whipped, banished, imprisoned and put to death. We have been driven from city to city, from state to state, for no just cause of complaint. . . . Shall we join the North to fight against the South? No! Shall we join the South against the North? As emphatically, No! Why? They have both . . . brought it upon themselves, and we have no hand in the matter. . . . We know no North, no South, no East, no West.[27]

"MY HEART IS FILLED WITH PAIN"—A SOFTENING OF ATTITUDE?

But as the war intensified, was there a softening in Mormon attitude? As news of the slaughters at Shiloh, Antietam, Chancellorsville, Fredericksburg, Vicksburg, and Gettysburg reached Utah almost instantaneously over the newly completed transcontinental telegraph lines, did such tragedies give the Saints pause to ponder and perhaps to recast their view of the war in a different hue? Did they see other, broader factors at work? Speaking at the Bowery in Salt Lake City the Sunday morning of August 31, 1862, President Young, after excoriating America once more for Carthage Jail, lamented the great destructions of human life and in a tone not yet heard before said, "My heart is filled with pain for the inhabitants of the earth. We desire with all our hearts to do them good. . . . It is our duty to pray for them and place before them the holy principles of the gospel by precept, and in the acts of our lives, rather than to hold prominently

forward their manifold corruptions. They are in the hands of God, and so are we."[28] The most meaningful expression of sympathy they could express would be to proclaim the gospel to America and to perform a lasting work of redemption for both their living and the dead. "We expect to . . . build hundreds and thousands of cities and magnificent temples and officiate for our forefathers and relatives . . . and for those ignorant thousands who are killing each other in the present war, and we will give them a salvation."[29]

By the middle of 1863, Brigham Young was referring to the war less as a punishment and more as an "unnecessary war," a "useless war" in which "more than a half million of the brave sons of our country now sleep in the dust."[30] "I do not think I have a suitable name for them," Brigham said later that year. "Shall we call them abolitionists, slaveholders, religious bigots, or political aspirants? Call them what you will, they are wasting away each other." Not anxious to take sides over the divisive issue of slavery and Lincoln's Emancipation Proclamation, the Mormon leader said: "Will the present struggle free the slaves? No, but they are wasting away the black race by the thousands. Many of the blacks are treated worse then [sic] we treat our dumb brutes, and they will be called to judgment for the way they have treated the negro."[31]

On receiving news of the bloodletting at Gettysburg, even Heber C. Kimball sounded less assured than he once had. "When the trouble will be at an end, is not for me to say. Now the Presbyterians of the North are preaching and praying against their Presbyterian brethren in the South; and this is precisely the condition of the Baptists, Methodists, Quakers and Shakers and I am real sorry that this is the case. There are many honorable and peaceable citizens who are moving west in consequence of the lamentable state of our once happy and peaceful country."[32] And from the *Millennial Star*, "We do not, however, allude to these events now, in a spirit of bitterness or revenge. Our hearts grieve over the sufferings of our misguided but obstinate brethren and sisters on the other side of the water. . . . How shall they be saved?"[33]

By 1864, the talk had turned to an invitation to repentance as the only solution to the stalemate of human suffering. "Can the inhabitants of our once beautiful, delightful, and happy country avert the horrors and evils now upon them?" asked Brigham Young. "Only by turning from their wickedness and calling upon the Lord. If they will turn unto the Lord and seek after him, they will avert this terrible calamity."[34]

"DO WE REJOICE OVER THEM?"

It is tempting to argue that there was a softening in Mormon attitudes toward America as the war progressed. Yet, such is hard to prove conclusively, since for every note of conciliation there were still cries of indignation. If there was one Latter-day Saint spokesman, however, who ever sounded a more conciliatory note, a more global view, and who gave a broader interpretation of America's present distress than the injustices of Carthage, it was the very man who was there with the Prophet when he died. Possibly because of his British and Canadian background and more global interests, John Taylor placed the causes of the war—of all wars—in the larger context of man's inhumanity to man and his recurring disobedience to God. Rarely did he place Mormon sufferings in the center of the cauldron, opting instead to see far greater forces of cause and effect at work. "When we

think of the trouble that is likely to overtake this nation," he said two weeks after the surrender of Fort Sumter,

as well as others, it is calculated to create a sympathetic feeling in the bosoms of all who reflect. For some weeks past I have been reviewing the events current in the nation, and I have felt a great deal of commiseration, and especially latterly. . . . If there is a cessation of open hostilities against us, it is not for want of a disposition, but owing to the peculiar situation in which they are placed relative to each other. . . . They are led captive by the Devil and are in a great measure controlled by him. This is truly a lamentable position, but the picture is not overdrawn. Do we rejoice over them? No, we do not; we have frequently offered to them the principles of life. . . . But who is this God of battles? Why, the Devil, the prince and power of the air. . . . What shall we do in the midst of these things that are now transpiring? Why, lean upon the Lord Our God, purify ourselves. . . . Let us also look at our position as Elders in Israel, clothed with the power of the Holy Priesthood, as men who hold the ministry of reconciliation. . . . This is the position we ought to occupy in relation to these matters.[35]

In a later address, Taylor saw the war less as punishment and more as the result of a depraved character of men: "The world has been full of darkness and wickedness, and has not understood the things of God; but many of the past as well as the present generations have been full of blood-thirstiness, fraud and oppression without any correct principles,

In 1862, Wilford Woodruff (1807–98), later the fourth LDS Church President, declared that the Civil War was "a hard dealing of the Almighty and we cannot help it." (Utah State Historical Society)

without the Spirit of the Lord to direct them. It is so now, and hence the wars and turmoils that at present exist in these United States."[36]

Elder Taylor also repeated his conviction that the war was but part of a rising tide of worldwide calamities and atrocities brought on by mankind because of their rejection of the principles of the gospel of Jesus Christ. "The Lord has begun to vex the nations," he said midway through the Civil War, "beginning with our own nation, he is vexing it and will vex other nations, and his judgments will go forth, and all the wicked nations of the world will feel the avenging hand of God and He will continue to overthrow nation after nation until he whose right it is will take the government into his own hand."[37]

"THE LORD IS PREPARING THAT END OF THE ROUTE"— THE RETURN TO ZION

There remains one final topic to discuss, and if it is not central to Latter-day Saint views of the war, then certainly it is at least a fascinating corollary to it. What impact did the war have on the view of many that Zion—Missouri—must be reclaimed by the returning Latter-day Saints? The topic is complicated, but this study would be incomplete if it did not attempt to show, at least in part, that there was lively Mormon interest in what was happening in western Missouri, especially Jackson County, during the Civil War. Was the time ripening for a return to Zion? Was there another purpose to the war?

There is little question that Mormon attention fastened more on Jackson County than on any other arena of the Civil War during these years. What skirmishes and troubles did take place there the *Deseret News* was quick to report. The following is but one of several news stories carried on the topic:

> The interest of the people of Utah in Jackson County, Missouri, prompts the publication of the following extracts: "Devastation in Jackson Co., Missouri."
>
> The depopulation of the counties in Jackson, Cass, Bates, and Vernon is thorough and complete. One may ride for hours without seeing a single inhabitant and deserted houses and farms are everywhere to be seen. The whole is a grand picture of desolation.[38]

Heber C. Kimball saw the impending conflict as a possible means of fulfilling another prophecy. "The United States will suffer, for they will be afflicted with wars and with trouble at home. While this is going on, the man who lives his religion and honours his calling will be prospered and go back to Jackson County, Missouri, with the faithful Elders, where they will receive their inheritances."[39]

Likewise, Brigham Young, at least in the early goings-on of the war, saw the possible return of his people and sounded the call of warning and preparation. "Just as soon as the Latter-day Saints are ready and prepared to return to Independence, Jackson County, in the state of Missouri," he said, "just as soon will the voice of the Lord be heard, 'arise now, Israel, and make your way to the center stake of Zion.' . . . Do you believe that we, as Latter-day Saints, are preparing our own hearts—our own lives—to return to take possession of the center stake of Zion, as fast as the Lord is preparing [it]? . . . We must be pure to be prepared to build up Zion. To all appearance the Lord is preparing that end of the route faster than we are preparing ourselves to go."[40] In 1862, Brigham Young returned to this same theme. Referring to the construction of the Salt Lake Temple, which was frustratingly slow for a host of reasons, he said, "I am afraid we shall not get it up until we have to go back to Jackson County which I expect will be in seven years. I do not want to quite finish this Temple for there will not be any temple finished until the one is finished in Jackson Co. [as] pointed out by Joseph

Smith. Keep this as a secret to yourselves, lest some may be discouraged."[41]

Come the end of 1863, with the war at fever pitch, a watchful Wilford Woodruff had also come to the conclusion that this might be the long-awaited time. "The Lord is watching over the interests of Zion and sustains his Kingdom upon the earth and [is] preparing the way for the return of his saints to Jackson County, Missouri to build up the waste places of Zion. Jackson County has been entirely cleared of its inhabitants during the year 1863 which is one of the greatest miracles manifested in our day and those who have driven the Saints out and spoiled them are in their turn now driven out and spoiled."[42]

Of course, the Saints never did return to Missouri, and the topic remains for further study. At long last, America's deadliest war ended at Appomattox in April 1865. With the waning of the war, Mormon statements about the conflict also lessened. The news of Lee's surrender was happily received in Utah, although celebrations were muted, as perhaps elsewhere throughout the land, by the reflection on the destruction of the South, Sherman's march through Georgia, and the horror and devastation of the past four years. Furthermore, the attention of Latter-day Saint leadership now began to shift to protect the institution of plural marriage the nation had already vowed to exterminate. That would be another war well worth watching.

Richard E. Bennett is a professor of Church history and doctrine at Brigham Young University.

NOTES

This chapter is reprinted, with permission, from *Mormon Historical Studies* 10, no. 1 (Spring 2009): 51–63.

1. "Editorial," *Deseret News*, May 18, 1861.

2. Some of the few works dedicated to the Civil War from a Mormon history perspective are E. B. Long, *The Saints and the Union: Utah Territory during the Civil War* (Champaign: University of Illinois Press, 1981); Gustive O. Larson, "Utah and the Civil War," *Utah Historical Quarterly* 33, no. 1 (Winter 1965): 55–67; and Ray C. Colton, *The Civil War in the Western Territories: Arizona, Colorado, New Mexico, and Utah* (Norman: University of Oklahoma Press, 1959). See also Robert J. Stott, "Mormonism and War: An Interpretative Analysis of Selected Mormon Thought Regarding Seven American Wars" (master's thesis, Brigham Young University, 1974).

3. Brigham Young to the Saints at Mt. Pisgah and Garden Grove, Iowa Territory, January 25, 1847, Brigham Young Papers, Church History Library, The Church of Jesus Christ of Latter-day Saints, Salt Lake City.

4. Brigham Young, in *Journal of Discourses* (London: Latter-day Saints' Book Depot, 1854–86), 8:325, February 10, 1861.

5. Orson Hyde to the editor of the *(St. Louis) Missouri Republican*, January 1, 1862, as found in the Journal History of the Church, January 1, 1862, Church History Library.

6. Wilford Woodruff, in Journal History, July 27, 1862.

7. Brigham Young, in *Journal of Discourses*, 9:5, April 6, 1861.

8. Brigham Young, in Journal History, May 15, 1864.

9. John Taylor, in Journal History, March 5, 1865.

10. Brigham Young, in *Journal of Discourses*, 8:324, February 10, 1861.

11. Heber C. Kimball, in *Journal of Discourses*, 9:55, April 14, 1861.

12. Heber C. Kimball, in Journal History, July 4, 1861.

13. Heber C. Kimball, in Journal History, May 4, 1862.

14. Orson Hyde, in Journal History, January 1, 1862.

15. Brigham Young, in *Journal of Discourses*, 9:4, April 6, 1861.

16. Wilford Woodruff, in Journal History, July 27, 1862. Albert Sidney Johnston, commander of the Utah expedition and later general in the Confederate Army, had only recently been killed in the Battle of Shiloh.

17. Brigham Young, in *Journal of Discourses*, 8:320–21, February 10, 1861.

18. "Emancipation of the Slaves—The Prophet Joseph Smith's Plan—Results of Its Rejection," *Millennial Star*, February 14, 1863, 101. The article was probably written by George Q. Cannon, editor of the *Millennial Star*.

19. George Q. Cannon, in Journal History, January 23, 1864.

20. George A. Smith, in *Journal of Discourses*, 9:69–70, March 10, 1861.

21. Heber C. Kimball, in *Journal of Discourses*, 9:134, May 12, 1861.

22. Brigham Young, in *Journal of Discourses*, 9:143, July 28, 1861.

23. George Q. Cannon to Brigham Young Jr. and Daniel H. Wells, September 18, 1864, in Journal History for the same date. Cannon, like most Mormon commentators, was likely referring to the prophecy on war (D&C 87), which told not merely of the American conflict but of the many "wars" that would ensue thereafter.

24. George A. Smith, in *Journal of Discourses*, 9:69, March 10, 1861.

25. George A. Smith, in *Journal of Discourses*, 8:360, July 4, 1861.

26. Brigham Young, in Journal History, January 26, 1862.

27. John Taylor, in Journal History, July 4, 1861.

28. Brigham Young, in Journal History, August 31, 1862.

29. Brigham Young, in Journal History, April 6, 1862. For a very modern twist on this earlier prediction, see the article "Civil War Relics Lead to Life of Research," by Therese Fisher, in the *Church News*, January 20, 1990, which details the account of a William Taylor submitting temple work on over twenty thousand Confederate soldiers killed during the war. According to remarks given by Thomas S. Monson in 1992, the numbers had increased to over one hundred thousand. See Thomas S. Monson, "The Priesthood in Action," *Ensign*, November 1992, 48.

30. Brigham Young, in Journal History, May 31, 1863.

31. Brigham Young, in Journal History, October 6, 1863.

32. Heber C. Kimball, in Journal History, July 19, 1863.

33. "National Crimes and Their Consequences," *Millennial Star*, September 12, 1863, 580. The article was probably written by George Q. Cannon, editor of the *Millennial Star*.

34. Brigham Young, in Journal History, May 15, 1864.

35. John Taylor, in *Journal of Discourses*, 9:234, 236–37, April 28, 1861.

36. John Taylor, in Journal History, April 13, 1862.

37. John Taylor, in Journal History, February 22, 1863.

38. From the *St. Joseph (MO) Herald*, as reprinted in the *Deseret News*, October 18, 1863.

39. Heber C. Kimball, in *Journal of Discourses*, 9:42, March 17, 1861.

40. Brigham Young, in Journal History, July 28, 1861.

41. Brigham Young, in Journal History, August 22, 1862. See also *Wilford Woodruff's Journal, 1833–1898*, ed. Scott G. Kenney (Midvale, UT: Signature Books, 1983–84), 6:71.

42. *Wilford Woodruff's Journal*, 6:147.

Great Salt Lake City as it appeared shortly after the end of the Civil War in 1868. The Beehive House (Brigham Young's residence) and the Young family schoolhouse are shown near the center of the photograph. (Library of Congress)

CHAPTER 7

Brett D. Dowdle

"WHAT MEANS THIS CARNAGE?"

THE CIVIL WAR IN MORMON THOUGHT

Few events have captured the country's attention with greater power than the American Civil War. Resulting in over six hundred thousand deaths, the Civil War remains, by far, the country's most devastating military conflict. The war reached well beyond the battlefield, affecting almost every aspect of American society and touching nearly every home. Throughout the four-year span of the Civil War, newspapers were filled with reports of the carnage. Beyond newspapers, the war made its way into personal diaries and letters, as well as the literature of the day. According to historian Drew Gilpin Faust, the Civil War carnage "transformed the American nation" and "created a veritable 'republic of suffering.'"[1] Indeed, because of the war, "death dominated the thoughts of many Americans" during the first five years of the 1860s.[2]

As it did to the rest of the nation, the Civil War left its mark upon Utah and the Church. Although very few Mormons actually participated in the war, reports of the difficulties regularly filled the pages of the *Deseret News.* Further, while Utah communities did not experience the high mortality rates that devastated Northern and Southern communities, Utahns were affected by the war in a variety of ways. Like other Americans, Mormon leaders struggled to understand the meaning of the war and its devastating effects, making it a familiar topic in their public sermons, private conversations, correspondence, and diaries. These glimpses into the thoughts and feelings of Mormonism's leaders provide valuable insights into the question of why an American community remained largely neutral during the greatest tragedy in American history.

THE MEANING OF THE WAR

The Civil War presented Americans with a scene of destruction that was unlike anything the country had ever seen. The numbers were staggering, almost beyond comprehension, and challenged the American populous to grapple with the painful landscape of death.

In their search for understanding, many Americans turned to religion and theological explanations. One reverend expressed the country's desire to understand the war in verse, writing,

> "Oh great god! What means this
>   carnage
> Why this fratricidal strife,
> Brethren made in your own image
> Seeking for each other's life?"
>
> Thus spoke a dying Federal soldier,
> Amid the clash of arms he cried;
> With hope he fixed his eyes on
>   heaven,
> Then bid adieu to earth—and died.[3]

For such religious seekers, theology yielded a number of answers. As historian Mark Noll has pointed out, the Civil War became something of a "theological crisis" for the United States.[4] While some lost faith in the ability of God and religion to provide them with answers, others continued to find "spiritual meaning in death."[5] Their pain of death eased, many Americans were cheered by the idea of a "steadfast hope in a joyous, eternal reunion" with their departed loved ones in heaven.[6]

Although somewhat disconnected from the day-to-day scenes of the war because of geography, Mormons likewise turned to religion as they grappled with news of the conflict. Similar to many Americans, Mormons saw the war as a result of the sins of the nation.[7] In defining which sins America was being punished for, Mormons differed drastically from their Christian counterparts. Whereas many Northerners attributed the carnage of the Civil War to the sin of slavery, Mormons saw it as the divine judgment for the nation's persecution of the Latter-day

Saints. Brigham Young suggested that war in general was "instigated by wickedness" and was "the consequence of a nation's sin."[8] For Saints like Wilford Woodruff, the country was "ripe for the Harvest" and worthy of "the Judgments of God . . . because of their wickedness."[9] Although acknowledging that the war would come at a tremendous cost to the nation, Brigham Young believed that America had contracted a substantial debt through its persecution of the Saints and that any result other than the "overthrow" of the nation "would rob justice of its claims."[10]

For Latter-day Saints, the Civil War was not only a divine response to their persecuted past but also a fulfillment of prophecy and a vindication of Joseph Smith's prophetic status. On Christmas Day in 1832, the Prophet received a revelation concerning a coming war between the states. The prophecy predicted that the deluge of blood and wars prior to the Lord's Second Coming would begin with "the rebellion of South Carolina," leading to a vicious war between the North and the South.[11] Due to the dramatic nature of this prophecy, both Joseph Smith and his followers occasionally referred to it during the following years, although at the time it was not formally published among the revelations.[12] When the Civil War finally came, the prophecy became a key tool by which Latter-day Saints interpreted the conflict. Most of the explanations for the war that were championed by Latter-day Saint leaders during the 1860s were first expressed within the prophecy's wording, which covers only one page in Revelation Book 1 of *The Joseph Smith Papers*. As Mormon leaders interpreted the Civil War, they stayed close to the ideas and concepts of Joseph Smith's revelatory language.

PAINFUL OLD WOUNDS

Viewed through contemporary eyes, the Mormon response to the beginnings of the Civil War seems harsh, uncaring, and even vindictive. Mormon leaders seemed to take a measure of satisfaction in the nation's struggle. While the correctness of such reactions is debatable, these sentiments must be viewed in the context of the early Mormon experience and their memories of persecution.[13] For Mormons, "the mystic chords of memory" stirred deep emotions and provided painful reminders of a country whose chief executive had responded to their plight, "Your cause is just but I can do nothing for you."[14] As the war clouds grew increasingly threatening, Brigham Young remembered this infamous statement by Martin Van Buren and said with feeling, "The Curse of God will be upon the Nation and they will have Enough of it. . . . They have persecuted the Saints of God and the Rulers would do nothing for us but all they Could against us and they will now get their pay for it."[15]

Even before the difficult experiences of Jackson County, Haun's Mill, and Carthage Jail, Latter-day Saint leaders had begun to see the coming civil strife in the context of the persecution of the Church. The Lord told Joseph Smith that the coming scourge and "the consumption decreed" were to be brought about so that "the cry of the Saints of the bloodshed of the Saints shall cease to come into the ears of the Lord of Sabaoth from the earth to be avenged of their enemies."[16]

The issues surrounding the Civil War were a frequent topic in Brigham Young's discourses throughout the early years of the war. This photograph was taken in 1876. (Utah State Historical Society)

Not long after Joseph's prophecy, the Saints experienced serious troubles with the larger American communities in both Missouri and Illinois. In 1833, Latter-day Saints were driven from their settlements in Jackson County and forced to seek refuge in neighboring counties. Then in 1838, the Church's struggles in Missouri erupted into war, leading to the imprisonment of Joseph Smith and other leaders, as well as the expulsion of the body of the Saints from the state. Little more than five years later, the Saints found themselves experiencing similar difficulties in Illinois, culminating in the martyrdom of Joseph and Hyrum Smith and prompting Church leaders to abandon Nauvoo and seek refuge in the sparsely populated West.

The experiences of Missouri and Illinois left many Mormons feeling betrayed by the American Republic and its promised freedoms. Latter-day Saints felt that these experiences had left an indelible stain upon the United States and that the country would have to pay for these transgressions. Pained by the tragedy at Carthage, W. W. Phelps penned a well-known tribute to Joseph Smith now entitled "Praise to the Man."[17] In its original language, the poem read, in part,

> Praise to his mem'ry,
>   he died as a martyr;
> Honor'd and blest
>   be his ever great name;
> Long shall his blood,
>   which was shed by assassins,

Stain Illinois,
　　while the earth lauds his fame. . . .
Sacrifice brings forth
　　the blessings of heaven;
Earth must atone
　　for the blood of that man!
Wake up the world
　　for the conflict of justice.
Millions shall know
　　"brother Joseph" again.[18]

Writing in a similar strain, John Taylor exclaimed,

Ye men of wisdom, tell me why—
No guilt, no crime in them were
　　found—
Their blood doth now so loudly cry,
From prison walls and Carthage
　　ground?[19]

The challenges of Haun's Mill and Carthage Jail, together with the irresponsiveness of both state and federal officials, convinced many Mormons of the justness of a divine punishment upon the nation. Less than three years after the Martyrdom, as the Church was preparing to leave Winter Quarters and go to the West, Brigham Young received a revelation in which he was told:

Thy brethren have rejected you and your testimony, even the nation that has driven you out, and now cometh the day of their calamity even the days of sorrow like a woman that is taken in travail, and their sorrow shall be great: unless they speedily repent; yea, very speedily! for they have killed the Prophets and them that were sent unto them; and they have shed innocent blood which crieth from the Ground

against them. . . . Many have marveled because of [Joseph Smith's] death, but it was needful that he should seal his testimony with his blood, that he might be honored, and the wicked might be condemned.[20]

At least for Brigham, such sentiments did not soften as time elapsed. In February 1861, with the secession crisis in full sway and the nation on the brink of war, Brigham stated that he "knew the reason why this Government was in trouble." He attributed the national problems to the fact that "they had killed Joseph Smith" and noted that the country would "have to pay for it as the Jews did in killing Jesus."[21] As the news of secession portended an eruption into civil war, one Haun's Mill Massacre survivor told a group of Saints that he dreamed two years prior to that time that "the U. S. Government & Army will all break to peaces [sic] as they are now doing."[22] Then, as the war ravaged Missouri, Brigham assured the Saints that their persecutions in the state "will not begin to compare with the misery and real suffering they are now receiving . . . in consequence of war."[23]

While Brigham believed that the war was at least partially the result of the persecutions in Missouri and Illinois, the war also provided him with a new perspective on the Missouri and Illinois experiences. As the conflict ravished the state of Missouri, Brigham noted that because the Saints had been "invited to sign away our property to pay the expenses of our persecutors" and to "take away as much of our moveable property as we could," the Saints had avoided the suffering brought on by the war.[24] Painful as the early persecutions had been, Mormon leaders began to see them as having been somewhat providential in that they had led the Saints to the Utah Territory, where they were able to avoid the war.

Drawing upon more recent experiences, Mormon leaders also attributed the Civil War to the 1857–58 campaign officially known as the "Utah Expedition," more commonly known as the Utah War, in which the United States Army was dispatched to put down a supposed Mormon rebellion in Utah. Occurring only three years prior to the outbreak of the Civil War, the Utah Expedition was a fresh and painful memory that had only deepened the rifts between Mormons and the federal government. During the Utah War, public opinion against the Church had been mean-spirited and even violent. Citizens throughout the country had written to James Buchanan declaring that "B. Young and fifty others, of the leaders [ought] to be hanged up by the 'neck.'"[25] When Buchanan finally sent a Peace Commission to investigate matters in Utah, the *New York Times* praised the decision but assured Buchanan that "the Government is not likely to be held to a very strict account for its acts towards [the Mormons]," even suggesting that "they should be utterly exterminated, or driven from their present resting-place."[26] Brigham later reminded a group of leaders that "when Buchanan sent the armey it was there intention to Hang the Leaders then send thousands of Gentiles here."[27]

Even though the Saints had been exonerated from the claims of rebellion, federal officials remained skeptical of the Mormons. In 1861, as the war was just under way, a California newspaper claimed, "Brigham Young . . . has nearly completed his preparations for withdrawing Utah from the Union."[28] Then, as the troops stationed at Camp Floyd prepared to leave Utah to fight in the Civil War, Mormons were allowed to purchase many of the army's supplies at a nominal price. On orders from Washington, DC, however, the army destroyed all of the munitions that could not be taken east. This display of continued mistrust angered Brigham, leading him to describe the perceived insult to several friends.[29] Writing to Walter Murray Gibson, Brigham described the destruction of the arms and ammunition as clear evidence of "the animosity still existing against us in the breasts of the would be 'powers that be' at Washington." For Brigham, the scene was "a fitting finale" to the government's "unholy . . . crusade" against the Mormons, tangible proof that the government had never abandoned its mistrust of the Utah community.[30]

To counter national distrust, Brigham made it known that "he did not wish Utah mixed up with the secession movement."[31] When someone asked if the Saints would secede if an undesirable man was appointed governor of the territory, Brigham responded, "No, we will keep our records Clean. . . . It is better for us to Submit to those things which are unplesant than for us to do wrong." He then promised, "For all the oppressions [the government] put upon us God will bring them into Judgment."[32] In answer to the continued questions of Mormon loyalty, Brigham noted that Utah was "preparing to appropriately celebrate our Nation's birthday" in 1861, while "commotion and war [were] rife in our land." Noting the irony of the circumstances, he commented that "when the nation that sought our destruction is disunited, we celebrate the day it asserted its independence against oppression." For Brigham, such actions proved the Saints' "constant loyalty to our Government correctly administered."[33] These displays of patriotism were important to Brigham Young, who was trying to convince government officials that

"Utah [had] not seceded but [was] firm for the constitution and laws" of the country.[34]

Although Latter-day Saint leaders were anxious to emphasize their loyalty to the United States, they had not forgotten the Utah War and frequently referred to it in speaking about the Civil War. For some Saints, it was a kind of poetic justice to see the army that had been sent to Utah divided and fighting each other. Brigham Young found it particularly fitting that the secession crisis happened at the end of "the reign of king James [Buchanan] the defunct."[35] Sharing similar feelings, some Saints prayed that Confederate general Albert Sidney Johnston, commander of the Utah Expedition, would "be hung as a traitor" or find himself involved in a battle where he would "be right well whipped."[36] Johnston died during the bloody fighting at the battle of Shiloh on April 6, 1862. In spite of the many hurt feelings that Johnston's name occasioned in Utah, his death was reported to the Saints in a matter-of-fact manner.[37]

A POLITICAL CRISIS

While the war provided Mormons with ample opportunity to see the judgments of God upon a sinful nation, Mormon leaders were likewise cognizant of the fact that the nation's volatile political circumstances had created the country's struggles. Sectional divisions plagued the country since its founding and had been an important issue in the 1830s, when Joseph Smith prophesied that

Wilford Woodruff (1807–98), an LDS Church Apostle and later President, frequently wrote about the Civil War in his journal. (Seminaries and Institutes)

the beginning of the bloodshed would "probably arise through the slave question" (D&C 130:13). During the three decades between 1832 and the beginning of the war in 1861, the slavery question became increasingly divisive, a fact of which Mormon leaders were particularly cognizant.

While representing the Church in Washington a year prior to the outbreak of the war, George Q. Cannon noted the political divisions. He reported to Brigham Young, "Party feeling runs high, and the interest of the country are completely lost sight of in the desire to benefit the party. The daily scenes in the halls of Congress present a wretched spectacle."[38] Using news from the Pony Express and the telegraph, the Saints in Utah likewise kept close tabs on the country's political situation during 1860 and 1861 and frequently discussed it in private conversations. Wilford Woodruff in particular kept a detailed record of the political chaos. As the election of 1860 progressed, Elder Woodruff seemed to sense that dramatic events were unfolding. Just weeks before the election, he read the news and wrote, "Politicks still occupy the attention of the united States."[39] Then, upon receiving news of Lincoln's election, Elder Woodruff wrote that he "spent [the] evening . . . at President Youngs. . . . Conversing upon the Election & governmentull affairs."[40] In the months prior to Lincoln's inauguration, Elder Woodruff paid close attention to the secession crisis and recorded the events in his diary.[41] On the day of Lincoln's inauguration,

Woodruff noted, "This day Abel [sic] Lincoln is Inaugurated as the President of the United States, or that portion of it which is left."[42] The day's simple entry spoke volumes about the chaos of the previous four months.

For Brigham Young, the cause of this sectional strife was clear: slavery. Since America's founding, no single issue had been more politically divisive than slavery. To appease the slaveholding colonies, the Continental Congress had eliminated several lines about slavery from the Declaration of Independence.[43] Then, during the Constitutional Convention of 1787, the debate over slavery became so strident that the founders finally agreed to leave it alone with hopes that the issue would eventually resolve itself "without intervention by the central government."[44] Such hopes, however, proved to be unrealistically optimistic as slavery and sectional strife increasingly plagued the country in the decades following the 1780s, eventually erupting into the Southern secession and the Civil War.

Since 1832, the Saints had suspected that a conflict would eventually arise in the States "through the slave question" (see D&C 87:1–4; 130:12–13). Mormons learned just how divisive the politics of slavery could be during their experience in Jackson County in the early 1830s and witnessed the contentious debate over the topic during 1850 with keen interest.[45] Between 1830 and 1860, the topic of slavery affected nearly every American, including Mormons. Although Brigham emphatically denied any connections to the abolitionist movement, he opposed the institution of slavery.[46] When some questioned whether Utah would "lay a foundation for Negro slavery" in the early 1850s, Brigham responded, "No[,] God forbid. And I forbid.

I say let us be free."[47] He then proclaimed his belief that "those who mistreat slaves will be damned."[48] But Brigham's opposition to slavery went beyond the well-founded concern that slaves were often mistreated. With his New England eyes, he saw the South's "peculiar institution" as a blight on America and "the ruin of the South." Brigham was convinced that "slavery ruins any soil," including the South with its "beautiful climate and rich soil."[49] His views reflected the views of most people with a New England upbringing who had challenged the institution of slavery. Hence, when he ascribed political reasons to the war, Brigham was quick to note that the war had begun "to give freedom to millions that are bound."[50] Given the significant historiographical debates since 1865 about the cause of the Civil War, it is significant that, at least for Brigham Young, the political origins of the war had everything to do with the question of slavery and its detrimental effects on the country.

Brigham noted a number of additional factors linked to the issue of slavery that led to the war. He felt that the war was at least partially due to the work of radical politicians who had been allowed to take center stage on the country's political scene, and he bemoaned the contributions of both the secessionists and abolitionists who had "set the whole national fabric on fire."[51] Brigham believed that the war might have been shortened if the government had "cast out the Seceders" when the secession crisis had begun.[52] Although many Mormons sympathized with the South, Brigham was emphatic that "South Carolina [had] committed treason" when it seceded, and he regretted that Buchanan had not "hung up the first man who rebelled" in the state.[53] When some suggested that peaceful secession was an option, Brigham scoffed at the idea and argued that eventually "the fierce spirit urging to civil war" would overwhelm the nation, resulting in "rapine, flame, and bloodshed."[54]

In addition to blaming the radicalization of American politics, Brigham correctly noted that "commercial interests" had helped to lay "the foundation of the war."[55] Wilford Woodruff concurred, journalizing that "the Banks & rich men throughout the whole Country were Consecrating there millions of Dollars to sustain the war."[56] Prior to the Civil War, the South was in the midst of an economic boom that was mostly due to the growth of the slave

George Q. Cannon (1827–1901) witnessed the nation's Secession Crisis firsthand in Washington, DC. Cannon served in the Church's First Presidency under four Presidents: Brigham Young, John Taylor, Wilford Woodruff, and Lorenzo Snow. (Utah State Historical Society)

economy and the cotton that the slaves produced.[57] Slavery was big business, and "the South—or more accurately, the slaveholders of the South—had a great deal at stake in the continuation of their peculiar institution."[58] For Southern slaveholders who had amassed their wealth by relying upon a system of slavery, the election of a Republican president spelled disaster. They accordingly pushed for secession and the protection of their "peculiar institution" and the wealth it created.

IT COMES AS NO SURPRISE

In some regards, the outbreak of the Civil War came as no surprise to Latter-day Saints. They had been expecting a war between the states since 1832 and almost immediately recognized the secession crisis and the Civil War as the fulfillment of Joseph

Smith's prophecy. Hearing some early calls for Southern secession at the end of 1859, William H. Hooper, Utah's representative to Congress, wrote a letter to Brigham predicting, "This union will be disolved within 18 month."[59] A month later, the country's political divisiveness led George Q. Cannon to conclude that "the glory of our nation is rapidly fading away" and that if such a course continued, "the destruction of the government . . . is inevitable."[60] As the volatile election of 1860 unfolded, W. W. Phelps discussed the prophecy with Brigham Young, both clearly demonstrating their confidence that the current political situation was part of its fulfillment.[61] Following Lincoln's election and the outbreak of secession talk, Wilford Woodruff recalled Joseph's prophecy and concluded, "1860 has laid the foundation for the fulfillment of these things."[62] Likely with Latter-day Saint involvement, the text of the prophecy subsequently appeared throughout American newspapers, where it received a mostly negative reception.[63]

While some individuals seemed certain of the meaning of the prophecy and of the course of national events, the *Deseret News* editorials were less definitive in their declarations of coming war. Following Lincoln's election, one editorial wrote that it was "hard to predict" what would happen and that many in Salt Lake were "anxious to know what the South will do, whether they will back down, or carry their threats into execution, by taking measures to establish a Southern Confederacy."[64] For the paper's editors, however, what seemed certain was that the crisis would cause plenty of political problems in Washington and that the federal government would "have enough business" to draw their attention away from "the annihilation of the Saints."[65]

Brigham Young was similarly cautious in his interpretation of the crisis. The divisive election of 1860 made it clear to him that there were "some great Events at the door of this generation which will effect both Zion & great Babylon," but he was careful about defining just what those events would be and when they would occur.[66] Brigham's use of the phrase "at the door" hearkened back to the scriptural language that taught both the closeness and the uncertain timing of the Second Coming.[67] Still pained by the persecutory events of earlier years, Brigham expressed some hope that the nation would be moved to war in fulfillment of Joseph's prophecy. Even as events seemed to make this hope likely, however, Brigham expected some change in national feelings to avert the crisis. On the day of Lincoln's election, Brigham commented to Wilford Woodruff, "I hope that Abe Lincoln was Elected Presidet of the United States yesterday & that the South meet in Convention & nominate Breckenride to day to be the presidet of the South but I am afraid they will not have pluck enough to do it."[68] As national events unfolded and Southern secession became a reality, however, Brigham became firmly convinced that the nation actually would soon tear itself apart just as Joseph had prophesied. In January 1861, he remarked that "the news from the States would be extremely interesting about the middle of next April."[69] In February 1861 he commented, "There is

no union in the North or in the South. The nation must crumble to nothing."[70] Although peace commissioners worked to mend the growing rift, Brigham placed "but little confidence" in their efforts because of the fact that the members of Congress had "done but little" and were "not likely to do much" to save the Union.[71] By early 1861, Brigham was convinced that a peaceful resolution was no longer an option; the secession crisis and the lackluster efforts of those in Congress could only end in war.

While the events of 1860 and 1861 likely led most Americans to conclude that some bloodshed between the North and the South was inevitable, most expected a short conflict, marked more by fanfare than by fury. In his Second Inaugural Address, Abraham Lincoln gave voice to these sentiments, noting that "neither party [had] expected for the war, the magnitude, or the duration" which the nation had by that point "already attained." On the contrary, both sides had "looked for an easier triumph, and a result less fundamental and astounding."[72] Northern soldiers expressed similar sentiments. One Wisconsin volunteer wrote, "Many were confident that the war would last but for a few months," with none anticipating "more than a year away from those happy homes to which so many were destined never to return."[73] Another volunteer reassured his mother that most believed "the contest [would] be a short and decisive one" and "comparatively bloodless."[74] So certain had most Northerners been of a quick and relatively bloodless war that some interested citizens, with "no understanding of the realities of war," traveled to Manassas, Virginia, in July 1861 to witness one of the Civil War's first battles.[75] Watching the fray, one spectator reportedly exclaimed, "Oh, my! Is not that first-rate? I guess we will be in Richmond this time tomorrow."[76]

In contrast to such perspectives, Latter-day Saints fully expected a long and bloody conflict. Joseph Smith's prophecy about the war had promised that it would lead to an "outbreak of general bloodshed" and would "eventually terminate in the death & misery of many Souls."[77] So certain had Joseph been of the reality and intensity of the coming war that he advised Emmanuel Murphy, an early convert from the South, "to go to South Carolina & Georgia & warn his friends of the wrath & desolation . . . & to gather out his Friends to Zion for the wars & rebelion would begin in South Carolina."[78] Concurring with Joseph's prophecy Heber C. Kimball a few years prior to the war prophesied that he would live to see a "division . . . between the North and South . . . and much Blo[o]d would be spilt on the ocation."[79] As events began to unfold, Latter-day Saints trusted Joseph's assessment, believing that secession would "gain bitterness" and that the events would "probably lay a foundation for a bloody war."[80]

Even the ebb and flow of the war would not change Brigham's mind that it was to be a prolonged conflict. In April 1862, while some were declaring that "the tide of war" had turned "most decidedly in favor of the Federal armies" and that "the rebellion will soon be put down and peace again prevail," Brigham emphatically stated that the South would not easily submit and that "the war has scarcely commenced."[81] Brigham had

A close friend of Brigham Young, Thomas L. Kane (1822-83) served as an officer in the Union Army during the Civil War and saw action in several major battles, including Gettysburg.

been there when Joseph "predicted that the time would come when slavery in the South, and abolitionism in the North would sever the Union, divide the slave States from the free States, and there would be a great war," and he refused to believe that the war would be any different than Joseph's prophecy predicted.[82] Early in the war, Brigham had hoped that his "voice [might] be . . . effectually heard in the strife" so that he could "most cheerfully endeavour to reciprocate the noble deeds" of Thomas L. Kane during the Utah War and help restore peace to the Union. To his dismay, however, he saw that "the roar of canon and the clash of arms drown the still, small voice of prudent counsel," making peaceful negotiations almost impossible.[83] At least by 1863, he was convinced that nothing could be done to stop the scourge. Speaking to a group of Saints, he said, "[Joseph's] prediction is being fulfilled, and we cannot help it."[84]

THE BEGINNING OF BLOODSHED

Part of the reason that the Saints were so certain that the crisis would be long and bloody lay in their beliefs about the timing of the Second Coming. Millennialism pervaded American religious thought throughout the nineteenth century and was particularly influential during the Civil War.[85] Expressions like "the Son of Man cometh" were commonly used to describe the "suddenness of death" during the Civil War years. The war's high death rates combined with these scriptural phrases encouraged soldiers to prepare their souls to meet God.[86] Yet such phrases also bespoke the common belief that the war's awful carnage was evidence that the Lord's return was near.

For Latter-day Saints, a millennial interpretation of the Civil War was embedded in the revelations as well as in the surrounding society. Joseph's prophecy about the war stated that "the day of the Lord . . . cometh quickly."[87] Joseph also prophesied that the "commencement of bloodshed" in South Carolina would be "preparatory to the coming of the Son of Man." Then, upon inquiring concerning the timing of the Second Coming, he was informed, "Joseph my son, if thou livest until thou art 85 years old thou shall see the face of the Son of Man."[88] Alluding to this revelation, Joseph's early feeling about the approaching Millennium was that "the coming of the Lord . . . was nigh" and that "fifty six years, should wind up the scene."[89] Although in later years Joseph began to see far more ambiguity in the prophecy's statement about the timing of the Second Coming, many Latter-day Saints continued to see the prophecy as an announcement of the imminence of the Lord's return.[90]

With such expectations for the Lord's immediate return, Latter-day Saints spoke of the Civil War in apocalyptic terms. As they observed the events of the day, it seemed to them that the nation was "going to peices fast" and that "Destruction was nigh there door."[91] Indeed, in the words of Wilford Woodruff, the Lord had "commenced a Controversy with the American Government and Nation in 1860 and he will never cease untill they are destroyed from under heaven, and the Kingdom of God Esstablished upon their ruins." Even if the full Second Coming was still some years away, the message of the Civil War was "Let the Gentiles upon this land prepare to meet their God."[92] Because of the nation's sins, "the Lord was about to Empty the Earth th[at?] men would be destroyed."[93]

While the war certainly brought unprecedented death and destruction to America, it did not bring the all-consuming devastation that some had expected. Joseph's prophecy, however, only stated that the Civil War would be "the first outbreak of general bloodshed" and "the commencement of bloodshed as preparatory to the coming of the Son of Man."[94] It was clear that there was more to come. Accordingly, Mormon leaders continued to emphasize the need for the Saints to prepare for the Second Coming. In the closing months of the war, as a Northern victory appeared to be the inevitable outcome, Brigham Young admonished the Saints in England to "be warned by the signs of the times, and be on the alert, that they be not overtaken by the evils which are coming upon Babylon." Such difficulties would only end when the Savior had come to "reign and sway an undisputed sceptre over the earth." He warned, however, that in order for the Saints to "participate in all the blessings of this glorious and happy future, they must be humble and faithful and diligently seek to obey every commandment which the Lord has given."[95]

A CASE FOR NEUTRALITY

Expectations that the war would roll into the events of the Second Coming helps to partially explain why Mormons remained mostly neutral throughout the Civil War. At the end of Joseph's prophecy on the war, the Saints had been admonished, "Wherefore stand ye in holy places & be not moved untill the day of the Lord come for Behold it cometh quickly saith the Lord."[96] Given the feelings that the Civil War was a part of God's wrath upon a wicked nation, most Latter-day Saints likely felt no inclination to participate in the war, preferring instead to remain "peacefully and prosperously progressing in [their] 'mountain retreat.'"[97]

Although Utah was connected to the Union by its territorial status, many of its citizens felt disconnected from the war and felt no real allegiance to either side of the controversy. As many Saints saw the matter, neither the North nor the South had been friendly to the Saints, and therefore they were under no obligation to desire the triumph of either side. Explaining his reasons for staying out of the war, Brigham compared himself to a "woman who saw her husband fighting with a Bear." When her "husband called upon her to assist him, she replied I have no interest in who whips [who]."[98] By his own account, Brigham "earnestly prayed for the success of both North & South," hoping that "both parties might be used up."[99]

Because of the Church's past history with the federal government, Brigham was determined not to raise volunteers for the war. Noting that the federal government had "sought our Destruction all the day long," he promised that they would not "get 1,000 men to go into the Armey" from Utah. He then declared, "I will see them in Hell before I will raise an army for them."[100] While Brigham's comments were certainly incendiary and had the potential to raise questions, Mormon neutrality and distance from the conflict seemed to suit Lincoln, whose avowed Mormon policy was "I will let them alone, if they will let me alone."[101]

Remaining neutral, the Saints continued the work of establishing the Church in the Intermountain West and in various other parts of the world. Church leaders believed that God was ordering the events of the war so as to allow the Church to grow and prosper in Utah while the rest of the nation was at war. Upon receiving news of secession, Brigham Young reportedly "seem[ed] pleased." Brigham's pleasure, however, was not in the idea of the total annihilation of America but only in that it would give God's Kingdom the opportunity of "being established upon the Earth."[102] God's purpose in "vex[ing] the nations" was to "break down the barriers that have prevented His Elders from searching out the honest among all peoples."[103] Some missionaries noted a change in the demeanors of the people they taught. George Q. Cannon noted that the war created "gloomy feelings" among the people of England, stirring many up to "a sense of their actual position, and to enquire of the origin of it."[104] Having properly established God's kingdom, in due time the Saints would "step in and rescue the Constitution and aid all lovers of freedom in sustaining such laws as will secure justice and rights to all, irrespective of creed or party."[105]

FURTHER STRUGGLES TO COME

Even as the Civil War allowed Latter-day Saints an opportunity to better establish God's Kingdom and afforded them a brief respite from the pressures of intense federal scrutiny, Church leaders warned that it would only be a short-lived reprieve from their problems. Although Lincoln's election and the ascendancy of the Republican Party spelled an immediate conflict over the issue of slavery, it likewise portended future problems for Mormonism over the other "twin relic of barbarism," polygamy.

Although the government had made some concessions toward the Mormons, Brigham cautioned that the mere fact that the government was "not yet quite ready to commence open war upon the other 'twin relic'" was "by no means an indication that their feelings toward us are any better."[106] By Brigham's account, some Americans had taken Lincoln to task "for not destroying both 'the twins' together."[107] While he expected that the Civil War would "keep [the government] busy . . . for a time longer," Brigham fully expected future campaigns against polygamy and the Mormons.[108]

John Milton Bernhisel (1799–1881) was the original delegate of Utah Territory in the U.S. House of Representatives, serving from 1851 to 1859 and 1861 to 1863. (Utah State Historical Society)

Although slavery and the Civil War were the immediate tasks at hand, the government also began a long legal campaign against polygamy during this same period. Little more than a year into the war, the Republican Congress passed the Morrill Anti-Bigamy Act, which specified a punishment by "a fine not exceeding $500, and by imprisonment for a term not exceeding five years," for "every person having a husband or wife living, who shall marry any other person, whether married or single, in a Territory of the United States."[109] Learning that the Senate had passed the act, Brigham wrote to William H. Hooper requesting a copy of the bill.[110] Although the war prevented the act's immediate implementation, antipolygamy prosecution became an important part of the postbellum era. Indeed, in the years following the war, both Northern and Southern politicians joined together to support and pass

antipolygamy legislation. This joint crusade thus "provided one set of bonds that helped reforge national unity after the Civil War and Reconstruction."[111]

THIS REPUBLIC OF SUFFERING AMONG THE MORMONS

Although most Church members were largely detached from the Civil War and the death and suffering it brought, the war's massive death rates moved Mormon leaders. Brigham Young, in particular, still had family and friends in the East. As the death count grew and the pain of the Civil War deepened, Mormon statements about the justness of the nation's destruction almost entirely disappeared. Brigham's correspondence revealed a growing sense of compassion toward those who were suffering as a result of the war.

It is likely that nobody affected Brigham's thinking about the war more than Thomas L. Kane, who for years served as Brigham's closest non-Mormon confidant. Throughout his life, Kane had been motivated by a deep sense of patriotism. This patriotism led Kane to broker agreements between the Saints and the government when the Saints left Nauvoo in 1846 and again during the Utah War in 1858. And although he was an avowed pacifist, this same patriotism led Kane to enlist as an officer in the Northern army to help restore order to the Union when the war began.[112] Throughout the course of the war, Kane was wounded numerous times and was eventually encouraged by his physicians to withdraw from the army.[113] After learning that Kane had been wounded in 1862, Brigham wrote to John Bernhisel, "I was much gratified to learn that our good Friend Col. Kane had entirely recovered from his wounds. When you again see him, please give him my kind regards and best wishes for himself, dear family, and all his father's house."[114] Although Kane's several battle wounds were not fatal, they affected him throughout the remainder of his life. The effect of the war upon Kane's health was so dramatic that upon seeing him in 1869, Brigham Young Jr. wrote to his father that he had found Kane "miserable in health" and that he "would not have recognised him had we met in the street."[115]

William H. Hooper (1813–82) was Utah Territory's second delegate to Congress and worked vigorously to promote the interests of the territory from 1859 to 1861. (Utah State Historical Society)

This close connection to the hellish effects of war only redoubled Brigham's resolves for peace and his desires for both family and friends to avoid the dangers of the war. His desire to protect loved ones went so far as to welcome willing and friendly gentiles to Utah, where they would be shielded from the reach of the draft. He encouraged one friend and her family "to sell out and remove to far off and peaceful Utah," where they would "assuredly meet a cordial welcome."[116] Brigham also became more cautious to ensure that missionaries sent to England did not find their way to the battlefields. While en route to England in 1862 for missionary service, Brigham Jr. visited Thomas L. Kane, who was recuperating from a wound in Philadelphia. Kane asked Brigham Jr. "to go

with him one month . . . as his aidde camp." In writing to his father, Brigham Jr. hoped to gain "one word of advice, to me on that point." Because of the delay in mail service, Brigham Jr. decided to continue his journey toward England, and his father's subsequent letter revealed his pleasure with the decision to turn down Kane's offer.[117] For his part, Brigham Jr.'s decision had likely been influenced by a trip to Washington, DC, during which he had seen "some hundreds of wounded" arrive in the city "minus arms, legs, heads tied up, blood dripping from the hind end of the waggons, as they went through the streets— others shot through the body and puking blood at every step." The experience had horrified Brigham Jr., who wrote in his diary, "I would rather be in Utah than anywhere else in the world."[118] In 1864, when Brigham Jr. was called to yet another mission in England, his father sent a letter to Kane formally asking that "no requests, wishes or solicitations be made or inducements held out to him to go into the war now raging in the States, for I cannot and shall not in the least degree consent to his so doing,—at least not before his return from his present mission to Europe."[119] Thus, while Brigham did not entirely reject the idea of his son serving in the army, he left little room for speculation as to his feelings about Brigham Jr.'s potential service.

As the horrors of war came closer to home, Brigham became far more sympathetic as he spoke about those who were fighting in the war. Acknowledging the goodness of many of the soldiers, he referred to them as "multitudes of good and honorable men" who, for various reasons, had chosen to "expose themselves upon the field of battle."[120] For Brigham, the loss of what he estimated to be "not less than one million men . . . in a little over two years" was the most shameful consequence of the "useless war."[121] Brigham laid most of the blame for these deaths at the feet of the "popular leaders, who have inaugurated war instead of arbitrating peace." He went so far as to label the deaths occasioned by the war as "murder" and suggested that the leaders who were responsible would be "held accountable to God for the lives of their subjects which they have caused to be destroyed on the battlefields." Furthermore, Brigham believed that the leaders of the nation would also be held accountable for "the thousands of hearts they have broken and for the destitution and suffering they have caused to exist outside the battlefields."[122] Thus, for Brigham, the devastation of the Civil War went far beyond the battlefield and the astronomical death rates occasioned by gunfire, and reached into the homes and families of the dead, leaving them emotionally and temporally shattered. Moved by such grief,

Brigham exhorted the members "not to boast over our enemies' downfall."[123]

CONCLUSION

A mixture of conflicting memories and emotions defined the Civil War experience of the Latter-day Saints. For Mormons, the war represented a fulfillment of prophecy and the just vengeance of God upon a nation that spurned the "innocent who [had] cried for redress."[124] Accordingly, Latter-day Saints had remained neutral in the dispute and at times even "seem[ed] pleased with the news" of secession and the war.[125] In some regards, the war even seemed to benefit the Saints, providing them with a few years of long-desired refuge. Yet in spite of all this, they were Americans, and they wept over the painful effects of the Civil War. Brigham pled for the nation to develop "the bonds of everlasting peace" that would "continue to grow stronger and stronger until all are sanctified."[126] Although "passion[s] [had] strained" and harsh rhetoric had been uttered, by the end of the war, the Saints had been "touched . . . by the better angels of [their] nature," causing them to mourn the fact that their "once happy country [had been] clothed in mourning [and] drenched in fratricidal blood."[127]

Brett D. Dowdle is a PhD student in American history at Texas Christian University.

NOTES

1. Drew Gilpin Faust, *This Republic of Suffering: Death and the American Civil War* (New York: Vintage Books, 2008), xiii.

2. Sean A. Scott, *A Visitation of God: Northern Civilians Interpret the Civil War* (New York: Oxford University Press, 2011), 193.

3. "My God! What Is All This For?," quoted in Faust, *Republic of Suffering*, 177.

4. Mark A. Noll, *The Civil War as a Theological Crisis* (Chapel Hill: University of North Carolina Press, 2006).

5. Scott, *Visitation of God*, 193.

6. Scott, *Visitation of God*, 194; see 213.

7. Such explanations were particularly prominent among Northerners, many of whom viewed the war as a divine punishment for Southern slavery. Scott, *Visitation of God*, 35–70.

8. Brigham Young, in *Journal of Discourses* (London: Latter-day Saints' Book Depot, 1854–86), 10:230.

9. Wilford Woodruff, diary, November 24, 1860, and January 1, 1861, in *Wilford Woodruff's Journal: 1833–1898 Typescript*, ed. Scott G. Kenney (Salt Lake City: Signature Books, 1983–85), 5:520, 533.

10. Brigham Young to Charles C. Rich, April 4, 1861, Brigham Young Office Files, Church History Library, The Church of Jesus Christ of Latter-day Saints, Salt Lake City (hereafter cited as CHL).

11. Joseph Smith, revelation, December 25, 1832, in Robin Scott Jensen, Robert J. Woodford, and Steven C. Harper, eds., *Manuscript Revelation Books*, facsimile edition, vol. 1 of the Revelations and Translations series of *The Joseph Smith Papers*, ed. Dean C. Jessee, Ronald K. Esplin, and Richard Lyman Bushman (Salt Lake City: Church Historian's Press, 2009), 291.

12. For a fuller treatment of the prophecy's history and usage, see Scott C. Esplin, "'Have We Not Had a Prophet among Us?': Joseph Smith's Civil War Prophecy," within this volume.

13. For an examination of how Mormons remembered and interpreted their persecutory past, see David W. Grua, "Memoirs of the Persecuted: Persecution, Memory, and the West as a Mormon Refuge" (master's thesis, Brigham Young University, 2008).

14. Abraham Lincoln, "First Inaugural Address," *The Collected Works of Abraham Lincoln*, ed. Roy P. Bassler (New Brunswick, NJ: Rutgers University Press, 1953), 4:271; Martin Van Buren, quoted in Church Historian's Office, History of the Church, February 6, 1840, CHL.

15. Wilford Woodruff, diary, April 28, 1861, in *Wilford Woodruff's Journal*, 5:570.

16. Joseph Smith, revelation, December 25, 1832, in Robin Scott Jensen, Robert J. Woodford, and Steven C. Harper, eds., *Manuscript Revelation Books*, 291.

17. There is some question as to whether "Praise to the Man" was written by W. W. Phelps or Eliza R. Snow. Not having a conclusive answer, I will follow the tradition that attributes the poem to Phelps.

18. "Joseph Smith," *Times and Seasons*, August 1, 1844.

19. "O, Give Me Back My Prophet Dear," in *The Gospel Kingdom: Selections from the Writings and Discourses of John Taylor*, ed. G. Homer Durham (Salt Lake City: Bookcraft, 1987), 386.

20. Brigham Young, "The Word and Will of the Lord Concerning the Camp of Israel in their Journeyings to the West, 1847 Jan. 14," CHL; see D&C 136: 34–36, 39.

21. Brigham Young, office journal, February 2, 1861, in Richard S. Van Wagoner, ed., *The Complete Discourses of Brigham Young* (Salt Lake City: Smith-Pettit Foundation, 2009), 3:1744.

22. Wilford Woodruff, diary, February 13, 1861, in *Wilford Woodruff's Journal*, 5:552.

23. Brigham Young, in *Journal of Discourses*, 9:320.

24. Brigham Young, in *Journal of Discourses*, 9:320.

25. J. Porter Brawley to James Buchanan, December 17, 1857, James Buchanan Papers, L. Tom Perry Special Collections, Harold B. Lee Library, Brigham Young University, Provo, UT; E. G. Butler to James Buchanan, July 1, 1858, James Buchanan Papers, L. Tom Perry Special Colletions; "The Utah Expedition," *New York Herald*, April 20, 1858, in Church Historian's Office, Historical Scrapbooks, CHL.

26. "Light Wanted on Mormon Difficulty," *New York Times*, January 28, 1858.

27. Wilford Woodruff, diary, March 10, 1861, in *Wilford Woodruff's Journal*, 5:559.

28. "The Mormons Seceding," *San Francisco Evening Mirror*, May 6, 1861, in Church historian's office, Historical Scrapbooks, CHL.

29. Wilford Woodruff, diary, December 11, 1861, in *Wilford Woodruff's Journal*, 5:605; Brigham Young to Dwight Eveleth, July 23, 1861, Brigham Young Office Files, CHL; Brigham Young to H. B. Clawson, July 26, 1861, Brigham Young Office Files, CHL; Brigham Young to Amasa Lyman and Charles C. Rich, July 26, 1861, Brigham Young Office Files, CHL.

30. Brigham Young to Walter Murray Gibson, September 18, 1861, Brigham Young Office Files, CHL.

31. Wilford Woodruff, diary, March 10, 1861, in *Wilford Woodruff's Journal*, 5:559.

32. Wilford Woodruff, diary, April 28, 1861, in *Wilford Woodruff's Journal*, 5:570.

33. Brigham Young to Walter Murray Gibson, July 2, 1861, Brigham Young Office Files, CHL.

34. Brigham Young to Abraham Lincoln, October 18, 1861, quoted in Leonard J. Arrington, *Brigham*

Young: American Moses (New York: Knopf, 1985), 294.

35. Brigham Young to Dwight Eveleth, January 1, 1861, Brigham Young Office Files, CHL.

36. Brigham Young, in *Complete Discourses*, 3:1733.

37. Journal History of The Church of Jesus Christ of Latter-day Saints, April 6, 1862, CHL; "Progress of the War," *Deseret News*, April 23, 1862.

38. George Q. Cannon to Brigham Young, January 18, 1860, Brigham Young Office Files, CHL.

39. Wilford Woodruff, diary, October 20, 1860, in *Wilford Woodruff's Journal*, 5:514.

40. Wilford Woodruff, diary, November 11, 1860, in *Wilford Woodruff's Journal*, 5:517.

41. See Wilford Woodruff, diary, November 22, 24, 26, 1860; December 15, 24, 28, 1860; January 1, 5, 7, 9–11, 24, 26, 1861; February 28, 1861, in *Wilford Woodruff's Journal*, 5:519–21, 523, 525, 533, 539–40, 542–43, 556.

42. Wilford Woodruff, diary, March 4, 1861, in *Wilford Woodruff's Journal*, 5:557.

43. Don E. Fehrenbacher, *The Slaveholding Republic: An Account of the United States Government's Relations to Slavery*, ed. Ward M. McAfee (New York: Oxford University Press, 2001), 17.

44. Fehrenbacher, *Slaveholding Republic*, 34.

45. In Missouri, the mostly Yankee-born population of Mormons found themselves accused of "tampering with . . . slaves, and endeavoring to sow dissentions and raise seditions among them" following W. W. Phelps's publication of abolitionist articles in the *Evening and Morning Star*. Nathaniel R. Ricks, "A Peculiar Place for the Peculiar Institution: Slavery and Sovereignty in Early Territorial Utah" (master's thesis, Brigham Young University, 2007), 26.

46. Brigham said, "I am neither an abolitionist nor a pro-slavery man. If I could have been influenced by private injury to choose one side in preference to the other, I should certainly be against the pro-slavery side of the question, for it was pro-slavery men that pointed the bayonet at me and my brethren in Missouri." Brigham Young, in *Journal of Discourses*, 10:111; see also 9:157.

47. Wilford Woodruff, diary, June 1, 1851, in *Wilford Woodruff's Journal*, 4:31.

48. Brigham Young, in *Complete Discourses*, 1:432.

49. Brigham Young, office journal, December 26, 1860, in *Complete Discourses*, 3:1720.

50. Brigham Young, in *Journal of Discourses*, 10:209.

51. Brigham Young, in *Journal of Discourses*, 10:110.

52. Brigham Young, in *Journal of Discourses*, 9:333.

53. Brigham Young, office journal, February 2, 1861, in *Complete Discourses*, 3:1744. Noting some of the pro-South loyalties, Brigham's clerk, George Sims, wrote to a friend, "The sympathies of our brethren are divided some for the Union and some for the South, but the south gets the greatest share." George Sims to William C. Staines, February 21, 1862, Brigham Young Office Files, CHL.

54. Brigham Young to W. H. Hooper, January 3, 1861, Brigham Young Office Files, CHL.

55. Brigham Young, in *Complete Discourses*, 3:1919.

56. Wilford Woodruff, diary, May 1, 1861, in *Wilford Woodruff's Journal*, 5:571.

57. See Roger L. Ransom, *Conflict and Compromise: The Political Economy of Slavery, Emancipation, and the American Civil War* (Cambridge: Cambridge University Press, 1989), 42–53.

58. Ransom, *Conflict and Compromise*, 49.

59. Wilford Woodruff, diary, December 28, 1859, in *Wilford Woodruff's Journal*, 5:405.

60. George Q. Cannon to Brigham Young, January 18, 1860, Brigham Young Office Files, CHL.

61. Brigham Young, office journal, October 9, 1860, in *Complete Discourses*, 3:1686.

62. Wilford Woodruff, diary, December 31, 1860, in *Wilford Woodruff's Journal*, 5:528.

63. George Q. Cannon to Brigham Young, June 15, 1861, Brigham Young Office Files, CHL; see "A Mormon Prophecy," *Philadelphia Mercury*, May 5, 1861, in Church Historian's Office, Historical Scrapbooks, CHL; "From Salt Lake City," *Los Angeles Star*, April 20, 1861, in Church Historian's Office, Historical Scrapbooks, CHL; "Ominous," *San Francisco Herald*, March 15, 1861, in Church Historian's Office, Historical Scrapbooks, CHL; "A Prophecy of Joe Smith," *Sacramento Bee*, January 7, 1863, in Church Historian's Office, Historical Scrapbooks, CHL. See also the chapter by Scott C. Esplin in this volume.

64. "Will the South Resist?," *Deseret News*, November 21, 1860.

65. "Prospective Dissolution," *Deseret News*, November 28, 1860.

66. Brigham Young, quoted in Wilford Woodruff, diary, November 7, 1860, in *Wilford Woodruff's Journal*, 5:513.

67. See, for instance, Matthew 24:33; Joseph Smith—Matthew 1:39; D&C 110:16; Joseph Smith, diary, April 3, 1836, in Dean C. Jessee, Mark Ashurst-McGee, and Richard L. Jensen, eds., *Journals, Volume 1: 1832–1839*, vol. 1 of the Journals series of *The Joseph Smith Papers*, ed. Dean C. Jessee, Ronald K. Esplin, and Richard Lyman Bushman (Salt Lake City: Church Historian's Press, 2008), 222.

68. Wilford Woodruff, diary, November 7, 1860, in *Wilford Woodruff's Journal*, 5:516.

69. Brigham Young, office journal, January 28, 1861, in *Complete Discourses*, 3:1742.

70. Brigham Young, office journal, February 2, 1861, in *Complete Discourses*, 3:1744.

71. Brigham Young to Walter Murray Gibson, March 5, 1861, Brigham Young Office Files, CHL.

72. Abraham Lincoln, "Second Inaugural Address," *Collected Works*, 8:332–33.

73. Quoted in Jeffrey D. Wert, *The Sword of Lincoln: The Army of the Potomac* (New York: Simon & Schuster, 2005), 5.

74. Frank L. Lemont, quoted in Wert, *Sword of Lincoln*, 15.

75. David Detzer, *Donnybrook: The Battle of Bull Run, 1861* (Orlando: Harcourt, 2004), 310. Detzer argues that this scene was not as dramatic as it has often been portrayed in later years. Most of those who went to see the battle were either politicians or civilians with family members in the army rather than entertainment seekers.

76. Quoted in Detzer, *Donnybrook*, 313. Detzer questions the accuracy of this wording.

77. William Clayton, diary, April 2, 1843, in *An Intimate Chronicle: The Journals of William Clayton*, ed. George D. Smith (Salt Lake City: Signature Books, 1995), 97; Joseph Smith, revelation, December 25, 1832, in *Manuscript Revelation Books*, 291.

78. Wilford Woodruff, diary, December 30, 1860, in *Wilford Woodruff's Journal*, 5:526.

79. Heber C. Kimball, memorandum book, March 27 [year unknown], in *On the Potter's Wheel: The Diaries of Heber C. Kimball*, ed. Stanley B. Kimball (Salt Lake City: Signature Books, 1987), 173.

80. Brigham Young to William H. Hooper, January 3, 1861, Brigham Young Office Files, CHL; Wilford Woodruff, diary, November 22, 1860, in *Wilford Woodruff's Journal*, 5:520.

81. "News from the East," *Deseret News*, April 9, 1862; Brigham Young, in *Journal of Discourses*, 10:33.

82. Brigham Young, in *Complete Discourses*, 4:2092.

83. Brigham Young to Thomas L. Kane, September 21, 1861, Brigham Young Office Files, CHL.

84. Brigham Young, in *Complete Discourses*, 4:2092.

85. See James H. Moorhead, *American Apocalypse: Yankee Protestants and the Civil War, 1860–1869* (New Haven: Yale University Press, 1978).

86. Scott, *A Visitation of God*, 196.

87. Joseph Smith, revelation, December 25, 1832, in *Manuscript Revelation Books*, 291.

88. Joseph Smith, diary, April 2, 1843, *An American Prophet's Record: The Diaries and Journals of Joseph Smith*, ed. Scott H. Faulring (Salt Lake City: Signature Books, 1989), 340; see also William Clayton, diary, April 2, 1843, *Intimate Chronicle*, 95–97.

89. Minutes, Kirtland, Ohio, February 14–15, 1835, Minute Book 1, CHL, accessed April 6, 2011, http://beta.josephsmithpapers.org/paperSummary/minutes-14%E2%80%9315-february-1835.

90. In 1896, Francis M. Lyman said, "*The prophet Joseph had foretold that some great event would transpire 56 years hence, which was figured out to be 1891.* And many of our people thought that the world would come to an end in that year, and were greatly disappointed when it did not." Francis M. Lyman, in *Collected Discourses Delivered by President Wilford Woodruff, His Two Counselors, the Twelve Apostles, and Others*, ed. Brian H. Stuy (Burbank, CA: BHS, 1991), 4:433; italics in original. Joseph Smith was far less certain about the timing implied in these revelations, remarking, "I was left thus without being able to decide w[h]ether this coming referred to the beginning of the Millennium, or to some previous appearing or w[h]ether I should die and thus see his face. I believe the coming of the son of man will not be any sooner than that time." William Clayton, diary, April 2, 1843, *Intimate Chronicle*, 95–96. Similar to Joseph, some members recognized the ambiguity within the prophecy and determined that it would "require further explanation, if not further revelation, to make [Joseph's statements on the matter] plain." Joseph E. Taylor, in *Collected Discourses*, 1:137. See also B. H. Roberts, in *Collected Discourses*, 2:105–6.

91. Wilford Woodruff, diary, February 1, 1861, in *Wilford Woodruff's Journal*, 5:547.

92. Wilford Woodruff, diary, December 31, 1860, in *Wilford Woodruff's Journal*, 5:529.

93. Brigham Young, quoted in Wilford Woodruff, diary, July 28, 1861, in *Wilford Woodruff's Journal*, 5:587.

94. William Clayton, diary, April 2, 1843, *Intimate Chronicle*, 97; Joseph Smith, diary, April 2, 1843, *American Prophet's Record*, 340.

95. Brigham Young to Daniel H. Wells and Brigham Young Jr., February 28, 1865, Brigham Young Office Files, CHL.

96. Joseph Smith, revelation, December 25, 1832, in *Manuscript Revelation Books*, 291.

97. Brigham Young to Erastus Snow, February 21, 1861, Brigham Young Office Files, CHL.

98. Brigham Young, office journal, December 28, 1860, in *Complete Discourses*, 3:1720.

99. Brigham Young, office journal, July 9, 1861, in *Complete Discourses*, 3:1884.

100. Wilford Woodruff, diary, December 11, 1861, in *Wilford Woodruff's* Journal, 5:605. It should be noted, though, that less than five months later, at the request of President Lincoln, Brigham Young authorized the enlistment of a cavalry company, under the command of Lot Smith. See Joseph R. Stuart and Kenneth L. Alford, "The Lot Smith Cavalry Company: Utah Goes to War," within this volume.

101. Abraham Lincoln, quoted in Brigham Young to George Q. Cannon, June 25, 1863, Brigham Young Office Files, CHL.

102. Brigham Young, office journal, May 1, 1861, in *Complete Discourses*, 3:1804.

103. Brigham Young to Charles C. Rich, November 28, 1861, Brigham Young Office Files, CHL.

104. George Q. Cannon to Brigham Young, September 7, 1861, Brigham Young Office Files, CHL.

105. Brigham Young to William H. Hooper, December 20, 1860, Brigham Young Office Files, CHL.

106. Brigham Young to George Q. Cannon, May 30, 1863, Brigham Young Office Files, CHL.

107. Brigham Young, in *Journal of Discourses*, 10:306.

108. Brigham Young to George Q. Cannon, May 30, 1863, Brigham Young Office Files, CHL.

109. Cong. Globe, 37th Cong., 2d Sess. 157 (1862).

110. Brigham Young to William H. Hooper, June 5, 1862, Brigham Young Office Files, CHL.

111. Patrick Q. Mason, *The Mormon Menace: Violence and Anti-Mormonism in the Postbellum South* (New York: Oxford University Press, 2011), 14.

112. See Matthew J. Grow, *"Liberty to the Downtrodden": Thomas L. Kane, Romantic Reformer* (New Haven: Yale University Press, 2009), 211.

113. See Grow, *"Liberty to the Downtrodden,"* 217–19, 222, 231.

114. Brigham Young to John Bernhisel, March 22, 1862, Brigham Young Office Files, CHL.

115. Brigham Young Jr. to Brigham Young, December 18, 1869, Brigham Young Office Files, CHL; quoted in Grow, *"Liberty to the Downtrodden,"* 237.

116. Brigham Young to Angeline E. Worden, June 10, 1862, Brigham Young Office Files, CHL.

117. Brigham Young Jr. to Brigham Young, July 11, 1862, Brigham Young Office Files, CHL; Brigham Young to Brigham Young Jr., August 6, 1862, in *Letters of Brigham Young to His Sons*, ed. Dean C. Jessee (Salt Lake City: Deseret Book, 1974), 25–26.

118. Brigham Young Jr., diary, July 4, 1862, quoted in *Letters of Brigham Young to His Sons*, 24.

119. Brigham Young to Thomas L. Kane, April 29, 1864, Brigham Young Office Files, CHL.

120. Brigham Young, in *Journal of Discourses*, 10:248.

121. Brigham Young, in *Journal of Discourses*, 10:250.

122. Brigham Young, in *Complete Discourses*, 4:2150.

123. Brigham Young, in *Journal of Discourses*, 8:324.

124. Brigham Young, in *Complete Discourses*, 4:2048.

125. Brigham Young, office journal, May 1, 1861, in *Complete Discourses*, 3:1804.

126. Brigham Young, in *Complete Discourses*, 4:2151.

127. Abraham Lincoln, "First Inaugural Address," *The Collected Works of Abraham Lincoln*, 4:271; Brigham Young, in *Complete Discourses*, 4:2048.

Erected on the grounds of the Utah State Capitol by the Daughters of Utah Pioneers in 1961, this monument honors the men who served in the Lot Smith Utah Cavalry. (Courtesy of W. Jeffrey Marsh)

CHAPTER 8

Joseph R. Stuart and Kenneth L. Alford

THE LOT SMITH CAVALRY COMPANY

UTAH GOES TO WAR

When the American Civil War is studied, it is almost always the major battles and campaigns that draw our attention and focus our interest—Manassas, Chancellorsville, Fredericksburg, Antietam, Gettysburg, and many others. In remembering a war that cost hundreds of thousands of lives, it is often easy to overlook lesser-known contributions to the war effort. This chapter is the story of one minor, but still important, story from the Civil War—an account of the only military unit from Utah Territory called to active duty during the war.

UTAH'S ATTITUDE REGARDING THE CIVIL WAR

With the outbreak of war, the federal government found itself, as President Lincoln noted, "in the midst of unprecedented political troubles."[1] As the national crisis began, communication between the eastern and western sections of the country was sometimes interrupted—with telegraph service sometimes out of operation for several days at a time.[2] Indian attacks on mail and telegraph stations left the nation without cross-country communication, threatening further confusion on both sides of the country.[3]

Given geographic realities and Washington's attitude, Utah's active participation in the Civil War was limited. While other states were seceding to the Confederacy, Utah sought to join the Union and become the thirty-fifth state. Utah's applications were denied, reinforcing the view that the Civil War was primarily a problem of "the states."[4] Shortly after the telegraph reached Salt Lake City in October 1861, President Brigham Young publicly declared that "Utah has not seceded [from the Union], but is firm for the Constitution and laws of our once happy country."[5] Church members often had mixed emotions regarding the war because they felt that the nation had denied them the protections of the Constitution, which the Saints considered to be divinely inspired. The Saints had made the best of their situation—settling in Utah rather than Texas, California, or Oregon—and had done herculean work to make the land habitable. Because of their hard work, the Saints hoped to be left alone by the United States—a welcome change from the torment and interference they had come to expect at the hands of the federal government.

ASKING FOR UTAH'S ASSISTANCE

After 1861, telegraph lines spanned the width of the United States and enabled news to be sent thousands of miles almost instantaneously. Then, as now, rapid communication was highly valued. Working telegraph lines and open mail routes supported Union victory and the well-being of the nation. After suffering several Indian attacks and fear of attack by the Confederate Army, the trail required increased protection.[6]

The Overland Trail—which carried people, mail, and telegraph lines—stretched from Atchison, Kansas, to Salt Lake City, Utah. General James H. Craig, brigadier general of volunteers, received orders on April 16, 1862, making him responsible for protecting the Overland Trail.[7] The trail had been plagued for months by Indian attacks that disrupted travel and communication.[8] Soldiers were now required to protect the Overland Trail.

Mustering a unit from Utah to protect the trail made good sense. Not only did the Union have access to people who wanted to prove their loyalty to the United States, but the Mormons were also largely frontier people, used to living on barren and unsettled land. Utahns were well suited for the job of protecting the mail, telegraph, and emigration routes.

THE CALL TO SERVE

In April 1862, three weeks after the Battle of Shiloh, President Lincoln turned to Brigham Young to muster men to protect the Overland Trail.[9] The idea may have originated in a letter from General Lorenzo Thomas to General James W. Denver, a brigadier general stationed at Fort Leavenworth. The letter, dated April 11, 1862, suggested that Brigham Young would be ideal to contact because of his interest "in the telegraphic communication with Salt Lake and from his known influence over his own people, and over the Indian tribes" around Salt Lake City. Thomas's letter acknowledged that Brigham Young was "not a functionary recognized by the United States Government" and that any formal request for troops should probably be sent to the governor of the territory.[10]

The idea for direct contact from Lincoln to Young, rather than to Governor Stephen Harding, also came from U.S. Congressman Milton Latham of California. In an April 26, 1862, letter, Latham proposed that Lincoln ask Brigham Young to provide soldiers to protect the Overland Trail. Latham suggested that because of recent trouble with Indians destroying mail stations and making the mail route unsafe, "authority [should] be given [to] Brigham Young to raise and equip one hundred men for ninety days' service in protecting the [telegraph] line."[11] In addition to Congressman Latham's suggestion, it was practical to ask Brigham Young for recruits because there was no official governor in the Utah Territory at that time. Governor John W. Dawson had fled the state, and Lieutenant Governor Frank Fuller was serving as the acting governor. The new governor, Stephen Harding, did not arrive until July.[12]

General Lorenzo Thomas, adjutant general of the U.S. Army, and the War Department recognized that the real power to get things accomplished in Utah lay in the hands of

Brigadier General Lorenzo Thomas served as the U.S. Army's adjutant general from March 7, 1861, until 1869. (Library of Congress)

Brigham Young and not the federally appointed leadership.[13] Young received a telegraph message asking for soldiers on April 28, 1862, two days after Congressman Latham's suggestion to President Lincoln.

Washington, April 28, 1862
Mr. Brigham Young,
Salt Lake City, Utah:

By express direction of the President of the United States you are hereby authorized to raise, arm, and equip one company of cavalry for ninety days' service. This company will be organized as follows:

One captain, 1 first lieutenant, 1 second lieutenant, 1 first sergeant, 1 quartermaster-sergeant, 4 sergeants, 8 corporals, 2 musicians, 2 farriers, 1 saddler, 1 wagoner, and from 56 to 72 privates. The company will be employed to protect the property of the telegraph and overland mail companies in or about Independence Rock, where depredations have been committed, and will be continued in service only till the U.S. troops can reach the point where they are so much needed. It may therefore be disbanded previous to the expiration of the ninety days. It will not be employed for any offensive operations other than may grow out of the duty hereinbefore assigned to it. The officers of the company will be mustered into the U.S. service by any civil officer of the United States Government at Salt Lake City competent to administer the oath. The men will then be enlisted by the company officers. The men employed in the service above named will be entitled to receive no other than the allowances authorized by law to soldiers in the service of the United States. Until the proper staff officer for subsisting these men arrive you will please furnish subsistence for them yourself, keeping an accurate account thereof for future settlement with the United States Government.

By order of the
Secretary of War:
L. Thomas, Adjutant-General.[14]

The message granted direct authority for President Young to recruit men for active duty military service. The soldiers called were to arm and equip themselves, as well as provide their own horses and firearms for the campaign. Perhaps such a small unit was mustered because General Thomas believed

Daniel H. Wells, an early Utah pioneer, apostle, and counselor in the First Presidency of the LDS Church, served as commander of the Nauvoo Legion in Utah and as the third mayor of Salt Lake City. His son, Heber Manning Wells, became the first governor of the state of Utah. (Utah State Historical Society)

that "so large a force is [not] necessary" and raising a small force from Utah "offer[ed] the most expeditious and economical remedy to the obstructions to the mail route."[15]

Brigham acted upon the message "within the hour."[16] Writing "at even date" to Daniel H. Wells, his first counselor and the commanding officer of the Utah militia (also known as the Nauvoo Legion), Brigham explained the situation.[17] Young and Wells decided to accept the government's call. The next order of business was to determine who would command the company. At that moment of military need, Colonel Robert T. Burton, commander of the elite Nauvoo Legion Lifeguards, was leading the Utah militia protecting the mail route from Indian attack in northern Utah and Wyoming at the request of Frank Fuller, the acting governor. General Wells contacted another officer,

Colonel Fullmer, but he too was unavailable.[18] With Colonel Burton and Colonel Fullmer unavailable to answer the call from President Lincoln, General Wells selected another experienced officer—Lot Smith.

LOT SMITH—UTAH FOLK HERO

Lot Smith was something of a folk hero in the Utah Territory. Described as a "red head [with] a red face, a straight form, a military bearing . . . and a gleam in the eyes that bespoke a high temper and an absolute absence of fear,"[19] Lot Smith looked the part of a soldier. According to one member of the Lot Smith Company, "He was gentle as a woman and as brave as a lion . . . a citizen . . . a soldier, and also . . . a missionary of the Church."[20] With prior service in Indian wars, in the Utah War, and as an active member of the Nauvoo Legion, Major Smith was well respected and admired within the territory. (Lot Smith, who served as a major in the Nauvoo Legion, will be referred to as Captain Smith throughout this essay because the letter requesting the active duty Utah Cavalry unit authorized only the rank of captain for the commander. Accepting the government's call was actually a demotion for Major Smith.[21]) His most important previous assignment came during the Utah War when he disrupted and delayed the progress of the United States Army under Colonel Albert Sidney Johnston. Lot Smith was a territorial hero and a man the Church could rely upon to get a job done.[22]

BRIGHAM'S RESPONSE

After General Wells and Captain Smith mustered local men into service (in less than two days) and borrowed animals,[23] President Young sent the following telegram to General Thomas:

Great Salt Lake City, April 30, 1862
Adjutant General Thomas, U.S.A.
Washington, D.C.

Upon receipt of your telegram of April 27, I requested General Daniel H. Wells, of the Utah militia to proceed at once to raise a company of cavalry and equip and muster them into the service of the United States army for ninety days, as per your telegram. General Wells, forthwith issued the necessary orders and on the 29th day of April the commissioned officers and non-commissioned officers and privates, including teamsters, were sworn in by Chief Justice John F. Kinney, and the company went into camp adjacent to the city the same day.

Brigham Young[24]

Lot Smith was a frontiersman and early Mormon Church member. Noted chiefly for his military exploits in the Utah War, he lived for nearly three decades in the Davis County town of Farmington and led a colonizing mission to Arizona in the late 1870s and 1880s. (Utah State Historical Society)

At first look, it may seem unusual that President Young took nearly two days to officially respond to the government's request for military service. The delay, though, was characteristic of Brigham Young. Rather than telegraphing the government with a promise of future action, he chose to respond after the action had already been completed.[25]

INSTRUCTIONS TO THE LOT SMITH COMPANY

The same day Brigham Young answered the government's request, the First Presidency, in a letter dated April 30, 1862, clarified and outlined the duties of the Lot Smith Company. The First Presidency directed the men under Lot Smith to "recognize the hand of Providence in [the Saints'] behalf" and to place the wages from the army as secondary to their purpose. The men were to act as emissaries of the Church, to "establish the influence God has given us . . . be kind, forbearing, and righteous in all your acts and sayings in public and private . . . that we may greet you with pleasure as those who have faithfully performed a work worthy of great praise." Doing so would enable the men to "again prove that noble hearted American citizens can don arms in the defense of right and justice, without descending one hair's breadth below the high standard of American manhood." Counsel was also given to abstain from "card playing, dicing, gambling, drinking intoxicating liquors, or swearing" and to "be kind to [their] animals." Expectations were expressed that the company would "improve the road as you pass along, so much so as practicable diligence in reaching your destination will warrant, not only for your own convenience but more particularly for the accommodation of the Mail Company and general travel," showing the First Presidency's concern for continued cross-country communication and future Mormon immigration.[26]

In a final piece of ecclesiastical advice, the company was directed that each "morning and evening of each day let prayer be publicly offered in the Command and in all detachments thereof, that you may constantly enjoy the guidance and protecting care of Israel's God and be blest in the performance of every duty devolved upon you." With the salutation "Your Fellow Laborers and Brethren in the Gospel," the First Presidency formalized their approval of the mission of the Lot Smith Company.[27]

DEMONSTRATING LOYALTY

Ben Holladay, proprietor of the stage and U.S. mail line that extended from St. Joseph to San Francisco, sent a telegram to Brigham Young thanking him for the service that the Mormons would provide. Holladay promised that "just as soon as these Utah volunteers are located along the line, I will proceed to replace my coaches, horses and drivers and rebuild and man the destroyed mail stations from the North Platte River and Independence Rock to Salt Lake City."[28] The mail and telegraph would be fully operational, pending the arrival of soldiers on the plains. The ability to communicate between the east and

Following his military service, Seymour Young served for several decades as a general authority in The Church of Jesus Christ of Latter-day Saints; he was one of the first Lot Smith company veterans to be accepted as a member of the Grand Army of the Republic.
(Juvenile Instructor)

west coasts of the United States would not be seriously interrupted again during the Civil War—in part because of service rendered by the Lot Smith Company.[29] The importance of cross-country communication should not be underestimated. Mail delivery in the 1860s was not the organized system our nation enjoys today. When mail and telegraph lines were interrupted, communication slowed to a crawl.

Mr. Holladay's motives for keeping the trail and telegraph lines open were not entirely patriotic. As owner of the Holladay Mail and Telegraph Company, Holladay's financial losses could have been severe, even crippling. During the spring of 1862, for example, Indians were held responsible for more than $50,000 worth of damage and destruction to animals, supplies, and wagons equipment, as well as the deaths of several employees.[30] Holladay had already been forced to alter his stagecoach route to accommodate the heavy losses he was incurring in Indian territory.[31]

But protection of the trail and delivery of the mail were not the sole incentives for accepting the invitation to serve; many Latter-day Saints believed that the government's call had a larger purpose. Less than two weeks after the Utah volunteers enlisted, President Wells publicly stated that the call of the Lot Smith Company was divinely inspired, and he reaffirmed that the Saints would continue to demonstrate their loyalty to the United

This painting by Frank Thomas shows Lot Smith and his company at the beginning of their military service in May 1862.
(Courtesy of Frank Thomas)

States—despite the government's past interactions with the Saints.

It is all right with regard to those expeditions going forth, and will result for the benefit of this people . . . and in this way we prove ourselves before God, that we are ready to do his will, and to do his bidding. The requisition was made by the proper authority at Washington, and was readily responded to, as has always been the case when a call has been made through the proper channel, and the compliance with this call will result in good. Our brethren will perform their duties and do honour to their country. It is our country; we are citizens of the American Government, and we have a right to act for the preservation of its institutions, and we have always done it whenever called upon, and we have

shown ourselves ready to respond to our duty as good citizens, no matter what usage we have received in return. This proves a weapon in the hands of this people for their defence. Let us feel contented to respond to every call that comes from the proper source, let us do it with full faith and confidence believing that it is right.[32]

THE MARCH TO FORT BRIDGER

At 1:00 p.m. on May 1, 1862, the Utah Cavalry (as the unit was later designated) embarked on their military assignment.[33] At nightfall the men gathered to pray. After a futile attempt to travel through Parley's Canyon the next day, the company traveled north and east through Emigration Canyon, east of Salt Lake City. At 9:00 a.m. the following day, they met with Brigham Young and Daniel H. Wells.[34] The two Church leaders spoke to the troops regarding spiritual as well as practical matters. This "Canyon Discourse" was largely a reiteration of the First Presidency's April 30 letter to the company. Brigham Young spoke to the men frankly regarding their mission: "I desire of the officers and privates of this company, that in this service they will conduct themselves as gentlemen, remembering their allegiance and loyalty to our government, and also not forgetting that they are members of the organization to which they belong." He again cautioned the soldiers to never indulge in intoxicants of any kind and warned them against "associating with bad men or lewd women."[35] President Young also counseled,

Harvey Coe Hullinger (1824–1926), who kept a handwritten pocket diary of his 1862 military service and served as the physician for the Lot Smith Cavalry Company. (Utah State Historical Society)

> Another thing I would have you remember is that, although you are United States soldiers you are still members of the Church of Jesus Christ of Latter-day Saints, and while you have sworn allegiance to the constitution and government of our country, and we have vowed to preserve the Union, the best way to accomplish this high purpose is to shun all evil. . . . Remember your prayers . . . establish peace with the Indians . . . [and] always give ready obedience to the orders of your commanding officers. If you will do this I promise you, as a servant of the Lord, that not one of you shall fall by the hand of an enemy.[36]

President Young wanted the Utah soldiers to be viewed as loyal, obedient, patriotic, and thoroughly American—not dependent on Church leaders for direction, counsel, or action. The Church leaders may have hoped that the company's good example would create positive impressions and some favorable press reports in the East.[37] Brigham also recalled the example of the Mormon Battalion and how their service had benefited the Church at large.[38]

The march to Fort Bridger was difficult. The company "encountered ten feet of newly fallen snow," and in many places the roads were almost impassable. Despite the fact that there were food shortages, Indian problems, snow, challenges crossing rivers and streams, and oceans of mud to contend with, "they did not complain."[39] Dr. Harvey C. Hullinger, the company's doctor and self-appointed diarist, noted that "only the Latter-day Saints could have surmounted these difficulties and remained cheerful."[40]

As they had been counseled, the Lot Smith Company improved the trail on their way to Independence Rock. One of their major contributions was bridge building: at one point they built three bridges in just four days. They traveled on many washed-out roads and had great difficulties in their travel to Independence Rock.[41] As the group followed the Bear River, they found "many of the Mail stations were still smouldering when [they] came upon them. Wagon-loads of United States mail had been scattered and destroyed by the Indians."[42] This provided the company somber firsthand evidence as to why they had been enlisted by President Lincoln. Ironically, at the same time the Lot Smith Company was actively protecting the Overland Trail, "Mormons" were being blamed for destruction of the mail.[43]

LIFE AT INDEPENDENCE ROCK

After a twenty-six-day march that tested the men physically, they arrived at Independence Rock, located in what is today south-central Wyoming. There they joined Lieutenant Colonel William O. Collins, commander of the Eleventh Ohio Cavalry (previously designated as the Sixth Ohio Cavalry), who had also been assigned to protect the Overland Trail.[44] The Eleventh Ohio Cavalry had met several Indian groups but had avoided military conflict to that point. The Eleventh Ohio and Lot Smith Cavalries were jointly responsible for protecting the Overland Trail and keeping peace with the Indians on the plains.[45]

The Utah Company's initial contact with army leadership created a favorable impression. The first days in camp provided them with several opportunities to demonstrate their ability to work and follow orders. The Latter-day Saint soldiers were soon ordered to investigate and rectify Indian horse thefts that had occurred three days earlier at Ham's Fork, Wyoming. Lot Smith, together with twenty men and four pack animals, was sent to Ham's Fork in late May. They traveled 150 miles in only two days. When the soldiers reached the Green River, Captain Smith decided that pursuing the Indians any further would entail a "very considerable risk of life," and he gave up the chase.[46]

The month of June was spent in camp at Independence Rock with no significant military action. Dr. Hullinger's diary recorded that

he "drew 2 sketches of devil's Gate," built "a bridge that the Church Trains coul[d] cross," and "Clean[ed] their Pistols and Guns."[47]

During June, Lot Smith sent several telegrams to Brigham Young. The first telegram, sent June 16, reported on many items of interest to the First Presidency. Captain Smith noted that General James Craig was "much pleased with the corral and Houses [the Lot Smith Company was] building at Devil's Gate . . . and desired us to contribute as much as possible to our own comfort, and render all the assistance possible to the Mormon Emigration." General Craig "was much pleased with the promptness of our people attending to the call of the General Government . . . spoke in high terms of our people generally . . . [and] informed me that he had telegraphed President Lincoln to that effect." Captain Smith quoted General Craig as having commented that the Utah Cavalry were "the most efficient troops he had for the present service" and recommended that the president "engage our Services for 3 Months longer."[48] General Craig, though, did not actually ask Secretary of War Edward Stanton to "re-enlist the Utah troops for a limited time" until August 23 (nearly a month after their initial ninety-day enlistment had expired).[49]

A subsequent telegram from Lot Smith, dated June 27, 1862, focused largely on the army's relations with the local Indians. Smith wrote that the army "is decidedly against killing Indians indiscriminately"; the army, he said, would not act against any Indians unless they had ample evidence and just cause for an attack. Lot also brought up the musings of the army concerning re-enlistment, saying Colonel Collins "allow[s] we are best suited to guard this road, both men and horses; they are anxious to return, and if they have

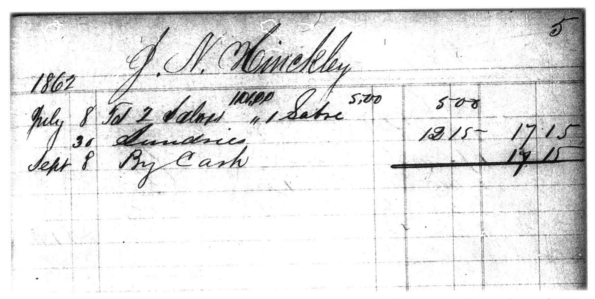

A ledger page showing purchases made by Ira N. Hinckley, grandfather of Gordon B. Hinckley, at the Fort Bridger sutlery in July 1862.

any influence, I imagine they will try to get [us] recalled and recommend [us] to Utah to furnish the necessary guard."[50] The men were desperately needed. General Craig wrote to General James G. Blunt, brigadier general of volunteers and given command of the Department and Army of Kansas on June 26, that he was "using the company of Utah troops in that region, but they are not sufficient."[51] On August 25, Edwin M. Stanton, secretary of war, authorized General Craig to "raise 100 mounted men in the mountains and re-enlist the Utah troops for a limited time."[52]

The Lot Smith Company did not have their enlistment extended, though. On August 25, General Craig received word from Stephen Harding, territorial governor of Utah, that Brigham Young would not extend the men's enlistment. General Craig was told to "not expect anything for the present. Things are not right."[53] That same day, President Young sent the following telegram to the adjutant general, Lorenzo Thomas, at Washington, DC:

Governor Harding has received a telegram from Brig. General Craig at Laramie, for the re-enlistment of Captain Lot Smith's Company and their being marched to Laramie. Please inform me whether the Government wishes the military of the Territory of Utah to go beyond her borders while troops are here from other states who have been sent to protect the mail and telegraph property.[54]

Brigham Young was not anxious to resend the Lot Smith Company to protect the Overland Trail when a similar order had been given to Colonel Patrick E. Connor and the California Volunteers who were en route to Utah.[55] It is not clear whether General Thomas answered President Young's telegram, but Young maintained his position, later stating that "if the Government of the United States should now ask for a battalion of men to fight in the present battle-fields of the nation, while there is a camp of soldiers from abroad located within the corporate limits of this city, I would not ask one man to go; I would see them in hell first."[56]

General Craig assigned the Lot Smith Company responsibility for "the 1st crossing of the Sweet Water to Green River, considering it would be more to [the company's] advantage to be near home."[57] The Lot Smith Company moved to Fort Bridger during June 1862 to protect the trail between Green River and Salt Lake City.[58]

TRACKING DOWN A HORSE THIEF

At the beginning of July, the company was ordered to pursue five U.S. Cavalry deserters. Captain Lot Smith and First Lieutenant J. Q. Knowlton deployed with a squad of nine men to apprehend the deserters. When they embarked on July 4, 1862, Captain Smith directed Lieutenant Knowlton to make contact with Washakie, chief of the Shoshoni Indians, who was rumored to live around Bear Lake. At the time, Chief Washakie was considered as being possibly hostile toward settlers.[59]

With the "persuasion . . . of a loaded revolver," the Utah soldiers convinced a passing Shoshoni warrior to direct them to Chief Washakie.[60] After entering the Indian's camp, the eleven-man group was informed they could meet with Chief Washakie, who lived across Bear Lake. While crossing the lake, it was discovered that Indians had stolen a horse from Samuel W. Richards, a citizen of Salt Lake City. Recognizing the stolen horse, Lieutenant Knowlton captured it and fought the Indian thief, who ultimately succeeded in stealing it back. Following that brief skirmish, the men continued south, entered the Indian camp, and were welcomed by the chief. Washakie told them "he was no

longer acknowledged as the Head Chief of the Snakes." Lot Smith and his men sought to improve relations with the Shoshoni, and from all appearances, the chief desired good relations with the army.[61]

When he heard that a horse had been stolen, Washakie ordered the horse be given to Lieutenant Knowlton. The chief showed his disapproval by having the thief severely whipped. In another show of good faith, Washakie provided provisions for the soldiers' return march to Fort Bridger. He placed a fifty-pound bag of flour on the ground and gave half to the soldiers. Washakie also entrusted the soldiers to take one of his relatives to Fort Bridger for medical attention.[62] After the detachment returned to Fort Bridger on July 13, Captain Smith reported to Brigham Young by telegram that the company had followed the First Presidency's counsel to "establish peace with the Indians."[63]

THE COMPANY'S LAST MISSION

The night of July 15, Indians raided the ranch of Jack Robinson, a prominent settler near Fort Bridger, and stole nearly three hundred of his horses and mules. The Lot Smith Company responded to a request to recover the animals. Sixty-one members of the company tracked the animals through the Snake River Valley.[64] The trip took longer than planned; the company ran out of provisions and was forced to live on wild strawberries. A group of twenty-one men under the direction of Lieutenant Joseph Rawlins returned home "by way of Fort Bridger" and arrived in Salt Lake City on August 2, 1862.[65]

The remaining members of the company continued their difficult and dangerous search through the Tetons.[66] While following the Snake River, they were forced to swim nearly two hundred yards in deep water with a swift current. As the detachment crossed the river, Private Daniel McNicol lost control of his horse, which was unwilling to swim across the strong current.[67] Suddenly, McNicol was pulled beneath the water's surface. To the horror of his fellow soldiers, his body was carried downstream.[68] After a desperate search, McNicol was declared drowned, but his body was never recovered. Because McNicol did not die in combat, President Young's promise that "not one of you shall fall by the hand of an enemy" was still fulfilled.[69]

In a somber mood, the soldiers continued their trek down the Snake River and toward Salt Lake City. Lot Smith felt particularly distraught by the loss of Private McNicol. He lost his appetite almost entirely and one night "walked the camp all night, broken-hearted, because of the death."[70] With their supplies nearly exhausted, the company passed their original federal service separation date—July 29, 1862. The company was ordered to return home "so that there may be no loss of . . . supplies used more than could be called for by the ninety days' service."[71] The soldiers under the direct command of Lot Smith returned to Salt Lake City on August 15, 1862—107 days after they initially left Salt Lake City. After reaching their destination, Captain Smith told his men that they had "filled the bil [sic] and as far as he was concerned [they] were dismissed."[72]

LEAVING A LEGACY OF SERVICE

Heber C. Kimball, Brigham Young's first counselor, spoke to the men upon their return. President Kimball reportedly and tearfully told the men that the company had been a "ram in the thicket," given as a sacrifice to prove the loyalty and love of the Latter-day Saints for the United States. Kimball told the company that they had "saved Israel" with their service.[73] The Latter-day Saints had shown good faith by protecting American interests and communication lines during a time of war.

The Lot Smith Company was honorably discharged on August 16, 1862. Together they earned more than $35,000 for wages, horseshoeing, blacksmithing, and other expenses incurred over their three and a half months of service—a boon for cash-deprived Utah.[74] Daniel H. Wells noted that Mormons "have always [served] whenever called upon, and we have shown ourselves ready to respond to our duty as good citizens, no matter what usage we have received in return."[75] Brigham Young agreed with General Wells, stating that he had agreed to send the men "to prove our loyalty to the Constitution and not to their infernal meanness . . . to fight the battles of a free country to give it power and influence, and to extend our happy institutions in other parts of this widely extended republic. In this way we have proved our loyalty. We have done everything that has been required of us."[76]

The Civil War continued for another three years and cost the nation dearly. The service of the Lot Smith Company did not influence the outcome of the war, but Utah's only official military contribution during the Civil War provided an opportunity to demonstrate the loyalty of the Latter-day Saints collectively and the members of the Lot Smith Company individually as they faithfully served their country.

Joseph R. Stuart is an American studies major at Brigham Young University.
Kenneth L. Alford is an associate professor of Church history and doctrine at Brigham Young University.

NOTES

1. Abraham Lincoln, "President's Message," *National Republican* (Washington, DC), December 4, 1861, 1.

2. Fred'k Steele to Major-General Halleck, April 22, 1862, in *The War of the Rebellion: A Compilation of the Official Records of the Union and Confederate Armies*, series 1 (Washington, DC: Government Printing Office, 1885), 23:365.

3. See Aurora Hunt, *The Army of the Pacific: Its Operations in California, Texas, Arizona, New Mexico, Utah, Nevada, Oregon, Washington, Plains Region, Mexico, etc. 1860–1866* (Glendale, CA: Arthur H. Clark, 1951).

4. Heber C. Kimball, in *Journal of Discourses* (London: Latter-day Saints' Book Depot, 1854–86), 9:7.

5. "The Completion of the Telegraph," *Deseret News*, October 23, 1861, 5.

6. Hunt, *Army of the Pacific*, 186.

7. Gen. S. D. Sturgis to Headquarters District of Kansas, April 16, 1862, in *War of the Rebellion*, series 1, 13:362.

8. Curtis P. Nettels, *A History of the Overland Mail* (Madison: University of Wisconsin, 1922), 146.

9. Latter-day Saints took notice that on April 6, 1862, Confederate General Albert Sidney Johnston was killed at the Battle of Shiloh (also known as the Battle of Pittsburg Landing).

10. General Lorenzo Thomas to General Denver, in *War of the Rebellion*, series 1, 50:1023–24.

11. Abraham Lincoln, endorsement, April 26, 1862, in Paul M. Angle, comp., *New Letters and Papers of Lincoln* (Boston: Houghton Mifflin, 1930), 291–92.

12. Hubert Howe Bancroft, *History of Utah, 1540–1886* (San Francisco: The History Company, 1889), 604–9.

13. The territorial governor of Utah, John W. Dawson, had fled the state on December 31, 1861, after an alleged attack on his life. See "Governor Dawson's Statement," *Deseret News*, January 22, 1862.

14. L. Thomas to Brigham Young, April 28, 1862, in *War of the Rebellion*, series 3, 2:27.

15. General Lorenzo Thomas to General Denver, in *War of the Rebellion*, series 1, 50:1023–24.

16. Edward W. Tullidge, in *History of Salt Lake City: by Authority of the City Council and under the Supervision of a Committee Appointed by the Council and Author* (Salt Lake City: Star Printing, 1886), 255.

17. Brigham Young to Daniel H. Wells, April 28, 1862, in *Brigham Young Letter Books*, Church History Library, Salt Lake City, Utah (hereafter refered to as Church History Library).

18. Letter to Colonel A. L. Fullmer, April 28, 1862, in Utah Military Files, Utah State Archives, Salt Lake City, Utah. Almon Linus Fullmer (1816–90) was colonel of the First Regiment of Infantry, Great Salt Lake Military District, Nauvoo Legion.

19. George H. Crosby, a newspaper clipping penciled "12-8-23," Lot Smith Papers, 1856–92, L. Tom Perry Special Collections, Harold B. Lee Library, Brigham Young University, Provo, Utah.

20. James Sharp, quoted in Margaret M. Fisher, ed., *Utah and the Civil War: Being the Story of the Part Played by the People of Utah in that Great Conflict, with Special Reference to the Lot Smith Expedition and the Robert T. Burton Expedition* (Salt Lake City: Deseret Book, 1929), 110.

21. Lot Smith had served as a major in the Nauvoo Legion since 1857. See Orson F. Whitney, *Popular History of Utah* (Salt Lake City: Deseret News, 1916), 145.

22. In a case of historical irony, in 1862 Lot Smith fought for the United States while Albert Sidney Johnston fought for the Confederacy. Surely this irony was not lost on Latter-day Saints. See "The Rank of General," *The Semi-Weekly Shreveport News*, February 7, 1862, 1.

23. Some animals were borrowed from the notable O. Porter Rockwell. See also letter from Daniel H. Wells to O. P. Rockwell, April 28, 1862, in Utah Military Files, Utah State Archives, Salt Lake City, Utah.

24. Quoted in Seymour B. Young, "Lest We Forget," *Improvement Era*, March 1922, 336.

25. Tullidge, *History of Salt Lake City*, 256.

26. First Presidency to Captain Lot Smith and Company, April 30, 1862, in Lot Smith Papers.

27. First Presidency to Captain Lot Smith and Company, April 30, 1862, in Lot Smith Papers.

28. Kate B. Carter, "Utah During Civil War Years," in *Treasures of Pioneer History* (Salt Lake City: Daughters of Utah Pioneers, 1956), 5:391.

29. See Young, "Lest We Forget."

30. See J. V. Frederick, *Ben Holladay, The Stagecoach King: A chapter in the development of Transcontinental Transportation* (Glendale, CA: Arthur H. Clark, 1940), 168.

31. Hunt, *Army of the Pacific*, 186.

32. Daniel H. Wells, in *Journal of Discourses*, 9:352–53.

33. Fisher, *Utah and the Civil War*, 24.

34. Harvey Coe Hullinger Journal, May 2, 1862; see also Fisher, *Utah and the Civil War*, 25.

35. Fisher, *Utah and the Civil War*, 25.

36. Fisher, *Utah and the Civil War*, 25–26.

37. For additional information, please see the "Utah and the Civil War Press" chapter herein.

38. Harvey Coe Hullinger Journal, May 2, 1862.

39. Fisher, *Utah and the Civil War*, 26; see also Harvey Coe Hullinger Journal, May 2–27, 1862.

40. Fisher, *Utah and the Civil War*, 40.

41. Harvey Coe Hullinger Journal, May 4–9, 1862.

42. Fisher, *Utah and the Civil War*, 37.

43. J. Downs, "To Whom it may Concern," May 10, 1862, MSS 2210, Utah Military Files, Utah State Archives, Salt Lake City, Utah.

44. David P. Robrock, "The Eleventh Ohio Volunteer Cavalry on the Central Plains, 1862–1866," *Arizona and the West* 25, no. 1, 23.

45. Fisher, *Utah and the Civil War*, 26–27; see also Horton and Teverbaugh, *A History of the Eleventh Regiment, (Ohio Volunteer Infantry)* (Dayton, OH: W. J. Shuey, 1866), 72–88.

46. Letter to Brigham Young, June 16, 1862, in Lot Smith Papers.

47. Harvey Coe Hullinger Journal, June 6–20, 1862.

48. Letter to Brigham Young, June 16, 1862, in Lot Smith Papers.

49. James Craig to Honorable E. M. Stanton, August 23, 1862, in *War of the Rebellion*, series 1, 13:592.

50. Tullidge, *History of Salt Lake City*, 257.

51. James Craig to Brigadier General James G. Blunt, June 26, 1862, in *War of the Rebellion*, series 1, 13:451.

52. Governor Stephen Harding to Adjutant-General James Craig, August 25, 1862. *War of the Rebellion*, series 1, 13:596.

53. Quoted in Major-General Halleck to Brigadier-General James Craig, August 25, 1862, in *War of the Rebellion*, series 1, 13:596.

54. Brigham Young Letter to Adjutant-General Thomas, August 25, 1862, *Brigham Young Letter Books*, Church History Library.

55. Patrick E. Connor's California volunteers arrived in Utah in July 1862. Leonard J. Arrington and Davis Bitton, "The Kingdom and the Nation," in *The Mormon Experience: A History of the Latter-day Saints*, 2nd ed. (Urbana: University of Illinois Press, 1992), 172. For additional information, please see the chapter herein regarding the establishment of Camp Douglas.

56. Brigham Young, in *Journal of Discourses*, 10:107.

57. Lot Smith to Brigham Young, June 16, 1862, in Lot Smith Papers.

58. James Craig to General James G. Blunt, July 11, 1862. *War of the Rebellion*, series 1, 13:469.

59. Brigham D. Madsen, *The Northern Shoshoni* (Caldwell, ID: Caxton Printers, 1980), 32.

60. Patrick E. Connor's California Volunteers arrived in Utah in May 1862. See Carter, "Utah During Civil War Years," 397.

61. Brigham Young Office Files, July 13, 1862, from Lot Smith, Microfilm (CR 1234-1), Church History Library.

62. Carter, "Utah During Civil War Years," 400.

63. See Fisher, *Utah and the Civil War*, 25.

64. Carter, "Utah During Civil War Years," 401.

65. Brigham Young Office Files, July 30, 1862, Joseph Rawlins, Microfilm (CR 1234-1), Church History Library; Harvey Coe Hullinger Letter Accompanying Transcript of his Journal, May 1–August 24, 1862, Church History Library.

66. Carter, "Utah During Civil War Years," 403.

67. The August 14, 1862 "Muster-Out Roll of Captain Lott Smith's Company of Mounted Volunteers" (MSS A 5238, Utah State Historical Society, Salt Lake City, UT) lists his name as Daniel McNicol. Fisher, reprinting an account by Seymour B. Young of the Snake River Expedition in which McNicol lost his life, lists his name as "Donald McNicol" (pp. 72–79). Fisher also lists his name as "Daniel McNicol" (p. 29). See Appendix E for additional information about this soldier.

68. "Captain Lot Smith's Company of Volunteers," *The Utah Genealogical and Historical Magazine*, January 1911, 138.

69. Fisher, *Utah and the Civil War*, 26.

70. Fisher, *Utah and the Civil War*, 109.

71. H. B. Clawson (Assistant Adjutant General) to Lot Smith, in Lot Smith Papers.

72. Harvey Coe Hullinger Journal, August 10, 1862.

73. Harvey Coe Hullinger (letter accompanying transcript of his journal), May 1–August 24, 1862.

74. Lot Smith Accounts 1862, in Lot Smith Papers.

75. Daniel H. Wells, in *Journal of Discourses*, 9:353.

76. Brigham Young, in *Journal of Discourses*, 10:107.

Colonel Robert T. Burton commanded the Nauvoo Legion's First Regiment of Cavalry and later served as a General Authority in The Church of Jesus Christ of Latter-day Saints. (Utah State Historical Society)

CHAPTER 9

Ephriam D. Dickson III

PROTECTING THE HOME FRONT

THE UTAH TERRITORIAL MILITIA DURING THE CIVIL WAR

In August 1861, the leader of the Utah Territorial Militia, Lieutenant General Daniel H. Wells, ordered district commanders to "quietly revive the military throughout the Territory." Utah's militia, better known as the Nauvoo Legion, had been established more than a decade earlier to protect frontier Mormon communities from Indian depredations and was reorganized in 1857 to defend those same communities from the approaching U.S. Army. But over the next three years, the Legion had largely languished. With the withdrawal of Federal troops to fight in the expanding Civil War and the departure of the territorial governor, the political situation in Utah Territory appeared to be on the cusp of change. "What we wish is to have our military organization as perfect as possible," General Wells communicated in his order, "and to have the implements of war on hand and in good order. Now is a favorable opportunity to obtain guns and ammunition. Let the brethren provide themselves with a good

supply of powder, ball and caps and then not shoot nor trade it away."[1]

Historical reviews of Utah during the Civil War inevitably discuss Captain Lot Smith's company, the only territorial militia unit sworn into Federal service. For three months, this company patrolled the main trail from Salt Lake City east to Independence Rock on the Sweetwater. To focus exclusively on the Lot Smith company, however, is to overlook the larger role of the Nauvoo Legion during the Civil War. The territorial militia continued to provide security on the frontier edges of the expanding Mormon kingdom, often negotiating with or fighting against Indian tribes. Echoing the militia's role during the Utah War, units were placed on alert when Federal troops returned in 1862 and assembled to guard Brigham Young's residence from possible army intervention. The Nauvoo Legion explored new areas for possible settlement and was called upon by the marshal's office to make arrests and provide security. The territorial militia also served in a ceremonial role, marching in parades, firing cannons during celebrations, and escorting visiting dignitaries. While not directly engaged in bloody battles against the Confederacy, the Nauvoo Legion nonetheless played an active role in Utah during the Civil War. The militia reveals another facet of the Latter-day Saint Church's continued efforts to direct the development of Utah Territory.

MILITIA ORGANIZATION

Descended from the earlier Mormon militia in Illinois, the Nauvoo Legion was formally reestablished in 1849 as part of the new State of Deseret.[2] The primary role of the militia was to provide security against Indian depredations to spreading Mormon settlements, which impacted native communities and their economic livelihoods. During the Latter-day Saints' first decade in the Salt Lake Valley, the Nauvoo Legion skirmished with the Utes near Fort Utah in 1850, fought in the Wakara War in 1853–54, and planned delaying tactics against the approaching U.S. Army during the Utah War in 1857. In 1861, as Federal troops withdrew from Fort Crittenden (or Camp Floyd, as it was originally known), Mormon leaders anticipated that the Civil War would be the next significant test of the territorial militia.[3]

White males between the ages of eighteen and forty-five were eligible for military service in Utah Territory; however, muster rolls reveal that enlistment was restricted to Latter-day Saints. Territorial militia records are incomplete, but surviving documents suggest that the force numbered between eight and ten thousand men during the Civil War period. By 1867, the Nauvoo Legion

had grown to over twelve thousand men. Three-quarters of the militia were listed as infantry, and about 20 percent were classified as cavalry (or "minute men"). Two units of light field artillery, one based in Salt Lake and the other in Ogden, made up about 1 percent of the total force. The remaining 1 percent included staff officers and military bands.[4]

Units of the Nauvoo Legion were mustered at least once a year. During the three- or four-day encampment, officers were elected to fill vacancies and the enlisted men received basic instruction and drill. Quality of the drill varied from community to community, depending upon the experience of the officers. One army veteran noted in 1863 that despite the annual musters, there was "a marked deficiency in many of the officers of the Legion with regard to tactics and drill."[5] To improve training, Colonel David J. Ross was promoted in 1864 to the senior staff with the responsibility to oversee drill instruction throughout the territory, and a standardized drill manual for the Nauvoo Legion was published in 1865.[6]

In most state militias, officers were nominated and elected by citizen soldiers in their respective units. In Utah, nominations for officers generally originated with Latter-day Saint Church leaders, with the men voicing a unanimous vote of confirmation ("sustaining"). Warren Foote, who served in the Legion's Second Regiment of Infantry in the Salt Lake Military District, described his election in 1862: "After drilling a short time, we marched into the schoolhouse and were seated. After making some remarks, General Richards nominated me for Major. It was seconded and voted unanimously."[7] Individuals selected as officers were often Church and community leaders, a merging

"Major Ladd's Artillery." On November 3, 1865, Charles R. Savage or possibly his partner, George Ottinger (both officers in the Nauvoo Legion), set up a camera to capture images of the annual muster of the Great Salt Lake District. (Church History Library)

of religious, civil, and military roles common in Mormon culture during this period.

While Utah militia regulations did not specify a required uniform, many regiments developed their own standardized attire modeled after other militia units or the U.S. Army. Officers sometimes purchased the Federal blue frock coat, to which were added brass Nauvoo Legion buttons. They also wore the standard army black hat with an ostrich feather. "In uniform, I saw a Captain, a Major and one Colonel," wrote an observer of the 1864 muster near Salt Lake City; "all the others were in the free and easy mountain habiliments of corduroys, homespun and broadcloth."[8] By 1865, a few companies in Salt Lake City were "neatly uniformed."[9]

Not only were officers and enlisted men expected to clothe themselves; they were also responsible for procuring their own weapons and maintaining at least forty rounds of lead,

powder, and percussion caps at all times. Soldiers assigned to cavalry units provided their own horses and saddles. Wagons and teams used for hauling baggage were often supplied by members of the community. The soldiers were generally expected to bring their own rations when deployed in the field.

Each of the regiments displayed locally made regimental standards, which often exhibited religious symbols and mottos such as "God and Our Rights" and "The Stone from the Mountain."[10] The American flag was also prominently displayed. Colonel Fullmer, commander of the First Regiment of Infantry in the Salt Lake Military District, was ordered in 1863 to procure and prominently display the national standard to show the militia's Union sympathies. "The presence of a National flag with your command would be palpable evidence of its loyalty to the Constitution and laws of the U.S.," noted

Officers of the Third Regiment of Infantry, Great Salt Lake Military District. This photograph has sometimes been misidentified as portraying pre-Civil War troops at Camp Floyd. (Church History Library)

his commander, "while its absence might, under some circumstances, seriously embarrass you."[11]

Headquarters of the Nauvoo Legion was based in Salt Lake City, with Lieutenant General Daniel H. Wells as overall commander. Having served in the Nauvoo Legion in Illinois, Wells was appointed to the committee charged with drafting legislation for organizing the militia in 1849 and selected as its first commander. When the Nauvoo Legion was reorganized in 1852 and again in 1857, his position was reconfirmed. In addition to militia duties, Wells also served as an Apostle in the Church, as Second Counselor in the First Presidency, and as superintendent of public works overseeing construction of public buildings in Salt Lake City. In 1862, after thirteen years in the militia, Wells submitted his resignation to Brigham Young. It was not accepted. Except for his absence on a mission

to Great Britain in 1864–65, Wells remained commander of the territorial militia until 1870, when the Nauvoo Legion was largely deactivated by Governor Shaffer.[12]

Salt Lake City lawyer James Ferguson served as the adjutant general on General Wells's staff, responsible for maintaining Nauvoo Legion records. Formerly a sergeant major in the Mormon Battalion, Ferguson served with distinction as adjutant general for nine years before problems associated with alcoholism forced Wells to suspend him in 1861. Hiram B. Clawson, General Wells's aide-de-camp and a son-in-law of Brigham Young, filled the vacancy for the next three years until he was officially appointed adjutant general in 1864.[13]

Other members of General Wells's staff included Lewis Robison, quartermaster general; Albert P. Rockwood, commissary general of subsistence; and Thomas W. Ellerbeck, chief of ordnance. Because the territorial militia lacked a centralized supply system, these officers had modest responsibilities compared to their counterparts in the Regular Army. Additional staff officers were tasked with overseeing medical care, military justice, and martial music.[14]

The Nauvoo Legion was organized into districts, which generally correlated with existing counties. Individual units such as companies, battalions, and regiments reported to their local district commander. Surviving records suggest that General Wells rarely issued specific directives, leaving many decisions to be made at the discretion of his district commanders. This somewhat decentralized system of command resulted in military districts being shaped differently depending upon local issues and the individual abilities of community leaders. A closer examination of two military districts can serve to illustrate these differences. Based in a growing urban center, the Great Salt Lake Military District was the largest in the territory, with most of its activities driven by local interactions with federal authorities. In contrast, the Cache Military District was located on the northern edge of the Mormon frontier, where new settlements struggled against a growing wave of Shoshone resistance. These very different roles for the legion reflect ways in which the militia was utilized throughout the territory during the Civil War.

GREAT SALT LAKE MILITARY DISTRICT

Major General George D. Grant was promoted to commander of the Great Salt Lake Military District in 1857 following the death of his brother, Jedediah Grant, the previous

commander and mayor of the city. A veteran of the Illinois Nauvoo Legion, George Grant had a leading role in early militia campaigns against Indians in the territory, including the fight at Fort Utah in 1850 and in the Tooele Valley in 1851. (The town of Grantsville was named in his honor.) He was also prominent in preparations for the Utah War in 1857.[15] By the beginning of the Civil War, General Grant commanded the largest component of the territorial militia, consisting of one regiment of cavalry, three regiments of infantry, and a light artillery company. These units were organized under two brigade commanders.[16]

Upon receipt of General Wells's order to revitalize the Nauvoo Legion in 1861, General Grant forwarded instructions to each of his two brigade commanders.[17] Brigadier General Franklin D. Richards, head of the Second Brigade, ordered each regiment to update rolls and conduct an inspection. "No particular danger is now felt that requires these orders to be issued," General Richards wrote in an explanatory note, "but the present is the first proper time that has presented itself, since our Territory was occupied by a Government Mob, to put our Militia in a state of self defense." Richards added that the militia might be called upon by the U.S. government to provide troops to fight in the Civil War or to act as a home guard. Richards added that he wanted the men "on a complete war-footing," ready for effective service "at home or abroad."[18]

The First Regiment of Cavalry was commanded by Colonel Robert T. Burton, one of the best-known officers in the Nauvoo Legion. As a young man, Burton had served briefly with the Nauvoo Legion in Illinois. In Utah, he had the reputation of a fearless Indian fighter. During the Utah War, his company shadowed the approaching U.S. Army,

Third Regiment of Infantry's martial band. At the far left stands the band's drum major, Dimick B. Huntington. This band later became known as the Beesley Martial Band, named for Ebenezer Beesley, who succeeded Huntington as director. (Church History Library)

reporting their position and strength. He was named colonel of the cavalry regiment in 1857. The regiment numbered about 265 men in 1863, about 62 percent of which Burton reported were available for deployment on short notice. His regiment included two battalions, one led by Major Lot Smith and the other by Major Andrew Cunningham.[19]

As part of the 1861 reorganization of the militia, Almon L. Fullmer was promoted from adjutant to colonel of the First Regiment of Infantry, replacing Jesse P. Harmon, who had moved to southern Utah. Fullmer's regiment was estimated at about 363 men in 1861, divided between four battalions.[20] Jonathan Pugmire Jr. was named the new commander of the Second Regiment of Infantry, in place of Thomas Callister, who resigned. Veteran of the Mormon Battalion, Pugmire helped oversee the construction of the fortifications in Echo Canyon during the Utah War and worked as the

foreman of the Public Works Blacksmith Shop in Salt Lake City. Colonel Pugmire served the regiment until 1864, when he was sent to the Bear Lake Valley and the command passed to Samuel W. Richards. At the 1861 muster, the regiment included 420 men divided among five battalions. A muster roll from the following year reveals that over one-third of his force did not possess a firearm.[21]

The Third Regiment of Infantry was commanded by Colonel David J. Ross, one of the most experienced officers in the district, having served in the British Army a decade earlier. He was promoted to General Wells's staff in 1864 and assigned as training officer for the militia throughout the territory. His regiment numbered about 319 men in 1863.[22]

The Salt Lake Military District also had one company of light artillery, with six cannons of various sizes. General Wells expressed concern about leadership of the battery following

In this group portrait, enlisted men from the Third Regiment of Infantry proudly display personal weapons and homemade uniforms.
(Church History Library)

an accident on July 4, 1861, that seriously wounded a militiaman. An investigation cleared the men of drinking but found contradictory testimony about whether the barrel had been properly swabbed and whether the gun captain had adequately supervised the crew. "Your attention is particularly directed to the organization and probably the entire reconstruction of the artillery," General Wells directed. As part of the 1861 reorganization, Major Samuel G. Ladd was named the new artillery commander. The company numbered about 140 men by 1865.[23]

One final unit was added to the Salt Lake Military District in 1862. With the significant advancement of firearms, General Wells established a sharpshooter company known as the Enfield Rifles under the command of Captain Thomas Jack. The new company was recruited in Salt Lake City and ordered to hone marksmanship "to the requisite efficiency."[24]

Important insights about Salt Lake City during the Civil War, including frequent mention of the territorial militia, were reported in weekly newspaper dispatches of Thomas B. H. Stenhouse. Baptized into the Latter-day Saint Church in 1841, Stenhouse had been an enthusiastic missionary in Europe for over a decade before immigrating to the U.S. in 1855. While in New York City, he served as editor of the *Mormon* and then as a reporter for the *New York Herald*. After his arrival in Salt Lake City in 1859, Stenhouse was employed as a clerk in the Church historian's office, opened a newsstand, and in 1862 was appointed postmaster. He submitted pro-Mormon letters to the *New York Herald* and several newspapers in California, including the *Sacramento Daily Union*, where he wrote under the pseudonym "Liberal."[25] "Had the territory of Utah possessed a minister of public information and propaganda,"

Third Regiment of Infantry. (Church History Library)

one historian noted, "Thomas Stenhouse would have been it. . . . His journalistic voice was undoubtedly the most powerful in the territory."[26] While Stenhouse's writings focused primarily on religion and politics in Salt Lake, he also frequently mentioned militia activities.

The reorganization of the Great Salt Lake Military District was completed in early 1862, just as word reached the territorial capital of a series of Indian attacks along the trail east of Fort Bridger near Independence Rock. In response, both Brigham Young and Acting Governor Frank Fuller ordered General Wells to assign a militia unit to patrol the trail, creating a conflict of jurisdiction. Colonel Burton was selected for the assignment, and on April 26, he departed with a hastily assembled detachment of twenty-three mounted militiamen. "The company is composed of picked men, the cream of the regiment that could be spared," Stenhouse noted. "Brigham has sent

two of his own sons and a son-in-law, and Heber has two of his sons in it."[27]

Burton's company escorted William H. Hooper, the former congressional delegate for Utah Territory, as he headed east to the States. While en route, his men examined damaged stage stations, two burned coaches, and numerous bags of looted mail, but they did not encounter any Indians. Rumors abounded throughout the region, but the identity of the raiding party could not be established with certainty, some suggesting Shoshone while others thought Arapaho or possibly Crow. After reaching the Deer Creek station near present Glenrock, Wyoming, Burton's company turned around and headed home.[28]

Meanwhile in Salt Lake City, just two days after Colonel Burton's departure, a telegram was received from the War Department addressed to Brigham Young. The communication authorized Young to raise one company of cavalry for ninety days of federal service

Photo is part of the November 1865 series, which remains the most significant photographic documentation of the Utah territorial militia during the Civil War. (Church History Library)

to protect property and personnel along the Overland Trail, especially in the Sweetwater country where Indian attacks had occurred. Rather than federalize Colonel Burton's company (they were only twenty-five miles away, having passed Parley's Summit), Brigham Young and General Wells recruited a second company for field service. "Young received the dispatch at nine o'clock on the evening of the 28th," observed Stenhouse, "and I am told that in fifteen minutes afterwards, there were three expresses at full speed in three counties for an equal division of men. Major Lot Smith, now in command, was down from his farm by early breakfast, and that evening the muster roll was nearly full with respondents."[29] Lot's company departed Salt Lake City on May 1 to begin their term of Federal service. Colonel Burton's company returned to Salt Lake City on May 31. Lot Smith returned with most of his company on August 15, 1862.[30] Both expeditions demonstrated that on a small

scale the territorial militia could be quickly mobilized and dispatched in an emergency even some distance from Salt Lake City.

In addition to serving along the Overland Trail, militias in the Salt Lake Military District assisted the judicial arm of the government. For example, on June 12, 1862, Governor Fuller ordered General Wells to provide the marshal with "a sufficient military force" to assist in the arrest of religious dissident Joseph Morris. Excommunicated from the Church a year earlier, Morris and his followers had gathered on the Weber River at Kingston Fort to await what he and his band of followers believed to be the imminent Second Coming. After several predicted dates for the millennial event passed, some followers doubted Morris's revelations and started leaving. Conflict erupted when three of the departing men seized a wagonload of wheat. They were chased down and brought back to the fort, though one escaped and reported the situation to officials in Salt Lake City. A writ of habeas corpus was issued for their release, but the Morrisites refused to comply. Governor Fuller wrote, "It appears that said Joseph Morris and his associates have organized themselves into an armed force to resist the execution of said writs, and are setting at utter defiances the law and its officers."[31]

The militia was dispatched under the command of Burton, who served as both county sheriff and colonel of the First Regiment of Cavalry. Nauvoo Legion records do not list which units were sent with Burton to make the arrests. Richard W. Young, in an 1890 article on the "Morrisite War," noted that the force from Salt Lake City consisted of "one skeleton company of riflemen, one full company and a detachment of artillery, in all about two hundred and fifty men." Young's description suggests that the units included Captain Jack's newly formed Enfield Rifles, a portion of Major Ladd's artillery with two cannons, possibly a portion of Colonel Burton's First Regiment of Cavalry, and part of Colonel Ross's Third Regiment of Infantry. An additional two hundred men from Davis County and about one hundred men from Weber County, representing militia units from these northern districts, also joined the posse early in the morning of June 13 near Kingston Fort. This represented the largest movement of militiamen since the Utah War.[32]

After sending a written demand to surrender, Burton ordered Major Ladd to fire two warning shots from the artillery battery. The first flew over the fort, while the second landed in front of the adobe walls, ricocheting into the structures and killing two women. Shots soon erupted from both sides, commencing a siege that lasted for three days. On June 15, the Morrisites raised a white flag.

But tragically, as the two parties met in the chaotic moments of the surrender that evening, Joseph Morris and several others were shot point blank and killed, the circumstance of which remains controversial to this day. The posse then returned to Salt Lake City with male prisoners charged with murder or resisting arrest. The militia was then released from service.

Another instance in which the Nauvoo Legion was called to support the legal system came in January 1864 with the execution of convicted murderer Jason R. Luce. A month earlier, Luce cut the throat of a man he claimed had previously beaten him unconscious for being a Mormon. Luce was convicted and sentenced to death for the murder. Robert T. Burton, as county sheriff, called upon the Nauvoo Legion for support in guarding the prisoner and maintaining peace on the day of the execution. When Stenhouse arrived at the courthouse where the prisoner was held in a cell, he found the building "entirely surrounded by the militia and the Minute Men (cavalry) were posted inside of the outer wall." Luce was executed by a five-man firing squad inside the courthouse grounds.[33]

While statutes directed the Nauvoo Legion to report to the territorial governor, the militia, in reality, answered to Brigham Young, evidence that the militia continued to operate as an extension of the LDS Church. No event emphasizes this allegiance better than the militia's reactions to the return of the Federal army to Utah in 1862.

Soon after closing Fort Crittenden, President Lincoln telegraphed the governor of California, requesting that the state raise two regiments to protect the main transportation corridor across the western interior. This assignment was originally given to Colonel

A skirmish line of the Third Regiment of Infantry shows the diversity of military hats worn by the men. The Sibley tent in the background to the right was probably purchased as military surplus when Camp Floyd was closed in 1861. (Church History Library)

James H. Carleton; however, his troops were diverted to southern California as the Confederacy appeared to advance across the Southwest. Following Lincoln's request for additional troops from California, Colonel Patrick Edward Connor was assigned to guard the trails. He departed in spring of 1862 with companies of the Third California Infantry and Second California Cavalry.

After establishing Fort Ruby in the Nevada Territory, Connor marched toward Salt Lake City in October 1862. Expecting the army to rebuild on the site of Fort Crittenden, Mormon leaders were surprised when Connor moved up to the bench overlooking the city and established Camp Douglas.[34] The proximity of Federal troops made a collision between the army and militia a real possibility.

In March 1863, following his plural marriage to Amelia Folsom, Brigham Young was charged with violating the new Morrill Anti-Bigamy Act. Rumors suggested that Connor's troops would accompany the territorial marshal to make the arrest. As a result, the Nauvoo Legion was placed on alert. Over a three-week period, activities at the post were misinterpreted and militiamen gathered to protect the Beehive House.[35] On the evening of March 29, a thirteen-gun salute celebrating Connor's promotion to brigadier general again prompted the militia to surround Brigham Young's home.[36]

Similarly in 1864, the militia was called upon to protect Temple Square. In an effort to retrieve disorderly soldiers and to ensure Union sympathies in the city, the army established a provost marshal's office in Salt Lake City. In a provocative move, the army rented a building directly across from the south entrance of Temple Square. Once again the Nauvoo Legion was called to protect Church leaders from a feared attack. After failing in

"Croxall's band." A noted fixture in Salt Lake City for many years, this band was led by Jonah Croxall (1822–84), probably the man standing in the front row center. The young men to his left and right are probably his sons, who also played brass instruments. (Church History Library)

court to force Connor to close his provost marshal's office, men bricked up the south gate of Temple Square. Such examples illustrate ways in which the Nauvoo Legion was utilized in Salt Lake City.

CACHE MILITARY DISTRICT

A copy of General Wells's August 1861 order to reorganize the Nauvoo Legion arrived in Cache Valley on the northern border of Utah Territory. For the past two years, settlers had borne the brunt of Shoshone aggressions against Mormon expansion in the region, and as a result, militia units were being actively developed.[37]

The militia in Cache County had been initially organized as part of the Weber Military District in 1859, the first year of significant migration into the valley. In November 1859, as religious leaders were being selected for the valley, the commander of the Weber

Military District, General Chauncey W. West, organized the local militia. In Wellsville, men were paraded on the public square and instructed in basic drill. Elections of officers were conducted. William H. Maughn, bishop of Wellsville, was selected to lead the new battalion with the rank of major. General West and his party then traveled to Logan, where they organized another battalion under the command of Major Israel J. Clark.[38]

In the fall of 1860, General Wells accompanied Brigham Young on his first visit to the Cache Valley settlements, which had grown threefold over the past year to more than 2,600 people. Young recognized that one of the most critical issues for Cache County was security. "You are very much exposed here," he noted at a public meeting in Franklin. "The settlements in this valley are, as it were, a shield to the other settlements." He encouraged settlers to build a strong fort capable of withstanding an Indian attack and to be vigilant. At a meeting in Logan the following day, Young again emphasized security. "Be at all times prepared to successfully resist Indian hostility," he instructed. "Keep minute men ready, that they can be in the saddle and off on short notice—enough to protect your settlement." During this trip, General Wells issued an order establishing the Cache Military District, though it was to remain subordinate to the Weber District. Wells also set the date for the formal muster and elections and echoed Brigham Young's instructions to fortify and protect settlers.[39]

For the 1860 muster held on June 14, General West again traveled to Logan to oversee the organization of the Cache Military District and individual militia units. Apostle Ezra T. Benson, who had recently moved to the valley to oversee its growth, was selected as colonel for the military district. Presiding Bishop Peter Maughn served as the militia chaplain. Nine battalions were established with a total of 601 men, each based in one of the Cache Valley communities. The original company of militia from Logan formed the First Battalion, commanded by Major Thomas E. Ricks, and the Wellsville unit formed the Second Battalion, led by Major William H. Maughn. To these was added battalions from Hyde Park, Providence, Richmond, Smithfield, Franklin, Hyrum, and a second one from Logan.[40]

The diary of Nauvoo Legionnaire George Barber of Smithfield highlights some of the activities of the militia in 1861. "Went to Logan in company with five other minute men to attend a meeting and review of all the minute men in Cache Valley," he recorded on May 11. Two weeks later, he attended a muster in Logan. When a large number of Shoshone

appeared in the valley that summer, he and several other men from Smithfield were ordered to assemble near the Indian camp. Together with a unit from Logan, these fifty militia men drilled and carefully scouted the village. "The Indians do not know what to make of a body of well-armed men encamped so near them watching their movements," Barber noted in his diary. "They made another demand for presents today, throwing out threats occasionally." Nine days later, the large Indian village moved near Wellsville, where other members of the Nauvoo Legion took over the vigil. When Barber's unit was released from duty, the men returned to their farms, some finding that crops had suffered from lack of water during their absence.[41]

General Wells's 1861 order to reactivate the Nauvoo Legion across the territory also established the Cache Military District as an independent command that reported directly to Salt Lake City. General West was ordered to assist Colonel Benson with the 1861 muster to create a "more effective and complete organization" in the Cache Valley.[42]

For three days in September 1861, the militiamen gathered from across the valley to a large encampment near Logan. Each day, they drilled under the leadership of two members of Colonel Benson's staff who had prior army service in the Mexican War. The structure of the Cache Valley militia was again reorganized. The First Battalion commanded by Major Ricks became the First Battalion Cavalry, with each company based in a community. The remainder of the militia was organized into six battalions of infantry. General West expressed satisfaction with the men's progress.[43]

Throughout the 1861–63 period, the militia was frequently called out to recover stolen horses. When the Shoshone passed through the valley each year, militia units camped nearby, visible and prepared to respond to any emergency. The Nauvoo Legion was also used to scout and explore areas for future settlements. In July 1861 and again in July 1862, detachments from the Cache Valley militia scouted east into the Bear Lake vicinity, reporting favorable conditions. When a portion of Lot Smith's federalized company traveled north to the Bear Lake area in pursuit of deserters, the Cache County militia was notified to assist if needed.[44]

The arrival of Colonel Connor in Utah in the fall of 1862 created turmoil as far north as Cache Valley. As Connor set out from Fort Ruby en route to Salt Lake City, he sent two companies of cavalry under Major Edward McGarry north to the Humboldt River in pursuit of Shoshones who had attacked an emigrant train near Gravelly Ford. McGarry then moved east to City of Rocks before turning south toward Salt Lake City, following the main road. They crossed the Bear River just west of Cache Valley as they continued south to rejoin Colonel Connor.[45]

McGarry's expedition, however, was apparently not widely known in Salt Lake City; thus, the approach of a second column of troops from a different direction caught some residents by surprise. On October 25, 1862, Colonel Benson sent a small detachment of militiamen from Logan to scout for evidence of federal troops in the area. The party traveled west to the upper ford of the Bear River, where they found McGarry's tracks heading south. At midnight, an express arrived in Mendon from Salt Lake City asking for twenty men to be prepared to start immediately to defend Salt Lake City, if needed. The Logan militia was also under similar marching orders.[46]

Major McGarry returned to Cache Valley several times in the coming months in pursuit of Shoshones. In late November 1862, he had a minor skirmish with a Shoshone band at the mouth of Providence Canyon during which a white child was rescued. After McGarry's departure, Shoshone retaliated by attacking Providence. Although the attack was repelled by the militia, local leaders were concerned that indiscriminate violence against the Shoshone would provoke further troubles for settlers in the Cache Valley.[47] McGarry returned in December to recover stolen stock but failed to engage the Shoshone in a decisive battle.[48]

In January 1863, Colonel Connor led a larger column of troops into the Cache Valley and attacked the village of Bear Hunter and Sagwitch, north of Franklin, killing hundreds of Shoshones. This attack sent shock waves throughout the tribe. In the wake of the Bear River Massacre, Cache Valley communities struggled with Shoshone retaliation. General Wells counseled Colonel Benson to distinguish the militia from the army and warned him not to get caught up in the Indian war started by Connor.[49]

In August 1865, Brigham Young visited Cache Valley and, in company with General Wells, reviewed the militia at their annual muster. By this time, the Shoshone had signed a series of peace treaties and had largely pulled back from the valley. As these Church leaders congratulated the assembled men under Benson, now promoted to brigadier general, they must have realized how indispensable the Nauvoo Legion had been in establishing the settlers' hold on the valley. This had been the same process in each of the Mormon frontier zones as they wrestled areas from native control. In fact, this process was just starting anew in southern Utah in what would become the largest Indian war fought by the territorial militia, the Black Hawk War of 1865–72.[50]

CONCLUSION

In November 1865, the territorial militia in the Great Salt Lake Military District gathered for its annual muster and review at a temporary encampment about four miles south of the city. The bloody American Civil War had ended seven months earlier, and the territory was entering its new period of growth. This muster was especially poignant. On the morning of the review, General Connor and several of his officers from Camp Douglas visited the encampment early and received a polite tour with the senior staff. Citing pressing business back at the post, Connor's party soon departed. Fifteen minutes later, the official review party from Salt Lake arrived, including Brigham Young, General Wells, and the new territorial governor, Charles Durkee. The two wagon cavalcades, Connor's heading back into the city and Young's heading out, must have passed each other on the road. As with all of their public appearances, these two men never actually met. They remained two powerful forces carefully revolving around each other's spheres of influence.

On the final day of the muster, militia troops marched back to Salt Lake City, stopping briefly at the governor's residence to render honors. As a visible symbol of the Nauvoo Legion's true allegiance, the militia next marched to the Beehive House, where it formed into columns. Brigham Young thanked the men for their years of faithful service to the territory and to the Church and officially dismissed the troops.[51] The Nauvoo Legion was truly a unique institution, an important element of the culture in the nineteenth-century Utah Territory.

Ephriam D. Dickson III is the curator at the Fort Douglas Military Museum in Salt Lake City.

NOTES

1. Wells to Gen. G. D. Grant, Salt Lake Military District, Special Orders #3, August 2, 1861, Nauvoo Legion Letterbook, MS 1370, Church History Library, The Church of Jesus Christ of Latter-day Saints, Salt Lake City. Similar orders were sent to each of the district commanders.

2. Richard E. Bennett, Susan Easton Black, and Donald Q. Cannon, *The Nauvoo Legion in Illinois: A History of the Mormon Militia, 1841–1846* (Norman, OK: Arthur H. Clark, 2010). A detailed examination of the Nauvoo Legion in Utah remains to be written. For general overviews, see Richard W. Young, "The Nauvoo Legion," *Contributor* 9 (1888), 121–27, 161–68, 201–12, 241–51, 281–86, 321–32, 361–73, 401–13, 441–54; Richard C. Roberts, *Legacy: The History of the Utah National Guard* (Salt Lake City: National Guard Association of Utah, 2003), 5–19; Hamilton Gardner, "Utah Territorial Militia," unpublished manuscript, Gardner Papers, MS B 113, Utah State Historical Society.

3. D. Robert Carter, *Founding Fort Utah: Provo's Native Inhabitants, Early Explorers, and First Year of Settlement* (Provo, UT: Provo City Corporation, 2003), 163–95; Ryan E. Wimmer, "The Walker War Reconsidered" (master's thesis, Brigham Young University, 2010); Brandon J. Metcalf, "The Nauvoo Legion and the Prevention of the Utah War," *Utah Historical Quarterly* 72 (2004): 300–321.

4. Abstract Return of the Nauvoo Legion the Militia of Utah Territory, 1867, document #4652, series 2210, Utah Territorial Militia Records, Utah State Archives.

5. H. W. Isaacson to Gen. Daniel H. Wells, March 19, 1863, document #738, UTMR. He may have been Private Henry W. Isaacson, age 22, who enlisted in Company E, 62nd New York Infantry, in 1861.

6. General Orders #4, Headquarters 2nd Brigade, Salt Lake Military District, July 2, 1864, *Record of Orders, Returns and Courts Martial &c of 2nd Brigade, Nauvoo Legion*, MS 357, Yale Collection of Western Americana, Beinecke Library, Yale University, 85; William B. Pace, *Rifle and Light Infantry Tactics* (Salt Lake City: Deseret News, 1865).

7. "Autobiography of Warren Foote of Glendale, Kane Co., Utah," unpublished manuscript, MS 1123, 174, Church History Library.

8. Thomas B. H. Stenhouse, "Letter from Salt Lake," dated May 29, 1864, *Sacramento Daily Union*, June 6, 1864.

9. "General Muster of the Militia of Great Salt Lake County," *Deseret News*, November 9, 1865, 4.

10. Stenhouse, *Sacramento Daily Union*, June 6, 1864.

11. Gen. Franklin D. Richards to Col. Almon L. Fullmer, December 12, 1863, *Record of Orders, Returns and Courts Martial &c of 2nd Brigade, Nauvoo Legion*, MS 357, Yale Collection of Western Americana, Beinecke Library, 81.

12. Bryant S. Hinckley, *Daniel Hamner Wells and Events of His Time* (Salt Lake City: Deseret News, 1942); Gen. Daniel H. Wells to Brigham Young, March 21, 1862, document #467, Utah Territorial Militia Records, Utah State Archives; Roberts, *Legacy*, 13–17.

13. Gen. Daniel H. Wells to Gen. James Ferguson, July 5, 1861, Nauvoo Legion Letterbook, MS 1370, Church History Library; Gen. James Ferguson to Gen. Daniel H. Wells, August 17, 1861, document #445, Utah Territorial Militia Records, Utah State Archives; Will Bagley, ed., *"A Bright, Rising Star": A Brief Life of James Ferguson, Sergeant Major, Mormon Battalion; Adjutant General, Nauvoo Legion* (Spokane, WA: Arthur H. Clark, 2000).

14. Ralph Hansen, "Administrative History of the Nauvoo Legion in Utah" (master's thesis, Brigham Young University, 1954).

15. Orson F. Whitney, *History of Utah* (Salt Lake City: George Q. Cannon & Sons, 1892), 1:426, 623; Edward W. Tullidge, *The History of Salt Lake City and Its Founders* (Salt Lake City: privately published,

1886), 69–70; Ouida Blanthorn, *A History of Tooele County* (Salt Lake City: Utah Historical Society, 1998), 78.

16. Registry Book, Great Salt Lake Military District, MS 9391, Church History Library.

17. J. M. Simmons to Gen. F. D. Richards and Gen. Wm. H. Kimball, Orders #1, Great Salt Lake Military District, August 23, 1861, Record and Order Book of the Major General Commanding G.S.L. Military District, Nauvoo Legion, Theodore A. Schroeder Papers, State Historical Society of Wisconsin.

18. Orders #1, Headquarters 2nd Brigade, September 7, 1861. Richards to Harmon, September 7, 1861.

19. Muster Roll, 1863, Utah Territorial Militia Records, Utah State Archives.

20. *Deseret News*, January 16, 1878, *Record of Orders, Returns and Courts Martial &c of 2nd Brigade*, Yale Collection of Western Americana, Beinecke Library, 44.

21. *Record of Orders, Returns and Courts Martial &c of 2nd Brigade*, Yale Collection of Western Americana, Beinecke Library, 44; muster roll, 1862, Utah Territorial Militia Records, Utah State Archives.

22. Muster roll, 1863, Utah Territorial Militia Records, Utah State Archives.

23. General Orders #1, NL HQ, June 25, 1861, document #675; R. H. Attwood to General Wells, July 5, 1861, document #677; Samuel G. Ladd to D. H. Wells, July 6, 1861, document #678, series 2210. Wells to Grant, August 2, 1861, Special Orders #3, document #679, series 2210, Utah Territorial Militia Records, Utah State Archives; Simmons to Ladd, September 28, 1861, Record and Order Book of the Major General Commanding G.S.L. Military District, Theodore A. Schroeder Papers, State Historical Society of Wisconsin.

24. Wells to Jack, March 2[?], 1862, NL Letterbook, Church History Library.

25. Mrs. T. B. H. Stenhouse, *An Englishwoman in Utah: The Story of a Life's Experience in Mormonism* (London: Sampson Low, Marston, Searle & Rivington, 1880), 213; Tullidge, *History of Salt Lake City*, 317.

26. Ronald W. Walker, *Wayward Saints: The Godbeites and Brigham Young* (Champaign: University of Illinois Press, 1998), 53.

27. Stenhouse, "Letter from Salt Lake," dated April 28, 1862, *Sacramento Daily Union*, May 9, 1862.

28. Burton to Wells, June 3, 1862, document 472, Utah Territorial Militia Records, Utah State Archives.

29. Stenhouse, "Letter from Salt Lake," dated May 5, 1862, *Sacramento Daily Union*, May 19, 1862.

30. See the Stuart-Alford chapter herein for additional details on the Utah cavalry commanded by Lot Smith.

31. Frank Fuller to Daniel H. Wells, June 12, 1862, series 242, Utah State Archives. For detailed narratives of these events, see Thomas B. H. Stenhouse, *Rocky Mountain Saints* (New York: D. Appleton, 1873), 593–601; Richard W. Young, "The Morrisite War," *Contributor* 11 (1890): 281–84, 348, 369, 428, 466; G. M. Howard, "Men, Motive, and Misunderstandings: A New Look at the Morrisite War of 1862," *Utah Historical Quarterly* 44 (1976): 112–32; C. LeRoy Anderson, *Joseph Morris and the Saga of the Morrisites* (Logan: Utah State University Press, 1988).

32. Young, "The Morrisite War," 370.

33. Burton to Wells, January 9, 1864; Order # 1, January 11, 1864; *New York Times*, February 14, 1864; Thomas B. H. Stenhouse, "Letter from Salt Lake," dated January 1 and January 12, 1864, *Sacramento Daily Union*, January 11 and January 22, 1864; R. Michael Wilson, *Legal Executions in the Western Territories, 1847–1911* (Jefferson, NC: McFarland, 2010), 166–67.

34. See the Alford-MacKinnon chapter herein for additional information about the establishment of Camp Douglas.

35. Stenhouse, "Letter from Salt Lake," dated March 18, 1863, *Sacramento Daily Union*, March 28, 1863.

36. Report of guard service rendered by 2nd Regt. 2nd Brigade at Brigham Young Residence, March 4–22, 1863; B. H. Roberts, *A Comprehensive History of the Church of Jesus Christ of Latter-day Saints* (Salt Lake City: Deseret News Press, 1930), 5:28–29.

37. Brigham D. Madsen, *The Shoshone Frontier and the Bear River Massacre* (Salt Lake City: University of Utah Press, 1985), 98–99, 127–30. John W. Heaton, "No Place to Pitch their Tepees: Shoshone Adaptation to Mormon Settlers in Cache Valley," *Utah Historical Quarterly* 63 (1995): 159–71.

38. *Deseret News*, November 30, 1859. *Tullidge's Histories*, 2:355. No records for this muster are known to have survived, with the possible exception of an undated list of men eligible for militia service.

39. Federal Census, 1860, Cache County, Utah Territory. *Deseret News*, August 1 and August 8, 1860; Special Orders, Headquarters Nauvoo Legion, June 11, 1860, Nauvoo Legion Records, MS 1370, Church History Library. Brigham Young followed up his speeches with similar written instructions to Benson on June 18, the bishop to read them to each of the settlements. Brigham Young Letter Press books, 5:536–37, Church History Library.

40. "Muster Roll of the Field and Staff of the Regiment," June 14, 1860, document #4868, Utah Territorial Militia Records, Utah State Archives.

41. Barber diary, MS A 20, Utah State Historical Society.

42. Wells to Chauncey W. West, August 2, 1861, Nauvoo Legion Records, MS 1370, Church History Library; Special Orders, June 11, 1860.

43. Donald G. Godfrey and Rebecca S. Martineau-McCarty, *An Uncommon Common Pioneer: The Journals of James Henry Martineau, 1828–1918* (Provo, UT: Religious Studies Center, Brigham Young University, 2008).

44. Special Orders #7, HQ NL, August 7, 1862, Utah Territorial Militia Records, Utah State Archives.

45. McGarry to Connor, October 31, 1862, *War of the Rebellion*, vol. 50 pt. 1, 178–79.

46. Godfrey and Martineau-McCarty, *Uncommon Common Pioneer*, 131.

47. *Deseret News*, November 19, 1862.

48. Ephriam D. Dickson III, "Prelude to Bear River: Confrontation at Empey's Ferry, December 6–8, 1862," *Post Dispatch*, newsletter of the Fort Douglas Museum, December 2008, 4–6.

49. Wells to Benson and Maughn, May 10, 1863, Utah Territorial Militia Records, Utah State Archives.

50. For an excellent account of this new Indian war, see John Alton Peterson, *Utah's Black Hawk War* (Salt Lake City: University of Utah Press, 1998).

51. "General Muster of the Militia of Great Salt Lake County," *Deseret News*, November 9, 1865, 4.

Stephen Arnold Douglas (1813–61), the deceased U.S. senator from Illinois for whom Patrick Connor named his new post outside Salt Lake City. Douglas was Connor's political hero but either a maladroit or deliberatively provocative choice for namesake in view of his status as former chief political rival to President Lincoln and bête noire to Brigham Young since his June 12, 1857, "loathsome ulcer" speech in Springfield at the beginning of the Utah War. (Library of Congress)

CHAPTER 10

Kenneth L. Alford and William P. MacKinnon

WHAT'S IN A NAME?

THE ESTABLISHMENT OF CAMP DOUGLAS

Since my arrival the people of the Territory have been treated kindly and courteously by both my officers and men, who have never given one of them cause for complaint, which the people freely acknowledge. But notwithstanding this, the courtesy we have given is returned with abuse.

—Colonel Patrick Edward Connor, U.S. Army
March 15, 1863[1]

Camp Douglas is the only military installation in the United States sited purposely so that soldiers could keep a watchful eye on the American citizens outside its gates. The establishment and naming of this post on the bench above Salt Lake City is a colorful, but little known, story of the American Civil War. Utah is generally viewed as a backwater of the Civil War, but events in the territory played an important supporting role and were surprisingly laced with conflict. While Camp Douglas (later renamed Fort Douglas) experienced a long and colorful history that has continued into the twenty-first century, this essay focuses on the short period between the camp's founding in October 1862 and the end of the Civil War.

BACKGROUND

Brigham Young and his Latter-day Saint pioneers first arrived in the Salt Lake Valley in July 1847. Folklore has it that Young said at that time, "If the United States will now let this people alone for ten years to come, we will ask no odds of them or any one else but God."[2] In 1857, exactly ten years later, President James Buchanan moved to replace Brigham Young as Utah's first governor and organized an expeditionary force of several thousand soldiers to escort his successor to Utah while restoring federal authority in a territory perceived as rebellious. After harassment of the approaching army by the territorial militia, the evacuation of northern Utah, discussions between Brigham Young and federal peace commissioners, and the issuance of a blanket presidential pardon for Utah's entire population, the conflict was settled peaceably with Brevet Brigadier General Albert Sidney Johnston's forces marching quietly through Salt Lake City in June 1858.[3]

The soldiers then established Camp Floyd (named after John B. Floyd, President Buchanan's secretary of war) forty miles southwest of Salt Lake City, the nation's largest garrison until the outbreak of the Civil War.[4] Civilian relations with Camp Floyd were sometimes strained, but they resulted in economic benefits for many Utah residents. Camp Floyd was renamed Fort Crittenden,[5] in honor of U.S. senator John J. Crittenden, after Secretary Floyd resigned in disgrace in December 1860 and joined the Confederacy. The camp's distance from Salt Lake City was probably viewed favorably by most of the city's residents.

In 1861, when the first shots in the Civil War were fired, Utah found itself at a strategic crossroads—mail, telegraph lines, gold from California, silver from the newly created Nevada Territory's Comstock Lode, and emigrants all needed to pass freely through Utah Territory, but regular U.S. troops were needed in the East far more than they were required at Fort Crittenden. In May 1861, the War Department "issued orders for the immediate withdrawal of all the regular troops from New-Mexico and Utah."[6] Auctions held in June and July disposed of reusable building materials (lumber, windows, doors, and so forth), and the remaining adobe walls were left to the elements.[7] Fort Crittenden was evacuated and closed. The soldiers garrisoned there marched east during July. One Salt Lake resident's August 1861 letter summed up the feelings of many Utah residents: "The troops are gone. Camp Floyd,

which for three years past has resounded with the orgies of the ungodly and become a nest for every unclean thing, has reverted to its wonted quietude and simplicity. Sometimes I regret that I never visited it; yet at other times I feel grateful that I have kept myself entirely aloof from Gentile influences and associations."[8]

While some residents celebrated the post's closing, others questioned the wisdom of the decision. A *New York Times* writer predicted that "the removal of the small force from Utah will prove a fatal blunder, as it will leave the great overland routes to California and Oregon unprotected, and invite aggression both from lawless Mormons and hostile Indians."[9] When increased Indian activity and attacks along the Overland Trail followed the withdrawal of soldiers from Fort Crittenden, it soon became apparent that military action was required to protect the trail. Brigham Young and territorial federal officials suggested that "a regiment of mounted men be raised"[10] to protect the mail, emigration, and telegraph routes. The government initially rejected their offer "because it is not supposed so large a force is necessary."[11] On April 28, 1862, though, by "express direction of the President of the United States," Brigham Young, then a private citizen but still President of the LDS Church, was authorized to "raise, arm, and equip one company of cavalry for ninety days' service."[12] The government's request specified that "the company will be employed to protect the property of the telegraph and overland mail companies in or about Independence Rock [Nebraska Territory], where depredations have been committed, and will be continued in service only till the U.S. troops can reach the point where they are so much needed. . . . It will not be employed for any offensive operations other than may grow out of the duty hereinbefore assigned to it."[13]

The requested soldiers mustered within two days, an extraordinary feat of organization. Under the command of Captain Lot Smith, who had won fame as a militia major during the Utah War, the company of about a hundred men left Salt Lake City in early May 1862 for three months of active duty military service. In late August 1862, after this volunteer company had returned to Utah, Union General James Craig, who was responsible for the overland mail and telegraph lines from the Missouri River to Utah Territory, telegraphed Secretary of War Stanton and requested either reinforcements from the States or permission to "re-enlist the Utah troops for a limited time."[14] Secretary Stanton answered the following day, "You are authorized to raise 100 mounted men in the mountains and re-enlist the Utah troops for three months as requested."[15] After conferring with Brigham Young, Utah's Governor Harding informed the army that reenlistment of Lot Smith's company was not possible because, as Harding cryptically phrased it, "Things are not right."[16] Consequently, federal military leaders determined that dispatching volunteer units from California would be a more permanent military solution to the need to protect commerce and emigration along the Overland Trail. The state of California was asked to recruit sixteen thousand volunteers, some of whom would be sent to Utah.[17]

In May 1862, Brigadier General George Wright, commander of the army's Department of the Pacific in San Francisco, appointed Patrick Edward Connor, a California militia officer, to command several companies of California volunteers (or CVs, as they were often called) to travel from Stockton, California, "to

Patrick Edward Connor, the Irish-born commander of California Volunteers who established Camp Douglas in October 1862 while incurring the enmity of Brigham Young in a way that Albert Sidney Johnston had not. After the Bear River Massacre of January 1863, the army promoted Connor from colonel to brigadier and in 1865 made him a major general in part to encourage his resignation after his controversial Powder River campaign. He remained in Utah to stimulate an inflow of non-Mormons motivated by mining opportunities. (Utah State Historical Society)

the vicinity of Salt Lake." According to orders received in July 1862, his primary mission as a newly commissioned colonel was "to protect the Overland Mail Route"[18] and "also the telegraph stations."[19] Connor's command arrived at Fort Churchill (near Reno, Nevada Territory) in August 1862, where Colonel Connor assumed command of the military district of Utah, which included Utah and Nevada Territories.[20]

ESTABLISHMENT OF CAMP DOUGLAS

Utah residents had done too good of a job dismantling Fort Crittenden after the army blew up its magazines and marched east. Nearly everything of value had been removed. Little did they know that the army

A prime mission of Connor's California Volunteers was to protect from Indian attack the transcontinental telegraph line, completed in Salt Lake City exactly a year before their arrival there. Although they tried to destroy the line, the tribes (and others) marveled at the way it worked as depicted in Henry Farney's classic 1904 painting, The Song of the Talking Wire. *(Wikimedia Commons)*

would return in strength at the end of the following year, and the poor condition of Fort Crittenden would influence the selection of the army's new encampment elsewhere.

In the fall of 1862, Colonel Connor traveled in advance of the army to the Salt Lake Valley from Fort Ruby, Nevada Territory, in order to select a route and scout out the best site for a military camp near the city. Wearing civilian clothing, he "took a stroll about town and looked around with an air of familiarity that indicated that after all Salt Lake City was something of a place, and might not be unpleasant notwithstanding its desert surrounding."[21] Apparently during this reconnaissance, Connor met with neither Governor Stephen Harding nor former governor Young.

When word reached Utah that the army would soon be returning, but this time from the west, there was great concern. A *New York Times* report from Salt Lake stated, "There may be still another jurisdiction conflict in our midst, and perhaps a very pretty quarrel. . . . Let us hope for the best, particularly in the present juncture of affairs, and that peaceable counsels will prevail."[22]

After visiting the former Fort Crittenden, Colonel Connor reported to his superiors several reasons for not reopening it. First, the camp was "in ruins" except for a few buildings (for which the owner wanted $15,000). Second, most of the few remaining buildings "would have to be torn down and removed." Third, "the post is badly located." His fourth, and most important, reason was that "I found another location, which I like better." That site was "on a plateau about three miles from Salt Lake City; in the vicinity of good timber and saw-mills, and at a point where hay, grain, and other produce can be purchased cheaper than at Fort Crittenden." Colonel Connor also revealed an additional unofficial rationale for the new location—keeping an eye on the Mormons. Connor reported to his superior that the site he selected was "a point which commands the city, and where 1,000 troops would be more efficient than 3,000 on the other side of the Jordan [River]. If the general decides that I shall locate there, I intend to quietly intrench my position, and then say to the Saints of Utah, enough of your treason; but if it is intended that I shall merely protect the overland mail and permit the Mormons to act and utter treason, then I had as well locate at Crittenden. The Federal [civilian] officers desire and beg that I will locate near the city."[23]

On October 1, 1862, a few days prior to entering the Salt Lake Valley with his soldiers, Colonel Connor reported that "the people of Utah are under the impression that I am to winter at Fort Crittenden."[24] He also informed his superiors that he had been "credibly informed by letter this morning that the flag-staff at Fort Crittenden was cut down since my visit and hauled away by Brigham's orders."[25] Connor quite likely viewed this as an affront to federal authority and a misuse of government property.[26]

Colonel Connor and his mixed command (five infantry and two cavalry companies) bivouacked at Fort Crittenden on October 17, 1862, and marched into Salt Lake City on October 22, 1862. The soldiers halted

HEADQUARTERS DISTRICT OF UTAH,
Camp Douglas, Utah Ter., November 9, 1862.
ADJUTANT GENERAL,
   Washington, D. C.:
   GENERAL: I have the honor to inform you that pursuant to orders from headquarters Department of the Pacific on the 26th day of October, 1862, I established a military post in Utah Territory, and which I have named Camp Douglas. It is situated at a distance of three miles east of Great Salt Lake City, at which place there is a post-office and telegraph office, with good facilities for communication both east and west daily. It is situated at the foot and on the west side of a range of mountains which form the divide between Weber River and the Great Salt Lake Valley. It is on an elevated spot which commands a full view of the city and the Great Salt Lake and Valley, with a plentiful supply of wood and water in its vicinity, and in the neighborhood of numerous quarries of stone adapted to building barracks. If it is contemplated to establish a permanent post in this Territory I know of no spot so desirable as this. Besides the above advantages, it is the center from which diverge three roads to California, two to Oregon, and the great Overland Mail Route to the east. The low price of forage for animals is an additional advantage which it possesses, and the health of the soldiers has also materially improved since their arrival here.
   I am, very respectfully, your obedient servant,
                                P. EDW. CONNOR,
   Colonel Third Infantry California Volunteers, Comdg. District.

Connor's first notification to army headquarters that he had established Camp Douglas. Here it is clear that the siting and naming of the post were solely his decision. Seeking a site within artillery range of Brigham Young's Lion House—soon a widely-believed myth—was not part of Connor's stated rationale.
(Cornell University Library)

and formed two lines in front of Governor Harding's residence. After being introduced by Colonel Connor, the governor addressed the troops. While standing in a carriage, he confessed to the soldiers, "I have been disappointed, somewhat, in your coming to this city," and noted somewhat disapprovingly that the federal government "knows not the spirit of the officers who represent it in this Territory."[27] Accordingly, he finished by telling them, "I do not know now what disposition is to be made of you, but I suppose you will be encamped somewhere, I know not where, but within a short distance of this city. I believe the people you have now come amongst will not disturb you if you do not disturb them."[28]

NAMING CAMP DOUGLAS

Following the governor's speech, the California soldiers marched to the base of the mountains east of the city "between Red But[t]e and Emmigration Kanyons [*sic*]."[29] On

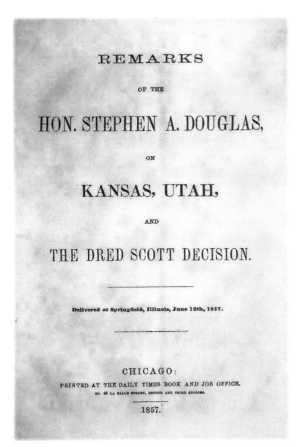

REMARKS

OF THE

HON. STEPHEN A. DOUGLAS,

ON

KANSAS, UTAH,

AND

THE DRED SCOTT DECISION.

Delivered at Springfield, Illinois, June 12th, 1857.

CHICAGO:

PRINTED AT THE DAILY TIMES BOOK AND JOB OFFICE.

NO. 45 LA SALLE STREET, SECOND AND THIRD STORIES.

1857.

The pamphlet published by Douglas in enormous quantity to broadcast his June 12, 1857, speech in Springfield, Illinois, on, among other subjects, "the Mormon problem." The speech, impromptu remarks originally intended to entertain a bored grand jury, triggered a rebuttal by Abraham Lincoln two weeks later—precursor to the 1858 Lincoln-Douglas debates—and long-lasting Mormon enmity when press reports reached Utah in late August 1857 as the Utah Expedition crossed the plains. (Internet Archive)

October 26, 1862, Colonel Connor formally announced that "pursuant to orders from department headquarters a military post is hereby established at this camp, to be called Camp Douglas." The boundaries of the camp began "at a post due north one mile distant from the garrison flag-staff, and running thence west one mile, thence south two miles, thence east two miles, thence north two miles, and thence west one mile, to the place of beginning, containing 2,560 acres more or less."[30]

Tensions between Salt Lake City and Camp Douglas began almost immediately and were possibly fueled by Connor's decision to name the new post as he did. The military correspondence for the fall of 1862 clearly indicates that the choice of names was Connor's—he dubbed the post Camp Douglas rather than being directed to do so by General George Wright in California or by an even higher authority in Washington. In fact, Wright did not even know at this point that Connor was establishing a new post, having assumed that he would be using the remnants of old Camp Floyd in distant Cedar Valley. So why would Colonel Connor—a man patently on the rise with even higher military aspirations—make such a politically maladroit name selection given the Democratic Party identification of Stephen A. Douglas vis-à-vis the prominent Republican Party affiliations of Secretary of War Stanton and President Lincoln? The late senator Stephen A. Douglas was the slave-holding Democrat who beat Abraham Lincoln in the 1858 Illinois senate race after nine face-to-face debates and against whom the Republican Lincoln ultimately triumphed in the presidential election of 1860. Connor's naming decision for Camp Douglas is even more astonishing when one considers that the three U.S. Army posts in Utah Territory established by Albert Sidney Johnston during the late 1850s prior to Camp Douglas were dubbed with political astuteness Camp Winfield and Camp Scott (after the general-in-chief) and Camp Floyd (in honor of the then-sitting secretary of war). For Connor to have honored Stephen A. Douglas in this way is akin to a scenario in which during 2003 General Tommy Franks would have named his Baghdad headquarters "Camp Al Gore."

The relatively meager collection of Connor's personal papers that have survived the ravages of fire, multiple relocations, and the passage of time offers little help in understanding his naming decision. In *Glory Hunter*, his 1990 biography of the general, Brigham D. Madsen notes that Connor had long been an admirer of Senator Douglas and even before entering the army had raised funds to finance the erection of a statue in his honor in Stockton. Madsen commented, "The new colonel never forgot his loyalties." With respect to the naming decision, Madsen's book comments without citation that Connor vetoed the desire of his men to name the post after himself, and that his choice of the admired Douglas's name was "understandable."[31] E. B. Long's 1981 account of Utah during the Civil War, *The Saints and the Union*, describes at length the initial tense approach and passage of Connor's unit through Salt Lake City to the site of Camp Douglas but is mute on why the post was so named, as was Major Fred B. Rogers's 1938 study *Soldiers of the Overland*.[32]

In his 1989 book *Brigham and the Brigadier*, James F. Varley discerns a motivation very different from Madsen's belief that Connor intended simply to honor the late Senator Douglas. Noting the uneven nature of relations between Douglas and the Mormons during their Illinois years and the fact that Mormon leaders were "incensed" by an anti-Mormon speech that Douglas had given at the very beginning of the Utah War, Varley speculates without supporting documentation that "the choice of names was undoubtedly a deliberate jab by Colonel Connor at the Mormons. . . . Patrick Connor thus could hardly have chosen a better name than Douglas for his new post if his object

was the daily chaffing of a few Mormon sensibilities."[33]

Logical as Varley's conjecture seems, an examination of Brigham Young's correspondence and the files of the *Deseret News* for the fall of 1862 yields no outbursts about the post's name, although there was a great deal of resentment and muttering about the more fundamental issue of its very establishment and siting without Mormon consultation.

But what of Varley's quite accurate point about a highly negative Mormon reaction to Douglas early in the Utah War? The cause of this rupture was a speech given by Douglas in Springfield, Illinois, on June 12, 1857, two weeks after the launch of the Utah Expedition and soon after his return from Washington. It was a strange speech—delivered in impromptu fashion at the invitation of a sitting grand jury in search of entertainment—in which Douglas ranged through three of the most volatile subjects of the day: the Supreme Court's Dred Scott decision, "bleeding" Kansas, and Utah affairs. When it came to Mormon matters, Douglas may have been stimulated by bitter private inputs from recently resigned Utah associate justice W. W. Drummond of Illinois, his constituent, as well as by the sting of Republican efforts to portray Douglas's pet doctrine of popular sovereignty (local choice) as a de facto defense of polygamy, if not slavery, in the territories. After reciting the then-current litany of accusations against Utah's Mormons—principally disloyalty and un-American backgrounds and tendencies—Senator Douglas's Springfield speech advocated the repeal of Utah's organic act and therefore her territorial obliteration. For the remedy, Douglas used graphic, surgical imagery: "When the authentic evidence shall arrive, if it shall establish the facts which

Major General Henry W. Halleck (1815–72) served for almost two years as general in chief of all U.S. armies. (Library of Congress)

are believed to exist, it will become the duty of Congress to apply the knife and cut out this loathsome disgusting ulcer. [Applause.] No temporizing policy—no half-way measure will then answer."[34]

With this political betrayal and provocative language, Douglas was immediately assigned to a place in the LDS pantheon of Utah War villains, second only to Judge Drummond, and he remains there. In the midst of the Utah War, First Counselor Heber C. Kimball stated publicly: "Many of you have sustained Judge Douglas as being a true friend to this people; and he is just as big a damned rascal as ever walked, and always has been. He has taken a course to

get into the [presidential] chair of State, and that is what he is after: he will try to accomplish that, if he goes to hell the next day; but he will not go into the chair of State; he will go to hell."[35]

Even with the passage of years, Brigham Young continued to brood over what he viewed as Senator Douglas's betrayal. In May 1861, he wrote a caustic, mocking unpublished letter to a gravely ill Douglas reminding him of his 1857 Springfield speech as well as of his role in the disruption of the Union then so violently in progress. With Douglas's failed 1860 presidential bid and Joseph Smith's apocalyptic 1843 prophecy about Douglas's political fate in mind, President Young closed, "Do you not begin to realize that the prediction of the Prophet Joseph Smith, personally delivered to you, has been and is being literally fulfilled upon your head? Why have you barked with the dogs, except to prove that you were a dog with them?"[36] The velvet glove which Brigham Young had earlier used in dealing with Douglas as chairman of the U.S. Senate's Committee on the Territories was off. Within a month—even before receiving this letter—Stephen A. Douglas lay dead in Chicago, with Fort Sumter in Confederate hands and Patrick Edward Connor of Stockton, California, about to join the Union Army.

Shortly after Senator Douglas's death, a *New York Times* correspondent reported from Salt Lake City that "last Wednesday the Pony [Express] told us of the death of Senator Douglas. The Mormon portion of the community entertain certain hard recollections of the Senator, on account of his 'loathsome ulcer' recommendations. So there are no flags at half mast, no mourning appears, no tears are shed, no tokens of respect for the memory

Camp Douglas (later designated Fort Douglas) shown in the busy 1860s. Later the post morphed from an installation for the regular army into the headquarters for the Utah National Guard, a POW camp, a troop processing/training base, Olympic Village for the 2002 Winter Games, and housing for the University of Utah. (Fort Douglas Military Museum)

of the illustrious Illinoisan are visible, though an old neighbor in Nauvoo days."[37]

TENSIONS BEGIN

Four days after Colonel Connor officially christened Camp Douglas, Brigham Young complained that "right in the time of war there could not be a greater insult offered" than the federal government sending another army to Utah. Strangely, Young suggested that with Connor's selection of the site for Camp Douglas overlooking Salt Lake City, "they are in the best place they can be in for doing the least injury. . . . Here they cannot do much hurt." He also quoted an associate as recently having said, "We are praying all the time for the Lord to make fools of them."[38]

In the months following the establishment and naming of Camp Douglas, the Overland Mail Company, the Post Office Department, and Department of the Interior all urged Connor's superiors, including General Henry W. Halleck (President Lincoln's general in chief), to move Connor's

soldiers from Salt Lake City to Fort Bridger, Utah Territory, presumably because of that post's proximity to the Overland Trail.[39] As a compromise, Connor was ordered to detach one or two companies from his command to occupy Fort Bridger. Echoing Colonel Connor's anti-Mormon sentiments, General Wright informed his superiors in Washington, DC, "Without entering into details I am well convinced that prudential considerations demand the presence of a force in that country [Salt Lake] strong enough to look down any opposition."[40] Utah governor Stephen S. Harding also recommended that Colonel Connor's command remain at Camp Douglas: "I have not a doubt but that it will be the last time that U.S. soldiers will have the privilege of entering this Territory peaceably if Colonel Connor is now ordered away. I do not say that Mormons would meet our troops openly in such an attempt, although there are strong reasons for believing that they would, yet I have no doubt but the Indians would be encouraged to do so, and all possible succor would be given them by the [Mormon] powers here. . . . The base of operations should be here. . . . In the [proposed] withdrawal of the troops the General Government virtually abandons her sovereignty over this Territory."[41]

The army's late arrival in 1862 required it to work hard throughout the winter building temporary facilities at the new camp. By February 1863, Colonel Connor reported that his troops had built thirteen small officers' quarters, a guard house, a bake house, a commissary, quartermaster offices, stores, stables, a blacksmith shop, and a hospital. The enlisted soldiers lived in "temporary shelters of tents placed over excavations four feet deep, with good stone and adobe fireplace."[42]

Camp Douglas proved to be a source of welcome income for many civilian residents. While many supply items were received from the States, the military purchased tons of locally produced hay, barley, oats, potatoes, and cattle, among other products. In accordance with Colonel Connor's strong Unionist views, all contractors supplying items to Camp Douglas were "required to take the oath of allegiance to the United States Government,"[43] to which Brigham Young reportedly replied, "I hope the brethren will keep their families from that camp [Douglas]. . . . Let them [soldiers] come and say, 'Will you sell me a bushel of potatoes?' Then come[s] the answer, 'Do you want me to take the oath of allegiance? If you do, go to hell for your potatoes.'"[44]

Soldiers found Salt Lake City the obvious location to spend their pay. In December 1862, the army "disbursed among them the snug sum of $74,000, so that they can now rejoice in being paid up. . . . The shopkeepers of this city are doing a heavy business. The stores are thronged most of the day, and 'greenbacks' are

more plentiful than blackberries in this Territory."[45] Businesses, some of a questionable nature, also began to spring up around the borders of the camp, and as the *New York Times* reported, "It is really too much to suppose that every officer and private is entirely unimpressible when Bacchus and Venus hang out their colors. . . . Col. Connor, at a dress parade on Monday, declared, by special order, that the military reserve [reservation] connected with the post above-named, was extended to embrace an area of four miles square."[46]

There were apparently few, if any, discussions between Colonel Connor and Salt Lake civic authorities regarding either the original location or expanded dimensions of Camp Douglas. Much of the newly extended camp boundaries were within the corporate limits of Salt Lake City—then being challenged by the Interior Department's General Land Office— which undoubtedly did not sit well with city authorities, but there was little they could do. Other problems arose during the next few months as the city and camp struggled to accommodate each other. Camp Douglas was just six months old when a grand jury of the U.S. District Court for the Third Judicial District of Utah Territory (with Latter-day Saint Apostles George A. Smith and Franklin D. Richards serving as the foreman and a jury member, respectively) was empanelled in Salt Lake City to consider Camp Douglas's "notoriously offensive or . . . obnoxious and revolting" water usage practices. The grand jury declared that Camp Douglas was abusing Red Butte Creek—the primary water supply for at least three thousand downstream Salt Lake City residents. Soldiers were accused of having "placed obstructions in the stream; [having] built privies on or close to one of said streams of water, and in divers other ways have the said troops and those [civilians] following them . . . fouled the water thereof, and rendered it extremely filthy and nauseous, to the great inconvenience of the people of the said city, and deleterious to their health."[47] The army also prevented residents from taking their livestock up Red Butte Canyon to graze during the summer months.

FRICTION BETWEEN CHURCH AND STATE

Economic tensions were exacerbated by historical and philosophical differences between the Church and the U.S. government. Relations between the two parties had been mixed since the Church's founding in 1830. Latter-day Saints viewed themselves as loyal Americans with a firm dedication to and belief in the Constitution of the United States. Several federal actions, though, were not viewed favorably by the Saints. With a likely eye to President Van Buren's unwillingness to protect Mormons in Missouri and President Polk's recruitment of the Mormon Battalion in 1846, a March 1863 article in the *Deseret News* proclaimed, "Ever since we as a people were driven from our homes in Illinois; traversed an almost trackless desert and settled in these distant valleys; a constant effort has been made by wicked and designing men to disturb our peace and interfere with those religious rights secured to us by the Federal Constitution. We have neither time, space, nor inclination to review the wrongs and insults that our bodies, and we as a people have suffered. They are all matters of history; delineating them will present one of the darkest pages ever recorded of any religious people."[48]

The early history of Camp Douglas may be viewed, in large measure, through the interaction between two strong personalities—Brigham Young and Patrick Connor. Connor was seen by himself and many others as a true patriot. A self-made Irish immigrant, he voluntarily left his family and a very comfortable life in California to serve his nation. Brigham Young's feelings regarding soldiers being sent again to Utah might be summed up in the opening words of the proclamation he issued to the "Citizens of Utah" in declaring martial law five years earlier, on September 15, 1857:

For the last twenty-five years we have trusted officials of the government, from constables and justices to judges, governors and presidents, only to be scorned, held in derision, insulted and betrayed. Our houses have been plundered and then burned, our fields laid waste, our principal men butchered while under the pledged faith of the government for their safety, and our families driven from their homes to find that shelter in the barren wilderness and that protection among hostile savages, which were denied them in the boasted abodes of christianity and civilization.

The Constitution of our common country guarantees unto us all that we do now, or have ever claimed. If the constitutional rights which pertain unto us as American citizens were extended to Utah, according to the spirit and meaning thereof, and fairly and impartially administered, it is all that we could ask, all that we have ever asked.[49]

As he had done during the Utah War, Brigham Young sought during the 1860s to demonstrate his loyalty to the Constitution, although that loyalty rarely extended to federal officials charged with administering the government that sprang from it. When the transcontinental telegraph reached Salt Lake City in October 1861, for example, one of the first messages sent by Brigham Young affirmed that "Utah has not seceded, but is firm for the Constitution and laws of our once happy country."[50]

Brigham Young had little patience for General Connor. Discussing the army's presence in Salt Lake City, Young once observed in a report to Utah's Legislative Assembly that "there is not one soul of them [Camp Douglas soldiers] that I would not take into my house if they were perishing in the street," and then he added "even Gen. Connor." He reportedly continued, "I do not know the man [Connor]; as a citizen I have nothing against him, he wants to kill the truth, and sacrifice every virtue there is upon the earth that God has established, that is what makes me hate him. He is nothing to me as a business man. . . . But as an individual I have not the least feeling against him."[51] The clash of temperament between Young and Connor was mutual—neither of them made much of an effort to disguise their dislike and distrust of the other.

Colonel Connor's superior, General Wright, reported, "Brigham Young was exceedingly anxious that the troops should

Brigham Young, former governor and de facto ruler of Utah Territory when Connor and the California Volunteers arrived. Offended by their unannounced arrival, Young considered them an unwanted, threatening alien presence in Utah's midst and refused to countenance further recruiting for the Union Army. (Photo by Charles William Carter, Harvard Art Museum)

reoccupy Fort Crittenden or some point remote from the city, but after mature consideration I came to the conclusion that the site of the present camp was the most eligible for the accomplishment of the objects in view. It is a commanding position, looking down on the city, and hence has been dreaded by the Mormon chief."[52]

Colonel Connor saw it as his responsibility to do something about the Mormons. As early as September 1862, his official reports began to include complaints about Mormons and Mormonism. According to Connor, Mormons were "a community of traitors, murderers, fanatics, and whores"[53] who were "composed chiefly of the very lowest class of foreigners and aliens . . . , hesitating at the commission of no crime."[54] He believed Mormons permitted an "unholy, blasphemous, and unnatural institution"[55] and that "if the crimes and designs of this people were known and understood by the people of the United States as I understand and know them, it would cause such a burst of indignation as would result in the utter annihilation of this whole people. . . . The sooner we are rid of the evil, and the nation of the stigma [of Mormonism], the better it will be for us. . . . Individually I would prefer to serve in another field. At the same time there is much to do here, and it would give me great pleasure to contribute my humble services to blot out this stigma on our national honor."[56]

It was not just the religious tenets of Mormonism that bothered Connor. He saw Mormons as "disloyal almost to a man, and treason, if not openly preached, [was] covertly encouraged."[57] In Connor's eyes, "the so-called President Young" was "engaged in mounting cannon for the purpose of resisting the Government."[58] He reported that the Mormons were "hard at work making cartridges" and that Brigham Young had placed a "guard of 300 men" at his home with which, from Connor's perspective, he could attempt to resist federal authority.[59]

Camp Douglas was a thorn in Brigham Young's side, and Connor knew it. In December 1862 Connor reported, "My present position [at Camp Douglas] was selected for its availability, and commanding as it does not only all the avenues to but even the town itself, it is an important one, and I am not surprised that Brigham Young considers its occupancy dangerous to his interests."[60] Connor's view was that "Mormonism as preached and practiced in this Territory is not only subversive of morals, in conflict with the civilization of the present age, and oppressive on the people, but also deeply and boldly in contravention of the laws and best interests of the nation"; therefore, he sought "by every proper means in my power to arrest its progress and prevent its spread."[61] He initially believed there were but two ways to resolve the problems and influence of Mormonism: "First, by dividing the Territory into four parts and adding the parts to the four adjoining Territories; second, by declaring martial law."[62] By dividing the territory, he hoped to weaken both Brigham Young and Salt Lake City's influence on the surrounding regions.

A few months later, he came to see a third way—"inviting into the Territory large numbers of Gentiles to live among and dwell with the people." To accomplish this end, he "considered the discovery of gold, silver, and other valuable minerals in the Territory of the highest importance," and he "instructed commanders of posts and detachments to permit the men of their commands to prospect the country in the vicinity of their respective posts, whenever such course would not interfere with their military duties, and to furnish every proper facility for the discovery and opening of mines of gold, silver, and other minerals."[63] Connor, who is recognized today as the "father of Utah mining,"[64] believed that by encouraging "gentiles" (non-Mormons) to settle and mine in Utah, "the Mormon question [would] at an early day be finally settled by peaceable means, without the increased expenditure of a dollar by Government."[65] His belief in this policy was so strong that by spring 1864, he directed some of his subordinate commanders to "devote most of [their] attention" to the discovery of new mines.[66] In a sense, Connor was filling a vacuum, given Brigham Young's well-known hostility to mining as an inappropriate activity for Latter-day Saints.

The military blamed increasing tensions with Salt Lake inhabitants on "the open declarations of hostility to the Government on the part of their public men, and their bold, continued, and unceasing teachings of disloyalty" which Patrick Connor stated "time and again tended to produce excitements leading to collision, which have only been avoided by the most temperate and moderate course of the officers and men of my command."[67]

March 1863 was a particularly tense period in the relationship between Salt Lake City and Camp Douglas. Several events and beliefs contributed to the heightening of tensions—chief among them was concern that the army was planning to arrest Brigham

Young.[68] Colonel Connor became alarmed on March 3 and again on March 4 when "Brigham caused to be removed from the Territorial arsenal to his residence all the ordnance and ordnance stores, and placed a large body of armed men in his yard, which is inclosed with a high stone wall."[69] Connor was uncertain whether Young's actions and intent were defensive or offensive. On March 8, Brigham Young spoke in the Tabernacle and discussed the loyalty of the Saints, relations with the federal government, the Civil War, and Camp Douglas:

> But if the Government of the United States should now ask for a battalion of men to fight in the present battle-fields of the nation, while there is a camp of soldiers from abroad located within the corporate limits of this city, I would not ask one man to go; I would see them in hell first. What was the result a year ago, when our then Governor . . . called for men to go and guard the mail route? Were they promptly on hand? Yes, and when President Lincoln wrote to me requesting me to fit out one hundred men to guard the mail route, we at once enlisted the one hundred men for ninety days. On Monday evening I received the instruction, and on Wednesday afternoon that hundred men were mustered into service and encamped ready for moving. But all this does not prove any loyalty to political tyrants.
>
> We guarded the mail route. . . . We do not need any soldiers here from any other States or Territories to perform that service, neither does the Government, as they would know if they were wise. . . .

> What can we do? We can serve God, and mind our own business; keep our powder dry, and be prepared for every emergency to which we may be exposed, and sustain the civil law to which we are subject. . . .
>
> Now, as we are accused of secession, my counsel to this congregation is to secede, what from? From the Constitution of the United States? No. From the institutions of our country? No. Well then, what from? From sin and the practice thereof. That is my counsel to this congregation and to the whole world.[70]

On March 9, Colonel Connor reported that Brigham Young "raised the national flag over his residence for the first time I am told since his arrival in the Territory, but not, however, from motives of patriotism or for any loyal purpose, but as a signal to his people to assemble armed, which they immediately did, to the number of about 1,500."[71] The following day, Connor reported that Brigham Young and the Mormons "are determined to have trouble, and are trying to provoke me to bring it on, but they will fail."[72]

Tension in the city continued to increase when Brigham Young was arrested on March 10 under the 1862 antibigamy law (Morrill Act) and quickly released on a two-thousand-dollar bond.[73] On March 12, the flag at Brigham Young's residence was raised again, causing 1,500 Mormon militia members to assemble. As before, the unofficial militia was dismissed, but Latter-day Saint guards patrolled the city each night. Connor clearly recognized the friction that existed but apparently felt he was not responsible for it. He notified General Wright that the only excuse his adherents give for this extraordinary proceeding is that he feared I would arrest him for uttering treasonable language. . . . There has been nothing in my conduct or language which could be construed so as to induce that belief. . . . Since my arrival the people of the Territory have been treated kindly and courteously by both my officers and men, who have never given one of them cause for complaint, which the people freely acknowledge. But notwithstanding this, the courtesy we have given is returned with abuse. They rail at us in their sermons in which we are also classed with cutthroats and gamblers, our Government cursed and vilified in their public speeches and meetings.[74]

While noting that his command was "in no immediate danger," he warned, "If the present preparations of the Mormons should continue I will be compelled for the preservation of my command to strike at the heads of the church. . . . If I remain in my present position (although a strong one) for them to attack me, I am lost, as they have about 5,000 men capable of bearing arms and cannon of heavier caliber than mine. . . . I will do nothing rashly or hastily, and my intercourse with them will be, as heretofore, courteous and firm."[75]

After hearing of the increased tensions in Salt Lake City, General Wright stepped back from his own anti-Mormonism and admonished Colonel Connor to "be prudent and cautious. Hold your troops well in hand. A day of retribution will come."[76] On March 29, 1863, with the approval of Edwin M. Stanton,[77] Secretary of War, Patrick Connor was promoted from colonel to brigadier general for his "heroic

conduct and brilliant victory on Bear River" over the local Indian population.[78] By the end of the month, General Wright notified Washington, DC, that "although the excitement at Great Salt Lake City, brought about by the treasonable acts of Brigham Young and his adherents, has somewhat subsided, yet I am fully satisfied that they only wait for a favorable opportunity to strike a blow against the Union."[79]

Continuing distrust and tensions between Salt Lake residents and soldiers caused General Wright to do a surprising about-face when he informed army headquarters during July 1863 that he was seriously considering "the propriety of removing the troops from the immediate vicinity of Great Salt Lake City to the old position at Camp Floyd. . . . It would obviate the irritations and complaints which are constantly arising between the soldiers and citizens." The district's headquarters would remain in Salt Lake City even if the soldiers were relocated, and no plans were entertained regarding the complete removal of soldiers from Utah Territory. According to Wright, "The presence of the force now there is indispensable for the protection of the Overland Mail Route and the general safety of the country."[80]

That same day, July 31, Wright notified Connor that he was contemplating reoccupying Fort Crittenden and ordered Connor "to make immediate preparations to this end. . . . Advise the general by telegraph . . . when the command at Camp Douglas can be moved to Fort Crittenden."[81] Any response to this order from General Connor has apparently been lost, but something caused General Wright to change his mind. On August 19, General Connor received new orders "to the extent that if, in your judgment, the withdrawal of the troops from Camp Douglas would produce an impression on the minds of the Mormons that the removal was in consequence of disapprobation of your course while in command, or in any manner injurious to the interests of the Government, you will retain Camp Douglas as your principal station"—which he did.[82]

Tension and misunderstanding between the Mormons and the military continued throughout the Civil War. In August 1863, Utah's somewhat more sympathetic new governor, James D. Doty, noted that "many of those difficulties arise from the mistaken notion that the interests of this people and those of the Government are at variance. I think they are not."[83] The Latter-day Saint perspective after the war ended was adequately summarized in a correspondent's November 1865 *New York Times* report:

> As to the graver matters of disloyalty and threatened difficulties, we may say that such accusations against the Mormons are not new, and perhaps are not now, any more than formerly, altogether without foundation. There may be two reasons for this—firstly, because more than half of the population of Utah consists of recent emigrants of foreign birth, gathered from all the lands under the sun, and from all the islands fixed in the sea; and secondly, because the long and terrible persecutions of the Mormons in Illinois and Missouri in the early days of the Church, have left behind them bitter memories of the power that failed to afford protection. Then, again, there have always been annoying quarrels in progress with the Mormons, which reached the very verge of war eight years ago, and the embers of which have been smouldering ever since. We do not see,

however, from anything that has been published, that there have been any new or menacing developments of late, or that things are in any worse condition than that in which they have been for the last eighteen or twenty years.

> Is it necessary for the government to take any action in the premises?

CAMP DOUGLAS AFTER THE CIVIL WAR

In the years following the Civil War, relations between Camp Douglas and Salt Lake City gradually softened from antagonism to grudging acceptance and finally to an embrace. In the space of a few short years, Camp Douglas became an important and uncontroversial part of Salt Lake City. Reflecting a personal example of the widespread change of attitude that occurred, General Patrick Connor left his family, returned to Salt Lake City in the later years of his life, and lived there until his death on December 16, 1891, when, as he had requested, he was buried in the military cemetery at Fort Douglas.[84]

In 1878, the year after Brigham Young's death, Camp Douglas was officially renamed Fort Douglas and designated as an army regimental post. Soldiers from Fort Douglas played a contributing role in American history from the Civil War through the Korean War. Prisoners of war were housed at Fort Douglas during both World War I and World War II. The fort was officially closed in 1991, although a small section of the original grounds continued to support elements of the Utah National Guard and Army Reserve for several years. During the 2002 Salt Lake Winter Olympic games, part of Fort Douglas—now an integral part of the University of Utah—was used as the Olympic Village, housing visiting athletes from many continents. Visitors to Fort Douglas today can tour a military museum and several historic buildings that help preserve its historic past.

Patrick Connor deliberately established Camp Douglas in the foothills above Salt Lake City so that his forces could dominate and command the city below and probably named the post to rub salt into the civil-affairs wound that resulted. During the Civil War, relations between the city and the soldiers were often marked by mutual mistrust and misunderstanding. Over time, though, Salt Lake residents came to accept the idea of federal forces in their midst and enjoyed the economic benefits that resulted from the army's presence. The local citizens recognized that most of the soldiers were simply trying to serve their country at the territorial outpost to which they had been assigned, and soldiers stationed at Camp Douglas learned that the local residents were people who had much in common with them. Their post is now viewed as a collection of quaint Victorian buildings owned by a university; the origins of its name are a cipher rather than a continuing source of Mormon bitterness about a long-dead Illinois politician.

Kenneth L. Alford is an associate professor of Church history and doctrine at Brigham Young University. William P. MacKinnon is an independent historian in Montecito, California.

NOTES

Parts of this chapter were previously published in *Salt Lake City: The Place Which God Prepared* (Provo, UT: Religious Studies Center, 2011) and are used by permission.

1. P. Edw. Connor to Lieut. Col. R. C. Drum, March 15, 1863, in *The War of the Rebellion: A Compilation of the Official Records of the Union and Confederate Armies*, series 1, vol. 50, pt. 2 (Washington, DC: Government Printing Office, 1897), 371 (hereafter cited as *WOTR2*).

2. Orson Hyde, in *Journal of Discourses* (London: Latter-day Saints Book Depot, 1854–86), 6:12; Brigham Young to Thomas L. Kane, September 12, 1857, Brigham Young Collection, Church History Library, The Church of Jesus Christ of Latter-day Saints, Salt Lake City.

3. There are numerous sources for additional reading on this subject. For example, see *Kingdom in the West: The Mormons and the American Frontier*, ed. Will Bagley, vol. 10, *At Sword's Point, Part I: A Documentary History of the Utah War to 1858*, ed. William P. MacKinnon (Norman, OK: Arthur H. Clark, 2008); LeRoy R. Hafen and Ann W. Hafen, eds., *Mormon Resistance: A Documentary Account of the Utah Expedition, 1857–1858* (Lincoln: University of Nebraska Press,

1958); David L. Bigler and Will Bagley, *The Mormon Rebellion: America's First Civil War, 1857–1858* (Norman, OK: University of Oklahoma Press, 2011); or Norman F. Furniss, *The Mormon Conflict: 1850–1859* (New Haven, CT: Yale University Press, 1960).

4. Since Utah's principal city was styled Great Salt Lake City until an official name change in 1868, that name is used here in documents, but for purposes of simplicity, the name Salt Lake City is used in the narrative.

5. Fort Crittenden was also sometimes referred to as Camp Crittenden. See, for example, "Report of Lieut. Anthony Ethier," April 6, 1863, in *The War of the Rebellion: A Compilation of the Official Records of the Union and Confederate Armies*, series 1, vol. 50, pt. 1 (Washington, DC: Government Printing Office, 1897), 200 (hereafter cited as *WOTR1*).

6. "The Secession Rebellion," *New York Times*, May 24, 1861, 1.

7. "Affairs in Utah," *New York Times*, August 2, 1861, 5. See also Thomas G. Alexander and Leonard J.

Arrington, "Camp in the Sagebrush: Camp Floyd, Utah, 1858–1861," *Utah Historical Quarterly* 34 (1966).

8. Gilbert Clements to W. G. Mills, August 25, 1861. Mills was then serving as a missionary in England. Cited in *History of the Church of Jesus Christ of Latter-day Saints*, ed. B. H. Roberts, 2nd ed. rev. (Salt Lake City: Deseret Book, 1957), 4:544n17.

9. "The Secession Rebellion," *New York Times*, May 24, 1861, 1.

10. L. Thomas, report on measures taken to make secure the Overland Mail Route to California, April 24, 1862, in *WOTR1*, 1023.

11. L. Thomas to Brigadier-General Wright, April 8, 1862, in *WOTR1*, 1023.

12. L. Thomas to Mr. Brigham Young, April 28, 1862, in *The War of the Rebellion: A Compilation of the Official Records of the Union and Confederate Armies*, series 3, vol. 2 (Washington, DC: Government Printing Office, 1899), 27 (hereafter cited as *WOTR3*).

13. L. Thomas to Mr. Brigham Young, April 28, 1862, in *WOTR3*, 27.

14. Jas. Craig to Honl. Edwin M. Stanton, August 23, 1862, in *WOTR3*, 449.

15. Edwin M. Stanton to General James Craig, August 24, 1862, in *WOTR3*, 453.

16. Jas. Craig to Gen. Halleck, August 25, 1862, in *WOTR3*, 596.

17. Richard H. Orton, ed., *Records of California Men in the War of Rebellion: 1861–1867* (Sacramento: State Office, 1890), 2.

18. Special Orders No. 115, Hdqrs. Department of the Pacific, San Francisco, Cal., July 5, 1862, Richard C. Drum, in *WOTR2*, 5–6.

19. G. Wright to Brig. Gen. L. Thomas, December 15, 1862, in *WOTR1*, 181.

20. P. E. Connor to Major Drum, August 5, 1862; R. C. Drum to Colonel Connor, August 5, 1862; and Orders No. 1, Fort Churchill, August 6, 1862, in *WOTR2*, 53–55.

21. "Memoranda in relation to Camp Douglas, U.T. furnished by Gen. P. E. Connor," quoted in Brigham D. Madsen, *Glory Hunter: A Biography of Patrick Edward Connor* (Salt Lake City: University of Utah Press, 1990), 65.

22. "Affairs in Utah," *New York Times*, September 7, 1862, 3.

23. P. Edw. Connor to Maj. R. C. Drum, September 14, 1862, in *WOTR2*, 119.

24. P. Edw. Connor to Maj. R. C. Drum, October 1, 1862, in *WOTR2*, 143–44.

25. P. Edw. Connor to Maj. R. C. Drum, October 1, 1862, in *WOTR2*, 143–44. Stenhouse states, "There is no truth in this." See T. B. H. Stenhouse, *The Rocky Mountain Saints* (London: Ward, Lock, and Tyler, 1874), 602.

26. The historian B. H. Roberts reported that Colonel Philip St. George Cooke, the last commander at Fort Crittenden, "presented to Brigham Young the flag staff of Camp Floyd–Fort Crittenden. . . . After the remnant of the army was departed, the flag staff was removed from Fort Crittenden, and planted on the hillcrest immediately east of the Beehive House." But Roberts did not mention the date when the actual removal occurred. See B. H. Roberts, *A Comprehensive History of the Church of Jesus Christ of Latter-day Saints* (Salt Lake City, Deseret News, 1930), 4:543. In a 1907 address to the Daughters of the Utah Pioneers, Hiram B. Clawson provided additional details regarding Brigham Young's flagpole. "One evening, while sitting in front of the general's tent [at the Camp]," he said, "I was attracted by a beautiful flag and staff and I was asked by the commanding officer [Colonel St. George-Cooke], if I thought President Young would accept it. I assured him that he would not only accept it, but place it on his Salt Lake home, the 'White House,' and that on all national occasions the flag would be unfurled. They presented it; it was accepted and placed as stated." Quoted in George D. Pyper, *The Romance of an Old Playhouse* (Salt Lake City: Seagull, 1928), 75.

27. "Affairs in Utah," *New York Times*, November 15, 1862.

28. "Arrival of Col. Connor's Command," *Deseret News*, October 22, 1862. Harding's appalling comments betrayed a significant lack of communications between the War Department and Utah's governor, while echoing Colonel Edmund B. Alexander's command disorientation during the early stages of the Utah War. MacKinnon, *At Sword's Point, Part I*, 339. Harding's comments parallel President Lincoln's facetious exposition of his Mormon policy—if Brigham Young "will let me alone, I will let him alone." George H. Hubbard, "Abraham Lincoln as Seen by the Mormons," *Utah Historical Quarterly* 31 (Spring 1963): 103.

29. "Arrival of Col. Connor's Command," *Deseret News*, October 22, 1862.

30. Orders, No. 14, Headquarters District of Utah, October 26, 1862, in *WOTR2*, 195.

31. Madsen, *Glory Hunter*, 41, 49, 71.

32. E. B. Long, *The Saints and the Union* (Champaign: University of Illinois Press, 1981); Fred B. Rogers, *Soldiers of the Overland* (San Francisco: Grabhorn, 1938).

33. James F. Varley, *Brigham and the Brigadier: General Patrick Connor and His California Volunteers in Utah and Along the Overland Trail* (Tucson, AZ: Western Lore, 1989), 70, 71.

34. Stephen A. Douglas, "Kansas, Utah, and the Dred Scott Decision," address at State House, Springfield, Illinois, June 12, 1857. The senator's impromptu remarks immediately drew substantial national attention in the newspapers and were rebutted formally by one attendee, local attorney Abraham Lincoln, who spoke in the same chamber on June 26. In a sense, these two speeches became the template, if not the inspiration, for the early rounds of the famous Lincoln-Douglas debates of the following year. Because of mail delays, word of Douglas's comments about the Mormons did not reach Utah until late summer, at which point the reaction was volcanic. See "Comments," editorial, *Deseret News*, September 2, 1857; MacKinnon, *At Sword's Point, Part I*, 136–37; "Stephen A. Douglas, Abraham Lincoln, and 'The Mormon Problem': The 1857 Springfield Debate," unpublished paper, 44th annual conference, Mormon History Association, Springfield, Illinois, May 23, 2009; and Mary Jane Woodger, "Abraham Lincoln and the Mormons," in this volume.

35. Heber C. Kimball, discourse, August 23, 1857, in *Journal of Discourses* (London: Latter-day Saints' Book Depot, 1854–86), 5:178.

36. Brigham Young to Stephen A. Douglas, May 2, 1857, Brigham Young Collection, Church History Library.

37. "Affairs in Utah," *New York Times*, July 8, 1861, 2.

38. Salt Lake City schoolhouse, October 30, 1862, in *The Complete Discourses of Brigham Young*, ed. Richard S. Van Wagoner, vol. 4, *1862 to 1867* (Salt Lake City: Smith-Pettit Foundation, 2009), 2076.

39. H. W. Halleck to Brigadier-General Wright, December 9, 1862, in *WOTR2*, 244.

40. G. Wright to Brig. Gen. L. Thomas, December 9, 1862, in *WOTR2*, 245.

41. S. S. Harding to General G. Wright, February 16, 1863, in *WOTR2*, 315. Utah's governor here overlooked the fact that Fort Bridger was in Utah until the formation of Wyoming Territory in 1868.

42. P. Edw. Connor to Lieut. Col. R. C. Drum, February 26, 1863, in *WOTR2*, 326–27.

43. "Affairs in Utah," *New York Times*, November 23, 1862.

44. Salt Lake City schoolhouse, in *Complete Discourses of Brigham Young*, 4:2076.

45. "Affairs in Utah," *New York Times*, December 21, 1862.

46. "Affairs in Utah," *New York Times*, February 8, 1863.

47. "Third District Federal Court," *Deseret News*, April 15, 1863.

48. "Arrest of Brigham Young for Polygamy," *Deseret News*, March 11, 1863.

49. *History of the Church*, 4:273.

50. "The Pacific Telegraph Line," *New York Times*, October 19, 1861.

51. George D. Watt, report, legislative assembly, January 23, 1865, in *Complete Discourses of Brigham Young*, 4:2260.

52. G. Wright to Brig. Gen. L. Thomas, March 30, 1863, in *WOTR2*, 369.

53. P. Edw. Connor to Maj. R. C. Drum, September 14, 1862, in *WOTR2*, 119.

54. P. Edw. Connor to Lieut. Col. R. C. Drum, February 19, 1863, in *WOTR2*, 319.

55. P. Edw. Connor to Lieut. Col. R. C. Drum, February 19, 1863, in *WOTR2*, 319.

56. P. Edw. Connor to Lieut. Col. R. C. Drum, February 19, 1863, in *WOTR2*, 319, 320.

57. P. Edw. Connor to Lieut. Col. R. C. Drum, February 19, 1863, in *WOTR2*, 319.

58. P. Edw. Connor to Lieut. Col. R. C. Drum, December 20, 1862, in *WOTR2*, 257.

59. P. Edw. Connor to Lieut. Col. R. C. Drum, March 8, 1863, in *WOTR2*, 342.

60. P. Edw. Connor to Lieut. Col. R. C. Drum, December 20, 1862, in *WOTR2*, 257.

61. P. Edw. Connor to Lieut. Col. R. C. Drum, October 26, 1863, in *WOTR2*, 656.

62. P. Edw. Connor to Lieut. Col. R. C. Drum, February 19, 1863, in *WOTR2*, 320. Connor's proposal for repealing Utah's Organic Act and redistributing its territory to neighboring states and territories echoed suggestions debated in Congress since the late 1850s. So too with the suggestion of martial law, which General William S. Harney, the Utah

Expedition's initial commander, had sought unsuccessfully in June 1857.

63. P. Edw. Connor to Lieut. Col. R. C. Drum, October 16, 1863, in *WOTR2*, 656–57.

64. "Utah: The Treasure House of the Nation," Utah Mining Association, accessed May 18, 2011, http://www.utahmining.org/brochure.htm.

65. P. Edw. Connor to Lieut. Col. R. C. Drum, October 26, 1863, in *WOTR2*, 657.

66. M. G. Lewis to Capt. N. Baldwin, May 11, 1864, in *WOTR2*, 846.

67. P. Edw. Connor to Lieut. Col. R. C. Drum, October 26, 1863, in *WOTR2*, 656.

68. See Stenhouse, *Rocky Mountain Saints* (London: Ward, Lock, and Tyler, n.d.), 422; and James F. Varley, *Brigham and the Brigadier* (Tucson, AZ: Westernlore, 1989), chapter 6, for additional information about the "March Madness," as Varley called it.

69. P. Edw. Connor to Lieut. Col. R. C. Drum, March 15, 1863, in *WOTR2*, 370–71.

70. Brigham Young, in *Journal of Discourses*, 10:107, 109, 111.

71. P. Edw. Connor to Lieut. Col. R. C. Drum, March 15, 1863, in *WOTR2*, 371. This may have been the first time that Colonel Connor or his soldiers saw the national flag flying at Brigham Young's residence, but it was clearly not the first time a flag had been flown there. See, for example, "Affairs in Utah," *New York Times*, April 6, 1862, which reports that "the Stars and Stripes were flung to the breeze from Brigham's bee-hive mansion."

72. P. Edw. Connor to Lieut. Col. R. C. Drum, March 10, 1863, in *WOTR2*, 344.

73. Andrew Jensen, *Church Chronology* (Salt Lake City: Deseret News, 1899), 69. According to historian Dean C. Jessee, "The circumstances in the 1863 arrest of Brigham Young were as follows: Rumor of an impending arrest of President Young by a military force from Camp Douglas for an alleged infringement of the anti-bigamy law of 1862 threatened a confrontation between civilian and military forces in Salt Lake City. To avoid this, a 'friendly complaint' was preemptively filed against the Mormon leader [in a territorial, non-federal court], charging him with violation of the anti-bigamy law. The President was subsequently arrested and appeared in court, where his case was bound over for the next term. However, when the grand jury sat in 1864 it found no indictment against him and he was discharged."

See *Letters of Brigham Young to His Sons*, ed. Dean C. Jessee (Salt Lake City: Deseret Book, 1974), 88–89.

74. P. Edw. Connor to Lieut. Col. R. C. Drum, March 15, 1863, in *WOTR2*, 371.

75. P. Edw. Connor to Lieut. Col. R. C. Drum, March 15, 1863, in *WOTR2*, 372.

76. G. Wright to Col. P. E. Connor, March 11, 1863, in *WOTR2*, 347.

77. Edwin M. Stanton to H. W. Halleck, March 29, 1863, in *WOTR1*, 185.

78. H. W. Halleck to Col. R. C. Drum, March 29, 1863, in *WOTR2*, 369. The action at Bear River occurred January 29, 1863, about 150 miles north of Camp Douglas and led to the greatest loss of Indian life in all of the nation's Indian wars. The army considered it a legitimate military action and used the description "battle." Connor's biographer, Madsen, and many other historians as well as tribal descendants use the term "massacre." For the latest scholarship, see Harold S. Schindler, "The Bear River Massacre: New Historical Evidence," *Utah Historical Quarterly* 67 (Fall 1999): 300–308; and John P. Barnes, "The Struggle to Control the Past: Commemoration, Memory, and the Bear River Massacre of 1863," *Public Historian* 30 (February 2008): 81–104. With Colonel Connor personally commanding, his soldiers killed at least 224 Indians and lost only 14 soldiers. See Col. P. Edward Connor, report, February 20, 1863, in *WOTR1*, 184–87. By July 1864, General Connor reported, "The policy pursued toward the Indians has had a most happy effect. That policy, as you are aware, involved certain and speedy punishment for past offenses, compelling them to sue for a suspension of hostilities, and on the resumption of peace, kindness and leniency toward the redskins. They fully understand that honesty and peace constitute their best and safest policy." See P. Edw. Connor to Lieut. Col. R. C. Drum, July 1, 1864, in *WOTR2*, 887. Yet by February 1865, General Connor was again reporting that Indians "have again returned in increased force. The troops are insufficient to contend with them." See P. E. Connor to Col. R. C. Drum, February 10, 1865, in *WOTR2*, 1131.

79. G. Wright to Brig. Gen. L. Thomas, March 30, 1863, in *WOTR2*, 369.

80. G. Wright to Adjutant-General U.S. Army, July 31, 1863, in *WOTR2*, 546.

81. R. C. Drum to Brig. Gen. P. E. Connor, July 31, 1863, in *WOTR2*, 547, 548.

82. R. C. Drum to Brig. Gen. P. E. Connor, August 19, 1863, in *WOTR2*, 581.

83. James Duane Doty to General [G. Wright], August 9, 1863, in *WOTR2*, 584.

84. "Death and Funeral of General P. E. Connor," *Deseret News*, December 26, 1891.

This March 1864 woodcut from Frank Leslie's Illustrated Newspaper *shows a Civil War recruiting station in New York City. (Library of Congress)*

This 1861 Currier & Ives lithograph, entitled "The Voluntary Manner in Which Some of the Southern Volunteers Enlist," portrays a facetious view of the Confederate states' early efforts to man a volunteer army during the Civil War. The placard on the right announcing the "Suicide of Abe Lincoln" and "Washington to be taken" is signed by Confederate general John B. Floyd. Floyd, who served as secretary of war under President Buchanan, was accused of secretly supplying arms and ammunition to the South from the federal arsenal before the war; Camp Floyd in Utah Territory (named in his honor) was renamed Fort Crittenden after he resigned on December 29, 1860 and joined the Southern cause. (Library of Congress)

CHAPTER 11

Brant W. Ellsworth and Kenneth L. Alford

MORMON MOTIVATION FOR ENLISTING IN THE CIVIL WAR

On April 12, 1861, shots fired between Union and Confederate soldiers at Fort Sumter officially ushered in the American Civil War—the most violent and devastating conflict in American history. The nation was torn apart as families, friends, and neighbors were divided against each other. There were over six hundred thousand casualties—approximately half the total number of combat deaths in the nation's history. An additional three hundred thousand men returned home with battle wounds. Today, visitors at Civil War sites pause to commemorate the soldiers, marvel at their bravery, honor their sacrifices, and consider their lives.

The impact of the Civil War engulfed the entire nation. Because the war was fought primarily in the East, historians have generally paid less attention to the war's impact on the western territories and states. Members of The Church of Jesus Christ of Latter-day Saints (hereafter referred to as Mormons or Latter-day Saints) distinctly felt the impact of the Civil War. Although Latter-day Saint leaders never directed Church members to enlist, several members did so. While it is unknown exactly how many Latter-day Saints actually served in the Civil War, the experiences of those who did serve provide insight into an important but generally overlooked period of Mormon history.[1]

Mormon soldiers who enlisted were different in some respects from the typical Union or Confederate soldier. Fresh in many minds at the time was President James Buchanan's 1857 request for Colonel Albert Sidney Johnston and approximately twenty-five hundred soldiers to quell a supposed Mormon rebellion in Utah and replace Brigham Young as governor. Although the Utah War concluded without significant bloodshed, the effects of that war were long lasting. At the start of the Civil War, the U.S. Army still occupied nearby Camp Floyd. The majority of Mormon men must have felt that they had understandable reasons for avoiding Civil

War military service. The purpose of this essay is to explore the motives of Latter-day Saints who chose to fight in the Civil War.

THE CHURCH'S POSITION ON THE CIVIL WAR

It is difficult to gauge past public sentiment in an effort to capture the mood and tenor of that time. Rhetoric used by Latter-day Saint Church leaders prior to the Civil War suggests that as the threat of war grew more pronounced, the Church and its members often grew more indignant of those who had abused them in the past. Wrathful tirades sometimes spilled from Mormon pulpits as Church leaders spoke regarding "when," not "if," war would come. Speaking in the Salt Lake Tabernacle in November 1860, Heber C. Kimball, a member of the Church's First Presidency, reminded his congregation that the "Lord then said, if [the governors, judges, and president of the United States] will not redress your wrongs, I will come out of my hiding place . . . and I will cut them off from the face of the earth." Kimball then asked the congregation, "Brethren, do you not think that day is right here?"[2] In February 1861, after receiving news that Alabama, Georgia, and Louisiana were the latest in the growing list of states that had seceded from the Union, Brigham Young cautioned Latter-day Saints about the calamity he expected to shortly befall the nation. Young admonished the Saints "not to boast over our enemies' downfall. Boast not, brethren.—God has come out of his hiding place, and has commenced to vex the nation that has rejected us."[3] Heber Kimball saw similar war clouds on the horizon. "I have never prayed for the destruction of this government," he said, "but I know that dissolution, sorrow, weeping and distress are in store for the inhabitants of the United States."[4]

In early 1861, with the threat of war growing more certain, Mormon leaders advised Church members against enlisting in the coming conflict. George A. Smith left little room for interpretation when he counseled: "[The Lord] does not wish us to go and slay our enemies."[5] Brigham Young placed his faith in God's power to protect his Saints. "As I often tell you," Young said, "if we are faithful, the Lord will fight our battles much better than we can ourselves."[6] John Taylor emphasized that the Latter-day Saints should remain neutral, as the coming war was not their fight. "It may now be proper to inquire what part shall we take in the present difficulties. . . . Shall we join the North to fight against the South? No! Shall we join the south against the north? As emphatically, No! Why? They have both . . . brought it upon themselves, and we have had no hand in the matter. . . . We know no north, no south, no east, no west." The Lord had other plans for them instead of fighting; Taylor counseled the Saints in April 1861, only days before the shots at Fort Sumter were fired, to keep God's commandments, live righteously, and focus on their spirituality. "What shall we do in the midst of these things that are now transpiring? Why, lean upon the Lord our God, purify ourselves. . . . Let us also look at our position as Elders in Israel, clothed with the power of the holy Priesthood, as men who hold the ministry of reconciliation. . . . This is the position that we ought to occupy in relation to these matters."[7] Considering Young's previous teachings, such a position of general neutrality made good sense for the Saints. For as Young taught: "When those who profess to be Saints contend against the enemies of God through passion or self will, it is then man against man, evil against evil, the powers of darkness against the power of darkness. But when men who are sanctified—purified—do anything, . . . they will do it with the power of the living God. If they are ever called to wipe out their enemies . . . they have to do it by the power of the Gods, or not at all."[8] Young, Kimball, and Taylor were not alone in their early opposition to the war effort; other Church leaders also urged the Saints to remain steadfast in Zion, wait out the storm in the safety of the valleys, and avoid the war whenever possible.[9]

As war continued during the next few years, Mormon rhetoric cooled. In a speech given on Sunday, August 31, 1862, President Young lamented the great destruction of human life: "My heart is filled with pain for the inhabitants of the earth. We desire with all our hearts to do them good. . . . It is our duty to pray for them. . . . They are in the hands of God, and so are we."[10]

MOTIVATION TO ENLIST

With Church leaders in such strict and synchronized opposition to the war, especially during 1861–62, why did some Mormons enlist as soldiers? To answer questions regarding enlistment motivation, soldier letters, diaries, and journals often reveal individual motives with clarity and candor.[11] Civil War armies were among the most literate in history. Scholars estimate approximately 90 percent of Union soldiers and 80 percent of Confederate soldiers were literate, and those soldiers had a proclivity to write.[12] As a result, Civil War records provide a window into wartime thoughts and experiences. Those letters, diaries, and journals are especially valuable to scholars trying to better understand

the attitudes of antebellum Americans and the factors that motivated soldiers to enlist. In spite of a general abundance of Civil War records, only a few accounts remain from Latter-day Saint soldiers, but from those records we can gain some insights into their varied motivations to enlist.

Despite contrasting ideological views and differing backgrounds, Northern and Southern soldiers offered the same general reasons for enlisting in the war. Likewise, notwithstanding differences in background and religious perspective, Mormon soldiers described the same motivations as non-Mormons for enlisting. Although Latter-day Saint soldiers may have interpreted the war somewhat differently than their Union and Confederate counterparts, most soldiers responded similarly to the war itself.[13]

After reading thousands of journals and letters from Union and Confederate soldiers, historian James McPherson outlined several enlistment motivations. He described the initial wave of volunteers enlisting because of the engrossing patriotic furor that swept across the nation—a *rage militaire*. The war's first volunteers chose to fight because of patriotic fervor—it was what their country expected of them. Later, soldiers often enlisted because of personal ideological convictions. Northern soldiers were often motivated to serve in order to preserve the Union from dissolution; Confederate soldiers fought for their concept of liberty and independence. Some soldiers served out of a sense of duty or honor; some fought to defend their personal honor.[14] Historian Bell Irvin Wiley suggested that "the dominant urge of many volunteers was the desire for adventure . . . the prevailing excitement, the lure of far places . . . the glory and excitement of battle."[15] Still other soldiers spoke of serving in order to defend more abstract concepts like "country, flag, Constitution, liberty, and [the] legacy of the [American] Revolution."[16]

Although we may gain some insights into individual reasons for Civil War service, a complete understanding will remain beyond our grasp. As historian John Demos wrote, "Proof is relative in any case—and scholars should never, in my opinion, dismiss an important problem because of 'insufficient data.' Particularly in the newer fields of research . . . , the framing of significant questions and of their probable answers may help to speed the recovery of the essential pieces of evidence."[17] Let us now, therefore, examine the lives of several Latter-day Saint Civil War veterans. Their wartime experiences are organized according to what appear in hindsight to be their primary motives for serving: *rage militaire*, a sense of duty, personal honor, and happenstance.

RAGE MILITAIRE

At 4:30 a.m. on April 12, 1861, Confederate Lieutenant Henry S. Farley fired a single ten-inch mortar round at Fort Sumter and the eighty-five troops within. The shot detonated over the fort, officially signaling the start of the general bombardment and the beginning of the war.[18] News spread rapidly from South Carolina—electrifying both the North and the South. The following morning newspaper headlines in New York City announced "War at Last."[19] An editorial in the *Chicago Tribune* declared, "By the act of a handful of ingrates and traitors, war is inaugurated in this heretofore happy and peaceful Republic! . . . Now, men of the North, for the struggle!"[20] In Virginia, the *Richmond Daily Dispatch* reported, "The 'irrepressible conflict' which has been

forced upon the peaceful homes and the unoffending citizens of the South, will be met by a people who will drench their native soil with the blood of their invaders, or perish, to the last man, in vindication of all that man holds dear."[21]

As the nation braced for war, President Abraham Lincoln called for seventy-five thousand men to put down the Southern insurrection. The response was immediate and overwhelming; people took to the streets vowing vengeance on the traitors. A Harvard professor wrote at that time, "I never knew what a popular excitement can be. . . . The whole population, men, women, and children, seem to be in the streets with Union favors and flags." During the first year of the war, men fought because they chose to do so. Overwhelming support from volunteers easily filled state quotas. Many were caught up in the wave of patriotic enthusiasm that swept the nation. Speaking of the impact of that impulse, one New York woman wrote that the "time before Sumter" was like another century. "It seems as if we never were alive till now; never had a country till now."[22]

Joseph Barlow Forbes, Union soldier. Patriotism seemed to know no bounds. Union enlistee Joseph Barlow Forbes spent the months prior to the start of the war away from newspapers and the reported threats of Southern secession. An avid sailor from a wealthy family with connections in the shipping trade, Forbes had been at sea, navigating a ship around the Cape of Good Hope. On this most recent trip, Forbes had decided on a career as a sailor. When he docked in March 1861, though, Forbes found himself in a nation on the edge of war. A month earlier, Texas had officially seceded, bringing the tally to seven.

In April, war transformed the nation and its citizens. Forbes answered Lincoln's initial call for volunteers and enlisted immediately. He recorded the specifics in his journal: "[I]n April through the excitement through the firing on Sumpter [sic] and secession of the South States I joined my old class mates, the Bangor City Cadets and enlisted in the 2d M[ain]e Vol[unteers] under the first call of Pres. Abraham Lincoln, April 26th, 1861, for six mo[nth]s." The Bangor Regiment was the first to march out of Maine. After briefly training at Willets Point on Long Island, they made their way to the District of Columbia. Forbes and the Second Maine Infantry engaged in eleven battles, including First Bull Run, the Peninsular Campaign, Antietam, and Chancellorsville. Forbes survived his tour of duty and the war; he was mustered out of service as a second lieutenant on June 9, 1863.[23]

David Crockett Stuart, Confederate soldier. After the bombardment of Fort Sumter, a similar patriotic furor swept through the Southern states as they prepared to meet the potential Union invaders. Early one Monday morning in April 1861, a twenty-six-year-old Alabama farmer named David Crockett Stuart walked into the local blacksmith shop and learned that war had been declared between the North and South. Stuart recorded, "I lost no time in getting home, . . . telling every one on the way of the bloody war that was coming on." "During that week," he wrote, the news stirred up "excitement all over the South, and I suppose it was the same in the North. How we all got through that week I don't know." Naturally, not everyone was excited by the prospect of war. Stuart captured the mixed emotions they felt: "We did not know whether to be scared or tickled; some of us seemed to want war, as it was something new, and might be quite interesting . . . , while many others wished for anything else before war, but there was no getting around it."[24]

The following Saturday, Stuart and his family rode ten miles to Falkville, Alabama, in order to purchase farm supplies. While in town, Stuart noticed a crowd gathered around an "old war horse by the name of Campbell." Campbell riled up the crowd with stories about the "Yanks" and "what they would do if we let them come down South." Stuart admitted that Campbell "told some allfired big stories" about how the Yanks would "take all the peoples land, put the men in bondage like the negroes and take their families, such as they wanted, for themselves." Campbell stood atop the "platform in his white shirt, coat and hat off, with the sweat running down his cheeks, while his shirt was wringing wet in places" and gave "one of the hotest war speeches that ever fell from the lips of any man." Campbell continued to electrify the crowd with promises that "one Southerner could whip from ten to twelve Yanks in no time, and could lick all of the North in from thirty to sixty days."[25]

Campbell's stories excited his listeners. Caught up in the enthusiasm of the moment, Stuart was among the first from his town to enlist. Of his enlistment, he wrote, "When [Campbell] saw that he had the people worked up to a pitch, he gave a sign to the leader of a Marshal band that he had hid out, to get to the front with their band and give us some old war music. . . . At the same time he came down from the platform roaring like a lion, calling for volunteers to go fight the Yankees." Campbell's enthusiasm was contagious and swept through the crowd, as both old and young lined up to volunteer. Stuart was third in line. In a short time, an entire brigade had been raised.[26]

By 1862, Stuart had tired of infantry life. Camping, drilling, and marching were exciting for a while, but Stuart wanted to ride with the cavalry. With his captain's permission, Stuart and a band of fellow soldiers returned home, obtained horses, and joined the Fourth Alabama Cavalry, commanded by Colonel Nathan Bedford Forrest. Under Forrest's command, Stuart fought for the Confederacy in battles at Fort Donelson, Nashville, and Shiloh. On December 31, 1862, Union forces attacked Stuart and the Confederates at the Battle of Parker's Crossroads in Tennessee. In a moment of confusion, Stuart and a small group of men became separated from their unit during a fire fight. Soon they were surrounded and forced to surrender to Union soldiers.

For the next few months, twenty-year-old Stuart was a prisoner of war at Camp Douglas, Illinois, where soldiers often suffered from smallpox, typhoid fever, and pneumonia. During his captivity, Stuart lost ninety pounds—nearly half his body weight. He was exchanged in a prisoner-of-war swap in 1863 and survived the war. Stuart waited until 1915 to record his wartime experiences—sharing them in a letter addressed to his son, Forrest (who was named after Nathan Bedford Forrest).[27]

A SENSE OF DUTY

Stuart and others quickly realized that Campbell's prediction of a short war was wildly inaccurate. As weeks became months and the conflict dragged on, initial enlistment enthusiasm faded as casualities increased and the war's end seemed increasingly farther away. Even though the North and the South instituted conscription in 1862, the preponderance of soldiers volunteered their service instead of being drafted. Many of those soldiers, Union and Confederate, joined the military out of a sense of duty—an understanding that citizens were bound by a moral obligation to set aside personal feelings, relationships, and fears in order to protect their country.[28]

David H. Peery, Confederate soldier. Prior to the Civil War, Mormon missionaries met with great success in Tazewell County, Virginia—so much so that it was locally known as "the nest" for its reputation as a religious stronghold for Mormons in the eastern United States. In 1839, the fiery missionary Elder Jedediah M. Grant baptized the first member of the Church in Virginia—Peter Gose Litz. Litz, a prominent member of his community, recorded that he was baptized after a visit from a "Heavenly Messenger who commanded him to 'Doubt no more.'"[29]

After the June 1844 martyrdom of Joseph and Hyrum Smith, a few members of the branch left Tazewell County to join the Saints in the West, but the majority remained behind, pledging themselves loyal to the Twelve Apostles and Brigham Young. Missionaries continued to serve in Tazewell until the 1860s, when the Civil War forced the Church to keep missionaries at home. From "the nest," at least four Latter-day Saints enlisted with the Confederacy: Colonel Peter Gose Litz (likely the highest-ranking Mormon in the Confederacy), his two sons John Tiffany and William Sawyers Litz, and local businessman David H. Peery. Peery is the only one of those four soldiers who is known to have left a wartime account.

After enlisting in 1862 as an officer under General Humphrey Marshall in the Confederate Army of Eastern Kentucky, Peery contracted typhoid fever. He was temporarily released from military service and sent to his father's

Camp Douglas, near Chicago, was a Union prisoner-of-war camp for captured Confederates. Pictured here in 1864, the camp was known for poor prisoner conditions and high rates of death and disease. (Library of Congress)

home to recuperate. While at home, his father, mother, and father-in-law died of typhoid. Although he was still sick, Peery returned in July 1862 to his home in Burke's Garden, Virginia. In September, his wife, Nancy, died of typhoid fever—followed in October by his one-month-old son. Within one year of joining the Confederate Army, Peery had lost his entire family except for his daughter, Louisa. Setting aside his personal grief, Major Peery returned to active service in the Confederate Army and served until 1864.[30]

Lorenzo Dow Watson, Union soldier. Union enlistee Lorenzo Dow Watson, or "Low" as he preferred to be called, was born on September 17, 1845, in Limerick, Maine.[31] In the winter of 1861, during his third year of schooling at a local academy in Maine, Low's father, David Watson Jr., "sent him to Portland [Maine], a seaport town sixty miles from his home, with a load of vegetables and pork to be shipped south to the Northern Armies." Low described the streets of Portland as "teeming with excitement, the shrill sound of the fife, the beat of drums, and the tramping of feet, for war was in the air." One of Low's cousins had previously enlisted with a local infantry regiment. Low wrote that as he walked through Portland, he was stopped by a man who offered him three hundred dollars as a substitute conscript. "Three hundred dollars! What a lot of money!" Low remembered thinking. He longed "for excitement, a chance to get out in the world, and here was [his] opportunity."[32] Low sent his team home with a neighbor who traveled with him and entered the army without the consent of his parents. He was only sixteen years old when he enlisted as an infantryman. His three-hundred-dollar bounty would shortly be stolen.

Low and his cousin took part in battles at Fort Henry and Fort Donelson. On April 5, 1862, they landed at Pittsburg Landing on the Tennessee River and marched two miles to the Shiloh Church log cabin. At the Battle of Shiloh, over ten thousand Confederate soldiers and thirteen thousand Union soldiers lost their lives. Low's cousin, John Watson of Limerick, Maine, was killed on April 6, 1862.[33] Years later, Low penned a poem about his cousin's death during the Battle of Shiloh.

Lorenzo Dow Watson, from Limerick, Maine, fought in several Civil War battles. After the war, he wrote a poem about watching his cousin be killed by his side during the Battle of Shiloh (Pittsburgh Landing). (Courtesy of Stevenson Genealogy Center)

> At night we lay together
> Near the waters of the Tennessee
> When before the dawn
> We woke at the alarm
> Of the advancing enemy.
>
> That day when forced from cover
> Under a merciless hail of lead
> Together we sank
> At the river's bank
> While all 'round us lay the dead.
>
> "Buell is coming," he shouted
> As I handed him my bruised canteen.
> He took it and drank,
> Returned it, and sank
> Suddenly down, the dead between.
>
> A red stream 'neath his visor
> Showed why he uttered no cry,
> I knelt in the sand
> As I grasped his hand
> And 'midst the dying watched him die.
>
> That night with a broken mess-pan
> I there hollowed his grave in the sand
> And at break of day
> I left him to lay
> At rest in peace in that southern land.[34]

Following the Battle of Shiloh, Low's family "felt that he would be much better off in school than in the army."[35] Low's parents, being very upset that their sixteen-year-old son was at war, contacted Mr. Bean, a local minister, to bring the boy home—which he did in June.

Low's military service, though, was not yet over. On December 9, 1863, at eighteen years old, Lorenzo Dow Watson enlisted in Company L of the Second Maine Volunteer Cavalry for a three-year term—this time with the permission of his parents. Written records are sparse from Low's second tour of duty. He contracted malaria, from which he would suffer the rest of his life, and developed scurvy while serving in the Florida Everglades. Yet, despite the "hardships of soldiering," Low had a "resiliency that enabled him to quickly overcome depression."[36]

Forbes, Stuart, Peery, and Dow were all from the eastern United States. Approximately one hundred Latter-day Saint Civil War soldiers enlisted in Utah as members of Lot Smith's Utah Cavalry. Although they were geographically separated from the war, remaining records generally cite duty as their primary reason for enlisting.

Soon after the start of the Civil War, Union soldiers stationed in Utah were withdrawn to the east, and the Utah Territory was left without a federal military presence. Without military protection, travel and communication on the Overland Trail became vulnerable to Indian attacks.[37] In April 1862, the federal government requested that Brigham Young raise a company of men to protect the mail and telegraph lines. The Utah Cavalry volunteers served under the command of Captain Lot Smith.[38] Unfortunately, few written records remain from those soldiers.

Lewis Albert Huffaker, Union soldier. Lewis Albert Huffaker enlisted in Lot Smith's Utah Cavalry. Born in Illinois during 1841, Lewis was six years old when he crossed the plains to Utah as a member of the Jedediah Grant and Willard Snow Company. He came to Utah as the son of a "well to do" father who "could furnish equipment for his sons at any time."[39] At the age of twenty-one, Huffaker "volunteered [in April 1862] at the call of President Abraham Lincoln to help keep open the line of communication." He acknowledged that due to his father's means, he felt an obligation to serve. He wrote that it was also his duty to "protect the people against marauding Indians."[40]

Huffaker related how Lieutenant Colonel William O. Collins, commanding the Eleventh Ohio Cavalry, approached Lot Smith and challenged his men to a friendly competition.

Huffaker reported that Collins said, "I would like to try a test and see whether your men or mine are best adapted to remain here in the West to protect the mail line." Collins "ordered a detachment of his men, double quick time, up the side of the mountain and down again." Collins's soldiers completed the task with "great confusion." Huffaker noted that Smith's unit completed the same tasks in "perfect order." "We gave our Indian ponies the reins and they knew how to avoid the sagebrush and gopher holes." After losing the challenge, Colonel Collins exclaimed, "Captain Smith, I would rather have ten of your men than my whole regiment. We will send the Eastern men to the front."[41]

Reuben Parley Miller, Union soldier. Reuben Parley Miller, born December 22, 1844, was the second son of Mormon pioneers Reuben and Rhoda Ann Letts Miller from Illinois. In 1849, as a four-year-old, he traveled the Mormon Trail to Salt Lake City with other Saints. At eighteen, Miller was one of the youngest members of the Utah Cavalry. Miller's motivation for military service was his sense of duty after he was "called upon to bear arms in defense of the U.S. government."[42] It is unclear if Miller felt he was responding to the "call" of Abraham Lincoln or Brigham Young—perhaps he felt a service obligation to both men.

Edwin Brown, Union soldier. Edwin Brown's account of his enlistment suggests that he volunteered for service in the Lot Smith Company only after President Young personally asked him to enlist. Brown was born in Berkshire, England, in 1841 and immigrated to Utah in 1853. His family settled in Murray, Utah, on a farm large enough to support their family of nine. Tragedy struck the family in 1860 when Edwin's father and younger brother died. The responsibility fell on Edwin and his older brother, Henry, to run the farm. In April 1862, after Lincoln's request for Utah soldiers, Brigham Young made a surprise visit to their farm. Young was brief; he requested that the Brown family send one of their remaining two sons to guard the trail. As was traditional for English families, the eldest son's primary responsibility was to the family and the farm. As Edwin's brother Henry was needed at home, the responsibility to enlist fell upon Edwin.[43] He served faithfully from April to August 1862, when he was mustered out of service with the rest of the Utah Cavalry and returned to his farm.

PERSONAL HONOR

Some Civil War soldiers admitted that their enlistment was motivated by a desire to honor their families. Such a mindset was derived, in part, from the era in which they lived. As McPherson noted, "Boyhood was a time of preparation for the tests and responsibilities of manhood. And there could be no sterner test than war. It quite literally separated men from boys."[44] As a representative of his family, a man fully embodied the values for which he fought; soldiering was the ultimate proving ground for a man to defend his family. Union soldier Saul Norman understood his role, although he needed a stern rebuke and reminder before he would enlist.

Saul Norman, Union soldier. Saul Norman was born the son of a Methodist minister in July 1836, and little is known about him, his family's connection to Mormonism, and how the family arrived in Utah. In 1848, when gold was discovered in California, prospectors rushed to claim their fortunes. Norman was late to the scene, trekking to California in 1857 at the age of twenty-one. When

the Civil War started, Norman was still in California. We do not know his initial attitude toward the war. In a letter written by his father in 1862, Norman was chastised for thinking only of himself and not of his responsibilities to his family or his country. That was unacceptable behavior. Norman's father demanded he "show his colors" and follow the example set by his four brothers and six nephews who were serving in the army.[45] The pressure worked. Reminded of his responsibility, Norman made his way in late 1862 to Camp Douglas, a small, newly established military garrison east of Salt Lake City. There he enlisted with the Third Regiment of the California Volunteer Infantry under the command of Colonel Patrick Edward Connor.

HAPPENSTANCE

Hans N. Chlarson, Union soldier. The end of the Civil War in April 1865 meant soldiers could return to their families. Such was the case for Union Lieutenant Hans Chlarson, who had not seen his wife and son for two years—since he watched them leave Sweden in March 1863 on their way to Utah. Chlarson had vowed to follow his family as soon as it was financially possible; he hoped to join them no later than the summer of 1864. At least that was his plan.

After meeting two Mormon missionaries in 1854, their teachings had a profound effect on him, and Chlarson "decided to lead a better life."[46] Chlarson was soon baptized a member of The Church of Jesus Christ of Latter-day Saints. He served as a missionary in his homeland until 1861, when he fell in love with Johanna, a young Mormon girl. They married, and a year later welcomed their first son, Heber. After sending Johanna and Heber to Utah in 1863, Hans remained behind, worked two jobs, and saved money for his voyage to America. By July 1864, he had saved over four thousand dollars and boarded a boat for New York City.

After arriving in America, Chlarson rented a hotel room in the city while he made preparations for his trip west. The first week in New York a thief broke into his room and stole his entire savings. Alone in a new country without money or means, Chlarson desperately sought for advice. A fellow Swede named Nicolas told Chlarson that his language skills (he was fluent in seven languages, but English was apparently not one of them) would make him an ideal candidate as a translator and officer at the army hospital in Washington, DC. Nicolas presented Chlarson with some paperwork to fill out, which he did, before boarding a troop train bound for Washington. After he arrived at camp, Chlarson discovered that his name was not on the officers' commissioning list. After describing his situation, the recruiting officers told Chlarson that the papers he had signed were conscription papers. By signing, Chlarson had agreed to fight in the Civil War as a substitute soldier for Nicolas. The officers explained that he had two options: either he could desert the army, evade authorities, and escape to Utah; or he could stay in camp, train to be a soldier, and fight in the war. He chose the latter, saying he "did not want to start his career as an American with that kind of a record."[47] Within just a few short weeks of arriving in his new country, Chlarson found himself training for combat in a war he never intended to join.

Chlarson wrote that he "stood in many bloody fights" as a lieutenant in General Philip Sheridan's cavalry until wounds to his shoulder and leg forced him to the hospital.[48] He was "unable to earn a support by reason of an

Hans Chlarson and his wife, Johanna, joined the Church in Sweden and desired to join with the Saints in America. The two were separated after Hans was tricked into enlisting as a soldier in the Union army. (Courtesy of Daniel K Judd)

injury of the left leg or thigh supposed to have been caused by a fragment of a shell which struck me in battle at Southside Rail Road rendering me insensible," an injury which left him with a limp the remainder of his life.[49] After the war ended, Chlarson made his way back to New York City, where his first order of business was to hunt down his erstwhile friend Nicolas and give him a beating.[50] After spending a few days in jail for attacking Nicolas, Chlarson made his way to Utah, where he "embraced [his] wife and son for whom [his] heart had longed."[51]

John Rozsa, Union soldier. Like Chlarson, John Rozsa was a European emigrant who served in the Civil War. Born in Hungary in 1820, Rozsa was a child of privilege. His father's military commission enabled him to have a

John Rozsa served in several European armies before emigrating to the United States and enlisting in the U.S. Army. Stationed at Camp Floyd following the Utah War, Rozsa fought for the Union in the Civil War and died after the war while returning to Utah. (Pleasant Grove Chapter, Daughters of Utah Pioneers)

childhood filled with excellent educational opportunities. After a few years of schooling, Rozsa took advantage of his father's goodness and used his money to patronize saloons and gambling halls.[52] Eventually, Rozsa fell deep into debt. His family expressed disappointment regarding his poor decisions. Unable to look into their disapproving eyes, Rozsa left home to live with his grandmother.

Rozsa worked in a variety of jobs in many cities. In 1838, while he prepared for employment as a notary public, he fell in love. Rozsa's parents expressed displeasure in his decision to marry and announced that they would not support him. Rozsa sold all of his possessions and decided to join the Hungarian Army. When his father learned

of his decision, he tried to talk him out of it, but Rozsa's mind was set. He enlisted on February 6, 1838. When Hungary and Italy declared war in 1847, it was a perfect chance for Rozsa to become an officer; however, he admitted that he behaved poorly, and soon after he lost his opportunity to become one. In August 1849, Rozsa deserted. He wrote, "I only had to go 18 miles to cross the Poo river and then I'd been free from getting arrested. It was a pleasant night, but never the less it wasn't very pleasing to me for fear of getting caught, then the bylaws at that time for deserters was to be shot inside of 24 hours."[53]

Unable to find meaningful employment, Rozsa next enlisted in the Austrian Army as a corporal. He served honorably for almost three years before taking a leave of absence to care for a woman and her child. While thus occupied, Rozsa traveled to a nearby town to pick up supplies where he was arrested and incarcerated. Eventually, he was transferred to a larger prison where he was housed with criminals who awaited execution. The prison director informed Rozsa that he was charged as a political offender—a charge Rozsa claimed was unfounded. The details are hazy, but on March 26, 1853, after three months of imprisonment, Rozsa was placed aboard a ship bound for the United States. On May 15, 1853, he arrived at New York City.

The first few months in America were particularly difficult as he drifted from job to job trying to find his place in the bustling city. First, Rozsa tried to use his language skills by working at a hotel frequented by immigrants.[54] The job was not what he expected, and he next moved to Baltimore, where he worked as a bartender. In December 1853, after getting into an argument with his boss's wife, Rozsa was fired. Spending his last few dollars on alcohol, drunk and down in spirit, on December 12, 1853, Rozsa stumbled into an enlistment office and signed a six-year contract to return to soldiering. Rozsa wrote that he had always loved life as a soldier and felt that the American Army gave "the best pay of a soldier in the whole world."[55]

Rozsa was stationed at Governor's Island, New York, for six months before asking to transfer to the Tenth Infantry at Carlisle Barracks, Pennsylvania, thinking he would be promoted more easily there. Rozsa said that in hindsight, it was one of the worst decisions in his life. After three months at Carlisle, Rozsa was overlooked for promotion and transferred to the Second Dragoons. This began a three-year period, from 1855 to 1858, during which Rozsa was constantly on the march, traveling through the Midwest. In June 1858, he arrived in Salt Lake City as a soldier in the Utah War under the command of Brevet Brigadier General Albert Sidney Johnston.[56]

Rozsa did not record much about his day-to-day experiences in Utah at Camp Floyd aside from mentioning that they "had a quiet easy life, where we had an abundance of all sorts of vegetables, butter, eggs, etc." Rozsa converted to Mormonism in 1858 after falling in love with Patience Loader, a Mormon girl he met while visiting Lehi, Utah. On December 8, 1858, the two were married by Able Evans, the same man who baptized Rozsa as a member of the Church five days earlier. Rozsa's decision to be baptized was met with the expressed displeasure of his commanding officer and friends.[57]

Alluding to the coming war, Rozsa wrote, "A sure storm will follow fine weather and Vice Versa."[58] Their easy life in Utah was soon shattered when the soldiers at Camp Floyd received news of the outbreak of the Civil War. Ordered to return to Washington, DC, Rozsa; his wife, Patience; and their newborn son, John James, left Utah and headed east to join the war.

The journey east was eventful. After a two-day stop at Fort Leavenworth in October, Rozsa's unit intended to cross a railroad bridge over the Platte River. Upon arriving, the troops found that the bridge had been destroyed. The enlisted soldiers were ordered to make their crossing at Easton, fifteen miles away, while the officers, staff, women, and children crossed by raft. Rozsa reported that when the raft crossed the second or third time, the rope broke and several children were thrown into the river. Attempts at rescue were in vain, and many lives were lost. Patience and their son had crossed before the incident; all they lost was their bedding. The remainder of the trip proved uneventful. Rozsa's family and his unit arrived in Washington, DC, in late October 1861.

After having fought in the Peninsular Campaign, Rozsa's years of military service finally caught up to him. He complained in August 1862, "I got broken down entirely in regard to my physical condition as I feel the palpitation of heart in the highest grade." Unable to march, he was evacuated on a vessel bound for Harrison Landing, Virginia. Separated from his unit, Rozsa decided, without permission, to return to his family. He found a position as a clerk in the office of Henry Halleck, general-in-chief of the Union armies, which increased his monthly pay from twenty-two to seventy-five dollars. His new position also gave him the opportunity to visit his family regularly.[59]

Rozsa returned to his previous unit on October 13, 1862, and was immediately placed under arrest for returning to

Camp Douglas, Illinois, in about 1863. Confederate soldiers David Crockett Stuart and William H. Norman (aka John Eugene Davis) were held as prisoners of war in wretched conditions at Camp Douglas. During his captivity, Stuart lost ninety pounds— nearly half his body weight. (Chicago History Museum, ICHi-01800)

Washington without official orders. The following week he was court-martialed. After years of military service, Rozsa was reduced in rank from first sergeant to private and was fined twenty dollars, and his pay was reduced to thirteen dollars per month. As a newly minted private, he was forced to stand guard during the cold and windy winter months.

Rozsa was never wounded during battle but suffered severe burns to his shoulders and back when a container of hot coffee was spilled on him in camp. In October 1863, he was honorably discharged from military service—for the first time in his life! On a return trip to Utah in 1866, Rozsa unexpectedly became ill and died near Fort Kearney, Nebraska, due to complications from lung disease.[60]

GALVANIZED YANKEES

A small number of Civil War soldiers served in both the Confederate and Union armies. Soldiers who fought first for the Confederacy and afterward for the Union were called "galvanized Yankees"—a reference to metal that has a thin galvanizing layer of zinc placed over steel. "In the process the surface color of the metal is altered, but underneath the coating the steel is unchanged. During the Civil War, in both Northern and Southern prison camps, soldiers sometimes decided to 'galvanize,' or change sides, to save themselves from the horrors of prison life. Like the metal, these galvanized soldiers in many cases were still 'Good old Revels,' or 'Billy Yanks,' underneath their adopted uniforms."[61]

William H. Norman, Confederate soldier (who changed his name to John Eugene Davis after the war). Shortly after the Civil War began, sixteen-year-old William H. Norman enlisted in the Confederate Army with the 1st Georgia Infantry Regiment. After serving, reenlisting, and fighting for several years, he was captured by Union forces on December 16, 1864, at Nashville, Tennessee, and sent to Camp Douglas, a prisoner-of-war

(CONFEDERATE.)

N | 1 | C.S.A.

W. H. Norman

Prt , { (2d) Co. E, 1 Confederate Reg't
Georgia Volunteers.

Appears on

Company Muster Roll

of the organization named above,

for *Sept + Oct* , 186 *2.*
dated Oct. 31 1862

Enlisted:
When *Apr. 14* , 186 *2*
Where *Macon Ga.*
By whom *Capt. Aderhold*
Period *The war*

Last paid:
By whom *Maj. Barnwell*
To what time *Aug. 31* , 186 *2*

Present or absent *Present*

Remarks:

The designation of the 36th (Villepigue's) Regiment
Georgia Infantry was changed to the 1st Regiment Confed-
erate Infantry (also known as the 1st Confederate Regiment
Georgia Volunteers) by S. O. No. 25, A. and I. G. O., dated
January 31, 1862.
About April 9, 1865, the 1st Regiment Confederate In-
fantry, the 25th, 29th, 30th, and 66th Regiments Georgia
Infantry, and the 1st Battalion Georgia Sharp Shooters were
consolidated and formed the 1st Confederate Battalion
Georgia Volunteers, which was paroled at Greensboro, N. C.,
May 1, 1865.

Book mark:

W. A. Brinkman

(642) *Copyist.*
3208

(Confederate.)

N | 1 | Ga.

W. H. Norman

Pri. Co. E, 1 Reg't Ga. Inf.

Appears on a

Roll of Prisoners of War

at Camp Douglas, Ill., applying for oath of allegiance, January —, 1865.

Roll not dated *

Where captured *Nashville, Tenn.*
When captured *Dec. 16* , 186 *4*
Remarks: *Claims to have been
loyal. Was conscripted.
Was captured & desires
to take the oath of alle-
giance to the U.S. & be-
come a loyal citizen.*

*Indorsement shows: "Rec'd (O. C. G. P.) Jan'y 28, '65."

Number of roll:
237; sheet *5* *J. B. Dowd*

(689b) *Copyist.*

*Left: Confederate Company Muster Roster record for William H. Norman for September and October 1862. (National Archives)
Right: January 1865 Union Prisoner of War Roll transcription from Camp Douglas, Illinois, in which William H. Norman (who later
changed his name to John Eugene Davis) applied for service in the Army of the United States. (National Archives)*

Confederate soldier William H. Norman became a "galvanized Yankee" when he enlisted at Camp Douglas, Illinois, as a Union soldier. He changed his name to John Eugene Davis after he deserted in 1865. This picture of Norman/Davis was taken around 1870. (Courtesy of Robert L. Davis)

camp near Chicago. In the early war years, such camps "were merely holding areas where men waited to be exchanged for equal numbers of prisoners held by the other side." After 1863, though, "the prisoner exchange system broke down, causing prison camps to become permanent areas of incarceration, where growing numbers of men had no hope of release until the end of the war." Life in prison camps, for both Union and Confederate soldiers, was generally filthy and horrible. "Soldiers were seldom issued new clothing, and often starved due to meager food allowances."[62]

There was a fairly easy way out of a prison camp, though—change your allegiance and enlist in the army of your former enemy. And that's exactly what Norman did. He swore an oath of allegiance to the United States on March 25, 1865, and enlisted as a "galvanized yankee." Like the majority of galvanized Yankees, whose true allegiance remained questionable, Davis's new unit, the 6th Regiment U.S. Volunteers, was ordered west to keep trails open and provide settlers with protection against Indian attacks. He reportedly deserted from the Union army on August 3, 1865, a few months after the war's end. Sometime after his desertion, William H. Norman changed his name to John Eugene Davis—the name he used for almost seventy years.

After the war, Davis travelled west with a Mormon freighter arriving in Utah in 1867. He lived in Utah for several years and later moved to Nevada. He was baptized a member of The Church of Jesus Christ of Latter-day Saints in May 1877 under the name John Eugene Davis. His children and grandchildren grew up unaware that he had changed his name. He often shared exciting stories of his Confederate military service but never mentioned that he had also briefly served as a "galvanized yankee" with the U.S. Volunteers or that he had changed his name after he deserted. His May 1935 obituary in the Richfield Reaper mentioned only his Confederate Civil War service. Several decades after his death—using family, military, and census records—one of his daughters slowly pieced together the story of his name change and dual military service.[63]

CONCLUSION

Latter-day Saint Civil War soldiers came from all walks of life and from varied backgrounds. They were men from all over the world—varying in age, experience, and occupation. Some soldiers were lifelong members of the Church, while others had recently converted to Mormonism. Some were multigenerational Americans; others were not citizens, having only recently arrived in America. Despite their differences, they all stepped forward to serve in the Civil War.

According to their journals, letters, and autobiographies, those Latter-day Saint soldiers served for a variety of reasons. Some of them were motivated primarily by patriotism. Others claimed it was their duty to serve. Some sought personal glory or honor. Still others joined because they were in the wrong place at the wrong time. Whatever their reasons for joining, the Civil War contributions of Latter-day Saint soldiers, however small, should not be overlooked. While many people were content to leave the fighting to others, those men believed that it was their fight too.

Brant W. Ellsworth is a PhD candidate in American studies at Pennsylvania State University, Harrisburg. Kenneth L. Alford is an associate professor of Church history and doctrine at Brigham Young University.

NOTES

1. See E. B. Long, *The Saints and the Union: Utah Territory during the Civil War* (Champaign: University of Illinois Press, 1981); Gustive O. Larson, "Utah and the Civil War," *Utah Historical Quarterly* 33 (Winter 1965): 55–67; Ray Colton, *The Civil War in the Western Territories: Arizona, Colorado, New Mexico, and Utah* (Norman: University of Oklahoma Press, 1959); and David F. Boone, "The Church and the Civil War," in *Nineteenth-Century Saints at War*, ed. Robert C. Freeman (Provo, UT: Religious Studies Center, Brigham Young University, 2006), 113–49.
2. Heber C. Kimball, "Remarks," *Deseret News*, February 20, 1861.
3. Brigham Young, "Remarks," *Deseret News*, February 27, 1861.
4. Heber C. Kimball, "Remarks," *Deseret News*, September 18, 1861.
5. George A. Smith, "Discourse," *Deseret News*, December 25, 1861.
6. Brigham Young, "Remarks," *Deseret News*, February 27, 1861.
7. Quoted in David F. Boone, "The Church and the Civil War," in *Nineteenth-Century Saints at War*, ed. Robert C. Freeman (Provo, UT: Religious Studies Center, Brigham Young University, 2006), 126–27.
8. Brigham Young, "Remarks," *Deseret News*, February 27, 1861.
9. The *Deseret News* recorded similar pronouncements by Church leaders in 1861. See comments by Brigham Young ("Remarks," *Deseret News*, February 13, 1861; "Remarks," *Deseret News*, February 27, 1861; and "Remarks," *Deseret News*, March 13, 1861), Heber C. Kimball ("Remarks," *Deseret News*, January 30, 1861; "Remarks," *Deseret News*, February 20, 1861; and "Remarks," *Deseret News*, April 3, 1861), Daniel H. Wells ("Remarks," *Deseret News*, April 24, 1861), and John Taylor ("Discourse," *Deseret News*, January 9, 1861).
10. Brigham Young, in *Journal of Discourses* (London: Latter-day Saints' Book Depot, 1854–86), 9:368–69.
11. See Bell Irvin Wiley, *The Life of Billy Yank: The Common Soldier of the Union* (Baton Rouge: Louisiana State University Press, 1971) and *The Life of Johnny Reb: The Common Soldier of the Confederacy* (Indianapolis: Bobbs-Merrill, 1943); and James I. Robertson Jr., *Soldier's Blue and Gray* (Columbia: University of South Carolina Press, 1998). A study that focuses on the ideological motivations of the Union soldier is Earl J. Hess, *Liberty, Virtue, and Progress: Northerners and Their War for the Union*, 2nd ed. (New York: Fordham University Press, 1997). Randall C. Jimerson, *The Private Civil War: Popular Thought during the Sectional Conflict* (Baton Rouge: Louisiana State University Press, 1988), and Reid Mitchell, *Civil War Soldiers* (New York: Penguin, 1988), describe the common experiences of the Union and Confederate soldiers. Reid Mitchell, *The Vacant Chair: The Northern Soldier Leaves Home* (New York: Oxford

University Press, 1993), describes the community's role in motivating soldiers. James M. McPherson, *For Cause and Comrades: Why Men Fought in the Civil War* (New York: Oxford University Press, 1997), explores the reason soldiers fought. Chandra Manning, *What this Cruel War Was Over: Soldiers, Slavery, and the Civil War* (New York: Alfred A. Knopf, 2007), argues for slavery's central role in motivating men to enlist.

12. McPherson, *For Cause and Comrades*, 11.

13. Earl J. Hess, *The Union Soldier in Battle: Enduring the Ordeal of Combat* (Lawrence: University Press of Kansas, 1997), xi.

14. McPherson, *For Cause and Comrades*, 14–29.

15. Quoted in McPherson, *For Cause and Comrades*, 26.

16. McPherson, *For Cause and Comrades*, 21.

17. John Demos, *A Little Commonwealth: Family Life in Plymouth Colony* (Oxford: Oxford University Press, 2000), xxi.

18. David Detzer, *Allegiance: Fort Sumter, Charleston, and the Beginning of the Civil War* (New York: Harcourt, 2001), 269–70.

19. "War at Last," *New York Times*, April 13, 1861.

20. "War Inaugurated," *Chicago Tribune*, April 13, 1861.

21. "The War Began," *Richmond Daily Dispatch*, April 13, 1861.

22. Quoted in James M. McPherson, *Battle Cry of Freedom: The Civil War Era* (Oxford: Oxford University Press, 1988), 274.

23. Autobiography of Joseph Barlow Forbes, 1840–1927, file MS 15909, Church History Library, The Church of Jesus Christ of Latter-day Saints, Salt Lake City.

24. Autobiographical letter by David Crockett Stuart, "A Few Lines from an Old Johnny Reb," file MS 8895, Church History Library, Salt Lake City, 4.

25. Autobiographical letter by David Crockett Stuart, 4–5.

26. Autobiographical letter by David Crockett Stuart, 5.

27. Autobiographical letter by David Crockett Stuart, 12–17.

28. McPherson, *For Cause and Comrades*, 22–23.

29. A. J. Simmonds, "'Thou and All Thy House:' Three Case Studies of Clan and Charisma in the Early Church," *Nauvoo Journal* 7, no. 1 (1995): 51, http://www.mormonhistoricsitesfoundation.org/publications/nj_spring1995/Simmonds.pdf; see also Tyler Jarvis, "Life Sketch of Peter Gose Litz," http://www.math.byu.edu/~jarvis/FamilyHistory/PeterGoseLitz-Bio.pdf.

30. For more information on the life and experiences of David H. Peery, see Robert Freeman's chapter herein.

31. Lorenzo Dow Watson may have been named after Lorenzo Dow (1777–1834), an influential preacher who was popular during the Second Great Awakening. Dow, who traveled and preached widely, is said to have preached to more people than anyone else at that time. See James Grant Wilson and John Fiske, eds., *Appletons' Cyclopædia of American Biography* (New York: D. Appleton, 1887), 2:218.

32. Alma Gertrude Watson McGregor, *Lorenzo Dow Watson* (Provo, UT: J. Grant Stevenson, 1970), 17.

33. John Watson, Low's cousin, died as a Union soldier on the same day and in the same battle that General Albert Sidney Johnston, a senior Confederate general and former commander of the Utah Expedition during the Utah War, died. McGregor, *Lorenzo Dow Watson*, 20.

34. McGregor, *Lorenzo Dow Watson*, 21.

35. McGregor, *Lorenzo Dow Watson*, 21.

36. McGregor, *Lorenzo Dow Watson*, 26.

37. Alvin M. Josephy Jr., *The Civil War in the American West* (New York: Alfred A. Knopf, 1991), 246.

38. For additional details regarding the background and service of the Utah Cavalry, see Joseph Stuart and Kenneth L. Alford's chapter in this volume.

39. Margaret M. Fisher, C. N. Lund, and Judge Nephi Jensen, eds., *Utah and the Civil War: Being the Story of the Part Played by the People of Utah in That Great Conflict, with Special Reference to the Lot Smith Expedition and the Robert T. Burton Expedition* (Salt Lake City: Deseret Book, 1929), 96–99.

40. Louis Huffaker Journal, in Kate B. Carter, "Utah during the Civil War Years," *Treasures of Pioneer History* (Salt Lake City: Daughters of Utah Pioneers, 1956) 5:425–26.

41. Louis Huffaker Journal, in Carter, *Treasures of Pioneer History*, 5:425–26.

42. Reuben Miller Journal, in Carter, *Treasures of Pioneer History*, 5:422–23.

43. Edwin Brown Journal, in Carter, *Treasures of Pioneer History*, 5:426–27.

44. McPherson, *For Cause and Comrades*, 25.

45. Saul Norman Journal, in Carter, *Treasures of Pioneer History*, 5:424.

46. Ida-Rose Langford Hall, "Johanna Charlotte Scherlin & Hans Nadrian Chlarson" (unpublished), accessed July 15, 2011, http://members.cox.net/juddclan/JuddHist/ChlrsnHJ/ChlrsnHJ.htm.

47. Hans Chlarson Journal in Carter, *Treasures of Pioneer History*, 5:430.

48. As quoted in Hall, "Johanna Charlotte Scherlin & Hans Nadrian Chlarson."

49. As quoted in Hall, "Johanna Charlotte Scherlin & Hans Nadrian Chlarson." Hall quotes from Chlarson's Civil War Invalid Pension Application #SO988484, February 11, 1891, Thatcher, Arizona.

50. Hans Chlarson Journal in Carter, *Treasures of Pioneer History*, 5:430.

51. As quoted in Hall, "Johanna Charlotte Scherlin & Hans Nadrian Chlarson."

52. John Rozsa, *Autobiography*, file MS 15389, Church History Library, Salt Lake City, 3.

53. Rozsa, *Autobiography*, 4.

54. John Rozsa claimed to have spoken seven languages.

55. Rozsa, *Autobiography*, 11.

56. Rozsa, *Autobiography*, 14.

57. Sandra Ailey Petree, *Recollections of Past Days: The Autobiography of Patience Loader Rozsa Archer* (Logan, UT: Utah State University Press, 2006), 98.

58. Rozsa, *Autobiography*, 16.

59. Rozsa, *Autobiography*, 21.

60. Petree, *Recollections of Past Days*, 139–40.

61. "The Galvanized Yankees," *The Museum Gazette* (Washington, DC: National Park Service, 1992), 1.

62. "The Galvanized Yankees," 1.

63. Interview with Robert L. Davis, grandson of John Eugene Davis, and Kenneth L. Alford, October 12, 2011, records in possession of the Davis family.

Washakie (1804?–1900) served as a Shoshone chief in the Utah–Wyoming–Idaho area for sixty years. Noted for his friendliness to whites, he considered Brigham Young, James Bridger, and General Albert Sidney Johnston as his friends. He was given a U.S. military funeral when he was buried at Fort Washakie, near Lander, Wyoming. (Utah State Historical Society)

CHAPTER 12

Kenneth L. Alford

INDIAN RELATIONS IN UTAH DURING THE CIVIL WAR

Native Americans[1] played a small, but interesting, role during the Civil War. During the first year of the war, the U.S. secretary of the interior reported that "our Indian affairs are in a very unsettled and unsatisfactory condition. The spirit of rebellion against the authority of the government, which has precipitated a large number of States into open revolt, has been instilled into a portion of the Indian tribes by emissaries from the insurrectionary States."[2] Both Union and Confederate armies courted tribe members in an effort to recruit additional soldiers and were met with some success. Confederate General Stand Watie, for example, the last Southern general to surrender to Union forces (in June 1865), was a Cherokee Indian.[3]

While most regions of the country experienced few Indian problems during the war, Utah had to contend with numerous challenges. What happened in Utah when settlers and Indians came into contact is the same story that occurred throughout the early

history of the United States. Settlers arrived; Indians were displaced. In Utah Territory it happened quickly. From the arrival of the first Mormon pioneers, it was just over thirty years until the last Indians were removed to government reservations. This essay provides an overview of the complicated and often violent relationships that existed in Utah Territory during the Civil War between Indians, settlers, and the federal government.

UTAH'S INDIANS

Several Indian tribes lived in Utah Territory during the nineteenth century with three tribes accounting for the majority—Utes (often referred to as Utahs—the namesake of Utah Territory), Shoshones (sometimes referred to as Snakes), and Paiutes (who lived in the central and southern parts of the territory).[4] Members of smaller and neighboring tribes, such as Bannock, Goshute, and Washoe, also lived within the territorial boundary. As Jacob Forney, a Utah Territory superintendent of Indian

Affairs who was later dismissed for misman-agement, explained in September 1858, "The principal tribes are, of course, divided into a great number of small bands but all submit to the authority of one or the other of the chiefs of their respective tribes."[5]

The exact number of Indians who lived in Utah Territory is unknown. An 1861 report from J. F. Collins, Utah superintendent of Indian Affairs, acknowledged that no one "had ever been able to obtain satisfactory information in regard to their numbers." Collins's estimate at the beginning of the Civil War suggested, though, that there may have been fifteen to twenty thousand Indians prior to the arrival of the first Mormon set-tlers.[6] The best approximation prior to the Civil War may be an estimate included in Superintendent Forney's 1859 annual report to the federal commissioner of Indian Affairs (see figure 1).

INDIAN TRIBE OR BAND	ESTIMATE
Sho-sho-nes or Snakes	4,500
Ban-nacks	500
Uinta Utes	1,000
Spanish Fork and San Pete farms	900
Pah-vant (Utes)	700
Pey-utes (South)	2,200
Pey-utes (West)	6,000
Elk mountain Utes	2,000
Wa-sho of Honey lake	700
Total	18,500

Figure 1. Supposed total number of Indians in Utah Territory (1858). Source: Report of the Commissioner of Indian Affairs, Accompanying the Annual Report of the Secretary of the Interior for the Year 1858 (Washington, DC: George W. Bowman, 1859), 365. ("Farms" were Indian reservations. Original spelling retained.)

Living conditions in Utah Territory were difficult for everyone—but especially so for Indians. According to Benjamin Davies, Utah Territory's superintendent of Indian Affairs in 1861, Utah's Indians were "unquestion-ably the poorest Indians on the continent."[7] In an 1850 Indian agent's annual report, Paiutes, for example, were categorized as "benumbed by cold, and enfeebled, intel-lectually and physically, by the food upon which they subsist; it consisting only of roots, vermin, insects of all kinds, and everything that creeps, crawls, swims, flies, or bounds, they may chance to overtake."[8] Many Indians struggled to stay alive and eagerly consumed "everything containing a life-sustaining ele-ment, such as hares, rabbits, antelope, deer, bear, elk, dogs, lizards [sic], snakes, crickets, grasshoppers, ants, roots, grass, seeds, bark, etc. . . . With some of the Indians stealing cattle, horses, mules, &c, is a matter of necessity—*steal* or *starve*."[9] While sent to Utah to serve both the government and the Indians, the personal prejudices of individual Indian agents often crept into reports to their superiors as evidenced by the 1850 report of Indian agent J. S. Calhoun, who charged that Indians "feed upon their own children. Such a people should not be permitted to live within the limits of the United States, and must be elevated in the scale of human existence, or exterminated."[10] Yet the same Indians were defined by other Indian agents as "very industrious," "honest, amiable," and "peaceable," who "conducted themselves well" and were "friendly disposed toward us [Indian agents] destitute as they are."[11]

PRIOR TO THE CIVIL WAR

Utah's first Mormon settlers arrived in the Salt Lake Valley in July 1847. Mormons iden-tified American Indians as a lost branch of the house of Israel and felt a sense of responsibil-ity to convert and civilize them. There were many Indian baptisms, but conflict occurred more frequently than conversion.

For security reasons, new Mormon settlements often began with the building of an enclosed fort. Lieutenant John W. Gunnison, a U.S. Army topographic engineer sent to Utah in the early 1850s to survey potential rail routes, described the first settlement in Salt Lake City: "A fort enclosing about forty acres was built, by facing log-houses inward, and picketing four gateways on each side of the square, making a line nearly a mile and a half in length—the timber being hauled several miles, and cut in the distant kanyons."[12]

Indians did not appear to be concerned with the initial arrival of Mormons in the Salt Lake Valley because that valley was a neutral buffer zone between the Ute, Goshute, and Shoshone tribes. Trouble began when the Mormons expanded into Utah Valley. The Mormon fort in Provo was built on a centuries-old Indian campsite that was near several major hunting trails.[13] During 1848, just one year after the first pioneers arrived, settlers suffered attacks by a band of Shoshones and sought to administer a "chastisement" of their own to the Indians.[14] The following year, in the winter of 1849, Indians "became insolent in Utah Valley, killed cattle and boasted of it, entered houses and frightened women and children, took provisions forcibly, and compelled those on the farms to retire within the fort."[15] In 1850, during what is sometimes termed the Timpanogos War, Mormon forces from Salt Lake and Utah Valleys attacked and killed dozens of Indians.[16] Additional Indian-settler skirmishes, such as the Walker War in 1853–54 (named after the Timpanogos Ute Indian chief Wakara), continued throughout the 1850s.[17] Gunnison wryly noted, "It is a curious matter of

reflection that those [Mormons] whose mission it is to convert these aborigines by the sword of the spirit should thus be obliged to destroy them."[18] (Gunnison himself was killed by Utes in October 1853 near Fillmore, then the capital of Utah Territory.)

Prior to the Utah War (1857–58), Indian relations and diplomacy had been a shared responsibility, divided by proximity and interest between the Mormon population and federal Indian agents. After the Utah War, Indian policy was most often made and enforced by the U.S. Army and the federal government's Indian agents. Among the many challenges this presented was that "army leaders and their volunteers often had little training in and patience for the protocols of Indian diplomacy."[19]

According to an 1861 government report, among the many causes of Indian hardship were "the natural poverty of the country, the destruction of the wild game by the introduction of white men, and the selfish policy of the Mormon people"—although exactly what that policy might have been was left unstated.[20] Perhaps it was the fact that the arrival of Mormon pioneers upset the delicate and fragile natural balance within the region. Indians were continually being displaced as the Mormons established new settlements. Competition for limited natural resources became "a constant source of irritation and vexation to the whites" as well as to the Indians.[21] Indians were soon "deprived of their accustomed means of subsistence" and were "driven to the alternative of laying violent hands upon the property of the whites or of perishing by want."[22]

Violence between Indians was another problem, with intermittent conflicts occurring within and between the numerous tribes

Paiutes, who were generally nonequestrian, tended to move to reservations and adopt settler ways more easily than other tribes within the territory (circa 1860). (Library of Congress)

and bands.[23] Lieutenant Gunnison observed that the "different tribes of the Utahs are frequently at war with each other."[24] Comparing Utah's local Indian wars to the Civil War, one *Deseret News* writer suggested in 1861, "In their way, and according to their numbers, they [warring Indians] may destroy as many lives as the armies of the North and South, in the civil war now raging in the States."[25] The fact that many Ute and Shoshone bands were equestrian, while Paiutes seldom had horses, influenced the relationship each tribe developed with Mormon settlers. Horses enabled a migratory lifestyle that made their owners less interested in farming on government reservations. Utes also captured and enslaved

nonequestrian Indians, which caused many Paiutes to seek protection from nearby Mormon settlements.[26]

Disease (including several new diseases introduced into Indian communities by contact with whites) and violent conflicts with settlers contributed to a decline in the Indian population.[27] Indians within Utah Territory did not fare well in the years immediately preceding the Civil War; they had "degenerated very rapidly during the last twelve years or since white men have got among them."[28] In 1860, Utah Indian agent A. Humphreys reported that "the sufferings of these poor Indians during the past winter were horrible, many of them dying from starvation and exposure. It was a common circumstance to find them frozen to death. . . . On several occasions I parted with my own blankets to bury them in."[29]

FEDERAL INDIAN OFFICIALS

Congress created the Utah Territorial Indian Agency in February 1851, just one year after Utah was organized as a territory.[30] Throughout much of its history as a territory, Utah had a difficult and strained relationship with many of the federal appointees sent to direct its affairs. Utahns wanted to govern themselves and viewed federal office holders as an unnecessary burden. The Utah War, which ended less than three years before the beginning of the Civil War, was caused in part by the role that disgruntled territorial federal officials played in shaping the Buchanan administration's view of Utah's perceived rebellion. Relations were particularly bad when it came to Utah's Indian superintendents and agents, many of whom recognized that a Utah appointment would do little to further their career. Problems ranged from apathy and incompetence to open corruption. Part of Utah's Indian difficulties must be laid at the feet of Utah's Indian officials.

In a lengthy October 1861 editorial, the *Deseret News* summarized the frustration Utahns had with many federal Indian agents. While recognizing that some "of the government officials who have been sent here within the last three or four years have been honorable men, and a few others might be called so without much perversion of language, having done no particular harm to any one excepting to themselves," the *News* categorized a "majority of the United States' officers" as being "neither moral, honest, or virtuous." Federal officials were generally categorized as alcoholics who "worship[ped] at the shrine of Bacchus." While the newspaper took most federal appointees to task, one category of government workers "who have come here since Buchanan's disastrous expedition was planned and executed [the Utah War]" was singled out for especially harsh rhetoric—"those connected with the Indian Department." Indian superintendents and agents were criticized for being "unbusinesslike," committing numerous "unlawful acts," and for seldom attending "to the duties of their office." The paper charged that Utah residents were left to feed and clothe "the Indians that were in their midst and around about them, and when the various bands have been hostile towards each other, or towards the whites, waged war upon them and committed depredations the superintendents and their subordinates, with few exceptions," the paper continued, the Indian Department took "little or no notice of their belligerent and lawless proceedings." In what might be an overstatement based on the emotion of the time, the editorial suggested that "superintendents and agents have held out inducements to the Indians to steal the stock of the settlers, informing them where they could find a market for all they stole which they did not need for their own use. It is notorious that when horses, mules and cattle have been stolen by the natives and known to have been thus taken and in their possession, but feeble or no efforts have been made, generally speaking, to recover the property and restore it to the owners; and seemingly the more lawless acts the Indians committed, the better were those government functionaries pleased with their doings." It was the opinion of the *Deseret News* that to list all of the "ridiculous and unlawful acts" committed "would require much time and space" and "would be exceedingly bulky." The only remedy available was to "sincerely hope that no other than honorable men will be appointed to or hold office in this Territory hereafter." If any more "miserable specimens of humanity be sent here in that capacity, it is hoped that they will be induced, shortly after their arrival, to retrace their steps or continue their journey across the continent."[31]

INDIAN TREATIES AND RESERVATIONS

The United States government officially recognized each Indian tribe as a separate nation, which meant that Indian relations were the responsibility of the federal government and not individual states or territories.[32] Legal issues, such as land titles, were usually determined through treaties. When Utah was established as a territory, though, the federal government "took over Utah without a single Ute land title settled and without any treaty of cession negotiated."[33] Land ownership was problematic from the earliest days of the territory. When Mormon pioneers arrived in 1847, the land they settled was claimed by Mexico and occupied by Indians—neither of whom could provide a transferable title. Further complicating the situation, when Mormon pioneers settled along the northern Wasatch Front, they chose land that was claimed by several tribes.[34]

Although each tribe was formally viewed as a separate sovereign nation, the treaty system never treated Indians equally or fairly. Indians were always "at a disadvantage. Treaties were written in English, and often the terms were not explained adequately to the Indians. Land ownership and government systems were concepts often foreign to Indians. And the government often negotiated

with persons whom it had selected but who were not the accepted leaders of the entire tribe."[35] Indians were viewed as a nuisance that needed to be contained, and treaties were the legal mechanism to do so. The first treaty—negotiated between Mormon leaders and Ute chiefs—was signed on December 30, 1849.[36] A second treaty, for which no record exists today, apparently followed in April 1850.[37]

The reality was that "the distressed condition of the Indians in this Territory" became worse each year as more settlers arrived and taxed the limited natural resources even further. Beginning in 1851, in an effort to both assist and contain Indians within the territory, Mormons established a series of Indian farms (reservations) to assist Indians in learning to feed themselves.[38] With Indian poverty and starvation increasing each year, the "extension of the farming system" was seen as "the proper remedy" to help Indians become self-sufficient again.[39] As Luther Mann Jr., one of Utah's numerous Indian agents, wrote, "Wild Indians, like wild horses, must be corralled upon reservations."[40] The government's goal was to "entirely reclaim them from savage life and cause them to become useful and good citizens."[41] To domesticate and feed the territory's Indian population, several government reservations were established in Utah before the Civil War. Using Mormon Indian farms as the foundation, three reservations—Spanish Fork reservation in Utah Valley south of Provo, the San Pete reservation in San Pete Valley, and the Corn Creek reservation located near Fillmore (approximately one hundred miles north of Mountain Meadows)—were established by the Utah Indian Agency in 1854. Two additional reservations, Deep Creek and Ruby Valley farms, were established during spring 1858, shortly before the Utah War's conclusion; those reservations became part of Nevada Territory in 1861.[42]

Living conditions on the reservations were always difficult as the newly minted Indian farmers battled drought, crickets, disease, hunger, government bureaucracy, and a host of cultural challenges, as well as the fact that the reservations themselves were often not maintained "in a promising condition."[43] In 1861, a Utah Indian agent complained that an army officer had "taken away many of the implements, such as ploughs, hoes, harrows, and wagons" from Indians at both the Corn Creek and San Pete reservations, which "quite discouraged the poor Indians" and caused them "to ask if the great father has thrown them away."[44] The result was that only a small percentage of Utah's Indians chose to relocate to a reservation by the beginning of the Civil War. Territorial Indian agents often sent optimistic annual reports regarding their efforts to alleviate Indian starvation and suffering, and those reports frequently had some version of the sentiment that the suffering, "I trust, will be obviated next year."[45] Indian agents appealed "in the sweet name of 'charity'" that something be done to better the condition of the Indians because their "present state is intolerable," but the agents recognized that genuine relief would not be forthcoming that year.[46]

In 1861, a few months after the Civil War began, Utah's three main Indian farms—Spanish Fork, Corn Creek, and San Pete—were declared as being deficient by Utah Indian agents. The Spanish Fork reservation was characterized as being "surrounded by a large Mormon population who have no particular regard for the welfare of the Indians from the fact that they have surveyed said reservation with the avowed intention

of taking possession of it." The Corn Creek reservation was "closely surrounded by white settlements which renders it very nearly valueless as an Indian reservation because of the Indians continually coming into contact with the whites," and the San Pete reservation was said to have been "worthless and abandoned by the superintendent in the spring of 1860."[47]

THE COMING OF THE CIVIL WAR

For most settlers in Utah Territory, Indian relations were probably more important than events in the distant civil war. As talk of Southern secession increased following Lincoln's November 1860 election to the presidency, a letter from Carson City, Utah Territory, published in January 1861 may have adequately summed up local residents' feelings regarding the coming war as well as their Indian problems. The writer stated, "We have nothing to do with Secession here, and it does not trouble us. When we want to fight all we have to do is to give one shot in the direction of an Indian camp, and then we got it [all the fighting we can handle]."[48]

The Civil War influenced Utah Territory's Indian policy in ways that could not have been envisioned at the beginning of the war. The last commander of the army's Department of Utah and Camp Floyd (renamed Fort Crittenden) was Colonel Philip St. George Cooke. A native of Virginia, Cooke (not to be confused with the similarly named and fellow Virginian Philip St. George Cocke—who served the Confederacy as a brigadier general) had ties to Mormons that stretched back to his service with the Mormon Battalion in the 1840s during the Mexican War.[49] Cooke's southern roots and secessionist family members—J. E. B. Stuart, the famous Confederate cavalry commander, was Cooke's son-in-law, and his own son, John Rogers Cooke, fought in the Army of Northern Virginia as an infantry brigade commander—caused some concern within the army, but Colonel Cooke declared his loyalty to the Union and earned the rank of brevet major general by the war's end. Under Cooke's command, Indian policy in Utah Territory had been dominated by frequently changing Indian superintendents and agents. That would change the following year with the arrival of Colonel Patrick Edward Connor and his California Volunteers.

In May 1861, hostile actions by Indians on the emigrant trails caused Utah's governor, Alfred Cumming, to request that a detachment of Union soldiers from Fort Crittenden be sent to guard the Overland Trail "for the protection of the Mail, Express, and emigrants,

Patrick Edward Connor (1820–91) advocated a disciplinarian approach toward Indians. Connor was promoted to brigadier general following the Bear River Massacre in January 1863. (Utah State Historical Society)

and, if need be, for the chastisement of the Indians."[50] Soldiers were not sent at that time but were ordered instead to leave Utah and join the growing fight in the East. In June, the *New York Times* reported that Utah's governor felt that removing the soldiers "would leave the inhabitants too much exposed to attacks from unfriendly Indians."[51] As the soldiers from Fort Crittenden marched east, Indians "helped themselves to a goodly toll of Army cattle"—stealing over one hundred head.[52] While a few Indians took advantage of the distraction offered by the Civil War, the majority did not. Some Indians even marched

in Salt Lake City with "Mormon pioneers and Nauvoo Legion militia" members during the city's 1861 Fourth of July parade.[53]

Utah's geographic isolation diminished in October 1861 when the telegraph reached Salt Lake City and linked the nation together. When the soldiers stationed in Utah were withdrawn in 1861 to fight the war in the East, the telegraph lines, mail lines, and emigrant trails, as well as the citizens who lived within the territory, were left with little protection. With the telegraph's arrival, Utah's new superintendent for Indian Affairs, Dyman S. Wood, warned Washington officials that the "establishment of the overland daily mail and telegraph lines and their recent completion through this Territory—consummations of such vital importance to the people throughout the Union—render it necessary that steps should be immediately taken by the government to prevent the possibility of their being interrupted by the Indians."[54]

Tensions in Utah continued to rise, and by mid-April 1862, Frank Fuller (acting governor), I. F. Kinney (Utah Supreme Court chief justice), Edward R. Fox (Utah's surveyor general), and officials from the Overland Mail Company and Pacific Telegraph Company appealed directly to Edwin M. Stanton, President Lincoln's secretary of war, for assistance in controlling "the Indians in Utah" who were robbing and destroying Overland Mail Company stations and killing cattle. They asked Secretary Stanton to "put in service" under the command of James D. Doty, Utah's superintendent of Indian Affairs, "a regiment [of] mounted rangers from inhabitants of the Territory."[55] Yet just three days later, Brigham Young informed John M. Bernhisel, Utah Territory's original delegate in the U.S. House of Representatives: "So far as I know, the Indians in Utah are unusually quiet and instead of 2,000 hostile Shoshones coming into our northern settlements, Washhekuk, their chief, has wintered in the city and near it, perfectly friendly, and is about to go to his band. Besides, the militia of Utah are ready and able, as they ever have been, to take care of all the Indians, and are able and willing to protect the mail line if called upon so to do. The statements of the aforesaid telegram are without foundation in truth so far as we know."[56]

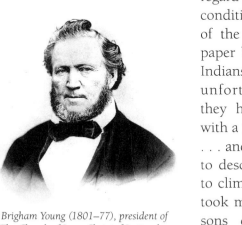

Brigham Young (1801–77), president of The Church of Jesus Christ of Latter-day Saints, advocated a gentler, more mentoring approach to Indian relations than the stern policies followed by the army. (Photo by Charles R. Savage, Harold B. Lee Library, Brigham Young University)

On April 28, Brigham Young received a telegram requesting that an active duty cavalry company be raised within Utah. During the ninety-day period (May–August 1862) that the Utah cavalry company, under the command of Captain Lot Smith, guarded a portion of the Overland Trail, the *New York Times* reported that Indians were "again troublesome" and had cut telegraph lines, stolen one hundred and fifty mail animals, killed employees of the mail company as well as some emigrants, and burned down one or two mail stations.[57] As the Utah Cavalry ended their active duty military service, the *Deseret News* reported that "during the past few weeks we have heard of several instances

of robbery and murder on Sublette's Cutoff [an alternate and fifty-three-mile shorter route on the Oregon Trail in Wyoming and southern Idaho], which exhibit[s] beyond all doubt that the Indians have thrown off all restraint, and indulge their thieving and murderous propensities without the slightest regard to the sex, age, or condition of the subjects of the attack." The newspaper blamed much of the Indians' behavior on "the unfortunate associations they had some years ago with a few renegade whites, . . . and as it is much easier to descend a hill than it is to climb one, the red skins took much easier their lessons of corruption than their lessons of right." The journalist was certain that until "another kind of relationship [is] established between the Indians and those who should see to them, no life will be secure on [the Sublette] road."[58]

In May 1862, after learning that soldiers would again be stationed in Utah, a *New York Times* reporter suggested that it was "much more likely that these Gentile Soldiers from California will create difficulties in Utah than that they will ever settle them. If the troops are designed to operate against the fragments of dying savages west of the Rocky Mountains, we are likely to have an Indian war on our hands this Summer, which, though barren enough of value, will be fertile enough of expenses."[59] At the beginning of August, an Indian chief named Little Soldier warned Doty and others that Shoshone and

Bannock Indians "inhabiting the northern part of this Territory and the southern portion of eastern Washington Territory have united their forces for the purpose of making war upon and committing depredations on the property of the white people." Little Soldier warned "very urgently" of a "great danger" and cautioned settlers to "have their guns with them at all times in the cañons and in their fields."[60] Also during August, James D. Doty, Utah's Indian Affairs superintendent and future governor, reported a series of Indian attacks: several immigrant wagon trains had been robbed; "many people killed;" "many murders committed;" and hundreds of head of livestock had been stolen.[61] Historian Brigham D. Madsen suggested that during that time perhaps "as many as 400 people lost their lives as a result of raids and murders at the hands of Shoshoni, Bannock, and Northern Paiute warriors on the Humboldt and Snake rivers."[62]

Chief Little Soldier, a Weber Ute, warned whites of a possible Indian uprising during the summer of 1862.
(Utah State Historical society)

Concern regarding real and potential Indian actions continued to build. By the end of August, Ben Holladay, who owned stage routes and the federal contract to deliver mail to Salt Lake City, reported, in a classic case of overstatement, that a "general war with nearly all the tribes of Indians east of the Missouri River is close at hand. I am expecting daily an interruption on my [mail] line, and nothing but prompt and decisive action on the part of government will prevent it."[63] Three weeks later, Charles E. Mix, acting commissioner of Indian Affairs in the Department of the Interior, issued an official warning to "all persons contemplating the crossing of the plains this fall, to Utah or the Pacific coast, that there is good reason to apprehend hostilities on the part of the Bannack and Shoshone or Snake Indians, as well as the Indians upon the plains and along the Platte river." Mix reported that those Indians were "numerous, powerful, and warlike" and could make crossing the plains "extremely perilous."[64] The following day, Luther Mann Jr., an Indian agent at Fort Bridger, charged Shoshone and Bannock Indians with "some of the most brutal murders ever perpetrated upon this continent" and stated he was certain "that a general outbreak of hostilities will take place throughout this entire region of country."[65]

It was into that tense environment that U.S. Army California Volunteers under the command of Colonel Connor entered Utah in late fall 1862 and established Camp Douglas on the foothills overlooking Salt Lake City. An eastern newspaper reported that Colonel Connor's "particular business is generally understood to be to keep the Western mail and emigrant route clear of Indians."[66]

DIFFERING POLICY APPROACHES

Connor's arrival brought into sharper focus two contrasting and coexistent philosophies regarding Indian relations. The first, epitomized by Brigham Young, might be termed a "welfare approach," and the second,

Chief Washakie (front, center) with members of his tribe. (Utah State Historical Society)

personified by Patrick Connor and the U.S. Army, was a "disciplinarian approach."

The welfare approach. Brigham Young taught that Indians should generally be treated with kindness. He believed that Indians did not commit aggressive acts "without provocation on the part of the whites."[67] His Indian philosophy may be summed up in an address he gave in the Salt Lake Tabernacle on March 8, 1863 (during a period of particularly tense relations with Colonel Connor and the soldiers stationed at Camp Douglas). From the Tabernacle podium, Young declared: "I will, comparatively speaking, take one plug of tobacco, a shirt and three cents' worth of paint, [give it to the Indians] and save more life and hinder more Indian depredations than they [the federal government] can by

expending millions of dollars vested in an army to fight and kill the Indians. Feed and clothe them a little and you will save life; fight them, and you pave the way for the destruction of the innocent. This will be found out after a while, but now it is not known except by comparatively a few."[68] Commenting on the federal government's poor record of honoring treaty obligations with Indians, Young stated:

I will ask every person who is acquainted with the history of the colonization of the Continent of North and South America, if they ever knew any colony of whites to get along any better with their savage neighbors than the inhabitants of Utah have done. Talk about making treaties with the

Indians! Has there been any one treaty with the Indians fulfilled in good faith by the Government? If there is one, I wish you would let me know. But we call them savages, while at the same time the whites too often do as badly as they have done, and worse, when difference of intelligence and training are taken into account. This has been so in almost every case of difficulty with the red skins. When soldiers have pounced upon these poor, ignorant, low, degraded, miserable creatures, mention a time, if you can, when they have spared their women and children. They have indiscriminately massacred the helpless, the blind, the old, the infant, and the mother.[69]

President Young suggested that his followers should "take the Indians, become acquainted with them and know their feelings and spirits and you will find as large a proportion that have good feelings and spirits as among the whites. . . . If you see an Indian give him a biscuit instead of half an ounce of lead, then they will be your friends."[70] In remarks made in Salt Lake City's public square to emigrants passing through Utah in July 1863, Young taught, "You have heard of Indian hostilities, . . . but you will have no trouble with them, if you will do right. I have always told the traveling public that it is much cheaper to feed the Indians than to fight them. Give them a little bread and meat, a little sugar, a little tobacco, or a little of anything you have which will conciliate their feelings and make them your friends. . . . I am satisfied that among the red men of the mountains and the forest you can find as many good, honest persons as among the Anglo Saxon race."[71]

Not surprisingly, Brigham Young's approach made him popular with many Indian bands. He was so popular, in fact, that O. H. Irish, Utah's superintendent of Indian Affairs, wrote in 1865, "The fact exists, however much some might prefer it should be otherwise, that he [Young] has pursued so kind and conciliatory a policy with the Indians that it has given him great influence over them."[72]

The disciplinarian approach. In contrast to Brigham Young's welfare-like approach, the U.S. army in general, and Colonel Connor specifically, often favored a strict policy of Indian correction and punishment. Connor's Indian policy was outlined to Major Edward McGarry, one of his subordinate officers, in a September 29, 1862, dispatch—issued even before his soldiers reached Salt Lake City. Connor instructed McGarry that if hostile Indians resisted capture "you will destroy them."[73] If any Indians were known to have committed murder, "immediately hang them, and leave their bodies thus exposed as an example of what evil-doers may expect while I command in this district. . . . This course may seem harsh and severe, but I desire that the order may be rigidly enforced, as I am satisfied that in the end it will prove the most merciful."[74] Connor also ordered McGarry, though, that in "no instance will you molest women or children."[75] Connor's views reflected those of General George Wright, commander of the Department of the Pacific and Connor's immediate supervisor, who wrote that Indian difficulties "have been growing worse and worse for years, and I am determined to settle them now for the last time. Every Indian you may capture, and who has been engaged in hostilities present or past, shall be hung on the spot. Spare the women and children."[76]

In 1863, Utah governor James D. Doty reflected the army's attitude when he shared with Colonel Connor that many Indians who were "suing for peace—protest that they are friendly to the whites and are afraid the soldiers will kill them. This is the condition in which I desire to see all the tribes in this Territory. They now realize the fact that the Americans are the masters of this country, and it is my purpose to make them continue to feel and to acknowledge it. Without this there can be no permanent peace here and no security upon the routes of travel. . . . Your troops have displaced the Mormon power over these Indians."[77]

James Duane Doty (1799–1865) filled several government appointments in Utah Territory—first as superintendent of Indian Affairs and then as governor (1863–65). He had previously served in the U.S. House of Representatives (from Wisconsin's Third Congressional District) and as governor of the Wisconsin Territory. (Utah State Historical Society)

INDIAN POLICY IN PRACTICE

Differences in the Indian policies of Colonel Connor and President Young quickly became apparent after the army's arrival. Neither the welfare approach nor the opposing disciplinarian approach, however, could resolve every trying situation. The reality was, of course, much more complicated. "The simple fact," as historian John Alton Peterson observed, "was that two honorable peoples were hopelessly trapped not only by their own cultures, goals, and interests but also by the larger political and national forces of their time. Both were victims of violent demographic and political changes that threatened their very existences as communities. . . . The simple truth is that, try as he [Brigham Young] might, he could not induce his people

to follow his policies,"[78] just as Patrick Connor recognized that force was not always justified. With few exceptions, though, once the army returned in 1862, the Mormons generally deferred to military authority regarding Indian relations and "the Saints tended merely to look on as bystanders."[79]

Little love was lost between Connor and Young. One contributing factor to Connor's dislike of almost all things Mormon is that he believed Latter-day Saints encouraged and instigated Indian raids throughout his area of responsibility. "Mormons," Connor complained to his superiors, "instead of assisting to punish Indians for bad conduct actually encouraged them. . . . From the evidence before me I am well satisfied that the Mormons are the real instigators [of trouble]."[80] He believed "the Indians are completely under his [Brigham Young's] control and do just as he tells them."[81]

Brigham Young, on the other hand, had little tolerance for the army's forceful and often violent Indian policy. Young was also a realist, though, and he recognized that "there are a few Indians that are wickedly disposed, just as it is among all white settlements" and encouraged his listeners to "keep your horses under a strong guard and then you will be safe."[82] Increasing Indian hostility throughout 1861 and 1862 meant that the optimistic "feed-rather-than-fight policy was given lip service" but there were increasing strains on adhering to it as settlers desired a

Looking east across the site of the Bear River Massacre. Colonel Connor and his soldiers came down the bank below where the ranch stands on the hill. (Utah State Historical Society)

more permanent resolution to their Indian problems.[83]

BEAR RIVER MASSACRE

Connor's disciplinarian Indian policy was forcibly demonstrated at the Battle of Bear River (now more frequently referred to as the Bear River Massacre) in January 1863 about 150 miles north of Camp Douglas near Preston, Idaho. Several historians have argued that given the circumstances of that time, the massacre was probably inevitable.[84] Six weeks before the battle, a report in the *Deseret News* expressed hope that "the Indians [will be] so thoroughly whipped that they will retire into the Bannock country [in Idaho], there to remain during the winter." If not, the reporter feared, settlements in northern Utah and southern Idaho "will not be as safe hereafter as they were before the expedition was sent out to punish them."[85] A few weeks

before the battle, thousands of Indians had assembled in the Bear River area to hold a Warm Dance—a gathering designed to "drive out the cold of winter and hasten the warmth of spring." Most of the Indians left the area following completion of the Warm Dance ceremonies.[86] If Connor had attacked earlier that month, many more Indians presumably would have been killed.

Two weeks before the battle, there were reports of murders committed by Indians "to avenge the blood of their comrades, who were killed by the soldiers" during the previous fall.[87] The day before the battle, the *Deseret News* reported that Colonel Connor and four companies of cavalry had marched through Salt Lake City "with the expectation, no doubt, of surprising the Indians." The report surmised that Connor's forces would "come up with the red skins about eighty or ninety miles from here on Bear River, and that with ordinary good luck the volunteers will 'wipe them out.' . . . The Indian has ever been a difficult subject to handle with nicety and justice."[88]

Some Indians reportedly escaped prior to the attack. During the night of January 27, 1863, an older Indian by the name of Tindup "foresaw the calamity which was about to take place. In a dream he saw his people being killed by pony soldiers. He told others of his dream and urged them to move out of the area that night." Some families believed him, left the area, and survived.[89]

Early in the morning of January 29, 1863, with Colonel Connor commanding, soldiers attacked and killed at least 224 Indians; only fourteen soldiers were lost.[90] The nineteenth-century Utah historian Hubert Howe Bancroft

observed, "Had the savages committed this deed, it would pass into history as a butchery or a massacre."[91] Commended by General Henry W. Halleck, U.S. army general-in-chief, for his "heroic conduct and brilliant victory on Bear River," Connor was promoted to brigadier general on March 29, 1863.[92]

FOLLOWING THE MASSACRE

Less than one week after the battle, the *Deseret News* reported that "Col. Connor and the Volunteers who went north last week to look after the Indians on the Bear River have, in a very short space of time, done a larger amount of Indian killing than ever fell to the lot of any single expedition of which we have any knowledge."[93] Had it occurred during a period of peace, the attack at Bear River

This painting, entitled Returning from the Battle of Bear River, *hangs in the Fort Douglas Officers Club. The man waving his hat is Orrin Porter Rockwell, and the other central figure on horseback is Colonel Patrick Edward Connor. (Utah State Historical Society)*

would have been front page news across the country. As it was, the battle received little notice in the American press outside of the West, because of more pressing news from the Civil War.

Connor worked quickly to capitalize on his victory. Shortly after the battle, which according to Bancroft "completely broke the power and spirit of the Indians,"[94] Connor held a conference with Indian leaders near Brigham City. His official dispatch to his superiors reported that he informed the Indians "that the troops had been sent to this region to protect good Indians and whites and equally to punish bad Indians and bad whites; that it was my determination to visit the most summary punishment—even to extermination—on Indians who committed depredations upon the lives and property of emigrants and settlers."[95] The prevalent popular sentiment regarding Indians was summed up in February 1863 by a *New York Times* report from Utah: "If an Indian be starving, he must and will steal. Notwithstanding, if Col. Connor succeeds in leaving a few of the really guilty Indians beneath the sod, it will be a good thing, and may teach a necessary and salutary lesson."[96] In April and May 1863, there were again reports of hostile Indian activity across northern Utah—west of Utah Lake, at Pleasant Grove, near Payson, outside North Ogden, five miles east of Brigham City, in southern Idaho, and along the Overland Trail mail routes.[97]

In December 1863, during his annual message to the legislative assembly of Utah, Amos Reed, the territory's acting governor, claimed that the soldiers had achieved a "termination of hostilities and depredations by the Indians," but he informed the legislature that the "condition of the Utah Indians in

this Territory will [still] require your future attention. Roaming as they do through all our settlements south of this City, they are and have been since the settlement of the Territory, a great annoyance to, and a continual, burthensome tax upon the people."[98]

News of the January 1863 massacre at Bear River spread quickly among both Indian and white populations, and it generally had the effect that General Connor desired. Several treaties were signed in rapid succession: a treaty at Fort Bridger with Shoshone Indians (signed July 2, 1863), a treaty of Box Elder (signed July 30, 1863), a treaty at Tuilla (Tooele) Valley (signed on October 12, 1863—that treaty contained a special provision that required that "Indians agree to give up their roving life and settle upon a reservation whenever the President of the United States shall deem it expedient for them"), and a treaty at Soda Springs (signed on October 14, 1863).[99]

Then, as now, Congress often moved slowly. Although President Lincoln had signed an executive order in October 1861 creating a large Indian reservation in Utah at Uintah Valley, it was not until May 5, 1864, that Congress formally designated Uintah Valley as a reservation—a location that the governor of Utah declared was "most admirably adapted to that purpose."[100] In February 1865, a few months before the end of the Civil War, Congress finally acted to extinguish the "Indian title to lands in the Territory of Utah suitable for agricultural and mineral purposes."[101] While the federal government normally moved "quickly to extinguish title through formal treaties before or in the early stages of white settlement," in this instance the government "as a result of Utah's unique situation, purposely allowed eighteen years

Two Native American Utes standing in front of a tepee wearing decorative clothing including hair pipe breastplates, chokers, and beaded leggings (between 1860–70). (Denver Public Library)

to pass before extinguishing native title and providing for Indian removal to reservations. Even then, Congress authorized the move only because of an expected massive influx of gentiles into the territory."[102]

Connor and others felt that subsequent events had justified the attack at Bear River. One year after the massacre, the *New York Times* reported that "the Bear River and other conflicts . . . [pre]pared the way for the subsequent treaties and the present burial of the tomahawk, and were, in short, the main causes of the peace which is now enjoyed in the Territory and around its borders."[103] During July 1864, General Connor reported: "The policy pursued toward the Indians has had a most happy effect. That policy, as you are aware, involved certain and speedy punishment for past offenses, compelling them to

sue for a suspension of hostilities, and on the resumption of peace, kindness and leniency toward the redskins. They fully understand that honesty and peace constitute their best and safest policy."[104] Yet by February 1865, just seven months later, General Connor reported that Indians had "again returned in increased force" and suggested that the "troops [stationed in Utah] are insufficient to contend with them."[105]

An 1865 article in the *New York Times* commented on the continuing cycle of violence between Indians and white settlers: "The Indian's wrath is poured out, with indiscriminate discrimination, upon the passing emigrant, or the industrious settler, and thus a general character is given in a murderous struggle which commenced with a few. . . . They will do a little stealing, get saucy, impudent, presuming, and when very 'mad' will be cruel and kill." The violent cycle sometimes escalated when "whites, irritated and provoked, even when the Indians do not murder, but steal only, shoot at the marauders, if a sight can be obtained of them."[106] Utah's 1865 superintendent of Indian affairs, Orsemus H. Irish, offered his view that the "cruelties practiced by hostile savages have prejudiced our people against the whole race. The emigrants . . . and the officers and soldiers who are here for their protection, are almost entirely in favor of the extermination of all Indians. . . . Under my observation and within my own experience, *I know of only one case of Indian outrage and depredation that has not commenced in the misconduct of the whites.*"[107]

In 1865 the federal government took action to resolve land ownership questions in Utah. William P. Dole, commissioner of Indian Affairs, directed Superintendent Irish in February 1865 to negotiate additional Indian treaties, as required, to place Utah's remaining Indians onto a reservation. The commissioner additionally instructed Irish that because the government had not previously accepted Indian titles to any land in Utah, he was to ensure that the resulting treaties were framed so that the Indians relinquished "the right of occupancy" to the lands identified by Congress and moved to the reservation land "reserved for their use."[108] Not all of the federal officers involved with the resulting treaty negotiations were pleased to resolve the confusion that existed in Utah regarding land titles. Some government officials "declared, that rather than associate with Brigham Young on such an occasion, they would [prefer to] have the negotiation fail; that they would rather the Indians, than the Mormons, would have the land."[109]

In the resulting Spanish Fork Treaty, signed on June 8, 1865, Indians relinquished the "right of possession to all of the lands within Utah Territory occupied by them . . . with the exception of the Uintah valley which [was] to be reserved for their exclusive use." The treaty required Indians to give up their Spanish Fork, San Pete, and Corn Creek reservations. It also gave the president of the United States authority to place other bands of "friendly Indians" on the Uintah reservation without prior Indian approval, and the Indian signatories agreed to move to the reservation "within one year after ratification of the treaty."[110] Indians were to receive annual payments of $25,000 for ten years, followed by $20,000 per year for the next twenty years, and finally $15,000 for an additional thirty years. The United States Congress did not ratify the treaty, though, and the government failed to pay the promised amounts.[111]

AFTER THE CIVIL WAR

While the Civil War ended in 1865, Utah's Indian problems did not. Toward the conclusion of the Civil War, a Utah-based *New York Times* reporter complained, "What to do with the red men is still a problem which, it appears, cannot be satisfactorily solved. For this Spring there seems to be as much chance of difficulties with them, all around, as ever. We hear of Indian troubles [in Utah] from every quarter nearly."[112] In the midst of the Civil War, an article about Utah in the *New York Times* proclaimed that the "Indians here, as elsewhere, dwindle away before the onward march of the white man. Chief after chief is passing away from the small Utah bands, until it is said to be difficult to find eligible and aspiring braves to fill the vacancies."[113] Indians found an able commander and strategist, however, in the Ute chief Antonga (called Black Hawk by the whites), who was able to consolidate factions of the Ute, Paiute, and Navajo tribes.[114] The same day—April 9, 1865—that General Robert E. Lee surrendered to General Ulysses S. Grant at Appomattox, Virginia, is often cited as the beginning of Utah's Black Hawk Indian War. The war continued off and on, primarily in central and southern Utah, for the next seven years. Most of the conflict and skirmishes between Indians and white settlers occurred between 1865 and 1867. In 1866, "Indian attacks were so damaging and threats so ominous" that Mormon militia leaders required settlers to vacate twenty-seven settlements in nine Utah counties.[115] Dozens of Utah settlers were killed during the Black Hawk War. The number of Indians killed is unknown, although it was no doubt higher than the number of settler deaths.

While there were continuing Indian problems in Utah Territory throughout the Civil War, they dramatically escalated in the years immediately after the war. By Civil War standards, the total deaths on both sides were insignificant, but the Black Hawk War had an influence on the history and settlement of central and southern Utah that was greater than the loss of life would imply. The war was

the last major challenge that Indians in Utah Territory mounted against white authority and encroachment. The last Utes were moved onto the Uintah Reservation by 1882, marking the completion of a thirty-five year effort to "reclaim and civilize the Indians" and place them on reservations "for their permanent and happy homes."[116] The Uintah reservation is still in existence (and is known today as the Uintah and Ouray Reservation). Covering over 4.5 million acres, it is the second-largest Indian reservation in the United States.[117]

Utah's Indian society went into a steady and irreversible decline after 1847 that culminated in marginalization on isolated reservations. The decades when white and Indian societies lived in close proximity to each other brought successes and failures. Charity and violence were both in evidence as the cultures intermingled and attempted to live with each other. Benjamin Davies, an 1861 superintendent of Indian Affairs in Utah, perhaps said it best when he inadvertently complimented the local Mormon population by noting that Utah's Indians were "not so demoralized and corrupted as those who have been brought into closer association with white men in other localities."[118] It is difficult to envision how things could have ended differently.

Kenneth L. Alford is an associate professor of Church history and doctrine at Brigham Young University.

NOTES

1. While current usage often favors the term "Native Americans" or "native peoples," the remainder of this article will use the term "Indians" to conform to common nineteenth-century usage. It was also common at that time to refer to settlers simply as "whites." See, for example, William P. Dole to O. H.

Irish, "Utah Superintendency," March 28, 1865, in *Report of the Commissioner of Indian Affairs for the Year 1865* (Washington, DC: Government Printing Office, 1865), 148–49.

2. The secretary's report continued: "The large tribes of Cherokees, Chickasaws, and Choctaws situated

in the southern superintendency have suspended all intercourse with the agents of the United States." See "Extract from the report of the Secretary of the Interior in relation to Indian affairs," in *Report of the Commissioner of Indian Affairs, Accompanying the Annual Report of the Secretary of the Interior, for the Year 1861* (Washington, DC: Government Printing Office, 1861), 3.

3. Edward E. Dale, "Some Letters of General Stand Watie," *Chronicles of Oklahoma* 1, no. 1 (January 1921): 30–59. See also Frank Cunningham, *General Stand Watie's Confederate Indians* (Norman, OK: University of Oklahoma Press, 1998).

4. Spelling of Indian names varied widely. An 1849 Indian history refers to the Utes as "Yutas." See John Frost, *Thrilling Adventures among the Indians: Comprising the Most Remarkable Personal Narratives of Events in the Early Indian Wars, as Well as of Incidents in the Recent Indian Hostilities in Mexico and Texas* (Philadelphia: J. W. Bradley, 1849), 294. The historian Hubert Howe Bancroft refers to the Ute Indians as "Yutas, Utaws, or Youtas" and notes that others also referred to them as the "Eutaws." Hubert Howe Bancroft, *The Works of Hubert Howe Bancroft: The Native Races*, vol. 1 (San Francisco: The History Company, 1882), 465. Duncan lists eleven major Ute bands. See Clifford Duncan, "The Northern Utes of Utah," in Forrest S. Cuch, ed., *A History of Utah's American Indians* (Salt Lake City: Utah State Division of Indian Affairs and Division of History, 2003), 176–78. See John Alton Peterson, *Utah's Black Hawk War* (Salt Lake City: University of Utah Press, 1998), xiv, for an additional listing of tribal lands in nineteenth-century Utah Territory. Also see Ned Blackhawk, introduction in *Violence Over the Land: Indians and Empires in the Early American West* (Cambridge, MA: Harvard University Press, 2006).

5. Jacob Forney to Hon. C. E. Mix, "Utah Superintendency," in *Report of the Commissioner of Indian Affairs, Accompanying the Annual Report of the Secretary of the Interior, for the Year 1858* (Washington, DC: Wm. A. Harris, 1858), 210. According to the 1861 Indian Affairs Report, the following Ute bands lived in Utah: "Wiminanches, Asivoriches, Sampuches, Cawaupugos, Tupanagos, Pa-uches and Povantes." J. F. Collins to Hon. Wm. P. Dole, "Indian Superintendency," in *Report of the Commissioner of Indian Affairs, . . . 1861*, 21, 125.

6. J. F. Collins to Hon. Wm. P. Dole, "Indian Superintendency," in *Report of the Commissioner of Indian Affairs, . . . 1861*, 21, 125.

7. Benjamin Davies to Hon. Wm. P. Dole, "Utah Superintendency," June 30, 1861, in *Report of the Commissioner of Indian Affairs, . . . 1861*, 132.

8. J. S. Calhoun to Orlando Brown, March 29, 1850, in *Annual Report of the Commissioner of Indian Affairs, Transmitted with the Message of the President at the Opening of the Second Session of the Thirty-Second Congress, 1850* (Washington, DC: Office of the Commissioner of Indian Affairs, 1850), 99.

9. J. Forney to Hon. A. B. Greenwood, "Utah Superintendency," September 29, 1859, in *Report of the Commissioner of Indian Affairs, . . . 1858*, 365.

10. J. S. Calhoun to Orlando Brown, March 29, 1850, 99.

11. See Dyman S. Wood to Major H. Martin, October 1, 1861, and J. F. Collins to Wm. P. Dole, October 8, 1861, in *Report of the Commissioner of Indian Affairs, . . . 1861*, 137, 125; see also A. Humphreys to Charles E. Mix, "Utah Agency," November 12, 1860, in *Report of the Commissioner of Indian Affairs Accompanying the Annual Report of the Secretary of the Interior, for the Year 1860* (Washington, DC: George W. Bowman, 1860), 170; and John C. Burche to James W. Nye, August 1, 1864, in *Report of the Commissioner of Indian Affairs, for the Year 1864* (Washington, DC: Government Printing Office, 1865), 144.

12. Lieut. J. W. Gunnison, *The Mormons, or, Latter-day Saints, in the Valley of the Great Salt Lake: A History of Their Rise and Progress, Peculiar Doctrines, and Present Condition, and Prospects, Derived from Personal Observation, During a Residence Among Them* (Philadelphia: Lippincott, Grambo & Co., 1852), 30.

13. Clifford Duncan, "The Northern Utes of Utah," in *A History of Utah's American Indians*, ed. Forrest S. Cuch (Salt Lake City: Utah State Division of Indian Affairs and Division of History, 2003), 187.

14. Gunnison, *The Mormons*, 147.

15. Gunnison, *The Mormons*, 146.

16. Blackhawk, *Violence Over the Land*, 244.

17. Chief Wakara is also known as Walkara. See Duncan, *Northern Utes*, 184.

18. Gunnison, *The Mormons*, 147.

19. Blackhawk, *Violence Over the Land*, 254.

20. Wm. P. Dole to Hon. Caleb B. Smith, "Report of the Commissioner of Indian Affairs," November 27,

1861, in *Report of the Commissioner of Indian Affairs, . . . 1861*, 21.

21. Wm. P. Dole to Hon. Caleb B. Smith, "Report of the Commissioner of Indian Affairs," November 27, 1861, 20.

22. Wm. P. Dole to Hon. Caleb B. Smith, "Report of the Commissioner of Indian Affairs," November 27, 1861, 21.

23. Gunnison, *The Mormons*, 150.

24. Gunnison, *The Mormons*, 150.

25. "War between the Cheyennes and Shoshone Indians," *Deseret News*, July 10, 1861, 1.

26. Blackhawk, *Violence Over the Land*, 231.

27. Gunnison, *The Mormons*, 146.

28. J. Forney to Hon. A. B. Greenwood, "Utah Superintendency," September 29, 1859, in *Report of the Commissioner of Indian Affairs, Accompanying the Annual Report of the Secretary of the Interior, for the Year 1859* (Washington, DC: George W. Bowman, 1859), 367.

29. A. Humphreys to Hon. Charles E. Mix, "Utah Agency," November 12, 1860, in *Report of the Commissioner of Indian Affairs, Accompanying the Annual Report of the Secretary of the Interior, for the Year 1860* (Washington, DC: George W. Bowman, 1860), 170.

30. Duncan, *Northern Utes*, 187.

31. "Federal Officials," *Deseret News*, October 23, 1861, 5.

32. The unique status of Indians was acknowledged in the Constitution of the United States. See U.S. Const. art. I, § 2 and 8; amend. XIV, § 2 (ratified in July 1868) also addresses Indians.

33. Duncan, *Northern Utes*, 188.

34. Blackhawk, *Violence of the Land*, 246.

35. Duncan, *Northern Utes*, 197.

36. "Appendix—Special Estimate of Funds, Etc." in *Annual Report of the Commissioner of Indian Affairs, . . . 1850*, 156.

37. Jared Farmer, *On Zion's Mount: Mormons, Indians, and the American Landscape* (Cambridge, MA: Harvard University Press, 2008), 76.

38. Duncan, *Northern Utes*, 189.

39. *Report of the Commissioner of Indian Affairs, . . . 1859*, 369.

40. Luther Mann Jr. to O. H. Irish, "Utah Superintendency," September 28, 1865, in *Report of the Commissioner of Indian Affairs . . . 1865*, 159.

41. Wm. P. Dole to Hon. Caleb B. Smith, "Report of the Commissioner of Indian Affairs," November 27,

1861, in *Report of the Commissioner of Indian Affairs, . . . 1861* (Washington, DC: U.S. Government Printing Office, 1861), 19.

42. *Report of the Commissioner of Indian Affairs, . . . 1859*, 367–69. An additional reservation, in Uintah Valley, was established by an act of Congress in 1864. See William P. Dole to O. H. Irish, "Utah Superintendency," March 28, 1865, in *Report of the Commissioner of Indian Affairs . . . 1865*, 148.

43. *Report of the Commissioner of Indian Affairs, . . . 1859*, 368.

44. Dyman S. Wood to Major H. Martin, "Utah Superintendency," October 1, 1861, in *Report of the Commissioner of Indian Affairs, . . . 1861* (Washington, DC: Government Printing Office, 1861), 137.

45. J. Forney to Hon. A. B. Greenwood, "Utah Superintendency," September 29, 1959, in *Report of the Commissioner of Indian Affairs, . . . 1859*, 369.

46. F. Dodge to Jacob Forney, "Carson Valley Agency," January 4, 1959, in *Report of the Commissioner of Indian Affairs, . . . 1859*, 377.

47. A. Humphreys to Wm. P. Dole, "Utah Superintendency," September 30, 1861, in *Report of the Commissioner of Indian Affairs, . . . 1861*, 140.

48. "From Utah," *The Columbus [Ohio] Gazette*, March 15, 1861, 2. The article notes that the letter was written January 28, 1861.

49. Philip St. George Cooke (June 13, 1809–March 20, 1895), Cullum number 492, graduated from the United States Military Academy (USMA) with the Class of 1827—twenty-third of thirty-eight cadets. Philip St. George Cocke (April 17, 1809–December 26, 1861), Cullum number 667, graduated from USMA in 1832—sixth in his class of forty-five cadets. Cocke committed suicide following the Battle of First Manassas (Bull Run). See Michael J. Krisman, ed., *Register of Graduates and Former Cadets of the United States Military Academy* (West Point, NY: Association of USMA Graduates, 1980), 223, 227.

50. "Affairs in Utah," *New York Times*, June 2, 1861, 2.

51. "News of the Day," *New York Times*, June 24, 1861, 4.

52. "Affairs in Utah," *New York Times*, August 24, 1861, 5.

53. "Affairs in Utah," *New York Times*, July 26, 1861, 3.

54. Dyman S. Wood to Major H. Martin, "Utah Superintendency," October 1, 1861, in *Report of the Commissioner of Indian Affairs, . . . 1861*, 135.

55. Frank Fuller, I. F. Kinney, Edward R. Fox, Frederick Cook, H. S. R. Rowe, E. R. Purple, Joseph Holladay,

and W. B. Hibbad to Edwin M. Stanton, April 11, 1862, in *Report of the Commissioner of Indian Affairs for the Year 1862* (Washington, DC: Government Printing Office, 1863), 212.

56. Brigham Young to John M. Bernhisel, April 14, 1862, in *Report of the Commissioner of Indian Affairs for the Year 1862* (Washington, DC: Government Printing Office, 1862), 213.

57. "The Indians in Utah Again Troublesome," *New York Times*, July 4, 1862; "Affairs in Utah," *New York Times*, July 4, 1862, 3.

58. "The Indians on Sublette's Cut Off," *Deseret News*, September 17, 1862, 5.

59. "A Needless War in Prospect," *New York Times*, May 26, 1862, 4.

60. James Duane Doty, August 5, 1862, in *Report of the Commissioner of Indian Affairs for the Year 1862*, 213–14.

61. James Duane Doty to W. P. Dole, "Utah Superintendency," August 13, 1862, in *Report of the Commissioner of Indian Affairs for the Year 1862*, 211.

62. Brigham D. Madsen, *The Shoshoni Frontier and the Bear River Massacre* (Salt Lake City: University of Utah Press, 1985), 17.

63. Ben Halladay to M. P. Blair, August 26, 1862, in *Report of the Commissioner of Indian Affairs for the Year 1862*, 215.

64. Charles E. Mix, "To the Public," September 19, 1862, in *Report of the Commissioner of Indian Affairs for the Year 1862*, 215.

65. Luther Mann Jr. to James D. Doty, September 20, 1862, in *Report of the Commissioner of Indian Affairs for the Year 1862*, 215.

66. "Affairs in Utah," *New York Times*, September 7, 1862, 3.

67. Brigham Young Office Journals, April 23, 1862, in Richard S. Van Wagoner, *The Complete Discourses of Brigham Young*, vol. 4 (Salt Lake City: The Smith-Pettit Foundation, 2009), 2004.

68. Brigham Young, in *Journal of Discourses* (London: Latter-day Saints' Book Depot, 1854–86), 10:104–11.

69. Brigham Young, in *Journal of Discourses,* 10:104–11.

70. Brigham Young Collection, June 30, 1863 (Salt Lake City: LDS Church Archives) in *The Complete Discourses of Brigham Young*, vol. 4, ed. Richard S. Van Wagoner (Salt Lake City: The Smith-Pettit Foundation, 2009), 2142.

71. "Remarks by President Brigham Young, to the Emigrants on the Public Square, in Salt Lake City, July 8, 1863," *Deseret News*, July 15, 1863, 2.

72. O. H. Irish to Wm. P. Dole, "Utah Superintendency," June 29, 1865, in *Report of the Commissioner of Indian Affairs . . . 1865*, 150.

73. P. Edw. Connor to Maj. Edward McGarry, September 29, 1862. *The War of the Rebellion: A Compilation of the Official Records of the Union and Confederate Armies*, series I, vol. L, part 2 (Washington, DC: Government Printing Office, 1880–1900), 144 (hereafter cited as *WOTR1*).

74. *WOTR1*, 144.

75. *WOTR1*, 144.

76. G. Wright to Col. Francis J. Lippitt, April 7, 1862. *The War of the Rebellion: A Compilation of the Official Records of the Union and Confederate Armies*, series I, vol. L, part 1 (Washington, DC: Government Printing Office, 1880–1901), 992 (hereafter cited as *WOTR2*.)

77. James Duane Doty to General [G. Wright], August 9, 1863. *WOTR1*, 583.

78. John Alton Peterson, *Utah's Black Hawk War* (Salt Lake City: University of Utah Press, 1998), 7, 12.

79. Madsen, *Shoshoni Frontier*, 176.

80. Report of Brig. Gen. P. Edward Connor, April 9, 1863. *WOTR2*, 198.

81. Report of Brig. Gen. P. Edward Connor, April 9, 1863. *WOTR2*, 199.

82. Brigham Young Collection, June 30, 1863 (Salt Lake City: LDS Church Archives), in *Complete Discourses of Brigham Young*, 4:2142.

83. Madsen, *Shoshoni Frontier*, 155.

84. See, for example, Madsen, *Shoshoni Frontier*, 24.

85. "Another Expedition after Indians," *Deseret News*, December 10, 1862, 4.

86. Duncan, *Northern Utes,* 33.

87. "More Indian Murders," *Deseret News,* January 14, 1863, 8. A December 1862 newspaper article reported that one of the Indians "who was thus shot was a Bannack, and is represented to be a truthful, faithful boy, who has rendered good service on more than one occasion in intercourse between the white, and the Bannacks and other Indian tribes." See "An Outrageous Occurrence," *Deseret News*, December 31, 1862, 4.

88. "Expedition for the Arrest of Indian Chiefs," *Deseret News*, January 28, 1863, 4.

89. Duncan, *Northern Utes*, 34.

90. Report of Col. P. Edward Connor, February 20, 1863. *WOTR2*, 184–87.

91. Hubert Howe Bancroft, *History of Utah* (Salt Lake City: Bookcraft, 1964), 631–32.

92. Report of Col. P. Edward Connor, *WOTR1*, 187.

93. "The Fight with the Indians," *Deseret News*, February 4, 1863, 5.

94. Bancroft, *History of Utah*, 632.

95. "Affairs in Utah," *New York Times*, August 2, 1863, 2.

96. "From Utah," *New York Times*, February 22, 1863, 8.

97. "Expedition After Indians," *Deseret News*, April 15, 1853, 8. "Indian War in Idaho," *Deseret News*, May 13, 1853, 4. "Another Fight with Indians," *Deseret News*, May 13, 1863, 4. "Indian Depredations in the Northern Counties," *Deseret News*, May 20, 1863, 3.

98. Amos Reed, "Governor's Message," December 14, 1863, in *Journals of the Legislative Assembly of the Territory of Utah. Thirteenth Annual Session, for the Years 1863–64* (Salt Lake City: Elias Smith, 1861), 18.

99. O. H. Irish to D. N. Cooley, "Utah Superintendency," September 9, 1865, in *Report of the Commissioner of Indian Affairs . . . 1865*, 143–48. See also Madsen, *Shoshoni Frontier*, 212.

100. "Governor's Annual Message," *Union Vedette*, December 18, 1863, 1; Duncan, *Northern Utes*, 190.

101. William P. Dole to O. H. Irish, "Utah Superintendency," March 28, 1865, in *Report of the Commissioner of Indian Affairs . . . 1865*, 148.

102. Peterson, *Utah's Black Hawk War*, 29.

103. "Affairs in Utah," *New York Times*, February 28, 1864, 2.

104. P. Edw. Connor to Lieut. Col. R. C. Drum, July 1, 1864. *WOTR1*, 887.

105. P. E. Connor to Col. R. C. Drum, February 10, 1865. *WOTR1*, 1131.

106. "From Utah," *New York Times*, June 30, 1865, 2.

107. O. H. Irish to D. N. Cooley, "Utah Superintendency," September 9, 1865, in *Report of the Commissioner for Indian Affairs . . . 1865*, 147; emphasis in original.

108. Wm. P. Dole to O. H. Irish, "Utah Superintendency," March 28, 1865, in *Report of the Commissioner of Indian Affairs . . . 1865*, 148.

109. O. H. Irish to Wm. P. Dole, "Utah Superintendency," June 29, 1865, in *Report of the Commissioner of Indian Affairs . . . 1865*, 150.

110. O. H. Irish to Wm. P. Dole, "Utah Superintendency," June 29, 1865, in *Report of the Commissioner of Indian Affairs . . . 1865*, 150.

111. Duncan, *Northern Utes*, 190.

112. "From Utah," *New York Times*, June 30, 1865, 2.

113. "Affairs in Utah," *New York Times*, January 27, 1862, 6.

114. Antonga "like hundreds of his people, evidently was baptized into the Mormon church." Peterson, *Utah's Black Hawk War*, 1, 10.

115. Carlton Culmsee, *Utah's Black Hawk War* (Logan, UT: Utah State University Press, 1973), 12–13, 27. The nine Utah counties involved were Summit, Wasatch, Sanpete, Sevier, Piute, Beaver, Iron, Kane and Washington. Using Utah's current county map, the total would be ten counties—as Garfield County was then part of Kane County. Culmsee notes (page 13): "At times Sevier and Piute Counties and the Long Valley Northern portion of Kane [County] were completely abandoned. Major or extensive portions of the other six counties were abandoned."

116. Wm. P. Dole to Hon. Caleb B. Smith, "Report of the Commissioner of Indian Affairs," November 27, 1861, in *Report of the Commissioner of Indian Affairs, . . . 1861*, 20. Duncan, *Northern Utes*, 195.

117. The website "The Ute Indian Tribe," http://www.utetribe.com/ states: "The Uintah and Ouray reservation is located in Northeastern Utah (Fort Duchesne) approximately 150 miles east of Salt Lake City on U.S. Highway 40. The reservation is located within a three-county area known as the "Uintah Basin." It is the second largest Indian Reservation in the United States that covers over 4.5 million acres. The Utes have a tribal membership [in 2011] of 3,157 and over half of its membership lives on the Reservation. They operate their own tribal government and oversee approximately 1.3 million acres of trust land."

118. Benjamin Davies to Wm. P. Dole, "Utah Superintendency," June 30, 1861, in *Report of the Commissioner of Indian Affairs, . . . 1861*, 133.

Patrick Edward Connor, shown after his promotion to general, established Camp Douglas in 1862 and commanded the soldiers who participated in the Bear River Massacre. (Photo by Flaglor, Utah State Historical Society)

CHAPTER 13

Harold Schindler

THE BEAR RIVER MASSACRE

NEW HISTORICAL EVIDENCE

Controversy has dogged the Bear River Massacre from the first.

The event in question occurred when, on January 29, 1863, volunteer soldiers under Colonel Patrick Edward Connor attacked a Shoshoni camp on the Bear River, killing nearly three hundred men, women, and children. The bloody encounter culminated years of increasing tension between whites and the Shoshonis, who, faced with dwindling lands and food sources, had resorted to theft in order to survive. By the time of the battle, confrontations between the once-friendly Indians and the settlers and emigrants were common.

So it was that "in deep snow and bitter cold"

Connor set forth from Fort Douglas with nearly three hundred men, mostly cavalry, late in January 1863. Intelligence reports had correctly located Bear Hunter's village on Bear River about 140 miles north of Salt Lake City, near present Preston, Idaho. Mustering three hundred warriors by

Connor's [p. 301] estimate, the camp lay in a dry ravine about forty feet wide and was shielded by twelve-foot embankments in which the Indians had cut firing steps. . . .

When the soldiers appeared shortly after daybreak on January 27 [sic], the Shoshonis were waiting in their defenses.

About two-thirds of the command succeeded in fording ice-choked Bear River. While Connor tarried to hasten the crossing, Major [Edward] McGarry dismounted his troops and launched a frontal attack. It was repulsed with heavy loss. Connor assumed control and shifted tactics, sending flanking parties to where the ravine issued from some hills. While detachments sealed off the head and mouth of the ravine, others swept down both rims, pouring a murderous enfilading fire into the lodges below. Escape blocked, the Shoshonis fought desperately in their positions until slain, often in hand-to-hand combat. Of those who broke free, many were shot while swimming the icy river. By mid-morning the fighting had ended.

On the battlefield the troops counted 224 bodies, including that of Bear Hunter, and knew that the toll was actually higher. They destroyed 70 lodges and quantities of provisions, seized 175 Indian horses, and captured 160 women and children, who were

A young Shoshoni brave. Shoshonis bore the brunt of the January 1863 attack. (Photo by William H. Jackson, Utah State Historical Society)

left in the wrecked village with a store of food. The Californians had been hurt, too: 14 dead, 4 officers and 49 men wounded (of whom 1 officer and 6 men died later), and 75 men with frostbitten feet. Even so, it had been a signal victory, winning Connor the fulsome praise of the War Department and prompt promotion to brigadier general.[1]

Controversies over the battle have tainted it ever since. For one thing, Chief Justice John F. Kinney of the Utah Supreme Court had issued warrants for the arrest of several Shoshoni chiefs for the murder of a miner. But critics have questioned whether the warrants could legally be served, since the chiefs were no longer within the court's jurisdiction.[2] The legality of the federal writs was irrelevant, however, to Colonel Connor, commander of the California Volunteers at Camp Douglas.

At the onset of his expedition against the Bear River band, he announced that he was satisfied that these Indians were among those who had been murdering emigrants on the Overland Mail Route for the previous fifteen years. Because of their apparent role as "principal actors and leaders in the horrid massacres of the past summer, I determined . . . to chastise them if possible." He told U.S. marshal Isaac L. Gibbs that Gibbs could accompany the troops with his federal warrants if he wanted, but "it [p. 302] was not intended to have any prisoners."[3]

However—and this is another controversy—there have been many who have questioned whether Connor's soldiers actually tangled with the guilty Indians.

Recently discovered evidence, while it resolves neither of those debates, does address a more fundamental aspect of the encounter that ultimately claimed the lives of twenty-three soldiers and nearly three hundred American Indians: that is, Bear River began as a battle, but it most certainly degenerated into a massacre. We have that information from a participant, Sergeant William L. Beach of Company K, 2nd Cavalry Regiment, California Volunteers, who wrote an account and sketched a map just sixteen days after the engagement, while he was recuperating from the effects of frozen feet.

The sergeant specifically describes a crucial moment in the four-hour struggle: the point at which the soldiers broke through the Shoshoni fortifications and rushed "into

Battle action superimposed on a picture of the battlefield. (Utah State Historical Society)

their very midst when the work of death commenced in real earnest." Having seen a dozen or so of his comrades shot down in the initial attack, Beach watched as the tide of battle fluctuated until a desperate enemy finally sought to surrender.

> Midst the roar of guns and sharp report of Pistols could be herd the cry for quarters but their was no quarters that day. . . . The fight lasted more than four hours and appeared more like a frollick than a fight the wounded cracking jokes with the frozen some frozen so bad that they could not load their guns used them as clubs.

The "cry for quarters" fell upon deaf ears as the bloody work continued.

In his account, the cavalry sergeant also provided valuable insights concerning the movement of troops as the attack took shape; he carefully recorded the position of each unit and located the Indian camp and its defenders on a map of the battlefield. He also charted the course of the river at the time of the engagement and pinpointed the soldiers' ford across the Bear. From his map, historians learn for the first time that some of the Shoshonis broke from the fortified ravine on horseback.[4] Beach traced the warriors' retreat on the map with a series of lowercase "i" symbols.

The manuscript and map came to light in February 1997 after Jack Irvine of Eureka, California, read an Associated Press story in the *San Francisco Chronicle* about Brigham D. Madsen, University of Utah emeritus professor of history, and learned that Madsen had written *The Shoshoni Frontier and the Bear River Massacre*.[5] Irvine, a collector of Northwest documents and photographs, telephoned Madsen that night and told him that he had collected Sergeant Beach's narrative and map. He sent the historian a photocopy and so opened a sporadic correspondence and telephone

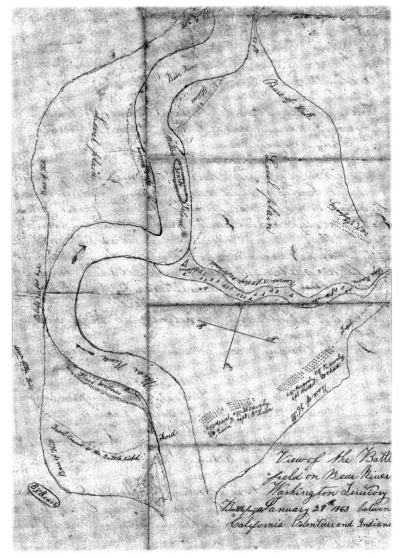

Map drawn by Sergeant William L. Beach shortly after the Bear River Massacre in 1863.
(Courtesy of Harold Schindler family, University of Utah Press)

and rancher. Harville had an abiding interest in local history and was a founding member of the Humboldt County Historical Society. He also owned a large collection of California memorabilia, which was put up for sale after his death in 1996.

Irvine found the narrative and map folded in an envelope and was intrigued because the documents referred to Bear River, which he at first took to be the Bear of Humboldt County. When he found that it was not the Northern California stream, he briefly researched the Connor expedition. Although he determined that Joseph Russ had been alive when the regiment was organized in 1861, he could find no connection between the pioneer and the soldier to indicate how the manuscript had come into Russ's possession. After his research, Irvine put the document away and thought no more of it until he saw the *Chronicle* article a year later.

Both Irvine and Madsen agreed that the document should be made available to scholars and researchers, preferably those in Utah. The only obstacle was in determining a fair exchange for the four-page manuscript.[6] When Irvine suggested a trade for Northwest documents or photos, Madsen contacted Gregory C. Thompson of the University of

dialogue that would continue over the span of some eighteen months.

The manuscript has an interesting, if not sketchy, pedigree. According to Irvine, he obtained the four pages from the estate of Richard Harville, a prominent Californian and a descendant of Joseph Russ, an early 1850s overland pioneer to Humboldt County who became fabulously wealthy as a landowner

Looking along the line of the old riverbank where Indians were camped the morning of the massacre. (Utah State Historical Society)

Utah's Marriott Library Special Collections. He also contacted me. Special Collections had nothing that fell within Irvine's sphere of interest, but after some months of dickering, Irvine and I were able to reach a mutually acceptable agreement.[7] Beach's narrative and map would return to Utah.

Madsen feels that the Beach papers are very important in resolving some of the issues surrounding the encounter. He also says the papers can "emphasize and strengthen the efforts of the National Park Service to bring recognition, at last, to the site of this tragic event, which was the bloodiest killing of a group of Native Americans in the history of the American Far West."

Madsen's comment points to the fact that, although Bear River has long been considered by those familiar with its details as the largest Indian massacre in the Far West, scholars and writers continue to deny the encounter its rightful place in frontier history. Yet, Beach

confirms the magnitude of the massacre when he cites the enemy loss at "two hundred and eighty Kiled." This number would not include those individuals shot while attempting to escape across the river, whose bodies were swept away and could not be counted.[8] While the fight itself has been occasionally treated in books and periodicals, Sergeant Beach's narrative and map are singularly important for what they add to the known record. Here is his account as he penned it:

This View Represents the Battlefield on Bear River fought Jan. 29th /63 Between four companies of the Second Cavelry and one company third Infantry California Volenteers under Colonel Conner And three hundred and fifty Indians under Bear hunter, Sagwich and Lehigh [Lehi] three very noted Indian chiefs. The Newspapers give a very grafic account of the Battle all of which is very true with the exception of the positions assigned the Officers which Cos K and M cavalry were first on the ground

When they had arrived at the position they occupy on the drawing Major McGeary [Edward McGarry] gave the commands to dismount and prepare to fight on foot which was instantly obayed. Lieutenant [Darwin] Chase and Capt. [George F.] Price then gave the command forward to their respective companies after which no officer was heeded or needed The Boys were fighting Indians and intended to whip them. It was a free fight every man on his own hook. Companies H and A came up in about three minutes and pitched in in like manner. Cavelry Horses were sent back to bring the Infantry across the River as soon as they arrived. When across they took a double quick until they arrived at the place they ocupy on the drawing they pitched in California style every man for himself and the Devil for the Indians. The Colonels Voice was occasionally herd encourageing the men teling them to take good aim and save their amunition Majs McGeary and Galiger [Paul A. Gallagher] were also loud in their encouragement to the men.

The Indians were soon routted from the head of the ravine and apparently antisipated a general stampede but were frustrated in thair attempt Maj McGeary sent a detachment of mounted cavelry down the River and cut of their retreat in that direction Seing that death was their doom they made a desparate stand in the lower

end of the Ravine where it appeared like rushing on to death to apprach them But the victory was not yet won. With a deafening yell the infuriated Volenteers with one impulse made a rush down the steep banks into their very midst when the work of death commenced in real earnest. Midst the roar of guns and sharp report of Pistols could be herd the cry for quarters but their was no quarters that day. Some jumped into the river and were shot attempting to cross some mounted their ponies and attempted to run the gauntlet in different directions but were shot on the wing while others ran down the River (on a narrow strip of ice that gifted the shores) to a small island and a thicket of willows below where they foung [found] a very unwelcome reception by a few of the boys who were waiting the approach of straglers. It was hardly daylight when the fight commence and freezing cold the valley was covered with Snow—one foot deep which made it very uncomfortable to the wounded who had to lay until the fight was over. The fight lasted four hours and appeared more like a frollick than a fight the wounded cracking jokes with the frozen some frozen so bad that they could not load their guns used them as clubs No distinction was made betwen Officers and Privates each fought where he thought he was most needed. The report is currant that their was three hundred of the Volenteers engaged That is in correct one fourth of the Cavelry present had to hold Horses part of the Infantry were on guard with the waggons While others were left behind some sick with frozen hands and feet. Only three hundred started on the expedition.

Our loss—fourteen killed and forty two wounded Indian Loss two hundred and eighty Kiled.

The Indians had a very strong natural fortification as you will percieve by the sketch within it is a deep ravine {with thick willows and vines so thick that it was difficult to see an Indian from the banks} runing across a smooth flat about half a mile in width. Had the Volunteers been been in their position all h—l could not have whiped them. The hills around the Valley are about six hundred feet high with two feet of snow on them. . . .

In the language of an old Sport I weaken

....	Trail in the snow
^^^^^^^^	Lodges or Wickeups in Ravine
iii iii iii	Retreating Indians
::: ::: :::	Co. K, 3rd Infantry
!!!!!!!	Cavelry four companies afterwards scattered over the field

Sergeant W. L. Beach. Co. K, 2nd c. C. V. Camp Douglas. Feb. 14th /63

I recieved six very severe wounds in my coat. W. L. Beach

Beach had enlisted in the California Volunteers on December 8, 1861, in San Francisco. After his hitch was up, he was mustered out at San Francisco on December 18, 1864.[9] After that, Sergeant William L. Beach may have faded away as old soldiers do, but his recollections of that frigid and terrible day in 1863 at Bear River will now live forever in Utah annals.

The late Harold Schindler was a member of the Advisory Board of Editors for the Utah Historical Quarterly *and an award-winning historian of Utah and the West.*

NOTES

This article originally appeared in the Fall 1999 issue of *Utah Historical Quarterly* and is reprinted by permission of the Utah State Historical Society.

1. Robert M. Utley, *Frontiersmen in Blue: The United States Army and the Indian, 1848–1865* (New York: Macmillan, 1967), 223–24. Other accounts tell of soldiers ransacking the Indian stores for food and souvenirs and killing and raping women. See Brigham D. Madsen, *The Shoshoni Frontier and the Bear River Massacre* (Salt Lake City: University of Utah Press, 1985), 192–93. Madsen's study is the best account of the expedition and of the circumstances surrounding it.

2. The Bear River Indian camp, located twelve miles north of the Franklin settlement, was in Washington Territory.

3. "Report of Col. P. Edward Connor, Third California Infantry, commanding District of Utah," *The War of the Rebellion: A Compilation of the Official Records of the Union and Confederate Armies* (Washington, DC: Government Printing Office, 1897), 185.

4. In the past, the belief was that the warriors had been cut off from their herd of ponies.

5. "Historian Delights in Debunking Myths of Old West," *San Francisco Chronicle*, February 8, 1997.

6. The manuscript was written in ink on a large sheet of letter paper folded in half to provide four pages measuring 19.3 cm by 30.6 cm. Beach's map covers the fourth page. There are two large tears in the paper,

one in the upper right corner of the first page and another across the bottom of the same leaf. Evidently, the paper was ripped before Beach began his narrative, for he wrote around the ragged edges, thus preserving the integrity of the account. His penmanship is quite legible though flavored with misspellings.

7. Schindler owned a California-related manuscript that Irvine was willing to trade for the Beach papers. The battle narrative and map are presently in the possession of the Schindler family.

8. Most histories of the American West mention the massacres at Sand Creek, Colorado, in 1864; Washita, Indian Territory, in 1868; Marias River in 1870; Camp Grant, Arizona, in 1871; and Wounded Knee, South Dakota, in 1890. Yet Bear River is generally ignored. Body counts vary widely in these histories, but typical numbers of Indian fatalities listed in traditional sources are Sand Creek, 150; Washita, 103; Marias River, 173; Camp Grant, 100–128; and Wounded Knee, 150–200.

Sergeant Beach's first-person assertion of at least 280 Shoshoni deaths lends additional support to Madsen's claim that the Bear River Massacre was the largest in the Far West. The toll would almost certainly have been even higher had Connor been able to press his two howitzers into action, but deep snow prevented the cannons from reaching the battlefield in time.

Madsen's book conservatively places the number of Shoshoni dead at 250. It also addresses the question of why Bear River has been generally neglected and advances three reasons: (1) at the time, the massacre site was in Washington Territory, some eight hundred miles from the territorial capital, so residents of that territory paid little attention; (2) the event occurred during the Civil War, when the nation was occupied with other matters; and (3) Mormons in Cache Valley welcomed and approved of Connor's actions, and some historians may have been reluctant to highlight the slaughter because of the sanction it received from the massacre that involved Mormons. See *Shoshoni Frontier*, 8, 20–24. Currently, Madsen says, some traditional military historians are still opposed to using the term "massacre" relative to Bear River.

9. Fortunately, none of Beach's "wounds" seems to have penetrated beyond the coat; officially the sergeant was listed among the men hospitalized with frostbitten feet. See Brigadier General Richard H. Orton, comp., *Records of California Men in the War of the Rebellion, 1861 to 1867* (Sacramento: State Printing Office, 1890), 178–79, 275.

ADDENDUM

By Ephriam D. Dickson III

When Hal Schindler first published Sergeant Beach's historic map of the Bear River Massacre in *Utah Historical Quarterly* in 1999, he noted that little was known of this soldier. Since then, however, much has been discovered about Sergeant Beach's background.

William Leake Beach was born in August 1832 in Abbeville County, South Carolina, the son of Chauncey and Huldah Beach. By 1840, the family had located in Upson County, Georgia. William Beach left home in 1849 at the age of seventeen, joining thousands of young men who headed west to the California gold fields, hoping to find their fortune. Failing in that, he worked at a variety of odd jobs until the outbreak of the Civil War. In 1862, Beach enlisted in Company K, Second California Volunteer Cavalry, and spent the next seven months at Camp Alert near San Francisco learning the basic skills of a soldier. He was promoted to corporal on March 1, 1862, and to sergeant five months later.

In July 1862, the Second California Cavalry joined Colonel Connor's column as they marched over the Sierra Nevada Mountains, bound for Utah Territory. In the Ruby Valley, they established Fort Ruby and then headed for Salt Lake City. As Connor led his column east, Sergeant Beach's company was assigned to Major McGarry as he swung north to punish the Shoshoni who had attacked a wagon train near Gravelly Ford. His company participated in several later Indian campaigns, including the attack at Bear River and a fight near Fort Ruby in which fifty-three Goshiute were killed.

Company K was transferred back to California in the summer of 1864 where Sergeant Beach was mustered out of the service in December that year. He returned

William L. Beach (center with beard) and his family, circa 1894. Photo by Charles H. Pautzke, taken at Auburn, Washington. (Courtesy of David Vandergriff)

home to Georgia after the war, but finding the area economically devastated, he soon headed back west. Beach operated a meat market in St. Louis and later in Salina, Kansas, before moving his family to Washington Territory. William Beach retired in Seattle, where he died on September 30, 1904. He is buried in the Grand Army of the Republic Cemetery—his grave marked with the white military headstone bearing his unit and years of service during the Civil War.

Sergeant Beach rarely spoke about his army experience, saying only that he remained haunted by what he witnessed during his Indian fighting service in Utah Territory. That he had been a participant at Bear River and had drawn a map of the battlefield was a surprise to his descendants. Hal Schindler died a year before the Beach map was published, and the original document appears to have once again disappeared. Despite a diligent search by his son through his father's papers, this important historical document could not be located. Perhaps one day, Sergeant Beach's map will once again reemerge and hopefully find its way into a public repository where it will be available for all those who wish to further explore this chapter of Utah history.

Ephriam D. Dickson III is the curator at the Fort Douglas Military Museum in Salt Lake City.

The Monarch of the Sea *was one of the sailing ships that brought Latter-day Saints to the United States from Europe during the Civil War. (Courtesy of the Mariners' Museum, Newport News, Virginia)*

This engraving, entitled "Pilgrims on the Plains," showing horses being driven into a corral formed by the covered wagons of a wagon train appeared in Harper's Weekly on June 12, 1869.

CHAPTER 14

William G. Hartley

LATTER-DAY SAINT EMIGRATION DURING THE CIVIL WAR

When the Civil War erupted, Latter-day Saints gathering to Zion had been flowing annually across America to Utah for fourteen years. By then, approximately forty thousand people had crossed the plains in more than two hundred wagon companies and ten handcart companies. As of 1860, the Church had in place a sail-rail-trail operation that resembled a rolling snowball. European converts crossed the Atlantic to New York or another eastern port. There, Eastern Seaboard Saints joined them for train rides to Chicago and on to Quincy, Illinois.[1] Riverboats took them down the Mississippi River twenty miles to Hannibal, Missouri. Aboard the Hannibal and St. Joseph Railroad, they crossed the width of the state of Missouri to St. Joseph, from where Missouri River steamers carried them upriver about 150 miles to wagon train outfitting camps at Florence, Nebraska Territory, near Omaha. Joining them there were emigrants from various parts of America and Canada.

At Florence, designated agents created the outfitting camp, rounded up wagons, usually from wagon makers in Chicago or St. Louis, stockpiled food and equipment, and organized and sent off wagon trains. Those rolled across the plains in about ten weeks, mostly on the north side of the Platte River to Fort Laramie, then on the well-worn Oregon-California-Mormon Trail to Fort Bridger and on into the Great Salt Lake Valley. Thus, by the time Fort Sumter fell in April 1861, the Church had a workable transportation network in place. For the system to work well, everything depended on scheduling, and the scheduling of ships, trains, and riverboats depended on their availability, costs, and the weather. But after that, the system's success hinged on what course the Civil War took.

How did the four-year-long war impact the Mormon emigration system? Did numbers shrink? Did they increase because of Joseph Smith's Civil War prophecy? Were ships available? Did departure and arrival

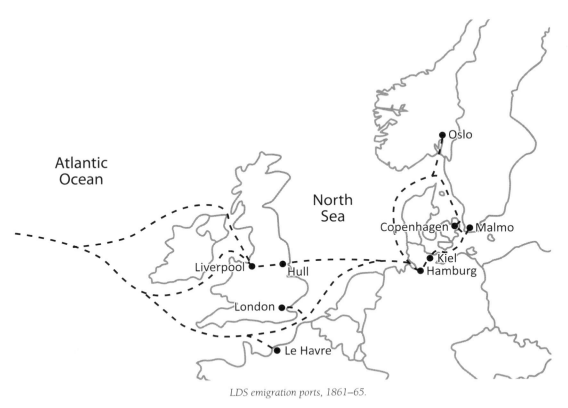

LDS emigration ports, 1861–65.

ports change? How available were railroad cars? Did routes across the States change? Did war conditions in Missouri disrupt rail travel there? Were emigrants considered secessionists because of perceived Mormon disloyalty that caused the Utah War? Given needs the armies had, how available were wagons and teams for emigrants at the outfitting camps? What encounters did Mormon emigrants have, if any, with Union or Confederate soldiers? The following yearly histories of Latter-day Saint emigration during the Civil War years provide answers to those questions.[2]

1861: WAR ANXIETY BOOSTS THE EMIGRATION FLOW

Church emigration plans for 1861 were drawn independent of whether or not war might break out.[3] Readers of the November 24, 1860, issue of the Church newspaper

Millennial Star found therein a letter from Brigham Young dated September 13. "After baptism, comes the gathering as rapidly as wisdom and circumstances will permit," the Prophet counseled, and then hinted that a new system to boost emigration was forthcoming.[4] In January 1861, the European Mission presidency, headquartered in Liverpool, consisted of Apostles Amasa Lyman, Charles C. Rich, and George Q. Cannon. That month, with the emigration season "close at hand again," they called for names, orders, and deposits without delay "to enable us to make timely arrangements on the other side of the water for the purchase of the outfit needed for the Plains." The *Star* provided cost estimates for oxen, wagons, handcarts, railroad fare, and baggage. "We trust that those of the Saints who have means will not delay their departure in the hope of by so doing of bettering their conditions for another season. Nothing can be gained by this." This was a typical annual admonition.[5] In January, the mission presidency sent Elders Nathaniel V. Jones and Jacob Gates to New York to make preparations for receiving the year's European emigration.[6] Thus, early in 1861, planners in Europe had in mind a repeat of the previous year's operations.

By March 1861, missionaries near Council Bluffs, Iowa, had "resurrected" over two hundred "old saints." Members "asleep for years" were "waking up" and exhibiting "a great desire" to head to Utah, stimulated by rising concerns about America becoming a war zone.[7]

In Utah, meanwhile, a revolutionary wagon train system was being launched.[8] During 1860, two handcart companies had crossed the plains, the last of ten created since 1856 to help the poor reach Utah. Because thousands of European Saints still needed low-cost transportation, Church leaders replaced handcarts with a new program: it would send wagon trains down from Utah to Florence to load up emigrants and haul them back to Utah. That way, hundreds would not need to buy wagon-and-team outfits but could ride in "down-and-back" wagons by promising to later repay a transportation fee. President Young announced this plan to Utah bishops in January 1861. It took time for news of it to reach England. Communication between Utah and Liverpool went east by Pony Express, then by telegraph across the States, and then by steamship to Liverpool— a month or two each way.

At the same time, in England, news of America's civil strife was worsening. On February 16 the *Star* published an article titled "Division of the United States—causes which have hastened it." It bluntly observed that "War—bloody, fratricidal war seems to be inevitable." The article reprinted Joseph Smith's 1832 revelation about war, reminding readers that it had been published "to the world" a number of years before and had widely circulated in the United States and Great Britain. Now, the prophesied rebellion in South Carolina and division of Southern and Northern states was happening. "How marvellously the prophecy uttered twenty-eight years ago is being fulfilled!" America's troubles, the report continued, "convey this warning—'Stand ye in holy places.'" For European Saints, war in America gave cause for increasing, not decreasing, emigration.

In Denmark, Scandinavian Mission president John Van Cott urged hopeful emigrants to collect at Copenhagen's docks by late April. That month he learned that war had started. He booked the Baltic Sea steamer *Waldemar* and ushered more than 550 Saints aboard on May 9, bound for Kiel, on Germany's north shore. He chartered for them a train from Kiel to Hamburg. There, he arranged for two North Sea steamers to transport them to Hull and Grimsby, on England's east coast. Trains next took them to Liverpool, where they joined other European Saints poised to cross the Atlantic.

In Liverpool, the world's busiest seaport, the European Mission presidency chartered three ships, filled them with supplies, supervised the emigrants' boarding, and appointed Mormon officers for each ship. On April 16, some 379 Saints set sail aboard the *Manchester*. One week later, 624 members followed on the *Underwriter*. Three weeks later, President Van Cott's Scandinavian company became part of the largest company yet to sail, 955 Saints, on the *Monarch of the Sea*. In total, about 2,000 European Saints made the five- to seven-week voyages to New York on the three ships.[9]

In New York City, agents prepared for the ships. Elders Jones and Gates arrived in the city on February 1 and found that Apostles Orson Pratt and Erastus Snow also had just arrived there.[10] With war clouds ready to burst, the two Apostles were finding cold Saints suddenly warming up:

> Many of those who once had a standing in the Church, but had fallen away, have been awakened to a sense of their position by the preaching of the Elders and the events now transpiring, which so strictly verify the truth of the prophecy and the near approach of those calamities they have been taught to expect when they first received the Gospel, and are coming back, repenting of their sins and being baptized for their remission. New members are also being added. Every exertion is being made by the Saints . . . to get away to Zion this season; and it is altogether likely that the migration to the Valley from the Eastern and Western States will be very large.[11]

By early 1861, missionary Bernhard Schettler had raised up a branch of German converts in Williamsburg (Brooklyn) New York, anxious to head for Zion.[12] In Philadelphia, Elder John D. T. McAllister warmed up several hundred Pennsylvania Saints. Elder Snow called the shots fired at Fort Sumter a "loud sermon" warning Saints to flee to Zion.[13] After war broke out, missionary Lucius Scovil, laboring in New York and New Jersey, mailed copies of Joseph Smith's 1832 prophecy to several of his non–Latter-day Saint relatives. President Lincoln's urgent call for troops, Scovil said, upset the citizenry: "War! War and blood! is the cry." He advised eastern Saints "to wind up their business and leave Babylon" that

spring. By April 26, an anonymous letter with anti-Mormon threats prompted Elders Pratt and Snow to cancel public Church meetings in the New York City area. Pro-South mobs tore up railroad tracks in Baltimore, making elders worry that war might prevent the Saints' departures.[14] Early in May, Elder Pratt spent several weeks in Philadelphia. "The Saints through these lands are using great exertions to emigrate," he reported, not so much from war fears, but because "it is very difficult for the poor to find employment."[15]

In New York City the two Apostles and agents Jones, Gates, and Thomas Williams awaited the Mormon ship companies. On April 19, one week after the war started, the bark *Race Horse* arrived in Boston from South Africa with thirty-three Saints on board. Told by telegraph of their arrival, agent Jones in New York said for them to stay in Boston until the first Mormon shipload from Liverpool reached New York. While they waited in Boston, Eli Wiggill said, "All was commotion with the bands of music fife and drum and recruiting parties and flags flying in every direction."[16]

The ships from Liverpool arrived in New York on May 14 (*Manchester*), May 21 (*Underwriter*), and June 19 (*Monarch of the Sea*). On May 21, agent Jones wrote to Elder George Q. Cannon of the Mormon emigrant situation in New York. After the *Manchester*'s arrival, he said, part of the company, with twenty-two Saints from the New York branch, boarded a train and left. A small company of about two dozen Saints had arrived from the Cape of Good Hope and were waiting to join the next group going by train. "The New York, Philadelphia, and Boston Saints, consisting of from three to four hundred, will start for the frontiers about the 12th of June."[17] The eastern company,

Map showing emigration routes across the states.

including teenager Thomas Griggs (who later composed the hymn "Gently Raise the Sacred Strain") and sixty Saints from Boston (via a steamer from Connecticut), and Elder Schettler's German flock, left on June 11. A day later, President McAllister and three hundred Pennsylvania Saints joined that train. Finally, on June 20, the *Monarch* passengers sailed into port.

Church agents funneled the four companies in separate departures, three thousand Saints total, onto harbor barges that chugged them to the Jersey City railroad depot. From there, they traveled by train northwest to Dunkirk, New York, west along Lake Erie and to Chicago, and southwest to the Mississippi River at Quincy. From Quincy the Saints traveled the

normal boat-train-boat route to Florence. This tiring, dirty, uncomfortable ten-day journey from New York required a half-dozen train changes and two riverboat transfers.

While crossing the States, the emigrants saw clear evidence of war. At the Jersey City train depot, the Boston Saints met and were harassed by "a regiment of New York soldiers on their way to war." Because of "the call of government for means of transporting the troops," Church agents had difficulty lining up enough railroad cars.[18] In Elmira, New York, George Ottinger, one of the Pennsylvania Saints (later a famous Utah artist), "had a row with a soldier" who was bothering two Latter-day Saint women.[19] Near Chicago the train passed "a gallows furnished with a noose and

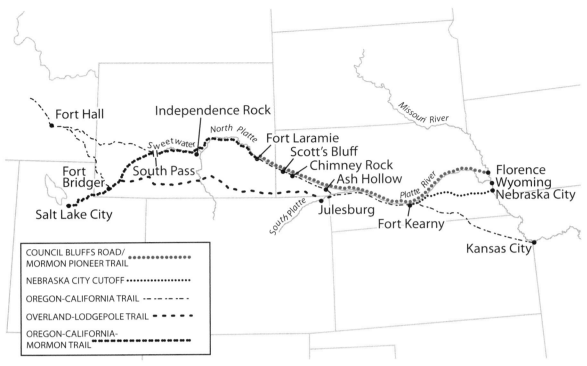

LDS pioneer companies used several routes to reach Utah Territory during the Civil War.

an inscription that read 'Death to traitors.'"[20] At Chicago, while the South African Saints waited to transfer, some "colored men" saw an African boy they had brought with them, Gobo Fango. "They accusing us of taking him away into Slavery and they thought to liberate him and caused great disturbance," Eli Wiggill said. But a lady in the company "hid him under her crinoline," so searchers never found him. After that, they kept the boy concealed as much as possible.[21]

Although the state of Missouri sided with the Union, it suffered its own private civil war. To harass Union forces, pro-Southern raiders tore up railroad tracks and occasionally fired on trains and riverboats.[22] When the eastern Saints reached Hannibal, they saw the "Home Guards protecting a cannon captured from secessionists, and learned that a rebel officer was imprisoned in the train depot." Nearly

every town and bridge they passed was under guard. Thomas Griggs wrote that Chillicothe, Missouri, "presented the appearance of a captured city, all business being entirely suspended and the streets patrolled by armed men of every conceivable character of drunkenness."[23] He found "the spirit of secession was prevalent" and American and rebel flags were alternately run up and down the town's flagpole.[24] By mid-July, when Lucius Scovil and Orson Pratt were hurrying to Florence to catch up with the last Mormon wagon companies, they found that no trains were running in Missouri because secessionists had burned railroad bridges and torn up tracks. So, the two elders rode by stagecoach to Florence. If the Mormon emigrant groups had reached Missouri a month behind schedule, it might have been impossible for that many people to find ways to reach Florence in time to cross the plains.[25]

War reduced Missouri River traffic, forcing emigrants to overload whatever steamboats going upriver were available. On George Ottinger's boat "the people piled in endways, sideways, crossings and every way all as thick as hops."[26]

In Utah on April 23, three days after Pony Express riders brought news of Fort Sumter's fall, about 200 wagons and 1,700 oxen, in four wagon trains loaded with flour, left the Salt Lake Valley for Florence to pick up needy emigrants. Assembling these "down-and-back" companies had taken three months of recruiting. In February, Brigham Young had asked Utah ecclesiastical wards for loans of wagons and teams for the six-month round trip in exchange for tithing credits. Seventy-five wards, nearly every ward in Utah, each donated one or more fully outfitted wagons and yokes of oxen. Mormon Trail veterans Joseph W. Young, John R. Murdock, Joseph Horne, and Ira Eldredge captained the four wagon trains. At four stations along the trail, the companies deposited tons of flour for use during the return trip.[27]

At Florence, between May and July, about 3,900 emigrants and 200 "down and back" wagons converged to form a massive, complex, busy outfitting campground centered around a provisions store, warehouse, corrals, weighing machines, and a bowery.[28] Agent Jacob Gates had set up the camp. He had arrived in New York City from England in February. There, he had made preliminary

Joseph W. Young was in charge of LDS wagon train outfittings in 1861, 1862, and 1864. (Church History Library)

railroad bookings for the May and June European emigrants. In Chicago, Gates bought 111 unassembled wagons from the Peter Schuttler wagon company for $7,300, to be delivered at Florence in June.[29]

Just after Gates reached Florence to set the campsite up, he heard about the fall of Fort Sumter. On April 24 he saw soldiers from Fort Kearny, Nebraska, heading east. "The war spirit is up," he wrote, "and fear seems to creep over the nation and a dread of something to come." On May 5 he learned how many Utah wagons were coming. Then, without knowing how many emigrants to expect, or if the war might cause delays, he opened a warehouse and stockpiled provisions and trail equipment.[30]

The first group of emigrants, mostly *Manchester* passengers, arrived in Florence on May 24. Elder Gates helped them obtain wagons, form into an independent train, and start west on May 29. The second emigrant company, *Underwriter* passengers, arrived on June 3, followed by Eastern States people on June 20. The Utah wagons rolled into Florence between June 16 and June 30, on schedule. The last emigrant company, those from the *Monarch*, showed up on July 2. While awaiting wagon assignments, emigrants assembled the prefab Schuttler wagons, built a public bowery, and sewed together wagon covers and tents. Elder Gates's agents procured bulk supplies from stores in the area, including 13,000 pounds of sugar, 3,000 pounds

Emigrant train in Echo Canyon en route to Salt Lake City in 1867. The poles are those used by the transcontinental telegraph line, completed in the fall of 1861. (Photo by C. W. Carter, 1867, Utah State Historical Society)

of apples, 3,300 pounds of ham, and 15,000 pounds of bacon.[31]

On July 2, the Florence outfitting camp contained more than 2,500 waiting emigrants, including Germans, Swiss, Italians, Danes, Swedes, Norwegians, Scots, Welsh, English, Irish, and Canadians. Saints unable to buy their own outfits signed up to travel in the down-and-back companies. For the four Church trains, Captain Joseph W. Young supervised the ticket sales and loading, freeing up Elder Gates to organize the independent trains. People in Church trains received wagon assignments, with six to twelve people per wagon. Fares were fourteen dollars for adults and seven for children under age eight. Each passenger was allowed fifty free pounds of baggage and was charged twenty cents for

each pound over fifty. On Perpetual Emigrating Fund Company ledgers, agents issued loans and credits for food, supplies, and wagon fares to passengers in the Church trains, including more than 600 heads of households.

During late June and early July, six more independent trains and the four down-and-back trains fitted out. Jacob Gates closed the campground and left it on July 17. By then, twelve main emigrant wagon trains with 624 wagons had left Florence, carrying 3,900 emigrants—1,000 from the Eastern states, 1,900 from Europe, and 1,000 "independents" who had reached Florence on their own.[32]

Mid-journey, the wagons passed U.S. army troops once stationed in Utah heading east for Civil War duty. During August, September, and October, the Mormon trains reached

Salt Lake City. The borrowed wagons and teams were returned to their Utah owners, who received more than $200,000 in tithing credits as pay. In practice, Church down-and-back companies averaged ten to twelve weeks to return to Utah.[33] They transported approximately 1,700 emigrants. Although the emigrants experienced some problems, the majority arrived healthy and in good spirits. "All in all it was a nice trip for the healthy and strong," English emigrant James H. Linford said; "all of the able-bodied emigrants walked." The new system had worked so well that Brigham Young increased the number of down-and-back wagons the next year.[34]

1862: MORE SHIPS, MORE WAGONS, MORE EMIGRANTS

As a result of the 1857–58 Utah War, some people in the States put Mormons on a par with Southern rebels. A Mormon elder working in Pennsylvania in September 1861 found "but little opportunity" for public preaching, "neither is it safe. Our enemies charge us with being Secessionists," which label became "a license for violence." Such hostility might have convinced some local Mormons to head for friendlier climes in Utah the next spring.[35]

In January 1862, Congress authorized President Lincoln to seize control of the railroads and telegraph for military use. In practice, the War Department restricted its authority to southern rail lines captured during the war. The military, needing the Northern railroad companies' expertise, counted on cooperation rather than coercion, and the railroads fell in line and cooperated, not wanting their lines seized.[36]

After news reached Europe in April 1861 of the war's outbreak, mission leaders preached with increased vigor the "warning voice" for

the next year's emigrants. The *Star*'s May 11, 1861, issue reminded readers that the revelation warned that war would "spread until all nations were involved in it," which meant that European nations "cannot escape from it, if they continue as they are." Therefore, "now is the time for the Saints" to exercise faith to emigrate. Prospects looked good "for a heavier emigration next year than we have had this," the *Star* editorialized on May 25. By mid-June, European members learned, belatedly, about the two hundred wagons sent from Utah to help the 1861 emigrants.[37] That news instilled hope for poorer Saints, if such trains would be available the next year. And poor there were. That month the *Star* bemoaned that the "division of the United States" was closing the American market, which "has had a depressing effect upon almost every branch of trade throughout the country [England]. There is no manufacturing district that does not groan under the loss of trade."[38]

Early in 1862, the *Star* told the Saints that "the condition of affairs in the States should not be any reason for those who have means delaying their departure till another season." Mission leaders surmised that the "cost of transit" wouldn't "differ much from that of last year."[39] However, for several weeks there was fear that Britain might become pulled into the war because of the "*Trent* Affair." On November 8, 1861, the USS *San Jacinto* intercepted the British mail packet *Trent* and removed, as contraband of war, two Confederate diplomats, James Mason and John Slidell. The envoys were bound for Great Britain and France to press the Confederacy's case for diplomatic recognition. In Britain, the public expressed outrage at this U.S. violation of neutral rights as an insult to their national honor. The British government

DATE	PORT	SHIP NAME	PASSENGERS
9 Apr	Hamburg	*Humboldt*	323
15 Apr	Hamburg	*Franklin*	413
18 Apr	Hamburg	*Electric*	336
21 Apr	Hamburg	*Athena*	484
23 Apr	Liverpool	*John J. Boyd*	702
6 May	Liverpool	*Manchester*	376
14 May	Liverpool	*William Tapscott*	807
15 May	Le Havre	*Windermere*	110
18 May	Liverpool	*Antarctic*	38
		Total	3,589

Table 1. Dates and ports of departure, with names and passenger counts of ships carrying LDS emigrants in the spring of 1862.

demanded an apology and the release of the prisoners, while it took steps to strengthen its military forces in Canada and for the Atlantic. English Mormon Thomas Memmott journalized on December 11, 1861, "Much excitement in England through an American ship's company taking two Southern commissioners . . . off a British Mail Steamer. Should war arise between the two countries I propose to get to Canada."[40] After weeks of tension and talk of war, the crisis resolved when the Lincoln administration released the envoys and disavowed its ship's actions. With obvious relief, the *Star* reported on March 8, "The prospect for an uninterrupted emigration of the Saints has become bright, in consequence of the peaceful settlement of the difficulty."[41]

That season, Church agents chartered ships to sail not only from Liverpool but also from Hamburg, Germany, and from Le Havre, France. See table 1 for the ships, departure dates and ports, and passenger numbers.

Ship passengers signed up before they knew for sure what to expect at the outfitting camps in America. Finally, word came late in April that the Church had called for three hundred Utah teams to go "down and back," so Saints boarding the last four or five of the Church-chartered ships had some assurance of that help.[42]

A May 17 report said "there are as many Saints leaving Great Britain alone this season as were numbered in the entire European emigration of last year, while the total emigration from Europe this year will, it is quite probable, outnumber last year's." In fact, the numbers almost doubled those in 1861. "Has there been a stronger desire, if as strong, manifested by the Saints to gather to Zion, than is exhibited the present season?" a *Star* editorial wondered. It then identified three causes for the enthusiasm: first, "the partial fulfillment of the revelation given to the Prophet Joseph"; second, the "hard times and misery" pervasive in England; and third, "the prospect they have of being able, with a small amount of means, to reach the place where they can be met by the oxen and waggons sent down from Zion to assist them in crossing the Plains. The amount being so small that they need to enable them to gather to

Emigrants boarding a ship, from Harper's Weekly, *June 26, 1858.*

Zion, and the prospects in these lands being so gloomy" naturally made Saints try to go.[43] Nothing in the *Star*'s pages during 1862 indicated worry about the Civil War interfering with the cross-America journeys.

For Scandinavians, a new departure port was picked, Hamburg. Four chartered ships left from there, possibly because Liverpool lacked a good supply of ships due to the Civil War, but also to help Scandinavians avoid the three transfers if going to Liverpool. "There were a larger number of Saints emigrating from Denmark that season than has ever been before or since," one said.[44] One of the German ships was the full-rigged, three-masted *Franklin*,

which sailed on April 15 carrying 413 Latter-day Saint Danes. Tragically, 48 died during the Atlantic crossing, nearly all children, from measles. In New York City, officials quarantined and kept the Saints from disembarking for two days. The *Athena*'s crossing also saw measles break out, which contributed to 35 deaths. The clipper ship *Electric* had little sickness.[45] One ship sailed from Le Havre, France, the *Windermere*, an old freighter. On board were Saints from Switzerland and France with such surnames as Hafen, Staeheli, Albrecht, and Zollinger. They sailed a long, fifty-four-day loop south past Portugal and then across the Atlantic to New York.[46]

At Liverpool docks and "just behind our ship," said Joseph C. Rich on the *John Jay Boyd*, "lay a Confederate clipper of a fine appearance which had just a short time before came in. She was captured while at sea by the Federals who placed sixteen men on her with 5 prisoners. . . . But the prisoners got loose, captured the sixteen federals, turned the ship" and docked her in Liverpool.[47] Four Latter-day Saint companies sailed from Liverpool.

Between May 20 and July 8, the nine ship companies sailed separately into New York harbor. When the measles-plagued *Franklin* docked, eighteen passengers with measles were taken to a hospital, and when the rest of the company cleared quarantine, Elders Charles C. Rich and John Van Cott met them. For those lacking means to go on, the two leaders raised donations, and then the company left on May 31.

During 1862, the emigrants' land route differed from that taken in 1861. Rather than diagonal across New York State, they first went to Albany, by train or by boat, and then went by train across New York to Niagara Falls. There, because of better rates and train schedules, the companies passed over a suspension bridge into Canada to reach Windsor. They took a steam ferry to Detroit, then resumed the usual train trip route via Chicago and Quincy, ferried across the Mississippi, and boarded the Hannibal and St. Joe train cars. In war-damaged Missouri, a *Franklin* passenger said, they "drove across flat, fertile and almost uninhabited plains where we saw American soldiers who had raised their tents, partly at the towns and partly at the bridges to prevent the Southern people to break up the railroad or the bridges." At St. Joseph his company transferred to the *Westwind*, a riverboat that deposited them at Florence on June 9.[48]

Passengers from the *Electric* and *Athena* left New York on June 9. "We boarded the train and rolled westward. This was during the Civil War and the railroad companies were not very particular what kind of cars they furnished. All kind of rolling stock was used for passengers. . . . There were no upholstered seats for our use."[49] *Electric* passenger Ola Stohl said that many soldiers came up to them at whistle stops when crossing Missouri but did them no harm.[50] When the *John Jay Boyd* docked in New York, horse cars took the passengers to the Hudson River, where a steamboat transported them to Albany. "There we were shut up in a railroad roundhouse," William Lindsay said, "until a train came to take us farther on our journey."[51] Regarding the Missouri war zone, William Ajax, a passenger from the *Antarctic*, noted that "there were quite a number of U.S. soldiers here, as well as every bridge on the Hannibal and St. Joseph railroad. The companies in each place numbered from about fifty to one hundred, and the majority of them were cavalry. Our company was divided into two at Hannibal (for the first time) and some of us packed in cattle cars as though we were but beasts."[52] Across Missouri, "in many places houses were burned down, fences destroyed, and crops unattended," one traveler said.[53]

One after another, the Mormon emigrants companies reached Florence. On June 10, for example, former *Franklin* passengers pitched their tents and then remained camped for several weeks, waiting for cattle and wagons.[54] Scandinavians who had means were organized into two independent companies, both with forty wagons, captained by Christian Madsen and Ola N. Liljenquist, with Elder John Van Cott as general leader. They pulled out on July 14.[55]

Three main differences marked the outfitting camp in 1862 compared to 1861. First, while emigrants waited, a tornado struck, causing damage and death and nearly killing agent-in-charge Joseph W. Young. Second, three hundred down-and-back wagons arrived, compared to two hundred. Third, the Church trains arrived very late. Florence and vicinity were visited by a terrible tornado, accompanied by rain and thunder. Lightning killed two men, and Joseph W. Young received severe wounds when a wagon box blew on top of him. He was knocked unconscious but recovered. Tents and wagon covers were torn and shattered.[56] "The volume of water washed gullies from ten to fifteen feet deep and in some instances washed away boxes and bags and buried them in the sand," William Wood said, "some of which were never found."[57]

Church trains pulled in well behind schedule because heavy winter snows and spring rains had swollen rivers, causing teamsters long waits while water levels lowered. About July 15 the companies reached Florence, one by one. "There was a string of sixty or seventy wagons, each drawn by three of four yoke of oxen," emigrant Olaf Larson wrote. The Utah teamsters "were ragged and dirty with broad brimmed slouchy hats, many wearing one shoe and one boot of which were often ragged. They had a brace of two or three pistols and a large bowie knife strapped to their waist and carried a 15 or 20 foot whip in their hands. Thus they came in a cloud of dust. This was a terrorizing sight for those who never before had seen such a thing," Larson said. Young girls expecting to meet some nice young men from Zion were "sadly disappointed."[58]

Campground officials partly loaded the Utah wagons with iron and heavy merchandise, and then a dozen or so people were assigned to each, luggage was weighed, excess discarded, and the wagons packed. Mormon Trail traffic in 1862 was heavier than in 1861. Down-and-back wagons totaled 262. The passenger company names and their departure dates are given in table 2 below:[59]

COMPANY	DATE
Lewis Brunson	14 Jun
James Wareham	ca. 8 Jul
Ola N. Liljenquist	14 Jul
Christian A. Madsen	14 Jul
Homer Duncan	22 Jul
Arba L. Lambson	23 Jul
John R. Murdock	24 Jul
Joseph Horne	27 Jul
James S. Brown	28 Jul
Isaac A. Canfield	30 Jul
Ansil P. Harmon	1 Aug
Henry W. Miller	5/8 Aug
Horton D. Haight	10 Aug
William H. Dame	14 Aug

Table 2. Emigrant companies that traveled on the Mormon Trail in 1862 and their departure dates.

William Lindsay, in the Homer Duncan train, said that "flour and bacon was furnished to everybody but of course every family had to do their own cooking." Bake skillets, frying pans, and camp kettles were provided. "In the evening with ox yokes for seats we sat around the camp fires & sang songs or told stories. . . . Some had violins, Accordions, Concertina's or other musical instruments so we had all kinds of entertainments," Lindsay said, "and forgot the hard traveling in the dust thru the day."[60] In the Ansel Harmon Train, measles killed a dozen. The Henry W. Miller company suffered a "devastating toll" from measles that killed

SHIP	PORT	DEPARTURE	ARRIVAL	PASSENGERS
Rowena	Port Elizabeth, S. Africa	14 Mar	22 May	15
Henry Ellis	Port Elizabeth, S. Africa	31 Mar	28 May	31
John J. Boyd	Liverpool	30 Apr	29 May	767
B. S. Kimball	Liverpool	8 May	15 Jun	657
Consignment	Liverpool	8 May	20 Jun	38
Antarctic	Liverpool	23 May	10 Jul	486
Cynosure	Liverpool	30 May	19 Jul	775
Amazon	London	4 Jun	18 Jul	895

Table 3. LDS emigrant ships that arrived in New York City in 1862.

twenty-eight children under age five. The Haight train had measles casualties, too.[61]

Construction crews had completed the overland telegraph the previous fall, so this was the first emigration season when wagon trains could send and receive telegrams. In Jens Weibye's diary he noted many telegraph stations that the Christian Madsen train passed. At the Sweetwater River telegraph station near Independence Rock he found "two houses and many soldiers; they stood and looked at us." On September 6, at a telegraph station where soldiers also were, John Van Cott sent a telegram to Brigham Young, reporting on Captain Madsen's and Captain Liljenquist's companies' progress. On September 9, Weibye's company continued to follow the telegraph line as they neared the Green River. Reaching Ham's Fork on the 13th, they found a telegraph station, and just beyond Fort Bridger they sometimes followed the telegraph road. Also, he noted, they were passed by mail stagecoaches driving east and west.[62]

The 1862 emigration season was a success. Looking ahead to 1863, European Mission leaders argued that terrible events taking place in America with "fearful rapidity" could close the way to Zion, so Saints should make "every effort" to go to Utah "before the storm overtakes them." The 1862 companies, they underscored, safely reached Utah, where "peace prevails."[63]

1863: ENCOUNTERING REALITIES OF THE WAR

During 1863, Latter-day Saint emigration had increased contact with Civil War realities. It dodged the New York draft riots. In Missouri the emigrants saw many soldiers and much war damage. On the plains, federal troops stopped some Mormon companies and required oaths of allegiance. At sea, Mormon-chartered ships faced interception by Confederate naval units. That year, Horace S. Eldredge, William C. Staines, and John W. Young oversaw the shipping of European and Eastern States emigrants to the frontier. In Florence, Feramorz Little and Jacob Bigler directed the outfittings.[64] Migrations to the west, other than by Mormons, were large-scale that year due to mining booms in California, Nevada, and Idaho.[65]

Millennial Star readers began in 1863 digesting "Seasonable Advice" for intending emigrants. The article lauded that "there never has been a time . . . when the spirit of emigration has rested more mightily upon the Saints" than at present. Events and working-class distress produced anxieties to

Wagon train assembled in the area of Coalville, Utah 1863. Photo by C. R. Savage, 1863. (Utah State Historical Society)

gather.[66] By late March, emigrants needed to sign up and place deposits so ships could be booked.[67] That year's ships, ports and dates of departure, arrival dates in New York City, and Latter-day Saint passenger numbers are shown in table 3.

Those aboard the *B. S. Kimball*, except for thirteen English, came from Scandinavia, who had trans-shipped to England from the port of Hamburg. Some thirty-eight Scandinavians couldn't fit aboard the *B. S. Kimball*, so they sailed the same day on the *Consignment*. The *Antarctic*'s Mormon company came from thirteen different countries: England, Scotland, Ireland, Wales, America, France, Holland, Switzerland, Germany, Italy, Denmark, Norway, and Sweden. During its voyage, passenger Thomas Henry White said that "the sailors were kept busy several hours each day, pumping water out of this ship, which leaked badly" and that "the drinking water was bad and we couldn't drink it without boiling it."[68]

No sailing ship carrying Mormons is better known now than the *Amazon*, which Charles Dickens immortalized in his *Commercial Traveler* account of his visit aboard it before it sailed from London. He termed the Mormon emigrants "the pick and flower of England." His long word-portrait contains no concern that, at journey's end, these people might be in danger in America because of the Civil War.[69] Latter-day Saint Atlantic crossings that year were judged "in every respect, satisfactory," even though some vessels sailed "at a much later date than has been customary" or desirable. The reason for such lateness was "the scarcity of ships."[70] After the ships had all sailed, mission leaders praised the results: "A larger number of Saints have left Europe this season . . . than have ever before sailed in any single years." The tally: within five weeks, they said, 3,650 had shipped through the Liverpool office.[71] (Our totals show 3,618.)

In New York City, Church agents had hands full processing the ship passengers. Fortunately, the ships' arrival times dodged the terrible July 13–16 New York City Draft Riots, when the city suffered "the largest civil insurrection in American history" other than the Civil War itself. That March, a federal act had authorized states to meet their assigned quotas of soldiers by conscription. But anyone drafted could avoid service by paying a commutation fee or finding a substitute, options the working classes couldn't tap. Violent antidraft riots exploded, causing arson, murder, and destruction of property. More than 120 civilians were killed (some estimates say 2,000) and 2,000 injured. The military suppressed the mob, using artillery and fixed bayonets.[72]

Fortunately, the last of the Church-chartered ships arrived in New York City just before and just after the riots: the *Antarctic* on July 10, the *Amazon* on July 18, and the *Cynosure* on July 19. *Cynosure* passenger David Stuart noted that "New York City was all upset upon our arrival. Ten thousand soldiers were there from the front to enforce the draft."[73] A *B. S. Kimball* passenger said that, once ashore, "some of our pockets were picked," some trunks robbed, and some vendors gave them "bogus money."[74]

Travel to Florence had its problems. Mary E. Fretwell, from the *Amazon*, said that "we rode three days shut up in cattle cars with nothing but straw to sit on." She and her female traveling companion "only had one dozen eggs to eat; that was all we could get. What little bread that there was to be got, the men got it for their wives and children." While their train was in Upper Canada, using the same routing as the 1862 companies used, "one of the luggage cars got on fire," passenger Elijah Larkin said; "it was soon uncoupled & the engine ran on ahead with it about a mile to where there was water, & the fire was soon put out & the luggage was got out about thirty bags & boxes were burned & two or three beds." The luggage was then put back in the car, which was run back and recoupled to the train.[75]

While passing through the Missouri war zone, William Freshwater, an 1862 *William Tapscott* emigrant who wintered in New York, said that "the rebels, or bushwhackers, fired two cannon balls through our train, one shot went through the passenger car exactly eight inches above three people's heads and the other through a baggage car destroying a great amount of baggage."[76] Thomas White, from the *Antarctic*, said that Union soldiers earned one dollar for every man or boy they could pin a ribbon on, meaning the recipient of such pinning was then in the army.[77] In St. Joseph, he said, soldiers were looking for recruits. No Mormon emigrants are known to have been pinned. One young boy asked a soldier to let him sit on his horse. "The soldier at once reported that the boy was stealing the horse. The boy was hidden three days or he would have been taken by the army."[78] At St. Joseph, some Union soldiers were "very drunk and shooting around and swearing about the Mormons."[79]

Not a part of the emigrant flow from New York, a riverboat carrying Mormons upriver from St. Louis had on board military supplies, a cannon, and five hundred mules and horses. To protect the cargo, soldiers on board created breastworks of grain and tobacco sacks around the deck.[80]

At Florence, thirteen Church-organized wagon trains, not counting freight companies, loaded up about four thousand emigrants for the trip west. Ten of those thirteen were down-and-back companies, containing more than five hundred teams of the nearly seven hundred total.[81] The wagon trains left from Florence later than usual, the first on June 29 and the last on August 16. Rough estimates show that company sizes averaged 54 wagons and 300 people. McArthur's was the largest, with

75 wagons, Canfield's the smallest, with 24. The trains reached Salt Lake City in 63 days on average, the fastest (Haight) in 56 days, the slowest (Young), 74 days.[82]

Thomas White, in the Nebeker company, said their wagons were loaded with telegraph wire and roofing for the Salt Lake Tabernacle.[83] Three young girls were walking together when "very bad" lightning struck and killed the middle girl. It also killed seven oxen in the train and flashed along the iron yoke chains. One teamster had skin taken off his nose while he was sitting on his front endgate.[84]

Telegraph stations let trail travelers sometimes hear war news, such as of the Battle of Gettysburg.[85] In Salt Lake City, Camp Douglas received a telegram saying that the Haight company at the Green River had two or three loads of gunpowder. Fears were that Mormons might use that powder to blow up Camp Douglas, so soldiers at Green River visited the company's camp to confiscate the powder. While Captain Haight served the soldiers dinner in his tent and talked with them for two or three hours, "the wagon with the powder crossed the river and up into the mountains." Men unloaded the powder into sacks and returned. The next day, soldiers came and searched the train, found no powder, and "told us to go on."[86]

On August 25, soldiers stopped the Patterson independent company near Fort Bridger. "Every male native or foreign from the age of 18 years and upwards took the Oath of alegiance [sic] to the Government of the U. S. of America." The troops' commander "acted very gentlemanly." Before taking the oath, the camp journal noted, "we gived three cheers for the Constitution of the U. S. of America."[87] Mary Elizabeth Lightner said the soldiers searched the wagons for powder.[88]

In a September 25 letter, E. L. Sloan described the McArthur company's encounter with troops. While traveling on the Muddy Road that bypassed Fort Bridger, he said, they were stopped by twenty-one mounted soldiers. These ordered Captain McArthur to move the company to Fort Bridger, where the men age eighteen or older must take an oath of allegiance if citizens, or an oath of neutrality if aliens, and the wagons would be searched for "freighted ammunition." So the train diverted and rolled nine hours to the fort on a difficult road. Soldiers jeered, made coarse jokes, and abused the Mormons. At Bridger the company had to wait till morning for a commanding officer to return. Finally, in a corral, the oaths were administered.[89]

All the trains arrived safely in Utah. A December report from the Valley termed the year "one of the most pleasant seasons for crossing the plains" on record.[90] With the 1863 emigration season concluded, European leaders noted that the flow had faced and survived three difficulties. First, the challenge to obtain ships and prepare them before the "season was too far advanced." Second, the South's rebellion aroused Northerners to a "fearful pitch of anger" that put them in "no mood to hesitate about using the most desperate measures" to punish Mormons for any breach of law or "rebellious symptoms." Third, through the "changing fortunes of war," the railroad through Missouri might have been stopped or destroyed. But the obstacles vanished because "the Lord removed the difficulties."[91]

1864: WAR PROBLEMS, NEW OUTFITTING CAMP, NEW ROUTES

Early in 1864, with a new emigration season upcoming, Saints in England "hailed

SHIP NAME	DEPARTURE	PORT	ARRIVAL	PORT	PASSENGERS
Echo	5 Apr	Port Elizabeth, S. Africa	12 Jun	Boston	9
Susan Pardew	10 Apr	Port Elizabeth, S. Africa	11 Jun	Boston	18
Monarch of the Sea	28 Apr	Liverpool, England	3 Jun	New York	974
General McClellan	21 May	Liverpool, England	23 Jun	New York	802
Hudson	3 Jun	London, England	19 Jul	New York	863

*Table 4. Names, departure dates and ports, arrival dates and ports, and passenger counts
of emigrant ships carrying Latter-day Saints in 1864.*

with joy" news that teams again were being sent from Utah to assist the poor.[92] By early March, word came that Utah trains would be sent, although fewer than before.[93] Joseph A. Young and William C. Staines were assigned to be the emigrant-receiving agents in New York City. While the largest company ever sent by sailing ship was boarding the *Monarch of the Sea* on April 30, mission leaders reported that "everything seems favorable" for the gathering but that "there is no room to doubt that there are times not far distant ahead, when it will require great faith, combined with wise management, to enable those who wish to escape from difficulty, to effect their purposes."[94]

In February, war broke out in Europe, pitting Denmark against Prussia and Austria, fighting for control of the Schleswig-Holstein region. Germanic forces drove the Danish army northward into Jutland, which meant that Mormon Danes could not emigrate via Kiel and Hamburg. Fortunately, at Copenhagen, steamers were booked that took the Mormons north around the top of Denmark and then south on to Hull, England. From there they went by train to Liverpool.[95] Swedes and Norwegians, however, still used the usual route through Hamburg, then to England.[96] We lack information about four ships that apparently brought some Mormon emigrants in 1864, but the ships for which there is data

regarding departure dates and ports, arrival dates and ports, and number of passengers are given in table 4.

That year's European and African transatlantic Saints numbered roughly 2,700, making 1864 yet another big emigration season.

Before the *Monarch* left Liverpool on April 28, weather and war had combined to make it hard for the mission to book ships in that port. "So many ships have been prevented from reaching the port by the strong easterly winds which have prevailed, and the bounty offered by the American navy inducing so many sailors to enter into their service, there has been a real scarcity of that class of men, of late, in this port."[97] The *Monarch's* Mormon company was the largest ever carried by sailing ship. About forty of them died of measles, mostly children. Sailing the Newfoundland Banks, they saw "a number of very large icebergs."[98]

The *General McClellan* crossed the Atlantic in a speedy thirty-two days.[99] The *Hudson* "sailed about seventeen days later than the time we wished to have the last of the emigrating Saints go." But she had been delayed leaving New York for England. The booked emigrants had no alternative but to wait and sail late, because "ships were so scarce that another could not be obtained that could leave earlier or be affordable."[100] The *Hudson* company was organized into fourteen wards. Passenger

George Careless (later a Tabernacle Choir director) organized a very proficient choir, which the ship captain let practice in his cabin.[101] On August 8, near America, the Confederate steam gunboat *Georgia* hailed the *Hudson* "and brought us to a standstill. After inquiries from our captain we were permitted to move on for they ascertained that eleven hundred British subjects were on board. Consequently, they had no means of handling that many persons and the would-be prize was given up, the gunboat's band playing a farewell."[102]

How the year's South African immigrants traveled from Boston to the plains is not known, but they probably linked up with those who left from New York City. The Europeans, who disembarked in New York, immediately boarded the magnificent Hudson River steamer *St. Johns* for Albany. There they loaded onto trains.[103] "Though every coach was full to its utmost," *Monarch* passenger H. N. Hansen recalled, "we were pleased with the cushioned seats and comfortable arrangements."[104] But when they changed trains, they next rode in boxcars with "temporary hard seats arranged even without any support for the back.[105] When they reached Missouri, they refused to ride again in box cars, so they had to wait a day, without shelter or access to baggage. However, sleeping in the woods with only shawls and overcoats was, Hansen said, "the most comfortable night spent for a week."[106]

Likewise, in New York City the ship *Hudson* passengers boarded the *St. Johns*, which packed 1,400 people on its lower deck, for an all-night cruise to Albany. From there the Mormons rode in twenty-four cars to Buffalo. During the Canadian stretch, they clattered over "track laid through a wood which was on fire for several miles and the wind carried the flames unpleasantly close to the train." In Chicago,

some army officers boarded their train, looking for deserters. The company left Chicago July 25 on the Illinois Central, suffering "much inconvenience" by frequent changes of cars. After ferrying the Mississippi to West Quincy's railroad spur, the people were told that a bridge and a station up ahead had been burned by rebels, so no train was available. They camped in the woods until a thunderstorm drove them into the depot for shelter.[107]

After a day's delay, on July 28 they loaded onto three trains and chugged only to the burned, impassable bridge. They climbed out and "forded the river, and camped again in the woods to wait the removal of the luggage which was carried over 3/4 of a mile, of very rough road mostly on men's backs, only three wagons available for the heavier boxes." The next afternoon, "3 trains of goods, cars, and cattle trucks very filthy were crammed to excess by the Saints."[108] A Union army officer walked through the trains to enlist young men into the army, causing one mother to put a bonnet on her son and disguise him as an old woman.[109] Effects of guerilla raids were "very apparent in the burnt buildings, the excitement of the inhabitants and the number of armed men at the stations who were sent to protect the line." During this final leg to St. Joseph, which was "dreadful rough," one engine and several cars went off the track, "the brethren having to get out to push the trains into the sidings."[110]

Deboarding in St. Joseph, the Saints took cover in a large railway shed. Some harassing soldiers questioned a Dutch girl, who knew but little English. Then they claimed the Mormons were forcing her to Utah against her will. When sent for, a provost marshal determined that the soldiers misunderstood her and ordered them to leave the grounds.

"The rabble then declared they would have her if they burnt the building, but by disguising her she was got safely on board the steamer 'Colorado.'" That steamer took the Saints upriver, stopping for each night at a woodyard on shore. On August 2, after "rubbing over sandbars and snags, feeling our way from bank to bank," the steamboat docked at the Church's new outfitting camp in Wyoming, Nebraska.[111]

Only one Mormon wagon company in 1864 did not outfit there. The William D. Pritchett company of Southerners left from the Florence-Omaha area. In the group was David H. Peery, a daughter, and some of his in-laws, all from Virginia. Perry had been a Confederate commissary officer serving in Kentucky. During the war he converted to his beloved deceased wife's Mormon religion. He then resigned from the army and took his family across Kentucky to the Ohio River. From there, steamboats took them to Florence. They headed west in a small wagon company headed by Captain Prichett, a Virginian and a Mormon. Some Missourians bound for Oregon joined them at Fort Kearny, at which point the train contained twenty wagons. But the Missourians broke off when Pritchett was elected captain over both groups, not wanting a Mormon captain. Some weeks later, the Pritchett company came upon the Missourians, who had lost their livestock during an Indian raid. Captain Pritchett's company gave them enough oxen to pull their wagons to Green River, where they could obtain more stock.[112]

All the other 1864 Mormon wagon trains outfitted at and left from the new outfitting site. Six were Church trains from Utah, containing 170 teams; three were independent companies. The Wyoming, Nebraska Territory, site, located on a bluff three hundred feet above the river, was forty-five miles downriver from Florence and seven above Nebraska City. A good location, it reduced the steamboat time from St. Joseph, provided ample space, was not hounded by apostate and criminal elements like Florence was, was near Nebraska City for supplies, and had access to overland trails on the Platte's south side, including the overland mail's stage-coach route to Salt Lake City, which opened in 1862.[113] As the campground chronology of table 5 shows, agent John W. Young dealt with busy comings and goings.[114]

COMPANY	ARRIVAL	DEPARTURE
John D. Chase	——	26 Jun
John R. Murdock	6 Jun	29 Jun
Monarch passengers		15–16 Jun
*William B. Preston	21 Jun	8 Jul
Joseph S. Rawlins	26 Jun	15 Jul
*William S. Warren	2 Jul	21 Jul
John Smith	——	by 15 Jul
Isaac A. Canfield	by 3 Jul	27 Jul
McClellan passengers		3 Jul
*William Hyde	3 Jul	9 Aug
Hudson passengers		1 Aug
*Warren S. Snow	——	17 Aug

Table 5. LDS wagon companies outfitted at and leaving from the Church's camp in Wyoming, Nebraska. Church trains are in boldface. Asterisks mark companies that chose to follow a new route, the Overland–Bridger Pass Trail.

Some emigrants had long waits at Wyoming. "We camped in some brush there for 3 wks. in the hot weather while we were waiting for the church teams to come," a young girl in the *Monarch* company recalled; "it was so hot the ground would burn our feet."[115] A few emigrants had tents, but most built huts of poles and brush, which gave shade but leaked rain.[116] The first train to leave, the John D. Chase independent company of twenty-eight mule-team wagons, included 102 people and much freight.[117] On July 3, just as William Hyde's final Church train arrived in camp, so did about eight hundred Saints from the *General McClellan* company. Agent Joseph W. Young (not to be confused with Joseph A. Young, the agent in New York) sent off wagon trains as fast as he could load them.[118] By July 27 all the down-and-back trains were on the trail. But on August 2 two steamboats unloaded more than eight hundred *Hudson* emigrants. Young sent the Hyde company off with 350 passengers and freight and then purchased more wagons and teams for a new train. He assigned returning missionary Warren S. Snow to captain it. The company left very late, about the same time as many wagon trains in the past were arriving in Salt Lake City. Four days after Snow's company pulled out, a weary Young and his assistants closed up the Wyoming buildings and left.

Traveling south of the Platte, the companies followed the Nebraska City Cut-off most of the way to Fort Kearny, then joined the Oregon Trail. Their route included Fort Kearny, Plumb Creek, Fremont Springs, O'Fallon Bluffs, "the Old California Crossing," and Julesburg.[119] That year the trail between Fort Kearny and Julesburg was unsafe because of what later was popularly termed the "Indian War of 1864."[120] After passing Fort Kearny, the Hyde company learned that "many of the people from Towns & Mail Stations in advance had been driven in by Indians & were now at Fort Kearney." Through this danger zone, he said, they traveled double file.[121] "Trains ahead and behind us were burned," a Preston company passenger noted.[122] (See map on p. 234.)

At Julesburg, half of the Mormon companies crossed the South Platte and headed north to join the main Oregon-California Trail at Fort Laramie. In the chart above, the four companies marked with an asterisk chose a different route, following the stagecoach mail route, called the Overland–Bridger Pass Trail.[123] The Hyde and Snow companies crossed the South Platte just below Julesburg, reached Pole Creek and followed it west about 180 miles to its head (the "Pole Creek route"[124]), passed over the Black Hills one hundred miles south of Fort Laramie, struck the head of Bitter Creek and followed it a few days, and moved on to Fort Bridger. "This is a new route," John Gerber wrote; "feed and water is more plentiful than on the old route via Fort Laramie."[125]

About 2,600 Mormon emigrants crossed the plains in 1864.

1865: STEEP DROP IN EMIGRATION NUMBERS

"We should not send teams . . . to Wyoming for the poor next season," Brigham Young announced in mid-1864, "for we wish to prosecute work upon the Temple, and we are not able to do both at the same time." The *Star*'s September 17 issue made that announcement public, saying that because of "great cost and little return," no Church trains would be provided in 1865. For four years, hundreds of wagons and teams had been thus engaged, receiving tithing credits as compensation. But unpaid debts by the emigrant beneficiaries necessitated belt tightening.[126]

Late in 1864, President Young counseled those intending to emigrate in 1865, who had their "own means" to reach America but not Utah, to plan to lay over in Canada

SHIP NAME	DEPARTURE	PORT	ARRIVAL	PORT	PASSENGERS
Mexicana	12 Apr	Port Elizabeth, S. Africa	18 Jun	New York	47
Belle Wood	29 Apr	Liverpool	31 May	New York	636
B. S. Kimball	8 May	Hamburg	15 Jun	New York	657
David Hoadley	10 May	Liverpool	19 Jun	New York	24
Bridgewater	7 Jun	Liverpool	14 Jul	New York	7

Table 6. Names, departure dates and ports, arrival dates and ports, and passenger counts
of LDS emigrant ships sailing in 1865.

where they could find "the best facilities for obtaining employment." Don't stop and work in the States, he said, "for the regions

Castle Garden, located at the southern end of Manhattan in New York City, served as an emigrant reception station prior to the opening of Ellis Island. (ca. 1880; repr., New York: Arno Press and the New York Times, 1969)

of strife are constantly enlarging." Sail to New York, he advised, because rates to there were cheaper than to Canadian ports, but then go to Buffalo and cross into Canada by July or August. However, those able to finance the full journey to Utah should go to the Wyoming outfitting site, if war conditions allowed, "where agents will be sent to furnish outfitting supplies as usual."[127]

The European Mission intended to "carry on the emigrating business as usual, under the same general plan and arrangements" as before. "Lose no opportunity of making your escape," mission leaders said, for they foresaw

"no prospect of bettering or advancing your condition by remaining here." Despite the war and bloodshed "so rapidly devastating the United States," a combination of caution, wisdom, and trusting "the Lord and his servants" could provide safety.[128]

When 1865 opened, Northern forces under Generals Grant and Sherman were turning the tide against the Confederacy's armies, but fierce Civil War battles continued. The European Mission sent Thomas Taylor, assisted by John G. Holman, and Joseph G. Romney, to supervise the 1865 emigrations in America.[129] The known Mormon emigrant ships that sailed that year, the approximate passenger numbers, their departure dates and places, and arrival dates and places are shown in table 6.

"Owing to no Church teams being sent down to Wyoming," which meant higher emigration costs, "the emigration from the Mission this year has been comparatively small," a June report said. It totaled 1,224. Unusual for Mormon ship companies, the *Belle Wood*, with 636 Saints on board, had so many aged, feeble, and sick, that they appointed a Female Sanitary Committee to attend to them, dispensing sago, tapioca, arrowroot, hot tea, coffee, soup, boiled rice, and dried

COMPANY	DEPARTURE	WAGONS	PASSENGERS
Miner G. Atwood	31 Jul	ca. 60	245
Henson Walker	12 Aug	50	200
William S. Willis	12, 15 Aug	35	200

Table 7. Names, departure dates, and wagon and passenger counts of LDS wagon companies traveling in 1865.

applesauce.[130] The brig *Mexicana* brought 47 Saints from South Africa.[131] The fine American packet ship *B. S. Kimball* carried 557, primarily Scandinavians. Passengers received good treatment, including three warm meals each day. Three adults died, as did twenty-five children, of measles and scarlet fever.[132] Details are lacking regarding the voyages of the *David Hoadley* and the *Bridgewater*.

On April 9, General Robert E. Lee surrendered his Confederate army to General Ulysses S. Grant at Appomattox Court House in Virginia. Then, on April 15, President Lincoln died after being shot by assassin John Wilkes Booth. When *Belle Wood* passengers landed at Castle Garden on June 2, they "found the country in deep mourning over the tragic death of Abraham Lincoln. Everywhere we saw soldiers who were returning home from the Civil War." They looked "ragged, tired and sick as they dragged themselves down the street to their quarters amid the sound of cheers and martial music."[133] Upsetting *Belle Wood* emigrants, railroad contractors refused for four days to honor their contract signed with agent Thomas Taylor. Frustrated, he initiated legal action, which quickly produced train space.[134] On June 6, the Mormons boarded a train to Albany. From there, they moved on to Niagara Falls, Chicago, and Quincy, and reached the outfitting camp at Wyoming on June 14.

The *Belle Wood*'s "English company" of nearly four hundred emigrants arrived at Wyoming on June 15, the Scandinavian company of about 550 on June 26.[135] There the emigrants waited until into July for chief agent Thomas Taylor to arrive. When he did, he still had to buy cattle and some wagons.[136] Three Mormon emigrant wagon trains headed west that season (as did four freight companies). The names, departure dates, and numbers of wagons and passengers in these companies are shown in table 7.

All three companies traveled on the south side of the Platte, crossed the South Platte near Julesburg, and joined the Oregon-California Trail near Court House Rock in western Nebraska. Because of Indian dangers, "it has been against the law for any small train to travel on this side of the Platte," Captain Atwood journalized, "but mine being a large train and having a number of men, we were allowed to cross over [the South Platte] without any trouble." His company of Scandinavians rolled over Scott's Bluff, passed by Fort Mitchell, and then, constantly encountering soldiers on patrol against Indians, they ran into trouble just beyond Fort Laramie. While camped for dinner at Cottonwood Creek, Captain Atwood said, "We had just unyoked and the mules and oxen were being driven to water when about fifteen Indians came riding down amongst the cattle from the hills, hooting and yelling. Some of them had fire arms and some arrows. They fired at the herders, trying the while to stampede the cattle but the cattle all ran for the corral, the mules

YEAR	SHIPS	SHIP EMIGRANTS	TRAIL EMIGRANTS	WAGON COMPANIES	WAGONS
1861	3	1,958	4,400	12	828
1862	9	3,589	5,200	14	664
1863	8	3,664	4,000	13	699
1864	5	2,466	2,600	10	523
1865	5	1,371	1,000	3	180
Totals	30	13,048	17,200	52	2,894

Table 8. Estimates of the totals for LDS emigration during Civil War years.

leading the way, and the Indians did not succeed in driving one away. Seven Danish men were wounded and one sister taken away."[137] The sister was Jensine Christine Hostmark Gruntvig. "We never heard from her any more," one passenger said; "they also threw a rope on a girl 18 years of age by the name of Stena Kemfy Jenson, but she managed to free herself from the ropes and in doing so she escaped from the Indians."[138]

Among the Henson Walker company, or English company, was the Kershaw family from South Africa. They had with them "two colored men from Africa, who strenuously objected to being called niggars and said they were Caffairs."[139] Passengers in the Willis company, also mostly English, had little wagon space for their use because chief agent Thomas Taylor, a merchant, had the wagons loaded with his merchandise. Late in September the Walker and Willis companies camped near each other and visited.[140] But the Willis company, so overloaded with freight, made slow progress. Food ran out, and winter approached. "The Captain had telegraphed to Utah that we were nearly out of provisions," one passenger recalled; "then one morning we heard whooping and yelling, we thought it was Indians, but it proved to be a train sent from Utah. And we were indeed glad to see them. They told us to hold our aprons

and they filled them with potatoes, onions, and other vegetables. They also brought fresh beef and I tell you we had a feast."[141] That relief train, a mule train captained by Orson Arnold, took the women, children, and elderly to Utah. It reached Salt Lake City on November 15, the Willis wagon train two weeks later.[142]

After the 1865 lull, a heavy flow of emigration resumed in 1866, involving nine ships and ten Church team trains transporting some 3,500 emigrants from the Wyoming outfitting camp.[143]

ASSESSMENT OF WARTIME EMIGRATION

Due to incomplete records, Mormon emigration totals during the Civil War years can only be roughly approximated. The ship and passenger totals in table 8 are based on Conway Sonne's encyclopedia of the ships that Mormon emigrants used. The trail passenger and wagon numbers are current estimates by Mel Bashore, the LDS Church History Library reference specialist whose work generated the Church's invaluable website *Mormon Pioneer Overland Travel*.[144]

This heavy flow of Mormon emigrants from abroad accords with strong national immigration totals for "Alien passengers arriving" at America's seaports during those years, as reported in the 2003 *Yearbook of Immigration Statistics* (see table 9).[145]

YEAR	TOTAL
1861	91,918
1862	91,985
1863	176,284
1864	193,418
1865	248,120

Table 9. Totals of U.S. immigrants for each year of the Civil War.

An 1863 explanation for this "great rush" to America said it was "caused chiefly by the great demand for laborers and consequent high prices and the large bounties offered by the Government for volunteers."[146] By comparison, Mormon emigration from overseas flowed vigorously, except in 1865, for three clearly identified causes: (1) Joseph Smith's prophecy about civil war in America and war spreading throughout the world made believers move to Zion for safety; (2) terrible employment conditions in Europe and manpower needs in America made people emigrate in order to better themselves; (3) the Church's down-and-back wagon train system made it possible for those otherwise financially unable to emigrate to do so. Clearly, the 1865 precipitous drop in Mormon emigration numbers correlates with suspensions that season of the Church trains option.

The Church's basic transportation system to the plains that was in place in 1860 continued through the war years. That is, agents continued to charter sailing ships, the ships arrived safely in New York or Boston, and the agents booked railroad and steamboat passage to Chicago, Quincy, and St. Joseph, and on to Florence, or, after 1862, to Wyoming, Nebraska. That the down-and-back Church train system characterized Mormon emigration during the Civil War years was coincidental. No concern about war engineered the system, which was set in motion before the war broke out. Rather, Church leaders hoped the war would not interfere with it.

War did cause the system difficulties. War demands meant ships were harder to charter and harder to staff. Ships tried to avoid Confederate raiders on the high seas. War drew off railroad cars, hence many Mormon emigrants had to ride in box or cattle cars, change trains more often than normal, and sometimes be routed a short distance into Canada. Missouri was a dangerous war zone, where trains were fired on, tracks were damaged, and bridges wrecked. The war's demand for goods and services forced prices up, including those for transportation tickets, wagons, oxen, and food. Depreciated dollars hurt agents and emigrants trying to stay within budgets. Emigrants' encounters with soldiers sometimes were ugly. Soldiers sometimes checked Mormon railroad passengers, looking for deserters. Soldiers stopped some Mormon wagon companies and required men to take oaths of allegiance or loyalty.

During the Civil War years, the Mormon emigration system continued to work very well, moving more than 17,000 Saints to Utah. That five-year total equals nearly half of the total for the previous fourteen years of Mormon Trail travel up to 1861.

William G. Hartley is a retired BYU history professor and founding president of the Mormon Trails Association.

NOTES

1. Stanley B. Kimball, "Sail and Rail Pioneers before 1869," *BYU Studies* 35, no. 2 (1995): 7–42, especially 23–29.

2. An introductory survey is Fred E. Woods, "East to West through North and South: Mormon Immigration to and through America during the Civil War," *BYU Studies* 39, no.1 (2000): 7–29.

3. This discussion about 1861 emigration is based on my essays, "The Great Florence Fitout of 1861," *BYU Studies* 24 (Summer 1984): 341–71; and "Down-and-Back Wagon Trains: Travelers on the Mormon Trail in 1861," *Overland Journal* 11, no. 4 (1993): 23–34.

4. "Instruction to the Saints Throughout the European Mission," *Millennial Star*, November 24, 1860, 744.

5. "Emigration," *Millennial Star*, January 5 and 19, 1861.

6. "Departures," *Millennial Star*, February 2, 1861.

7. "Correspondence," W. A. Martindale to George Q. Cannon, *Millennial Star*, April 13, 1861, 238–39.

8. William G. Hartley, "Brigham Young's Overland Trails Revolution: The Creation of the 'Down-and-Back' Wagon Train System, 1860–61," *Journal of Mormon History* 28, no. 1 (2002): 1–30; John K. Hulmston, "Mormon Immigration in the 1860s: The Story of the Church Team Trains," *Utah Historical Quarterly* 58 (Winter 1990): 32–48.

9. Ship passenger totals used in this paper are those presented in Conway B. Sonne, *Ships, Saints, and Mariners: A Maritime Encyclopedia of Mormon Migration 1830–1890* (Salt Lake City: University of Utah Press, 1987).

10. "Correspondence," N. V. Jones and Jacob Gates to George Q. Cannon, February 8, 1861, *Millennial Star*, March 23, 1861.

11. "News from the United States," *Millennial Star*, April 6, 1861, 219.

12. Bernhard Schettler, memorandum book, 1861, Church History Library, The Church of Jesus Christ of Latter-day Saints, Salt Lake City, Utah (hereafter cited as Church History Library); "Rosine Wilhelmina Aust Bitter," and "Traugott Bitter," life sketches in possession of Constance Brown, Rexburg, Idaho.

13. Erastus Snow to George A. Smith, June 26, 1861, in Journal History of the Church, that date, Church History Library; John D. T. McAllister to George Q. Cannon, July 30, 1861, in Journal History, that date.

14. Diary of Lucius Scovil, April 27, 1861, Church History Library.

15. "Correspondence," Orson Pratt to George Q. Cannon, May 24, 1861, *Millennial Star*, June 15, 1861, 395.

16. Eli Wiggill, Autobiography, MS 8344, Church History Library.

17. "Correspondence," N. V. Jones to George Q. Cannon, May 21, 1861, *Millennial Star*, June 15, 1861, 396.

18. Thomas Cott Griggs's summary of Boston Saints' trip to Florence and of the Joseph Horne wagon train, in Journal History, September 13, 1861.

19. George M. Ottinger, reminiscences and journal, June 12, 1861, in possession of Susanna Helbling, Salt Lake City.

20. Griggs, summary.

21. Eli Wiggill Autobiography; M. Dean Garrett, "The Controversial Death of Gobo Fango," *Utah Historical Quarterly* 57 (Summer 1989), 265.

22. Kimball, "Sail and Rail Pioneers," 15.

23. Griggs, summary.

24. Griggs, summary.

25. Hartley, "Great Florence Fitout of 1861," 365–66.

26. Ottinger Journal, June 18, 1861.

27. Hartley, "Great Florence Fitout of 1861."

28. Hartley, "Great Florence Fitout of 1861." Unless cited otherwise, the discussion about Florence operations that follows is from that article.

29. Jacob Gates, reminiscences and diaries, April 24, 1861, Church History Library.

30. Gates, reminiscences and diaries.

31. Hartley, "Great Florence Fitout of 1861."

32. A thirteenth company led by Ira Reid had forty-five wagons in it but split up and merged into other companies, whose wagon counts probably included their wagons. See "Mormon Pioneer Overland Travel, 1847–1868," Church History website, http://lds.org/churchhistory/library/pioneercompany search/1,15773,3966-1,00.html, 1861 Ira Reed or Reid company.

33. John K. Hulmston, "Transplain Migration: The Church Trains in Mormon Immigration, 1861–1868" (master's thesis, Utah State University, 1985), 61.

34. Regarding Church trains during the rest of the 1860s, see Hulmston, "Mormon Immigration in the 1860s: The Story of the Church Trains."

35. "New from America," J. McKnight, letter, September 22, 1861, *Millennial Star*, October 26, 1861, 693.

36. Bob Ansler, "Railroads in the Civil War," www.gateway nmra.org/articles/civil-war1.htm.

37. "What the Saints Are Capable of Doing," *Millennial Star*, June 15, 1861, 393.

38. "What the Saints Must Do Who Want to Emigrate," *Millennial Star*, June 8, 1861, 361.

39. "To Presidents and Emigrating Saints," *Millennial Star*, February 22, 1862.

40. H. Kirk Memmott, ed., *Thomas Memmott Journal* (Provo, UT: J. Grant Stevenson, 1976), 1:31.

41. "How Many Elders Shall Be Released to Go to Zion," *Millennial Star*, March 8, 1862, 155.

42. "Correspondence," William Clayton to George Q. Cannon, February 20, 1862, *Millennial Star*, April 26, 1862, 270.

43. "The Best Policy for the Saints to Pursue," *Millennial Star*, May 17, 1862, 312–14.

44. Autobiography of Hans Christian. Excerpt posted on the LDS Church's Mormon Immigration Index, ship *Franklin* 1862 account. This index is a ship emigration CD database. It is also online at various genealogy database websites.

45. John Hansen Hougaard, autobiography and journal, excerpt on Mormon Immigration Index, ship *Electric* 1862 accounts.

46. Jacob Zollinger, autobiography, excerpt on Mormon Immigration Index, ship *Windermere* 1862 accounts.

47. Joseph Coulson Rich, journal, excerpt on Mormon Immigration Index, ship *John Jay Boyd* 1862 accounts.

48. Jens Christian Andersen Weibye, reminiscences and journals, excerpt on Mormon Immigration Index, ship *Franklin* 1862 accounts.

49. Oluf Christian Larson, autobiography, excerpt on Mormon Immigration Index, ship *Electric* 1862 accounts.

50. Ola Nelson Stohl, diaries, excerpt on Mormon Immigration Index, ship *Electric* 1862 accounts.

51. William Lindsay, autobiography, excerpt on Mormon Immigration Index, ship *Antarctic* 1862 accounts.

52. William Ajax, diary, excerpt on Mormon Immigration Index, ship *John Jay Boyd* 1862 accounts.

53. Joseph Coulson Rich, journal diary, excerpt on Mormon Immigration Index, ship *John Jay Boyd* 1862 accounts.

54. Andrew Jenson, *History of the Scandinavian Mission* (Salt Lake City: Deseret News, 1927), 162–67.

55. Jenson, *History of the Scandinavian Mission*, 162–67.

56. Jenson, *History of the Scandinavian Mission*, 162–67.

57. William Wood, autobiography, in *Our Pioneer Heritage* (Salt Lake City: Daughters of Utah Pioneers, 1970), 13:273–77.

58. Oluf Christian Larson, autobiography.

59. Hulmston, "Transplain Migration," 79.

60. William Lindsay, autobiography.

61. Hulmston, "Transplain Migration," 74–75.

62. Jens Weibye, reminiscences and journal.

63. "Blessings to Be Obtained by Gathering," *Millennial Star*, October 4, 1862, 633–35; "Why Are So Many of the Saints Not Gathered?" *Millennial Star*, October 11, 1862, 649–52; "News from Home," *Millennial Star*, November 8, 1862, 714.

64. "The Immigration to Utah," *Deseret News*, July 14, 1863, reprinted in the *Millennial Star*, September 5, 1863, 564–65.

65. "Emigration," *Millennial Star*, July 25, 1863, 476.

66. "The Intending Emigrants—Seasonable Advice," *Millennial Star*, January 10, 1863, 25.

67. "To the Saints and Intending Emigrants," *Millennial Star*, March 21, 1863, 184.

68. Thomas Henry White, autobiography, excerpt on Mormon Immigration Index, ship *Antarctica* 1863 accounts.

69. Charles Dickens, *The Uncommercial Traveler* (Oxford: Oxford University Press, 1987), 220–32.

70. "Emigration—Prosperity of the Past Season—Counsel for the Future," *Millennial Star*, August 29, 1863, 552.

71. "Close of the Emigration Season," *Millennial Star*, June 20, 1863, 392.

72. "New York City Draft Riots," Wikipedia, http://en.wikipedia.org/wiki/New_York_City_draft_riots; see also "New York City Draft Riots," *Shotgun's Home of the American Civil War*, www.civilwarhome.com/draftriots.htm.

73. David M. Stuart, autobiography, excerpt on Mormon Immigration Index, ship *Cynosure* 1863 accounts.

74. Daughters of Utah Pioneers, "They Came in 1863," in *Our Pioneer Heritage* (Salt Lake City: Daughters of Utah Pioneers, 1964), 7:35.

75. Elijah Larkin, diaries, excerpt on Mormon Immigration Index, ship *Amazon* 1863 accounts.

76. William H. Freshwater, diary, excerpt on Mormon Immigration Index, ship *William Tapscott* 1862 accounts.

77. White, autobiography.

78. White, autobiography.

79. Thomas Wright Kirby, autobiography, excerpt on Mormon Immigration Index, ship *Antarctic* 1863 accounts.

80. Kimball, "Sail and Rail Pioneers before 1869," 16.

81. *Deseret News*, April 29, 1863, 1.

82. Author's calculations based on *Deseret News* reports and data for the 1864 wagon companies posted on the "Mormon Pioneer Overland Travel" website.

83. White, autobiography.

84. White, autobiography.

85. Mary Charlotte Jacobs Soffe, "The Story of My Life," excerpt posted on "Mormon Pioneer Overland Travel, 1847–1868," 1863 John R. Murdock company accounts.

86. William Richardson, autobiography, excerpt on "Mormon Pioneer Overland Travel," 1863 Horton D. Haight company accounts.

87. Martin A. Zyderlaan, A. H. Patterson camp journal, in Journal History, September 4, 1863, 1–12.

88. Mary Elizabeth Rollins Lightner diary, excerpt on "Mormon Pioneer Overland Travel," 1863 Alvus H. Patterson company accounts.

89. E. L. Sloan Letter, September 25, 1863, in Journal History, that date. Also see Elijah Larkin Diary.

90. "Correspondence," [E. L. Sloan to George Q. Cannon], December 14, 1863, *Millennial Star*, February 20, 1864, 122.

91. "The Past Season's Emigration—Potency of Faith and Prayer," *Millennial Star*, October 31, 1863, 696–98.

92. "Emigration and the Motives Which Prompt It," *Millennial Star*, January 23, 1864, 58.

93. "Emigration Deposits, Etc.," *Millennial Star*, March 13, 1864, 168–69.

94. "The Emigration of the Scandinavian Saints," *Millennial Star*, April 30, 1864, 282.

95. Andrew Christian Nielson, autobiography, excerpt on Mormon Immigration Index, ship *Monarch of the Sea* 1864 accounts; and "The Emigration of Scandinavian Saints," *Millennial Star*, April 30, 1864, 281.

96. John Johnson [Johan Johanssen], reminiscences, excerpt on Mormon Immigration Index, ship *Monarch of the Sea* 1864 accounts.

97. "Departure," *Millennial Star*, May 7, 1864, 298.

98. John Smith, autobiography, excerpt on Mormon Immigration Index, ship *Monarch of the Sea* 1864 accounts.

99. Thomas Evans Jeremy to President Cannon, July 2, 1864, *Millennial Star*, August 13, 1864, 524.

100. "Departure," *Millennial Star*, June 18, 1864, 395.

101. Mary Ann Ward Webb, autobiography, in "The Year of 1864," *Our Pioneer Heritage* (Salt Lake City: Daughters of Utah Pioneers, 1965), 8:39–43.

102. Charles William Symons, autobiography, excerpt on Mormon Immigration Index, ship *Hudson* 1864 accounts.

103. John Smith, autobiography.

104. H. N. Hansen, "An Account of a Mormon Family's Conversion to the Religion of the Latter-day Saints and their Trip from Denmark to Utah," *Annals of Iowa* 41, no. 1 (Summer 1971): 712–26.

105. Hansen, "Account of a Mormon Family's Conversion."

106. Hansen, "Account of a Mormon Family's Conversion."

107. John Lyman Smith, diaries, excerpt on Mormon Immigration Index, ship *Hudson* 1864 accounts; Mary Ann Ward Webb, autobiography. She was on the ship *Hudson*.

108. John Lyman Smith, diaries.

109. Elizabeth Edwards, reminiscences, excerpt on "Mormon Pioneer Overland Travel," 1864 William S. Warren company accounts.

110. John Lyman Smith, diaries.

111. John Lyman Smith, diaries.

112. "Life History of Elizabeth Letitia Higginbotham Peery," "David H. Peery on Honesty and Thrift," and "Life Story of David Harold Peery," in Mormon Biographical Sketches Collection, Church History Library; "David H. Peery," in Andrew Jenson, *Biographical Encyclopedia*, 1:756–58; William G. Hartley, "The Confederate Officer and 'That Mormon Girl,'" *Ensign*, April 1982, 52–54.

113. Craig S. Smith, "Wyoming, Nebraska Territory: Joseph W. Young and the Mormon Emigration of 1864," *BYU Studies* 39, no. 1 (2000): 31–51; Andrew Jenson, "Latter-day Saint Emigration from Wyoming, Nebraska, 1864–1866," *Nebraska History Magazine* 17 (April–June 1936): 113–27; Stanley B. Kimball, "The Nebraska City Cutoff, 1864–66," in "A Forgotten Trail and Mormon Settlements," *Ensign*, February 1980.

114. Church Emigration Book, 1862–1881, Church History Library.

115. Matilda Christina Ohlson Sprague, autobiographical sketch, excerpt on "Mormon Pioneer Overland Travel," 1864 William B. Preston company accounts.

116. Hansen, "Account of a Mormon Family's Conversion."

117. John D. Chase Company Summary on "Mormon Pioneer Overland Travel," 1864 John D. Chase company accounts.

118. Joseph A. Young was Brigham Young's son; Joseph W. Young was Brigham Young's nephew, the son of Lorenzo Dow Young.

119. Henry Ballard, journal, excerpt on Mormon Immigration Index, ship *Hudson* 1864 accounts.

120. William E. Lass, *From the Missouri to the Great Salt Lake: An Account of Overland Freighting* (n.p.: Nebraska State Historical Society, 1972), 145. These Indian attacks were not due to opportunities opened by a weakened federal government but stemmed from specific recent army activity against plains Indians (p. 147).

121. John Lyman Smith, autobiography and journals. He was in the William Hyde wagon company.

122. John T. Gerber, diary, in Journal History, October 26, 1864.

123. "The Overland–Bridger Pass Trail" and "The Overland–Bridger Pass Trail Mountain Division Variant in Colorado and Wyoming," in Stanley B. Kimball, *Historic Sites and Markers along the Mormon and Other Great Western Trails* (Urbana and Chicago: University of Illinois Press, 1988), 153–59, 160–66, and Kimball, "Another Route to Zion: Rediscovering the Overland Trail," *Ensign*, June 1984, 34.

124. "Emigration," *Salt Lake Daily Telegraph*, September 7, 1864.

125. John T. Gerber, diary.

126. "Emigration and the Temple," *Millennial Star*, September 17, 1864, 600–602.

127. "Emigration," *Millennial Star*, January 21, 1865, 40–41.

128. "Emigration," *Millennial Star*, January 21, 1865, 42–43.

129. "Departure," *Millennial Star*, February 25, 1865, 124.

130. "Correspondence, June 24, 1865, from W. H. Shearman and others to Presidents Wells and Young," *Millennial Star*, July 1, 1865, 398. The committee was Sisters Cecelia Campbell, Maria Wixley, and Elisebeth Savage.

131. "Correspondence," M. G. Atwood and others to President Wells, June 15, 1865, *Millennial Star*, July 15, 1865, 443.

132. Jenson, *History of the Scandinavian Mission*, 183–86.

133. Mary Ann Greenhalgh Mace, autobiography, in *Our Pioneer Heritage* (Salt Lake City: Daughters of Utah Pioneers, 1972), 15:125–27.

134. W. [William] H. Shearman, et al. [Letter], *Millennial Star*, July 22, 1865, 461–63.

135. John G. Holman [Letter], *Deseret News Weekly*, August 2, 1865, 351.

136. Robert Pixton, autobiography, excerpt on Mormon Immigration Index, ship *Belle Wood* 1865 accounts.

137. Miner G. Atwood, journal, in Journal History, November 8, 1865, 8–22.

138. James P. Anderson, autobiographical sketch, excerpt on "Mormon Pioneer Overland Travel," 1865 Miner G. Atwood company accounts.

139. Thomas Alston, autobiography, excerpt on "Mormon Pioneer Overland Travel," 1865 Henson Walker company accounts. The term "kaffir" was a pejorative term for a South African black person.

140. Miner G. Atwood, journal, in Journal History, November 8, 1865, 8–22.

141. "History of Annie Maria Kershaw Thompson," excerpt on "Mormon Pioneer Overland Travel," 1865 William S. S. Willis company accounts.

142. *Deseret News*, November 23, 1865.

143. Jenson, "Latter Day Saint Emigration from Wyoming, Nebraska, 1864–1866," 124–25.

144. Sonne, Ships, Saints, and Mariners, and Melvin L. Bashore files, pioneer companies statistics, electronic file, Church History Library.

145. Office of Immigration Statistics, 2003 *Yearbook of Immigration Statistics*, http://www.dhs.gov/xlibrary/assets/statistics/yearbook/2003/2003Yearbook.pdf.

146. *New York Observer and Chronicle*, October 29, 1863.

The connecting of the transcontinental telegraph wires took place on Main Street in Salt Lake City during October 1861. This photo shows Utah Territory's first telegraph office at the northeast corner of 100 South and Main Street. (Utah State Historical Society)

Photographic teams, such as the one pictured here that traveled with General Meade's Army in November 1863, helped to document much of the Civil War. Newspapers often printed woodcut images that were based on photographs. (Library of Congress)

CHAPTER 15

Kenneth L. Alford

UTAH AND THE CIVIL WAR PRESS

Shortly after the Civil War ended, the *New York Times* suggested that "in the Spring of 1861 South Carolina was more loyal to the Union than Utah is today"[1]—a truly staggering statement, considering that South Carolina had seceded from the Union in December 1860 and the following spring South Carolinian artillery units fired the first shots of the Civil War, a war that led to the death of over six hundred thousand people. What was it about Utah Territory that caused newspapers to express such strong views?

To understand what interested American newspapers about Utah and Mormons during the Civil War, we must look at the decade before the war. While the Latter-day Saints had never been popular in the American press, reporting took a negative turn following Apostle Orson Pratt's public announcement on August 29, 1852, regarding the practice of polygamy.[2] Interest and reports about Utah reached new heights during the Utah War (1857–58). Mormons and the Utah War captured the popular imagination of the nation and were among the most frequent news stories,

second only to articles about slavery and the Kansas Territory. In 1857–58, the *New York Times*, for example, printed over 1,200 articles that mentioned Utah, Mormons, or the Utah Expedition—an average of almost two stories a day.[3] Throughout the Utah War, American newspapers reported a steady stream of "Mormon outrages" regarding polygamy, Brigham Young, and Utah's perceived disloyalty.[4]

The Utah War essentially ended on June 26, 1858, when Brevet Brigadier General Albert Sidney Johnston and his soldiers marched through Salt Lake City.[5] With the nation's interest piqued during the Utah War, news reporting about Utah Territory and Mormonism continued after the war. Camp Floyd, located forty miles outside of Salt Lake City, became the largest military post in the country and served as a Civil War training ground for military leaders on both sides of the conflict. Utah and Mormonism continued to receive harsh treatment from the press during the Civil War.

While the artillery barrage of Fort Sumter in Charleston Harbor during April 1861 is

This photograph shows the Confederate flag flying at Fort Sumter on April 15, 1861, following the surrender of Major Anderson and his Union soldiers. (Library of Congress)

generally credited as the official beginning of the Civil War, the first hostile Confederate artillery fire actually occurred on January 9, 1861, when a Southern battery fired upon the *Star of the West*, a commercial ship carrying needed supplies to soldiers stationed at Fort Sumter.[6] Those opening shots of the war occurred just two and a half years after the Utah War ended; it should come as no surprise, therefore, that Civil War newspapers continued to reflect the same anti-Mormon bias exhibited during the Utah War.

As should be expected, reporting of the Civil War dominated the American press from 1861 to 1865. While newspapers were focused on bringing war news to their readers, reporting also continued on a host of other issues of national and local concern. Continuing interest in Utah Territory and

Mormonism ensured a steady stream of news reports on those subjects during the war.

Newspapers and weekly news magazines were the most common source of news in the nineteenth century.[7] Newspapers were hungry for news and printed much, if not most, of what they received. In the 1860s, information reached newspapers several ways—by mail, reporters, dispatches, and express riders.[8] The immediacy with which news could be delivered changed when the first transcontinental telegraph lines met in Utah in late 1861.[9] For the first time in American history, newspapers could quickly share news from across the nation.

Nineteenth-century journalism standards were different from today's standards. It was not uncommon for rumors, speculation, and editorial comments to appear intermingled in the same article. News reporters and editors were more open with their views. And there was little attempt to hide political opinions. Stories were often published without any confirmation. Some Confederate news reporters, for example, tried to encourage rebellion and secession in Utah. This helps explain why the North Carolina *Fayetteville Observer* printed the false report in August 1861 that "Brigham Young has thrown off his allegiance to Lincoln's rump government, and declared the independence of the territory. The Mormons are arming in every direction to maintain their independence at all hazards."[10]

Brigham Young was the subject of great curiosity during the Civil War.
(Utah State Historical Society)

Newspapers regularly sent bundles of previous editions to other papers so they could borrow and reprint articles of interest. Journalism standards required newspapers only to acknowledge the source of a story. There was so much borrowing between newspapers that it was sometimes difficult to determine where an individual article originated. Reports regarding the conduct and progress of the war often carried a political bias, so they were not readily reprinted between Northern and Southern newspapers, but articles and reports about Mormonism, polygamy, Brigham Young, and Utah Territory were generally outside of wartime politics. Consequently, they were easily printed and reprinted by both sides of the conflict; Utah was a good source of news. While the nation held divergent views regarding slavery, polygamy was a source of moral outrage on which most of the nation agreed. Articles about Utah Territory and Mormonism tended to focus on several recurring themes—loyalty, Utah's

quest for statehood, polygamy, and Brigham Young. This essay provides an overview of Civil War reporting on those four themes.

Mormon loyalty was a national concern throughout the nineteenth century. During the Utah War, Latter-day Saints were portrayed as disloyal to the nation, and as the Civil War began, there were lingering and sincere doubts among Americans regarding the true loyalties of Utah Territory. Mormons were usually portrayed in the press as being "openly inimical to the Government of the United States" while considering themselves "steadfast adherents to the Constitution."[11] Difficult relations between Utahns and Federal officials, an important cause of the Utah War, continued during the Civil War, which reinforced previous perceptions.

Ten days after Confederate artillery fired upon the *Star of the West*, the *Daily Dispatch* in Richmond, Virginia, published a comparison of the Federal government's response to Utah in 1857 and South Carolina's secession. When Utah, "that abominable nest of murder, incest and polygamy . . . was in open rebellion against the General Government, Mr. Buchanan sent Peace Commissioners with the Army," but to South Carolina, "a sovereign State, one of the most civivilized [*sic*], virtuous, and exemplary of Christian communities," the government "sen[t] no Peace Commissioners . . . only the Sword."[12]

At the beginning of the Civil War, there were seven United States territories—Washington, Nebraska, Utah, New Mexico,

Some of the wives and daughters of Brigham Young. Newspapers across the country were fascinated by the practice of polygamy. (Utah State Historical Society)

Colorado, Nevada, and Dakota. The Southern press predicted that "in all probability they [the territories] will, with the exception, perhaps of Utah, be admitted into the Union in the course of a few years."[13] The Congress of Confederate States, which met at Montgomery, Alabama, in 1861, recognized that Utah had aligned itself with the Union. The "permanent Constitution of the Confederacy," debated in March 1861, proposed that "south of Kansas and Utah[,] slavery shall be established beyond the power of Congress or of the Northern States ever to abolish it."[14]

Southern papers often reported events and stories differently than their Northern neighbors. Following the outbreak of hostilities in 1861, the Union War Department ordered

army units stationed in Utah to return east for service against the Confederacy. A month after Fort Sumter, the *New York Times* expressed the Northern concern that "the removal of the small force from Utah will prove a fatal blunder, as it will leave the great overland routes to California and Oregon unprotected, and invite aggression both from lawless Mormons and hostile Indians."[15] Southern newspapers reported in a different light the long-standing perception that Utah Territory was disloyal to the national government. After commenting on Utah's assumed disloyalty, a Georgia paper added this Southern sentiment: "We hope Father Brigham will give the Yankees as much trouble as possible." And not wishing to miss an opportunity to malign their Northern enemies as well, the reporter added, "They [the North] are no better than the Mormons, though they conceal their rascality a little more."[16] Even though the South was at war with the North, Mormons were still viewed as being less trustworthy.

After defining the Confederacy as the "self-appointed champions of the institution of slavery," a correspondent for the North Carolinian paper the *Weekly Raleigh Register* complained that under President Buchanan "the Mormons who were to be thrashed into good behavior are still as obdurately determined as ever to set at defiance the laws of God, and man, and decency" and that "the army of the United States, sent to the Mormon territory at an enormous expense, has not been permitted to carry out, or attempt to carry out, the object of the expedition."[17] Again, even while involved in a war of secession with the North, many Southern newspapers could not bypass an opportunity to publicly complain about Utah Territory.

Many political observers in the States watched closely to see how Utah Territory celebrated the nation's birthday in 1861. Explaining Fourth of July celebration events, a Utah-based reporter for the *New York Times* discussed the clearly patriotic observance of Independence Day in Salt Lake City: "The procession might have been a mile and a half long, nearly one-half of which consisted of school-children from the various Wards in the city. Flags and banners were numerous, and with varied inscriptions and devices, all intensely Mormon and strongly conservative

Eliza R. Snow, a Utah Mormon poetess, wrote war-related poetry that was published in eastern newspapers during the Civil War. (Utah State Historical Society)

of the 'Constitution' and the 'spirit of '76' . . . [which] magnified the 'Declaration of Independence.'" After reciting numerous patriotic events in Salt Lake City, the reporter still concluded, though, that it was "difficult to judge whether the 'North' or the 'South' ha[d] the preponderance in the scale of Mormon sympathy."[18] Newspapers across the country seemed united in the popular belief that Mormons were disloyal and could not be trusted.

In July 1861, two weeks before the First Battle of Bull Run (Manassas), the first major military engagement of the war, the *New York Times* reminded readers of the federal government's reaction to Utah's perceived rebellion in 1857 by noting that "three years ago, when the authority of the nation was contemptuously defied by the Mormons in Utah, the only safe policy consistent with the dignity of the Government was the prompt employment of such an overwhelming force for the suppression of the rebellion as removed all possibility of failure." The writer then recommended "the same vigorous and merciful policy now" to deal with Confederate secession.[19]

Reinforcing the national stereotype regarding Utah's disloyalty, Henry Martin, Utah Territory's Superintendent of Indian Affairs, announced in October 1861 in the *New York Times* that "the Mormons are seceding on their own hook, and won't have anything to do more with the National Union, and are declaring vengeance on Government trains which may be caught in this Territory hereafter, and several other things of that sort." Several Mormon leaders "called on the Superintendent, and represented their view of matters so strongly to him, that after a great deal of unwillingness he has consented to a public acknowledgment that he told the Government a little more or less than he now considers strictly warranted by the facts in the case."[20] Occasionally, alternative viewpoints would also appear in print. In early 1862, the *New York Times* reported that "the 'crusade of '57' [the Utah War] was now generally acknowledged to have been the result of slander."[21] Stories of that nature were an exception, though, rather than the rule.

In the fall of 1861, after hostilities between the opposing Union and Confederate armies had increased, William Cullen Bryant wrote a patriotic poem entitled *Our Country's Call*. The last stanza of his poem proclaimed the correctness and ultimate triumph of the Union's cause:

> Few, few were they whose
> swords of old
> Won the fair land in which we dwell;
> But we are many, we who hold
> The grim resolve to guard it well.
> Strike, for that broad and goodly land,
> Blow after blow, till men shall see
> That Might and Right move
> hand in hand,
> And glorious must their triumph be!

Eliza R. Snow, a Mormon poet, wrote a poetic reply a few months later. Portions of Snow's poem were published by the *New York Times* in January 1862. The reporter interspersed political commentary and criticism with lines from Snow's poem as he mocked Utah's apparent neutrality regarding the war:

Perhaps this lady's effort may be taken as a fair index of the views of the more orthodox Mormons on the present National civil struggle. Bryant is asked reproachfully why his "gifted pen" should "move to scenes of cruel war." Eliza thinks the effort vain to save the country, for

> *"Its fate is fixed—its destiny*
> *Is sealed—its end is sure to come;*
> *Why use the wealth of poesy*
> *To urge a nation to its doom?"*

The cause of the distress and calamity which now afflict the nation is perspicaciously revealed:

> *"It must be so, t'avenge the blood*
> *That stains the walls of Carthage jail."*

That is, the blood of the original "Joseph, the Prophet." It appears there is little hope for the country, for war, pestilence and famine are to rage

> *"Till every hope and every charm*
> *Shall that ill-fated land forsake."* . . .

North and South are eventually to make the discovery that

> *"Protection is not made of steel."*

Salt Lake is to be and remain the single cheering oasis amid the universal National desolation in the years to come.[22]

The American press, North and South, eagerly embraced negative reports about Utah. In August 1862, the Utah Cavalry completed ninety days of Federal service protecting the Overland Trail. This military unit was mustered by Brigham Young at the request of President

Lincoln and was commanded by Lot Smith. At the same time as the completion of this service, a Mississippi newspaper reported that the "robberies and murders on the stage route heretofore ascribed to hostile Indians, have in reality been instigated, if not actually committed by the Mormons."[23] In actuality, Mormon soldiers from Utah guarded the trail that summer.

A few months after the military abandoned Fort Crittenden (formerly Camp Floyd) outside of Salt Lake City, the government ordered Colonel Patrick Edward Connor and the California Volunteers he commanded to establish a wartime garrison in Utah Territory.[24] Soon after the War Department announced that soldiers would return to Utah, the *New York Times* asked, "What are these troops needed for in Utah? There are no rebels there. . . . The Mormons and Indians are, as things go, doing respectably well at present; and it would not be bad policy to let well enough alone."[25] Connor selected a site in the Salt Lake City foothills in late 1862 and established Camp Douglas.

Northern papers portrayed Utah—not entirely without cause—as sitting on the sidelines during the war. In January 1863, Utah's governor, Stephen Harding, was quoted in the eastern press as saying that "he was sorry that he had heard so very little in the Territory, in public or in private, which sympathized with the Government in its present unhappy struggle with the rebels."[26] In May 1864, the Northern press reported that Lieutenant

In June 1862, as Utah Territory's request for statehood languished on Capitol Hill, President Abraham Lincoln signed the Anti-Bigamy Law. (Wikimedia)

General Daniel H. Wells (commander of Utah's Nauvoo Legion militia and counselor in the First Presidency to Brigham Young) "thinks the present a good time to be watchful that the 'disunion, secession, direful war and general discord,' which are 'filling the land with devastation, crime and misery,' be not permitted to creep into Utah. . . . The folks up in this Territory have no idea of themselves being drawn into the vortex of war, for they think of fighting to keep out."[27]

Utahns were generally pleased with Lincoln's November 1864 reelection. During March 1865, "in common, as is presumed, with the whole of the northern portion of the Union, on the 4th inst., the reinauguration of Mr. Lincoln, was celebrated here [Utah] in grand style."[28] Mormons still considered themselves loyal to the Union. The war's end and President Lincoln's assassination shortly thereafter in April 1865 did not bring an end, though, to the questioning of Mormon sympathies as American newspapers continued to report Utah's perceived disloyalty. A November 1865 report in the *New York Times* suggested that "as to the graver matters of disloyalty and threatened difficulties, we may say that such accusations against the Mormons are not new, and perhaps are not now, any more than formerly, altogether without foundation." The news report suggested two possible reasons for Mormon disloyalty, "firstly, because more than half of the population of Utah consists of recent emigrants of foreign birth . . . and secondly, because the long and terrible persecutions of the Mormons in Illinois and Missouri in the early days of the Church, have left behind

Sample headlines about Utah and Mormonism from Northern Civil War newspapers.

them bitter memories of the power that failed to afford protection." The reporter suggested that "there have always been annoying quarrels in progress with the Mormons, which reached the very verge of war eight years ago, and the embers of which have been smouldering ever since." Even though the nation was weary from four years of Civil War that killed over half a million people, the reporter noted that "there are folks who think the only thing to do is to fight the Saints, and reduce them to loyalty and monogamy at the point of the sword."[29]

With the end of formal hostilities between the North and South, Utah Territory returned once again to the front pages of many newspapers. In November 1865, a large front-page article in the *New York Times* announced that the Mormons "are preparing for resistance, even to war. . . . They anticipate no interference except from the United States. The burden of their speeches and sermons everywhere is to arm for the coming contest. They are arming."[30]

The physical distance between Utah Territory and the States—both east and west—as well as the religious distance between Latter-day Saints and the majority of Americans made it difficult, if not impossible, for Mormons to be perceived and portrayed as they saw themselves. An 1865 *New York Times* article showed the depth of distrust within the nation. Negatively comparing Mormons in Utah to secessionists in the Confederacy, the paper suggested that "Utah was the first to go through with the solemn farce of declaring its little self independent of the United States . . . [in] August, 1857, when Brigham Young . . . declared . . . that the umbilical cord that united this Territory with the United States was then and there cut. . . . The so-called State of Deseret . . . is in open rebellion against the United States; and the people, under the command of their leaders, are in open rebellion against the laws of the United States."[31]

Utah's extended quest for statehood was a second topic that received frequent coverage during the Civil War. Utah first applied for statehood in 1849 and submitted other unsuccessful requests prior to the Civil War. Beginning with South Carolina's secession in December 1860, eleven states eventually left the Union. A year after the Southern states formed the Confederate States of America, Utah Territory again formally applied for statehood. As William H. Hooper, Utah's territorial delegate to Congress, noted in a letter to George Q. Cannon, "We show our loyalty by trying to get in while others are trying to get out."[32]

Unlike their Northern counterparts, Southern newspapers seldom mentioned Utah's application for statehood. By January 1862, Confederate papers grudgingly announced that "Utah desires admission into the Federal Union" and two weeks later reported "Utah demands admission into the Union."[33] Utah's 1862 statehood convention occurred in a brief period between January and July when Utah was without a federally appointed governor in residence.[34] Utah's governor, John W. Dawson (Lincoln's first appointment for Utah), was "accused of making improper advances to one of the Mormon women" and fled the territory on New Year's Eve 1861.[35] The state convention in Salt Lake City three weeks later drafted a constitution and appealed to the U.S. Congress for statehood.[36] When two associate federal judges, Thomas J. Drake and Charles B. Waite, left Utah a month after Governor Dawson, Northern reporters asked, "What is to be done with Utah? Shall she become one of the sisterhood of States, or shall she be kept out here in the cold a little longer?"[37] That question was answered in an earlier news story: "We shall have to tell Utah to wait."[38]

When news of Utah's statehood request reached the east, the *New York Times* commented that "in the stirring events of the rebellion, the Mormon territory out in the Great Salt Lake region has probably been the last thing thought of; and it is a little startling

to hear that Utah is knocking at the door of the Union, and asking to be let in . . . during the present session [of Congress]." The article further observed that "Utah had dropped as completely out of mind as Pompeii or Palmyra, when, all of a sudden, a few weeks ago, a message was flashed over the wires, by the just completed telegraph from Salt Lake City, announcing to the Government that Utah was loyal to the Union, and her people ready to fight for its preservation."[39]

In February 1862, a news report observed that "Utah had for years petitioned every session of Congress for admission as a State, in vain; while Oregon, with half the population, got a State Government." The rejection came, according to the reporter, because "they were poor, d—d Mormons, and that was sufficient."[40]

Northern readers were informed of the prevalent view in Utah that "they were going to become a State" and that if their application was approved by Congress, "they would be as faithful and true as the sun to the Constitution and the Union."[41] Utahns wanted statehood. That same article concluded, "There are two things which the Mormons seem bent upon doing—entering into the Union, and erecting their wonderful temple."[42]

In spring 1862, Brigham Young was elected governor of the proposed state of Deseret. The *New York Times* reported that within Utah Territory "the feeling [was] freely expressed, that it [was] the duty of Congress to acknowledge the present initiatory steps and to straightway admit 'Deseret' into the Union 'on an equal footing with the original States.'" Writing from Salt Lake City in May 1862, the Utah-based newspaper correspondent asked, "What are we? Are we a Territory or are we a State? We have a Territorial organization, and we have a State organization. We have a Territorial Acting Governor, and we have a State Governor beginning to act. . . . So you see the questions of 'to be, or not to be,' and what to be, are assuming an actual importance in this Territory."[43] Congress, however, took little serious action regarding Utah's statehood request. In January 1863, Brigham Young acknowledged that "Congress, during its last session, was heavily burdened with duties pertaining to the conduct of the war . . . [and] took no action upon our petition."[44] In November 1863, a week before President Lincoln's Gettysburg Address, Young was quoted as asking, "Who is it that calls us apostates from our Government, deserters, traitors, rebels, Secessionists?"[45] The article provided no answer.

During the 1864 Northern presidential election, the *Daily South Carolinian* predicted that "four new States will be admitted this session [of Congress] . . . Nevada, Colorado, New Mexico and Utah." With the addition of those four states, Lincoln's reelection would "be a fraud, but, as they say, a justifiable one." The reporter recognized, though, that "there may be a hitch in admitting Utah, owing to her polygamy institutions."[46] Utah's application was again denied. The general tone of reporting was clearly against granting statehood to Utah: polygamy was too large of a problem. An 1865 *Boston Herald* editorial stated, "In our judgment the nation would never sanction it [polygamy] by receiving Utah as a State until the whole thing was wiped out. The law of Congress on this subject, as all other laws, we assure them must be obeyed."[47]

Polygamy, the third major topic of wartime reporting about Utah and the Mormons, was a source of continuing fascination and disgust for the rest of the divided nation.

During the first Republican National Convention, held at Philadelphia in 1856, slavery and polygamy were jointly designated as the "twin relics of barbarism."[48] The Civil War provided the North with the opportunity to eliminate the "first pillar"—slavery—but the "second pillar"—polygamy—remained a topic of great interest, debate, and action throughout the war.

In March 1861, the month before Fort Sumter surrendered, the *Boston Herald* reported that "the doctrine of the Mormons is blasphemous in the extreme. . . . The effects of polygamy [are] extremely horrible. Woman is degraded, all her finer qualities being sunk to give place to licentiousness. . . . Most of the Mormons have two wives, but six appears to be a favorite number with the leaders. . . . The effect upon the children . . . is still more horrible to contemplate."[49]

During the spring of 1862, as Utah's latest petition for statehood was debated on Capitol Hill, antipolygamy legislation passed both houses of Congress. A June 1862 editorial in the *New York Times* suggested that "the purpose of the bill is entirely right, and commends itself to every true friend of morality and civilization, [it] will scarcely be questioned anywhere outside the circles of Mormondom. . . . A National Republican Convention has also declared war against the institution, as one of the 'twin relics of barbarism.' The duty of the Government to exert its power for the extermination of this great social evil is almost universally recognized, and we may consider that question to have passed beyond the field of discussion."[50] President Lincoln signed the Morrill Anti-Bigamy Act in July 1862.

However, the same *Times* editorial expressed "grave reasons for doubting the policy" of openly confronting polygamy "at [that] precise period of time." Only two courses of actions were envisioned—either "the law will remain a dead letter on the statute book," or if the law was enforced, there would be "another Mormon rebellion and another civil war." The editorial affirmed that civil war with the Mormons "under ordinary circumstances would be a less evil" than not enforcing the law. The *Times* noted, however, that because the nation was "engaged in a grand struggle of much larger importance," it was probably not "prudent to break up or endanger our overland communications" by going to war with the Mormons "unless the Mormons [were] insane enough to begin the struggle by harassing overland emigration, exciting the Indians to mischief, oppressing or driving out the few Gentiles residing among them, interrupting the mails and telegraphs, or in some other way compelling active military operations for the protection of American citizens and interests."[51]

The *Times* concluded that "if the sacred duty of suppressing Polygamy is so immediately upon us as to justify all these risks, it is the clear duty of Congress to anticipate the consequences, and at once provide the means necessary for the enforcement of the new law."[52] A Tennessee newspaper similarly predicted that "serious trouble may yet grow out of the condition of affairs among the Mormons in Utah" because "the whole church is in deadly rebellion against this law [the Anti-Bigamy Act]."[53]

Polygamy was also used as an instrument of social satire. A February 1862 letter to the editor in North Carolina's *Semi-Weekly Raleigh*

Register complained that if a proposal of the Confederate Congress to draft only single men for military service was enacted, then

The Story of a Mormon Woman—Effects of Polygamy.

The New Mormon Complication.

From the New York Post, April 30th.

Insurrection among the Mormons in Utah.
The following important news is contained in a telegraphic dispatch dated Great Salt Lake City, June 16th:

Utah and South Carolina.

Sample headlines about Utah and Mormonism from Southern Civil War newspapers.

the remaining married men could be forced to "introduce Mormonism [polygamy] for the benefit of that portion of the community, and the good of the State."[54]

In June 1865, as the last Confederate forces were surrendering in the South, Schuyler Colfax, Speaker of the U.S. House of Representatives (and future vice president during Ulysses S. Grant's first term), visited Utah and met with Brigham Young. Of his visit, the *New York Times* reported:

> Mr. Colfax remonstrated earnestly against the barbarous institution of polygamy. The Prophet said in reply that it was no essential part of Mormonism; that it did not exist in the early days of the Mormon church; that it was not enjoined in the Book of Mormon, and that if the Lord were to give him a revelation that it should be

stopped, he would cheerfully enforce the divine injunction. It seemed, from the Prophet's remarks, that he was in expectation of receiving such a revelation. We hope he will get it before next session of Congress, though we hardly know how he will dispose of his three score and ten wives.[55]

The *Boston Herald* reported that Mr. Colfax and his party did not hesitate "to express their condemnation of the system, and to say that it [polygamy] is under the ban of the entire civilized world."[56] The article equated polygamy with slavery, noting that just as slavery was practiced "by the wealthy and influential, so this peculiar vice [polygamy] is indulged in mainly by the leading and wealthy men among the Mormons. . . . Whatever opinions we may form of the men, all who know anything of the misery they suffer, must pity the Mormon women." The article concluded that "like all festering sores, the longer it [polygamy] is endured, the more difficult of removal and the more dangerous it becomes."[57]

As illustrated by a November 1865 newspaper article, the question of Mormon loyalty often boiled down to one issue—polygamy: "Our correspondent in Utah . . . declared that Young and the other hierarchs are treasonably disposed toward the United States Government; and not only this, but the Mormon people, under the advice of their leaders, are preparing . . . against any interference with what they call their religious faith—which

A vocal opponent of polygamy, Schuyler Colfax Jr. (1823–85), Speaker of the U.S. House of Representatives, visited Utah and met with Brigham Young in 1865. He later served as Ulysses S. Grant's vice president. (Wikimedia)

. . . as appears from all they say and do, is reduced to but one item—polygamy."[58] The press correctly recognized the importance faithful Latter-day Saints placed on the practice of polygamy. "This [polygamy] is the only thing they talk of fighting for, and it is the only item the leaders care a rush for."[59]

Brigham Young, a fourth major topic of Civil War news reporting about Utah and Mormonism, was a larger-than-life character, and the press was fascinated by him. The unique combination of prophecy, polygamy, and power exercised in a desert kingdom hundreds of miles from the States made him a figure of great curiosity and interest. No wonder he was the subject of many profiles and articles during the war.

Much of the nation viewed Young more as a despot than a religious leader. According to the *Boston Herald*, "Unlimited obedience to Brigham Young and enmity of the Federal Government are topmost in the obligations taken" by Mormons. Readers were told Latter-day Saints considered that "this prophet has been re-elected by God, and that the three [the First Presidency] represent the Trinity. Brigham dictates the only law known among the Mormons."[60] If the Saints "would 'do as Brigham says,' they would soon become the wealthiest and most powerful people on the face of this mundane sphere."[61]

Each semiannual Latter-day Saint general conference brought renewed interest in Brigham Young. According to a November 1862 report,

Brigham was "in the habit of giving the speakers a text to "'spound and 'splain [expound and explain] during the Conference." After hearing talks on a variety of subjects—from taking care of immigrants to hauling rock for the rising temple—Brigham turned his attention to the war and reportedly commented that "the people of the States were pitied for the fix they had got into, but of course it all came of rejecting the 'Prophet Joseph Smith.'"[62]

In summer 1862, Southern papers crowed that "Northern papers are predicting that their Government will soon have some trouble with the Mormons."[63] Newspapers reported in March 1863 that Young was indicted and released on bail "to answer for a violation of the polygamy act" and that "a collision is anticipated between the Mormons and the yankee military."[64] A Savannah, Georgia, paper noted that one of Lincoln's cabinet members called for "relentless severity" in dealing with Brigham Young.[65]

Southern papers reprinted Northern news reports of Mormon activities, especially those that portrayed Brigham Young as a thorn in the Union's side. A June 1863 reprint in a North Carolina paper reported that "Brigham Young, in a speech in his Salt Lake Tabernacle recently, said if the United States asked for a battalion of soldiers for the war he would see it in h—ll first. Too much female society, says the Boston Post, is impairing Brigham's sense of discretion."[66]

The *Natchez (Mississippi) Courier* reprinted an 1863 interview with Brigham Young that originally appeared in the *New York Evening Post.* The author claimed that "old women have been known to go tottering out of their cabins and touch Brigham's clothes, believing that it would restore their eyesight." The interviewer personally found "President Young

an agreeable, affable gentleman, apparently not over forty-five years of age, although he is really upward of sixty. . . . Brigham sleeps alone and eats his meals alone. Whenever he wants one of his wives he sends for her."[67] President Young "conversed upon any and all subjects very freely. . . . The war, he thinks, will be continued till a great part of the North and South is used up, or, to speak more plainly, till they are annihilated, when the 'Saints' will be the people to occupy the country in peace and quietness. The desolation caused by the war, he regards as the judgment of the Lord for the persecution of the 'Saints.'"[68]

As the war entered its fourth year, the press reported that "Brigham expresses himself of the opinion that the folks eastward will make war their all-engrossing business for years to come, neglecting even the very necessary and fundamental labors of agriculture, and thus bringing upon themselves the necessity of crossing the barren plains to the deserts of Utah for bread, or at least that the widows and orphans and teetotal peace lovers will make this long and dreary pilgrimage."[69] Interest in Brigham Young remained high during the war; he was described in one 1865 newspaper account as follows:

> Brigham Young is a man of about medium height, with an immense chest, giving assurance of tremendous vital energy. His head is large, forehead high, round and broad, his hair and whiskers incline to auburn, and though he is sixty-four years of age, scarcely a gray hair can be seen and not a wrinkle detected upon his red and expressive face. His nose resembles the hawk's bill, and his lips, firmly closing, with his blue and at times flashing eyes, betoken

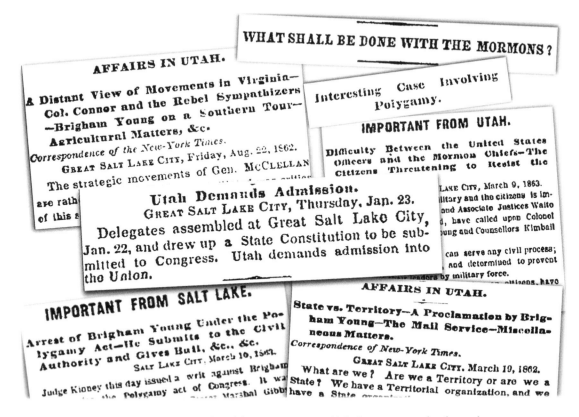

During the Civil War, Union and Confederate newspapers published numerous articles about polygamy, Utah's presumed disloyalty and request for statehood, and Brigham Young.

the great force and indomitable energy which he has always manifested. As some one said of Napoleon, "He is one of the favored few, born to command." He is also one of the shrewdest and most cunning of men, and sensible to the power money gives, and withal possessed of business talents of the highest order, he is now, it is believed, one of the wealthiest men in the nation.[70]

Regarding his reported wealth, one newspaper reported that "it is a mistaken idea that the keeping of so many wives is rendered expensive. The case is quite different, as husbands are frequently supported by their wives. Brigham Young keeps in operation quite a large workshop, with sewing machines, &c. The women were described as representing the lower order of servant girls."[71]

The *New York Times* discussed the role that Brigham Young played in Utah. "I must say," the reporter wrote, "that the tourist visits few places where more undefined impressions and emotions rush upon him than here . . . the land of the Latter Day Saints—the land of many wives and many children . . . the land of obedience, temperance and order—the land where Democracy and Republicanism are not known—the land of the one-man power."[72] The article continued by complaining that

there are three governments in Utah, . . . in form, if not in fact—the Territorial

Government, . . . the government of the so-called State of Deseret, of which Brigham Young is Governor; and the government of the Church, of which Brigham Young is First President. . . . The Church . . . extends to all the relations of life and business; to family affairs. . . . Nothing is beneath its care and nothing is above its power. This Church has larger and more positive powers than were ever claimed by the Church of Rome in the dark ages, . . . the voice of Brigham being the voice of God.[73]

A few months prior to the war's end, a Chattanooga newspaper humorously reported that "the prettiest girls in Utah generally marry Young."[74] Some reports claimed Brigham Young had eighty wives, sixty children, "and a prospect of more."[75]

An article in the *Boston Herald* predicted in July 1865 that "when Brigham Young sleeps with his fathers then will come the searching test before which we predict the whole Mormon fabric will be crumbled to the dust. It may, and doubtless will continue to exist as a religious sect, but as a compact and tremendously effective organization, its power will cease when Brigham Young's heart is forever still"—one of the less prescient statements made by that publication.[76]

CONCLUSION

From 1861 to 1865, even while the nation was locked in a bitter civil war, Union and Confederate newspapers continued to feed their readers a steady diet of articles about Utah, Mormonism, and polygamy. The numerous reports about Utah Territory and Mormonism that appeared in national and local newspapers across the country had no influence on the outcome of the war, but collectively they helped to set the stage for the national preoccupation with polygamy that followed the Civil War.

Americans remained curious and cautious about Utah and Mormonism throughout the remainder of the nineteenth century. After Appomattox and the formal ending of the Civil War, newspapers continued to portray Utah and the Mormons much as they had throughout the war. The general views expressed were that Mormons remained disloyal, that Utah Territory should not be granted statehood, and that polygamy must be eliminated. Brigham Young also remained a powerful and interesting enigma who continued to be a source of widely read news stories until his death in 1877. The tone of news reports changed little in the decades following the Civil War, as this excerpt from an 1875 address in the Salt Lake Tabernacle by Elder George Q. Cannon illustrates: "We [Latter-day Saints] are accused, you know, of being disloyal. This has been a story told of us, a charge repeated against us from the very beginning. . . . The idea prevails in many quarters that we are scarcely as true to the government as we should be. I have heard it stated that were it not for these troops at Camp Douglas, Utah Territory would rebel. By such nonsense as this do men who oppose us seek to deceive the world at large respecting us and our motives and feelings."[77] While most news stories were negative, occasionally there was grudging recognition and puzzlement over Mormonism's success and the fact that "the means of the Mormons to convert others to their faith are as great as those of all the Christian sects put together."[78]

Kenneth L. Alford is an associate professor of Church history and doctrine at Brigham Young University.

NOTES

This chapter originally appeared in the *Utah Historical Quarterly*, Winter 2012, and is reprinted with permission of the Utah State Historical Society.

1. "Affairs in Utah," *New York Times*, November 27, 1865.
2. Orson Pratt, in *Journal of Discourses* (London: Latter-day Saints' Book Depot, 1854–86), 1:53.
3. Based on research by the author, for the years 1857 and 1858 more than 2,200 articles regarding Kansas and slavery appeared in the *New York Daily Times* and the *New York Times*. (The *New York Daily Times* changed its name to the *New York Times* on September 14, 1857.)
4. For example, see "The Mormon Outrages," *New York Daily Times*, May 1, 1857, and "War with the Mormons," *New York Daily Times*, May 13, 1857.
5. Salt Lake City was named Great Salt Lake City until 1868, but it will be referred to as Salt Lake City in this essay.
6. In one of the many ironies of the Civil War, Fort Sumter was commanded by Major Robert Anderson. The Confederate artillery battery that fired upon the fort was commanded by P. G. T. Beauregard, who had been Anderson's artillery student at the United States Military Academy at West Point. Beauregard also has the distinction of being West Point's shortest-serving superintendent—from January 23 to 28, 1861. See Stephen E. Ambrose, *Duty, Honor, Country: A History of West Point* (Baltimore: Johns Hopkins University Press, 1999), 167, 170; and William M. Davidson, *A History of the United States* (Chicago: Scott, Foresman, 1902), 382.
7. Although there were popular weekly and monthly publications, such as *Harper's Weekly*, *Harper's New Monthly*, and *Leslie's Illustrated Magazine*, this essay will focus exclusively on period newspaper articles.
8. The Associated Press began sending telegraphic news in 1851. See Associated Press, "AP History—1846–1900: The News Cooperative Takes Shape," http://www.ap.org/pages/about/history/history_first.html.

9. While the telegraph shortened the time taken to disseminate the news, it did not eliminate a problem that had plagued newspapers since their creation—identifying which month a specific event occurred. This problem was solved by adding an extra word—*ultimate* or *ult.* (for references to dates in the previous month), *instant* or *inst.* (dates in the current month), or *proximo* (for dates in the following month). Readers could then read and understand, without confusion, statements such as "our correspondent at Great Salt Lake City gives us details of news from Utah to the 10th inst." ("General News," *New York Times*, October 28, 1861) or "we have details of affairs in Utah to the 12th ult., in a letter from our correspondent" ("News of the Day," *New York Times*, October 3, 1861).
10. *Fayetteville (North Carolina) Observer*, August 29, 1861.
11. "Telegraph to the Herald: From Washington," *Boston Herald*, February 14, 1863.
12. "Utah and South Carolina," *Daily (Richmond) Dispatch*, January 19, 1861, 2.
13. "Three New Territories," *Weekly Raleigh (NC) Register*, March 27, 1861.
14. "Important from the South," *Evening (Alexandria) Virginia Sentinel*, March 5, 1861.
15. "The Secession Rebellion," *New York Times*, May 24, 1861.
16. "The Mormons," *(Savannah, GA) Daily Morning News*, June 12, 1862.
17. "Ex-President Buchanan," *Weekly Raleigh (NC) Register*, March 13, 1861.
18. "Affairs in Utah," *New York Times*, July 26, 1861.
19. "The War Department," *New York Times*, July 7, 1861.
20. "Affairs in Utah," *New York Times*, November 3, 1861.
21. "Affairs in Utah," *New York Times*, February 3, 1862.
22. "Affairs in Utah," *New York Times*, January 20, 1862; emphasis added.
23. "The Mormons," *Hinds County (Raymond, MS) Gazette*, August 20, 1862.

24. Camp Floyd, established in 1858 by Albert Sidney Johnston, was renamed Fort Crittenden in honor of U.S. Senator John J. Crittenden after secretary of war John B. Floyd (after whom Camp Floyd was named) resigned to join the Confederacy in December 1860. The Utah military outpost is identified as both Camp Crittenden and Fort Crittenden in military dispatches.

25. "A Needless War in Prospect," *New York Times*, May 26, 1862.

26. "Affairs in Utah," *New York Times*, January 4, 1863.

27. "Affairs in Utah," *New York Times*, May 28, 1864.

28. "Affairs in Utah," *New York Times*, April 27, 1865.

29. "The Mormon Question—Its Easy and Peaceful Solution," *New York Times*, November 28, 1865.

30. "Affairs in Utah," *New York Times*, November 27, 1865.

31. "Affairs in Utah," *New York Times*, November 27, 1865.

32. William H. Hooper to George Q. Cannon, *Millennial Star*, December 16, 1860, 30.

33. "Late Northern and European News," *Weekly Raleigh (NC) Register*, January 15, 1862; and "Northern News," *Fayetteville (NC) Observer*, February 3, 1862.

34. Frank Fuller, Utah Territory secretary and a close friend of Mark Twain's, served as acting governor until Governor Stephen S. Harding arrived in July 1862. See "Frank Fuller Dead; Utah War Governor," *New York Times*, February 20, 1915.

35. Hubert Howe Bancroft, *History of Utah* (San Francisco: History Company, 1889), 604.

36. B. H. Roberts, *A Comprehensive History of The Church of Jesus Christ of Latter-day Saints* (Salt Lake City: Deseret News, 1930), 5:3–7.

37. "Affairs in Utah," *New York Times*, February 28, 1862.

38. "Utah Applying," *New York Times*, January 9, 1862.

39. "Utah Applying," *New York Times*, January 9, 1862.

40. "Affairs in Utah," *New York Times*, February 3, 1862.

41. "Affairs in Utah," *New York Times*, February 3, 1862.

42. "Affairs in Utah," *New York Times*, February 28, 1862.

43. "Affairs in Utah," *New York Times*, May 4, 1862.

44. "Affairs in Utah," *New York Times*, February 15, 1863.

45. "Brigham Young on the War," *New York Times*, November 8, 1863.

46. "The Northern Presidential Race," *Daily (Columbia) South Carolinian*, April 2, 1864.

47. "Utah," *Boston Herald,* July 19, 1865.

48. "Polygamy and a New Rebellion," *New York Times*, June 19, 1862; and "First National Convention," *Chicago Tribune*, June 17, 1856.

49. "The Mormons, Their Doctrine and Their Social Condition," *Boston Herald,* March 1, 1861.

50. "Polygamy and a New Rebellion," *New York Times*, June 19, 1862.

51. "Polygamy and a New Rebellion," *New York Times*, June 19, 1862.

52. "Polygamy and a New Rebellion," *New York Times*, June 19, 1862.

53. "The Mormons and Their Positions," *Chattanooga (TN) Daily Gazette*, December 30, 1864.

54. "The Military Ordinance," *Semi-Weekly Raleigh (NC) Register*, February 12, 1862.

55. "Polygamy," *New York Times*, July 18, 1865.

56. "Utah," *Boston Herald*, July 19, 1865.

57. "Utah," *Boston Herald*, July 19, 1865.

58. "The Mormon Question—Its Easy and Peaceful Solution," *New York Times*, November 28, 1865.

59. "Affairs in Utah," *New York Times*, November 27, 1865.

60. "The Mormons, Their Doctrine and Their Social Condition," *Boston Herald*, March 1, 1861.

61. "Affairs in Utah," *New York Times*, May 7, 1861.

62. "Affairs in Utah," *New York Times*, November 2, 1862.

63. "The Mormons," *(Savannah, GA) Daily Morning News*, June 12, 1862.

64. "Telegraphic: Late Northern News," *(Savannah, GA) Daily Morning News*, March 18, 1863; and "From the North," *Fayetteville (NC) Observer*, March 23, 1863.

65. "Affairs in Utah," *(Savannah, GA) Daily Morning News*, April 1, 1863.

66. "Brigham Young," *Raleigh (NC) Register*, June 24, 1863.

67. "Life Among the Mormons," *Natchez (MS) Courier*, November 17, 1863.

68. "Life Among the Mormons," *Natchez (MS) Courier*, November 17, 1863.

69. "Affairs in Utah," *New York Times*, July 3, 1864.

70. "Utah," *Boston Herald*, July 19, 1865.

71. "The Mormons, Their Doctrine and Their Social Condition," *Boston Herald*, March 1, 1861.

72. "Affairs in Utah," *New York Times*, November 27, 1865; emphasis removed.

73. "Affairs in Utah," *New York Times*, November 27, 1865.

74. "News Items," *Chattanooga (TN) Daily Gazette*, February 3, 1865.

75. "All About—Ghosts," *Natchez (MS) Courier*, December 30, 1865; and *Daily Richmond (VA) Examiner*, November 18, 1863.

76. "Utah," *Boston Herald*, July 19, 1865.

77. George Q. Cannon, in *Journal of Discourses*, 18:6.

78. "The Mormons, Their Doctrine and Their Social Condition," *Boston Herald*, March 1, 1861.

Emanuel Thompson served during the Civil War as a private in Company A, 69th Regiment, Ohio Infantry. He was baptized as a Latter-day Saint following the war. See Appendix E for additional information about this soldier. (Courtesy of Shirley Williams)

CHAPTER 16

Robert C. Freeman

LATTER-DAY SAINTS IN THE CIVIL WAR

The American Civil War (1861–65) was the most tragic event that has occurred in the history of the United States. Not only was it the war in which the most Americans died, but it was also the only experience, military or otherwise, that truly brought this nation to the brink of destruction.[1] Yet, historically speaking, the overt impact of the Civil War upon The Church of Jesus Christ of Latter-day Saints and its members has generally been viewed as relatively minimal.[2] This may explain why there has been little written on this subject.

The war occurred fourteen years after the arrival of the Saints in the Great Basin. It may be argued that the colonization of the Church in the West was actually aided by the war as the full attention and energy of national leadership was consumed by the events of the war, thus allowing for the continued establishment of the Church in the valleys of the Rocky Mountains.[3]

For many Latter-day Saints, the outbreak of the Civil War was seen as a fulfillment of a prophecy made by the Prophet Joseph Smith nearly thirty years before (D&C 87).[4] Of course, most of the fighting occurred over a thousand miles away. Still, for many Church members whose roots were from the northeastern region of the nation, there was great interest in the conflict as well as concern for the safety of loved ones who were living in the midst of the violence.[5]

The war was historically significant for the Church. It was the first time Latter-day Saints served in war where a chief motivation for service was patriotic in nature.[6] This was the first war in which members of the Church were to be found on both sides of a military conflict. And finally, this was the first national American conflict in which a Latter-day Saint died from wounds sustained in battle.[7]

Perhaps the greatest example of Latter-day Saint participation in the war was the response by two Utah cavalry units to the Union call in April 1862 to maintain open transportation and communication lines on the Overland Trails. The smaller of those units was led by Colonel Robert T. Burton, whose commission was from the Nauvoo Legion in Utah, and the larger by Captain Lot Smith, whose commission was from the United States Army.[8] Burton's unit did not meet the criteria for a federalized unit, but Smith's company did. The soldiers commanded by Lot Smith qualified for federal veterans' pensions after the war.

Locating the names of Latter-day Saints who served poses a challenge for researchers as religious affiliations were not officially listed on military induction or enlistment papers during the Civil War. Given that the total membership of the Church during the 1860s was about 70,000, it is believed that no more than several hundred served in the conflict. This is a very small number when compared to the total number of Union (approximately 2,200,000) and Confederate (600,000–1,500,000) soldiers.[9]

The modest number of soldier Saints is partially due to the decided lack of enthusiasm demonstrated by Mormon leadership regarding the conflict. Strong and able young men were not encouraged to fight for a nation that only a few years earlier had essentially banished the Mormon people from her borders. Church leaders spoke out often about the war, and the opinions expressed were generally negative toward both the North and the South.[10] Still, many of the Church's members, including those in key positions of Church leadership, had their family roots in the fertile soil of the northeastern United States. Most Mormons maintained a keen interest in the events in the States. While relatively few Saints engaged in the fighting, the experience of the war left an indelible mark on the lives of those who did fight. What follows are short sketches of Latter-day Saints who are known to have participated in the battles of the Civil War. For purposes of this chapter, soldiers whose baptisms occurred after the war have not been included.[11]

HENRY WELLS JACKSON

Perhaps the most compelling story of a Latter-day Saint who participated in the war is one of a soldier who did not return home. Henry Wells Jackson was born on March 10, 1827, in Chemung, New York.[12] His mother died when he was eleven years old. This imposed great difficulties on the family—he being the seventh of thirteen children. Jackson grew to adulthood, and along the way he was introduced to The Church of Jesus Christ of Latter-day Saints together with his brother, James. He was baptized at Nauvoo on January 28, 1844, by John Hicks.[13]

Henry Wells Jackson may have been the first Latter-day Saint to die in an American conflict as a result of battle wounds. (Saints at War Collection, L. Tom Perry Special Collections, Harold B. Lee Library)

Following the Saints' departure from Illinois, young Jackson enlisted as a musician in the Mormon Battalion in the summer of 1846. He marched from Iowa to Los Angeles. When his initial enlistment with the battalion expired, he reenlisted for six months and participated in the discovery of gold in California.[14] Jackson eventually made his way to the Rocky Mountains to reunite with the Saints in the Salt Lake Valley.

Soon after arriving in the Utah Territory, he met Eliza Ann, a daughter of the early and influential Church leader Philo Dibble.[15] The two were married by Brigham Young on February 3, 1850. Shortly after their marriage, the couple moved to Tooele, Utah, where their first child was born. From there they relocated to San Bernardino, California. The family returned to Utah in 1857. Henry went to work carrying mail from Utah to California, a route with which he had become very familiar. The mail service was discontinued after a few years, but his final wages were never paid. Jackson was determined to go east and file a claim to get his money as well as to visit his aged father and other relatives. While on his journey, Jackson ran out of money and hired out as a wagon master in order to support himself while he waited to receive his back pay.

While delivering provisions as a wagon master, he was captured by Confederate forces and placed in a Southern prison camp for about three months. Prisoner-of-war camps were notorious for inflicting death and disease on the unfortunate incarcerates. Following his release, Jackson determined to protect himself and enlisted in the First District of Columbia Cavalry. His enlistment began on January 6, 1864, and he agreed to serve for three years or for the duration of the war, whichever came first. Because of his military experience with the Mormon Battalion, he was commissioned as a first lieutenant.

On May 8, 1864, the First District of Columbia Cavalry began its march toward the Nottaway railroad bridge above Jarrett's Station. The soldiers encountered an entrenched enemy unit on the opposite end of the bridge. The rebels came forward, and a fierce battle followed in which the enemy force was driven through the woods and down the tracks for half a mile.

During this battle for the bridge, Lieutenant Jackson was shot. The bullet entered his breast, passed through his lung, and exited through his shoulder blade. He was taken first to Fort Jackson, then to Chesapeake General Hospital in Hampton, Virginia, where he died about two weeks later on May 24, 1864. His body was laid to rest in Hampton National Cemetery.[16] Having served in two national conflicts, Henry Wells Jackson represents an important example of an early soldier-Saint who made great sacrifices. As previously stated, it is likely that Jackson was the first Latter-day Saint soldier to die in consequence of injuries sustained in action during a U.S. war.

An immigrant from England, William Rex was a Latter-day Saint at the time of the war and later settled with his family in Randolph, Utah. (Saints at War Collection, L. Tom Perry Special Collections, Harold B. Lee Library)

WILLIAM REX

Despite being born on foreign soil (in November 1844 at Sherborne, Dorset, England), William Rex served in the Union Army.[17] His family joined The Church of Jesus Christ of Latter-day Saints in England when he was just a boy. Shortly afterward, the family immigrated to America to join with the Saints in Zion. They traveled up the Mississippi River, arriving at St. Louis in December 1850. Rex's father died a year and a half later, leaving behind his widow, Mary, and their five children. Life was difficult for them, so Rex and his brothers helped provide for the family. Among the jobs listed in his journal was swimming the Mississippi River in search of driftwood, which was sold to local families to heat their homes. Rex was baptized in May 1854.

When war broke out between the Northern and Southern states, William Rex was just fifteen years old. In 1863, two years into the conflict, he ran away from home and joined the Union Army—enlisting as a private in the 145th Illinois Infantry Regiment. His first assignment was to guard the freight wagons.[18] Much to his dismay, his mother soon discovered his whereabouts and insisted he return home.

Rex resumed his military service in May 1864—again serving with the 145th Illinois Infantry Regiment. Family records report that he served in Georgia under General William Tecumseh Sherman and participated in victories over Confederate forces there.[19] Rex served from June 9, 1864, until September 23, 1864, and received an honorable discharge.

The remainder of Rex's life was spent in the Rocky Mountains. In 1869, his family moved to Utah via the newly completed transcontinental railroad. Rex worked for the Overland Telegraph Company. Five years after his arrival, he married Mary Elizabeth Brough in the Endowment House at Salt Lake City. Most of Rex's life was spent in Randolph, Utah, where he and his family endured many hardships associated with frontier living. In 1884, Rex was called to serve a mission to his beloved England. After his return, he lived out his life in Utah and died on April 6, 1927.

DAVID HAROLD PEERY

David Harold Peery's story is unique because he joined the Church during the time of the war.[20] Born May 6, 1824, he was raised in Tazewell County, Virginia. As a boy, he worked on his father's farm alongside family slaves, attended common school during the winter months, and later enrolled at Emery and Henry College. In 1846, when he was only twenty-two years old, Peery began a merchandising

business with his brother, John. He later purchased his brother's share of the business.

Peery was a handsome young man, but it was not until Nancy Campbell Higginbotham (1835–62) walked into his life that he fell in love. Following a brief courtship, David and Nancy were married. The young couple was in love but disagreed over religion. David was an agnostic, but Nancy was a devout Latter-day Saint. In an effort to turn her against Mormonism, David enlisted two trained ministers to persuade Nancy against the gospel that she so fully believed. Both ministers were bested by his young bride.

David H. Peery is a rare example of a Latter-day Saint who converted to the Church during the war and served in the Confederate Army. (Saints at War Collection, L. Tom Perry Special Collections, Harold B. Lee Library)

The secession of Virginia from the Union took place in April 1861. This marked the beginning of a long sequence of sad events that would ultimately compel Peery to turn toward his wife's religion. On May 1, 1861, the couple's two-year-old son, Thomas Carnahan, died from typhoid fever.[21] In early 1862, David enlisted in the Confederate Army and served as an assistant commissary officer for General Humphrey Marshall's forces in Kentucky. While serving in the Army, he was likewise struck with typhoid fever and returned home to recover. He recovered, but soon several others in his family were ravaged by the deadly disease. David's mother died on May 17, 1863. His father died soon after on

July 8. Next his father-in-law succumbed to the disease. Eventually, Nancy and their son, William, died in the fall of that year. All were victims of disease, not of the war.

Heartbroken, Peery began an earnest search for comfort and spiritual answers. How could God allow such a tragedy to strike so many of those he loved? Ironically, it was within his wife's religion that he found the answers. Apostle Parley P. Pratt's pamphlet *Voice of Warning* and some writings by Orson Pratt about eternal family relationships were among the gospel treasures left behind by his wife. The concept of eternal families was especially attractive to him. In November 1862, Peery asked his mother-in-law, Louisa, where he could find the nearest Mormon elder, and she directed him to Absalom Young, who lived twenty-five miles away. The two men cut a hole through six-inch-thick ice, and Peery was baptized as a member of The Church of Jesus Christ of Latter-day Saints.[22]

The following month (December 1862), Peery returned to the army to serve under General Williams in Kentucky; he left his daughter, Louisa Letitia, in the care of his mother-in-law and sister-in-law. Once again he caught typhoid fever, and for weeks he lay on the verge of death. During his absence from home, the Union army swept through his homestead and destroyed his home, store, outer buildings, and all the provisions and property therein.

By 1864, the war was going poorly for the South. Discouraged and disheartened, Peery and his brother-in-law, Simon, who had also been serving in the Confederate Army, returned home to Virginia, gathered remaining family members, and prepared to join the Saints in the West. They arrived there safely on August 31, 1864. Once in Utah, Peery

began to farm and teach school. That winter, romance grew again in Peery's heart, this time for Elizabeth Letitia Higginbotham (1846–1938), his late wife's sister. Elizabeth had cared for his daughter since Nancy's death. The two became engaged and were married the following spring on April 10, 1865.[23] Seven months later, they were sealed in the Salt Lake Endowment House by President Heber C. Kimball. That same day, Elizabeth served as a proxy for Nancy, so Nancy too was sealed to Peery for time and all eternity.

The new couple moved to Ogden, where David, despite having his business destroyed at least three times, prospered in merchandising, milling, publishing, and banking. He and Elizabeth had ten children together. Much of Peery's remaining life was spent in Church leadership positions. He participated in various business endeavors, family events, and other opportunities that demonstrated his energetic and hardworking nature as well.

Peery left Utah in 1875 to serve a mission in Texas, Tennessee, and Virginia. In 1877, President Brigham Young called Peery to be a stake president, saying, "The name I propose to be your stake president is a man you all know and like. He is not known as a religious man, not a long praying man, but a man who will make you all rich if you will let him." He was well liked, and the people were not only satisfied but pleased by this announcement. David Peery was elected mayor of Ogden in 1883 and again in 1885. Peery additionally served as a territorial legislator for many years and actively worked for Utah's statehood. After he retired, he built "the Virginia"—a beautiful home where he lived the rest of his days. Peery passed away unexpectedly on September 17, 1901, and was buried in the Ogden City Cemetery.[24]

JOHN DAVIS EVANS

John Davis Evans was born March 4, 1841, in Aberdare, Glamorganshire, South Wales.[25] His parents joined the Church when he was four years old, and John was baptized a few days before his ninth birthday in 1850. His family immigrated to America in October that year. John's younger brother, Edward, died before they reached New Orleans in November 1850, and his father died shortly after reaching St. Louis, which left his pregnant mother with the responsibility to care for four small children. From June to September 1859, Evans crossed the plains from Nebraska to the Salt Lake Valley. He ultimately crossed the plains as part of a wagon team two additional times in order to help immigrants.

As the Civil War began, Evans returned to St. Louis, Missouri, to enlist—one of only a few Latter-day Saints from Utah who did so. John volunteered as a private in the 7th Missouri Infantry and was mustered in on June 1, 1861.[26] He trained with a broom handle because his unit did not have enough money to buy rifles. At the Battle of Gettysburg, he was wounded in his left leg and was hospitalized. He was honorably discharged in June 1864 after three years of active duty service.[27]

Evans returned to Utah and married Margaret Williams on July 16, 1870. They were married in the Endowment House at Salt Lake City by Daniel H. Wells, a member of the First Presidency. At different points in his life, Evans hauled salt from the shores of the Great Salt Lake, quarried canyon rock for the Salt Lake Temple, and made charcoal from cedar trees. He also helped lay tracks for the first rail line into Pleasant Valley, Utah. His wife accompanied him and brought their children; she cooked for all of the men who worked on the tracks. Later, Evans moved with his family

to Nevada and worked in the mines until he got lead poisoning. At one point, he weighed only ninety-six pounds, and Margaret had to take in boarders to provide for the family.

They moved back to Utah, where Evans bought property in Salt Lake City and started one of Utah's first ice cream businesses—called "Evans Union Ice Cream." It flourished for eighteen years until his death. He cut ice from a canal during the winter and saved it in shacks with sawdust between the blocks. He sold milk as well as ice cream. Originally, they made their ice cream turning it all by hand.

John and Margaret Evans were parents to ten children. During John's life, he assisted in building several Latter-day Saint houses of worship. After a long and useful life, he died on July 30, 1908, in Salt Lake City.[28]

JOHN ROZSA

John Rozsa was born on foreign soil in Hungary on November 7, 1820. He grew up in a good home with parents who tried to give him the best in life. As a youth he found friends who got him into trouble. His family relationships were strained because of his choices. At the age of eighteen he joined the Sixth Hungarian Linize Regiment without telling his parents. When his parents found out, they tried to stop him, but Rozsa would not listen. He enjoyed life as a soldier, although it was very difficult. He was made a field captain when the Italian war broke out and was in line to become an officer until he deserted on August 21, 1849.[29]

He traveled and lived reasonably well during the next few years until he was arrested in March 1853 for being present at an armed expedition in Switzerland. Not long after being jailed, the prisoners were shipped to America. Upon their arrival in New York on

These Civil War–era pen and ink drawings by John Rozsa are entitled Christmas in the City *and* Christmas in the Country. *(Courtesy of Drucilla Smith)*

May 15, they were set free. There Rozsa found work as a barkeeper in an Italian hotel, and after a few months of working he decided to become a soldier again. On December 12, 1853, he enlisted in the United States Army.

While with the military, Rozsa participated in a march west. In May 1857, he received orders to march to Salt Lake, where the Mormons were allegedly not cooperating with the federal government. The winter months of travel were extremely cold and difficult. Rations were cut due to the difficulty of finding food. In June 1858, they marched through Salt Lake City, which was nearly abandoned. In July, the soldiers were paid and given a leave of absence. Rozsa had the opportunity to explore Utah. He visited Lehi, south of Great Salt Lake City. While there he learned about The Church of Jesus Christ of Latter-day Saints and was baptized on December 8, 1858. During that time he met and married Patience Loader, who was also a Latter-day Saint.[30]

Shortly after his marriage, his unit was ordered to leave Utah. He arrived in Washington, DC, in October 1861 and stayed for the winter. During the spring and summer of 1862, he lived on the battlefield. His unit marched to Fort Monroe, Yorktown, Williamsburg, and Richmond as part of the Peninsular Campaign. After several battles, they marched back to Alexandria, Virginia, to await new orders. During this period he visited his family and was given a position as a clerk at the Army headquarters. This eased his soldier life and tripled his pay. The pay increase was a blessing to his family as his wife was close to giving birth.

By October, he was ordered to rejoin his company and was reduced to the rank of private because he had left his company for the clerk job without permission. This rank made it hard for him to support his wife and two children, but he was grateful to be near his wife during a period of confinement. Eventually he was able to assist in issuing rations and received a small increase in wages that helped his family.[31]

John Rozsa died on May 24, 1866, while returning with his wife to Utah. His health had been slowly failing for some time. He was buried along the trail about three days beyond Fort Kearney.[32]

CONCLUSION

The accounts in this chapter represent some of those Latter-day Saint soldiers who fought during the American Civil War for whom we have detailed records. The number of Latter-day Saints who fought was statistically insignificant, but their service was anything but insignificant—not only for them individually but for the nation as well.

As mentioned in the introduction of this chapter, very little has been published about the actual participation of Latter-day

Saints in the Civil War other than perhaps the experience of the expedition led by Lot Smith. Understandable as this may be, it is important to share these profiles of Civil War Saints who were present and who sacrificed in some measure for the cause they believed in. The Sesquicentennial of the war provides a fitting anniversary to memorialize these few Church members that we know of. It is hoped that perhaps additional research will come to light so that others may be added to this roster.

In the discovery of these stories, the goal is to preserve the details of their contributions so that these soldiers of long ago will be remembered and added to the long roster of other Latter-day Saints who have served in each of the wars of the latter days. For any and all that can be found, it will be a privilege to pay tribute to their service.

Robert C. Freeman is a professor of Church history and doctrine at Brigham Young University.

NOTES

1. If one combines deaths in consequence of injury and illness, Civil War losses eclipse those of World War II. Some sources maintain that World War II saw more deaths resulting from fighting than the Civil War. See John Whiteclay Chambers II, ed., *American Military History* (Oxford University Press, 1999), 210.

2. There has been little published on the subject of Latter-day Saints in the Civil War. One modest attempt is the volume Margaret M. Fisher, ed., *Utah and the Civil War* (Salt Lake City: Deseret Book, 1929). Fisher's book provides excerpts of journal accounts and a listing of the Lot Smith and Robert T. Burton Expeditions.

3. See Eugene Moehring, "The Civil War and Town Founding in the Intermountain West," *Western Historical Quarterly*, Autumn 1997, 316–41.

4. This section, received on December 25, 1832, has been one of the most frequently cited prophecies of Joseph Smith that saw clear fulfillment. Some Church members felt that the Civil War heralded the promised return of Christ. See Scott C. Esplin's chapter on this subject herein.

5. James B. Allen and Glen M. Leonard, *The Story of the Latter-day Saints* (Salt Lake City: Deseret Book, 1976), 299.

6. While about five hundred Latter-day Saints served in the Mormon Battalion during the Mexican-American War, economic motives are generally agreed to have been the primary purpose of their enlistment.

7. Henry Wells Jackson is very likely the first Latter-day Saint to perish in an American conflict. The author is indebted to the Jackson family for personal papers and images relating to his life and ultimate demise.

Particular thanks are expressed to Paul Hoffman, Marilyn and Celia Smith, and LaMar Taft Merrill Jr., as well as to Don Smith, who has conducted substantial research into Henry Jackson's life. Saints at War Collection, L. Tom Perry Special Collections, Harold B. Lee Library, Brigham Young University, Provo.

8. In brief, the unit commanded by Burton was composed of approximately twenty-four soldiers, and they served for about thirty days. Smith's company was composed of approximately one hundred and six soldiers that included officers, privates, and teamsters. Their service was for ninety days. See Fisher, *Utah and the Civil War*. See also chapter by Stuart and Alford and chapter by Dickson herein.

9. *American Military History*, vol. 1 (Washington, DC: Center of Military History, 2005), 849.

10. See Richard E. Bennett, "'We Know No North, No South, No East, No West': Mormon Interpretations of the Civil War, 1861–65," *Mormon Historical Studies* 10, no. 1 (2009); reprinted herein.

11. An example of a Latter-day Saint Civil War veteran who was baptized following the war is Joshua Clark, father of J. Reuben Clark (an LDS Apostle and member of the First Presidency), who served for almost two years in the Union Army and was baptized in 1868.

12. Henry Wells Jackson Papers (unpublished manuscript), Saints at War Collection, L. Tom Perry Special Collections.

13. Don Smith, "Life Sketch: Henry Wells Jackson" (unpublished manuscript).

14. Smith, "Life Sketch: Henry Wells Jackson."

15. For more on Philo Dibble, see Arnold K. Garr, Donald Q. Cannon, and Richard O. Cowan, eds., *Encyclopedia of Latter-day Saint History* (Salt Lake City: Deseret Book, 2000), 295.

16. Major Baker, Jackson's commanding officer, said Henry was a "brave and noble young officer." A picture of Jackson's headstone is in the possession of the author.

17. William Rex papers (unpublished manuscript), Saints at War Collection, L. Tom Perry Special Collections.

18. William Rex Papers, Saints at War Collection, L. Tom Perry Special Collections. His headstone, located in the Randolph City Cemetery in Wyoming, indicates he served as a private in the 145th Illinois Infantry.

19. David Boone, *Nineteenth-Century Saints at War* (Provo, UT: Religious Studies Center, Brigham Young University, 2006), 123.

20. See William Hartley, "The Confederate Officer and 'That Mormon Girl': A Nineteenth-Century Romance," *Ensign*, April 1982. See the Saints at War Collection, L. Tom Perry Special Collections. See also Julina Peery Parker, interviewed by author via telephone, June 16, 2011.

21. See William Hartley, "The Confederate Officer and 'That Mormon Girl,'" *Ensign*, 1982. See also Julina Ward Higginbotham (great-granddaughter of David Peery), interviewed by author via telephone, June 16, 2011.

22. Liliu Davis Peery, comp., "History of David Harold Peery" (unpublished manuscript, February 1941), 2. Peery's baptismal date is only identified as November 1862. In Hartley's article the date given is 1863.

23. They were married by Elder Winslow Farr in Holladay, Utah. See *Life History of Elizabeth Letitia Higginbotham Peery* (unpublished manuscript), Saints at War Collection, L. Tom Perry Special Collections.

24. A picture of David Peery's headstone is in the possession of the author.

25. Thomas, "John Davis Evans."

26. Thomas, "John Davis Evans."

27. Jerry Crouch Evans, *Silencing the Vicksburg Guns: The Story of the 7th Missouri Infantry Regiment* (Victoria, Canada: Hither & Yon, 2005).

28. Some of the notes for this profile are courtesy of Diane Tague as part of a contribution to the Saints at War Project, December 2005. Papers in the possession of the Saints at War Project, Brigham Young University.

29. *John Rozsa's Autobiography: A Sure Storm Will Follow Fine Weather and Vice Versa*, Americana Collection, L. Tom Perry Special Collections, 3–4.

30. Patience Loader Rozsa Archer, *Recollections of Past Days: The Autobiography of Patience Loader Rozsa Archer* (Logan: Utah State University Press, 2006), 98.

31. *John Rozsa's Autobiography*.

32. Archer, *Recollections of Past Days*.

The Soldiers' National Cemetery at Gettysburg marks the final resting place for many soldiers, mostly Union, killed during the battle. Many of the Confederate dead were moved to cemeteries in Virginia, Georgia, North Carolina, and South Carolina in the 1870s. (Courtesy of Kenneth L. Alford)

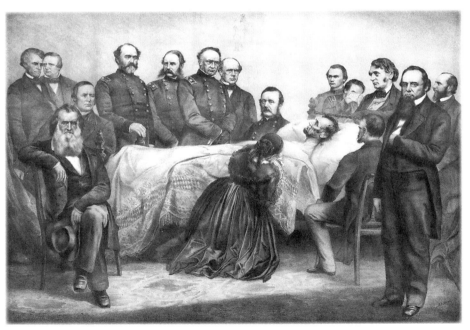

The death of President Abraham Lincoln on April 15, 1865, significantly altered the aftermath of the Civil War. (Library of Congress)

CHAPTER 17

Andrew C. Skinner

CIVIL WAR'S AFTERMATH

RECONSTRUCTION, ABOLITION, AND POLYGAMY

By late 1864, the physical fighting of the American Civil War was moving toward a final resolution. In December, General William T. Sherman (of "war is hell" fame) completed his infamous and devastating march to the sea in Georgia. In early April, the Confederate capital of Richmond, Virginia, fell to Union forces. On April 9, 1865, General Robert E. Lee, commander of the army of Northern Virginia, surrendered his forces to Union general Ulysses S. Grant at Appomattox Court House, Virginia—the rebellion more "worn out rather than suppressed," as Union artillery colonel Charles Wainwright put it.[1] Though skirmishes would continue for some weeks, the war was essentially over.

The period following the Civil War (1861–65) is known in U.S. history as Reconstruction. It lasted from 1865 to 1877 and has been called "one long referendum on the meaning and memory of the verdict reached at Appomattox."[2] That is to say, the Union had won the war on the battlefield. But what would be the long-term meaning of victory in the face of the abolition of slavery and the

nature of future government in the Southern states? Reconstruction was marked by efforts to rebuild the war-torn nation, to readmit the Confederate states into the Union, to help those states in particular to rebuild in the face of the war's near-total destruction of certain areas, to facilitate the reenfranchisement of white voters in the eleven secessionist states, to determine and guarantee the rights of the approximately four million freed slaves in the South, and to somehow try to help ease human suffering.

These were challenges of which President Abraham Lincoln was well aware. On April 11, just two days after Lee's surrender at Appomattox Court House, Lincoln gave a speech from a second-story window of the White House to the assembled crowds below, who were in a celebratory mood. But the president "was not interested in gloating or cheering about the victory, as perhaps many in the crowd would have wanted." Rather, "he wanted to caution people to think carefully about how the Union would be rebuilt—reconstructed—peacefully, how

The war left much of the South in ruins. This photograph shows the Norfolk Navy Yard in December 1864. (National Archives)

North and South could come back together again and be one friendly nation. He knew people disagreed about how to proceed and talked about how difficult it would be to rebuild the nation. Lincoln also put forth the idea of giving African Americans the right to vote."[3]

But such noble and important goals as Lincoln and other reconstructionists contemplated were easier said than done. The shooting may have ended by late spring of 1865, but the suffering and destruction were just beginning to be realized. Six months after the surrender at Appomattox, Confederate vice president Alexander H. Stephens was released from prison in Boston. As he

rode a slow train southward toward his home in Georgia, he witnessed a landscape everywhere in ruin. Of northern Virginia he said the "desolation of the country . . . was horrible to behold." And in northern Georgia he lamented the "desolation [to be] . . . heart-sickening. Fences gone, fields all a waste, houses burnt."[4] In many regions of the South, ex-Confederates faced not just crushing material poverty but "spiritual hopelessness."[5]

The most costly aspect of the Civil War, by far, was the human life taken and the suffering inflicted—the greatest, in fact, that the United States has *ever* seen. This was also the most tragic dimension of this massive and wrenching conflict. The estimated number of soldiers alone who died between 1861 and 1865, both North and South, is over 620,000. This is "approximately equal to the total American fatalities in the Revolution, the War of 1812, the Mexican War, the Spanish-American War, World War I, World War II, and the Korean War combined."[6] Furthermore, the percentage of the U.S. population killed during the Civil War is the equivalent of six million lives in our day.

CIVIL WAR SHAPED THE NATION

In one sense, it is impossible to comprehend the suffering that this human destruction generated and therefore monotonous to continue describing it; yet, in another sense, it is impossible to speak too much about it because of the way it has shaped the United States. Professor Drew Faust has written:

In the Civil War the United States, North and South, reaped what many participants described as a "harvest of death." By the midpoint of the conflict, it seemed that in the South, "nearly every household mourns some loved one lost." Loss became commonplace; death was no longer encountered individually; death's threat, its proximity, and its actuality became the most widely shared of the war's experiences. As a Confederate soldier observed, death "reigned with universal sway," ruling homes and lives, demanding attention and response. The Civil War matters to us today because it ended slavery and helped to define the meanings of freedom, citizenship, and equality. It established a newly centralized nation-state and launched

it on a trajectory of economic expansion and world influence. But for those Americans who lived in and through the Civil War, the texture of the experience, its warp and woof, was the presence of death. At war's end this shared suffering would override persisting differences about the meanings of race, citizenship, and nationhood to establish sacrifice and its memorialization as the ground on which North and South would ultimately reunite.[7]

Indeed, "death transformed the American nation as well as the hundreds of thousands of individuals directly affected by loss."[8] The effect of death resulting directly from the Civil War on the psyche of individuals and the whole nation was monumental. Death, as well as the maiming that resulted from the horrendous fighting that occurred in gargantuan battles of the war, "created a veritable 'republic of suffering,' in the words that Frederick Law Olmsted chose to describe the wounded and dying arriving at Union hospital ships on the Virginia Peninsula."[9] As if to emphasize this point, only days after the Confederate surrender at Appomattox, Abraham Lincoln was assassinated by John Wilkes Booth the evening of April 14, 1865, and the Union was plunged into a grief more profound than could have been imagined beforehand. "On April 19, 1865, an estimated twenty-five million people attended memorial services around the country for the slain leader."[10] Southern reaction to Lincoln's death varied according to geographical region as well as the social and political position of individuals. Though some were genuinely saddened, many hated Lincoln and were glad for his death.[11] Of course, the irony was that

The Civil War left hundreds of thousands of men sick and wounded. This is probably Carver Hospital near Washington, DC. (National Archives)

with the assassination of President Lincoln, the South lost one of its best, most thoughtful allies in the arduous tasks of Reconstruction—rebuilding life in the South.

When word of the president's murder reached Utah, citizens of the territory felt a genuine sense of loss and joined the nation in mourning the death of the great man. The *Union Vedette*, a newspaper started by soldiers at Camp Douglas, Utah, in order to provide an opposing voice to the Mormon-controlled *Deseret News*, announced the tragedy on April 17, 1865: "The wing of the Death angel broods over the Capitol and his shadow has fallen upon all the land. There

is consternation in the public places and the hearts of the people are appalled with a sadness that is something more than sorrow. Our banners droop low and the cities are clothed in the habiliments of woe. Nature herself is hushed to silence as though in sympathy with the National bereavement."[12] By the events of April 14, 1865, Utah became part of the republic of suffering, even though the territory's involvement in the war was minimal by design. As Brigham Young once indicated, one of the very reasons the Church had moved west was to enjoy insulation against the growing storms of war: "The whispering of the Spirit to us have [*sic*] invariably been . . . to depart, to go hence, to flee into the mountains . . . that we may be secure in the visitation of the Judgments that must pass upon this land . . . while the guilty land of our fathers is purifying by the overwhelming scourge."[13]

On April 18, the *Vedette* reported that the theater as well as businesses in Salt Lake City had been closed, flags flown at half-mast, and many houses outfitted with emblems of mourning. It then paid a sincere compliment aimed at the Latter-day Saints: "The citizens have done themselves lasting honor on this sad occasion, and we acknowledge the display of deep feeling on their part with the gratitude it deserves."[14] On April 21, the same newspaper described the ceremonies held at the old Salt Lake Tabernacle, whose pulpit had been draped in black, where a large congregation had gathered, and where "religious differences for the time were ignored and soldiers and civilians all united as fellow citizens in common observance of the solemn occasion."[15]

This significant turn of events, which saw Abraham Lincoln elevated to a place of respect and then veneration among the Latter-day Saints, came about during the war itself. The majority of Utahns (Latter-day Saints) started out being both suspicious and critical of Lincoln during the earliest days of his presidency. In fact, one historian notes that "it is possible that they held him in even greater disfavor than remaining written documents indicate."[16] However, a change in attitude seems to have occurred and accelerated after a reported favorable comment made by Lincoln gained circulation in the Utah Territory. Apparently, when asked by T. B. H. Stenhouse about the policy he intended to pursue in regard to the Mormons, Lincoln replied, "I propose to let them alone." He further illustrated what he meant: "Stenhouse,

when I was a boy on the farm in Illinois there was a great deal of timber on the farms which we had to clear away. Occasionally we would come to a log which had fallen down. It was too hard to split, too wet to burn and too heavy to move, so we ploughed around it. That's what I intend to do with the Mormons. You go back and tell Brigham Young that if he will let me alone I will let him alone."[17]

It is also probable that as time went on, the noble character of Lincoln, his genuine selfless concern over preserving the United States, his act of ultimately freeing millions of human beings from the bondage of slavery, and his helping the country heal from the wounds of war through a program of Reconstruction began to distill upon the Latter-day Saints. That is, through his speeches and actions, they saw the righteous intent of the president's desires. After all, had the Lord not said through his inspired servant that "it is not right that any man should be in bondage one to another" (D&C 101:79), and was it not the case that the Civil War was fought, at least in part, to prevent the institution of slavery from continuing unabated on this chosen land which had been redeemed by the shedding of blood (D&C 101:80)?

LINCOLN, SLAVERY, AND RECONSTRUCTION

President Lincoln's personal views on slavery were a matter of public record. In April 1864, he came out with his clearest articulation: "If slavery is not wrong, nothing is wrong. I can not remember when I did not so think, and feel."[18] One of Lincoln's leading biographers called him "colorblind." Personally, he "thought of the black man first of all as a man."[19] But as the president, he knew that he could not govern simply by personal preference or fiat; he could not free the slaves and expect their immediate and unimpeded assimilation into the fabric of society. Declarations of freedom alone would not solve their problems. He was president not just of "antislavery forces but of a disunited and divided people," and he had to "serve the general welfare."[20] Therefore, "he approached the difficult problems of reconstruction with an open mind and an absence of commitment"[21] as his own views changed and different pressures influenced him.

The first comprehensive effort at reconstruction is generally regarded as Lincoln's Proclamation of Amnesty and Reconstruction, issued on December 8, 1863. It was a carefully crafted plan that would begin to ease the nation into repair, unification, and healing. He had worked on it during a period of recuperation from smallpox after returning in November from Gettysburg, where he had delivered one of the most powerful addresses in American history using only 272 words! Though the proclamation was issued only halfway through the war, it is clear the president wanted the conflict to be over. Indeed, the "republic of suffering" was taking its toll on Lincoln and making him more sensitive, not less, to the increasing carnage. For example, as the war entered its final phase under the Union command of General Grant and the losses became ever more devastating, "Lincoln was horrified. He remembered his childhood days of hating even to see an animal killed." At one point he exclaimed, "Could we have avoided this terrible, bloody war! . . . Is it ever to end!"[22]

The Proclamation of Amnesty and Reconstruction required residents of the South, rebels and Confederates, to take an oath to faithfully support, protect, and defend the Constitution and the Union. In addition, they had to accept the abolition of slavery. They could resume rights of property, except as pertaining to slaves. The proclamation provided for Southern state governments to be reconstituted and established by only one-tenth of the number of voters that had participated in the 1860 presidential election. The states' constitutions had to abolish slavery, but not all states were required to give free blacks the right to vote (Louisiana, Arkansas, and Tennessee were exempted for a time).[23]

Lincoln's plan stirred up controversy. Some wanted him to drop emancipation in exchange for immediate peace with the Confederacy. Others—the Radical Reconstructionists—considered the plan to be too lenient on the rebels. In 1864, Congress proposed that Reconstruction not be inaugurated until 50 percent of a state's voters had sworn the oath of loyalty. A national debate ensued over who should establish Reconstruction policies.[24] In the meantime, the Senate approved the Thirteenth Amendment to the U.S. Constitution, abolishing slavery throughout the Union: "Neither slavery nor involuntary servitude, except as a punishment for crime . . . shall exist within the United States, or any place subject to their jurisdiction."[25] Sometimes the Civil War is referred to as the Second American Revolution because, with the abolition of slavery formalized in the Thirteenth Amendment, America began to fulfill the promise of the Declaration of Independence that "all men are created equal."[26] On January 30, 1865, the amendment was approved by the House of Representatives and forwarded to the states for ratification. Antislavery Congressman Cornelius Cole subsequently declared, "The one question of the age is *settled*."[27] But,

Weapons introduced during the Civil War caused death and destruction of property on a scale previously unseen in the United States. (National Archives)

like so much else about the Civil War, new questions arose—among them was the question of what a new president might do.

However, on March 4, 1865, once more under heavy guard, the newly reelected Abraham Lincoln walked out onto the inaugural platform at the east face of the Capitol. He delivered the address which, more than any other, both captured the essence of his feeling toward all citizens, North and South, and expressed his earnest desire to repair the nation. The last paragraph stands as Lincoln's watchwords of Reconstruction: "With malice toward none; with charity for all; with firmness in the right, as God gives us to see the right, let us strive on to finish the work we

are in; to bind up the nation's wounds; to care for him who shall have borne the battle, and for his widow, and his orphan—to do all which may achieve and cherish a just and lasting peace, among ourselves, and with all nations."[28]

Unfortunately, John Wilkes Booth was among the onlookers to Lincoln's Second Inaugural Address that day. But so was Frederick Douglass, black abolitionist. That evening, Douglass came to the White House reception to offer his congratulations to the president. Ironically, he was first refused admittance but subsequently let in upon Lincoln's order. When asked by the president what he thought of the speech earlier that day, "Douglass described it as a 'sacred effort.'"[29] Indeed!

For Lincoln, there should be no more slaves, no subhumans, no more North versus South, no unbound wounds, no more second-class citizens, no united states in the plural. Rather, his vision, as God gave him "to see the right," contemplated a United States—a single entity succoring those in need of help and guaranteeing inalienable rights to all. In parallel fashion, another president—of a different kind—two years earlier had summarized his view of those engaged in the great national conflict. In October 1863, Brigham Young said:

> I care for the North and the South and if I had sufficient power with the Lord, I would save every innocent man, woman and child from being slaughtered in this unnatural and almost universal destruction of life and property. . . . I care for the North and South more than I do for gold, and I would do a great deal, if I had the power, to ameliorate the condition of suffering thousands. I care enough for them to pray that righteous men may hold the reins of the government, and that wicked, tyrannical despotism may be wiped away from the land.[30]

RECONSTRUCTION CONTINUES

In March 1865, Congress created the Bureau of Refugees, Freedmen, and Abandoned Lands (simply called the Freedmen's Bureau), "an unprecedented agency of social uplift"[31] to look out for the interests of Southern blacks. With the abolition of slavery, most of them had no homes, no money, and no education. The Bureau sought to obtain jobs, set up schools, and create hospitals for blacks.

It also helped to protect white interests by providing services to blacks in a structured way and thus curtailing the outright clash of white landowners and black farmers, many of whom were eager to test the parameters of their newly bestowed freedom.

The following provides an example:

> In Appomattox County itself, Freedmen's Bureau agents, as well as Union officers, confronted problems of social disorder in the immediate wake of the surrender. A horseman passing through the country on April 29, 1865, described "one eternal scene of desolation & destruction" along a 13-mile route. The armies had left hundreds of dead horses and mules and burned every fence rail for miles. A Freedmen's Bureau post was established in Lynchburg to try to settle disputes over remaining livestock, to stop plundering and marauding in the countryside, and especially to try to establish new labor arrangements for the freedmen.[32]

How blacks could acquire land remained one of the great unanswered questions of the Reconstruction period.

In May 1865, Lincoln's successor, President Andrew Johnson, announced his Reconstruction plan. Being a Southerner and a "thoroughgoing white supremacist,"[33] he attempted to institute policies that would help the South recover as quickly as possible and not punish it for its stance on slavery or its secession. Reaction among very conservative or radical elements of the Republicans in Congress was outrage toward Johnson's perceived lenient approach to Reconstruction. Even before he was killed, Lincoln himself had to deal with these "Radicals" in his own party. Led in the

Senate by Charles Sumner of Massachusetts, and in the House of Representatives by Thaddeus Stevens of Pennsylvania, the Radical Reconstructionists saw an opportunity in the post–Civil War era "to convert black freedom into genuine citizenship, economic self-reliance, and political liberty. They viewed the former Confederate states as 'conquered provinces,' which had to be re-invented as states and readmitted to the Union by Congress."[34] They also conceived of greatly expanded federal power—which Andrew Johnson did not! And they wanted to wield that power.

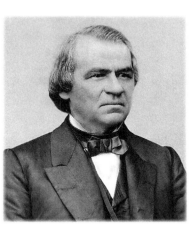

Prior to becoming Abraham Lincoln's running mate in the 1864 presidential election, Andrew Johnson (1808–75) had served as a mayor, U.S. congressman, and governor (winning all his elections as a Democrat). His political background and views caused tremendous friction with the Republican-controlled Congress, who impeached him in 1868. (Library of Congress)

Johnson's plan of Reconstruction offered amnesty to all but the main Confederate leaders. Southern states had to abolish slavery and take a loyalty oath to the United States (much like Lincoln's earlier plan) in order to be readmitted to the Union. The plan offered no legislative role to blacks to work out Reconstruction policy. The Southern states themselves, under white leadership, were to determine what role blacks would play in Reconstruction. Thus, toward the end of 1865, Southern states, Mississippi and South Carolina being the first, began to enact a series of laws called the Black Codes. In some cases, blacks were treated little differently than when slavery was in full operation:

Mississippi required all blacks to possess, each January, written evidence

of employment for the coming year. Laborers leaving their jobs before the contract expired would forfeit wages already earned, and, as under slavery, be subject to arrest by any white citizen. A person offering work to a laborer already under contract risked imprisonment or a fine of $500. To limit the freedmen's economic opportunities, they were forbidden to rent land in urban areas. Vagrancy—a crime whose definition included the idle, disorderly, and those who "misspend what they earn"—could be punished by fines or involuntary plantation labor; other criminal offenses included "insulting" gestures or language, "malicious mischief," and preaching the Gospel without a license. . . . Florida's code, drawn up by a commission whose report praised slavery as a "benign" institution deficient only in its inadequate regulation of black sexual behavior, made disobedience, impudence, and even "disrespect" to the employer a crime. Blacks who broke labor contracts could be whipped, placed in the pillory, and sold for up to one year's labor, while whites who violated contracts faced only the threat of civil suits.[35]

Again, reaction by Radical Reconstructionists to these measures was outrage. In

Two guards stand in Jefferson Davis's cell, in Fort Monroe, Virginia, while the prisoner sits on his bed. (Library of Congress)

December 1865, the Republican leadership of Congress refused to readmit Southern states to the Union. For two years, the executive and legislative branches of the U.S. government engaged in an epic struggle over Reconstruction policy. The Radicals won but in the process fueled a backlash of Southern white resentment that took a toll on blacks. In 1865 and 1866, whites murdered about five thousand blacks in the South. In 1866, the Ku Klux Klan was founded in Tennessee, motivated by opposition toward Radical Reconstruction. Ostensibly organized as a "social club," it spread rapidly in nearly every Southern state, launching a "reign of terror" against blacks as well as white sympathizers and supporters of Republican policies. By 1870, the Klan and kindred organizations such as the White Brotherhood and the Knights of the White Camelia had become deeply entrenched in every Southern state.[36]

Congressional response to violence against blacks and their supporters did not really appear until 1870. It came in the form of a series of Enforcement Acts, which forbade discrimination toward voters and outlawed fraud, bribery, intimidation, or conspiracies that prevented citizens from exercising their constitutional rights. When violence persisted, the Ku Klux Klan Act of April 1871 was enacted, which designated crimes that deprived citizens of the right to vote, hold office, or enjoy the equal protection of the law as punishable by federal law. States failing to act effectively against perpetrators could be subject to military intervention and the suspension of the writ of habeas corpus.[37]

RADICAL RECONSTRUCTION

By 1866, the Republican-dominated Congress was certain President Johnson's plan was a failure. Led by the Radicals, they took the extraordinary step of passing the nation's first Civil Rights Act and then overriding the president's veto to make it the law of the land. This gave certain legal rights to former slaves. In June of that year, they proposed the Fourteenth Amendment to the Constitution, which conferred citizenship upon "all persons born or naturalized in the United States."[38] This included black Americans. Since none of the defeated Southern states had yet been readmitted into the Union, Congress declared that no state could be readmitted until it ratified the amendment. President Johnson actually encouraged the states to reject it. All did so at first, except for Tennessee, which became the first of the former Confederate states to ratify the amendment and be readmitted to the Union. The Fourteenth Amendment officially became law in 1868.[39]

This was monumental. In 1857, the U.S. Supreme Court had ruled in *Dred Scott v. Sanford* that "African Americans, free or slave, could never be citizens of the United States. The Fourteenth Amendment overturned this decision by defining citizenship in the Constitution for the first time."[40]

In 1867, Congress increasingly challenged President Johnson's authority. First, they enacted a series of laws called the Reconstruction Acts, which abolished Southern state governments formed or proposed under Johnson's plan, divided the South into five military districts, and outlined the "approved" steps by which former Confederate states could be joined to the Union. Next, Congress passed laws forbidding the president from firing certain government officials or dismissing any commander of one of the Southern military districts without the approval of the Senate. When the president defied Congress and the recently passed Tenure of Office Act by dismissing Secretary of War Edwin Stanton, a supporter of Radical Reconstruction, the Radical Republicans began to demand Johnson's removal from office.[41] On February 24, 1868, the House of Representatives voted to impeach him (126 to 47)—a first in American history. He was tried in the Senate, but their vote fell one short (35 to 19) of removing him from office, and Andrew Johnson remained president until 1869, when Ulysses S. Grant succeeded him.

In 1869, other significant developments affected the course of Reconstruction. In February, Congress approved the Fifteenth Amendment to the Constitution, which prohibited federal and state governments from depriving any citizen of voting because of their race: "The right of citizens of the United States to vote shall not be denied or abridged by the United States or by any State on account of race, color, or previous condition of servitude."[42] It became part of the Constitution a little over a year later.[43] However, the practical implementation of the terms of this amendment, as well as those of the Fourteenth, was a long time in coming. One Southern newspaper declared in 1875 that these amendments "may stand forever; but we intend . . . to make them dead letters on the statute-book."[44] Such sentiments could openly bubble to the surface at that time because Southern Democrats began to regain control of the South beginning in 1869.

New state governments had begun to form under the provisions of the Reconstruction Acts of 1867. Southern whites protested the terms of the acts by refusing to vote in new

Libby Prison, shown here, was a Confederate prison at Richmond, Virginia. It became infamous for the poor living conditions provided for the Union prisoners. (National Archives)

elections. This allowed Republicans to take control of these state governments. But economic problems, coupled with corruption among legislators in the South, plagued these governments. Agriculture, the economic backbone of the South, was slow to recover after the devastation of the Civil War. In addition, Reconstruction governments immediately opened the political process to former slaves. Therefore, most Southern whites refused to support the Reconstruction governments. Republicans were eventually defeated in the South: first in Tennessee and Virginia in 1869; then in North Carolina in 1870; in Georgia in 1871; in Alabama, Arkansas, and Texas in 1874; and in Mississippi in 1876.

Latter-day Saints were not unaffected by these developments. Indeed, the end of the Civil War and the era of Reconstruction elevated the visibility of the Mormons on the stage of American religion and politics.

RECONSTRUCTION AND THE LATTER-DAY SAINTS

A significant consequence of the Civil War and Reconstruction was that the government of the United States became more centralized, and more intrusive, affecting the lives of individual Americans as never before. "The expanded role of the federal government to fight a total war brought similar expansion in its control over . . . a centralized monetary system, agricultural policy, the creation of land-grant colleges, homesteading on federal lands, immigration laws, and the building of the transcontinental railroad."[45] The authority of the government to affect so many aspects of life was solidified under, but not limited to, the era of the Radical Reconstructionists.

While the nation worked to rebuild the Southern states and restructure and expand the federal government, the Latter-day Saints, by contrast, sought to retrench and strengthen themselves without federal interference. They sought ways to insulate themselves against expanding government in general. For example, Church leaders were initially very interested to see how the railroad could aid in building up the kingdom of God and bringing more Saints to Utah. But they seem to have become increasingly worried that the expanding railroad system would bring more "gentiles" into their territory and eventually undermine their way of life. The completion of the transcontinental railroad system was not a deliberate, calculated assault on LDS culture, but rather a natural consequence of the ending of the Civil War and subsequent Reconstruction. The nation could, and really had to, turn its energies to other endeavors after four years of total war—the transcontinental railroad being one. Among its main workers were army veterans. Many of its engineers were ex-army men who had learned their trade keeping the trains operating during the Civil War. The first transcontinental railroad system was officially connected on May 10, 1869, with the ceremonial driving of the last rail spike at Promontory Summit in Utah.

But well before the event, the anticipated completion of the transcontinental rail system constituted a significant rationale for the organization or reestablishment of the School of the Prophets by Church leaders in 1867. This was "a confidential forum of leading high priests" who met to discuss religious ideas, economic policies, and political problems impacting the Church.[46] The expanding rail system was an important and vital issue for discussion because of its expected effect. Then, in the October 1868 general conference, President Brigham Young delivered a forceful address committing the Saints who met in the new Tabernacle to ameliorate the potential threat of outsiders by a renewed movement of cooperation and self-sufficiency. Among other things, President Young said, "If this is the Kingdom of God and if we are the Saints of God . . . are we not required to sustain ourselves and to manufacture that which we consume, to cease our bartering, trading, mingling, drinking, smoking, chewing and joining with all the filth of Babylon? . . . We want you henceforth to be a self-sustaining people. . . . What do you say brethren and sisters? All of you who say that we will be a self-sustaining people signify it by the show of your right hands." Everyone in the new Tabernacle raised his or her hand. "Let us govern our wants by our necessities, and we shall find that we are not compelled to spend our money for nought. Let us save our money to enter and pay for our land, to buy flocks of sheep and improve them, and to buy machinery and start more woolen factories. We have a good many now, and the people will sustain them."[47] President George Q. Cannon also warned the Saints of the outside threat to their institutions.[48]

The ultimate purpose of this new movement, largely directed by the School of the Prophets, was to curtail, as much as possible, contact with worldly elements; to avoid trade with outsiders; and even to boycott non-Mormon establishments—which Church leaders encouraged the Saints to do from 1868 until 1882. As James B. Allen and Glen M. Leonard explained:

The most controversial part of the plan was the proposition that Latter-day Saints should not trade with outsiders. If they were to keep the kingdom from being too strongly influenced or controlled by non-Mormon merchants, they must support their own cooperative institutions, and from 1868 until 1882 Church leaders encouraged the Saints to boycott "gentile" merchants and trade only with Mormon-owned establishments. In retrospect this may seem harsh and unfriendly, but most Latter-day Saints genuinely felt that incoming non-Mormons posed a threat to their economic well-being, and there was evidence that some outside merchants actually were trying to undermine the Church.[49]

Such plans and behavior on the part of Church leaders and members caused non-Latter-day Saints to become even more suspicious of and antagonistic toward the Mormons. These circumstances, combined with the expanding and controlling role of central government in the United States, impacted the Latter-day Saints in even more direct and severe ways than just the influx of "gentiles" resulting from the construction of the transcontinental railroad.

RADICAL RECONSTRUCTION AND POLYGAMY

Early in the Church's history, polygamy became a contentious issue with non-Latter-day Saints. It intensified after the Civil War. In 1856, the first platform of the new Republican party adopted at the National Convention declared that it was the duty of Congress to "prohibit in the Territories those twin relics

of barbarism, polygamy and slavery."[50] During the Civil War, the Latter-day Saints were not treasonous or rebellious or proslavery, but they were polygamous and remained so. This was a major reason they were not only harassed but also denied statehood. As one historian put it, had the Church disavowed the institution of plural marriage when federal antipolygamy legislation was passed in 1862, "Utah would have become a state during the war; with polygamy intact statehood was impossible."[51] Perhaps. Certainly after the war, individuals both in and out of the federal government, from the North and the South, again turned their attention to Utah, the Latter-day Saints, and polygamy.

The renewed campaign to eradicate polygamy from society after the Civil War seems to have been part of the general reform plan inaugurated by the Radical Republicans who were working so hard to establish civil and political rights for blacks. These Radical Republicans and Reconstructionists sought to reform not only the South but also the social structure of Utah. In the late 1860s, these reformers introduced into Congress three bills that show both the level of hostility the federal government possessed toward plural marriage and the Church as well as the power they believed it had acquired under Radical Republican leadership. These three legislative measures have been summarized: "In 1866 Senator Wade introduced a bill designed to destroy not only plural marriage but, in fact, the very strength of the Church in Utah. It was unsuccessful but was soon followed by the Cragin Bill, which would have eliminated trial by jury in Utah in cases involving polygamy. In 1869 a different approach was tried in the House of Representatives through the Ashley Bill, which proposed completely dismembering the Territory of Utah and dividing the area among surrounding states and territories."[52]

Antipolygamy sentiment intensified in 1870 owing to several developments. First was the publication of J. H. Beadle's book *Polygamy; or, the Mysteries and Crimes of Mormonism*.[53] The title says it all. In addition, that same year new legislation was proposed: the Cullom Bill, which would have required all cases involving plural marriage to be prosecuted exclusively by federal judges with juries selected by federally appointed marshals and attorneys. A huge protest by three thousand women in Salt Lake City caused legislators in Washington, DC, to think twice about this proposed law. It seems that such protest, plus the fear of another civil war now involving the Mormons, caused the bill to be defeated.

Sadly, the newly elected president of the United States who succeeded Andrew Johnson, Ulysses S. Grant, was no friend to the Latter-day Saints. He, along with his vice president, Schuyler Colfax, denounced Mormon practices and then appointed General John Wilson Shaffer as governor of the Utah Territory in 1870. Shaffer, an ally of the Radical Republicans in Congress, helped establish harsh federal rule in the Southern states as Radical Reconstruction unfolded. Known as an ardent foe of rebellion against the U.S. federal government, his appointment increased anxiety among Utah residents and antagonism against the administration in Washington.[54] He died unexpectedly before the year was out, but his home had become "virtual headquarters for the anti-Mormon group that conspired to destroy the Church's power."[55]

Shaffer helped to get the Utah territorial chief justice, Charles C. Wilson, removed from office so that President Grant could appoint James B. McKean in Wilson's place. He became chief justice of the Superior Court of the Utah Territory in 1870 and served until 1875. McKean, a Republican, had worked as a teacher and a judge, served in Congress, and fought in the Civil War as a colonel in the 77th Regiment of the New York Volunteers. President Grant sent McKean to Utah with instructions to root out polygamy. Both men believed this practice to be wrong. By contrast, the Latter-day Saints believed antipolygamy legislation to be wrong since it violated freedom of religion and was, therefore, unconstitutional.[56] When a showdown came, it centered on the person of Brigham Young.

Once in Utah, Judge McKean began denying citizenship to immigrants who practiced polygamy. He granted it only if applicants agreed to heed strictly the Anti-Bigamy Law of 1862. He even denied citizenship to those who expressed verbal support for the correctness of the right to practice polygamy though they themselves did not actually practice it. He then went after Mormonism's greatest symbol of polygamy, Brigham Young, by indicting him on charges of adultery. He was arraigned in court on January 2, 1872, but released on bail to await trial. The trial was never held because ultimately the United States Supreme Court intervened and dismissed this indictment as well as other charges against President Young.[57] However, this episode did not diminish the federal government's efforts to eliminate polygamy among the Latter-day Saints. Subsequent legislation against the Church and its members was enacted, and more immediate anti-Mormon activity in other parts of the country intensified.

As Radical Republicans began to lose power in the South, and Southern Democrats gained control of their states in the mid-1870s, many Northerners began to lose interest in Reconstruction. Federal troops that were placed in Southern states to facilitate Reconstruction on Republican terms were eventually withdrawn, and in 1875 the LDS Church organized the Southern States Mission.[58] Ironically, this led to a new wave of anti-Mormon violence. Not surprisingly, its ultimate cause was rooted in a fear of and revulsion over polygamy.

It has been argued persuasively that virtually all Southerners during the post–Civil War era, including blacks, believed "that polygamy was a menace to Christian civilization and that Mormonism was a heretical and sensual imposter that required a united Christian response."[59] Southern violence that had been leveled against blacks in the Reconstruction-era South was redirected against Church members, particularly missionaries.

> Proselytizing efforts throughout the region by representatives of the Church of Jesus Christ of Latter-day Saints stoked the fears of white southerners, who widely regarded Mormon missionaries as transient outsiders who imported heterodox religious beliefs and disrupted family ties and communities. Furthermore, southerners commonly saw missionaries as recruiting agents for Mormonism's most infamous practice: polygamy. The most common portrayal of the Latter-day Saint (LDS) missionary in the postbellum South was as a scheming sexual predator who seduced young women and lured them away to his polygamous harem in the West. Although of a different type than the

so-called black beast rapist who forced himself on unwilling white women, the image of the Mormon seducer tapped into many of the same fears that captivated southern white men in the late nineteenth century and provided their rationale for lynching.[60]

Vigilante violence was the most dramatic expression of Southern anti-Mormon sentiment. However, newspaper articles, pamphlets, sermons, and legislation also revealed how deep the bias against Mormons ran, and it almost always came back to the issue of polygamy. The St. Louis *Christian Advocate* of September 17, 1879, spoke of the "Mormon Question" as "one and the same thing" with polygamy.[61] Perhaps it is difficult for modern readers to comprehend the pervasive nature of anti-Mormon sentiment, but when Elder Joseph Standing was seized in rural Georgia in 1879, along with his companion, Elder Rudger Clawson, one of their captors stated, "There is no law in Georgia for Mormons, and the Government is against you."[62] Sadly, this was profoundly true of the U.S. government as well.

THE "SECOND RECONSTRUCTION"

By 1876 only three Southern states were still operating under Reconstruction governments. The presidential election that year resulted in the victory of Republican candidate Rutherford B. Hayes, but only after a compromise was reached whereby the federal government promised to withdraw all remaining federal troops from the South. For all intents and purposes, Reconstruction ended after Hayes took office in 1877 and carried out the terms of the compromise. Unfortunately, anti-Mormon and antipolygamy activity did

Little of value was left standing in the heart of Columbia, South Carolina, by the end of the Civil War in 1865. (National Archives)

not end. In fact, the end of Reconstruction led directly to even greater anti-Mormon sentiment, and the Latter-day Saints had many rough years ahead of them.

The failure of Judge McKean's crusade against polygamy in the Utah Territory was followed by the passage of federal legislation in 1874 that strengthened the Morrill Anti-Bigamy Act of 1862 and led to the prosecution of polygamy cases in federal courts. Named the Poland Bill for its sponsor, Luke P. Poland of Vermont, the new legislation emboldened the federal judiciary to reengage proceedings against polygamists. Church leaders believed antipolygamy legislation was unconstitutional—that it deprived them of their First Amendment right to practice their religion freely—and that a higher law, God's will, compelled them to violate federal law. It seems they designated George Reynolds, secretary to Brigham Young, to stand as a test case in order to

confirm the unconstitutionality of antipolygamy legislation as they saw it. Reynolds generally cooperated with the government prosecution, but he lost his case. He was convicted of bigamy, sentenced to two years of hard labor, and fined five hundred dollars. Through the appeals process, his case finally came before the U.S. Supreme Court. In the landmark decision of *Reynolds v. United States* in January 1879, the court ruled to uphold the lower court's decision. Antipolygamy law, specifically the Morrill Anti-Bigamy Act of 1862, was affirmed as the constitutional law of the land.[63]

The Church and its leaders were stunned. "Mormons could no longer claim shelter for their alternative marriage system as a form of religious expression protected under the First Amendment."[64] But more than that, just when Radical Republicans, Reconstructionists, and moral reformers had grown weary of their efforts to reform and rebuild the American

South, the decision of the U.S. Supreme Court breathed new life into the underlying impulse to restructure and rebuild society. This new antipolygamy crusade sparked what legal historian Sarah Barringer Gordon has called "a second 'Reconstruction' in the West."[65]

Antipolygamy sentiments specifically, and Anti-Mormonism sentiments generally, took on "a decidedly bipartisan and national character from the 1870s" onward. Significantly, "it was precisely because of the end of Reconstruction in the South that the federal government could turn its gaze—and direct its increased regulatory powers—toward problems in the West, including Indians and Mormons."[66] But Americans from every economic strata and political persuasion joined the campaign against Mormon polygamy. The "anti-polygamy movement cut across political, religious, and sectional lines" after Reconstruction in the South wound down.[67]

Ironically, Southern white participation in the national antipolygamy movement of the 1870s and 1880s served to soften somewhat the strained, even antagonistic, relationship between Southerners and Northern Republicans "by giving them common cause as moral and legislative reformers."[68] African Americans felt similar distaste toward polygamy, but their own problems, namely civil rights, kept them from participation in organized antipolygamy activities. Furthermore, many blacks "were quick to point out the hypocrisy of those who called for moral reform [among Mormons] while countenancing Jim Crow,"[69] a reference to laws enacted in the South to discriminate against African Americans.

CONCLUSION

Reconstruction proved to be a mixed "blessing." It produced the Thirteenth,

Fourteenth, and Fifteenth Amendments to the U.S. Constitution—landmark legislation to be sure. But on many counts, Reconstruction was a failure. It failed to solve the economic disasters engulfing the South after the Civil War. It failed to ease suffering, as President Lincoln seemed to envision. And it failed to bring racial harmony to the South and real equality to black Americans. Many blacks continued to work the land owned by whites. Most blacks in the South were prohibited from going to schools, attending churches, or entering hospitals where whites participated. Indeed, after Reconstruction ended, black Americans gradually lost all the rights they had gained during Reconstruction. This regression laid the foundation for the modern Civil Rights Movement one hundred years later, in the 1960s. Truly, Reconstruction was, in the words of Eric Foner, "America's unfinished revolution."[70]

Neither did Latter-day Saints fare so well after the Civil War as a result of what historians have called the "Second Reconstruction." They struggled to find what they regarded as fair treatment under an originally inspired Constitution. For a long time it seemed as though even friendly association beyond their Rocky Mountain home was out of the question. The "Second Reconstruction"—the national antipolygamy campaign of the 1870s and 1880s—treated them worse than they thought probable or possible. President Hayes did all he could to strengthen antipolygamy legislation, to recommend "more comprehensive and more searching methods for preventing as well as punishing" polygamy, as well as stripping its Mormon practitioners of their civil rights and privileges under U.S. citizenship.[71]

President Hayes's immediate successor, James A. Garfield, was no more conciliatory toward the Latter-day Saints than Hayes had been, nor any more realistic about the achievements of Reconstruction. As Garfield congratulated the government in his inaugural address for elevating "the negro race from slavery to the full rights of citizenship," he also declared that "the Mormon Church not only offends the moral sense of manhood by sanctioning polygamy, but prevents the administration of justice through ordinary instrumentalities of law."[72] Thus the national consciousness was led to embrace the notion that the Latter-day Saints were less than those possessing real manhood and that they obstructed justice to boot. They were, ironically, regarded as "that class which destroy the family relations and endanger social order."[73] In other words, now that blacks could no longer be held culpable by constitutional amendment of endangering the social order, the Latter-day Saints filled that role.

The agendas of Presidents Hayes and Garfield laid the foundation for the Edmunds Acts of 1882, which declared the practice of polygamy a felony and disenfranchised convicted polygamists. Five years later, the Edmunds-Tucker Act enacted even harsher measures to eliminate polygamy. While the legal maneuvering was occurring, individual Latter-day Saints, especially in the South, were enduring the physical indignities, insults, trauma, and violence perpetrated against them by an American public caught up in a national crusade against their religious beliefs.

Blessed with hindsight, the parallels between two groups of people targeted by two eras of Reconstruction are not lost on us. Though their trials were not nearly as profound, pervasive, or longlasting as the injustices and the travesties experienced by black Americans, the Latter-day Saints have endured experiences that make them more appreciative of the trials and tribulations of blacks living in the South after the Civil War. Such histories of mistreatment ought to make all of us more vigilant to injustice in our day and more willing to combat it. To an extent, there are some Americans who have never gotten over the "barbarism" of Mormonism. It remains one of the last great biases existing in this country.

Andrew C. Skinner is a professor of ancient scripture at Brigham Young University.

NOTES

1. Gary W. Gallagher, "An End and a New Beginning," in *Appomattox Court House: Appomattox Court House National Historical Park*, Handbook 160 (Washington, DC: National Park Service, Government Printing Office, n.d.), 76–77.

2. David W. Blight, "An America Transformed," in *Appomattox Court House,* 89.

3. Tanya Lee Stone, *Abraham Lincoln* (New York: DK Publishing, 2005), 110–11.

4. Quoted in Blight, "An America Transformed," 86.

5. Blight, "An America Transformed," 86.

6. Drew Gilpin Faust, *This Republic of Suffering: Death and the American Civil War* (New York: Vintage Books, 2008), xi.

7. Faust, *This Republic of Suffering*, xiii.

8. Faust, *This Republic of Suffering*, xiii.

9. Faust, *This Republic of Suffering*, xiii.

10. Harry R. Rubenstein, *Abraham Lincoln: An Extraordinary Life* (Washington, DC: Smithsonian Books, 2008), 80.

11. See the summary in Carolyn L. Harrell, *When the Bells Tolled for Lincoln: Southern Reaction to the Assassination* (Macon, GA: Mercer University Press, 1997), 103–7.

12. Quoted in E. B. Long, *The Saints and the Union: Utah Territory during the Civil War* (Urbana: University of Illinois Press, 1981), 261.

13. Brigham Young, quoted in Richard E. Bennett, *We'll Find the Place: The Mormon Exodus, 1846–1848* (Salt Lake City: Deseret Book, 1997), 7.

14. Long, *Saints and the Union*, 261–62.

15. Long, *Saints and the Union*, 262.

16. Long, *Saints and the Union*, 271.

17. Long, *Saints and the Union*, 191–92.

18. Rubenstein, *Abraham Lincoln*, 51; David Donald, *Lincoln Reconsidered: Essays on the Civil War Era* (New York: Vintage Books, 1989), 133.

19. Donald, *Lincoln Reconsidered*, 135.

20. Donald, *Lincoln Reconsidered*, 133–34.

21. Donald, *Lincoln Reconsidered*, 138.

22. Quoted in Stone, *Abraham Lincoln*, 90.

23. Eric Foner, *A Short History of Reconstruction, 1863–1877* (New York: Harper & Row, 1990), 16–18.

24. Stone, *Abraham Lincoln*, 88–89; Foner, *Short History of Reconstruction*, 18–30.

25. U.S. Const. amend. XIII, §1.

26. Linda R. Monk, *The Words We Live By: Your Annotated Guide to the Constitution* (New York: Hyperion, 2003), 209.

27. Quoted in Foner, *Short History of Reconstruction*, 30.

28. John Grafton, ed., *Great Speeches—Abraham Lincoln* (New York: Dover, 1991), 107–8.

29. Grafton, *Great Speeches*, 106.

30. Brigham Young, in *Journal of Discourses* (London: Latter-day Saints' Book Depot, 1854–86), 10:272–73.

31. Blight, "An America Transformed," 93.

32. Blight, "An America Transformed," 93.

33. Blight, "An America Transformed," 92.

34. Blight, "An America Transformed," 91.

35. Eric Foner, *Reconstruction: America's Unfinished Revolution, 1863–1877* (New York: Harper & Row, 1988), 199–200.

36. Foner, *Reconstruction*, 342–43, 425–44.

37. Foner, *Reconstruction*, 454–55.

38. U.S. Const. amend. XIV, § 1.

39. See the discussion in Monk, *Words We Live By*, 212–15.

40. Monk, *Words We Live By*, 213.

41. Monk, *Words We Live By*, 86.

42. U.S. Const. amend. XV, § 1.

43. Foner, *Reconstruction*, 446–49.

44. Quoted in Foner, *Reconstruction*, 590.

45. Blight, "An America Transformed," 88–89.

46. James B. Allen and Glen M. Leonard, *The Story of the Latter-day Saints*, rev. ed. (Salt Lake City: Deseret Book, 1992), 338.

47. Brigham Young, in *Journal of Discourses*, 12:284–85, 289.

48. George Q. Cannon, in *Journal of Discourses*, 12:290–91, 297.

49. Allen and Leonard, *Story of the Latter-day Saints*, 341.

50. Quoted in Long, *Saints and the Union*, 9.

51. Long, *Saints and the Union*, 273.

52. Allen and Leonard, *Story of the Latter-day Saints*, 351–52.

53. This book was published in Philadelphia.

54. Miriam R. Murphy, "Territorial Governors," *Utah History Encyclopedia*, ed. Allan Kent Powell (Salt Lake City: University of Utah Press, 1994), 549.

55. Allen and Leonard, *Story of the Latter-day Saints*, 353.

56. Allen and Leonard, *Story of the Latter-day Saints*, 353–54.

57. Allen and Leonard, *Story of the Latter-day Saints*, 354–55.

58. Allen and Leonard, *Story of the Latter-day Saints*, 397.

59. Patrick Q. Mason, "Opposition to Polygamy in the Postbellum South," *Journal of Southern History* 76, no. 3 (August 2010), 545.

60. Mason, "Opposition to Polygamy," 543.

61. Quoted in Mason, "Opposition to Polygamy," 543.

62. Mason, "Opposition to Polygamy," 543.

63. Allen and Leonard, *Story of the Latter-day Saints*, 363–65.

64. Mason, "Opposition to Polygamy," 547.

65. Sarah Barringer Gordon, *The Mormon Question: Polygamy and Constitutional Conflict in Nineteenth-Century America* (Chapel Hill, NC: University of North Carolina Press, 2002), 144.

66. Mason, "Opposition to Polygamy," 547.

67. Mason, "Opposition to Polygamy," 544.

68. Mason, "Opposition to Polygamy," 544.

69. Mason, "Opposition to Polygamy," 544.

70. This is the full title of Eric Foner's tour de force: *Reconstruction: America's Unfinished Revolution, 1863–1877*.

71. Quoted in Mason, "Opposition to Polygamy," 547–48.

72. *Inaugural Addresses of the Presidents of the United States from George Washington 1789 to George Bush 1989*, bicentennial ed. (Washington, DC: United States Government Printing Office, 1989), 163, 167.

73. *Inaugural Addresses*, 167.

LOYALTY

FRATERNITY

CHARITY

THE THREE CARDINAL PRINCIPLES OF THE GRAND ARMY OF THE REPUBLIC.

Organized shortly following the end of the Civil War, the Grand Army of the Republic promoted veteran causes for over eighty years.
(Courtesy of Kenneth L. Alford)

CHAPTER 18

Kenneth L. Alford

MORMONS AND THE GRAND ARMY OF THE REPUBLIC

"Fraternity, charity, and loyalty."

Motto of the Grand Army of the Republic

After achieving a tremendous victory at the battle of Austerlitz in 1805, Napoleon ordered a commerative medal made for the participants. On the obverse was the image of the emperor; on the reverse was the name of the battle and the simple words "I was there."[1] When the Civil War ended in 1865, there were over one million men serving in the United States armed forces; during the entire war, over two and a half million men served the nation.[2] They viewed themselves as soldiers who had seen "all the vicissitudes of war and had triumphed in the greatest cause that had ever brought happiness to the civilized world."[3] As the soldiers, sailors, and marines were discharged, it was natural to "desire that the friendships formed should be maintained through life,"[4] as bonds forged in combat can be "the most enduring of any

in this world, outside of the family circle."[5] Many of its members accorded the Grand Army of the Republic (GAR) "the same loyalty and devotion that they did to the regiments in which they once fought."[6] The GAR—which grew from humble beginnings to become "one of the most powerful organizations of the country"[7]—helped to fill that need and gave each Union veteran an opportunity to proclaim that "I, too, was there."[8]

OVERVIEW OF THE GAR

Like earlier American wars, the Civil War spawned a variety of veteran organizations.[9] The first Civil War veteran's society, the Third Army Corps Union, was organized during the war in March 1862. Similar societies were organized throughout the war and during the sometimes awkward peace that followed.[10]

STATE OR GROUP	TOTAL	STATE OR GROUP	TOTAL
New York	467,047	Rhode Island	23,609
Pennsylvania	366,107	Kansas	20,151
Ohio	319,659	District of Columbia	16,872
Illinois	259,147	California	15,725
Indiana	197,147	Delaware	13,670
Massachusetts	152,048	Arkansas	8,289
Missouri	109,111	New Mexico Territory	6,561
Colored Troops	99,337	Louisiana	5,224
Wisconsin	96,424	Colorado Territory	4,903
Michigan	89,372	Indian Nation	3,530
New Jersey	81,010	Nebraska Territory	3,157
Kentucky	79,025	North Carolina	3,156
Iowa	76,309	Alabama	2,576
Maine	72,114	Texas	1,965
Connecticut	57,379	Oregon	1,810
Maryland	50,316	Florida	1,290
Vermont	35,262	Nevada	1,080
New Hampshire	34,629	Washington Territory	964
West Virginia	32,068	Mississippi	545
Tennessee	31,092	Dakota Territory	206
Minnesota	25,052	**Total**	2,865,028

Figure 1. Number of men furnished for the Union Army by state, territory, and District of Columbia (from April 15, 1861, to the end of the Civil War). Note that Utah's total (just over 100) is not listed. (Source: D. A. Ellis, Grand Army of the Republic: History of the Order in the U.S. by Counties *[n.p.: Press of Historical Publishing, 1892], 22)*

The Grand Army of the Republic was officially organized in 1866 as a fraternal organization for everyone "who, on land or sea, honorably served their country" during the Civil War.[11] The first GAR post was created on April 6, 1866, at Decatur, Illinois, and additional posts followed in rapid succession.[12] A total of almost nine thousand local GAR posts were organized, and by 1890 there were over four hundred thousand members.[13] (As shown in figure 1, the number of potential GAR members was extremely large—based on the number of Civil War veterans in the nation. Note that Utah's Civil War veterans were not included.)

GAR membership was for male[14] Union veterans—"a membership drawn only from the limited number who were privileged to wear the uniform of their country in the days of its great peril."[15] Any veteran who honorably served between April 12, 1861, and April 9, 1865, "in the war for the suppression of the rebellion" in the United States Army, Navy, Marine Corps, or a state regiment "called into active service" was eligible to join.[16] While officially it "countenanced nothing of personal animosities against those who . . . so wrongfully arrayed themselves against their country,"[17] former Confederate soldiers and sailors were not eligible and needed not apply.[18] Latter-day Saint Civil War veterans from Utah's Lot Smith Cavalry Company would learn that initially they were not welcome to join the GAR either.

Beginning at Indianapolis in November 1866, the Grand Army of the Republic held an annual National Encampment, providing an opportunity for veterans from across the nation to assemble.[19] During the first few years of its existence, the GAR played an active political role as well— nominating and supporting candidates for national, state, and local political offices. At the National Encampment in 1868, many GAR members recognized that the organization needed to remove itself from politics and be "placed upon a purely nonpartisan basis." In 1869, the GAR's *Rules and Regulations* were amended to require that

Members of the Grand Army of the Republic wore badges like this one to identify themselves as Civil War veterans. Many members replaced the metal emblem at the top with a rectangular emblem that included their highest military rank. (Robert B. Beath, History of the Grand Army of the Republic)

called Decoration Day) as a national holiday.[20] With help from the GAR, five of its members became president of the United States: Grant, Hayes, Garfield, Harrison, and McKinley.[21]

The GAR was a quasi-military organization. Members wore a uniform—"a double-breasted, dark blue coat with bronze buttons, and a black wide-brimmed slouch felt hat, with golden wreath insignia and cord. A bronze star badge hung from a small chiffon flag. The star in relief depicted a soldier and sailor clasping hands in front of a figure of Liberty. Members wore these insignia in their lapels, so they could be easily identified."[22] The GAR had enough political clout that Congress modified the U.S. Code to authorize that "a member of the Army, Navy . . . or Marine Corps

"no officer or comrade of the Grand Army of the Republic shall in any manner use this organization for partisan purposes, and no discussion of partisan questions shall be permitted at any of its meetings." The party politics that so marked the GAR's earliest years slowly dissipated, and the organization was later able to report that it had "outgrown the mistakes of its infancy." The GAR actively lobbied for military benefits—especially education legislation for widows and orphans as well as pension increases—and was the key force behind the establishment of Memorial Day (originally

who is a member of a military society originally composed of men who served in an armed force of the United States during . . . the Civil War . . . may wear, on occasions of ceremony, the distinctive badges adopted by that society."[23] (The GAR's bronze star badge looked strikingly similar, though, to the military's Medal of Honor and sometimes led to confusion regarding which award was being worn.[24])

Military vocabulary and motifs found their way into the organization in a variety of ways. New members did not simply join the organization; they were mustered in. Meetings were called encampments. Local organizations were described as posts rather than chapters and were named after Union Army heroes or prominent officers. Announcements and bulletins were issued as general or special orders. National and local leadership positions mimicked the military command and staff structure with commanders, adjutants general, chiefs of staff, aides-de-camp, surgeons, chaplains, quartermasters, quartermaster-sergeants, inspectors-general, officers of the day, judge advocates general, and guards.[25] In recognition of the comradery that veterans felt during the war, GAR members referred to each other as "comrade" in correspondence and conversation. GAR posts provided companionship, a chance to reminisce, and opportunities to serve.

Ladies of the Grand Army of the Republic auxiliary members wore membership badges like this. "F.C.L." stands for "Fraternity, Charity, and Loyalty," the motto of the Grand Army of the Republic. (Courtesy of Kenneth L. Alford)

The constitution of the GAR specified it was to be loosely patterned after the organization of the United States Army during the Civil War with a national headquarters, departments (usually found at the state or multistate level), districts (often created at the county level), and posts (established in cities and towns). District organizations were "composed of one delegate for every ten members. . . . Each District was entitled to one delegate in the Department Organization, which [met] once in each year. The National Organization was to be composed of two delegates from each Department."[26]

GAR activity occurred primarily at the local level; district and department organizations actually existed for only a few days each year during state and national encampments.

Beginning in 1868, there were three degrees of GAR membership: recruit, soldier, and veteran. Each grade had its own "ritual, signs, grips, and passwords." Recruits, for example, could not speak, vote, or hold office.[27] The multitier membership system substantially reduced membership, though, and was generally abandoned after a few years. The GAR did not need an artificial rank system because all of its members had served in military units and earned real ranks.[28] Rank earned during their military service "played no small part in determining rank in the GAR."[29]

So that women, especially the wives and children of Civil War veterans, could participate in activities to promote fraternity, charity, and loyalty, two GAR women's organizations were established. The "Woman's Relief Corps, Auxiliary to the Grand Army of the Republic," was organized in Denver, Colorado, on July 25–26, 1883.[30] The Woman's Relief Corps was open to "the mothers, wives, daughters and sisters of Union soldiers, sailors and marines who aided in putting down the Rebellion." Members were to be "women of good moral character and correct deportment, who have not given aid and comfort to the enemies of the Union" and at least sixteen years old. Local units were called corps (instead of posts).

Each corps was to be associated with a GAR post and "must bear the name of the Post to which it is auxiliary."[31] In 1896, the year Utah was granted statehood, the Ladies of the Grand Army of the Republic was established on a national basis.[32] Similar to the Woman's Relief Corps but with broader membership eligibility, the preamble of the new group's *Rules and Regulations* stated that the organization was established for "the loyal mothers, wives, sisters, daughters, granddaughters and blood kin nieces of soldiers, sailors and marines, who served honorably in aiding and maintaining the integrity and supremacy of the National Government during the Rebellion, and ex-army [n]urses, and all lineal female descendants."[33] Local units of the Ladies of the Grand Army of the Republic were called circles (instead of posts), and five or more circles could be organized into a Ladies Department. Ladies circles could associate with a GAR post but were not required to do so. Unlike the Woman's Relief Corps, Ladies of the Grand Army of the Republic circles could select their own name.

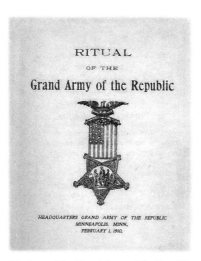

Meetings of the Grand Army of the Republic included formal rituals, handshakes, and passwords. (Courtesy of Kenneth L. Alford)

THE GAR IN UTAH

The first Civil War veterans' fraternal group organized in Utah—the Improved Order of Red Men—was established with seventy-one charter members on March 4, 1872, in Salt Lake City.[34] The observation by historian John Gary Maxwell that "formal Grand Army of the Republic (GAR) posts in Utah did not exist until 1878" may be incorrect.[35] The first GAR post in Utah was reportedly established at Camp Douglas prior to 1878 and was "composed of United States soldiers on garrison duty"; it was closed due to "a change of stations of the regiment."[36] If anyone recorded the date that the Camp Douglas GAR Post was established, that fact awaits discovery. One of the earliest references to GAR members in Utah, though, is a May 27, 1873, newspaper article in the *Salt Lake Tribune* regarding the observance of Decoration Day (Memorial Day) on May 30. The news report referred to GAR members and GAR committees but did not clearly state whether or not they were acting under the auspices of an organized Utah GAR post. It seems likely, though, that they could have been members of the GAR Post at Camp Douglas.

During the spring of 1873, GAR members solicited funds from the Salt Lake community at large to "decorate the graves of their fellow comrades" on the upcoming Decoration Day. Brigham Young and other Latter-day Saint leaders made donations which offended some of the GAR members. A "committee of three appointed from the Grand Army of the Republic," chaired by Patrick Edward Connor (the first commander of Camp Douglas), resolved to return all donations received from "Brigham Young and other leading Mormons."[37]

In a general committee meeting the previous evening "called by members of the Grand Army of the Republic at Independence Hall [in Salt Lake City]," General Connor declared that he desired "all loyal citizens to participate in the [grave-decorating]

STATES	POSTS	MEMBERS	STATES	POSTS	MEMBERS
Alabama	14	381	Missouri	428	20,326
Arizona	10	456	Montana	21	794
Arkansas	66	3,749	Nebraska	282	8,012
California	126	6,973	New Hampshire	93	5,162
Colorado & Wyoming	84	3,272	New Jersey	119	7,843
Connecticut	92	7,241	New Mexico	10	356
Delaware	23	1,474	New York	656	39,885
Florida	21	893	North Dakota	33	859
Georgia	11	487	Ohio	723	47,273
Idaho	23	946	Oregon	49	1,784
Illinois	621	34,315	Pennsylvania	607	45,273
Indiana	527	27,043	Rhode Island	22	2,762
Iowa	436	21,382	South Dakota	14	407
Kansas	492	19,326	Tennessee	74	3,371
Kentucky	148	6,027	Texas	34	914
Louisiana & Mississippi	19	1,443	Utah	3	168
Maine	161	10,851	Vermont	109	5,378
Massachusetts	207	22,453	Virginia	39	1,416
Maryland	45	2,326	Washington & Alaska	54	1,994
Michigan	407	21,817	West Virginia	95	3,017
Minnesota	181	8,003	Wisconsin	272	14,581
			Totals	7,441	432,510

Figure 2. Membership of the Grand Army of the Republic as of September 30, 1890. (Source: Ellis, Grand Army of the Republic, *12)*

ceremony, and those of the audience who chose to come he would like to meet him at his office after adjournment" (presumably to ensure that they met his definition of being a loyal citizen). The prevailing attitude of Utah's GAR members toward The Church of Jesus Christ of Latter-day Saints can be seen in the resolution passed by that committee on May 26, 1873:

Inasmuch as the Grand Army of the Republic is about to commemorate the day [Decoration Day 1873], and decorate the graves of their fellow comrades, and it appearing that Brigham Young, the President of the Mormon Church,

and other leaders of said church, *which is disloyal, and in its principles and practices opposed to Republican Government,* for the defense of which our fallen brethren gave their lives, have contributed certain sums of money to assist in defraying the expenses of such decoration, and *it further being self-evident that said contributions were not made in good faith, but to subserve the ulterior sinister motives of said Brigham Young,* and whereas the *acceptance of said contributions would be an insult to the memory of our fellow comrades,* Therefore it is *Resolved,* That the General Committee be and are hereby ordered to refund to Brigham Young and all other Mormon leaders, all moneys contributed by them for the purpose.[38]

The first permanent post in Utah—James B. McKean Post 1, whose namesake served as a colonel of New York Volunteers during the Civil War and as chief justice of the Superior Court of Utah Territory from 1870 to 1875—was mustered in at Salt Lake City on September 18, 1878, with George R. Maxwell, a former federal marshal and distinguished Civil War veteran, commanding.[39] The George R. Maxwell Post 2 was created in Salt Lake City shortly thereafter.[40] A third Utah GAR post, the John A. Dix Post 3 in Ogden (whose namesake was a well-known major general of New York Militia and former U.S. senator), was organized in a doctor's office by General Paul Van Der Voort, GAR's vice commander in chief, on April 25, 1879. The *Ogden Standard* newspaper noted that "all honorably discharged federal soldiers" were "cordially invited to be present."[41] It is doubtful that any Latter-day Saint veterans attended. In the nineteenth century, GAR members in Utah consisted of men "who had immigrated, usually men who had come to join mining or business ventures or who had arrived in Utah as appointed federal officers."[42] By 1888, there were still just three GAR posts in Utah Territory.[43] In 1890, Utah had the smallest GAR membership and

A former U.S. Congressman and Union colonel during the Civil War, James Bedell McKean (1821–79), was appointed chief justice of the Superior Court of the Utah Territory by President Ulysses S. Grant in 1870 and served until 1875. The first GAR post in Utah was named in his honor. (Beath, History of the Grand Army of the Republic)

least number of posts of any state or territory in the nation.[44] (See figure 2.)

While an exhaustive search of GAR membership in Utah is yet to be conducted, it appears that GAR members in Utah during the nineteenth century consisted exclusively of non-Mormon veterans. There are many possible reasons why non-Mormons may not have wanted to offer GAR membership to Latter-day Saints. First, Utah's few Civil War soldiers were not viewed as authentic veterans. Utahns generally were perceived, not without cause, as having watched the Civil War from the sidelines. The Lot Smith Cavalry Company, Utah Territory's only active duty Civil War military unit, faced no Confederate forces in battle and lost no soldiers in combat—plus they served for only ninety days. Even today, most Utahns are unaware of Utah's limited military participation during the Civil War. Second, Utah GAR members generally believed that Mormons were disloyal to the Union—a charge which, if upheld, would have made them ineligible for GAR membership. Article IV of the GAR *Rules and Regulations* specified that "no person shall be eligible to membership who has at any time born arms against the United States,"[45] and many Utah GAR members felt that rule excluded from membership any Mormon, such as Lot Smith, who had taken up arms during the Utah War, even if they later served honorably in the Union Army.

The Utah GAR saw itself as an organization which "stood up to maintain the honor of the flag on the picket line between two civilizations"—American and Mormon.[46] A third reason was that the GAR was openly against the practice of polygamy.

THE GAR AND POLYGAMY

The GAR dedicated itself to the defense of freedom and the abolition of any form of slavery, which included, from the perspective of many GAR members, polygamy. Politically, GAR membership leaned toward the Republican Party, which may partially explain the antithesis many GAR members felt toward polygamy—the remaining vestige of the "twin relics of barbarism" denounced at Philadelphia during the first Republican National Convention in 1856.

From its earliest beginnings, the GAR officially invited "all honorably discharged soldiers and sailors . . . desirous of becoming members of the Grand Army of the Republic" to join its ranks. For an organization "whose cardinal principles [were] Fraternity, Charity and Loyalty" and which viewed itself "as one of the noblest in its works and purposes of any fraternal and charitable association known,"[47] the Grand Army of the Republic in Utah took a dim view regarding extending membership to veterans who served during 1862 in the Lot Smith Utah Cavalry. Although it defined itself as an organization that welcomed "all who were among the Nation's defenders, demanding no vows of allegiance except to the country and the flag,"[48] the reality was more complicated when it involved Utah's Latter-day Saint veterans.

Article I in the Declaration of Principles, GAR's constitution, affirmed that "soldiers of the Volunteer Army of the United States during the Rebellion of 1861–5" had a responsibility to actively preserve "the grand results of the war, the fruits of their labor and toil, so as to benefit the deserving and worthy."[49] To many GAR members, this meant that they felt duty bound to oppose, as both oppressive and un-American, the Mormon practice of polygamy. Utah Civil War veterans who were Mormon were viewed as being neither eligible nor deserving of GAR membership. At the first National Encampment in 1866, E. W. H. Ellis, a member from Indiana, introduced the "Rallying Song of the Grand Army of the Republic" sung to the tune of "The Battle Hymn of the Republic." The first and last verses expressed the righteous indignation that many non-Mormon GAR members in Utah would later express against the Latter-day Saints:

[Stanza 1]
There's a mighty army gathering
    throughout the East and West,
With banners gaily flaunting
    they speed along with zest,
And the motto they are shouting,
    "We fight for the oppressed,
As we go marching on."

[Stanza 6]
The glorious hour is coming;
    the day is drawing nigh,
When slavery and oppression
    shall lay them down and die,
And universal freedom
    shall be echoed through the sky,
As they go marching on.[50]

In a July 1883 address to the National Encampment in Denver, GAR commander in chief Paul Van Der Voort[51] directly identified polygamy as "a crime as hideous as treason, and as damnable as slavery." He explained that he and the GAR's national surgeon general had visited the GAR Provisional Department of Utah on April 21 and 22 earlier that year as part of an 1883 Grand Army tour. After observing that he was "cordially received by as gallant a band of comrades as ever wore our badge," Van Der Voort expressed his belief that "the organization in Utah have had many difficulties to contend with. They are upholding the banner of the Grand Army in what is practically a foreign and hostile community. They are in the front of an enemy, treacherous and defiant, and who are trampling daily under foot the laws of the land with perfect impunity." Making direct reference to the practice of polygamy, Van Der Voort continued his verbal assault: "The Grand Army in Utah are the natural protectors of the glory and honor of the flag. They here . . . grandly illustrate the shining glories of our Order. Let us demand that earnest, true men who know and have faced the evil and sin day and night, shall be designated to codify the laws heretofore passed through the dictates of the leaders of this unholy Church. That it shall be written and declared that no Mormon shall vote or hold any office whatever . . . and that the emigration of recruits to build up this damning crime shall be stopped at once and forever."[52] Van Der Voort saw the Grand Army of the Republic "as a factor on the side

The Grand Army of the Republic and the auxiliary women organizations associated with it considered themselves the guardians of the American flag and patriotism. The singing of patriotic songs played a large part during meetings and rallies.
(Courtesy of Kenneth L. Alford)

of the government in the contest waging against treason [polygamy]."[53]

Following Commander in Chief Van Der Voort's 1883 address, the national GAR Committee on Resolutions recommended that the National Encampment adopt the following resolution: "*Resolved,* That we heartily endorse and concur in the views so forcibly and eloquently expressed in the address upon the barbaric crime of polygamy, and we most earnestly invite Congress to devise such measures as will speedily and effectually remove that blot upon the morals and purity of the nation."[54]

Relations between Mormons and GAR members became particularly tense during 1885 and 1886. On the Fourth of July, 1885, many American flags in Salt Lake City were lowered to half-staff at locations across the city, including City Hall, the County Court House, the Salt Lake Theater, the *Deseret News* office, John Taylor's home, the Garden House, and the Tithing Office.[55] The July 8 issue of the *Deseret News* included a lengthy article entitled "Loyalty of the Latter-day Saints" in which Mormons were declared "the most loyal community within the pale of the Republic of the United States," but "they have no reason for engaging in expressions of joy under existing circumstances." Flags were flown at half-staff, the article reported, as a symbol of mourning for lost freedoms.[56]

To Mormons, displaying the flag at half-staff represented their distress and frustration regarding the 1882 Edmunds Act and other laws aimed at curtailing polygamy. To GAR members, flying the nation's flag at half-staff was, as the *Salt Lake Tribune* labeled it, "the mark of treason" and a "day . . . never [to] be forgotten."[57] The American flag was held in extreme symbolic and emotional esteem by GAR veterans, and the GAR went to great lengths to honor and venerate the flag. Historian Stuart McConnell called the flag "the object of a sudden and intense cult that would ultimately produce Flag Day and the Pledge of Allegiance."[58] To illustrate the depth of feeling members felt for the American flag, for many years GAR posts ended each meeting with a closing ceremony that included this exchange:

> Commander.—Junior Vice-Commander, how may our country be kept undivided and our flag maintained unsullied?
>
> Junior Vice-Commander.—By eternal vigilance, which is the price of liberty.
>
> Commander.—Officer of the Day, what should be the doom of all traitors?
>
> Officer of the Day (*stepping in front of the Commander, smartly drawing his sword, and assuming the position of "guard," as do all the officers.*)—The Penalty of Treason is Death!

Paul Van Der Voort (1846–1902), eleventh commander in chief of the Grand Army of the Republic (1882–83), was an outspoken critic of polygamy. During his GAR command, the National Women's Relief Corps (NWRC) was designed as an official GAR auxiliary, and he was made an honorary NWRC member. (Beath, History of the Grand Army of the Republic)

> All the Comrades Respond.—*The penalty of Treason is Death.*[59]

The tensions created on July 4 lingered for several days. On July 11, George R. Maxwell spoke during a meeting in the federal court house at Salt Lake City and vowed that "never again, so long as a member of the G.A.R. is alive in Utah will that flag be trailed (lowered) again." The *Tribune* reported that several "Mormon hoodlums" tried unsuccessfully to interrupt and "hoot" him.[60] The *Deseret News* responded the following week by commenting that "the idea of the *Tribune* being mad over the alleged insult by 'Mormons' to the American flag, is as supremely ridiculous as the assumption by the irresponsible blatherskites who turn the crank of that organ, that any insult whatever was intended."[61] Intended or not, GAR veterans were deeply offended by the action and remembered it for many years.

The following summer, as a partial response to the July 4 half-staff flag incident in 1885, Utah GAR members organized a series of "camp fires" (July 24, 29, 30, 31, and August 1) in a large skating rink in Salt Lake City and invited national GAR leaders to speak. GAR leaders traveling to the national encampment in San Francisco passed through Utah, so it was an easy adjustment to their schedule. Salt Lake City saw "delegation after delegation arrive by rail, proceed from the depot to the Grand Army headquarters in the city, and there give utterance to the most pronounced opposition to what the Mormons are doing."[62] Characterizing the meetings as "anti-'Mormon' rabies," the *Deseret News* reported that "the skating rink was filled to overflowing by members of the G.A.R. and others curious to witness the antics of the anti-'Mormon' ring."[63] Mormon historian B. H. Roberts reported that "a bitter anti-Mormon flavor was imparted to each camp-fire gathering—hatred and rage chiefly characterized what was said."[64] During one campfire meeting, Reverend Doctor Dunning, of Boston, said that "the boys in blue . . . would do it (fight) again, and bring freedom to the slaves of Utah—*the women*." The U.S. district attorney for Utah declared that "the Mormon Church was steeped in disloyalty. . . . One of its prime purposes was the overthrow of the American home. . . . He had it from good authority that when Lincoln was assassinated and the news reached here (i.e., Utah) that Brigham Young then governor [*sic*] could not repress his exultation"—Roberts added in a footnote that it was "the revamping of an old slander many times refuted."[65] Charles W. Bennett, an attorney, charged that the citizens of Utah experienced less liberty "than anywhere else, [even] than in Russia, or in Ireland. . . . The people in Utah were as un-American as were Fiji Islanders." One speaker, identified only as Colonel Jones from New York, declared that "a greater Power than man put slavery down, and the boys in blue were his chosen instruments for the work. He sent the boys in blue here [to Salt Lake City] to say to the country they would put polygamy down."[66] Many other GAR members spoke in a similar vein.

During the 1886 Twentieth National Encampment held at San Francisco soon afterward, the GAR's national Committee on Resolutions considered and adopted a resolution that had originated with the James B. McKean GAR post in Salt Lake City and was forwarded to the national headquarters "with the hearty approval" of the GAR department of Utah:

> *Whereas*, The preservation of the unity of the Government is the highest duty of all; and
> *whereas*, it is the duty of citizens everywhere to try and enforce the laws; and
> *whereas*, any interference by a so-called ecclesiastical authority with temporal affairs is a menace to the institutions of the country; and
> *whereas*, the Mormon leaders have for years taught, and continue to teach, their people to look upon the Government as an enemy, and continue an organization by and through which the laws are nullified and the flag insulted; now
> *therefore*, we, the members of the Grand Army of the Republic, in encampment assembled, recognizing the facts, demand that the flag be everywhere respected, and do resolve that it is the duty of the American people to require their representatives in Congress to pass such laws as will effectually release the Territories of the United States from the control of said organization, and will insure to every one the protection of the laws.[67]

That same day, at a meeting of the Women's Relief Corps, Mrs. Ida L. Lincoln, president of the department of Utah, introduced this companion resolution that was also adopted:

> *Whereas*—There exists in these United States an organization professedly

independent of and hostile to the Government, known as "The Church of Jesus Christ of Latter-day Saints," which already holds absolute political control of one great Territory, and is rapidly gaining ascendancy in two others.

Whereas, This organization by its public teaching of the right to violate national law, when it conflicts with their religious practices, by its doctrines of State sovereignty so fully tested and settled by the civil war; by its overt acts of dishonoring the flag by trailing it in the dust, in contempt of national authority, and by half-masting the same on our national holiday, expressive of the sentiment, "Liberty is dead in Utah;" by these things it has inculcated disloyalty and arrayed itself against the principles of American unity; . . .

Resolved, That we deem it imperative upon us to enter our protest against the vile practices and the continued disloyalty of Mormonism, and call upon the loyal women of this Nation to encourage such legislation as shall most effectually suppress the evil.[68]

The following year during the 1887 national encampment, the same GAR committee debated an additional resolution regarding Mormonism:

Resolved, That the Grand Army of the Republic now, as in the past, views with detestation the determined purposes of the polygamous leaders of the Mormon majority of Utah to continue the nullification of National Laws. And we warn Congress and the country against the pending attempt to enlarge the powers of fugitives from justice by creating a

State out of that Territory; which, if successful, would be rewarding treason for continued insult to the flag and nullification of wholesome laws; place in the Union a theocratic State antagonistic to good order and the welfare of the nation, and an enemy to the cherished principles of free government. All of which is at variance with every sacred principle of our Order.

After a vigorous debate, during which the national commander affirmed that "the Grand Army has repeatedly set its stamp of disapproval on such a treasonable organization [the Latter-day Saints], such a damnable outrage on society [polygamy] as exists in the Territory of Utah to-day,"[69] the committee tabled that resolution because "its discussion would be foreign to the work and objects of the Grand Army of the Republic"—not because they disagreed with it.[70]

The Mormon practice of polygamy was a continuing irritant to Utah's GAR members. Throughout the 1880s, Kate Field of New York City—described by the Washington *National Tribune* as "one of the most rarely gifted women of this or any other country"—was an outspoken critic of polygamy. The *Salt Lake Tribune* gushed that "it is no exaggeration to say that among the American women writers of today . . . no one has the breath, the vigor, the originality and the power of Kate Field."[71] Her "crusade against the Mormon iniquity [polygamy]" received the endorsement of the GAR's national commander in chief and a "large portion of the G.A.R." In September 1886, the McKean post in Salt Lake City unanimously adopted a preamble and resolution condemning Mormonism. The preamble asserted that their post "has been on outpost duty for years, and during all that time has been surrounded by people of a community opposed to our government, at enmity with American institutions, hostile to our flag, and as in all human probability the unequal contest between the minority of citizens of Utah who are loyal and the majority of the Mormon Church will, without outside assistance, be protected until no soldier of 1865 will be alive." The preamble continued by noting that the "careful, long continued, and intelligent study by Kate Field of the issues between the government of the United States and the Mormon power in Utah is well known to us as comrades and citizens . . . [and] invites the admiration of all good citizens, and richly entitles her to the gratitude of all members of the Grand Army of the Republic." The McKean post formally resolved that "with gratitude to her we cordially and earnestly commend Kate Field to our commander-in-chief as the one especially fitted to present the facts . . . to the country; and we respectfully request that he commend her in her good work to our comrades everywhere."[72] GAR opposition to polygamy continued until Latter-day Saint Church President Wilford Woodruff issued the Manifesto in 1890.

Kate Field (1838–96) was an influential American journalist, lecturer, actress, and businesswoman. The Washington National Tribune *called her "one of the most rarely gifted women of this or any other country." In 1886, the McKean GAR Post in Salt Lake City passed a resolution commending Field for her stance against polygamy. (Library of Congress)*

MORMON MEMBERSHIP IN THE GAR

A resolution passed during the 1904 GAR state encampment extended to Utah's Congressional delegation the "grateful appreciation of their kindly services" in "procuring the allowance and increase of pensions from the government for many of our worthy comrades" and hoped that "the patriotic efforts of our friends [in Congress] will be continued until every soldier in Utah who deserves and needs a pension shall have [the] same allowed him."[73] Little did they recognize

that Utah's major Civil War pension conflict would involve Mormon veterans from the Lot Smith Utah Cavalry who served just ninety days in the spring and summer of 1862.

Based on the war of words that existed between the GAR and Latter-day Saints during the 1880s, it is not surprising that there were apparently no nineteenth-century Latter-day Saint GAR members who served during the Civil War from Utah. There are many possible factors that may have contributed to Mormons finally applying for membership in Utah GAR posts—the end of polygamy, Utah's receiving statehood, or a desire to secure a federal pension. Sentimentality may also have played a role, as expressed in this poem that was popular among GAR members:

> There are bonds of all sorts
>   in this world of ours,
> Fetters of friendship and ties
>   of flowers,
> And true lovers' knots, I wean;
> The boy and the girl are bound
>   by a kiss,
> But there is never a bond, old friend,
>   like this—
> We have drank from the same
>   canteen[74]

Regardless of what the actual motivations were, Mormon Civil War veterans in Utah began applying for GAR membership after the turn of the twentieth century.

In 1907, Seymour B. Young, a nephew of Brigham Young who served as a corporal in the Lot Smith Utah Cavalry and was then serving as senior president of the Presidents of the Seventy in the Church, applied for GAR membership with the George R. Maxwell Post in Salt Lake City. His application was referred to a three-man investigating committee, which reported his application favorably "without having made such an investigation as is required by the rules and regulations" (according to the Department of Utah's 1909 annual encampment record). The GAR post members voted on his application; his application was rejected, and his membership fee was returned to him. In 1908, the George R. Maxwell Post commander "ordered a new ballot on the same application," and his application was "declared favorable." Other post members questioned the legality of the second vote and demanded that the matter be "brought before

the Department Commander, asking that the ballot be declared illegal and be set aside." The Utah department commander referred the case to the department judge advocate for a legal decision. The judge advocate held that the second ballot "was void, and that the Commander should set it aside."[75]

The historian Margaret Fisher claimed that by the summer of 1909 "although many [Mormon Utah Civil War veterans] had applied for membership, only two, Charles Crismon, Jr., and Dr. Harvey C. Hullinger, had been allowed admittance into the Utah G.A.R. Posts, which were comprised of men who had enlisted in other states but had later taken up residence in Utah. . . . The Lot Smith Company, Utah Volunteers, who although eligible to become members of the Grand Army of the Republic, had been denied that privilege because of religious differences."[76]

To complicate the issue regarding eligibility of Lot Smith Company veterans to join the GAR, an earlier ruling by the federal pension bureau board declared that Utah Cavalry veterans were ineligible to receive federal Civil War pensions. However, in December 1909, X. J. L. Davenport, commissioner of the federal Bureau of Pensions, reinstated veteran status when he announced that "at one time it was held that this company [Lot Smith's cavalry] was not organized for service in connection with the war of the rebellion. Recently the secretary has reversed his former holding and now holds that the company was enlisted for service in that war, and that this last decision gives pensionable status to the members of the organization under the act of February 6, 1907. This would seem to place them in the same position as soldiers who actually served at the front during the war."[77] The pension

Members of the GAR went to great lengths to honor and respect the American flag. The GAR was responsible, in large measure, for the establishment of Memorial Day as a national holiday and the widespread adoption of the Pledge of Allegiance. (Courtesy of Kenneth L. Alford)

bureau's reversal meant that veterans of the Lot Smith Company would be "restored to a pensionable status . . . with back pension from [the] date of [their] rejection."[78]

Controversy regarding the GAR membership eligibility of Lot Smith company veterans climaxed after Harvey C. Hullinger and Charles Crismon attended the 1910 GAR State Encampment in Salt Lake City as delegates from the O. O. Howard Post in Salt Lake City.[79] Thomas Harris, a fellow Utah GAR member, "questioned their rights to membership."[80] The Department of Utah convened a Court of Inquiry to determine whether Lot Smith Company veterans were eligible for membership in the Grand Army of the Republic.[81] After conducting an investigation into the military records of Crismon and Hullinger, the Utah Court of Inquiry concluded that "all charges were unfounded, and the Lot

Smith men have an equal standing with any honorably discharged Union soldier."[82]

Unhappy with the ruling, the commander of the Department of Utah, Thomas Lundy, appealed the decision of his own Court of Inquiry to the national commander in chief in February 1911. The appeal included testimony provided by R. Oehler, commander of the Maxwell Post in Salt Lake City, that "no member of the Lott [sic] Smith Company is eligible to membership in the G.A.R. . . . for the reason they were only emergency men, called out to protect the property of the Telegraph and Overland Mail Co., and not commanded by an officer of the United States Army." Oehler admitted that Crismon and Hullinger were receiving United States Civil War pensions, but he requested that their GAR membership should be voided because they "testified before the Court of Inquiry that they were under the command of Gen. Cregg of the 6th Iowa Cavalry. You will see," Oehler continued, "by the enclosed letter from the Adjt. [Adjutant] Gen. of Iowa, that no such man as Gen. Cregg ever received any commission from the State of Iowa."[83] Harvey C. Hullinger was a poor speller, as his original diary confirms; the general to whom the Lot Smith Utah Cavalry reported was General Craig—not Cregg, a small point indeed. Oehler pleaded for "a square deal" and called the commander in chief's attention "to the fact that Utah never furnished a man for the suppression of the Rebellion." He emphatically denied that the actions taken against Crismon and Hullinger were "a political or religious fight, as there are a number of Mormon members belonging to the G.A.R. of this Department who have settled in Utah since the Civil War . . . men [who] have honorable records of service in the Civil War and they are not objected to."[84] (Who those Mormon GAR members could have been has yet to be determined.)

The GAR's national judge advocate general, Thomas S. Hopkins, reviewed the appeals file and issued his decision on July 7, 1911. In his "Statement of the Case," Hopkins reported the facts "as nearly as I can make out from the record." Summarizing the call of the Lot Smith Company "by express direction of President Lincoln," Hopkins noted that

> Charles Chrisman [sic], Jr., and Harvey C. Hullinger . . . were discharged upon the expiration of their terms of service.
>
> These comrades were subsequently admitted to membership in one of the Grand Army Posts in Salt Lake City.

After the lapse of considerable time, the question as to their eligibility was raised, and, if I may judge by the record, considerable bitterness of feeling has grown out of the case. There have been numerous proceedings, including appeals and a Court of Inquiry. . . . Most of the facts alleged and denied in the record of the case, . . . are immaterial, and need not be considered. I have examined the official records in the War Department and find the determination of the question very simple. In fact, the confusion in these proceedings from first to last has arisen because no one has taken the pains to go to the root of the matter by examining the official records, which, of course, are conclusive in a case of this kind.

The records of the War Department show that Lott [sic] Smith's Company of Utah Cavalry was duly mustered into the military service of the United States and thus became a part of the United States Army. . . .

This organization was not a militia company, and the question as to whether or not it was in "active service and subject to the orders of the United States general officers," has no bearing upon the case.[85]

Hopkins concluded that "this organization [Lot Smith's Utah Cavalry] was just as much a part of the Army of the United States as were any of the regiments that formed the great armies of the east and west," and then rendered his decision, as follows: "I, therefore, advise you that inasmuch as the official records of the government show that these men were duly mustered into the military service of the United States on April 30, 1862, and were honorably discharged therefrom on the 14th day of August, 1862, they are eligible to membership in the Grand Army of the Republic."[86]

The 1911 Proceedings of the Twenty-Ninth Annual Encampment of the Department of Utah acknowledged the ruling by the GAR's national judge advocate general, and the department commander sent Utah Department Headquarters General Order Number 5 to each post in Utah declaring both Crismon and Hullinger to be members of the GAR. The matter was declared as "now finally settled and put at rest, and it is the duty of all Comrades to acquiesce in and obey the said decision and order."[87]

With the Civil War veteran status of Utah's Lot Smith Company volunteers firmly and finally established, many of the Lot Smith Cavalry veterans worked to establish their own GAR post within the Department of Utah; the John Quincy Knowlton Post was organized on October 9, 1911.[88] It was "customary in the Organization of the Grand Army to name a newly formed Post after a departed officer, who served in the Civil War. The Utah volunteers were very anxious to call their Post after the name of their captain, 'Lot Smith,'" but the names of both Lot Smith and First Lieutenant Joseph S. Rawlins (second in command of the Lot Smith Company) were unacceptable to the Utah GAR organizations because of their active involvement during the Utah War. As a compromise, the new post was named after John Quincy Knowlton, who served with Lot Smith during 1862 as

This special issue United States postage stamp was issued in 1949 to commemorate the final National Encampment of the Grand Army of the Republic. (Courtesy of Kenneth L. Alford)

a second lieutenant. The first commander of the John Quincy Knowlton GAR Post was Seymour B. Young.[89]

UTAH WOMEN AND THE GAR

Prior to 1909, only two GAR ladies circles had been established in Utah (one in Salt Lake City and the other in Ogden). During the 1909 National Encampment in Salt Lake City, Della R. Henry, a female delegate from Missouri, was elected national president of the Ladies of the Grand Army of the Republic. While in Utah, Mrs. Henry met and befriended Nellie L. Lyon (an active Utah Ladies GAR member) and appointed Mrs. Lyon as the Ladies GAR National Organizer. Within two days of her appointment, Mrs. Lyon established two additional ladies circles in Utah. Early in 1910, she organized the Lot Smith Circle No. 5, which immediately created a great furor "in the state between those who favored the new organization of the wives and daughters of the [Lot Smith] Utah volunteers, and those who were opposed to giving the 'Mormons' recognition."[90]

In June 1910, Mrs. Henry visited Utah for the purpose of creating the Ladies of the GAR Department of Utah. While visiting Salt Lake City, Mrs. Henry "was made the object of a bitter attack by the *[Salt Lake] Tribune* for declaring the women of the Lot Smith [GAR ladies] circle eligible to admission to the state department. However, Mrs. Henry stood by her guns and is quoted as saying that she is surprised that a newspaper in a city like Salt Lake would deliberately resort to false and misleading statements to cause friction in an organization like the Ladies of the G.A.R." Mrs. Henry proclaimed, "I know nothing of local conditions, religious, political or otherwise, which may have prompted the attack upon me and the Ladies of the G.A.R. but I do know that it was unjust and unwarranted. Anyone who will take the pains to inquire must know that religion and politics are eliminated in the affairs of the Grand Army of the Republic, as well as in the Ladies of the G.A.R. . . . Our constitution and fundamental principles do not discriminate against religious sects, and any good woman who comes within the requirements, whether she be Jew, Mormon or Gentile, is acceptable, and, in fact, solicited."[91] Anti-Mormon elements within the GAR asked Mrs. Henry to delay admitting the Lot Smith Circle until an investigation could be held. The Lot Smith Ladies Circle was organized in November 1910, but only after it was renamed the General George Washington Circle in order to satisfy political sensitivities within Utah's GAR membership.[92] The spouses of several Lot Smith Utah Cavalry soldiers, such as Margaret Fisher (wife of Joseph Armstrong Fisher, who served as a private in the Lot Smith Utah Cavalry), actively participated in Utah circles of the Ladies of the Grand Army of the Republic. The John Quincy Knowlton GAR Ladies Circle was organized at Farmington, Utah, in June 1912, and additional Utah Department ladies circles were named after Seymour B. Young (February 22, 1926) and Joseph S. Rawlins (April 1, 1926)—members of the Lot Smith Company.[93]

THE 1909 GAR NATIONAL ENCAMPMENT

The first decade of the twentieth century contained small indications that the general GAR attitude toward Latter-day Saints may have begun to thaw a little. The Department of Utah's 1907 report to the national organization about the observance of Flag Day in Utah, for example, included the generally positive comment that "on that day the Mormon forgot who was Brigham Young and the Gentile turned from his alleged wrongs and with one accord all the people in their hearts sang hosannahs to 'the flag that makes us free.'"[94]

Following the turn of the century, an idea took root and grew regarding the desirability of Utah hosting a GAR national encampment. Serious discussion and planning for Salt Lake City to host the 1909 National Encampment began in 1907.[95] During the Forty-Second National GAR Encampment at Toledo, Ohio, in September 1908, Comrade George B. Squires from Salt Lake City, who had served during the Civil War as a colonel in the Fifteenth Connecticut Infantry, made an impassioned plea for the 1909 National Encampment to be held at Salt Lake City.[96] Squires said he came bearing the invitation of the Governor of Utah, the County of Salt Lake, the City of Salt Lake, the Commercial Club of Salt Lake, and "a telegram from the President of the Mormon Church. They [non-Mormons] tell you that Utah is not loyal. It is loyal from the crown of its head to the soles of its feet, from the tops of its mountains to the depths of its mines—Utah is loyal. . . . I tell you boys, we are in earnest, in deadly earnest. We want you to come to us; we want to open our hearts and our homes to you. Every home in Salt Lake City will be at your disposal." A counterproposal was made to hold the 1909 National Encampment in the District of Columbia, but when the vote was taken, Salt Lake City received 461 of the

565 votes cast; the 1909 GAR encampment would be held at Salt Lake City.[97] Considering the GAR's anti-Mormon rhetoric during much of the nineteenth century, it was somewhat surprising that the organization's leadership voted to hold the August 1909 annual convention in Utah.[98] The 1909 National Encampment was a tremendous success. (The story of the GAR's 1909 gathering in Salt Lake City is related in the following chapter.)

SUMMARY

In the decades following the Civil War, hundreds of thousands of Civil War veterans joined the GAR; "the camp fires of the Grand Army [burned] from ocean to ocean. Thousands and tens of thousands . . . of soldiers [met] nightly in fraternal greetings."[99] Sadly, though, it took almost half a century for Latter-day Saint Civil War veterans from the Lot Smith Utah Cavalry to be accepted as GAR members.

The Grand Army of the Republic considered itself "the grandest association of soldiers and sailors ever formed."[100] Many members felt a deep emotional attachment to the GAR—feelings that were captured in the first and last stanzas of a poem published in 1893 entitled "When We Were Boys in Blue":

> O comrades of the battle years,
> When lighting was our trade;
> O, you who charge with loyal cheers
> 'Gainst many a gay brigade!
> 'Tis joy to grasp again the hand
> O' rare and cherished few—
> Frail remnant of the mighty band

> Who once were Boys in Blue.
> And soon these glad reunions here
> Will be forever past—
> The broken ranks that close the rear
> Will cross the ford at last;
> But on the world's illustrious page
> Of heroes tried and true,
> Will live enshrined from age to age,
> The glorious Boys in Blue.[101]

Each passing year brought "an ever-increasing death-rate among the survivors."[102] As the historian Margaret Fisher wrote in 1929, "Relentless time is thinning the ranks. One by one they are answering the call of the Great Commander. One by one they fail to respond to the reveille. Taps are sounded above them, and life's battles for them are ended; peace comes to the soldiers' weary heart. A few years more and the last member of the G.A.R. will have received his final marching orders; will have gone to witness the last grand review."[103]

With GAR membership restricted to Civil War veterans, the organization had a limited lifespan. Individual posts were closed upon the death of the last living member. When the final member of the Grand Army of the Republic, Albert Woolson, died in 1956, nearly thirty years after Mrs. Fisher's writing, the organization died with him.[104] There have been many veterans' organizations in our nation's history, but as an August 1909 issue of the *Young Woman's Journal* concluded, "There has never been such an organization [as the Grand Army of the Republic] and there will never be another."[105]

Kenneth L. Alford is an associate professor of Church history and doctrine at Brigham Young University.

NOTES

1. B. F. Bair, "The Grand Army of the Republic," *Davis County (Utah) Clipper*, July 2, 1909, 5.

2. John E. Gilman, "The Grand Army of the Republic," in *The Photographic History of the Civil War*, ed. Francis Trevelyan Miller and Robert Sampson Lanier, (New York: Review of Reviews, 1911), 10:290.

3. "The G.A.R. Gush Continues," *Deseret News*, August 11, 1886, 2.

4. Robert B. Beath, *History of the Grand Army of the Republic* (New York: Willis McDonald, 1888), 11.

5. *Journal of the Twenty-Third Annual Session of the National Encampment Grand Army of the Republic* (St. Louis, MO: A. Whipple, 1889), 34.

6. "Founding the Grand Army of the Republic," *Salt Lake Telegram*, May 29, 1909, 10.

7. D. A. Ellis, *Grand Army of the Republic: History of the Order in the U.S. by Counties* (n.p.: Press of Historical Publishing, 1892), 5.

8. By the mid-twentieth century, with an attendant proliferation of military decorations and the wars that generated them, soldiers sometimes came to view this phrase more cynically than proudly, dubbing awards for the nonvalorous aspects of service like the Good Conduct Ribbon and even some campaign medals negatively as "I was there" decorations.

9. Examples of American veteran organizations for wars prior to the Civil War are the Patriots of the American Revolution (http://www.patriotsar.com/), the General Society of the War of 1812 (http://www.societyofthewarof1812.org/), and the National Association of Veterans of the Mexican War (http://www.dmwv.org/mwvets/mexvets.htm).

10. Societies such as the Army of the Tennessee (1865), the Army of the Cumberland (1868), the Army of the Ohio (1868), the Army of the James (1868), the Burnside Expedition and the Ninth Corps (1869), the Army and Navy of the Gulf (1869), the Army of the Potomac (1869), and many others. See Beath, *History of the Grand Army of the Republic*, 12–32.

11. Beath, *History of the Grand Army of the Republic*, 11, 35. "The Advance Guard of America" and "The Grand Army of Progress" were two of the early names suggested.

12. William H. Ward, *Records of Members of the Grand Army of the Republic* (San Francisco: H. S. Crocker, 1886), 6. See also Beath, *History of the Grand Army of the Republic*, 36, 53–67.

13. Grand Army of the Republic Records Project, http://suvcw.org/garposts/index.htm; and Glenn B. Knight, "Brief History of the Grand Army of the Republic," http://suvcw.org/gar.htm.

14. Interestingly, one woman, Sarah Emma Edmonds (born Sarah Emma Edmondson in New Brunswick, Canada; December 1841–September 5, 1898) was granted GAR membership. Passing herself off as a man, Edmonds enlisted as "Private Franklin Thompson" on May 25, 1861, and was "mustered into the 2nd Michigan Infantry as a 3 year recruit." Acting primarily as a mail carrier, she saw action at the Battles of Second Manassas and Fredericksburg in 1862. "In the spring of 1863, Edmonds and the 2nd Michigan were assigned to the Army of the Cumberland and sent to Kentucky. Edmonds contracted malaria and requested a furlough, which was denied. Not wanting to seek medical attention from the army for fear of discovery, Edmonds left her comrades in mid-April, never to return. 'Franklin Thompson' was subsequently charged with desertion. After her recovery, Edmonds, no longer in disguise, worked with the United States Christian Commission as a female nurse, from June 1863 until the end of the war." She later married Linus Seelye and had three children. "In 1876, she attended a reunion of the 2nd Michigan and was warmly received by her comrades, who aided her in having the charge of desertion removed from her military records and supported her application for a military pension. After an eight year battle and an Act of Congress, 'Franklin Thompson' was cleared of desertion charges and awarded a pension in 1884. In 1897, Edmonds was admitted into the Grand Army of the Republic, the only woman member." See "Sarah Emma Edmonds," http://www.civilwar.org/education/history/biographies/sarah-emma-edmonds.html.

15. Beath, *History of the Grand Army of the Republic*, 31.

16. Beath, *History of the Grand Army of the Republic*, 202.

17. Beath, *History of the Grand Army of the Republic*, 31–32.

18. It was not until June 10, 1889, that a similar fraternal organization, the United Confederate Veterans, was organized in New Orleans for veterans who served in the armed forces of the Confederate States of America. The purpose of that organization was to provide "a general organization of Confederates on

the order of the Grand Army of the Republic." See S. A. Cunningham, "The United Confederate Veterans," in *Photographic History of the Civil War*, 296.

19. Except for 1867, a National Encampment was held every year from 1866 through 1949. The last National Encampment, the eighty-third, was held at the site of the first National Encampment—Indianapolis (August 28–September 1, 1949). There were just sixteen living GAR members; six were able to attend. Library of Congress, "National Encampments: Bibliography," http://www.loc.gov/rr/main/gar/national/natlist .html. See also http://suvcw.org/gar50.htm.

20. Beath, *History of the Grand Army of the Republic*, 30–31, 90–91.

21. Library of Congress, "The Grand Army of the Republic and Kindred Societies," http://www.loc.gov/rr/main /gar/garintro.html.

22. Library of Congress, "The Grand Army of the Republic and Kindred Societies."

23. U.S. Code; Title 10, Subtitle A, Part II, Chapter 57, Section 1123, "Right to wear badges of military societies," http://www.law.cornell.edu/uscode/10/1123 .html.

24. Images of both the Medal of Honor and the Grand Army of the Republic bronze star badge may be viewed online at http://www.homeofheroes.com/moh /corrections/purge_army.html.

25. *Ritual of the Grand Army of the Republic* (Zanesville, OH: n.p., 1907), 7.

26. Beath, *History of the Grand Army of the Republic*, 44.

27. Beath, *History of the Grand Army of the Republic*, 99; and Robert B. Beath, *The Grand Army Blue-Book Containing the Rules and Regulations of the Grand Army of the Republic and Official Decisions and Opinions Thereon, with Additional Notes* (Philadelphia: Burk and McFetridge, 1884), v.

28. McConnell, *Glorious Contentment*, 39.

29. McConnell, *Glorious Contentment*, 33.

30. *Rules and Regulations for the Government of the Woman's Relief Corps, Auxiliary to the Grand Army of the Republic* (Boston: Griffith-Stillings, 1916). See also Mary M. North, *Patriotic Selections for Memorial Day, Flag Day and other Patriotic Anniversaries: Woman's Relief Corps* (Boston: Griffith-Stillings, 1909); and "The National Women's Relief Corps," http://www.suvcw.org/WRC/index.htm.

31. *Rules and Regulations for the Government of the Women's Relief Corps*, 3–4.

32. Library of Congress, "The Grand Army of the Republic and Kindred Societies," http://www.loc.gov/rr/main/gar/garintro.html. See also "Ladies of the Grand Army of the Republic," http://suvcw.org/ LGAR/index.php.

33. *Rules and Regulations of the Ladies of the Grand Army of the Republic* (Scranton, PA: Reeser Bros., 1909), 7.

34. John Gary Maxwell, *Gettysburg to Great Salt Lake: George R. Maxwell, Civil War Hero and Federal Marshal among the Mormons* (Norman, OK: Arthur H. Clark, 2010), 269.

35. Maxwell, *Gettysburg to Great Salt Lake*, 269. Maxwell's related statement on page 271 that "the judgment of GAR historian Mary Dearing that 'prior to 1883 efforts to give the society a foothold in Utah had failed' is incorrect" appears to be a disagreement over Dearing's use of the word "failed." Dearing's statement reads, "Before 1883, efforts to give the society a foothold in Utah had failed; only two posts existed there." See Mary R. Dearing, *Veterans in Politics: The Story of the G.A.R.* (Baton Rouge: Louisiana State University Press, 1952), 288. Although her count of Utah GAR posts established before 1883 is incorrect, Dearing correctly acknowledged that GAR posts were established in Utah prior to 1883.

36. Beath, *History of the Grand Army of the Republic*, 610.

37. "Soldiers Meeting," *Salt Lake Tribune*, May 27, 1873, 3.

38. "Soldiers Meeting," *Salt Lake Tribune*, May 27, 1873, 3; emphasis added.

39. Beath, *History of the Grand Army of the Republic*, 610. For a detailed account of George R. Maxwell's interesting life, see John Gary Maxwell's 2010 book, *Gettysburg to Great Salt Lake*.

40. Maxwell, *Gettysburg to Great Salt Lake*, 271. The Maxwell post was closed prior to 1888. See Beath, *History of the Grand Army of the Republic*, 612–13.

41. "Grand Army of the Republic" and "G.A.R.," *Ogden Standard*, April 26, 1879, 2.

42. Maxwell, *Gettysburg to Great Salt Lake*, 272.

43. *Proceedings of the First to Tenth Meetings 1866–1876 (Inclusive) of the National Encampment Grand Army of the Republic with Digest of Decisions, Rules of Order and Index* (Philadephia: Samuel P. Town, 1877), 43, 401. See also Beath, *History of the Grand Army of the Republic*, 198, 604, 610, 613, 618.

44. D. A. Ellis, *Grand Army of the Republic: History of the Order in the U.S. by Counties* (n.p.: Press of Historical Publishing, 1892), 12.

45. Beath, *Grand Army Blue-Book*, 4.

46. "The G.A.R. Gush Continues," *Deseret News*, August 11, 1886, 2.

47. Beath, *History of the Grand Army of the Republic*, v.

48. Ellis, *Grand Army of the Republic*, 8.

49. Mary Simmerson Cunningham Logan, *Reminiscences of a Soldier's Wife* (New York: Charles Scribner's Sons, 1913), 216.

50. Oliver Morris Wilson, *The Grand Army of the Republic under Its First Constitution and Ritual* (Kansas City, MO: Franklin Hudson, 1905), 30–32.

51. Dearing spells his name "Vandervoort." Beath spells his name "Van Der Voort."

52. Beath, *History of the Grand Army of the Republic*, 256.

53. Dearing, *Veterans in Politics,* 288.

54. Beath, *History of the Grand Army of the Republic*, 262.

55. "At Half Mast," *Salt Lake Tribune*, July 5, 1885, 4.

56. "Loyalty of the Latter-day Saints," *Deseret News*, July 8, 1885, 9.

57. "At Half Mast," *Salt Lake Tribune*, July 5, 1885, 4; "Patriotic Meeting," *Salt Lake Tribune*, July 5, 1885, 4.

58. McConnell, *Glorious Contentment*, 208; and Dearing, *Veterans in Politics*, 475. Dearing notes that "in the ceremony recommended by the G.A.R., the students rose as a leader brought the flag forward. With right hand uplifted in salute they repeated, 'I pledge allegiance to my flag and to the republic for which it stands, one nation, indivisible, with liberty and justice for all.' Then the hand was extended, palm upward, and the pupils sang 'America.' In primary classes the tots repeated, more or less in unison, 'I give my hand, my head, my heart to my country. One country, one people, one flag.'" For additional information regarding the GAR's veneration of the American flag, see Maxwell, *Gettysburg to Great Salt Lake*, 283–87; and McConnell, *Glorious Contentment*, 228–29.

59. *Ritual of the Grand Army of the Republic* (Zanesville, OH: n.p., 1907), 31–32.

60. "Loyal Indignation," *Salt Lake Tribune*, July 12, 1885, 4.

61. "Twin Relics of Absurdity," *Deseret News*, July 15, 1885, 4. Concern over whether or not celebration of the 24th of July would bring similar flag-related problems disappeared when "on July 24, flags in Utah—and across the nation—flew at half-mast with the death of Ulysses S. Grant." See Maxwell, *Gettysburg to Salt Lake City*, 287.

62. "The Lesson," *Salt Lake Tribune*, August 1, 1886, 2.

63. "Anti-'Mormon' Rabies," *Deseret News*, August 4, 1886, 1; "The G.A.R. Gush Continues," *Deseret News*, August 11, 1886, 2.

64. Brigham H. Roberts, "History of the Mormon Church: Chapter CXIX," *Americana (American Historical Magazine)* 10, May 1915, 433.

65. Roberts, "History of the Mormon Church," 434–35.

66. "Anti-'Mormon' Rabies," *Deseret News*, August 4, 1886, 1.

67. William H. Ward, ed., *Records of Members of the Grand Army of the Republic* (San Francisco: H. S. Crocker, 1886), 116; emphasis added.

68. "The G.A.R. and the 'Mormons,'" *Deseret News*, August 18, 1886, 1.

69. *Journal of the Twenty-first Annual Session of the National Encampment Grand Army of the Republic* (Milwaukee: Burdick & Armitage, 1887), 198–99.

70. Beath, *History of the Grand Army of the Republic*, 342.

71. "Miss Kate Field," *Salt Lake Tribune*, April 29, 1883, 3. The *Tribune* quotes or makes frequent mention of Kate Field during the 1880s and 1890s. See, for example, "Kate Field's Monologue," *Salt Lake Tribune,* September 7, 1884, 5; or "The Mormon Evil," *Salt Lake Tribune,* December 7, 1884, 3.

72. "Honors to Kate Field," *The (Chicago) Daily Inter Ocean*, November 8, 1886, 4.

73. "G.A.R. Resolves," *Deseret News*, June 23, 1904, 5.

74. *Journal of the Twenty-third Annual Session of the National Encampment Grand Army of the Republic* (St. Louis: A Whipple, 1889), 34.

75. *Twenty-Sixty and Twenty-Seventh Annual Encampments, Grand Army of the Republic, Department of Utah* (Salt Lake City: Grand Army of the Republic, 1909), 40–41.

76. Margaret M. Fisher, ed., *Utah and the Civil War; Being the Story of the Part Played by the People of Utah in That Great Conflict with Special Reference to the Lot Smith Expedition and the Robert T. Burton Expedition* (Salt Lake City: Deseret Book, 1929), 144–45. Margaret Fisher was the wife of Joseph Armstrong Fisher, a soldier in the Lot Smith Utah Cavalry.

77. "G.A.R. Controversy Settled at Last," *Deseret News*, June 13, 1910, 6.

78. "Pensions, Lot Smith Co.," *Washington County (Utah) News*, December 30, 1909, 1.

79. Fisher suggested that Harris's objection to Crismon and Hullinger's GAR membership was raised during the 1909 GAR National Encampment in Salt Lake City and not the 1910 GAR Utah State Encampment. See Fisher, *Utah and the Civil War*, 144.

80. "Findings of Court of Inquiry Just Made Public in Crismon-Hullinger Cases," *Vernal (Utah) Express*, September 9, 1910, 1.

81. *Journal of the Forty-Fifth Annual Encampment, Department of Massachusetts, Grand Army of the Republic* (Boston: Griffith-Stillings, 1911), 155.

82. "Lot Smith Veterans Eligible in G.A.R.," *Deseret News*, August 29, 1910, 5; and "Findings of Court of Inquiry Just Made Public in Crismon-Hullinger Cases," *Vernal (Utah) Express*, September 9, 1910, 1.

83. *Proceedings of the Twenty-eighth and Twenty-ninth Annual Encampment, Department of Utah* (Salt Lake City: Grand Army of the Republic, 1911), 49–51. Oehler served as Commander of the Department of Utah in 1913.

84. *Proceedings of the Twenty-eighth and Twenty-ninth Annual Encampment*, 50–51.

85. *Journal of the Forty-Fifth Annual Encampment*, 155–56.

86. *Journal of the Forty-Fifth Annual Encampment*, 156.

87. *Proceedings of the Twenty-eighth and Twenty-ninth Annual Encampment, Department of Utah* (Salt Lake City: Grand Army of the Republic, 1911), 34–35.

88. "John Quincy Knowlton G.A.R. Post Organized," *Salt Lake Herald*, October 10, 1911, 3; and "Smith Veterans Organize," *Salt Lake Telegram*, October 10, 1911, 10.

89. Fisher, *Utah and the Civil War*, 150–55.

90. "Lot Smith Circle Is Duly Organized," *Deseret News*, April 6, 1909, 5; and Fisher, *Utah and the Civil War*, 144–47. Margaret Fisher was the first president of the Lot Smith Circle of the Ladies of the Grand Army of the Republic.

91. "G.A.R. Controversy Settled at Last," *Deseret News*, June 13, 1910, 6.

92. Fisher, *Utah and the Civil War*, 146–47.

93. Fisher, *Utah and the Civil War*, 150–55.

94. *Journal of the Forty-First National Encampment of the Grand Army of the Republic* (Zanesville, OH: Courier, 1907), 178–79.

95. "Out After Encampment," *Deseret News*, September 6, 1907, 1.

96. "Veteran Hosts at Next GAR Encampment," *Deseret News*, December 19, 1908, 20.

97. *Journal of the Forty-Second National Encampment of the Grand Army of the Republic, at Toledo, Ohio* (Kansas City, MO: John C. Bovard, n.d.), 241–53.

98. The following table lists known Utah GAR membership figures for the years surrounding the 1909 GAR National Encampment in Salt Lake City. (These figures are extracted from the official GAR National Encampment Journals for the year following each date; not all journals were available for review.)

It is worth noting that in 1909, the year Salt Lake City sponsored the GAR National Encampment, a GAR member from Utah was elected to national GAR leadership for the first time; William M. Bostaph was elected national "Senior Vice-Commander-in-Chief." See *Journal of the Forty-Fifth National Encampment*, 121.

DATE	UTAH POSTS	UTAH MEMBERSHIP
Jun 1904	5	238
Jun 1905	5	254
Jun 1906	5	276
Jun 1907	5	282
Dec 1910	6	299
Dec 1912	5	329

Please see the following chapter by Ardis Parshall for a discussion of the GAR's 1909 National Encampment in Utah.

99. Beath, *History of the Grand Army of the Republic*, 51.

100. Beath, *History of the Grand Army of the Republic*, 31.

101. Captain Charles E. Nash, "When We Were Boys in Blue," in *Canteen and Haversack of the Grand Army of the Republic. The Largest and Most Complete Collection of Choice Recitations, Readings and Veteran War Songs, Also, Statistics, Records, Historical Events, etc. etc.*, comp. Isaac C. Tyson, vol. 1, nos. 19 and 20 (March 1893): 42–43.

102. Beath, *History of the Grand Army of the Republic*, 31.

103. Fisher, *Utah and the Civil War*, 140.

104. "In 1881 the GAR formed the *Sons of Veterans of the United States of America* (SV) to carry on its traditions and memory long after the GAR had ceased to exist. Membership was open to any man who could prove ancestry to a member of the GAR or to a veteran eligible for membership in the GAR In later years, men who did not have the ancestry to qualify for hereditary membership, but who demonstrated a genuine interest in the Civil War and could subscribe to the purpose and objectives of the SUVCW, were admitted as Associates. This practice continues today." See Grand Army of the Republic Records Project, http://suvcw.org/.

105. Emma Ramsey Morris, "What the Grand Army of the Republic Means to Us," *Young Woman's Journal*, August 1909, 369.

Official attendees to the Forty-Third National Encampment of the Grand Army of the Republic held in Salt Lake City, Utah, in August 1909 wore this ribbon to signify their delegate status. The flower in the middle is a sego lily, Utah's state flower. The medal at the bottom honored the centennial year of Abraham Lincoln's birth.
(Courtesy of David Safranski)

CHAPTER 19

Ardis E. Parshall

"THIS SPLENDID OUTPOURING OF WELCOME"

SALT LAKE CITY
AND THE 1909 NATIONAL ENCAMPMENT
OF THE GRAND ARMY OF THE REPUBLIC

Thirty-eight men and seven women left Salt Lake City in August 1908 with a mission: to capture an army and bring it back to Utah. Their targets were the quarter million members of the Grand Army of the Republic, meeting in national encampment at Toledo, Ohio, and their mission was to convince that army to hold its 1909 convention in Salt Lake City. The ranks of that association of Union veterans of the Civil War were thinning by the passing of aged veterans, but the Grand Army was still a formidable political and social power. Its national encampments—1909 would be its forty-third such annual gathering—were prizes eagerly sought by cities that competed with promises of unsurpassed hospitality.[1]

Salt Lake City may have seemed an unlikely host for an encampment: Utah had played a negligible role in the Civil War, and twenty years earlier Mormons were refused Grand Army membership even though they may have given honorable military service years before religious conversion. Utah's Grand Army enrollment was barely 350, nearly all of whom had moved to Utah after service elsewhere. Yet Salt Lake held undeniable attractions for the largely eastern organization: the romance of the Wild West was in full flower in those years before the First World War. The natural wonders of the Great Salt Lake and curiosity about Mormons were almost irresistible draws. And finally, the timing was right: most surviving veterans were past seventy years of age and conscious that if they did not visit the West at this invitation, they might never have another opportunity. Utah boosters played off that sentiment by repeating the story of the Grand Army man who was turned away from the gates of heaven

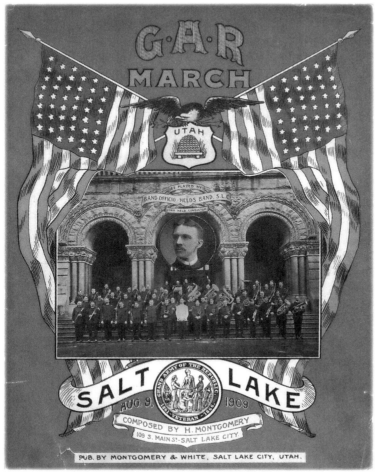

"GAR March," with photo of John Held's Band. (Library of Congress)

on the wooden prostheses that replaced the legs he had lost at the Second Battle of Bull Run and endorsed the bid. His emotional speech recalled an earlier trip west, when a group of gaunt and weathered miners, learning that Civil War veterans were on the train, lined the tracks near a nameless desert water stop, bared their heads, and gave "three cheers for the boys what did."[3]

Salt Lake City won the encampment by a vote of 461 to 104 over Washington, DC, its only competitor. Within hours of Salt Lake's selection as host city and his own election as commander in chief, Henry M. Nevius of New Jersey, who had lost his left arm defending Washington, DC, in July 1864, made plans to visit Salt Lake. To minimize expenses, only four of his staff living west of Chicago were appointed to accompany him. Before their tickets were bought, however, they received an invitation from Fisher Harris, secretary of the Salt Lake Commercial Club, enclosing an unsolicited check to cover travel expenses of Commander Nevius and his entire staff. With that first action, Salt Lake gave proof of its pledge to take care of the old soldiers as no city had ever done before.[4]

Something under one year—from the September 1 award to the opening of the encampment on August 9—was all the time given to Salt Lake to prepare. Most of the

because he had never visited Salt Lake. "You had your chance at paradise," Saint Peter told him, "and you let it get away."[2]

George B. Squires, a Massachusetts native who had served with a Connecticut unit at Gettysburg before moving to Salt Lake, extended the formal invitation at Toledo: "There will be no trouble that we are not willing to go to, there will be no obstacle which we will not overcome; we will take care of you, and we will make you think you have had the time of your lives before you get out of Utah." New Yorker James Tanner, national GAR commander in 1905–6, stood work would be organized by the Commercial Club, which was also responsible for raising the sixty-thousand-dollar cost of the encampment from government, business, and private subscriptions. Overall supervision belonged to the one-armed Commander Nevius. Realizing the plans of the executive committee fell to Salt Lake citizens—mostly volunteers, largely members of the Women's Citizens Committee, who promptly organized subcommittees on accommodations, music, decorations, medical care, entertainment, security, and every other needful thing.[5]

Time may have been short, but Salt Lake used it to advantage and by the first days of August was ready to welcome the Grand Army and all their accompanying organizations: the Ladies of the GAR, the Woman's Relief Corps, the Sons of Veterans, the Daughters of Veterans, and the Associations of Army Nurses, Ex-Union Prisoners of War, Naval Veterans, and Civil War Musicians—an estimated sixty thousand in all.[6]

Yet, as short as the interval of time was between winning the encampment and hosting the veterans, it proved too long for some. Amanda Ross Ramsey, a Salt Lake member of the GAR auxiliaries Woman's Relief Corps and Ladies of the GAR, had been a nurse during the Civil War while her husband served with the 130th Illinois Volunteers. Mrs. Ross served on the citizens' committee preparing entertainments for women visitors, but she died on April 28. Her daughter Emma Ramsey Morris stepped in to fill her mother's assignments, as well as singing at numerous events during the encampment itself: her solo performances of "The Flag Without a Stain" and "The Star-Spangled Banner" became signature features of the August campfires and church services.[7]

Then on August 4, just as the veterans began to arrive in Salt Lake, Frank Hoffman died. Hoffman, a veteran of the 29th Ohio Infantry, was a member of Salt Lake's McKean post of the GAR and a past commander of the Utah Department. A Utah resident and lawyer since 1869, Hoffman had planned to greet his comrades as a member of the official welcoming committee; instead, thousands of early-arriving veterans stood at attention in the streets or marched in a funeral procession for Hoffman on August 8, with music provided by the visiting Ladies' GAR band, as he was laid to rest at Mount Olivet.[8]

The first veteran arrived unexpectedly, coming not over the Denver & Rio Grande but down Emigration Canyon. Corporal John W. DeHaas and his wife had set out from Oklahoma in April by horse and buggy, camping along the road. The unorthodox appearance of the old "Bucktail," former member of the 149th Pennsylvania Volunteer Infantry who had fought at Gettysburg, delighted Salt Lake, and the couple were welcomed as guests in a private home.[9]

Among the tens of thousands attending the encampment were a number who had close ties to Utah residents or who were of more than usual interest to local people. Among these were Gilbert H. Pulver of Villisca, Iowa, originally of New York, who saw Civil War service at Shiloh, Vicksburg, and Corinth with the Third Iowa Volunteers. Pulver, who still carried a bullet in his right shoulder as a souvenir of Shiloh, stayed with his son Charles S. Pulver in Salt Lake's Avenues district. Another visitor of interest to Salt Lake residents was DeLos Robinson, a veteran of the 129th Illinois Infantry, visiting from Sheridan, Illinois. Robinson was a grandson of John Young, the oldest brother of Brigham Young; he had spent part of his childhood with the Mormons in Kirtland and had known or had ties by blood and marriage to many Utahns. This was his first visit to Utah. A prominent returning visitor was the Reverend Thomas C. Iliff, former pastor of Salt Lake City's Methodist Church and past chaplain of both the Utah Department of the GAR and of the national organization. Iliff had enlisted in the Ninth Ohio Cavalry when he was only fifteen, serving throughout the war, and had been with Sherman in Georgia. He had attended the Toledo encampment in 1908, speaking on behalf of Utah's bid to host the 1909 event, and would speak at several of the campfires and in church services while in Salt Lake.[10]

The bulk of the visitors, of course, arrived via railroad. What began as a corporal's guard on Saturday, August 7, became battalions on Monday, August 9, as train after train—some scheduled but mostly specials—stacked up at the railroad terminals. Every train was greeted by a brass band, at first either the Ladies' GAR Band or John Held's official encampment band. Along with military marches and patriotic songs, the bands all played the official "GAR March" composed by Salt Lake resident Harry Montgomery especially for this encampment. As the hours passed and bands arrived from Price, Ogden, and Springville, carloads of veterans were escorted to their hotels by marching bands. Some delegations brought their own music with them—Cook's Fife and Drum Corps from Denver, the Lyndonville Band from Vermont, the Modoc Singers from Topeka—and impromptu parades were held in the streets. For the entire week of the encampment, these bands serenaded organizational headquarters and played on street corners. The

Salt Lake music committee, headed by Tabernacle organist John J. McClellan, had hired twenty-five bands and singing groups, while additional bands arrived with the visitors.[11]

As Salt Lake's guests marched with the bands, they paraded through streets that were dressed especially in their honor. Most public and business buildings were decorated inside and out with flags, bunting, and huge portraits of presidents and Union generals. Downtown streets were crisscrossed by wires from which flapped American flags and the banners of the army and navy signal services.[12]

A minor scandal concerning those street decorations had rocked Salt Lake a week earlier. The proposal had looked quite promising: rows of closely packed flags alternating with electric lights creating a canopy along several downtown streets. But when the eastern decorators arrived, they were stunned to find streets twice as wide and blocks twice as long as any they had encountered before; they had nowhere near enough banners to decorate as promised. The local committee understood the error and quickly revised their expectations but rebelled when decorations began to go up. Many of the flags were old, ragged, and water-stained. Salt Lake residents unfamiliar with military signal flags were indignant that American heroes should be asked to march under "foreign" banners. They threatened to tear them down, declaring that "God's blue sky" was a more fitting tribute. The decorators quickly removed the worn and dirty American flags, explained the nature of the signal flags, and asked to decorate a sample intersection. Thousands visited that intersection, and with general approval decorating went forward.[13]

Salt Lake was especially proud of its electrical decorations, including the strings of bulbs

Marching band and street decorations, Salt Lake City. (Deseret News, *August 10, 1909*)

across the streets and the illuminated flag attached to the Brigham Young monument.

Newly arrived visitors queued up at information booths where they were directed to available rooms. About five thousand were lodged in hotels and rooming houses. A few thousand found free lodgings in elementary schools, where Salt Lake provided all-night janitors to regulate the ventilation: windows were opened to catch cool evening breezes and were gradually lowered throughout the night to protect guests from cold desert mornings. Another five thousand camped in their side-tracked Pullman cars. One enterprising veteran checked himself into the hospital, where he could have room and board and be waited on by a trained nurse, all for twenty dollars for the week.[14]

The greatest number by far, however, were directed to guest rooms in ten thousand private homes. For weeks, the housing committee had canvassed the town, soliciting rooms, urging

families to free their best beds for guests. Mrs. W. H. Jones, with the help of a single stenographer, had prepared cards for all offered rooms, noting address, streetcar line, whether bath or breakfast was included, and price—which in no case was allowed to exceed fifty cents per night or one dollar with private bath. Prices were suggested for meals as well, but families were encouraged to act as hosts rather than innkeepers whenever possible.[15]

Wherever the visitors stayed, they were given directions and very often escorted to their rooms by the high school military cadets, who quickly became the heroes of all. These boys, neatly uniformed and organized into around-the-clock shifts, answered questions, gave directions, carried luggage, and helped lost souls find their rooms again when the Salt Lake street-naming system confounded them. They served as runners when bands were summoned to receptions. They helped visitors on the street who needed spectacles left in their rooms or medicine left in Wisconsin. In short, they became the willing hands, eyes, and feet of every needy visitor, and virtually every farewell letter published in Salt Lake's newspapers

Lighted flag at Brigham Young monument.
(Deseret News, August 11, 1909)

expresses gratitude for the unfailing courtesy of Salt Lake's army of high school boys.[16]

Hospitality had been urged upon Salt Lakers for weeks before the encampment. They were determined to be known not just for cordiality but for honesty and fairness. Profiteering would not be tolerated—the menu of every eatery in town was collected, and threats were issued that should profiteering occur, a uniformed policeman would be stationed by the restaurant door to warn patrons against entering.[17]

While overcharging for a meal was not precisely a crime, Salt Lake knew that genuine criminals were certain to follow the Grand Army crowds. Known local criminals were ordered out of town the week before

the encampment. With little formality, suspicious persons apprehended during the week were given twenty minutes to leave town or be jailed. Detectives were borrowed from cities throughout the country to help Salt Lake detectives spot pickpockets at train depots and turn them back. Seventy-five temporary policemen were hired for crowd control— and while editorial cartoons teased that the duties of the special policemen were likely to be limited to helping ladies straighten their hats, they were needed to guard nearly deserted neighborhoods during the most popular events of that week.[18]

And there were certainly numerous events to entertain the old soldiers and their friends. Besides the scheduled business meetings of all groups associated with the Grand Army, there were receptions to the commander in chief, to the old army nurses, to visiting Eagles and Odd Fellows, and to guests from the former homes of transplanted Salt Lakers. There was sightseeing on the streetcar lines—which donated ten thousand free tickets—and personal tours for army nurses, arranged by a committee who solicited the loan of every available automobile, especially if the owner could also furnish a driver. Saltair admitted veterans and their wives free, as did the Salt Palace's bicycle racetrack. Utah's Hawaiian Troubadours performed. There were campfires every evening in both the assembly hall and the armory building, with speakers, music, and war reminiscences. The Tabernacle Choir gave free concerts. There were fireworks atop Ensign Peak each night and a parade featuring cowboys and Indians from the Wild West show that performed all that week. Then, too, there was visiting with old comrades and spinning war tales

Former Civil War nurses attending 1909 encampment. (Forty-Third Annual G.A.R. National Encampment Souvenir Book of Views)

for wide-eyed children who followed the visitors everywhere.[19]

Thirsty visitors could drink at the newly installed water fountains on Main and State Streets or find a saloon for more serious refreshment. (Bars, closed by law at midnight, in fact stayed open later as long as everyone was discreet.) Veterans could pick up their mail at a temporary post office established in a downtown hotel. They could chat with friends on lawn furniture placed on the sidewalks by local businesses. Public "comfort stations," plumbed to empty directly into the sewers, were set up over manhole covers on many downtown streets. For guests wearied by heat or altitude, the Lion House and other downtown Latter-day Saint buildings were furnished with couches and electric fans, ice water and lemonade, and hostesses who could double as nurses. Banners draped across the buildings urged visitors to come in and rest.[20]

Guests could stroll through Temple Square, where they could view floral designs created especially in their honor. If they were curious about Mormon matters, they could chat with the twenty-five additional guides deployed by the Church to handle the crowds. Should they be so inclined, they could purchase copies of an anti-Mormon pamphlet published by the *Tribune* and offered for sale outside the gates on South Temple.[21]

Some of the Grand Army men indulged passionately in the fad of collecting and trading badges. Many wore ribbons and medals proclaiming earlier encampments they had attended. Street merchants hawked buttons identifying hundreds of military units. The Utah committees contributed their share to this hobby by providing souvenir badges commemorating the Salt Lake encampment. The official badge came in three parts: a gold top bar with eagle and cannon, a silver drop featuring a blue-enameled sego lily, and a final bronze drop celebrating the centennial of Abraham Lincoln's birth. This basic design was modified as needed: the badge for the Association of Civil War Musicians, for instance, replaced the Lincoln pendant with one carrying the image of a harp. For a few very distinguished guests, the badges were molded of Utah gold, Utah silver, and Utah copper.[22]

Other souvenirs were distributed. The official souvenir booklet featured photographs of Salt Lake scenes and portraits of prominent Grand Army and Utah personages. A "bootleg" booklet—one bitterly protested by the concession holder of the official souvenir—was available by the end of the week and featured scenes of the encampment. Visiting ladies were presented with souvenir autograph albums, fans, and postcards. The Salt Lake schools presented Commander Nevius with a large silk flag sewn by the children themselves.[23]

The visitors returned these favors with gifts of their own. The Ladies of the GAR donated an oil portrait of Abraham Lincoln for the City and County Building. The Association of

Civil War Musicians, who, along with most of the other bands, had been quartered at Lafayette Elementary, presented a six-foot panorama photograph to that school.[24]

The centerpiece of every Grand Army encampment was the grand parade of veterans. Salt Lake hosts were concerned for the safety of marching soldiers—especially after noting that two years earlier, in Milwaukee, five veterans had dropped dead while on parade. The soldiers were older, the altitude higher, the August sun hotter, and the visitors more tired by a longer journey than in previous encampments.[25]

Before the parade on Wednesday, August 11, the soldiers needed to be fortified by a good meal—ham sandwiches, pickles, and a cup of sweetened coffee. Miss Lucy Van Cott, head of the university's Domestic Science Department, had charge of the lunch. She secured donations of ham from Salt Lake packing houses and pickles from ZCMI. Ogden pledged one thousand loaves of bread. Cache Valley provided the butter, and Park City donated sugar. There was one snag— some things haven't changed in one hundred years, and Miss Van Cott should have known better than to ask Provo to donate the coffee. The city council refused, but private citizens, eager to be as patriotic as the rest of the state, came up with four hundred pounds.[26]

To aid any marcher who was overcome during the parade, Red Cross nurses were stationed along every block. A wave of their flags would bring a waiting horse-drawn or automobile ambulance, and the fallen marcher would be rushed to the emergency hospital set up on the sixth floor of the Boston Building, which Dr. W. F. Beer had equipped with an operating room and cots for recovering from heat exhaustion. The Sons of Veterans would circulate among the marchers as well with buckets of water and lemonade.[27]

The soldiers assembled early on Wednesday morning. The parade began upon three blasts from the *Tribune* whistle. Prominent Grand Army officers on horseback preceded carriages carrying distinguished Utah officials and honored guests including a few surviving veterans of the 1846 Mexican War. Following them came the active duty soldiers from the 15th Infantry stationed at Fort Douglas, who the week earlier had practiced their drills downtown to accustom their horses to the newly asphalted Main Street. Following these preliminary groups came all the units in the Grand Army of the Republic, organized by state delegation and interspersed with the dozens of visiting bands. Crowd estimates varied, but, on the conservative side, 100,000 onlookers lined the one-mile parade route down Main Street.[28]

These onlookers cheered as the passing soldiers were pelted by flowers. While Salt Lake homeowners had planted thousands of packets of flower seeds that spring, a late frost

Army musicians headquartered at Lafayette School. (Forty-Third Annual G.A.R. National Encampment Souvenir Book of Views)

Cover of official encampment souvenir booklet. (Courtesy of Ardis E. Parshall)

followed by heavy flooding had destroyed most of Salt Lake's crop—but Garland in Box Elder County had shipped in a full train-car load. Park City children had combed the hills for wildflowers; the Blind School at Ogden had grown gardens especially for the encampment. As the parade passed down Main Street, the crowds laughed at the Oklahoma soldiers carrying oversized baby bottles signaling their status as the Union's newest state. They were moved by the sight of the long-haired Montana veteran who was supported by the stronger arm of his best friend—a man wearing an old Confederate uniform. They cheered for the Iowa men who carried ears of corn, and dozens of Salt Lake girls ran out to kiss the one who carried a red ear. The spectators who cheered themselves hoarse during most of the parade fell silent in respect when the former prisoners of war marched by, carrying banners identifying the Southern prisons they had survived.[29]

The old soldiers marched from the Brigham Young monument at the head of Main Street down to Seventh South, where, because of the width of the streets, they were able to turn around and march up the other side of the road—the first time in their history they were able to watch their own parade. During their march they waved to the crowds, danced with each other during short delays, and possibly stood their tallest as they passed cameras making one of the first motion pictures of any Salt Lake parade. The movie film was processed overnight and displayed for the rest of encampment week,

Living Flag, Main Street at 700 South. Postcard. (Courtesy of Ardis E. Parshall)

and copies were soon distributed to movie houses around the country.[30]

Among the groups of parading soldiers who received special notice from the crowds of onlookers were a few black veterans, marching with delegations either from the states where they now lived or with whom they had once served. The Grand Army had been a remarkably egalitarian organization from its beginning, with black veterans accepted into the same posts with their white comrades. Ferdinand Shavers, a former servant of Abraham Lincoln, marched with the Colorado delegation; seven black veterans marched with the Louisiana soldiers ("only seven black men, but what a message their presence bore!" noted a journalist), one with Arkansas, and several more with Mississippi.[31]

Before turning back at Seventh South, the old soldiers paused to view what was billed as the greatest single feature of encampment

week: the Living Flag, composed of seventeen hundred Salt Lake children, posed on a grandstand the width of Main Street, dressed in ankle-length capes and mobcaps of red, white, or blue cheesecloth, some carrying silver paper stars above their heads. These costumes had been sewn by the local Woman's Relief Corps and by the women of the Church's Relief Societies. The children sang patriotic songs and recited the Pledge of Allegiance and, directed by Professor W. A. Wetzell of the Salt Lake School District, danced to mimic the waving of a flag in the breeze. Even allowing for excess of sentiment expressed by the newspapers, the Living Flag was without doubt an emotional, spectacular success.[32]

Plans called for the Living Flag to fall into the line of march when the last group of soldiers turned to retrace their steps up Main Street. The mid-August day, however, was clear and sunny, with little breeze, and temperatures soon climbed to ninety-seven

Living Flag parade, Main Street, August 15, 1909. Postcard. (Courtesy of Ardis E. Parshall)

degrees. The children, with no protection from the sun and despite the water and lemonade constantly passed to them, began to droop and finally to drop. The flag continued singing as one child after another passed out and was carried to the ambulances. But when the children began to faint in numbers too large for the ambulances to keep up with, and as their watching parents broke through restraining ropes and threatened to collapse the grandstand as they reached for their children, Professor Wetzell dismissed them, many being then carried to the shady lawn of a nearby house reserved especially for the Living Flag. In all, some sixty children and forty marching veterans were taken to the emergency hospital, while an untold number of others fell out but revived with medical attention on the parade route.[33]

Because so many were disappointed by not seeing the Living Flag, a parade was held the following Friday in the cool of early evening, the only performers being the costumed children of the Living Flag and the bands that accompanied them.[34]

While most visitors came for the parade, the campfires, and the camaraderie, the encampment was, technically, a business meeting for the Grand Army and for many of its affiliated organizations. Delegates from state organizations met in conference at their temporary headquarters established in hotels, churches, and civic buildings throughout the city. Delegates to the GAR meeting heard Commander Nevius report his year's efforts to influence national legislation regarding soldiers' pensions, the maintenance of "old soldiers' homes" and cemeteries, the funding and design of a monument to Benjamin F. Stephenson (a surgeon who had served with the 14th Illinois Infantry and who had founded the Grand Army in 1866), and other issues of particular interest to the organization. Delegates to the

A group of GAR men and women pose for a photograph with the Wisconsin group drum corps on, August 11, 1909, in Salt Lake City. The man at the right of the image is holding a sign which says, "The Badgers Come / With Fife and Drum / To make things hum / As in 1861 to 1865 / With Gun, Drum & Fife / We are still alive." (Utah State Historical Society)

business meetings of the various organizations also elected officers for the coming year.[35]

One business meeting of particular interest to Utahns was that of the National Association of Army Nurses. Time had reduced that association's ranks to a mere twenty-six members, twenty-two of whom attended the encampment in Salt Lake City. That organization elected as their president for 1909–10 Mrs. Mary Roby Lacey, a resident of Salt Lake City since 1906, who, as a seventeen-year-old bride, had nursed her soldier-husband John Roby in a Pennsylvania military hospital early in 1861 and had gone on to serve as an army nurse until the

close of the war. She had worked with Clara Barton on the still-smoking Antietam battlefield and recalled later presidential visits to the hospital: "Lincoln would come to our ward, and bending over the cots where the wounded soldiers lay, would speak words of encouragement." Mrs. Lacey had been one of the Utahns to present Salt Lake's invitation to the Toledo encampment in 1908 and had worked tirelessly as a member of a committee dedicated to ensuring that her sister nurses would enjoy their visit to Utah in 1909, including personalized souvenirs, a visit to the Saltair resort, automobile tours of the Salt Lake Valley and nearby canyons, and construction of a special grandstand from which the nurses could watch the parade in comfort.[36]

The campfires, receptions, and business meetings of the encampment continued until Saturday, August 14, and some groups, notably the old musicians, were having such a good time that they stayed another full week. Most soldiers, though, left within a day or two of the parade. Salt Lake City quickly turned its attention to other matters, beginning with the dedication of the Cathedral of the Madeleine the day after the encampment closed. But before closing this chapter of its history, Salt Lake tallied the costs and the gains: sixty thousand visitors had been welcomed and entertained within budget and to all reports beyond everyone's expectations. Those visitors, assured the editors of the *Deseret News*, "know now that the people of Utah are as patriotic, as loyal, and as warm-hearted . . . as any citizens anywhere. They know that Utah, notwithstanding slander, is an American state in every sense of that word."[37]

Corporal James Tanner reminded his hosts that "if it had not been for the fight I made at Toledo, Salt Lake would not have had the encampment, and I went to Salt Lake feeling that I had considerable at stake. . . . I came home perfectly satisfied and glad

that I had done as I did." The Grand Army's chaplain in chief reported to his Tennessee newspaper that "they treated us . . . royally. . . . I am quite sure they have been abused more than they deserve."[38]

Five years later, an encampment visitor wrote to a Salt Lake friend, "We will never forget you people and what you did for us while in your city during the G.A.R. encampment. We haven't had such good treatment before we came there and never expect such a good time again. The old veterans have a warm spot in their hearts for you and your people." Commander Nevius declared that it was "not in words alone that the welcome has come to the hosts of the Grand Army. This splendid outpouring of welcome, of hospitality by the people of this city and state has filled our hearts with delight. . . . We feel that on the shores of the great lake we have a home."[39]

Three generations have passed since Salt Lake's Main Street witnessed the marching of 7,500 Civil War veterans, half a continent away from the scenes of their battles. Salt Lake City has played host to a number of gatherings since then—but few, perhaps, involved such wholehearted support by the citizens of Utah as did that week in 1909 when the Grand Army was welcomed to Zion.

Ardis E. Parshall is an independent historian and researcher.

NOTES

1. "Utah Delegates Go East to Win for Salt Lake City Best Advertisement Yet," *Telegram*, August 19, 1908, 3; "Old Soldiers Start Out," *Deseret News*, August 25, 1908, 2; "Will Work for the G.A.R. Encampment," *Telegram*, August 27, 1908, 2;

"Mayor J. S. Bransford's Invitation to Veterans," *Deseret News*, September 4, 1908, 1. Preparations for Salt Lake City's successful 1908 bid (city leaders had discussed the possibility of bidding in earlier years) are reported in "G.A.R. Men to Fight for an

Encampment," *Tribune*, January 29, 1908; "Reasons Why Grand Army Should Hold Encampment Here," *Tribune*, February 19, 1908; "Estimated Cost of G.A.R. Encampment," *Tribune*, March 4, 1908; "Get the Veterans Here," *Telegram*, August 21, 1908, 10; "Local Grand Army Men Will Be Hosts," *Telegram*, August 24, 1908, 4; "Visitors Turn into Boosters," *Telegram*, August 25, 1908, 1; "Salt Lake in Line for Next Encampment," *Tribune*, September 1, 1908; "Seattle and Salt Lake to Fight for G.A.R. Meeting," *Telegram*, March 5, 1908; "Salt Lake May Get Next Encampment," *Deseret News*, September 1, 1908, 1; "Salt Lake to Win G.A.R. Encampment," *Tribune*, September 2, 1908, 1; "Good News from Toledo Arouses Much Enthusiasm," *Tribune*, September 2, 1908, 1; "Opposition to Salt Lake City," *Deseret News*, September 3, 1908, 1; "Carnival Plans for Convention," *Salt Lake Republican*, September 4, 1908; "Commander Royce Here," *Deseret News*, September 16, 1908, 2. For reports of competing bids for the 1909 encampment, see "Hustling for G.A.R. Prizes," *Toledo Daily Blade*, August 31, 1908; "Salt Lake City Leads for 1909," *Toledo Daily Blade*, September 2, 1908; "Nevius and Utah Seem Winners," *Toledo Daily Blade*, September 3, 1908; "Salt Laker on G.A.R.," *Deseret News*, September 8, 1908, 2; "Enthused Over Encampment," *Deseret News*, September 11, 1908, 3.

2. *Grand Army of the Republic, Utah Membership Records*, Utah State Archives. "Visitors Turn into Boosters," *Telegram*, August 25, 1908; "G.A.R. Leaders Expect Crowd of 60,000 for Encampment," *Telegram*, July 23, 1909, 10.

3. "Salt Lake to the Front!" *Tribune*, September 2, 1908, 4; "G.A.R. Encampment Coming," *Telegram*, September 2, 1908, 1; "Grand Army Will Come to Salt Lake," *Telegram*, September 3, 1908, 1; "Salt Lake Gets '09 Encampment," *Toledo Daily Blade*, September 4, 1908; "Salt Lake City Gets G.A.R. Encampment," *Deseret News*, September 4, 1908, 1; "Salt Lake Defeats All Competitors for Honor of Entertaining G.A.R.," *Telegram*, September 4, 1909, 1; "Salt Lake City Wins Next Encampment of G.A.R.," *Tribune*, September 5, 1908, 1; "How Utah Delegation Won the Encampment," *Deseret News*, August 7, 1909, 13.

4. "Salt Lake City Wins Next Encampment of G.A.R.," *Tribune*, September 5, 1908, 1; "Great Contract Confronts City," *Salt Lake Herald*, September 10, 1908, 12;

"Ample Salt Lake Accommodations," *Deseret News*, December 9, 1908, 2; "Women Are Again Urged to Respond," *Tribune*, March 19, 1909, 14; "Numerous Bands Will Be Present," *Tribune*, August 1, 1909, 3; "Commander Nevius Reviews Year's Work," *Telegram*, August 12, 1909, 1; "Good News from Toledo Arouses Much Enthusiasm," *Tribune*, September 2, 1908, 1; "G.A.R. Officials Are on Way to This City," *Deseret News*, December 7, 1908, 1.

5. "Hotels Are Preparing for Great Encampment," *Tribune*, July 3, 1909, 16; "All Ready but the Cream," *Deseret News*, July 10, 1909, 1; "Shaping Up Plans for Encampment," *Tribune*, July 13, 1909, 11; "Cots and Tents Ready for Camp," *Deseret News*, July 29, 1909, 5; "All About Ready," *Tribune*, August 5, 1909, 4; "Food Supply on Hand for Encampment," *Telegram*, August 6, 1909, 6; "Ready for the Veterans," *Telegram*, August 7, 1909, 4; "Doors Swing Wide to Welcome G.A.R.," *Deseret News*, August 7, 1909, 1; "Salt Lake Ready to Welcome Nation's Saviors," *Telegram*, August 7, 1909, 11; "Ogden City Is Ready to Care for Visitors," *Tribune*, August 9, 1909, 1; "Stands and Booths Ready," *Deseret News*, August 9, 1909, 5; "Great G.A.R. Encampment Opens in Earnest Today," *Tribune*, August 9, 1909, 1; "Fire Precautions Were Exceedingly Elaborate," *Telegram*, August 11, 1909, 10; "Cash on Hand to Entertain," *Herald-Republican*, August 25, 1909, 2.

6. "Hotels Are Preparing for Great Encampment," *Tribune*, July 3, 1909, 16; "All Ready but the Cream," *Deseret News*, July 10, 1909, 1; "Shaping Up Plans for Encampment," *Tribune*, July 13, 1909, 11; "Cots and Tents Ready for Camp," *Deseret News*, July 29, 1909, 5; "All About Ready," *Tribune*, August 5, 1909, 4; "Food Supply on Hand for Encampment," *Telegram*, August 6, 1909, 6; "Ready for the Veterans," *Telegram*, August 7, 1909, 4; "Doors Swing Wide to Welcome G.A.R.," *Deseret News*, August 7, 1909, 1; "Salt Lake Ready to Welcome Nation's Saviors," *Telegram*, August 7, 1909, 11; "Ogden City Is Ready to Care for Visitors," *Tribune*, August 9, 1909, 1; "Stands and Booths Ready," *Deseret News*, August 9, 1909, 5; "Great G.A.R. Encampment Opens in Earnest Today," *Tribune*, August 9, 1909, 1; "Fire Precautions Were Exceedingly Elaborate," *Telegram*, August 11, 1909, 10; "Cash on Hand to Entertain," *Herald-Republican*, August 25, 1909, 2.

7. "Salt Lake Women Served as Nurses in the Civil War," *Deseret News*, January 2, 1909, 24; "Installation of

Veteran Society," *Deseret News*, January 25, 1909, 8; "Noble Woman to Be Buried Sunday," *Deseret News*, April 30, 1909, 4; "Gather at Morris Home," *Deseret News*, July 27, 1909, 2; "Music Will Cheer Hearts of Veterans," *Telegram*, July 31, 1909, 16; "Campfire Programs Announced," *Telegram*, August 3, 1909; "Campfires During Encampment Week," *Tribune*, August 4, 1909, 8; "Entertainment Provided for Ex-Prisoners of War," *Tribune*, August 4, 1909, 3; "Patriotic Exercises to be Held Next Sunday," *Tribune*, August 7, 1909, 9; "Patriotic Exercises in M. E. Church," *Telegram*, August 7, 1909, 12; "Visiting Veterans Attend Services," *Tribune*, August 9, 1909, 12; "Patriotic Service at First Methodist Arouses Enthusiasm," *Telegram*, August 9, 1909, 6; "Campfires Are Feature for Tonight," *Telegram*, August 9, 1909, 12; "Campfire Is Held in the Darkness," *Tribune*, August 10, 1909, 16; "Old Veterans Hold Campfire in Dark," *Telegram*, August 10, 1909, 6; "Busy Day for G.A.R. Visitors," *Telegram*, August 10, 1909, 1; "Army Nurses Have Session Tuesday," *Tribune*, August 11, 1909, 2; "Outing of G.A.R. Ladies at Saltair," *Tribune*, August 24, 1909, 14; "Resolutions by the Army Nurses," *Herald-Republican*, August 26, 1909, 6.

8. "Death of G.A.R. Veteran," *Deseret News*, August 5, 1909, 5; "Comrades Perform Last Rites for Frank Hoffman," *Herald*, August 9, 1909, 10; "Civil War Veteran Honored in Death," *Tribune*, August 9, 1909, 2; "Salute Comrade Who Has Passed Before," *Telegram*, August 9, 1909, 3.

9. "Veteran Drives from Oklahoma," *Deseret News*, July 27, 1909; "Corporal De Hass and His Outfit," *Deseret Evening News*, July 28, 1909; "Redman 'Is For' De Hass," *Deseret News*, July 29, 1909; "By Campfire in Peaceful Evening of Life He Tells of Bivouacking on Battle Fields," *Telegram*, August 3, 1909.

10. "Will Work for the G.A.R. Encampment," *Telegram*, August 27, 1908, 2; "Long Time It Was Between the Drinks," *Tribune*, August 9, 1909, 2; "Dr. Iliff Visits Old Home in Zion," *Tribune*, August 6, 1909, 9; "Rev. T.C. Ilioff Here to See Old Comrades," *Telegram*, August 6, 1909; "Patriotic Exercises to Be Held Next Sunday," *Tribune*, August 7, 1909, 7; "First Patriotic G.A.R. Services," *Deseret News*, August 7, 1909, 5; "Visiting Veterans Attend Services," *Tribune*, August 9, 1909, 12; "Patriotic Service at First Methodist Arouses Enthusiasm," *Telegram*, August 9, 1909, 6; "An Illinois Veteran,"

Deseret News, August 12, 1909, 5; "Dr. Iliff Thaws Out," *Deseret News*, August 11, 1909, 11; "An Illinois Veteran," *Deseret News*, August 12, 1909, 5; *Biographical and Genealogical Record of La Salle County, Illinois* (Chicago: Lewis, 1900) 1:217.

11. For arrival of veterans, see "Old Soldiers Already Arriving in Town," *Telegram*, July 21, 1909, 2; "Many Specials to Bring Veterans Here," *Telegram*, July 29, 1909, 3; "Rio Grande Announces Coming of Delegations," *Tribune*, August 6, 1909, 2; "Further List of Special Trains," *Deseret News*, August 6, 1909, 2; "Time of Arrival of Special G.A.R. Trains," *Tribune*, August 7, 1909, 9; "Veterans Are Here in Force," *Salt Lake Evening Telegram*, August 7, 1909, 1; "Care of Visitors Important Matter," *Tribune*, August 7, 1909, 12; "Grand Army Camps in Utah," *Chicago Daily Tribune*, August 8, 1909, 4; "Encampment of the G.A.R.," *Great Falls (Montana) Daily Tribune*, August 8, 1909, 1; "Great G.A.R. Encampment Opens in Earnest Today," *Tribune*, August 9, 1909, 1; "Thousands on the Streets," *Deseret News*, August 9, 1909, 1; "Delegates Arrive Over the Oregon Short Line," *Tribune*, August 9, 1909, 1; "Fifteen Thousand Reach City Sunday," *Telegram*, August 9, 1909, 6; "Prominent Members of the Ladies of the G.A.R.," *Tribune*, August 9, 1909, 1; "Veterans Meet by Hotel Campfires," *Tribune*, August 9, 1909, 2; "Distinguished Soldiers Reach Salt Lake City," *Tribune*, August 9, 1909, 3; "Oklahoma Delegates Here in Force," *Telegram*, August 9, 1909, 8; "G.A.R. Veterans at Salt Lake City," *Indiana (Pennsylvania) Evening Gazette*, August 9, 1909; "Department of Potomac Delegates have Arrived," *Tribune*, August 9, 1909, 3; "Thousands of Veterans Invade Salt Lake City," *Tribune*, August 10, 1909, 1; "Still Arriving in Squads and Battalions," *Deseret News*, August 10, 1909, 1; "Visitors Are Still Pouring into City," *Tribune*, August 10, 1909, 16; "Arrival of Delegates Is About at an End," *Tribune*, August 11, 1909, 8; "12,000 More Come to Encampment; Trains Crowded to Guards," *Telegram*, August 11, 1909, 1. For bands in attendance, see "Many Bands to Be Here for G.A.R.," *Telegram*, July 16, 1909, 2; "Twelve Bands Have Been Engaged for G.A.R. Encampment," *Inter-mountain Republican*, July 17, 1909, 10; "Band Concerts Will Be Given G.A.R. Visitors," *Inter-mountain Republican*, July 22, 1909, 3; "Music Will Cheer Hearts of Veterans," *Telegram*, July 31,

1909, 16; "Twenty-Five Bands in Line," *Deseret News*, July 31, 1909, 5; "Numerous Bands Will Be Present," *Tribune*, August 1, 1909, 32; "Music in Air, and Everywhere," *Inter-mountain Republican*, August 1, 1909, 10; "Cook's Drum Corps Here for Meet," *Telegram*, August 9, 1909, 6; "Famous Drum Corps in Special Train," *Telegram*, August 3, 1909, 3; "Plenty of Bands," *Telegram*, August 7, 1909, 11; "Martial Music for Encampment Week," *Deseret News*, August 7, 1909, 5; "Band Concert with Two Hundred Pieces," *Telegram*, August 9, 1909, 6; "Concert Wednesday," *Deseret News*, August 9, 1909, 9; "Music Big Feature at Encampment," *Telegram*, August 10, 1909, 12; "Wednesday Evening Concert at the Reviewing Stand," *Tribune*, August 10, 1909, 3; "Drum Corps to March in Cross Formation," *Telegram*, August 10, 1909, 12; "Vermont's Band Men of Many Professions," *Telegram*, August 10, 1909, 2; "Lyndonville Band Is in Zion from Old Vermont," *Tribune*, August 10, 1909, 3; "Fine Railway Band from Kansas Here," *Telegram*, August 10, 1909, 7; "Encampment Notes," *Tribune*, August 11, 1909, 3; "Topeka Military Drum Corps All Star Band," *Telegram*, August 11, 1909, 1; "Strains of Music Palpitating Air," *Deseret News*, August 11, 1909, 3; "Mass Band Concert Will Be Enjoyable," *Tribune*, August 11, 1909, 3; "Musicians at Lafayette Building," *Tribune*, August 11, 1909, 3; "Arrangements of Bands for the Great Parade," *Tribune*, August 11, 1909, 4; "Payson Band in Line," *Deseret News*, August 11, 1909, 8; "There Is Music in the Air All This Week in Salt Lake City," *Deseret News*, August 11, 1909, 3; "Music in the Air," *Deseret News*, August 11, 1909, 11; "G.A.R. Notes," *Telegram*, August 12, 1909, 2; "Four Fine Bands Will Play at Concerts," *Telegram*, August 13, 1909, 1; "Encampment Notes," *Deseret News*, August 13, 1909, 3; "Final Band Concert," *Deseret News*, August 14, 1909, 8; "Idaho Band Appreciative," *Herald-Republican*, August 22, 1909, 10.

12. "A Noted Decorator Arrives to Prepare for Big Encampment," *Inter-mountain Republican*, June 4, 1909, 3; "Display in View for Encampment," *Tribune*, June 30, 1909, 14; "Plans for Decoration for Encampment Week," *Deseret News*, July 2, 1909, 12; "City to Decorate Elaborately for G.A.R. Encampment," *Telegram*, July 17, 1909, 8; "Decoration Work Started in City," *Telegram*, July 21, 1909, 2; "Decorations in Large Quantities

Received," *Inter-mountain Republican*, July 21, 1909, 10; "Decorations Now Well Under Way in City Streets," *Telegram*, July 29, 1909, 10; "Decorators at Work," *Deseret News*, July 29, 1909, 1; "Every Resident Should Decorate," *Tribune*, August 1, 1909, 1; "Encampment Notes," *Tribune*, August 1, 1909, 3; "Joint Building to Be Prettily Decorated," *Tribune*, August 1, 1909, 10; "Decorators Wield Tack Hammers Well," *Deseret News*, August 3, 1909, 3; "Federal Officials Decorate Building," *Telegram*, August 5, 1909, 10; "Federal Building Now Gaily Decorated," *Tribune*, August 6, 1909, 2; "Railroad Notes," *Tribune*, August 6, 1909, 9; "Beautiful Decorations," *Telegram*, August 7, 1909, 11; "Decorator Gets Busy," *Deseret News*, August 7, 1909, 5; "View of the Decorations on Main Street, Showing Those on Tribune Building," *Tribune*, August 9, 1909, 3; "The Man Who Did Not Go to Church Yesterday Decorated," *Deseret News*, August 9, 1909, 3; "Bewildering Mass of Color," *Deseret News*, August 9, 1909, 5; "Decorations and Bunting on Main Street," *Deseret News*, August 10, 1909, 5; "Infirmary Is Decorated," *Deseret News*, August 11, 1909, 12; "Denver Man Is Pleased with the Decorations," *Tribune*, August 12, 1909, 3.

13. "Business Men Are in Rage," *Telegram*, July 30, 1909, 1; "Bedraggled Flags Cause Resentment," *Deseret News*, July 30, 1909, 2; "Decorating Firm Makes Promise," *Deseret News*, July 31, 1909, 12; "Accept Decorations for the Encampment," *Telegram*, August 2, 1909, 10; "Revised Decoration Scheme Approved," *Telegram*, August 4, 1909, 10; "Encampment Notes," *Tribune*, August 5, 1909, 2; "G.A.R. Decorators Repudiate Contract," *Deseret News*, August 5, 1909, 2.

14. "G.A.R. Accommodations," *Deseret News*, May 15, 1909, 2; "Hotels Draw Comment," *Deseret News*, May 29, 1909, 1; "Will Likely Loan Cots," *Deseret News*, June 22, 1909, 5; "Local Hotel Men Slowly Working Up," *Telegram*, July 2, 1909, 9; "Hotels Are Preparing for Great Encampment," *Tribune*, July 3, 1909, 16; "G.A.R. Veterans to Have Cots of War Department," *Telegram*, July 5, 1909, 10; "Hotel Possible at Saltair Resort for the Veterans," *Telegram*, July 14, 1909, 10; "Salt Lake Hotels Hurting the City," *Deseret News*, July 28, 1909, 2; "How Hotel Men Can Avoid Much Censure," *Telegram*, July 29, 1909, 3; "Plan Tented City for Liberty Park," *Telegram*, July 30, 1909, 12; "Music in Air, and

Everywhere," *Inter-mountain Republican*, August 1, 1909, 10; "Housing Problem for Encampment Is Practically Solved," *Telegram*, August 2, 1909, 1; "Many Inquiries as to Quarters," *Tribune*, August 5, 1909, 1; "Further List of Special Trains," *Deseret News*, August 6, 1909, 2; "Free Accommodations for Many Veterans," *Telegram*, August 7, 1909, 11; "Wise Old Veteran," *Deseret News*, August 9, 1909, 1; "Plenty of Rooms and Beds for the Visitors," *Tribune*, August 11, 1909, 8; "Veterans Pleased with Quarters in School Houses," *Telegram*, August 13, 1909, 3.

15. "Ample Salt Lake Accommodations," *Deseret News*, December 9, 1908, 2; "Reasons Why Grand Army Should Hold Encampment Here," *Tribune*, February 19, 1909; "Hotels Cannot Handle Throng," *Deseret News*, April 14, 1909, 1; "Appeal to People for Hospitality," *Deseret News*, April 28, 1909, 10; "Citizens Asked to Offer Rooms," *Inter-mountain Republican*, May 18, 1909, 10; "Citizens Responding to G.A.R. Appeal," *Inter-mountain Republican*, May 19, 1909, 8; "People of Salt Lake Must Extend Welcome," *Tribune*, June 22, 1909, 14; "Accommodations Are Still Badly Needed," *Telegram*, July 1, 1909, 3; "Have You a Room for G.A.R. Visitor?" *Telegram*, July 3, 1909, 10; "Accommodations Are Somewhat Scarce," *Telegram*, July 6, 1909, 3; "Accommodations Are Coming in Slowly," *Telegram*, July 6, 1909, 12; "Call for Quarters Rapidly Increasing," *Tribune*, July 7, 1909, 14; "The Grand Army," *Deseret News*, July 10, 1909, 4; "People Should Charge Only $1 for Room," *Telegram*, July 13, 1909, 2; "Accommodations Are Coming in Rapidly," *Telegram*, July 15, 1909, 10; "Rooms for Visitors at Low Rates," *Telegram*, July 16, 1909, 1; "Plans Under Way for Encampment," *Deseret News*, July 27, 1909, 1; "Former Residents of Eastern States Asked for Help," *Telegram*, July 29, 1909, 10; "All Getting in Line," *Tribune*, August 2, 1909, 4; "Housing Problem Big One," *Telegram*, August 4, 1909, 10; "Many Inquiries as to Quarters," *Tribune*, August 5, 1909, 1; "G.A.R. Encampment Notes," *Tribune*, August 6, 1909, 2; "Housing Problem Is Solved," *Telegram*, August 6, 1909, 1; "Ogden City Is Ready to Care for Visitors," *Tribune*, August 9, 1909, 7; "Ten Specials Yet to Come," *Deseret News*, August 10, 1909, 1; "Wisconsin Delegation Being Well Entertained," *Tribune*, August 11, 1909, 8.

16. "Plan of Entertainment Most Extensive on Record," *Deseret News*, September 4, 1908, 1; "Choir Will

Sing for the Veterans," *Deseret News*, July 12, 1909, 1; "Old Soldiers Already Arriving in Town," *Telegram*, July 21, 1909, 2; "Music in Air, and Everywhere," *Inter-mountain Republican*, August 1, 1909, 10; "Numerous Bands Will Be Present," *Tribune*, August 1, 1909, 32; "Housing Problem for Encampment is Practically Solved," *Telegram*, August 2, 1909, 1; "Preparations to Receive Visitors," *Tribune*, August 3, 1909, 12; "Encampment Notes," *Deseret News*, August 5, 1909, 5; "Care of Visitors Important Matter," *Tribune*, August 7, 1909, 12; "First Patriotic G.A.R. Services," *Deseret News*, August 7, 1909, 5; "Grand Army Men Are Salt Lake's Guests," *Telegram*, August 9, 1909, 1; "Fifteen Thousand Reach City Sunday," *Telegram*, August 9, 1909, 6; "Advance Guard Arrived Early," *Deseret News*, August 9, 1909, 5; "Stands and Booths Ready," *Deseret News*, August 9, 1909, 5; "High School Cadets Doing Great Work," *Deseret News*, August 9, 1909, 16; "Encampment Notes," *Tribune*, August 10, 1909, 2; "Cadets Render Efficient Services," *Telegram*, August 10, 1909, 6; "The Forty-Third Encampment," *Inter-mountain Republican*, August 10, 1909, 4; "G.A.R. Indorses Cadet Corps Work," *Telegram*, August 10, 1909, 7; "Good Work of High School Cadets," *Tribune*, August 11, 1909, 2; "Get Into Line for the Great G.A.R. Parade," *Tribune*, August 11, 1909, 4; "Parade Comprises Imposing Spectacle," *Tribune*, August 12, 1909, 2; "High School Cadets Did a Magnificent Work," *Tribune*, August 14, 1909, 3; "Visitors Appreciate Hospitality of City," *Tribune*, August 15, 1909, 15; "Veterans March in Great Review," *Stevens Point (Wisconsin) Gazette*, August 18, 1909; "Pride of Salt Lake Now Speeding to Seattle for Utah Day," *Herald-Republican*, August 22, 1909, 5.

17. "Salt Laker on G.A.R.," *Deseret News*, September 8, 1908, 2; "Committee Will Meet on Tuesday," *Inter-mountain Republican*, January 4, 1909, 5; "Reasons Why Grand Army Should Hold Encampment Here," *Tribune*, February 19, 1909; "Salt Lakers Must Protect G.A.R.," *Telegram*, July 10, 1909, 1; "Salt Lake Must Head Off Raise in Prices During Encampment," *Telegram*, July 12, 1909, 1; "Combines Control the Prices in Salt Lake," *Telegram*, July 12, 1909, 10; "Storm of Public Sentiment Against High Prices Grows," *Telegram*, July 13, 1909, 1; "Fisher Harris Will Help Get Square Deal," *Telegram*, July 13, 1909, 2; "People Should Charge Only $1 for Room,"

Telegram, July 13, 1909, 2; "Prominent Citizens in Fight for Square Deal," *Telegram*, July 13, 1909, 2; "He Ate Hardtack Then So Give Him a Good Meal Now, and Make the Price Right, Too," *Telegram*, July 14, 1909, 1; "Officials to Demand Square Deal," *Telegram*, July 14, 1909, 1; "Increase in Business Should Satisfy Them," *Telegram*, July 14, 1909, 1; "No Grafting of Veterans," *Telegram*, July 14, 1909, 4; "Governor to Help Keep Prices Down," *Telegram*, July 15, 1909, 1; "Increase in Business Is Enough Pay," *Telegram*, July 15, 1909, 1; "Rooms for Visitors at Low Rates," *Telegram*, July 16, 1909, 1; "Council Will Punish Every Greedy One," *Telegram*, July 20, 1909, 1; "Councilmen Will Compel a Square Deal for Veterans," *Telegram*, July 30, 1909, 8; "Hotel Men on G.A.R. Outlook," *Deseret News*, July 31, 1909, 1; "License Department Helping Encampment," *Tribune*, August 1, 1909, 3; "Encampment Will Jam the Hotels," *Tribune*, August 1, 1909, 32; "Able to Care for the Crowds," *Inter-mountain Republican*, August 2, 1909, 2; "To Protect the Visitors," *Deseret News*, August 2, 1909, 4; "Police Will Keep Prices at Old Rate," *Telegram*, August 4, 1909, 1; "Policemen Will Inspect Menus," *Deseret News*, August 4, 1909, 2; "Oppose Advance in Price of Food," *Deseret News*, August 5, 1909, 2; "Prices Boosted Yet Once More," *Deseret News*, August 5, 1909, 10; "G.A.R. Encampment Notes," *Tribune*, August 6, 1909, 2; "Restaurant Men to Keep Same Prices," *Telegram*, August 6, 1909, 10; "Famine in Cots Reported Today," *Deseret News*, August 6, 1909, 1; "Give Them a Square Deal," *Telegram*, August 10, 1909, 1; "No Changes in Retail Prices," *Herald-Republican*, August 19, 1909, 12; "Prices Were Not Raised," *Deseret News*, August 19, 1909, 5.

18. "Extra Policemen Are Arranged for During Encampment," *Telegram*, July 20, 1909, 1; "Twenty-Five Extra Police for G.A.R. Week," *Deseret News*, July 27, 1909, 2; "Clever Sleuths Here to Guard Visitors Encampment Week," *Telegram*, July 31, 1909, 1; "Scat!" *Telegram*, August 4, 1909, 1; "Good Police Protection," *Telegram*, August 7, 1909, 11; "Plain Clothes Men Protect G.A.R. Visitors," *Inter-mountain Republican*, August 10, 1909, 10; "Ten Specials Yet to Come," *Deseret News*, August 10, 1909, 1; "Encampment Visitor Is Victim of Assault," *Tribune*, August 10, 1909, 12; "Encampment Visitor Bests a Highwayman," *Tribune*, August 10, 1909, 16; "Touched for $400,"

Deseret News, August 11, 1909, 2; "'This My Busy Day' Policeman's Motto," *Telegram*, August 11, 1909, 10; "Saloons Did Not Close," *Deseret News*, August 11, 1909, 12; "Youths Suspected of Picking Pockets," *Telegram*, August 11, 1909, 2; "Report Few Cases of Lost Visitors," *Inter-mountain Republican*, August 11, 1909, 10; "Mitchell Accused of Pocket Picking," *Tribune*, August 11, 1909, 9; "Heber Man Is Arrested for Attempted Robbery," *Inter-mountain Republican*, August 13, 1909, 10; "Grand Army Veterans Homeward Bound," *Deseret News*, August 14, 1909, 1; "Badges Presented to Salt Lake Officers," *Deseret News*, August 14, 1909, 6; "Much-Needed Order Issued by Police Chief," *Tribune*, August 15, 1909, 5; "Visitors Appreciate Hospitality of City," *Tribune*, August 15, 1909, 15; "Good Work Done by Police Force," *Tribune*, August 16, 1909, 12.

19. "Trips in Carriages for Old Soldiers," *Telegram*, July 21, 1909, 3; "Eight Big Camp Fires at G.A.R. Encampment," *Inter-mountain Republican*, July 22, 1909, 8; "Ogden Citizens to Entertain Veterans," *Inter-mountain Republican*, July 23, 1909, 3; "One More Week of Preparation," *Deseret News*, August 2, 1909, 2; "Campfire Programs Announced," *Telegram*, August 3, 1909, 10; "Campfires During Encampment Week," *Tribune*, August 4, 1909, 8; "Veterans' Daughters Planning Reception," *Telegram*, August 4, 1909, 3; "Encampment Notes," *Tribune*, August 4, 1909, 8; "Extend Hospitality to Civil War Nurses," *Telegram*, August 5, 1909, 3; "Many Events Scheduled for G.A.R.," *Telegram*, August 5, 1909, 1; "Pretty Display at Tabernacle," *Deseret News*, August 6, 1909, 10; "G.A.R. Encampment Notes," *Tribune*, August 6, 1909, 2; "Campfires Will Be Attractive Feature of Week's Program," *Telegram*, August 7, 1909, 12; "Monday's Program," *Deseret News*, August 7, 1909, 1; "Resorts to Give Visitors Tickets," *Telegram*, August 7, 1909, 11; "Great G.A.R. Encampment Opens in Earnest Today," *Tribune*, August 9, 1909, 1; "Veterans Meet by Hotel Campfires," *Tribune*, August 9, 1909, 2; "Veterans to Be Guests of Heagren," *Telegram*, August 9, 1909, 9; "Campfires Are Feature for Tonight," *Telegram*, August 9, 1909, 12; "Veterans Free Tomorrow," *Deseret News*, August 9, 1909, 10; "Thousands on the Streets," *Deseret News*, August 9, 1909, 1; "Veteran Vocalists Sing at Campfire," *Telegram*, August 9, 1909, 11; "Campfire Is Held in the

Darkness," *Tribune*, August 10, 1909, 16; "Veterans Meet in Capital of Utah," *Idaho Daily Statesman*, August 10, 1909, 1; "Old Veterans Hold Campfire in Dark," *Telegram*, August 10, 1909, 6; "Campfire Program at Assembly Hall," *Telegram*, August 10, 1909, 12; "Fine Camp Fire in Armory Hall," *Deseret News*, August 10, 1909, 3; "Nevius and Staff Given a Reception," *Tribune*, August 10, 1909, 1; "Reception Tendered to Commander Allen," *Tribune*, August 10, 1909, 3; "Gathering Held in Armory Hall," *Tribune*, August 10, 1909, 16; "Two Interesting Campfires Held," *Tribune*, August 11, 1909, 8; "Joyous Reunion Held by Naval Veterans," *Tribune*, August 11, 1909, 11; "Campfire at Armory a Brilliant Success," *Telegram*, August 11, 1909, 2; "Day of Pleasure for G.A.R. Ladies," *Telegram*, August 11, 1909, 2; "Receptions by W.R.C. Departments," *Tribune*, August 11, 1909, 11; "Rousing Campfire Is Held at Armory Hall," *Tribune*, August 11, 1909, 8; "Ex-Prisoners Hold Rousing Campfire," *Tribune*, August 12, 1909, 2; "Among the Stars in Glory's Field," *Deseret News*, August 12, 1909, 12; "Horrors of Dixie's War Prisons Told by Former Inmates," *Telegram*, August 12, 1909, 2; "Campfire Tales Amuse G.A.R. Men," *Telegram*, August 12, 1909, 9; "Veterans Shut Out of Concert," *Deseret News*, August 12, 1909, 3; "Assembly Hall Camp Fire," *Deseret News*, August 13, 1909, 3; "Of War Survivors Not Half Enrolled," *Deseret News*, August 13, 1909, 5; "New Officers Are Elected by Women," *Tribune*, August 14, 1909, 8; "Pleasant Reception Is Held by Eagles," *Tribune*, August 14, 1909, 11; "Hawkeye Club Has Pretty Reception," *Tribune*, August 14, 1909, 8; "Knights of Pythias Have a Busy Time," *Tribune*, August 15, 1909, 15; "Excursion to Saltair," *Deseret News*, August 23, 1909, 2.

20. "Drinking Fountains Will Be Installed When Veterans Meet," *Inter-mountain Republican*, June 18, 1909, 2; "Encampment Details Crowd Present Force," *Deseret News*, June 22, 1909, 2; "Rest Rooms Planned for Encampment," *Telegram*, July 24, 1909, 8; "Sanitary Fountains Here for Encampment," *Telegram*, July 30, 1909, 12; "G.A.R. Notes," *Deseret News*, July 31, 1909, 12; "Encampment Notes," *Tribune*, August 1, 1909, 3; "Rest Rooms Provided," *Telegram*, August 7, 1909, 11; "Business Men Show Kindness to Visitors," *Telegram*, August 9, 1909, 6; "Notes," *Tribune*, August 10, 1909, 2; "Saloons Did Not Close," *Deseret News*, August 11, 1909, 12;

"Visitors Appreciate Hospitality of City," *Tribune*, August 15, 1909, 15; "Nothing but Praise for Salt Lake," *Tribune*, August 23, 1909, 2.

21. "G.A.R. Floral Designs," *Deseret News*, June 17, 1909, 1; "Additional Guides for Temple Square," *Deseret News*, August 5, 1909, 1; "Pretty Display at Tabernacle," *Deseret News*, August 6, 1909, 10; "Attempts to Make a Good Impression," *Tribune*, August 9, 1909, 2; "Temple Block Thronged," *Deseret News*, August 9, 1909, 5.

22. "Committee to Be Named," *Deseret News*, January 11, 1909, 1; "The Fame of Utah to Be Told in Booklet," *Deseret News*, March 4, 1909, 5; "Grandstands for G.A.R. Review," *Deseret News*, May 1, 1909, 1; "Encampment Badges Will Soon Be Ready Says Manufacturer," *Inter-mountain Republican*, May 22, 1909, 12; "Prisoners of War to Meet in August," *Deseret News*, June 21, 1909, 2; "Excellent Work Done by Women," *Tribune*, July 4, 1909, 28; "G.A.R. Badge Is Handsome Affair," *Telegram*, July 16, 1909, 12; "G.A.R. Sample Badges Are Received Here," *Inter-mountain Republican*, July 17, 1909, 10; "Badges Are Ready for Distribution," *Tribune*, August 3, 1909, 3; "Can Get Badges," *Telegram*, August 3, 1909, 3; "G.A.R. Encampment Notes," *Tribune*, August 7, 1909, 9; "Harvest Time for Hawkers of Badges," *Telegram*, August 9, 1909, 6; "The Forty-Third Encampment," *Inter-mountain Republican*, August 10, 1909, 4; "Entertainment Given by the Ohio Society," *Tribune*, August 11, 1909, 2; "Unique Badge Flag Glorifies Lincoln; 30 Years in Making," *Telegram*, August 11, 1909, 2; "Badge Lost," *Deseret News*, August 13, 1909, 2; "Encampment Notes," *Tribune*, August 14, 1909, 2; "Prof. J. J. M'Clelland Presented with Badge," *Tribune*, August 15, 1909, 15; "Thomas & Lynch Are Given Credentials," *Tribune*, August 19, 1909, 8; "Credentials for G.A.R. Official Souvenir," *Telegram*, August 19, 1909, 3.

23. "Committee to Be Named," *Deseret News*, January 11, 1909, 1; "Grand Army Program to Be Full of Data," *Deseret News*, March 2, 1909, 1; "Booklet Nearly Ready," *Deseret News*, April 2, 1909, 5; "Souvenir Tells about Salt Lake," *Deseret News*, July 23, 1909, 2; "G.A.R. Souvenir," *Deseret News*, July 28, 1909, 4; "Encampment Notes," *Tribune*, August 4, 1909, 8; "G.A.R. Encampment Notes," *Tribune*, August 6, 1909, 2; "Pretty Souvenir for Woman Visitors," *Telegram*, August 6, 1909, 10; "Harvest Time

for Hawkers of Badges," *Telegram*, August 9, 1909, 6; "Visiting Photographer to Issue Souvenir Book," *Tribune*, August 10, 1909, 3; "Thomas Indignant," *Deseret News*, August 14, 1909, 2; "Credit Thomas & Lynch," *Herald-Republican*, August 18, 1909, 2; "Credentials for G.A.R. Official Souvenir," *Telegram*, August 19, 1909, 3; "Thomas & Lynch Are Given Credentials," *Tribune*, August 19, 1909, 8; "Official Book Is Designated," *Herald-Republican*, August 19, 1909, 9; "Outing of G.A.R. Ladies at Saltair," *Tribune*, August 24, 1909, 14.

24. "Encampment Notes," *Tribune*, August 11, 1909, 3; "Lafayette School to Get Musicians' Photo," *Telegram*, August 12, 1909, 2; "Encampment Notes," *Deseret News*, August 13, 1909, 3; "Interesting Souvenir Will Remain in City," *Inter-mountain Republican*, August 13, 1909, 3.

25. "Many Safeguards Are Planned for G.A.R. Parade," *Telegram*, July 9, 1909, 1; "Grand Army Veterans to Be Well Cared For," *Tribune*, July 10, 1909, 16; "Ready for the Veterans," *Telegram*, August 7, 1909, 4; "Hospitals to Care for Sick," *Telegram*, August 7, 1909, 11; "No Fatalities in Encampment," *Herald-Republican*, August 20, 1909, 5.

26. "Women Preparing to Serve Luncheon Day of G.A.R. Parade," *Inter-mountain Republican*, June 20, 1909, 3; "Woman's Committee Is Doing Good Work," *Tribune*, June 27, 1909, 24; "No Outside Help to Feed Veterans," *Inter-mountain Republican*, July 4, 1909, 3; "Junction City Will Help Encampment," *Telegram*, July 8, 1909, 5; "The Grand Army," *Deseret News*, July 10, 1909, 4; "All Ready but the Cream," *Deseret News*, July 10, 1909, 1; "Refreshments to Be Furnished Veterans," *Deseret News*, July 10, 1909, 1; "Public Is Warned Against Imposter," *Tribune*, July 11, 1909, 32; "Cities of State Come Forth with Supplies," *Inter-mountain Republican*, July 11, 1909, 3; "That Veterans May Eat," *Telegram*, August 2, 1909, 12; "'Snack' Provided for Veterans Who March in Parade," *Telegram*, August 4, 1909, 2; "Nice Little Lunch for the Veterans," *Tribune*, August 4, 1909, 14; "Delicate Refreshments for Veterans," *Tribune*, August 11, 1909, 3; "Ten Thousand Good Sandwiches for G.A.R.," *Deseret News*, August 11, 1909, 3; "Miss L. Van Cott's Bill for Services Astonishes Women," *Telegram*, August 17, 1909, 10; "Sterrett 'Raps' Salt Lake; Utahns Answer Colonel," *Telegram*, August 27, 1909, 1.

27. "Medical Corps Now Organized," *Tribune*, July 9, 1909, 14; "Nurses for Encampment," *Deseret News*, July 9, 1909, 5; "Announces Completion of Extensive Plans," *Inter-mountain Republican*, July 18, 1909, 10; "G.A.R. Parade Has Right of Way," *Telegram*, July 21, 1909, 3; "Final Details of Great Procession," *Telegram*, July 22, 1909, 12; "Rest Rooms Planned for Encampment," *Telegram*, July 24, 1909, 8; "Hospitals to Care for Sick," *Telegram*, August 7, 1909, 11; "Women Physicians to Attend to Wants of Women Visitors," *Telegram*, August 7, 1909, 1; "Ten Specials Yet to Come," *Deseret News*, August 10, 1909, 1; "'First Aid' Girls," *Deseret News*, August 11, 1909, 2; "Doctors and Nurses of Hospital Corps Win Crowd's Praise," *Telegram*, August 12, 1909, 3; "Light Day at Hospital," *Deseret News*, August 12, 1909, 6; "Knights of Pythias Have a Busy Time," *Tribune*, August 15, 1909, 15; "No Fatalities in Encampment," *Herald-Republican*, August 20, 1909, 5.

28. "Final Details of Great Procession," *Telegram*, July 22, 1909, 12; "Line of March of Big G.A.R. Parade on Wednesday, August 11," *Deseret News*, July 31, 1909, 5; "Final Plans for Big Parade Are Commenced," *Telegram*, August 5, 1909, 10; "Parade of Veterans to Be Week's Big Event," *Telegram*, August 7, 1909, 11; "Route of Tomorrow Morning's Parade," *Telegram*, August 10, 1909, 1; "Wednesday's Program," *Deseret News*, August 10, 1909, 3; "Largest Veteran Drum Corps in World Will Lead Grand Parade," *Telegram*, August 10, 1909, 7; "Green Mountain Boys in Parade," *Telegram*, August 10, 1909, 6; "Soldiery of State to Parade," *Telegram*, August 10, 1909, 12; "Get Into Line for the Great G.A.R. Parade," *Tribune*, August 11, 1909, 4; "Tribune Whistle Starts Parade," *Tribune*, August 11, 1909, 1; "Arrangements of Bands for the Great Parade," *Tribune*, August 11, 1909, 4; "The Parade Today," *Tribune*, August 11, 1909, 6; "Spanish War Veterans," *Tribune*, August 11, 1909, 8; "Silver Grays March Erect," *Deseret News*, August 11, 1909, 1; "Veterans' Parade is 3-3/4 Miles Long," *Telegram*, August 11, 1909, 1; "Everybody Came to See the Doings," *Deseret News*, August 11, 1909, 1; "Uncle John Beesley to Be In Parade," *Tribune*, August 11, 1909, 8; "Comrades March to Strains of Martial Airs," *The (Canton, Ohio) Evening Repository*, August 11, 1909, 1; "Guard Is Getting in Condition for Parade," *Tribune*, August 11, 1909, 8; "Veterans of Civil War in an Inspiring Parade,"

Tribune, August 12, 1909, 1; "Humorous Features of Grand Army Pageant," *Tribune*, August 12, 1909, 2; "Mexican War Veteran Walked in Parade," *Telegram*, August 12, 1909, 8; "Parade Comprises Imposing Spectacle," *Tribune*, August 12, 1909, 2; "Great Parade as Seen from Reviewing Stand," *Tribune*, August 12, 1909, 2; "Franklin Post No. 220 Makes Good Showing," *Tribune*, August 12, 1909, 2; "Yesterday," *Telegram*, August 12, 1909, 4; "Many People Come to See Great Parade," *Tribune*, August 12, 1909, 3; "Famous Old Relic Is Seen in G.A.R. Parade," *Tribune*, August 12, 1909, 3; "Great Heat Mars Big G.A.R. Parade," *Chicago Daily Tribune*, August 12, 1909, 4; "Heroes of Old in Annual Parade," *Idaho Daily Statesman*, August 12, 1909, 1; "The March of Boys in Blue," *Great Falls (Montana) Daily Tribune*, August 12, 1909, 1; "The Grand Parade," *Deseret News*, August 12, 1909, 4; "An Illinois Veteran," *Deseret News*, August 12, 1909, 5; "Oldest Veteran in G.A.R. Parade," *Inter-mountain Republican*, August 13, 1909, 10; "South Dakota Vets Carry an Odd Emblem," *Inter-mountain Republican*, August 13, 1909, 10; "No Confetti Throwing," *Deseret News*, August 14, 1909, 6.

29. "Flowers for Soldiers," *Deseret News*, February 13, 1909, 1; "Flowers for G.A.R. Week," *Deseret News*, March 31, 1909, 2; "To Distribute Flower Seed," *Deseret News*, April 14, 1909, 5; "New Quarters Now in Shape," *Deseret News*, April 15, 1909, 2; "Women to Watch Beds of Flowers," *Inter-mountain Republican*, April 16, 1909, 10; "G.A.R. Accommodations," *Deseret News*, May 15, 1909, 2; "Flowers Will Be Used Lavishly in Decoration Plan," *Telegram*, July 21, 1909, 10; "Final Details of Great Procession," *Telegram*, July 22, 1909, 12; "Millions of Flowers Will Be Available for Encampment Use," *Inter-mountain Republican*, July 22, 1909, 8; "Decorating Firm Makes Promise," *Deseret News*, July 31, 1909, 12; "Flower Committee Issues an Appeal," *Tribune*, August 1, 1909, 10; "One More Week of Preparation," *Deseret News*, August 2, 1909, 2; "Request Flowers for Encampment," *Inter-mountain Republican*, August 2, 1909, 2; "Flowers for Encampment," *Telegram*, August 2, 1909, 2; "To Receive Flowers Early Next Monday," *Telegram*, August 7, 1909, 10; "Doors Swing Wide to Welcome G.A.R.," *Deseret News*, August 7, 1909, 1; "Flowers for Veterans," *Telegram*, August 7, 1909; "Flower Problem Is Becoming Serious," *Tribune*, August 9, 1909, 3; "Flowers a Plenty,"

Deseret News, August 11, 1909, 2; "Nimble Fingers Busy," *Deseret News*, August 11, 1909, 12.

30. "Moving Picture of G.A.R.," *Deseret News*, July 28, 1909, 3; "'Bry' Young Enters Picture Business," *Telegram*, July 30, 1909, 5; "Will Make Pictures of the G.A.R. Parade," *Tribune*, August 1, 1909, 11; "Pictures of Parade," *Telegram*, August 2, 1909, 3; "Moving Pictures of G.A.R. Parade to Be Shown All Over Country," *Deseret News*, August 14, 1909, 7.

31. "Lincoln's Bodyguard is Visitor in City," *Telegram*, August 10, 1909, 6; "Veterans' Parade Is 3-3/4 Miles Long," *Telegram*, August 11, 1909, 1; "Two Left of First Negro Soldiers," *Telegram*, August 11, 1909, 2; "Veterans of Civil War an Inspiring Parade," *Tribune*, August 12, 1909, 1; "Humorous Features of Grand Army Pageant," *Tribune*, August 12, 1909, 2; "Parade Comprises Imposing Spectacle," *Tribune*, August 12, 1909, 2.

32. "G.A.R. Living Flag," *Deseret News*, June 7, 1909, 5; "Living Flag Plans Under Good Headway," *Deseret News*, June 9, 1909, 5; "More Arrangements for Big Living Flag," *Tribune*, June 9, 1909, 2; "Work Is Progressing on Great Living Flag," *Tribune*, June 25, 1909, 5; "Salt Lake Ladies Assume Big Task," *Telegram*, June 26, 1909, 20; "Children to Drill for Living Flag," *Telegram*, June 28, 1909, 10; "Captains of Flag Are Getting Busy," *Telegram*, June 29, 1909, 3; "Children Are Being Instructed in the 'Living Flag' Drill," *Inter-mountain Republican*, July 10, 1909, 12; "Auditorium for Living Flag Drill," *Telegram*, July 17, 1909, 14; "Change Is Made in the Costuming of Children," *Inter-mountain Republican*, July 18, 1909, 10; "Committee Has Big Job on Hands," *Telegram*, July 21, 1909, 10; "Dress Parade of G.A.R. Living Flag," *Deseret News*, July 22, 1909, 5; "Rehearsals for the G.A.R. Living Flag," *Telegram*, July 23, 1909, 6; "Living Flag to Be Big Feature of Encampment," *Telegram*, July 24, 1909, 8; "Living Flag Drill Promises Success," *Telegram*, July 29, 1909, 10; "Rehearsal Shows Living Flag Drill Will Be Inspiring," *Telegram*, July 31, 1909, 16; "Big Living Flag to Be a Success," *Tribune*, August 1, 1909, 32; "Living Flag Will Be Great Success," *Inter-mountain Republican*, August 1, 1909, 2; "Living Flag Meeting to Be Held Thursday," *Tribune*, August 5, 1909, 2; "G.A.R. Encampment Notes," *Tribune*, August 6, 1909, 2; "Moving Living Flag," *Telegram*, August 7, 1909, 11; "The Living Flag as It Will Appear to the Veterans in Parade Today," *Tribune*, August 11, 1909, 4; "Veterans' Parade is

3-3/4 Miles Long," *Telegram*, 11 August 1909, 1; "The Living Flag of Salt Lake's Children," *Deseret News*, August 11, 1909, 5; "Living Flag Stirs Hearts of Veterans," *Telegram*, August 11, 1909, 1; "Veterans of Civil War in an Inspiring Parade," *Tribune*, August 12, 1909, 1; "Living Flag Waves Patriotic Welcome," *Tribune*, August 12, 1909, 2; "Living Flag Joins Grand Army Men," *Christian Science Monitor*, August 12, 1909, 1; "Living Flag Should Live, It Is Declared," *Tribune*, August 16, 1909, 12; "D. of C. Helped to Drill Living Flag," *Telegram*, August 16, 1909, 10; "Nothing But Praise for Salt Lake," *Tribune*, August 23, 1909, 2.

33. "Children of Living Flag Faint in Sun," *Telegram*, August 11, 1909, 1; "Children Faint from the Heat," *Deseret News*, August 11, 1909, 1; "Living Flag Sings On Amid Ambulance Calls," *Deseret News*, August 11, 1909, 2; "Living Flag Waves Patriotic Welcome," *Tribune*, August 12, 1909, 2; "Sixty Children Are Overcome," *Tribune*, August 12, 1909, 3; "Children Faint on Living Flag Stand," *Intermountain Republican*, August 12, 1909, 1; "Too Busy to Care for the Children," *Deseret News*, August 12, 1909, 5; "Great Heat Mars Big G.A.R. Parade," *Chicago Daily Tribune*, August 12, 1909, 4; "Like Old War Days," *Fort Wayne (Indiana) Journal-Gazette*, August 12, 1909, 1; "Old Sol Puts Veterans Out," *Marion (Ohio) Weekly Star*, August 14, 1909.

34. "Living Flag May Be Put on Friday," *Telegram*, August 12, 1909, 1; "Living Flag Spectacle Will Again Be Presented to Guests of Salt Lake," *Telegram*, August 13, 1909, 1; "Living Flag Is to Be Repeated," *Deseret News*, August 13, 1909, 1; "'Living Flag' Will March Streets Saturday Evening," *Tribune*, August 14, 1909, 3; "Immense Throng Sees Living Flag," *Tribune*, August 15, 1909, 32.

35. *Journal of the 43d National Encampment of the Grand Army of the Republic at Salt Lake City, Utah, August 12th–13th* (G.A.R., 1909). "Business Sessions of Encampment in First Methodist," *Telegram*, August 3, 1909, 9; "Union Ex-Prisoners Meet Next Tuesday," *Telegram*, August 4, 1909, 3; "Entertainment Provided for Ex-Prisoners of War," *Tribune*, August 4, 1909, 3; "Great G.A.R. Encampment Opens in Earnest Today," *Tribune*, August 9, 1909, 1; "Thousands of Veterans Invade Salt Lake City," *Tribune*, August 10, 1909, 1; "Atlantic City Hustling for Next Encampment," *Tribune*, August 10, 1909, 3; "Army Nurses Demand Increase in Pensions,"

Telegram, August 10, 1909, 12; "Prisoners of War Are Meeting Today," *Deseret News*, August 10, 1909, 1; "Women's G.A.R. Camp Scene of Activity," *Deseret News*, August 10, 1909, 6; "It Looks Like Van Sant for Commander-in-Chief," *Tribune*, August 11, 1909, 1; "Women Enjoying Salt Lake Resorts," *Tribune*, August 11, 1909, 2; "Joyous Reunion Held by Naval Veterans, *Tribune*, August 11, 1909, 11; "Vansant Slated to Head the G.A.R.," *Idaho Daily Statesman*, August 11, 1909, 1; "Day of Pleasure for G.A.R. Ladies," *Telegram*, August 11, 1909, 2; "Union Ex-Prisoners of War Assemble," *Tribune*, August 11, 1909; "Grand Army Head Is Chief Topic at Salt Lake Today," *Christian Science Monitor*, August 11, 1909, 1; "Gettysburg Highway Will Be Considered," *Tribune*, August 11, 1909, 8; "Army Nurses Have Session Tuesday," *Tribune*, August 12, 1909; "Flying Squadron Lauds Navy in War," *Telegram*, August 12, 1909, 12; "Proud and Only G.A.R. Auxiliary," *Deseret News*, August 12, 1909, 3; "Naval War Veterans," *Deseret News*, August 12, 1909, 6; "Makes His Last Report," *Deseret News*, August 12, 1909, 1; "Van Sant Leads for the Honor," *Evening Repository (Canton, Ohio)*, August 12, 1909, 10; "Commander Nevius Reviews Year's Work," *Telegram*, August 12, 1909, 1; "Officers of Signal Corps Exhibit Few Relics of Rebellion," *Telegram*, August 12, 1909, 2; "Relief Corps Will Elect President," *Telegram*, August 12, 1909, 2; "Horrors of Dixie's War Prisons Told by Former Inmates," *Telegram*, August 12, 1909; "Ladies of G.A.R. Hold Services," *Telegram*, August 13, 1909, 1; "Ocean Wins Over Valley," *Deseret News*, August 13, 1909, 1; "Gallant Leaders for Ensuing Year," *Deseret News*, August 13, 1909, 5; "Veterans to Name Chaplain and Next Convention Today," *Christian Science Monitor*, August 13, 1909, 1; "Salt Lake Woman Is Highly Honored," *Tribune*, August 14, 1909, 3; "New Officers Are Elected by Women," *Tribune*, August 14, 1909, 8; "Closing Session W.R.C.," *Deseret News*, August 14, 1909, 5; "Ladies of G.A.R. Elect New Officers," *Deseret News*, August 14, 1909, 8; "Big Encampment Is Thing of Past," *Tribune*, August 15, 1909, 15; "Col. Sterrett to Direct Atlantic City Encampment," *Telegram*, August 20, 1909, 10.

36. "Old Soldiers Start Out," *Deseret News*, August 25, 1908, 2; "Salt Lake Women Served as Nurses in the Civil War," *Deseret News*, January 2, 1909, 24; "General Nevius Will Attend Utah Meeting," *Deseret*

News, April 16, 1909, 8; "Hospitable Welcome for War Time Nurses," *Telegram*, August 3, 1909, 3; "Encampment Notes," *Salt Lake Tribune*, August 4, 1909, 8; "Grandstands to Be Safely Constructed," *Tribune*, August 9, 1909, 3; "Army Nurses Demand Increase in Pensions," *Telegram*, August 10, 1909, 12; "Army Nurses Have Session Tuesday," *Salt Lake Tribune*, August 11, 1909, 2; "Utah Woman Heads Nurses," *Deseret Evening News*, August 12, 1909, 2; "Veterans Elect Commander in Chief," *Idaho Daily Statesman*, August 13, 1909, 1; "Army Nurses," *Deseret News*, August 13, 1909, 2; "Officers Elected by the Daughters," *Tribune*, August 14, 1909, 16; "Resolutions by the Army Nurses," *Herald-Republican*, August 26, 1909, 6; "Two Civil War Army Nurses Left a Lasting Legacy in Utah," *Tribune*, August 31, 2008.

37. "Veterans, Farewell!" *Deseret News*, August 14, 1909, 4; "G.A.R. Entertainment Closes," *Deseret News*, August 14, 1909, 3; "G.A.R. Finishes Up All Its Business," *Great Falls (Montana) Daily Tribune*, August 14, 1909, 1; "Guests of Zion Leave for Home," *Tribune*, August 15, 1909, 32; "Flags Come Down and City Assumes Every Day Aspect," *Telegram*, August 16, 1909, 1.

38. "Corporal Tanner Rebukes Sterrett," *Deseret News*, September 9, 1909, 8; "G.A.R. Chaplain Praises Salt Lake," *Deseret News*, September 15, 1909, 3.

39. "Grand Army Veteran Highly Appreciative," *Deseret News*, August 25, 1914, 14.

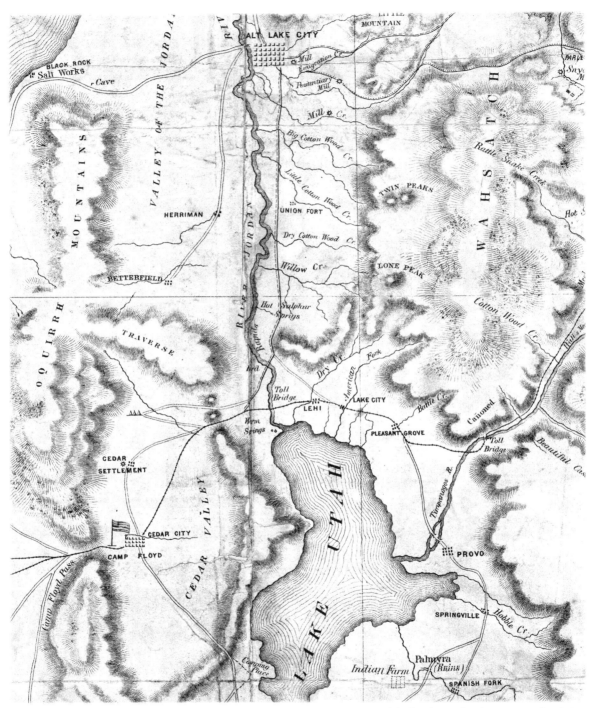

*This detail of a map of Utah Territory, entitled "Preliminary map of routes reconnoitred [sic] and opened in the Territory of Utah /
by Captain J. H. Simpson . . . under the orders of Brigadier General, A. D. [sic] Johnston, commanding the Department of Utah," was
completed in 1859 by the U.S. Army Corps of Engineers and published by the Government Printing Office in Washington, DC.
(L. Tom Perry Special Collections, Brigham Young University)*

BIBLIOGRAPHY

OFFICIAL RECORDS

An Act to Establish a Territorial Government for Utah. 9 Statute 453.

Annual Report of the Commissioner of Indian Affairs, Transmitted with the Message of the President at the Opening of the Second Session of the Thirty-Second Congress, 1850. Washington, DC: Office of the Commissioner of Indian Affairs, 1850.

Charles D. Beckwith Pension File. National Archives Records Administration. Washington, DC.

Congressional Globe, 46 vols. Washington, DC, 1834–73.

Descriptive Book. Company M, 2nd California Cavalry. National Archives Records Administration. Washington, DC.

Headstones Provided for Deceased Military Veterans. (Microcopy 1845). National Archives Records Administration. Washington, DC.

Journals of the Legislative Assembly of the Territory of Utah. Thirteenth Annual Session, for the Years 1863–64. Salt Lake City: Elias Smith, 1861.

Nauvoo Legion Letterbook, MS 1370, Church History Library, Salt Lake City.

Report of the Commissioner of Indian Affairs, Accompanying the Annual Report of the Secretary of the Interior for the Year 1858. Washington, DC: Wm. A. Harris, 1858.

Report of the Commissioner of Indian Affairs, Accompanying the Annual Report of the Secretary of the Interior for the Year 1859. Washington, DC: George W. Bowman, 1859.

Report of the Commissioner of Indian Affairs, Accompanying the Annual Report of the Secretary of the Interior for the Year 1860. Washington, DC: George W. Bowman, 1860.

Report of the Commissioner of Indian Affairs, Accompanying the Annual Report of the Secretary of the Interior, for the Year 1861. Washington, DC: Government Printing Office, 1861.

Report of the Commissioner of Indian Affairs, Accompanying the Annual Report of the Secretary of the Interior, for the Year 1865. Washington, DC: Government Printing Office, 1865.

Report of the Commissioner of Indian Affairs for the Year 1862. Washington, DC: Government Printing Office, 1862.

Report of the Commissioner of Indian Affairs for the Year 1864. Washington, DC: Government Printing Office, 1865.

Report of the Secretary of War. 35th Congress, 1st Session, 1857–58, Senate Executive Document.

Right to Wear Badges of Military Societies. United States Code. Title 10, Subtitle A, Part II, Chapter 57, Section 1123.

Special Order #49. Headquarters, 2nd California Cavalry. National Archives Records Administration. Washington, DC.

Special Order #66. January 18, 1862, National Archives Records Administration. Washington, DC.

Special Order #184. Headquarters, 2nd California Cavalry. National Archives Records Administration. Washington, DC.

United States Constitution. Amendment XIII, section 1.

United States Constitution. Amendment XIV, section 1.

United States Constitution. Amendment XV, section 1.

United States Constitution. Article 1, section 2.

United States Constitution. Article 1, section 8.

United States Constitution. Amendment XIV, section 2.

U.S. Census Bureau. *Ninth Census of the United States.*

———. "Special Schedule. Surviving Soldiers, Sailors, Marines, and Widows, etc." *Eleventh Census of the United States.*

———. *Twelfth Census of the United States.*

Utah Military Files. Utah State Archives. Salt Lake City.

Utah Territorial Militia Records. Utah State Archives. Salt Lake City.

The War of the Rebellion: A Compilation of the Official Records of the Union and Confederate Armies. Series 1, vol. 13. Washington, DC: Government Printing Office, 1885.

The War of the Rebellion: A Compilation of the Official Records of the Union and Confederate Armies. Series 1, vol. 50, part 1. Washington, DC: Government Printing Office, 1897.

The War of the Rebellion: A Compilation of the Official Records of the Union and Confederate Armies. Series 1, vol. 50, part 2. Washington, DC: Government Printing Office, 1897.

The War of the Rebellion: A Compilation of the Official Records of the Union and Confederate Armies. Series 1, vol. 58, part 2. Washington, DC: Government Printing Office, 1897.

The War of the Rebellion: A Compilation of the Official Records of the Union and Confederate Armies. Series 3, vol. 2. Washington, DC: Government Printing Office, 1899.

MANUSCRIPTS

Agnew, James B. "'A Day of Sorrow and a Day of Glory': A Brief Chronicle of the Career of Brigadier General Barnard E. Bee, CSA." Unpublished paper in the collections of U.S. Army Military History Institute, Carlisle Barracks, Pennsylvania.

Americana Collection, L. Tom Perry Special Collections. Harold B. Lee Library, Brigham Young University, Provo, UT.

Beauregard, Captain P. G. T. "Letter to Senator John Slidell, February 9, 1858." Huntington Library, San Marino, CA.

Becker, Charles. "With Johnston's Army, 1857." 4, typescript, Merrill-Cazier Library, Utah State University, Logan.

Brigham Young Collection. Church History Library, Salt Lake City.

Brigham Young Letter Books. Church History Library, Salt Lake City.

Brigham Young Letters. Bienecke Rare Book and Manuscript Library, Yale University, New Haven, CT.

Brigham Young Letterpress Copybooks. Church History Library, Salt Lake City.

Brigham Young Office Files. Church History Library, Salt Lake City.

Brigham Young Papers. Utah State Historical Society, Salt Lake City.

Church Emigration Book. Church History Library, Salt Lake City.

Delana R. Eckels to Sen. Jesse Bright, December 13, 1857. Copy in possession of William P. MacKinnon.

Foote, Warren. "Autobiography of Warren Foote of Glendale, Kane Co., Utah." Unpublished manuscript. MS 1123, 174, Church History Library, Salt Lake City.

Forbes, Joseph Barlow. "Autobiography of Joseph Barlow Forbes, 1840–1927." Unpublished manuscript. MS 15909, Church History Library, Salt Lake City.

Frank Fuller to Daniel H. Wells, June 12, 1862. Series 242. Utah State Archives, Salt Lake City.

Gardner Papers. Utah State Historical Society, Salt Lake City.

Gates, Jacob. *Reminiscences and Diaries*, April 24, 1861. Church History Library, Salt Lake City.

Grand Army of the Republic. Utah Membership Records. Utah State Archives, Salt Lake City.

Harper, John Claiborne. Diary. http://lib.byu.edu/digital/mmd/diarists/Harper_John_Claiborne.php.

Harvey Coe Hullinger Journal. Church History Library, Salt Lake City.

Heyward and Ferguson Family Papers. Southern History Collection. Wilson Library, University of North Carolina, Chapel Hill.

Historian's Office Journal. Church History Library, Salt Lake City.

Inaugural Addresses of the Presidents of the United States from George Washington 1789 to George Bush 1989. Bicentennial Edition. Washington, DC: United States Government Printing Office, 1989.

Interview with Robert L. Davis, grandson of John E. Davis, and Kenneth L. Alford, October 17, 2011. Records in possession of the Davis family.

James Buchanan Papers. L. Tom Perry Special Collections, Harold B. Lee Library, Brigham Young University, Provo, UT.

Joel E. Ricks Cache Valley History Collection. Utah State University, Logan.

Journal History of the Church of Jesus Christ of Latter-day Saints. Church History Library, Salt Lake City.

Leonard J. Arrington Papers. Merrill-Cazier Library, Utah State University, Logan.

Lot Smith Papers. L. Tom Perry Special Collections. Harold B. Lee Library, Brigham Young University, Provo, UT.

Melvin L. Bashore Files. Church History Library, Salt Lake City.

Mormon Biographical Sketches Collection. Church History Library, Salt Lake City.

"Muster-out Roll of Captain Lott Smith's Company of Mounted Volunteers . . . , 14 August 1862." MSS A 5238, Utah State Historical Society, Salt Lake City.

Nauvoo Legion Records. Church History Library, Salt Lake City.

Newell, Robert ("Doc"). "Letter to Ingalls, December 31, 1857." Photocopy in possession of William P. MacKinnon.

Ottinger, George M. "Reminiscences and Journal, 12 June 1861." In possession of Susanna Helbling.

Peery, Liliu Davis, comp.. "History of David Harold Peery." Unpublished manuscript, February 1941.

Pulsipher, John. "John Pulsipher Journal." MS 1045, LDS Church Archives.

Record and Order Book of the Major General Commanding G. S. L. Military District. Nauvoo Legion. Theodore A. Schroeder Papers. State Historical Society of Wisconsin, Madison.

Registry Book, Great Salt Lake Military District, MS 9391, Church History Library, Salt Lake City.

"Rosine Wilhelmina Aust Bitter." Life sketch in possession of Constance Brown.

Saints at War Collection. L. Tom Perry Special Collections, Harold B. Lee Library, Brigham Young University, Provo, UT.

Samuel Wragg Ferguson Papers. Special Collections, Hill Memorial Library, Louisiana State University, Baton Rouge.

Scovil, Lucius. *Diary of Lucius Scovil.* April 27, 1861. Church History Library, Salt Lake City.

Schettler, Bernhard. *Memorandum Book, 1861.* Church History Library, Salt Lake City.

Smith, Don. "Life Sketch Henry Wells Jackson." Unpublished manuscript.

Southern Historical Collection. Wilson Library, University of North Carolina, Chapel Hill.

"Stephen A. Douglas, Abraham Lincoln, and 'The Mormon Problem:' The 1857 Springfield Debate." Unpublished paper.

Stuart, David Crockett. "A Few Lines from an Old Johnny Reb." Autobiographical letter. MS 8895, Church History Library, Salt Lake City.

Thomas, Mary A. Evans. "John Davis Evans." Unpublished manuscript.

"Traugott Bitter." Life sketch in possession of Constance Brown.

Utah Military Files. Utah State Archives, Salt Lake City.

Utah Territorial Militia Records. Utah State Archives, Salt Lake City.

Wiggill, Eli. "Autobiography." MS 8344, Church History Library, Salt Lake City.

William Clarke Quantrill Research Collection. McCain Library, University of Southern Mississippi, Hattiesburg.

Yale Collection of Western Americana. Beinecke Rare Book and Manuscript Library, Yale University, New Haven, CT.

Young, Brigham. "The Word and Will of the Lord Concerning the Camp of Israel in their Journeyings to the West, 1847 Jan. 14." Church History Library, Salt Lake City.

NEWSPAPERS

Bangor Daily Whig & Courier, Bangor, ME.

Boston Herald, Boston.

Chattanooga Daily Gazette, Chattanooga, TN.

Chicago Daily Tribune, Chicago.

Christian Science Monitor, Boston.

Church News, Salt Lake City.

The Columbus Gazette, Columbus, OH.

Daily Evening Bulletin, San Francisco.

Daily Inter Ocean, Chicago.

Daily National Intelligencer, Washington, DC.

Daily South Carolinian, Columbia, SC.

Daily Morning News, Savannah, GA.

Davis County Clipper, UT.

Deseret News, Salt Lake City.

The Duchesne Courier, Duchesne, UT.

El Paso Times, El Paso, TX.

Evening Repository, Canton, OH.

Evening Virginia Sentinel, Alexandria, VA.

Fayetteville Observer, Fayetteville, NC.

Fort Wayne Journal-Gazette, Fort Wayne, IN.

Great Falls Daily Tribune, Great Falls, MT.

Herald-Republican, Salt Lake City.

Hinds County Gazette, Raymond, MO.

Idaho Daily Statesman, Boise, ID.

Illinois State Register, Springfield, IL.

Indiana Evening Gazette, Indiana, PA.

Inter-Mountain Republican, Salt Lake City.

Kalamazoo Gazette, Kalamazoo, MI.

Kansas City Times, Kansas City, MO.

Liberty Weekly Tribune, Liberty MO.

Livingston County Press, Howell, MI.

Los Angeles Star, Los Angeles, CA.

Marion Weekly Star, Marion, OH.

Natchez Courier, Natchez, MS.

National Republican, Washington, DC.

New York Herald, New York City.

New York Observer and Chronicle, New York City.

New York Times, New York City.

News Advocate, Carbon County, UT.

News and Observer, Raleigh, NC.

Philadelphia Mercury, Philadelphia.

Post Dispatch, Salt Lake City.

Ogden Standard, Ogden, UT.

Raleigh Register, Raleigh, NC.

Richmond Daily Dispatch, Richmond, VA.

Sacramento Daily Union, Sacramento, CA.

Sacramento Bee, Sacramento, CA.

Salt Lake Daily Telegraph, Salt Lake City.

Salt Lake Herald, Salt Lake City.

Salt Lake Republican, Salt Lake City.

Salt Lake Telegram, Salt Lake City.

Salt Lake Tribune, Salt Lake City.

San Francisco Chronicle, San Francisco.

San Francisco Herald, San Francisco.

Seer, Washington, DC.

St. Joseph Herald, St. Joseph, MO.

Stevens Point Gazette, Stevens Point, WI.

Sunday Mercury, Philadelphia.

Times and Seasons, Nauvoo, IL.

Toledo Daily Blade, Toledo, OH.

The Semi-Weekly Shreveport News, Shreveport, LA.

Tri-Weekly Miner Register, Central City, CO.

Union Vedette, Camp Douglas, UT Territory.

Vernal Express, Vernal, UT.

Washington County News, St. George, UT.

BOOKS

Adams, George Rollie. *General William S. Harney: Prince of Dragoons*. Lincoln: University of Nebraska Press, 2001.

Adams, Henry. *The Education of Henry Adams: An Autobiography*. Boston: Houghton Mifflin, 1918.

Alder, Lydia Dunford. *The Holy Land*. Salt Lake City: Deseret News, 1912.

Alexander, Thomas G. *Mormonism in Transition: A History of the Latter-day Saints, 1890–1930*. Urbana: University of Illinois Press, 1986.

Allen, Howard W. and Vincent A. Lacey, eds. *Illinois Elections, 1818–1992*. Carbondale, IL: Southern Illinois University Press, 1992.

Allen, James B. and Glen M. Leonard. *The Story of the Latter-day Saints*, rev. ed. Salt Lake City: Deseret Book, 1992.

Allred, Lee. *For the Strength of the Hills*. n.p.: Bridge Publications, 1997.

Alter, J. Cecil. *Jim Bridger*. Norman: University of Oklahoma Press, 1979.

Ambrose, Stephen E. *Duty, Honor, Country: A History of West Point*. Baltimore: The John Hopkins University Press, 1999.

American Military History. Vol. 1. Washington, DC: Center of Military History, 2005.

Anderson, C. LeRoy. *Joseph Morris and the Saga of the Morrisites*. Logan: Utah State University Press, 1988.

Angle, Paul M., comp. *New Letters and Papers of Lincoln*. Boston: Houghton Mifflin, 1930.

Appel, Theodore. *The Life and Work of John Williamson Nevin, D.D., L.L.D.* Philadelphia: Reformed Church Publication House, 1889.

Appomattox Court House: Appomattox Court House National Historical Park. Handbook 160. Washington, DC: National Park Service, Government Printing Office, n.d.

Archer, Patience Loader Rozsa. *Recollections of Past Days: The Autobiography of Patience Loader Rozsa Archer*. Logan, Utah: Utah State University Press, 2006.

Arrington, Leonard J. *Brigham Young: American Moses*. New York: Knopf, 1985.

———. *Charles C. Rich: Mormon General and Western Frontiersman*. Provo, UT: Brigham Young University Press, 1974.

Arrington, Leonard J. and Davis Bitton. *The Mormon Experience: A History of the Latter-day Saints*. New York: Alfred A. Knopf, 1979.

Bagley, Will, ed. *"A Bright, Rising Star": A Brief Life of James Ferguson, Sergeant Major, Mormon Battalion; Adjutant General, Nauvoo Legion*. Salt Lake City: Prairie Dog Press, 2000.

———, ed. *Kingdom in the West: The Mormons and the American Frontier*. Vol. 10. Spokane, WA: Arthur H. Clark, 2000.

Bancroft, Hubert Howe. *History of Utah 1540–1886*. San Francisco: History Company., 1889.

———. *The Works of Hubert Howe Bancroft: The Native Races*. Vol. 1. San Francisco: History Company, 1882.

Baskin, Robert Newton. *Reminiscences of Early Utah*. n.p.: R. N. Baskin, 1914.

Bassler, Roy P., ed. *The Collected Works of Abraham Lincoln*. New Brunswick, NJ: Rutgers University Press, 1953.

Beath, Robert B. *The Grand Army Blue-Book containing the Rules and Regulations of the Grand Army of the Republic and Official Decisions and Opinions Thereon, with Additional Notes*. Philadelphia: Burk and McFetridge, 1884.

———. *History of the Grand Army of the Republic*. New York: Willis McDonald, 1888.

Bennett, John C. *History of the Saints; or, an Exposé of Joe Smith and Mormonism*. Boston: Leland & Whiting, 1842.

Bennett, Richard E. *We'll Find the Place: The Mormon Exodus, 1846–1848*. Salt Lake City: Deseret Book, 1997.

Bennett, Richard E., Susan Easton Black, and Donald Q. Cannon. *The Nauvoo Legion in Illinois: A History of the Mormon Militia, 1841–1846*. Norman, OK: Arthur H. Clark, 2010.

Beveridge, Albert J. *Abraham Lincoln*. New York: Houghton Mifflin, 1928.

Bigler, David L. and Will Bagley. *The Mormon Rebellion: America's First Civil War, 1857–1858*. Norman: University of Oklahoma Press, 2011.

Biographical and Genealogical Record of La Salle County, Illinois. Chicago: Lewis, 1900.

Birkner, Michael J. and John W. Quist, eds. *Disrupted Democracy: James Buchanan and the Coming of the Civil War*. Gainesville: University of Florida Press, forthcoming.

Bitton, Davis. *Guide to Mormon Diaries and Autobiographies*. Provo, UT: Brigham Young University Press, 1977.

———, ed. The *Reminiscences and Civil War Letters of Levi Lamoni Wight*. Salt Lake City: University of Utah Press, 1970.

Black, Susan Easton, comp. *Membership of the Church of Jesus Christ of Latter-day Saints, 1830–1848*, 50 vols. Salt Lake City: LDS Church, 1990.

———. *Who's Who in the Doctrine and Covenants*. Salt Lake City: Bookcraft, 1997.

Blackhawk, Ned. *Violence Over the Land: Indians and Empires in the Early American West*. Cambridge, MA: Harvard University Press, 2006.

Blanthorn, Ouida. *A History of Tooele County*. Salt Lake City: Utah Historical Society, 1998.

Bringhurst, Newell G. *Brigham Young and the Expanding American Frontier*. Boston: Little, Brown, 1986.

Buell, Augustus. *"The Cannoneer": Recollections of Service in the Army of the Potomac*. Washington, DC: National Tribune, 1890.

Bullock, Richard H. *Ship Brooklyn Saints: Their Journey and Early Endeavors in California*. Sandy, UT: ShipBrooklyn.com, 2009.

Canning, Ray R. and Beverly Beeton, eds. *The Genteel Gentile: Letters of Elizabeth Cumming, 1857–1858*. Salt Lake City: University of Utah Library, Tanner Trust Series, 1977.

Carmichael, Peter S., ed. *Audacity Personified: The Generalship of Robert E. Lee*. Baton Rouge: University of Louisiana Press, 2004.

Carter, D. Robert. *Founding Fort Utah: Provo's Native Inhabitants, Early Explorers, and First Year of Settlement*. Provo, UT: Provo City Corporation, 2003.

Carter, Kate. *Treasures of Pioneer History*. Salt Lake City: Daughters of Utah Pioneers, 1952.

———, comp. *Our Pioneer Heritage*. Vol. 15. Salt Lake City: Daughters of Utah Pioneers, 1972.

Catton, Bruce. *The Civil War*. New York: Fairfax Press, 1980.

Chambers, John Whiteclay, II, ed. *American Military History*. Oxford University Press, 1999.

Child, Paul W., ed. *Register of Graduates and Former Cadets of the United States Military Academy*. West Point, NY: Association of USMA Graduates, 1990.

Civil War Papers Read before the Commandery of the State of Massachusetts, Military Order of the Loyal Legion of the United States. Wilmington, NC: Broadfoot, 1993.

Coddington, Edwin B. *The Gettysburg Campaign: A Study in Command*. New York: Scribner's Sons, 1968.

Colton, Ray C. *The Civil War in the Western Territories: Arizona, Colorado, New Mexico, and Utah*. Norman: University of Oklahoma Press, 1959.

Commager, Henry Steele, ed. *Churchill's History of the English-Speaking Peoples*. New York: Barnes & Noble Books, 1995.

Connelley, William Elsey. *Quantrill and the Border Wars*. Lawrence: Kansas Heritage Press, 1992.

———. *War with Mexico, 1846–1847: Doniphan's Expedition and the Conquest of New Mexico and California*. Topeka, KS: n.p., 1907.

Cook, Lyndon W., ed. *Aaron Johnson Correspondence*. Orem, UT: Center for Research of Mormon Origins, 1990.

———. *The Revelations of the Prophet Joseph Smith*. Salt Lake City: Deseret Book, 1985.

Cooling, Benjamin Franklin. *Forts Henry and Donelson: The Key to the Confederate Heartland*. Knoxville: University of Tennessee Press, 1987.

Corbin, Annalies. *The Material Culture of Steamboat Passengers*. New York: Springer, 2000.

Cowley, Matthias F. *Wilford Woodruff*. Salt Lake City: Bookcraft, 1964.

Cozzens, Peter. *Shenandoah 1862: Stonewall Jackson's Valley Campaign*. Chapel Hill: University of North Carolina Press, 2008.

Cresswell, Stephen E. *Mormons, Cowboys, Moonshiners & Klansman: Federal Law Enforcement in the South and West*. Tuscaloosa: University of Alabama Press, 1991.

Cuch, Forrest S., ed. *A History of Utah's American Indians*. Salt Lake City: Utah State Division of Indian Affairs and Division of History, 2003.

Culmsee, Carlton. *Utah's Black Hawk War*. Logan, Utah: Utah State University Press, 1973.

Cunningham, Frank. *General Stand Watie's Confederate Indians*. Norman: University of Oklahoma Press, 1998.

Daniel, Larry J. *Shiloh: The Battle That Decided the Civil War*. New York: Simon & Schuster, 1997.

Davidson, William M. *A History of the United States*. Chicago: Scott, Foresman, 1902.

Davis, Burke. *Sherman's March*. New York: Vintage Books, 1988.

Dearing, Mary R. *Veterans in Politics: The Story of the G.A.R.* Baton Rouge: Louisiana State University Press, 1952.

Demos, John. *A Little Commonwealth: Family Life in Plymouth Colony*. Oxford: Oxford University Press, 2000.

Detzer, David. *Allegiance: Fort Sumter, Charleston, and the Beginning of the Civil War*. New York: Harcourt, 2001.

———. *Donnybrook: The Battle of Bull Run, 1861*. Orlando: Harcourt, 2004.

Dew, Charles B. *Apostles of Disunion: Southern Secession Commissioners and the Causes of the Civil War*. Charlottesville: University of Virginia Press, 2001.

Dickens, Charles. *The Uncommercial Traveler*. Oxford: Oxford University Press, 1987.

Donald, David Herbert. *Lincoln's Herndon*. Cambridge, MA: Da Capo Press, 1989.

———. *Lincoln Reconsidered: Essays on the Civil War Era*. New York: Vintage Books, 1989.

Durham, G. Homer, ed. *The Gospel Kingdom: Selections from the Writings and Discourses of John Taylor*. Salt Lake City: Bookcraft, 1987.

Eakin, Joanne Chiles and Donald R. Hale, comps. *Branded as Rebels: A List of Bushwhackers, Guerrillas, Partisan Rangers, Confederates and Southern Sympathizers from Missouri during the War*. Independence, Wee Print, 1993.

Ellis, D. A. *Grand Army of the Republic: History of the Order in the U.S. by Counties*. n.p.: Press of Historical Publishing, 1892.

Ellsworth, S. George. *Dear Ellen: Two Mormon Women and Their Letters*. Salt Lake City: University of Utah Tanner Trust Series, 1974.

Esshom, Frank. *Pioneers and Prominent Men of Utah*. Salt Lake City: Utah Pioneers Book, 1913.

Etcheson, Nicole. *Bleeding Kansas: Contested Liberty in the Civil War Era*. Lawrence, KS: University of Kansas Press, 2004.

Evans, Jerry Crouch. *Silencing the Vicksburg Guns: The Story of the 7th Missouri Infantry Regiment*. Victoria, Canada: Hither & Yon, 2005.

Farish, Thomas Edwin. *History of Arizona*. Vol. 3. San Francisco: Filmer Brothers Electrotype, 1915.

Farmer, Jared. *On Zion's Mount: Mormons, Indians, and the American Landscape*. Cambridge, MA: Harvard University Press, 2008.

Faulring, Scott H., ed. *An American Prophet's Record: The Diaries and Journals of Joseph Smith*. Salt Lake City: Signature Books, 1989.

Faust, Drew Gilpin. *This Republic of Suffering: Death and the American Civil War*. New York: Vintage Books, 2008.

Faust, Patricia L., ed. *Historical Times Illustrated Encyclopedia of the Civil War*. New York: Harper & Row, 1986.

Fehrenbacher, Don E. *The Slaveholding Republic: An Account of the United States Government's Relations to Slavery*, ed. Ward M. McAfee. New York: Oxford University Press, 2001.

Fellman, Michael. *Inside War: The Guerrilla Conflict in Missouri during the American Civil War*. New York: Oxford University Press, 1989.

Fisher, Margaret M. *Utah and the Civil War. Being the Story of the Part Played by the People of Utah in That Great Conflict with Special Reference to the Lot Smith Expedition and the Robert T. Burton Expedition*. Salt Lake City: Deseret Book, 1929.

Fleek, Sherman L. *History May be Searched in Vain: A Military History of the Mormon Battalion*. Spokane, Washington: Arthur H. Clark, 2008.

Flood, Charles Bracelen. *Grant and Sherman: The Friendship That Won the Civil War*. New York: Farrar, Straus and Giroux, 2005.

Foltz, Charles S. *Surgeon of the Seas: The Adventurous Life of Jonathan M. Foltz in the Days of Wooden Ships*. Indianapolis: Bobbs-Merrill, 1931.

Foner, Eric. *A Short History of Reconstruction, 1863–1877*. New York: Harper & Row, 1990.

———. *Reconstruction: America's Unfinished Revolution, 1863–1877*. New York: Harper & Row, 1988.

Frederick, J. V. *Ben Holladay, The Stagecoach King: A Chapter in the Development of Transcontinental Transportation*. Glendale, CA: Arthur H. Clark, 1940.

Freehling, William W. *Prelude to Civil War: The Nullification Controversy in South Carolina, 1816–1836*. New York: Harper & Row, 1965.

Freeman, Robert C., ed. *Nineteenth-Century Saints at War*. Provo, UT: Religious Studies Center, Brigham Young University, 2006.

Frost, John. *Thrilling Adventures among the Indians: Comprising the Most Remarkable Personal Narratives of Events in the Early Indian Wars, as well as of Incidents in the Recent Indian Hostilities in Mexico and Texas*. Philadelphia: J. W. Bradley, 1849.

Furniss, Norman F. *The Mormon Conflict, 1850–1859*. New Haven, CT: Yale University Press, 1960, rept. 1966.

Garr, Arnold K., Donald Q. Cannon, and Richard O. Cowan, eds. *Encyclopedia of Latter-day Saint History*. Salt Lake City: Deseret Book, 2000.

Garrett, H. Dean, ed. *Regional Studies in LDS History: Illinois*. Provo, UT: Brigham Young University, 1995.

Gates, Zethyl. *Mariano Medina: Colorado Mountain Man*. Boulder, CO: Johnson, 1981.

Giese, Dale F., ed. *My Life with the Army in the West: The Memoirs of James E. Farmer, 1858–1898*. Santa Fe, NM: Stagecoach, 1967.

Godfrey, Donald G. and Rebecca S. Martineau-McCarty. *An Uncommon Common Pioneer: The Journals of James Henry Martineau, 1828–1918*. Provo, UT: Religious Studies Center, Brigham Young University, 2008.

Gordon, Sarah Barringer. *The Mormon Question: Polygamy and Constitutional Conflict in Nineteenth-Century America*. Chapel Hill, NC: University of North Carolina Press, 2002.

Gowans, Fred R. and Eugene E. Campbell. *Fort Bridger: Island in the Wilderness*. Provo, UT: Brigham Young University Press, 1975.

Grafton, John, ed. *Great Speeches—Abraham Lincoln*. New York: Dover, 1991.

Greene, Jerome A., ed. and comp. *Lakota and Cheyenne: Indian Views of the Great Sioux War, 1876–1877*. Norman: University of Oklahoma Press, 1994.

Gregg, Thomas. *The Prophet of Palmyra*. New York: John B. Alden, 1890.

Grow, Matthew J. *"Liberty to the Downtrodden": Thomas L. Kane, Romantic Reformer*. New Haven: Yale University Press, 2009.

Guelzo, Allen C. *Abraham Lincoln, Redeemer President*. Grand Rapids: William B. Eerdmans, 1999.

Gunnison, Lieut. J. W. *The Mormons, or, Latter-day Saints, in the Valley of the Great Salt Lake: A History of Their Rise and Progress, Peculiar Doctrines, and Present Condition, and Prospects, Derived from Personal Observation, during a Residence among Them*. Philadelphia: Lippincott, Grambo & Co., 1852.

Hafen, LeRoy R., ed. *The Mountain Men and the Fur Trade of the Far West*. Glendale, CA: Arthur H. Clark, 1969.

Hafen, LeRoy R. and Ann W. Hafen, eds. *Mormon Resistance: A Documentary Account of the Utah Expedition, 1857–1858*. Lincoln: University of Nebraska Press, 2005.

Hardoff, Richard G., comp. *The Death of Crazy Horse: A Tragic Episode in Lakota History*. Lincoln: University of Nebraska Press, 2001.

Harper, Steven C. *Making Sense of the Doctrine and Covenants: A Guided Tour through Modern Revelations*. Salt Lake City: Deseret Book, 2008.

Harrell, Carolyn L. *When the Bells Tolled for Lincoln: Southern Reaction to the Assassination*. GA: Mercer University Press, 1997.

Hartshorn, Leon R. *Powerful Stories from the Lives of Latter-day Saint Men*. Salt Lake City: Deseret Book, 2011.

Heidler, David S. and Jeanne T. Heidler, eds. *Encyclopedia of the American Civil War: A Political, Social, and Military History*. New York: W. W. Norton, 2000.

Hess, Earl J. *Liberty, Virtue, and Progress: Northerners and Their War for the Union*, 2nd ed. New York: Fordham University Press, 1997.

———. *The Union Soldier in Battle: Enduring the Ordeal of Combat*. Lawrence: University Press of Kansas, 1997.

Hilton, Hope A. *"Wild Bill" Hickman and the Mormon Frontier*. Salt Lake City: Signature Books, 1988.

Hinckley, Bryant S. *Daniel Hamner Wells and Events of His Time*. Salt Lake City: Deseret News Press, 1942.

History of the Union Pacific Railroad. Ogden, UT: Union Pacific Railroad, 1919.

Horton J. H. and S. Teverbaugh. *A History of the Eleventh Regiment (Ohio Volunteer Infantry)*. Dayton, OH: W. J. Shuey, 1866.

Howe, Daniel Walker. *The Transformation of America, 1815–1848*. New York: Oxford University Press, 2007.

Hunt, Aurora. *The Army of the Pacific: Its Operations in California, Texas, Arizona, New Mexico, Utah, Nevada, Oregon, Washington, Plains Region, Mexico, etc. 1860–1866*. Glendale, CA: Arthur H. Clark, 1951.

Jensen, Robin Scott, Robert J. Woodford, and Seven C. Harper, eds., *Manuscript Revelation Books*, facsimile edition, first volume of the Revelations and Translations series of *The Joseph Smith Papers*, edited by Dean C. Jessee, Ronald K. Esplin, and Richard Lyman Bushman. Salt Lake City: Church Historian's Press, 2008.

Jackson, Hester Bartlett. *Surry County Soldiers in the Civil War*. Surry, VA: Surry County Historical Society, 1992.

Jenson, Andrew. *Church Chronology: A Record of Important Events*. Salt Lake City: Deseret News, 1899–1914.

———. *History of the Scandinavian Mission*. Salt Lake City: Deseret News, 1927.

———. *LDS Biographical Encyclopedia*. Salt Lake City: Deseret Book, 1936.

Jessee, Dean C., ed. *Letters of Brigham Young to His Sons*. Salt Lake City: Deseret Book, 1974.

———, ed. *Personal Writings of Joseph Smith*. Salt Lake City: Deseret Book, 2002.

Jessee, Dean C., Mark Ashurst-McGee, and Richard L. Jensen, eds. *Journals, Volume 1: 1832–1839*, vol. 1 of the Journals series of *The Joseph Smith Papers*, edited by Dean C. Jessee, Ronald K. Esplin, and Richard Lyman Bushman. Salt Lake City: Church Historian's Press, 2008.

Jimerson, Randall C. *The Private Civil War: Popular Thought during the Sectional Conflict*. Baton Rouge: Louisiana State University Press, 1988.

Johannsen, Robert W. *Stephen A. Douglas*. New York: Oxford University Press, 1973.

Johnson, Alan P. *Aaron Johnson: Faithful Steward*. Salt Lake City: Publishers Press, 1991.

Johnston, William Preston. *The Life of Gen. Albert Sidney Johnston, Embracing His Services in the Armies of the United States, the Republic of Texas, and the Confederate States*. 1878; repr., Austin: State House Press, 1997.

Josephy, Alvin M., Jr. *The Civil War in the American West*. New York: Alfred A. Knopf, 1991.

Journal of Discourses. London: Latter-day Saints' Book Depot, 1854–86.

Journal of the 43d National Encampment of the Grand Army of the Republic at Salt Lake City, Utah, August 12th–13th. n.p.: Grand Army of the Republic, 1909.

Journal of the Forty-Fifth National Encampment Grand Army of the Republic. Boston: Griffith-Stillings, 1911.

Journal of the Forty-First National Encampment of the Grand Army of the Republic. Zanesville, OH: Courier, 1907.

Journal of the Forty-Second National Encampment of the Grand Army of the Republic, at Toledo, Ohio. Kansas City, MO: John C. Bovard, n.d.

Journal of the Twenty-first Annual Session of the National Encampment Grand Army of the Republic. Milwaukee: Burdick & Armitage, 1887.

Journal of the Twenty-third Annual Session of the National Encampment Grand Army of the Republic. St. Louis: A. Whipple, 1889.

Kenney, Scott G., ed. *Wilford Woodruff's Journal, 1833–1898*, 9 vols. Midvale, UT: Signature Books, 1983–84.

Kimball, Stanley B. *Historic Sites and Markers along the Mormon and Other Great Western Trails*. Urbana and Chicago: University of Illinois Press, 1988.

———, ed. *On the Potter's Wheel: The Diaries of Heber C. Kimball*. Salt Lake City: Signature Books, 1987.

La Jara Stake of The Church of Jesus Christ of Latter-day Saints. *The Mormons: 100 Years in the San Luis Valley of Colorado, 1883-1983*. La Jara, CO: n.p., 1982.

Larson, Gustive O. *The "Americanization" of Utah for Statehood*. San Marino, CA: Huntington Library, 1971.

Lass, William E. *From the Missouri to the Great Salt Lake: An Account of Overland Freighting*. n.p.: Nebraska State Historical Society, 1972.

Leslie, Edward E. *The Devil Knows How to Ride: The True Story of William Clarke Quantrill and His Confederate Raiders*. New York: Random House, 1996.

Linn, William Alexander. *The Story of the Mormons from the Date of Their Origin to the Year 1901*. New York: Macmillan, 1902.

Logan, Mary Simmerson Cunningham. *Reminiscences of a Soldier's Wife*. New York: Charles Scribner's Sons, 1913.

Long, E. B. *The Saints and the Union: Utah Territory during the Civil War*. Urbana: University of Illinois Press, 1981.

Lowrey, James Marvin. *Samuel Wragg Ferguson: Brig. General, CSA, and Wife Catherine Lee, Featuring Selections from Their Writings*. Sulphur, LA: n.p., 1994.

MacKinnon, William P., ed. *At Sword's Point, Part 1: A Documentary History of the Utah War to 1858*. Norman, OK: Arthur H. Clark, 2008.

Madsen, Brigham D. *Glory Hunter: A Biography of Patrick Edward Connor*. Salt Lake City: University of Utah Press, 1990.

———. *The Northern Shoshoni*. Caldwell, ID: Caxton Printers, 1980.

———. *The Shoshoni Frontier and the Bear River Massacre*. Salt Lake City: University of Utah Press, 1985.

Manning, Chandra. *What this Cruel War Was Over: Soldiers, Slavery, and the Civil War*. New York: Alfred A. Knopf, 2007.

Marcy, Randolph B. *Thirty Years of Army Life on the Border*. New York: Harper & Brothers, 1866.

Mason, Patrick Q. *The Mormon Menace: Violence and Anti-Mormonism in the Postbellum South*. New York: Oxford University Press, 2011.

Maxwell, John Gary. *Gettysburg to Great Salt Lake: George R. Maxwell, Civil War Hero and Federal Marshal among the Mormons*. Norman, OK: Arthur H. Clark, 2010.

McConnell, Stuart. *Glorious Contentment*. Charlotte: University of North Carolina Press, 1997.

McGill, James W. *Rediscovered Frontiersman: Timothy Goodale*. Independence, MO: OCTA, 2009.

McGinnis, Ralph Y. and Calvin N. Smith, eds. *Abraham Lincoln and the Western Territories*. Chicago: Nelson-Hall, 1994.

McGregor, Alma Gertrude Watson. *Lorenzo Dow Watson*. Provo, UT: J. Grant Stevenson, 1970.

McPherson, James M. *Battle Cry of Freedom: The Civil War Era*. New York: Oxford University Press, 1988.

———. *For Cause and Comrades: Why Men Fought in the Civil War*. New York: Oxford University Press, 1997.

Memmott, H. Kirk, ed. *Thomas Memmott Journal*. Provo, UT: J. Grant Stevenson, 1976.

Miers, Earl Schenck, ed. *Lincoln Day by Day: A Chronology*, 3 vols. Washington, DC: Lincoln Sesquicentennial Commission, 1960.

Miller, Francis Trevelyan and Robert Sampson Lanie ed., *The Photographic History of the Civil War*, 10 vols. New York: Review of Reviews, 1911.

Millet, Alan R. and Peter Maslowski. *For the Common Defense: A Military History of the United States of America*. New York: Free Press, 1994.

Millet, Robert L. and Kent P. Jackson, ed. *Studies in Scripture, Vol. 1: The Doctrine and Covenants*. Sandy, UT: Randall Book, 1984.

Mitchell, Reid. *Civil War Soldiers*. New York: Penguin, 1988.

———. *The Vacant Chair: The Northern Soldier Leaves Home*. New York: Oxford University Press, 1993.

Monk, Linda R. *The Words We Live By: Your Annotated Guide to the Constitution*. New York: Hyperion, 2003.

Moorhead, James H. *American Apocalypse: Yankee Protestants and the Civil War, 1860–1869*. New Haven: Yale University Press, 1978.

Mumey, Nolie. *The Life of Jim Baker, 1818–1898: Trapper, Scout, Guide and Indian Fighter*. Denver, CO: World Press, 1931.

Nettels, Curtis P. *A History of the Overland Mail*. Madison: University of Wisconsin, 1922.

Nibley, Preston. *Brigham Young: The Man and His Work*. Salt Lake City: Deseret Book, 1936.

Nicolay, John G. and John Hay. *Abraham Lincoln: A History*. New York: Century, 1914.

Noll, Mark A. *The Civil War as a Theological Crisis*. Chapel Hill: University of North Carolina Press, 2006.

North, Mary M. *Patriotic Selections for Memorial Day, Flag Day and other Patriotic Anniversaries: Woman's Relief Corps*. Boston: Griffith-Stillings, 1909.

Orton, Richard H., ed. *Records of California Men in the War of Rebellion: 1861–1867*. Sacramento: State Office, 1890.

Pace, William B. *Rifle and Light Infantry Tactics*. Salt Lake City: Deseret News Print, 1865.

Palmquist, Peter E. and Thomas R. Kailbourn, *Pioneer Photographers of the Far West: A Biographical Dictionary, 1840–1865*. Stanford, CA: Stanford University Press, 2000.

Perret, Geoffrey. *Lincoln's War: The Untold Story of America's Greatest President and Commander in Chief*. New York: Random House, 2004.

Peterson, H. Donl. *The Pearl of Great Price: A History and Commentary*. Salt Lake City: Deseret Book, 1987.

Peterson, John Alton. *Utah's Black Hawk War*. Salt Lake City: University of Utah Press, 1998.

Pinnegar, Charles. *Brand of Infamy: A Biography of John Buchanan Floyd*. Westport, CT: Greenwood, 2002.

Powell, Allan Kent, ed. *Utah History Encyclopedia*. Salt Lake City: University of Utah Press, 1994.

Proceedings of the First to Tenth Meetings 1866–1876 (Inclusive) of the National Encampment Grand Army of the Republic with Digest of Decisions, Rules of Order and Index. Philadephia: Samuel P. Town, 1877.

Proceedings of the Twenty-eighth and Twenty-ninth Annual Encampment, Department of Utah. Salt Lake City: Grand Army of the Republic, 1911.

Pyper, George D. *The Romance of an Old Playhouse*. Salt Lake City: Seagull, 1928.

Randall, J. G. and David Donald. *The Civil War and Reconstruction*. Boston: D. C. Heath, 1961.

Ransom, Roger L. *Conflict and Compromise: The Political Economy of Slavery, Emancipation, and the American Civil War*. Cambridge: Cambridge University Press, 1989.

Reeve, W. Paul and Ardis E. Parshall, eds. *Mormonism: A Historical Encyclopedia*. Santa Barbara, CA: ABC-Clio, 2010.

Richardson, Arthur M. *The Life and Ministry of John Morgan*. n.p.: Nicholas G. Morgan Sr., 1965.

Ripley, George ed. *The New American Cyclopædia: A Popular Dictionary of General Knowledge*. New York: D. Appleton and Company, 1863.

Ritual of the Grand Army of the Republic. Zanesville, OH: n.p., 1907.

Roberts, B. H. *A Comprehensive History of the Church of Jesus Christ of Latter-day Saints*. Salt Lake City: Deseret News, 1930.

———, ed. *History of the Church of Jesus Christ of Latter-day Saints*, 2nd ed. rev. Salt Lake City: Deseret Book, 1978.

Roberts, Richard C. *Legacy: The History of the Utah National Guard*. Salt Lake City: National Guard Association of Utah, 2003.

Robertson, James I., Jr. *Soldier's Blue and Gray*. Columbia: University of South Carolina Press, 1998.

Robinson, Stephen E. and H. Dean Garrett. *A Commentary on the Doctrine and Covenants*. Salt Lake City: Deseret Book, 2004.

Rogers, Fred B. *Soldiers of the Overland*. San Francisco: Grabhorn, 1938.

Roland, Charles P. *Albert Sidney Johnston: Soldier of Three Republics*, rev. ed. Lexington: University Press of Kentucky, 2001.

———. *Jefferson Davis's Greatest General: Albert Sidney Johnston*. College Station: Texas A&M Press Consortium, 2000.

Rubenstein, Harry R. *Abraham Lincoln: An Extraordinary Life*. Washington, DC: Smithsonian Books, 2008.

Rules and Regulations for the Government of the Woman's Relief Corps, Auxiliary to the Grand Army of the Republic. Boston: Griffith-Stillings Press, 1916.

Rules and Regulations of the Ladies of the Grand Army of the Republic. Scranton, PA: Reeser Bros., 1909.

Schindler, Harold. *Orrin Porter Rockwell: Man of God, Son of Thunder*, rev. ed. Salt Lake City: University of Utah Press, 1983.

Scott, Sean A. *A Visitation of God: Northern Civilians Interpret the Civil War*. New York: Oxford University Press, 2011.

Seegmiller, Janet Burton. *"Be Kind to the Poor": The Life Story of Robert Taylor Burton*. n.p.: Burton Family Organization, 1988.

Sketches of War History. Columbus, OH: Military Order of the Loyal Legion of the United States, 1893.

Smith, Andrew F. *The Saintly Scoundrel: The Life and Times of Dr. John Cook Bennett*. Urbana: University of Illinois Press, 1997.

Smith, George D., ed. *An Intimate Chronicle: The Journals of William Clayton*. Salt Lake City: Signature Books, 1995.

Smith, Hyrum M. and Janne M. Sjodahl. *Doctrine and Covenants Commentary*. Salt Lake City: Deseret Book, 1967.

Smith, Joseph Fielding, comp. *Life of Joseph F. Smith, Sixth President of the Church of Jesus Christ of Latter-day Saints*. Salt Lake City: Deseret News, 1938.

Sonne, Conway B. *Ships, Saints, and Mariners: A Maritime Encyclopedia of Mormon Migration, 1830–1890*. Salt Lake City: University of Utah Press, 1987.

Standifird, John Henry. *Life and Journals of John Henry Standifird 1831–1924*. Provo, UT: BYU Press, 1979.

Stanwood, Edward. *A History of the Presidency*, 2 vols. Boston and New York: Houghton Mifflin, 1904.

Starr, John William, Jr. and others. *Lincoln & the Railroads*. New York: Ayer Printing, 1981.

Stenhouse, T. B. H. *The Rocky Mountain Saints*. London: Ward, Lock, and Tyler, 1874.

Stone, Tanya Lee. *Abraham Lincoln*. New York: DK Publishing, 2005.

Stuy, Brian H., ed. *Collected Discourses Delivered by President Wilford Woodruff, His Two Counselors, the Twelve Apostles, and Others*. Burbank, CA: BHS, 1991.

Townsend, George A. *The Mormon Trials at Salt Lake City*. New York: American News, 1871.

Tullidge, Edward W. *The History of Salt Lake City and Its Founders*. Salt Lake City: privately published, 1886.

———. *History of Salt Lake City: by Authority of the City Council and under the Supervision of a Committee Appointed by the Council and Author*. Salt Lake City: Star Printing, 1886.

———. *Life of Brigham Young; or, Utah and Her Founders*. New York: n.p., 1877.

———. *Tullidge's Histories*, 2 vols. Salt Lake City: Juvenile Instructor, 1889.

Twenty-Sixth and Twenty-Seventh Annual Encampments, Grand Army of the Republic, Department of Utah. Salt Lake City: Grand Army of the Republic, 1909.

2012 Church Almanac. Salt Lake City: Deseret News, 2012.

Tyler, Sergeant Daniel. *A Concise History of the Mormon Battalion in the Mexican War 1846–1847*. Glorieta, New Mexico: Rio Grande, 1969.

Tyson, Isaac C., comp., *Canteen and Haversack of the Grand Army of the Republic, the Largest and Most Complete Collection of Choice Recitations, Readings and Veteran War Songs, also Statistics, Records, Historical Events, etc. etc.*. Vol. 1, nos. 19 and 20. n.p.: n.p., 1893.

Underwood, Grant. *The Millenarian World of Early Mormonism*. Urbana: University of Illinois Press, 1993.

Urwin, Gregory J. W. *The United States Infantry: An Illustrated History, 1775–1918*. New York: Sterling, 1991.

Utley, Robert M. *Frontiersmen in Blue: The United States Army and the Indian, 1848–1865*. New York: Macmillan, 1967.

Van Wagoner, Richard S., ed. *The Complete Discourses of Brigham Young*. Vol. 4. Salt Lake City: Smith-Pettit Foundation, 2009.

Varley, James F. *Brigham and the Brigadier: General Patrick Connor and His California Volunteers in Utah and along the Overland Trail*. Tucson, AZ: Western Lore, 1989.

Vetterli, Richard. *Mormonism, Americanism and Politics*. Salt Lake City: Ensign, 1961.

Vinovskis, Maris A. *Toward a Social History of the American Civil War: Exploratory Essays*. New York: Cambridge University Press, 1990.

Waite, C. V. *The Mormon Prophet and His Harem; or, an Authentic History of Brigham Young, His Numerous Wives and Children*. Chicago: J. S. Goodman, 1868.

Walker, John P., ed. *Dale Morgan and Early Mormonism: Correspondence and a New History*. Salt Lake City: Signature Books, 1986.

Walker, Ronald W. *Wayward Saints: The Godbeites and Brigham Young*. Champaign: University of Illinois Press, 1998.

Walker, Ronald W., Richard E. Turley Jr., and Glen M. Leonard. *Massacre at Mountain Meadows*. Oxford, New York: Oxford University Press, 2008.

Ward, William H. *Records of Members of the Grand Army of the Republic*. San Francisco: H.S. Crocker , 1886.

Weigley, Russell F. *The American Way of War: A History of the United States Strategy and Policy*. Bloomington: University of Indiana Press, 1973.

Wells, James M. *"With Touch of Elbow," or, Death Before Dishonor: A Thrilling Narrative of Adventure on Land and Sea*. Philadelphia: John C. Winston, 1909.

Wert, Jeffry D. *The Sword of Lincoln: The Army of the Potomac*. New York: Simon and Schuster, 2005.

White, Owen P. *Out of the Desert: A Historical Romance of El Paso*. El Paso, TX: McMath, 1923.

Whitney, Orson F. *History of Utah*. Salt Lake City: George Q. Cannon, 1892–1904.

———. *Popular History of Utah*, 4 vols. Salt Lake City: Deseret News, 1916.

Williams, T. Harry. *Lincoln and His Generals*. New York: Knopf, 1952.

Wiley, Bell Irvin. *The Life of Billy Yank: The Common Soldier of the Union*. Baton Rouge: Louisiana State University Press, 1971.

———. *The Life of Johnny Reb: The Common Soldier of the Confederacy*. Indianapolis: Bobbs-Merrill, 1943.

Wilford Woodruff's Journal: 1833–1898. Typescript. 9 vols. Salt Lake City: Signature Books, 1983–85.

Wilson, James Grant and John Fiske, eds. *Appletons' Cyclopædia of American Biography*. New York: D. Appleton, 1887.

Wilson, Oliver Morris. *The Grand Army of the Republic under Its First Constitution and Ritual*. Kansas City, MO: Franklin Hudson, 1905.

Wilson, R. Michael. *Legal Executions in the Western Territories, 1847–1911*. Jefferson, NC: McFarland, 2010.

Winik, Jay. *April 1865, The Month That Saved America*. New York: HarperCollins, 2001.

JOURNALS AND PERIODICALS

Agnew, James B. "General Barnard Bee." *Civil War Times Illustrated* 14 (December 1975): 4–9, 45–47.

Alexander, Thomas G. and Leonard J. Arrington, "Camp in the Sagebrush: Camp Floyd, Utah, 1858–1861." *Utah Historical Quarterly* 34 (1966): 3–22.

Alford, Kenneth L. "Utah and the Civil War Press." *Utah Historical Quarterly* 80, no. 1 (2012): 73–90.

Arrington, Leonard J. "Willard Young: The Prophet's Son at West Point." *Dialogue: A Journal of Mormon Thought* 4 (Winter 1969): 37–46.

Auchampaugh, Philip G. "John B. Floyd and James Buchanan." *Tyler's Quarterly Historical and Genealogical Magazine* 4 (April 1923): 381–88.

Barnes, John P. "The Struggle to Control the Past: Commemoration, Memory, and the Bear River Massacre of 1863." *Public Historian* 30 (February 2008): 81–104.

Belohlavek, John M. "The Politics of Scandal: A Reassessment of John B. Floyd as Secretary of War, 1857–1861." *West Virginia History* 31 (April 1970): 145–60.

Bennett, Richard E. "'We Know No North, No South, No East, No West': Mormon Interpretations of the Civil War, 1861–65." *Mormon Historical Studies* 10, no. 1 (2009): 51–63.

"The Best Policy for the Saints to Pursue." *Millennial Star*. May 17, 1862, 312–14.

Bigler, David L., "The Aiken Party Executions and the Utah War, 1857–1858," *Western Historical Quarterly* 38, no. 4 (Winter 2007): 457–76.

"Blessings to be Obtained by Gathering." *Millennial Star*. October 4, 1862, 633–35.

Bray, Robert. "What Abraham Lincoln Read: An Evaluative and Annotated List." *Journal of the Abraham Lincoln Association* 28, no. 2 (Summer 2007): 28–81.

Bullough, Vern L. "Polygamy: An Issue in the Election of 1860?," *Utah Historical Quarterly* 29 (April 1961): 119–26.

Bush, Lester E., Jr. "Brigham Young in Life and Death: A Medical Overview." *Journal of Mormon History* 5 (1978): 79–103.

"Captain Lot Smith's Company of Volunteers." *The Utah Genealogical and Historical Magazine*, January 1911, 138–39.

Carroll, Murray L. "Robert Foote: A Forgotten Wyoming Pioneer." *Annals of Wyoming* 74 (Winter 2002): 9–23.

Clarke, Henry S. "W. C. Quantrill in 1858." *Kansas Historical Collections* 7 (1901–2): 218–23.

"Close of the Emigration Season." *Millennial Star*, June 20, 1863, 392.

Cook, Lyndon W. "James Arlington Bennet and the Mormons." *BYU Studies* 19 (Winter 1979): 244–49.

"Correspondence." E. L. Sloan to George Q. Cannon, December 14, 1863. *Millennial Star*, February 20, 1864, 122.

"Correspondence." M. G. Atwood and others to President Wells, June 15, 1865. *Millennial Star*, July 15, 1865, 443.

"Correspondence." N. V. Jones and Jacob Gates to George Q. Cannon, February 8, 1861. *Millennial Star*, March 23, 1861.

"Correspondence." Orson Pratt to George Q. Cannon, May 24, 1861, *Millennial Star*, June 15, 1861, 395.

"Correspondence." Thomas Evans Jeremy to George Q. Cannon, July 2, 1864. *Millennial Star*, August 13, 1864, 524.

"Correspondence." W. A. Martindale to George Q. Cannon. *Millennial Star*, April 13, 1861, 238–39.

"Correspondence." William Clayton to George Q. Cannon, February 20, 1862. *Millennial Star*, April 26, 1862, 270.

"Correspondence." William H. Hooper to George Q. Cannon, December 16, 1860, *Millennial Star,* July 27, 1861.

Crouch, Barry A. "A 'Fiend in Human Shape'? William Clarke Quantrill and His Biographers." *Kansas History* 22 (Summer 1999): 143–56.

Dale, Edward E. "Some Letters of General Stand Watie." *Chronicles of Oklahoma*. Vol. 1, no. 1 (January 1921), 30–59.

"The Dark Day of the United States." *Millennial Star*, January 28, 1860, 52–53.

"Departure." *Millennial Star*, February 25, 1865, 124.

"Departure." *Millennial Star*, May 7, 1864, 298.

"Departure." *Millennial Star*, June 18, 1864, 395.

"Departures." *Millennial Star*, February 2, 1861.

"Division of the United States—Causes Which Have Hastened It." *Millennial Star*, February 16, 1861, 100–101.

Ellis, Charles (Mrs.) "Robert Foote." *Annals of Wyoming* 15:150–62.

"Emancipation of the Slaves—The Prophet Joseph Smith's Plan—Results of its Rejection." *Millennial Star* 25, no. 7 (February 14, 1863): 101.

"Emigration." *Millennial Star,* January 5 and 19, 1861.

"Emigration." *Millennial Star*, January 21, 1865, 40–41.

"Emigration." *Millennial Star*, July 25, 1863, 476.

"Emigration and the Motives Which Prompt It." *Millennial Star*, January 23, 1864, 58.

"Emigration and the Temple." *Millennial Star*, September 17, 1864, 600–602.

"Emigration Deposits, Etc." *Millennial Star*, March 13, 1864, 168–69.

"The Emigration of the Scandinavian Saints." *Millennial Star*, April 30, 1864, 282.

"Emigration—Prosperity of the Past Season—Counsel for the Future." *Millennial Star*, August 29, 1863, 552.

Esplin, Ronald K. "'A Place Prepared': Joseph, Brigham and the Quest for Promised Refuge in the West." *Journal of Mormon History* 9 (1982): 85–111.

Evans, David. "Personal Testimony." *Improvement Era*, June 1910.

Ferguson, Samuel W. "With Albert Sidney Johnston's Expedition to Utah, 1857." *Collections of the Kansas State History Society* 12 (1912): 303–12.

Garrett, M. Dean. "The Controversial Death of Gobo Fango." *Utah Historical Quarterly* 57 (Summer 1989), 264–72.

Gaylor, George R. "The Mormons and Politics in Illinois: 1839–1844." *Journal of the Illinois State Historical Society* 59 (Spring 1956): 28–66.

Gilbert, Benjamin F. "The Mythical Johnston Conspiracy." *California Historical Society Quarterly* 28 (June 1949): 165–73.

Gray, John S. "Fact Versus Fiction in the Kansas Boyhood of Buffalo Bill." *Kansas History* 8 (Spring 1985): 2–20.

Hansen, H. N. "An Account of a Mormon Family's Conversion to the Religion of the Latter-day Saints and their Trip from Denmark to Utah," *Annals of Iowa* 41, no. 1 (Summer 1971): 709–28.

Hansen, Lorin K. "Voyage of the Brooklyn." *Dialogue: A Journal of Mormon Thought* 21, no. 3 (Fall 1988): 47–72.

Hartley, William G. "Brigham Young's Overland Trails Revolution: The Creation of the 'Down-and-Back' Wagon Train System, 1860–61." *Journal of Mormon History* 28, no. 1 (2002): 1–30.

———. "The Confederate Officer and 'That Mormon Girl.'" *Ensign*, April 1982, 52.

———. "The Great Florence Fitout of 1861." *BYU Studies* 24 (Summer 1984), 341–71.

———. "Down-and-Back Wagon Trains: Travelers on the Mormon Trail in 1861." *Overland Journal* 11, no. 4 (1993): 23–34.

Heaton, John W. "No Place to Pitch their Tepees: Shoshone Adaptation to Mormon Settlers in Cache Valley." *Utah Historical Quarterly* 63 (1995): 158–71.

"Hiram B. Clawson." *Tullidge's Quarterly Magazine* 1 (July 1881): 678–84.

"History of Joseph Smith." *Millennial Star*, July 3, 1852, 296.

Holland, Matthew S. "With Charity for All." *Clark Memorandum* (Fall 2008): 18–26.

"How Many Elders Shall Be Released to Go to Zion." *Millennial Star*. March 8, 1862, 155.

Howard, G. M. "Men, Motive, and Misunderstandings: A New Look at the Morrisite War of 1862." *Utah Historical Quarterly*, 44 (1976): 112–32.

Hubbard, George U. "Abraham Lincoln as Seen by the Mormons." *Utah Historical Quarterly* 31, no. 2 (Spring 1963): 91–108.

Hulmston, John K. "Mormon Immigration in the 1860s: The Story of the Church Team Trains." *Utah Historical Quarterly* 58 (Winter 1990): 32–48.

"Instruction to the Saints Throughout the European Mission." *Millennial Star*, November 24, 1860, 744.

"The Intending Emigrants—Seasonable Advice." *Millennial Star*, January 10, 1863, 25.

Jackson, W. Turrentine. "Administration of Governor Thomas Moonlight." *Annals of Wyoming* 18 (1946): 139–62.

Jenson, Andrew. "Latter-day Saint Emigration from Wyoming, Nebraska–1864–1866." *Nebraska History Magazine* 17 (April–June 1936): 113–27.

Kimball, Stanley B. "A Forgotten Trail and Mormon Settlements." *Ensign*, February 1980: 33–35.

———. "Another Route to Zion: Rediscovering the Overland Trail." *Ensign*, June 1984, 34–45.

———. "Sail and Rail Pioneers before 1869." *BYU Studies* 35, no. 2 (1995): 6–42.

Larson, Gustive O. "Utah and the Civil War." *Utah Historical Quarterly* 33, no. 1 (Winter 1965): 55–77.

MacKinnon, William P. "125 Years of Conspiracy Theories: Origins of the Utah Expedition of 1857–58." *Utah Historical Quarterly* 52 (Summer 1984): 212–30.

———. "Albert Gallatin Browne Jr., Brief Life of an Early War Correspondent: 1832–1891." *Harvard Magazine* 111 (November/December 2008): 48–49.

———. "Buchanan's Thrust from the Pacific: The Utah War's Ill-Fated Second Front." *Utah Historical Quarterly* 34 (Fall 2008): 226–60.

———. "Epilogue to the Utah War: Impact and Legacy." Journal of Mormon History 29, no. 2 (2003): 186–248.

———. "'Lonely Bones': Leadership and Utah War Violence." *Journal of Mormon History* 33 (Spring 2007): 121–78.

———. "Review Essay." *New Mexico Historical Review* 76 (October 2001): 431–37.

———. "Sex, Subalterns, and Steptoe: Army Behavior, Mormon Rage, and Utah War Anxieties." *Utah Historical Quarter* 76 (Summer 2008): 227–46.

———. "'Who's in Charge Here?': Utah Expedition Command Ambiguity." *Dialogue: A Journal of Mormon Thought* 42 (Spring 2009): 30–64.

Mason, Patrick Q. "Opposition to Polygamy in the Postbellum South." *The Journal of Southern History* 76, no. 3 (August 2010): 541–78.

McKinney, Francis F. "The Last Act at Gettysburg, The Death of Farnsworth." *Quarterly Review of the Michigan Alumnus* 65 (Autumn 1959): 75–79.

McKnight, J. "New from America." *Millennial Star*, October 26, 1861, 693.

Metcalf, Brandon J. "The Nauvoo Legion and the Prevention of the Utah War." *Utah Historical Quarterly* 72 (2004): 300–321.

Moehring, Eugene. "The Civil War and Town Founding in the Intermountain West." *Western Historical Quarterly* (Autumn 1997): 316–41.

Monson, Thomas S. "Pathways to Perfection." *Ensign*, May 2002, 99.

———. "The Priesthood in Action." *Ensign*, November 1992, 48.

Morgan, Wanda. "The Pony Express Rider and the President." *Signal Mountain* 1 (Fall 1998): 4–9.

Morris, Emma Ramsey. "What the Grand Army of the Republic Means to Us." *Young Woman's Journal*, August 1909, 369–74.

"National Crimes and Their Consequences." *Millennial Star* 25, September 12, 1863, 580.

"New from America." J. McKnight, letter, September 22, 1861. *Millennial Star*. October 26, 1861, 693.

News Department. "Journal of Indian Treaty Days." *Washington Historical Quarterly* 11, no. 1 (January 1920): 75–76.

"News from Home." *Millennial Star*, November 8, 1862, 714.

"News from the United States." *Millennial Star*, April 6, 1861, 219.

"Passing Events." *Improvement Era*, April 1924.

"The Past Season's Emigration–Potency of Faith and Prayer." *Millennial Star*, October 31, 1863, 696.

Peterson, Charles S. "'A Mighty Man Was Brother Lot': A Portrait of Lot Smith, Mormon Frontiersman." *Western Historical Quarterly* 1 (October 1970): 393–414.

Phipps, Kelly Elizabeth. "Marriage and Redemption: Mormon Polygamy in the Congressional Imagination, 1862–1887." *Virginia Law Review* 95, no. 2 (April 2009): 441–51.

Pinney, Marie. "Charles Becker, Pony Express Rider and Oregon Pioneer." *Oregon Historical Quarterly* 67 (September 1966): 213–56.

Poll, Richard D. and William P. MacKinnon. "Causes of the Utah War Reconsidered." *Journal of Mormon History* 20 (Fall 1994): 16–44.

Read, B. M. "Ben Ficklin, 1849, and the Pony Express." *Virginia Military Institute Alumni Review* 50 (Summer 1973): 13–14.

Roberts, Brigham H. "History of the Mormon Church: Chapter CXIX." *Americana (American Historical Magazine)*, May 1915, 433.

Robinson, John C. "The Utah Expedition." *Magazine of American History* 11 (January–June 1884): 335–41.

Robrock, David P. "The Eleventh Ohio Volunteer Cavalry on the Central Plains, 1862–1866." *Arizona and the West* 25 (Spring 1983): 23–48.

Rosenberger, Homer T. "Two Monuments for the Fifteenth President of the United States." *Journal of the Lancaster County Historical Society* 78 (1974): 29–48.

Schindler, Harold S. "The Bear River Massacre: New Historical Evidence." *Utah Historical Quarterly* 67 (Fall 1999): 300–308.

Seifrit, William C. "Charles Henry Wilcken: An Undervalued Saint." *Utah Historical Quarterly* 55 (Fall 1987), 308–21.

Shearman, William H., and others. "Letter." *Millennial Star*, July 22, 1865, 461–63.

Simmonds, A. J. "'Thou and All Thy House:' Three Case Studies of Clan and Charisma in the Early Church." *Nauvoo Journal* 7, no. 1 (1995): 48–55.

Smith, Craig S. "Wyoming, Nebraska Territory: Joseph W. Young and the Mormon Emigration of 1864." *BYU Studies* 39, no. 1 (2000): 30–51.

Stuy, Brian H. "Wilford Woodruff's Vision of the Signers of the Declaration of Independence." *Journal of Mormon History* 26 (Spring 2000): 64–90.

Thompson, Jerry. "When Albert Sidney Johnston Came Home to Texas: Reconstruction Politics and the Reburial of a Hero." *Southwestern Historical Quarterly* 103 (April 2000): 453–80.

"To Presidents and Emigrating Saints." *Millennial Star*, February 22, 1862.

"To the Saints and Intending Emigrants." *Millennial Star*, March 21, 1863, 184.

Vitale, Gary C. "Abraham Lincoln and the Mormons: Another Legacy of Limited Freedom." *Journal of the Illinois State Historical Society* 101 (Fall–Winter 2008): 260–271.

Waldrip, William. "New Mexico During the Civil War." *New Mexico Historical Review* 27 (1953): 163–82.

Walker, Ronald W. "Sheaves, Bucklers and the State: Mormon Leaders Respond to the Dilemmas of War." *Sunstone Review* 7 (July/August 1982): 43–56.

"What the Saints Are Capable of Doing." *Millennial Star*, June 15, 1861, 393.

"What the Saints Must Do Who Want to Emigrate." *Millennial Star*, June 8, 1861, 361.

"Why Are So Many of the Saints Not Gathered?" *Millennial Star*, October 11, 1862, 649–52.

Woods, Fred E. "East to West through North and South: Mormon Immigration to and through America during the Civil War." *BYU Studies* 39, no.1 (2000): 7–29.

Young, Richard W. "The Morrisite War." *Contributor* 11, 1890, 281.

———. "The Nauvoo Legion." *Contributor* IX, 1888, 42.

Young, Seymour B. "Lest We Forget." *Improvement Era*, March 1922, 334-38.

Youngreen, Buddy. "'Sons of the Martyrs' Nauvoo Reunion—1860," *BYU Studies* 20, no. 4 (Summer 1980): 351–370.

Zamonski, Stanley. "Border Ruffian and the Gold Nugget Race." *Wild West* 12 (April 2000): 28–34.

ONLINE RESOURCES

Ansler, Bob. "Railroads in the Civil War." www.gatewaynmra.org/articles/civil-war1.htm.

"American Civil War Soldiers Database." http://www.ancestry.com/civilwar_sub?o_xid=21837&o_lid=21837&o_sch =Search.

"AP History—1846–1900: The News Cooperative Takes Shape." *Associated Press.* http://www.ap.org/pages/about /history/history_first.html.

Bagwell, Grace. "Old Manassa Cemetery, Manassa, Conejos, Colorado." http://files.usgwarchives.net/co/conejos /cemeteries/manassa.txt.

Blake, Kellee. "'First in the Path of the Firemen': The Fate of the 1890 Population Census, Part 1." *Prologue Magazine* 28:1 (Spring 1996). http://www.archives.gov/publications/prologue/1996/spring/1890-census-1.html.

"Civil War and Later Veterans Pension Index." http://www.fold3.com/title_57/civil_war_and_later_veterans_pension _index/.

"Civil War Soldiers & Sailors System." National Park Service Civil War Registry. http://www.itd.nps.gov/cwss/.

"Company B Muster Roll, 14th Missouri State Militia Volunteer Cavalry." http://www.cwnorthandsouth.com/1862 _MR_F.html.

"Confederate Soldiers Buried in the State of Colorado." http://www.coloradoscv.org/interment/interment.htm.

U.S. Navy. "Ship Histories: Dictionary of American Naval Fighting Ships." http://www.history.navy.mil/danfs/.

"Evans, John Davis." http://evansfamilyhistory.org/index.php?option=com_content&view=article&id=79:evans-john -davis&catid=81&Itemid=131.

"Family Search." *Church of Jesus Christ of Latter-day Saints.* http://familysearch.org.

"Find a Grave." http://findagrave.com.

"Fire, water, ice destroy the 1890 Census." The Ancestry Insider. February 25, 2009. http://ancestryinsider.blogspot .com/2009/02/fire-water-ice-destroy-1890-census.html.

"1st Confederate Regiment Infantry, Bibb County, 'Brown Infantry.'" http://www.ranger95.com/civil_war/georgia/infantry/rosters/roster2/1st_confed_inf_regt_rost_1st_c.html.

"The Grand Army of the Republic and Kindred Societies." *Library of Congress*. http://www.loc.gov/rr/main/gar/garintro.html.

"Grand Army of the Republic Records Project. http://suvcw.org/.

"The General Society of the War of 1812." http://www.societyofthewarof1812.org/.

Hall, Ida-Rose Langford."Johanna Charlotte Scherlin & Hans Nadrian Chlarson." http://www.fieldinglangford.org/FamilyTree/descendants/fieldingandsarah/jamesharveylangfordsr/jamesharveylangfordjr/chlarson/chlarsonbook.pdf.

Hamer, John. "Cemetourism: William B. Smith (1811–1893)." February 8, 2011. http://bycommonconsent.com/2011/02/08/cemetourism-william-b-smith-1811%E2%80%931893/.

"Illinois Civil War Muster and Descriptive Rolls Database." http://www.cyberdriveillinois.com/departments/archives/datcivil.html.

Jarvis, Tyler. "Life Sketch of Peter Gose Litz." http://www.math.byu.edu/~jarvis/FamilyHistory/PeterGoseLitz-Bio.pdf.

"Joseph Smith Papers." *Church History Library*. http://josephsmithpapers.org.

"Journal History, October 10, 1880, 4." http://ldsarch.lib.byu.edu/CD%20Volume%202/Disc8/v135-137/seg25.htm.

"Journal History of The Church of Jesus Christ of Latter-day Saint, April 10, 1896." *Church History Library*. http://ldsarch.lib.byu.edu/CD%20Volume%202/Disc19/v322-323/seg8.htm.

Knight, Glenn B. "Brief History of the Grand Army of the Republic." http://suvcw.org/gar.htm.

"Ladies of the Grand Army of the Republic." http://suvcw.org/LGAR/index.php.

"LDS Conference Reports." *Mormon Literature Database*. http://mormonlit.byu.edu/lit_work.php?w_id=3000.

"Mormon Immigration Index." *Harold B. Lee Library*. http://lib.byu.edu/mormonmigration/.

"Mormon Pioneer Overland Travel Database." *Church History Website*. http://www.mormontrail.lds.org.

"The National Association of Veterans of the Mexican War." http://www.dmwv.org/mwvets/mexvets.htm.

"National Encampments: Bibliography." *Library of Congress*. http://www.loc.gov/rr/main/gar/national/natlist.html.

"National Park Service Civil War Registry." www.itd.nps.gov/cwss/.

National Park Service. "The Galvanized Yankees." *The Museum Gazette*, July 1992. http://www.nps.gov/jeff/historyculture/upload/galvanized_yankees.pdf.

"The National Women's Relief Corps." http://www.suvcw.org/WRC/index.htm.

"New Family Search." *The Church of Jesus Christ of Latter-day Saints*. http://new.familysearch.org.

"New York City Draft Riots." *Wikipedia*. http://en.wikipedia.org/wiki/New_York_City_draft_riots.

"New York City Draft Riots." *Shotgun's Home of the American Civil War.* www.civilwarhome.com/draftriots.htm.

"Office of Immigration Statistics, 2003 Yearbook of Immigration Statistics." http://www.dhs.gov/xlibrary/assets/statistics/yearbook/2003/2003Yearbook.pdf.

"Old Manassa Cemetery." http://files.usgwarchives.org/co/conejos/cemeteries/manassa.txt.

"Pacific Railroad Act of July 1, 1862, 12 Stat. 489, (1862)." http://cprr.org/Museum/Pacific_Railroad_Acts.html.

"Patriots of the American Revolution." http://www.patriotsar.com/.

"Pension Records." Ancestry.com. http://search.ancestry.com/cgi-bin/sse.dll?rank=0&db=dbatitles&ctx=%2fMercury%2fPages%2fCardCatListBoolean.aspx&hco=100&_F0003A49=1&o_iid=5910&o_lid=5910&o_sch=Web+Property&offerid=0%3a679%3a0&_F0003A49-int=1#ccat=hc%3D25%26dbSort%3D1%26filter%3D0*39%7C0*129%26.

"People of Ft. Douglas." http://www.fortdouglas.org/fdpeopleGentile.htm.

Peterson, Charles S. "Lot Smith." http://www.media.utah.edu/UHE/s/SMITH,LOT.html.

"The Purge of 1917." http://www.homeofheroes.com/moh/corrections/purge_army.html.

"Remembering the Grand Army of the Republic Fifty Years Later." http://suvcw.org/gar50.htm.

"Sarah Emma Edmonds." http://www.civilwar.org/education/history/biographies/sarah-emma-edmonds.html.

"A Sketch of Henry W. Jackson and Some of His Ancestors." http://www.allenbutlerhistory.com/pdf/jackson_henry -wells_history.PDF.

"Utah Digital Newspapers." http://digitalnewspapers.org/.

"Utah: The Treasure House of the Nation." *Utah Mining Association.* http://www.utahmining.org/brochure.htm.

"The Ute Indian Tribe." http://www.utetribe.com/.

"Veterans Buried in Utah Database." https://www.familysearch.org/search/collection/show#uri=http:// hr-search-api:8080/searchapi/search/collection/1542862.

Wittenberg, Eric. "A Bold and Fearless Rider: Brig. Gen. Elon J. Farnsworth." http://www.gdg.org/Research/OOB/Union /July1-3/efarnswo.html.

ADDITIONAL RESOURCES

Douglas, Stephen A. "Kansas, Utah, and the Dred Scott Decision." Address at State House, Springfield, Illinois, June 12, 1857.

Grua, David W. "Memoirs of the Persecuted: Persecution, Memory, and the West as a Mormon Refuge." Master's thesis, Brigham Young University, 2008.

Hansen, Ralph "Administrative History of the Nauvoo Legion in Utah." Master's thesis, Brigham Young University, 1954.

Higginbotham, Julina Ward (great-granddaughter of David H. Peery). Interviewed by Robert C. Freeman via telephone, June 16, 2011.

Hulmston, John K. "Transplain Migration: The Church Trains in Mormon Immigration, 1861–1868." Master's thesis, Utah State University, 1985.

Ismert, Martin E. "Quantrill–Charley Hart?" Paper presented at the Posse of the Westerners of Kansas City, October 13, 1959.

MacKinnon, William P. "The Utah War's Impact: A Military Campaign's Legacy for Both Utah and the Nation." Paper presented at the Symposium Commemorating the 140th Anniversary of Fort Douglas's Founding, October 26, 2002.

Parker, Julina Peery (great-granddaughter of David and Elizabeth Peery). Interviewed by Robert C. Freeman via telephone, June 16, 2011.

Rea, Bob. "Ben Clark: Chief of Scouts." Paper delivered at the symposium "Through the Eyes of History." Washita, OK, November 2002.

Ricks, Nathaniel R. "A Peculiar Place for the Peculiar Institution: Slavery and Sovereignty in Early Territorial Utah." Master's thesis, Brigham Young University, 2007.

"Speech of the Hon. Abram Lincoln, in Reply to Judge Douglas, Delivered in Representatives' Hall." Springfield, IL, June 26, 1857.

Stott, Robert J. "Mormonism and War: An Interpretative Analysis of Selected Mormon Thought Regarding Seven American Wars." Master's thesis, Brigham Young University, 1974.

Wimmer, Ryan E. "The Walker War Reconsidered." Master's thesis, Brigham Young University, 2010.

Woodford, Robert J. "Historical Development of the Doctrine and Covenants." PhD diss., Brigham Young University, 1974.

George Henry Thomas was appointed a major general in the regular army and received a formal "Thanks of Congress" for his success in driving Confederate forces from Tennessee in 1864. (Library of Congress)

During the Civil War, Rufus Ingalls was appointed a brevet major general in both the regular and volunteer Union forces. (Library of Congress)

P. G. T. (Pierre Gustave Toutant) Beauregard was one of only seven "full" generals in the Confederate Army. (National Archives)

William Clarke Quantrill, in Confederate uniform, was not only a notorious Civil War guerrilla but a former civilian teamster, gambler, and camp cook with the Utah Expedition. (Kansas Historical Society.)

William P. MacKinnon

ROOTED IN UTAH

CIVIL WAR STRATEGY AND TACTICS, GENERALS AND GUERRILLAS

In addition to chapter 1, another way to illustrate the connection between the Utah and Civil Wars (and the impact of the former on the latter) is to probe the extent to which three very prominent West Point–trained Civil War generals had earlier tried to influence prosecution of the Utah campaign. They did so by gratuitously sending long memos to their military superiors or, in one case, to influential politicians. These documents contained information about alternate approaches to the Great Basin accompanied by strategic recommendations for military action. All of these men—Major Generals George H. Thomas and Rufus Ingalls of the Union Army and General Pierre G. T. Beauregard of the Confederate service—were valorous veterans of the Mexican War serving as mid-level U.S. Army officers during 1857–58, but in widely differing roles and locations. Each attempted to influence the conduct of the Utah War for a variety of professional and personal reasons—a selfless desire to contribute, anti-Mormon bias, and unmistakable self-promotion. Two of the three

officers—Thomas and Ingalls—displayed some nervousness over the "irregular" nature of their communications; the more flamboyant Beauregard was unabashedly assertive.

It may be helpful to provide a brief biography for each of these three officers, though it will not do justice to their distinguished and varied service careers. General George Henry Thomas (July 31, 1816–March 28, 1870) was one of the Union army's principal commanders in the Western Theater and won Union victories across Kentucky and Tennessee. Because of his dogged, determined personality and command style his nicknames included "Slow Trot" as well as "Rock of Chickamauga." He rose to major general, notwithstanding the doubts, if not prejudice, harbored by some northern politicians about his Virginia birth. Union General Rufus Ingalls (August 23, 1818–January 15, 1893) began the Civil War as a captain and ended the war as a brevet major general; he is perhaps best remembered for his outstanding logistical skills. During the war he was quartermaster for the Army of Potomac under first McClellan and later Grant; after the war he became the army's quartermaster general. Confederate General Pierre Gustave Toutant Beauregard (May 28, 1818–February 20, 1893) was known as "The Little Napoleon." He commanded the artillery units that opened fire on Fort Sumter in April 1861 and served in important command positions in both the western and eastern theaters during the Civil War. He became one of only seven full generals in the Confederate Army, and while considered one of the keenest minds in that service, he limited his effectiveness with prickly and abrasive behavior that produced poor relations with President Jefferson Davis as well as a number of peer and subordinate generals.

None of their reports have been published and, because of space limitations, are only excerpted here. Accordingly, this appendix seeks to lay down "markers" by providing scholars with a description of this material and where to find it. Armed with these memos and hindsight, it is possible to consider the linkages between the early strategic thinking of these three officers about a complex, sprawling, multibrigade military campaign in Utah and about the campaign they would soon encounter on a more daunting scale in Tennessee and Virginia.

Turning from generals to lowlifes, this appendix then explores the notion that some of the guerrillas nominally under Confederate and Union command, if not control, also honed the most atrocious of their tactical skills during the Utah War. It does so by focusing on a single, admittedly spectacular case, that of William Clarke Quantrill (July 31, 1837–June 6, 1865), a civilian Utah Expedition teamster, gambler, and camp cook during 1857–58. Later, Quantrill was easily

the Confederacy's most notorious guerrilla as he scourged with impunity the Missouri-Kansas border and ranged from Kentucky to Texas. To him falls responsibility for leading the Civil War's worst atrocity, the August 21, 1863, raid on Lawrence, Kansas, a slaughter of 150 largely unarmed civilians even more destructive than the Mountain Meadows Massacre in Utah six years earlier.

GEORGE H. THOMAS

At the outbreak of the Utah War in the spring of 1857, Thomas was a thrice-brevetted, forty-one-year-old major serving at Fort Mason, Texas, with the Second U.S. Cavalry.[1] His was a regiment established two years earlier and led by an elite group of officers hand-picked by then Secretary of War Jefferson Davis to include Colonel Albert Sidney Johnston as its commander and Lieutenant Colonel Robert E. Lee as its executive officer. These were staffing appointments that served the Second Cavalry well when Johnston, but not his regiment, was ordered north to lead the Utah Expedition.

On July 7, 1857, Thomas wrote to Colonel Samuel Cooper, the army's adjutant general in Washington, to share his knowledge of the Colorado River acquired during a previous posting to Fort Yuma, California. Because of Colonel Cooper's proximity to Secretary of War John B. Floyd, Davis's successor, Major Thomas probably hoped that his unsolicited memo would reach Floyd and would prove useful either to the prosecution of the Utah War or to the ascent of the Colorado River about to be undertaken by army First Lieutenant Joseph C. Ives, husband of the secretary's niece. Thomas's tactic worked, and on September 2, 1857, after a delay attributable to Floyd's prolonged struggle with medical problems, the secretary sent this memo to Ives en route to the Gulf of California. At this juncture, the Ives Expedition and the Utah Expedition were separate undertakings. They became linked when word reached Washington in mid-November of Lot Smith's devastating raid on the Utah Expedition's supply trains, an upset and threat that forced the Buchanan administration to consider reinforcing Johnston from the Pacific Coast. In late November, Floyd rushed orders west to Ives reorienting his mission from an expedition of exploration and scientific discovery to one tasked with determining whether the river would facilitate the insertion of large bodies of troops and supplies into southern Utah Territory. It is difficult to believe that Major Thomas's earlier recommendations about the navigability of the Colorado River and the attitudes of adjacent tribes did not enter the discussions in Washington during the third week of November 1857 on how best to redirect Ives's expedition.[2]

MAJ. GEORGE H. THOMAS, LETTER TO COL. SAMUEL COOPER, JULY 7, 1857[3]

Whilst stationed at Fort Yuma I made repeated inquiries of the Indians living on the Colorado river above the post as to the navigability of that stream, and am of the opinion from what they have told me, and from what I could learn from other sources, that small steamers can ascend it very nearly to the point where the whites suppose the Rio Vergen [sic] empties into it.

If upon examination the Colorado proves to be navigable [up to the confluence with the Rio Virgin], it will be not only the most direct but the most convenient and safest route to convey supplies to the troops [to be] stationed in Utah Territory. Such being my belief I recommended its exploration to the Commanding Officer of the Dept of the Pacific in 1854. The Hamok-an Indians . . . say there is no stream of any size emptying into the Colorado from the west, but one which comes in from the east, about the size of the Gila, far above. This I understood, from their description of it, to be the Little Colorado. It is inhabited on its south bank by a tribe which they call Huallo-pay or pine woods people. The Huallo-pays are now at war with their neighbours on the north side of this small stream. These they call Havisoh-pays or *Blue* people, because their favorite color is blue. The Havisoh-pays are represented as being wealthy in horses, sheep & goats and have frequent intercourse with the whites.[4] Judging from this circumstance and from the similarity of sound I think the Navahoes and Havisoh-pays are the same people. When asked if they knew of the Pay-Utahs they informed me that they were the next tribe above them on the West bank of the river. If this [Indian] story be true they are well acquainted with the Colorado as far north as the Pay-Utah country, and from their account of the river I believe it will be found to be navigable to within one or two hundred miles of Salt Lake City.[5] Believing this information of some importance at this time I have taken the liberty of communicating it in this irregular manner.

RUFUS INGALLS

Rufus Ingalls spent the Utah War posted to Fort Vancouver, Washington Territory, a former Hudson's Bay Company installation on the north bank of the Columbia River (opposite Portland). He was then a once-brevetted quartermaster captain, age thirty-nine. During the fall of 1857, as the Utah War unfolded to his southeast, Ingalls heard reports that senior officers with western commands like Brevet Major General Persifor F. Smith and Brevet Brigadier General William S. Harney were offering solicited and gratuitous military advice about a move on Utah from the Pacific Coast to James Buchanan. The president was then grappling with what to say and recommend to an ill-informed Congress about prosecution of the Utah War. At the end of December 1857 Captain Ingalls seized the initiative and, without being requested to do so, sent a long memo addressing the rumored thrust against Utah from the Pacific Coast to his superior at headquarters, Department of the Pacific in San Francisco, Lieutenant Colonel Thomas Swords.

There is logic to Ingalls's initiative, for he had spent the winter of 1854–55 in the Salt Lake Valley as the Steptoe Expedition's quartermaster, and at that time had crossed the plains to Utah from Fort Leavenworth as well as traversed a new route from Salt Lake Valley to San Francisco Bay. He knew the region. What neither this record nor Ingalls's memorandum to Swords indicated, however, was that he was grinding a substantial anti-Mormon axe relating to his April 1855 indictment in Salt Lake City for attempting to abduct and impair the morals of a thirteen-year-old Mormon girl and related armed confrontation with an angry Mormon apostle.[6]

CAPT. RUFUS INGALLS, LETTER TO LT. COL. THOMAS SWORDS, DECEMBER 29, 1857[7]

Events may render it necessary to dispatch troops in the early Spring to Utah from this Military Department, and I trust you will not hold me as being too forward or officious if I enclose you descriptive lists of some of the immigrants routes from this Coast to the Great Salt Lake City as observed by us in 1855, and further give you some hints of other routes . . .

The enclosed lists will be sufficiently explanatory.[8] From them you will observe that it will be difficult to find *any* road leading from *California* to the Great Salt Lake of less than 900 or 1000 miles in length. I am of opinion that quite *all the routes* that lead from *Central* California are impracticable from the Sierra Nevada across the [Great] Basin earlier than the middle of June for a column of troops. The Humbolt River Valley, I should say, would certainly be so, and [wagon] trains cannot pass to the south of the Lake by Carson's river earlier than July, unless a route has been discovered since we were there. . . .

The [southern] route, via San Bernardino and the Mohave is by no means a short one. I do not believe it possesses rescources [sic] for animals *in any numbers*. It answers well enough for expresses &c for it is open all the year though the best season to pass over it is in February and March. San Pedro [California] is the terminus on the Coast. Were it practicable, it [the road] would answer well, for it touches the most southern Mormon settlements, where I think there are more better disposed people than nearer the chief city.[9]

Were the Colorado River already explored I think it would be found that it is navigable for small steamers to the Great Bend which is only some 25 miles from Los Vegas, a Mormon town just south of the southern rim of the Basin, and about 500 miles from Salt Lake City, over a good road. The facts, however, cannot be made known until Lt Ives has made explorations; but *in any event*, the route via the Gulf of California [and Colorado River] would be a long and expensive one, answering perhaps the wants of commerce, but no way at all for troops.[10]

[Brevet] Major [John S.] Hatheway and myself sent a train in 1849 from the Umpqua Valley, Oregon, to Fort Hall, under Lieut [George W.] Hawkins—the distances, character of country &c are not now with me but Genl [Joel] Palmer, late Superintendent of Indian Affairs here, was the guide, and in a few days will furnish me notes of the route—It is not, probably, worth attention for any purposes now under consideration.[11]

The distance from Fort Leavenworth to the Great Salt Lake City by the nearest road is over 1200 miles—If the detour by Sublette's cutt off, and Soda Springs at the Great Bend of Bear River, is made, the distance must be over 1400 miles—Soda Springs, you will observe, is near (40 Miles) to Fort Hall, and the latter place is 196 miles from Salt Lake City. This leads me, Colonel, to suggest *the* line, that probably (and for aught I know, the one already decided upon

at Head Quarters) is the *shortest, most open defensible*, and practicable earlier in spring than any other. That is the line of the Columbia River to Walla Walla—thence by Boise and the southern tributary of the Columbia—the Snake—to near Fort Hall—thence over the northern rim of the Basin (there very low) to Bear River into the settlements of Utah. Walla Walla is about 350 miles from Astoria, and *I think, not to exceed* 600 miles, by a wagon road practicable from March, or April, (dependant on the winter preceding) to Great Salt Lake City. The Hudson's Bay Company people have usually called it 600 miles from Walla Walla to Fort Hall; but they think the distance much over estimated. But I see no reason for going as far *north* and *east* as Fort Hall. I know of no obstacle in turning down on the Humbolt road where it crosses Raft, or Cache river, *though I am not personally acquainted with this country*. See descriptive list of my route.

With this point for a Deposit [Depot], and the Dalles, Walla Walla and (perhaps) Boise for Entrepots, the line would appear to be the most eligible in every point of view. By it Utah can be more *easily accessible*, and the troops there *more cheaply supplied* than from any other point.

All supplies can be put at Walla Walla *by water*, and from thence transported in ox and mule trains, probably *cheaper* than by the South Pass, and more rapidly.

In former years we had a *monthly mail* from this point to Great Salt Lake City the year round, and were it necessary communication might be had with that City from this river any month by expressmen who know the country.

For all offensive operations, I regard the entrance into the Valley of the Salt Lake by Bear river *on the north* as far the most easy and eligible in every respect. Should the Rebels attempt an escape to British or Russian America, which, by the way, I do not believe they think of, they might be cut off by a force from this quarter.[12] This force *should be a regular one,* if possible, though from the present prospect the regulars now in the Country will be required here to hold the Indians in check. If Volunteers are called upon I have no doubt a good description of men could be raised in California.

The Mormons, in my opinion, are mad and crazy with religious fanaticism. You mark if events do not show it. Brigham Young *does not see the end* [consequences] of his insensate conduct. He believes he is right and that he is going to *conquer* by aid of God, and he and his devotees will probably fight with unexampled fierceness and perseverance, unless something unforeseen shall arrest them.

It is not clear what impact, if any, Ingalls's advice eventually had on the Utah War because, unlike Major Thomas and Captain Beauregard, he communicated within the army's tortuous chain of command instead of using shortcuts to reach key decision makers. Also, at Fort Vancouver, Rufus Ingalls was located at the end of a daunting communications arrangement by which mail traveled for a month or more from the Columbia River

by steamer to San Francisco, transferred to a packet boat destined for Panama's Pacific Coast, crossed the isthmus by rail, and then resumed a long, multi-leg journey north by sea and rail to reach whichever officer Colonel Swords intended to share this memo at the war department in Washington or at either of the two seasonal headquarters that General Scott maintained in Manhattan and West Point, New York.

PIERRE G. T. BEAUREGARD

At the onset of the Utah War, Beauregard was a twice-brevetted captain of engineers, age thirty-nine. In early February of 1858, at about the time the Buchanan administration was planning to pressure Brigham Young through a major thrust from the Pacific Coast, Beauregard wrote from New Orleans to criticize this strategy. He ridiculed it as overly complex and risky. His memo commenting on the administration's plans reflected Beauregard's well-developed self-confidence, keen interest in strategy, knowledge of European military history, the strong French-Creole influence of his Louisiana plantation upbringing, and contempt for Mormon Utah leavened with a shrewd appreciation of its desperation and potential military capabilities in what was likely to become a guerrilla campaign. Also at work was probably Beauregard's boredom with his responsibility for a long-term, unglamorous army engineering effort to rescue the sinking U.S. Custom House from the instability of the local soil. He wrote to John Slidell, who was a U.S. senator from Louisiana as well as his brother-in-law and James Buchanan's 1856 presidential campaign manager. For good measure, Beauregard also sent a copy of this document to Jefferson Davis and John A.

Quitman, both of Mississippi and chair-men of the senate and house committees on military affairs, respectively. Not excerpted in Beauregard's Utah-related passages presented below are his strong comments in defense of the South and slavery as well as his view of the region as unfairly beleaguered by a grasping, oppressive North—sentiments unrelated to Mormon Utah but undoubtedly congenial to the political opinions of Slidell, Davis, and Quitman, if not Buchanan.

In so writing, Beauregard hoped to influence strategy while displaying his knowledge of the field. He also wanted to obtain appointment as a colonel commanding one of the new volunteer regiments then being contemplated by President Buchanan and Secretary Floyd for prosecution of the Utah War.

CAPT. P. G. T. BEAUREGARD, LETTER TO SEN. JOHN SLIDELL, FEBRUARY 9, 1858[13]

I see it stated in the newspapers that Genl Scott is about to repair to California to take command of a Corps d'Armée to move from thence on to Utah! I wonder if this is to be done upon the recommendation of the Genl?[14] If so, it is contrary to all "strategic" principles, if to be executed in conjunction with a similar movement on this side of the mountains—for it is impossible that two operations, from such distant initial points—should be performed with such precision & regularity as to arrive at the Utah Valley within a few days of each other—at any rate such a favorable result would be against all probabilities—It would then follow, if the Mormons are ably commanded, that they would concentrate their forces in succession against each of said columns & crush them before they could unite—in other words, do what Napoleon the Great did so beautifully in Italy in 1796 around & about Lake Guarda & the city of Verona, when he destroyed after a series of the most brilliant victories, in a few months, with an Army of only 30,000 men—two Austrian Armies of 85,000 & 60,000 men each—commanded by two of the *oldest* and best Generals of the Empire—Wurms and Alvingi![15]

How do we know but that the Mormons may have amongst themselves a great Captain *in embryo*! Are not volunteers considered *by many* as equal if not superior to regulars in a Mountainous War?—then how much the more superior would they not be, when defending their religion & their own firesides! look at the interminable war the Russians have been waging for over a quarter of a century with her best troops, against the Circassians—are they any nearer to success now than they were when they first commenced?[16] I believe not—May we not be about to commence our "Circassian War"—with even greater difficulties to contend against than the Russians have had—If I were a Mormon and amply supplied with provisions & ammunitions, I would defy ~~five~~ three times the number of troops you could send against me on the system now adopted—not one of them would ever set foot within the valley of Utah!

The first principle in war, as laid down by the Greatest Captain that ever lived, is "never to despise your enemy" the next "always to act against his main or strategic points with concentrated masses superior if possible to those he has in position there"—& then where practicable "to endeavor to cut off his lines of communication, so as to strike at his bases of operations without exposing your own."[17]

Now with regard to that Mormon war we ought first to know, what are their resources, and how many effective men they can bring into the field—let us say about 5,000—the rest acting as scouts, guarding the passes &c not being counted but still effective to recruit from or as a force in reserve, in case of reverses—then it becomes evident from what I have already stated—that if we march two *converging* forces against them thus: [diagram: a right angle with the points marked "a" "b" and "c"]—from *a* to *c* & from *b* to *c*—the Mormons occupying the central or strategic point *c*—we must *to be certain of success*, send each column of at least 7,000 men, for by the time they would get to *c*—besides being nearly exhausted by their long and fatiguing marches—they would probably be reduced to about 5,000 fighting men each—then success would very much depend upon the nature of the ground they are operating upon, the relative discipline of the opposing forces—the abilities of their commanding officers & other contingencies not necessary to mention here.—Now, as all the probabilities are that the offensive forces, would not reach the point *c* within several weeks of each other—they would necessarily

be fought in succession, & the chances are, that they would get whipped all other things being equal—for the Mormons would be fresh for the fray; & fighting for their religion and their homes, would be the more desperate; whereas, if *the best* of these two lines of operations, were selected for the offensive march—a force calculated to arrive at *c*, a little stronger in numbers & discipline than the enemy's forces, would have all the probabilities of success on its side—whether it would succeed or not would be "for the Gods to decide"—and the same object would then be effected with a great economy in treasure, men & materials.

The above are but crude ideas, roughly put down—but they are based upon the true principles of the "Art of War"—which, whenever departed from—sooner or later assert their supremacy by some disastrous calamity to the offending party.[18]—[Because of its flaws] I am glad to see that the committee's bill for the increase of the Army has been voted down.—Do Legislators believe that field officers of Regts are less necessary on a distant or prolonged campaign than company officers & men? If so,—they are much mistaken, particularly in our [American] service, where most of those field officers are weighed down with age and infirmities.[19]—In time of active service particularly, our complement of officers ought to be kept up to the full standard, and our companies to about 96 rank & file—which is the French system based upon long standing & dearly bought experience.—Is it not surprising that so much opposition should be shown in Congress to an increase of an Army, so lamentably small in comparison to the duties it is called upon to perform—when in the last few years—(since the War with Mexico) —we have added so much to its area of operations. . . .

Should the Army be increased by two or more Regts, and I succeed to be appointed the Col. of one of said Regts (the Zouaves if possible), could not the Lt Colonelcy & two majorities be conferred on ex-Capts G. W. Smith[,] George McClelland [sic] of the Engrs & ex-Lieut I. [J.] K. Duncan of the Artillery—they are all now in civil life, but have seen considerable hard service whilst in the Army—the two former served with distinction in the company of sappers & miners during the War with Mexico—the second one is the officer who was sent to Europe by the Govt lately & who has written a very interesting & instructive work containing his observations whilst there—they are all in the prime of life & of the highest intelligence & gallantry—a Regiment having such men for its field officers would soon be equal if not superior to any other in our service.[20]

"TAKE A TAP, PARD": THE UTAH EXPEDITION AS FINISHING SCHOOL FOR CIVIL WAR HARD CASES

That the federal side of the Utah War produced no known atrocities was a function more of regular army discipline and seasoned, effective military leadership than any inherent good behavior of the troops and camp followers commanded by Colonel Albert Sidney Johnston. Delana R. Eckels, Utah's chief justice, described to a U.S. senator the discharged civilian teamsters swarming about him at Fort Bridger and Camp Scott, Utah, as St. Louis "wharf rats." U.S. Army Quartermaster Stewart Van Vliet reported to Secretary of War Floyd that Brigham Young "informed me that he had no objection to the troops themselves entering the Territory; but if they allowed them to do so, it would be opening the door for the entrance of the rabble from the frontiers, who would, as in former times, persecute and annoy them"[21]

Lounging in that group was William C. Quantrill, a young Ohioan barely out of his teens, who within six years would become the most notorious guerrilla of the American Civil War—the leader of the Confederate atrocity dubbed the sack of Lawrence, Kansas. Serving with Quantrill on the Utah Expedition as teamsters were David Poole and George Sheppard, both future members of "Captain" Quantrill's guerrilla band. Poole had witnessed the October 1857 raid by Lot Smith and the Nauvoo Legion on the Utah Expedition's undefended supply trains. Sheppard was a subsequent rider with the postwar gang led by Jesse James and Cole Younger until captured and imprisoned following an unsuccessful Kentucky bank robbery. Quantrill was mortally wounded in Kentucky by a Union Army patrol in June 1865 at age 27. Until relatively recently his skull was kept in the refrigerator of an Ohio household, a fate appropriate for a man whose band rode roughshod over the Missouri-Kansas border region with human ears and scalps dangling from their horses' bridles.[22]

Ironically, among the corpses that Quantrill's band left in the smoking ruins of

Lawrence was that of Lemuel Fillmore, a local realtor who during the Utah War had served as a field reporter in Salt Lake City and Provo for the *New York Herald* until becoming embroiled in a knife fight with a rival correspondent for the *New York Times*. As a direct consequence of Quantrill's Lawrence raid came the Union Army's punitive "Order No. 11," which in the fall of 1863 ordered the depopulation of three western Missouri countries. It was a mass exodus from the border area on a scale comparable to the Utah War's Move South of March–June 1858, the largest hegira of civilian refugees since the expulsion of the Acadians and British Loyalists in connection with the French and Indian War and American Revolution.

For a glimpse of the raw, volatile behavior that Col. Johnston and his provost marshal strained to control in 1858, one should turn to a description of Quantrill in action at a Fort Bridger gambling den provided in 1907 in his old age by former cavalry private Robert M. Peck:[23]

I was a soldier in one of the two companies of 1st Cav. that formed a part of the command of Lieut. Col. Wm. Hoffman, 6th Inf., which command was sent out from Fort Leavenworth early in the spring of '58 to escort several trains— some mule teams and some of oxen— loaded with supplies for the command of Brvt. Brig. Gen. Albert Sidney Johnston, Commanding the Mormon Expedition, who had been snowed in all winter at Fort Bridger, or Camp Scott, as it was officially designated.

We arrived at Camp Scott in the first days of June. A paymaster who had followed us arrived about the same time and paid the soldiers off. As

there were few ways of spending the money outside of Judge [William A.] Carter's sutler store, where prices were outrageously high, during the few days that intervened between our arrival at Fort Bridger and the departure of Gen. Johnston's forces for Salt Lake City, gambling was rife throughout the camp, and, as usually happens, in a short time, a few sharpers had nearly all the soldiers' money.

Among the celebrities of the camp I had frequently heard the name of Charley Hart[24] mentioned, whose notoriety seemed to be derived from his reckless bettings and phenomenal winnings. I heard it stated that he had come out from Kansas with Gen. Johnston's troops the previous fall, working as a teamster in one of the six-mule trains.

While sauntering through a big gambling tent a day or so after pay-day, watching the fluctuations of fortune at the various tables where chance games were being operated, I heard some one remark, "There comes Charley Hart", and having heard his fame as a wild plunger in gambling, I took a good look at him. I could see nothing heroic in his appearance, but considerable of the rowdy, as I now recall the impression I then got of him.

He was apparently about twenty-two or twenty-three [twenty] years of age; about five feet ten inches in height; with an ungraceful, slouchy walk; and by no means prepossessing in features. He had evidently been patronizing Judge Carter's store, since he "struck it rich," for his clothes all seemed new. A pair of high-heeled calf-skin boots of small size;

bottoms of trousers tucked into boot-tops; a navy [Colt] pistol swinging from his waist belt; a fancy blue flannel shirt; no coat; a colored silk handkerchief tied loosely around his neck; yellow hair hanging nearly to the shoulders; topped out by the inevitable cow-boy hat. This is the picture of Charley Hart, as my memory presents him now.

As he entered the tent he carried in his left hand a colored silk handkerchief, gathered by the four corners, which apparently contained coin. Advancing to one of the tables where the operator, or banker, as the dealer of a chance game is usually called, was dealing "Monte", he set the handkerchief on the table and opened it out, showing the contents to be gold coins, and seemingly in bulk about equal to the stacks of gold coins tiered upon the table in front of the banker.

Hart then asked, "Take a tap, pard?" meaning would the banker accept a bet of Hart's pile against the dealer's, on the turn of a card. The banker accepted the challenge, shuffled the cards, passed the deck to Hart to cut, then threw out the "lay-out" of six cards, in a "column-of-twos" style. Hart then set his handkerchief of gold on a card, at the same time drawing his pistol, "Just to insure fair play," he remarked, seeing that the banker had his gun lying on the table convenient to his right hand. Keeping his eye on the banker's hands, to make sure that the deal was done "on the square", Hart said, "Now deal."

Turning the deck face up the banker drew the cards off successively. Hart's card won. As the dealer looked up with a muttered oath he found himself looking into the muzzle of Hart's pistol.

"Back out", said Hart quietly. "Don't even touch your pistol. I'll give it back to you when I rake in the pot."

The banker did as directed, while Hart, without showing any nervousness, still holding his pistol in one hand, reached across the table and with the other arm swept the banker's money and pistol over to him. Picking out the twenties, tens, fives and two-and-a-half pieces, he tossed them into his handkerchief. There still remained on the table about a double handful of small silver, (there were very few silver dollars in circulation then, the little one-dollar gold pieces being largely used in their stead), and a handful of gold dollars. Sweeping this small stuff into his hands, Hart said, "I don't carry such chicken feed as that," as he tossed the small coins up in the air and let the crowd scramble for them.

Then handing the dejected looking banker his pistol and a twenty-dollar gold piece, he said: "There, pard, is a stake for you," and gathering up his plethoric handkerchief, he meandered on seeking new banks to "bust."

The next day, so I was told, Hart's marvelous luck deserted him, and he lost every dollar he had; and after trying in vain to "strike it up again", he became discouraged and disgusted with gambling, joined some outfit going back to the states, and went back to Kansas dead broke.[25]

I never heard the name Quantrill used till the summer of '61, when his depredations along the borders of

Missouri and Kansas were bringing the name into unpleasant notoriety. I then heard that Quantrill, the bloody-handed guerrilla leader, and Charley Hart, the reckless gambler of Fort Bridger, were identical.

William P. MacKinnon is an independent historian in Montecito, California.

NOTES

1. To brevet an officer was to confer an additional (higher) rank in recognition of either valor in battle or service of ten years in grade. Absent a system of decorations or awards until the Civil War, brevets were used by the U.S. Army as a means of honoring such officers without permitting them to wear the insignia of their brevet rank or receive its pay unless specifically ordered to a duty that allowed it. Hence, after his promotion in 1858 by brevet, Albert Sidney Johnston wore a single star and styled himself as "brevet brig. gen. and col., Second U.S. Cavalry."

2. MacKinnon, *At Sword's Point, Part 1*, 423–24.

3. Yale Collection of Western Americana, Beinecke Library, New Haven, Connecticut.

4. Here Thomas presumably means Mormons.

5. Thomas was almost as inaccurately optimistic about such distances in the region as was Brigham Young. Captain Rufus Ingalls's estimate of about five hundred miles was closer to the mark.

6. MacKinnon, "Sex, Subalterns, and Steptoe: Army Behavior, Mormon Rage, and Utah War Anxieties," *Utah Historical Quarterly* 76 (Summer 2008): 227–46.

7. Yale Collection of Western Americana, Beinecke Library, New Haven, Connecticut.

8. Not printed here for reasons of brevity.

9. When Ingalls departed Utah in the spring of 1855, it was via the northern route. His brother officer, First Lieutenant Sylvester Mowry, led a detachment to California through Utah's southern settlements and would have disagreed vigorously with Ingalls about the disposition of the settlers based on the hostility he encountered.

10. At this time Ives was just beginning his ascent of the Colorado River from the Gulf of California to Fort Yuma.

11. In addition to seeking his old field notes from Palmer, on December 29 Ingalls also sent an urgent note across the Columbia River to Robert ("Doc") Newell, one of the region's most experienced mountaineer-guide-interpreters. From Newell, Ingalls wanted advice as to the best route and season for funneling troops into the Salt Lake Valley from Oregon. Remarkably, within two days Newell responded from Champoeg, Oregon, with a long letter. Although he had dated his letter to Swords on December 29, Ingalls held it back until hearing from Palmer and Newell. Ingalls then revised it, constructed an appendix of routes and distances, and mailed all of this material to San Francisco on January 7, 1858. Newell to Ingalls, December 31, 1857; photocopy in author's possession.

12. Both coastal destinations were under consideration in at least some passing fashion by Brigham Young during the war.

13. The holograph original of this letter is at the Huntington Library, San Marino, California, and a holograph copy is included in the Papers of John A. Quitman, Southern Historical Collection, Wilson Library, University of North Carolina, Chapel Hill. When an additional copy (now lost) addressed to Jefferson Davis was captured with the baggage of a Confederate officer following the evacuation of Jackson, Mississippi, in August 1863, excerpts appeared in newspapers throughout the North. A typescript of Beauregard's letter made from the version at the Huntington is in Leonard J. Arrington Papers, Merrill-Cazier Library, Utah State University, Logan.

14. For a summary of these events swirling around General Winfield Scott, the army's general in chief, see MacKinnon, "Buchanan's Thrust from the Pacific: The Utah War's Ill-Fated Second Front," *Utah Historical Quarterly* 34 (Fall 2008): 226–60.

15. This was the battle of Arcole, Italy, November 15–17, 1796. Beauregard means Austrian generals

Dagobert Sigmund von Wurmser and Joseph Frei-
herr Alvin(c)zy de Berberck.

16. The Russians had been fighting to subjugate the Circassians in the northwest Caucasuses since 1763. The war would not end in a Russian victory until 1864, with the mass deportation of 500,000 Circassians in its aftermath.

17. Beauregard's "Greatest Captain" was the eighteenth-century Russian general Alexander Suvorov, author of the *Manual of Victory*.

18. Baron Antoine-Henri de Jemini's *The Art of War*, a text on military strategy and the Napoleonic campaigns, had an enormous influence on nineteenth-century military officers in the United States.

19. Field officers were majors, lieutenant colonels, and colonels; company-grade officers were lieutenants and captains. Beauregard's assessment of the U.S. Army's officer corps was accurate.

20. The army was not expanded for the Utah War, and Beauregard remained a captain of engineers until his resignation in 1861. The U.S. Army would have no units of Zouaves, a flamboyantly uniformed infantry corps in the French North African service, until the Civil War. This reference and several others in his letter reflect Beauregard's French-Louisiana background and proclivities, affectations that fellow Louisianan Slidell would understand, if not appreciate. McClellan's eagerness to return to the army for the Utah campaign from an engineering vice presidency at the Illinois Central Railroad was well known among his friends, including those still in the service. Beauregard refers to McClellan's army-sponsored role as a military observer during the recent Crimean War with two other officers and to their joint report published as a congressional document. First Lieutenant and Brevet Captain Gustavus Woodson Smith of Kentucky never returned to the U.S. Army after his 1854 resignation, although he rose to major general in the Confederate service. First Lieutenant Johnson Kelly Duncan of Ohio had resigned in 1855 and was a Confederate brigadier

when he died in 1862. All three men, as well as Beauregard, were West Pointers.

21. Delana R. Eckels to Sen. Jesse Bright, December 13, 1857, copy in author's possession. Capt. Stewart Van Vliet, Report to Sec. of War John B. Floyd, November 20, 1857, U.S. Secretary of War, *Report of the Secretary of War*, 35th Cong., 1st Sess., 1857–58, Senate Ex. Doc. 11, 38.

22. For an account of Quantrill's and Shepherd's lives, including their participation in the Utah and Civil wars, see Henry S. Clarke, "W.C. Quantrill in 1858," *Kansas Historical Collections* 7 (1901-2): 218-23; William Elsey Connelley, *Quantrill and the Border Wars* (Lawrence: Kansas Heritage Press, 1992), 1–7, 66, 75–81, 87, 94–96, 99–100, 103–4, 100–110; Barry A. Crouch, "A 'Fiend in Human Shape'? William Clarke Quantrill and His Biographers," *Kansas History* 22 (Summer 1999): 143–56; Edward E. Leslie, *The Devil Knows How to Ride: The True Story of William Clarke Quantrill and His Confederate Raiders* (New York: Random House, 1996), 52–63; and Martin E. Ismert, "Quantrill-Charley Hart?," paper presented at the Posse of the Westerners of Kansas City, October 13, 1959, William Clarke Quantrill Research Collection, McCain Library, University of Southern Mississippi, Hattiesburg; also Gilbert Cuthbertson, "Shepherd Was Name to Fear in Border War Era," *Kansas City [Missouri] Times*, September 9, 1965, 140.

23. Peck's reminiscences are found in Connelley, *Quantrill and the Border Wars*; Leslie, *The Devil Knows How to Ride*, 56–57.

24. Quantrill assumed the alias "Charley Hart" in Kansas Territory during 1856–57 to cover his participation in a spree of thefts and involvement with the violent disturbances then wracking the region over the slavery issue.

25. Actually, after leaving Fort Bridger in the summer of 1858, Quantrill followed the Utah Expedition west and worked as a civilian cook at its enormous garrison at Camp Floyd, Utah, until returning east in late 1859.

Figure 1. Camp Douglas, "View of Post Head Quarters and Officers' Quarters, East side of Parade."
Probably by Private Charles Beckwith, 1864. (111-SC-106908)

DAGUERREAN GALLERY.

C. D. BECKWITH, has the pleasure of announcing to the public, that he is now prepared to take pictures, of all kinds in the daguerrean art, at prices to suit.
☞ Gallery opposite the Commissary Store, at
Camp Douglas, U. T.   nov20-1m*

Charles D. Beckwith's advertisement for his photography studio at
Camp Douglas, from the Union Vedette. *This ad ran in late 1863*
and 1864. (Utah Digital Newspapers)

Ephriam D. Dickson III

CAMP DOUGLAS'S FIRST PHOTOGRAPHER

PRIVATE CHARLES D. BECKWITH

In May 1864, First Lieutenant Thomas B. Gately received orders from the army's quartermaster general instructing him to submit a map of Camp Douglas, together with descriptions and views of buildings at the post. Five months later, Gately submitted his detailed map together with seven photographs, the earliest known images of Camp Douglas. While he did not specifically mention the name of the artist responsible for these photographs, it is likely that they were taken by Private Charles D. Beckwith, a soldier in the Second California Cavalry who had opened a photographic studio at Camp Douglas. These images provide our first glimpse of the Civil War post as it was built by the California Volunteers. In August 1861, as the Civil War raged in the East, the secretary of war wrote to the governor of California asking that his state raise several additional regiments. Within several months, the Second California Volunteer Cavalry was formed, soon assigned to Colonel Patrick Edward Connor's column bound for Utah.

One of the soldiers who decided to enlist in the cavalry regiment was Charles D. Beckwith.

Born in about 1832 or 1833 in Broom County, New York, Beckwith left home in 1849 at the age of sixteen to try his luck in the California gold fields. Rather than making the long and difficult trek overland as many did, Beckwith chose to travel by sea. In Boston, he boarded the *Areatus* together with 21 crew members and 138 other miners as part of the Bay State and California Mining Company, departing in April. After 171 days at sea, rounding Cape Horn, he finally arrived in San Francisco in September 1849. Presumably, Beckwith worked in the gold fields but, like many, eventually decided to find other employment. He probably apprenticed in a photography studio. By 1858, he was operating his own daguerreian gallery in Yreka, California. He reportedly also did some work in Oregon and opened a studio briefly in Crescent City, California. In June 1859, he returned to Yreka, where he reopened his gallery, offering to produce portraits as daguerreotypes, ambrotypes, and melainotypes, along with "all the latest style of pictures."[1]

With the Civil War now under way and California raising volunteer regiments, Beckwith decided to enlist. In September 1861, he turned over his Yreka studio to another photographer named S. T. Feen and headed for Fort Jones. On September 25, he raised his right hand and was sworn into the military for three years. He was assigned to Company M of the Second California Volunteer Cavalry. For the next eight months, the regiment drilled and trained at Camp Alert on the edge of San Francisco. In December 1861, Private Beckwith was transferred to the regimental band and designated as a musician third class.[2]

Headquarters and five companies of the Second California Volunteer Cavalry were assigned to the Utah column commanded by Colonel Patrick Edward Connor to protect the Overland Trail. Musician Beckwith was probably with regimental headquarters, commanded by Colonel Columbus Sims, when it departed Camp Alert in July 1862 and reached Fort Churchill the following month. About this time, Beckwith was seriously wounded. Many years later, he recalled that while watering his horse it suddenly jumped and threw him onto the pommel of his saddle; on another occasion, he said that as the horses rushed to water, his horse fell and rolled over him. In September 1862, he rejoined his original company at Camp Ruby in Nevada Territory, but his injury haunted him for the remainder of his life.[3]

Colonel Connor departed Camp Ruby with his column (including Company M with Private Beckwith) on October 2 and continued east along the Overland Trail, arriving in Salt Lake City on October 20, 1862. On the bench about three miles east of the city, the troops established Camp Douglas. Company M, under the command of Captain George F. Price, participated in the Bear River Massacre in January 1863 and three months later was transferred to Fort Bridger. Rather than departing with his company, Private Beckwith was temporarily assigned to regimental headquarters and remained behind at Camp Douglas. By November 1863, he was operating a photographic studio at the post. His advertisement in the garrison's newspaper, the *Union Vedette*, advertised that he was "now prepared to take pictures, of all kinds in the daguerrean art, at prices to suit." In the spring of 1864, as Lieutenant Gately prepared his map of Camp Douglas, Private Beckwith was probably contracted to produce a series of photographic images of the post.[4]

Private Beckwith remained at Camp Douglas until he was mustered out of the service on October 4, 1864, having completed his three-year enlistment. He initially went home to New York but returned to Salt Lake City two years later. In March 1867, Beckwith moved to Montana, where he worked as a prospector, a painter, and finally a bartender. In January 1886, Beckwith located in Littlefield, Idaho, and again took up his camera as a commercial photographer. He applied for a pension two years later, and by 1890 his health had deteriorated to such a degree that he was no longer able to work. Beckwith finally moved to Murray, Idaho, where he died on July 13, 1891.[5]

Charles D. Beckwith was one of thousands of soldiers who served at Fort Douglas. As the garrison's first photographer, he left an important pictorial legacy for future generations. Perhaps one day additional photographs will come to light, but for now these seven images are all that we have of Camp Douglas as it appeared in 1864.

DESCRIPTION OF PHOTOGRAPHS

The original 1864 photographs are pasted onto Gately's report accompanying Map #47, Fort Douglas, Miscellaneous Forts File, Record Group 77, National Archives. Duplicates of the images were made by the U.S. Army Signal Corps and are part of their collection now also at the National Archives. Copy prints of the Signal Corps photographs are available at many archives, including the Utah State Historical Society. They can be recognized by the Signal Corps numbers written in the bottom left corner of each image.

Figure 1, page 398, top. In this photograph, most of officers' row is shown. The Post Headquarters, visible in the center, was a large whitewashed adobe building built in the fall of 1862 to serve both as the offices and as the residence for the post commander. Quarters for other commissioned officers in the command can also be seen. The partial dugouts were the first quarters, built in the fall of 1862, shortly after Camp Douglas was established. These primitive buildings were slowly replaced during the 1860s by more substantial above-ground log structures, each a duplex housing two officers and their families.

Figure 2, page 401, top. The enlisted men endured their first winter in tents. The following year, log barracks were constructed on the north and south side of the parade field, each housing one company. The frame structure visible in front of the barracks served as a warehouse for both the quartermaster and commissary stores at the post. Trees were planted around the parade field, many of which still survive today.

Figure 2. "View of Company Quarters, south side of Parade." (111-SC-106909)

Figure 3. "View of Quarters of Comdg. Officer of District and head Quarters of District of Utah." (111-SC-106912)

Figure 4. "View of Non-Comd. Staff and Laundress' Quarters." (111-SC-106913)

Figure 5. "View of Ordnance Store House, Guard House and Magazine, east side of Parade" (111-SC-106911)

Figure 6. "View of Sutler's Store and Company Quarters, north side of Parade." (111-SC-106910)

Figure 7. "View of Quarters of Comdg. Officer of Post, Hospital and Surgeon's Quarters." (111-SC-106914)

Figure 3, page 401, middle. Among the new buildings added to Camp Douglas in the fall of 1863 were two large adobe structures to serve as the offices and residence for the commander of the Department of Utah, Brigadier General P. Edward Connor. A third wing and a porch was later added. This building was later used as the post commander's house until new quarters were built in 1875. One wing of the original adobe building survives today as an extension on the back of the new 1875 commanding officer's quarters.

Figure 4, page 401, bottom. To the east of officer's row stood another line of buildings, rude single-room log cabins to house the laundresses and the families of noncommissioned officers.

Figure 5, page 402, top. Along the western edge of the parade ground were three buildings: the guardhouse in the center, flanked by the ordnance storehouse and magazine. One of the enlisted barracks on the north side of the parade field can be seen in the background. The structure at the left edge of this photograph was the blacksmith shop.

Figure 6, page 402, middle. In this photograph, the additional enlisted barracks located on the north side of the parade ground are shown. The framed building on the left belonged to the civilian post sutler who operated a general merchandise store at the post. Private Beckwith's studio was probably located near the sutler store but is apparently out of view in this image.

Figure 7, page 402, bottom. The easternmost row of buildings at Camp Douglas, built in the fall and winter of 1863, included the post hospital in the center, flanked by the surgeon's quarters on the left and the commanding officer's quarters on the right. This last building, also known as Building 55, became the quarters for the post quartermaster by 1866 and as NCO quarters in the 1890s. It still stands today, with minimal changes to its basic structure beyond a couple of later additions.

Ephriam D. Dickson III is the curator at the Fort Douglas Military Museum in Salt Lake City.

NOTES

Adapted, with permission, from the *Fort Douglas Vedette*, Winter 2008–9, 4–6.

1. Peter E. Palmquist and Thomas R. Kailbourn, *Pioneer Photographers of the Far West: A Biographical Dictionary, 1840–1865* (Stanford, CA: Stanford University Press, 2000), 106–7.

2. Richard H. Orton, *Records of California Men in the War of the Rebellion, 1861 to 1867* (1890). Descriptive Book, Company M 2nd California Cavalry; Special Order #49, Headquarters, 2nd California Cavalry, December 30, 1861; Special Order #66, January 18, 1862, National Archives.

3. Beckwith Pension File; Special Order #184, Headquarters 2nd California Cavalry, National Archives.

4. Special Order #57, 2nd California Cavalry, April 10, 1863, *Union Vedette*, November 20, 1863–March 12, 1864.

5. Beckwith Pension File, 1870 Census, Cedar Creek Mines, Missoula County, Montana. Headstones provided for Deceased Military Veterans (Microcopy 1845), National Archives.

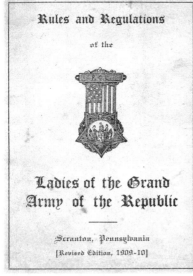

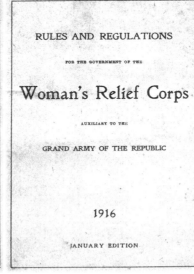

The Grand Army of the Republic (GAR) was the largest, most influential, and longest-lived Civil War veteran organizations. The Ladies of the Grand Army of the Republic and the Women's Relief Corps were auxiliary organizations for veteran spouses, daughters, and other interested women. (Courtesy Kenneth L. Alford)

Kenneth L. Alford

IDENTIFYING LATTER-DAY SAINT CIVIL WAR VETERANS

Soon after this project began, I was surprised to learn that no thorough search for Latter-day Saint Civil War veterans had been undertaken and published. Over a century and a half has passed since the beginning of the Civil War, and we felt it was past time to identify and celebrate Latter-day Saints who served both the North and the South during the Civil War. The results of our efforts are found in Appendix E. The purpose of this appendix is to briefly explain how we found and attempted to document both membership in The Church of Jesus Christ of Latter-day Saints and Civil War veteran status.

DEFINING A "LATTER-DAY SAINT"

To identify someone as both a Latter-day Saint and Civil War veteran required us to define both terms. For the purpose of this research, a Latter-day Saint is defined as an individual who was baptized as a member of The Church of Jesus Christ of Latter-day Saints during his or her lifetime. This definition defines as a "Latter-day Saint" individuals who were baptized prior to the Civil War, during the war, as well as after the war. It also includes individuals who were excommunicated during the course of their lifetime. (It does not, of course, include individuals who have been baptized vicariously.)

DEFINING A "CIVIL WAR VETERAN"

Identifying someone as a "Civil War veteran" required slightly different definitions for Union and Confederate soldiers. In order to be included in this study, Union soldiers, sailors, and marines must have served on active federal service between January 9, 1861 (when Confederate artillery opened first on the *Star of the West* in Charleston Harbor, South Carolina), and June 23, 1865 (the date that General Stand Watie surrendered the last Confederate soldiers). Active federal service is defined as service that qualified for federal pension benefits—a definition similar to that used by the Grand Army of the Republic to qualify applicants for membership. Applying that definition to soldiers who served in Utah Territory during the Civil War means that soldiers who served in the Utah Cavalry under Lot Smith's command are considered Civil War veterans; their ninety-day active-duty service was valid for pension and Grand Army of the Republic membership purposes. However, teamsters who served with the Lot Smith Utah Cavalry were not on active duty military service, did not receive federal pension credit, and are not considered Civil War veterans. Likewise, members of the Nauvoo Legion in Utah who served with Colonel Robert T. Burton are also not considered Civil War veterans as their service did not qualify them for federal pension benefits. The Confederate States of America did not employ the same service definitions as their Union counterparts. Any soldier or sailor who fought for the Confederacy is considered a Civil War veteran for the purpose of this research. There was no active duty versus militia distinction for wartime military service in the Confederate States of America.

RESEARCH METHODOLOGY

Part of the reason that no thorough Latter-day Saint Civil War veterans list has been published previously is because the tools to find and document both Church membership and veteran status have been largely unavailable or difficult to obtain. The recent proliferation of Internet databases related to both LDS Church membership and Civil War veterans has made the accompanying LDS Civil War veterans list in Appendix E possible. The resulting list was made possible through the efforts of numerous people who assisted in its preparation—from student research assistants to independent historians and history

buffs. (Please see Acknowledgments for the names of those who directly contributed to this effort.) While there are certainly exceptions, here is the basic process used to add individuals to the Latter-day Saint Civil War veterans list:

- Find the name of a possible LDS Civil War veteran
- Confirm that the individual was a baptized Latter-day Saint
- Confirm that the individual qualified as a Union or Confederate veteran
- Double-check that the LDS member and the veteran identified were the same individual

The first step—finding the name of a possible LDS Civil War veteran—proved to be the most challenging and difficult step in the process. Federal service as a member of the Lot Smith Utah Cavalry provided almost one hundred individuals who were added to the final list. The second most fruitful source for LDS Civil War veterans was the veteran schedule that was prepared as part of the 1890 U.S. Census. Census, cemetery, and other records from the San Luis Valley in Colorado proved to be an excellent source for finding almost three dozen LDS Civil War veterans (most of whom served in the Confederate armed forces.) Additional names for potential veterans came from a variety of sources, most notably Margaret Fisher's 1929 *Utah and the Civil War*, Frank Esshom's 1913 *Pioneers and Prominent Men of Utah*, newspaper obituary articles found in the online database *Utah Digital Newspapers*, lists from amateur historians and genealogists, federal pension and service records, records obtained through the Church History Library in Salt Lake City, other books,

How many Latter-day Saints served in the Union and Confederate military forces during the American Civil War, and who were they? Student research assistants at Brigham Young University, some of whom are pictured here (left to right: Joseph R. Stuart, Dr. Kenneth L. Alford, Mary E. Moberly, and Ian S. Lindsay), have worked for several years in an effort to answer those questions. Assistance was also provided by several independent researchers and historians. Appendices D-H share the results of their hard work.
(Courtesy of Brent R. Nordgren)

tips from friends and acquaintances, and even *Improvement Era* articles from the early part of the twentieth century.

The second step—confirming that the individual was baptized as a Latter-day Saint during his lifetime—was often frustrating but was generally a straightforward process. The available databases were a great help, but they are not complete. To confirm soldiers as Latter-day Saints, we used the LDS Church family history website http://new.familysearch.org, public records, newspaper obituaries, journals, biographical encyclopedias, and occasionally information obtained through Internet searches. In a few instances (which are noted in the list) where it can be reasonably inferred that a person was LDS (for instance, records that note the individual was an elder or a bishop), their name has been included in the list (with an explanatory note). When LDS membership has been confirmed through New Family Search, the accompanying individual identification number is included to enable readers to check our work. If baptismal information was unavailable in New Family Search, we checked Susan Easton Black's *Membership of the Church of Jesus Christ of Latter-day Saints, 1830–1848*. In a few instances, LDS membership could not be confirmed through New Family Search or early membership records, but was accepted based on published accounts that mentioned the individual's LDS Church membership.

The third step—confirming veteran status—required a variety of research skills. At this time, there is no complete online database of everyone who gave Civil War service, but the *Civil War Soldiers and Sailor System* database (sponsored by the National Park Service, http://www.itd.nps.gov/cwss/) and the *Veterans with Federal Service Buried in Utah, Territorial to 1966* database (available online from Family Search) proved to be the most helpful. Obituaries obtained from Utah Digital Newspapers were also an additional resource for identifying Civil War veterans. Diaries and journals were also consulted, if available. Where that was not possible, a newspaper reference to that person's Civil War veteran status was accepted on good faith. Biographical encyclopedias, *Improvement Era* articles, and other sources were researched in a similar manner. Ancestry.com's *U.S. Civil War Collection,* Civil War records collections available online at FamilySearch.org, and http://findagrave.org were also helpful.

The fourth step—double-checking (and in many cases, triple-checking) the accuracy of the previous steps—engendered both confidence and frustration. The easiest way to confirm that an LDS member and a soldier of the same name were the same person was through pension records. If biographical data obtained through New Family Search, obituaries, findagrave.com and other sources identified the name of the soldier's wife, we could frequently locate the veteran in Ancestry.com's *Civil War Pension Index* which often listed the soldier's wife, the regiment he served in, and sometimes additional identifying information which could be compared against the New Family Search records. In the absence of pension files, we relied on biographical information found in sources such as obituaries

and biographical histories. We are grateful to have so many wonderful resources available but, at the same time, have frequently been frustrated that they are not more complete.

One of the chief difficulties discovered during this process is that federal military records from the Civil War do not always contain vital records information such as birth, marriage, or death dates. In many instances, there were no overlapping data fields that could confirm, without any doubt, that the "John Q. Doe" who was baptized as a member of The Church of Jesus Christ of Latter-day Saints in 18xx was the same individual as the "John Q. Doe" who served during the Civil War in the Xth Regiment from the great state of Y. We have made every effort to verify that the individuals who appear on our list were Latter-day Saint Civil War veterans. For every person who appears on the final list, we screened and eliminated over fifty other individuals during the course of this research. Sometimes, quite honestly, we just had to make a best guess and assume the Church member and the soldier with the same name were the same person. We have made every effort to so identify those veterans.

During the course of our research, we discovered several individuals who, while failing to meet both criteria to be included in Appendix E, deserve to be mentioned on their own account. They are listed in Appendix F as "Special Interest" veterans. This list includes soldiers in the Lot Smith Utah Cavalry whose LDS membership could not be confirmed (but there is a high probability that they were baptized Latter-day Saints), the teamsters who served with them, and a few other Civil War veterans who had a special or unique relationship with The Church of Jesus Christ of Latter-day Saints, such as Levi

Lamoni Wight, son of the excommunicated LDS apostle Lyman Wight, who fought for the Confederacy.

We are pleased to recognize the military contributions of these individuals and have included source information with each individual's listing so that readers can, if desired, check and confirm or correct our work. We are not under the illusion, though, that our list as published is complete nor, unfortunately, even completely accurate. It is, though, a multiyear first effort to create a reproducible list of Latter-day Saint Civil War veterans. We invite readers to submit additions, suggestions, and corrections to improve upon our initial work. Please send list-related information (including as much documentation and source information as possible) to:

Dr. Kenneth L. Alford
Civil War Saints Project
c/o 375 JSB
Brigham Young University
Provo, Utah 84602

I, CERTIFY, That the within named *William H. Norman* a *Private* of Captain *Lieut. L. L. Nixon* Company (*C*) of the *1st Confederate* Regiment of *Georgia Volunteers*, born in *Twiggs Co* in the State of *Georgia*, aged *16* years, *5* feet, *5* inches high, *Dark* complexion, *Blue* eyes, *Dark* hair, and by a *Farmer* was enlisted by *Capt. Geo. A. Smith* at *Camp Walker, Florida* on the *22* day of *July*, 1861, to serve *Three 2L Days years*, and is now entitled to discharge by reason of *Expiration of term of Enlistment*.

The said *William H. Norman* was last paid by *Capt. L. S. Johnson* to include the *31st* day of *October*, 1861, and has

C. M. BROWN
NEW YORK
LDS U.S. NAVY
CIVIL WAR
APRIL 13 1847   MARCH 16 1934

Death Takes Respected Veteran

Monday morning the scores of friends and acquaintances of John W. ... respected citizen

JOSEPH H. CRAWFORD
ALABAMA
PVT CO E HILLIARD'S LEGION
CONFEDERATE STATES ARMY
APRIL 1 1836   AUG 24 1922

PIONEERS AND PROMINENT MEN OF UTAH   739

MEMORY OF
MAJOR
LOT SMITH
OF THE
NAUVOO LEGION
BORN MAY 15 1830
AT WILLIAMS
TOWNSHIP
OSWEGO CO., N.Y.
KILLED
JUNE 21 1892
BY NAVAJO INDIANS
AT TUBA CITY, ARIZ.
BODY EXHUMED
AND BURIED HERE
APR. 8 1902

Special Schedule.—Surviving Soldiers, Sailors, and Marines, and Widows, etc.

Page 2   S.D.: 1 ; E.D.: 77 : Minor Civil Division: Utah

HON. D. H. PEERY IS DEAD

Death Comes Suddenly to One of Utah's Most Prominent Citizens Early This Morning— He Was a Leader Among Men.

Death came suddenly to Hon. D. H. Peery this morning and one of Utah's most prominent citizens is now at rest, mourned by all who knew him. Not alone is grief felt and expressed in Utah but from prominent men all over the country...

NAME: MORGAN, JOHN   SERIAL NUMBER
RANK: Pvt   ORGANIZATION: Co E 123rd Inf.   BRANCH: Army
PERIOD OF SERVICE: Civil War
DATE OF ENLISTMENT: 14 December 1863   PLACE: Rush Co., Indiana
DATE OF DISCHARGE
DATE OF BIRTH
DATE OF DEATH
PLACE OF BURIAL: CI...
CEMETERY: City
NEXT OF KIN

JAMES M. BARLOW
QM SGT UTAH CAVALRY
CIVIL WAR
JULY 9 1812   FEB 8 1895

Smith's Co. Cav.   Utah.

Joseph W. Taylor, Capt. Smith's Co., Utah Cavalry.

Age ... years.
Appears on Co. Muster-out Roll, dated
Muster-out to date
Last paid to
When enrolled
Where enrolled
Period 3 months.
Mustered in
Where
Clothing account:

Harris Thomas H.

Smith's Co. Utah Cavalry.
(3 Months, 1862.)

Private   Private

CARD NUMBERS.

VETERAN OF THE CIVIL WAR CALLED

John T. Pribble Died Wed. Morning at His Home in This City.

John T. Pribble, age 82, veteran of the Civil War, died at 11 o'clock Wed. morning at the family home on South Main street of ailments incident to old age. The aged gentleman had been enjoying good health until about a month ago.

Some of the many sources used to verify Latter-day Saint Civil War military service—including enlistment documents, newspaper obituaries, the "Surviving Soldiers, Sailors, and Marines, and Widows, etc." schedule from the 1890 U.S. Census, the Veterans Buried in Utah database, Pioneers and Prominent Men of Utah, and muster rosters—are illustrated above.
(Utah Digital Newspapers, FindAGrave.com, National Archives)

INTERPRETING THE LDS CIVIL WAR VETERAN RECORDS

The following tables provide summary information for better understanding the Latter-day Saint Civil War Veterans and Special Interest Civil War Veterans appendices that follow. Both appendices contain summary records for Civil War veterans and use the same basic record format, codes, and abbreviations. The LDS Veteran Records Table, below, discusses the individual fields in those records. The Research Source Table lists and explains codes and acronyms (found primarily in the Military Service Source(s), LDS Membership Source(s), and Notes fields) in the veteran records.

LDS VETERAN RECORDS TABLE

LDS Civil War veteran records in Appendices E and F appear in tables like the one below.

VETERAN'S NAME (MILITARY AFFILIATION)   *When baptized.*

Rank:	Unit(s): Military Service Source(s):
Birth Date:	Birth Place:
LDS Membership Date:	LDS Membership Source(s):
Death Date:	Death Place: Find A Grave: Burial Location:
Notes:	

FIELD	EXPLANATION
VETERAN'S NAME	Spelling of names was not always standardized in the nineteenth century. Alternate ways of spelling the first or last names (as evidenced in various record sources) may be reflected either on the first line (with an alternate method of spelling being listed in parenthesis) or in the Notes field. In several instances, one record source (such as New FamilySearch or an obituary) may contain a partial name (first and last name only, with no middle name) while other record sources may contain middle initials or names for the same individual.
MILITARY AFFILIATION	The military affiliation (Union or Confederate) and branch of the service (Army, Navy, Marines) for each service member, when known, will be shown. The qualifier "(presumed)" has been added when veteran status has been confirmed but specific military affiliation cannot be identified (for example, the soldier's obituary may have simply stated that he was "a Civil war veteran" without mentioning for which side he fought). The military affiliation of three soldiers (John Eugene Davis, John W. Lawson, and William Pinkney Sargent) is listed as "Galvanized Yankee"; a galvanized Yankee was a soldier who served in both the Union and Confederate military forces during the Civil War. (Additional information about galvanized Yankees can be found in the Ellsworth-Alford chapter herein.)
WHEN BAPTIZED	Individuals are identified as having been baptized before, during, or after the Civil War. In a few instances the qualifier "(presumed)" has been added, when questions regarding an individual's LDS baptism exist.
RANK	The rank displayed is generally the highest or final rank earned by the veteran. Military rank information has been obtained from a variety of the sources listed in the Research Source Table, especially 1890 Census, NPS, and FOLD3.
UNIT(S)	Unit information was obtained from a variety of sources. When soldiers were known to have served with more than one unit, both units have been included. Unit designations may reflect the source from which they were obtained (for example, the same unit might be listed as "Company G, 26th Massachusetts," "Company G, 26th Regiment, Massachusetts," "Company G, 26th Massachusetts Infantry Regiment," "Company G, 26th Massachusetts Infantry," or "Company G, 26th Regiment, Massachusetts Infantry").

FIELD	EXPLANATION
MILITARY SERVICE SOURCE(S)	This field lists the sources where unit information was found. (Please see the following table for an explanation of the individual codes used.)
BIRTH DATE	With few exceptions, the birth date listed has been obtained from New FamilySearch (NFS). Additional information regarding birthdate discrepancies can sometimes be found in the Notes field.
BIRTH PLACE	Place of birth information was usually recorded from the same source as the date of birth (which is most often New FamilySearch).
LDS MEMBERSHIP DATE	For most veterans, the date listed is their baptismal date. LDS membership records for the nineteenth century remain incomplete. Most baptismal dates included were obtained from New FamilySearch (NFS). In several instances the NFS baptismal date listed online was clearly for vicarious ordinance work, but a confirmation or temple ordinances date was listed within the lifetime of the individual. In those instances, we have entered the "(confirmation)" or "(LDS temple ordinances)" NFS date—with the appropriate parenthetical notation. There are also a few individuals for whom no LDS membership dated records could be discovered, but additional sources (such as diaries or obituaries) refer to their LDS membership. For those individuals, the word "Uncertain" appears in this field.
LDS MEMBERSHIP SOURCE(S)	The primary source of LDS membership information was New FamilySearch (NFS). When an individual has a record in New FamilySearch, the NFS Identification Number (a unique seven-character alphanumeric code for each individual record in NFS, for example: "KWJK-4HP") has been included so that readers can quickly identify which LDS membership record was matched against the veteran record.
DEATH DATE	A veteran's date of death was generally obtained from New FamilySearch and/or FindAGrave.com.
DEATH PLACE	A veteran's place of death was generally obtained from New FamilySearch and/or FindAGrave.com.

FIELD	EXPLANATION
FIND A GRAVE	FindAGrave.com (FGC) was an extremely useful online resource to link an LDS member's record with a Civil War veteran's record. Each record on the Find A Grave website is given a unique identifying number (which has been included here, when available). In additional to name, death, and burial information, many Find A Grave record entries also have one or more photographs of the headstone, grave marker, and/or the cemetery where the deceased is buried. (Please note that new Find A Grave records are being added every day. Veterans on this list without Find A Grave entries may have been entered since the publication of this book.)
BURIAL LOCATION	A veteran's burial location was generally obtained from New FamilySearch and/or FindAGrave.com.
NOTES	This field often contains pertinent as well as general interest information about the veteran's military service and life. Information appears from a wide variety of sources. The original source of the information or the source code is generally enclosed in brackets. Some Notes sections contain historical information regarding the unit in which the veteran served; information for other units is generally available at [NPS]. When appropriate (such as when quoting from Esshom's *Pioneers and Prominent Men of Utah*), page numbers have also been included, for example: [PPMU, 1096]

RESEARCH SOURCE TABLE

In an effort to publish information thoroughly, but concisely, acronyms and codes have been used within individual veteran records for repeated data sources. Sources that are used once or sparingly are entered in whole within the appendix. Here is an example LDS veteran record illustrating where the research codes generally appear:

ABBOTT, CHARLES ENOCH (UNION ARMY)   *Baptized after the war.*

Birth Date: 22 December 1847	**Birth Place:** Fulton, White Side, Illinois
LDS Membership Date: 11 November 1878	**LDS Membership Source(s):** NFS (ID #: KWJK-4HP)
Death Date: 10 January 1927	**Death Place:** Los Angeles, California **Find A Grave:** 82343710 **Burial Location:** Wasatch Lawn Cemetery, Salt Lake City, Salt Lake, Utah
Notes: [MLM] "CIVIL WAR VETERAN" is carved on his grave marker [FGC]. [NPS] lists an additional "Charles E. Abbott" who served in Company E, 14th Regiment, Illinois Infantry.	

The table below provides the key to acronyms used throughout appendices E and F. When research codes are used within the Notes field, most of those are enclosed in brackets (for example, [FGC]).

CODE	EXPLANATION
1862 MOR	"Muster-out Roll of Captain Lott [*sic*]Smith's Company of Mounted Volunteers . . . , 14 August 1862." MSS A 5238, Utah State Historical Society, Salt Lake City. A typed transcript of the August 14, 1862, muster-out roll of the Lot Smith Utah Cavalry is on file at the Utah State Historical Society. A note on the bottom of the typed list states: "This list copied from the one in the possession of Margaret Fisher of the George Washington Circle of the G.A.R. Her copy was taken from the original at Washington D.C. thru the courtesy of Senator Smoot. Received August 6, 192[?]. Information about the Lot Smith Utah Cavalry is available in the Stuart-Alford chapter herein.
1890 Census	"Special Schedules of the Eleventh Census (1890) Enumerating Union Veterans and Widows of Union Veterans of the Civil War"; National Archives Microfilm Publication M123, 118 rolls; Records of the Department of Veterans Affairs, Record Group 15; National Archives, Washington, DC. "United States of America, Bureau of the Census." *Twelfth Census of the United States, 1900*. Washington, DC: National Archives and Records Administration, 1900. T623, 1854 rolls.
1900 Census	The following information is from Ancestry.com's online description of this database: "This database is an index to all individuals enumerated in the 1900 United States Federal Census, the Twelfth Census of the United States. In addition, the names of those listed on the population schedule are linked to actual images of the 1900 Federal Census, copied from the National Archives and Records Administration microfilm, T623, 1854 rolls. . . . "Enumerators of the 1900 census were instructed to record the names of every person in the household. Enumerators were asked to include the following categories in the census: name; address; relationship to the head of household; color or race; sex; month and year of birth; age at last birthday; marital status; number of years married; the total number of children born of the mother; the number of those children living; places of birth of each individual and the parents of each individual; if the individual was foreign

CODE	EXPLANATION
1900 Census (continued)	born, the year of immigration and the number of years in the United States; the citizenship status of foreign-born individuals over age twenty-one; occupation; whether the person could read, write, and speak English; whether the home was owned or rented; whether the home was on a farm; and whether the home was mortgaged."
ACWS	American Civil War Soldiers Database (Ancestry.com). The following information is from Ancestry.com's online description of this database: "The American Civil War Research Database is a historic effort to compile and link all available records of common soldiers in the Civil War. . . . Historical Data Systems has compiled and linked a wide array of record types including state rosters, pension records, regimental histories, photos, and journals. The genealogical value of this record is immeasurable. More than authoritative names and dates, this database connects researchers with the history their ancestors lived. "The collection is divided into four sections: soldier records, regiment records, battle histories, and officer records. . . . soldier records, may contain any of the following information about an individual soldier: the soldier's name, residence, date of entry, regiments, companies, rank, promotions, transfers, events (such as POW, wounded, etc.) and how and where the soldier exited the military (discharge, desertion, muster out, or death). Some states also include in their official records a soldier's birthplace, age at enlistment, occupation, and physical description."
CSC	Confederate Soldiers Buried in the State of Colorado (http://www.coloradoscv.org/interment/interment.htm). This online electronic database contains the following information: name, rank, state served, unit, cemetery, city, picture, and registration with the Sons of Confederate Veterans. This database was used to identify Civil War veterans who were later checked against LDS membership records to determine if they were baptized into the LDS Church during their lifetime.
FGC	Find A Grave (FindAGrave.com). This free online database documents the burial information for millions of individuals. Pictures and information may be uploaded. When the Notes field for an individual references information on their grave marker, almost without exception

CODE	EXPLANATION
	a photo of that grave marker is available on FindAGrave.com. Any Find A Grave reference numbers that were available at the time of publication have been included for your convenience
Fisher	Fisher, Margaret M. *Utah and the Civil War. Being the Story of the Part Played by the People of Utah in That Great Conflict with Special Reference to the Lot Smith Expedition and the Robert T. Burton Expedition.* Salt Lake City: Deseret Book, 1929. Margaret M. Fisher, who was married to Joseph A. Fisher (a member of Lot Smith's Utah Cavalry), was active in the Women's Grand Army of the Republic Auxiliary. An amateur historian, she dedicated her 1929 book to "the memory of the heroic men who volunteered and answered the call of Abraham Lincoln in the hour of the nation's peril from the state of Utah" and explained that the "purpose of this book is to preserve the record of the brilliant military achievemnts [*sic*] of these loyal American soldiers; and also to furnish a standing refutation of the false charge which has been made, by the uninformed that Utah in the early days of her history was lacking in loyalty to the United States" (10).
FOLD3	Civil War Service Records Database (http://fold3.com). This database consists of two major titles: Confederate Records and Union Records. Confederate Records includes sixteen subtitles: Virginia, Georgia, North Carolina, Mississippi, Alabama, South Carolina, Tennessee, Texas, Louisiana, Arkansas, Officers, Missouri, Florida, CSA, Kentucky, and Maryland. Union Records includes these subtitles: Missouri, Kentucky, West Virginia, Maryland, Tennessee, Delaware, Arkansas, New York (index cards), New York 1st Volunteer Engineers, Ohio, Louisiana, New Mexico, Nebraska, North Carolina, Oregon, Pennsylvania, Texas, Alabama, Nevada, Florida, Virginia, Massachusetts, Mississippi, Dakota, Georgia, and Utah.
LDSBE	Jenson, Andrew. *LDS Biographical Encyclopedia.* Salt Lake City: Deseret Book, 1936. This book contains biographical sketches, sometimes accompanied by a photo, of influential men and women from early Utah history.
LOT SMITH TEAMSTER	Teamsters who served with the Lot Smith Utah Cavalry were not considered Civil War veterans (nor were they eligible for federal pension benefits or membership in the Grand Army of the Republic following the war).

CODE	EXPLANATION
MCL	Manassa Cemetery List (http://files.usgwarchives.net/co/conejos/cemeteries/manassa.txt). Grace Bagwell's "Old Manassa Cemetery, Manassa, Conejos, Colorado" list contains the following information about individuals buried in the old Manassa (Colorado) cemetery: surname, given name, birth date, death date, spouse, marriage date, father's name, and mother's name.
MDA	Bitton, David. *Guide to Mormon Diaries and Autobiographies*. Provo, UT: Brigham Young University Press, 1977. This book provides some veteran information within diary or autobiography summaries.
MLM	"Most Likely Match." While Civil War and Latter-day Saint membership online resources have improved in recent years, positively matching an individual veteran's record with a Latter-day Saint membership record for that same individual cannot always be done with absolute certainty. Frequently, there are several Civil War veterans or baptized Latter-day Saints who shared the same name. While we have a high degree of confidence that the individuals who appear in the following appendices belong to Civil War veterans and to baptized Latter-day Saints with the same name, we cannot always be certain that the veteran and the Latter-day Saint are the same person. In cases where there is no cross-linked information between veteran and LDS records, we have selected the "most likely matched" records. This code appears in the Notes field to inform readers that, despite our best efforts, some uncertainty remains regarding whether we have matched this soldier and an LDS member's records correctly.
NARA	National Archives and Records Administration, Washington, DC. NARA houses original and microfilm military records for the Civil War. NPS usually lists the microfilm roll number where confirming veteran information can be found.
NFS	New.FamilySearch.org. This family history website is sponsored by The Church of Jesus Christ of Latter-day Saints. Each individual receives a unique identification number, referenced here

CODE	EXPLANATION
	as the "NFS ID #." NFS ID numbers have been provided so that you can easily see which person we linked to a particular Civil War veteran. It is important to note that while NFS contains a wealth of genealogical and historical information, not all of the information found on NFS is accurate nor, in many cases, has it been verified. NFS was, though, the most extensive source of LDS membership information available at the time of publication.
NPS	National Park Service Civil War Registry (http://www.itd.nps.gov/cwss/). This database lists the name, unit affiliation, rank, and National Archives microfilm roll numbers for numerous Civil War veterans (both Union and Confederate). Individual records include the following fields: name, regiment (unit), side (Union or Confederate), company, soldier's initial rank, soldier's rank upon termination of military service, alternate name (if used), notes, and film number (referencing NARA microfilm records). This database, while sometimes finicky to use, was the most frequently used resource to verify Civil War military service. When NPS listed several individuals with the same name—all of whom were Civil War veterans, but who served in different military units—our research team selected the most likely NPS listing (which opens the possibility that, while we have confirmed veteran status, we may have identified an incorrect unit affiliation). NPS also includes a searchable regimental database that provides information about most Civil War regiments (often including the unit's date of organization, campaigns and history, commanders, and losses).
Obituary	Please see the notes for a source citation and additional information about that service member's obituary.
PI	Pension Index records. Maintained by the National Archives and Records Administration, electronic copies are also available on Ancestry.com.
PPMU	Esshom, Frank. *Pioneers and Prominent Men of Utah*. Salt Lake City: Utah Pioneers Book Publishing, 1913. This book contains biographical sketches, often accompanied by a photo, of numerous early settlers of Utah Territory.

CODE	EXPLANATION
SBS	Bullock, Richard H. *Ship Brooklyn Saints: Their Journey and Early Endeavors in California*. Sandy, Utah: ShipBrooklyn.com, 2009. http://shipbrooklyn.com/passengers.html. Additional information is also available online at http://www.dialoguejournal.com/wp-content/uploads/sbi/articles/Dialogue_V21N03_49.pdf. According to Richard H. Bullock, all "238 passengers on the ship Brooklyn have been identified by several sources as all being members of the LDS Church. There were four exceptions to this: Edward Kemble—newspaperman, Edward Von Pfister—businessman, Howard Oakley—businessman, and Frank Ward—businessman. There were 100 children aboard the ship, 50 under six years of age, that would not have been baptized. I made a general assumption that they would have eventually been members. Many were baptized by John M. Horner, William Glover, Addison Pratt, and Parley P. Pratt, among others, in the San Francisco Bay and other locations in the gold fields. Many of these baptisms were never reported to Church headquarters, but appear in personal journals." (Email correspondence between Kenneth L. Alford and Richard H. Bullock, September 19, 2011.)
SEB	Susan Easton Black, comp. *Membership of The Church of Jesus Christ of Latter-day Saints, 1830–1848*. 50 vols. Salt Lake City: The Church of Jesus Christ of Latter-day Saints, 1990. "Susan Easton Black and associates researched LDS historical resources and compiled a 50-volume set of information on early members of the church. It is a good beginning point to identify available information and sources for an early LDS" member. "While this compilation is massive, it is not complete" (https://www.familysearch.org/learn/wiki/en/Early_Church_Membership_Records_by_Susan_Easton_Black). Entries generally contain the following relevant information: names and name variations, birth date and place, father's name, mother's name, marriage date and place, spouse's name, children's names, death date and place, burial date and place, baptism date, confirmation date, and temple ordinances. "It does not include—All sources about Latter-day Saints to 1848, Every early LDS membership record, All Latter-day Saint sources available at the Family History Library, Information on members who joined the Church after 1848, even if they were included in the sources indexed, [or] References to every major Latter-day Saint index" (http://www.familysearch.org/Eng/Search/RG/frameset_rg.asp?Dest=G1&Aid=&Gid=&Lid=&Sid=&Did=&Juris1=&Event=&Year=&Gloss=&Sub=&Tab=&Entry=&Guide=Membersh.ASP).

CODE	EXPLANATION
SLV	"San Luis Valley" (La Jara Stake of The Church of Jesus Christ of Latter-day Saints. *The Mormons: 100 Years in the San Luis Valley of Colorado, 1883–1983.* La Jara, CO: n.p., 1982). This book provides biographical information including veteran status, some vital record information (birth and death), and a history of The Church of Jesus Christ of Latter-day Saints in Colorado's San Luis Valley.
VBU	Veterans with Federal service buried in Utah. Utah State Archives, Salt Lake City, Utah. (https://www.familysearch.org/search/collection/show#uri=http://hr-search-api:8080/searchapi/search/collection/1542862). According to the FamilySearch Wiki: "These records cover the time period from the earliest territorial time to 1966. . . . [This database consists] of thousands of cards arranged by county, then by city, and then by the veteran's name. Only in Salt Lake City were the records filed by cemetery and then by veteran's name." The following veteran information is recorded: name of veteran, serial number, rank, organization (military unit), branch, date and place of enlistment, date and place of discharge, date and place of birth, date and place of death, city and county of burial, cemetery and plot location; name, address, and relationship of next of kin (which is often left blank). Additional information about this database is available online at https://wiki.familysearch.org (search for "Utah Veterans Burial Records).

These song sheets illustrate two of the many patriotic songs that were composed and sung during the Civil War. Most songs were published in the Northern states. Left: "Hail! Glorious banner of our land. Spirit of the Union" was published in 1861 by Gibson & Company in Cincinnati, Ohio. Right: "Our Confederate National Anthem" was composed in Richmond, Virginia, in 1862. (Library of Congress)

Union soldiers in the 8th New York State Militia Drums Corps pose at Arlington, Virginia in June 1861. (Library of Congress)

LATTER-DAY SAINT CIVIL WAR VETERANS

This appendix lists Civil War veterans who joined The Church of Jesus Christ of Latter-day Saints during their lifetime. (Appendix C contains information regarding how this list was researched and created. Appendix D provides explanatory information for each field in the record below as well as an explanation for the various codes and acronyms used. Please note that the inclusion of the [MLM] code in the Notes field indicates that the Civil War veteran with that name and the LDS member with that name may not be the same person.)

See Appendix G (Baptism Summary) and Appendix H (Military Service Summary) for synopsis information about the Latter-day Saint Civil War veterans listed below.

ABBOTT, CHARLES ENOCH   (UNION ARMY)   *Baptized after the war.*

Birth Date: 22 December 1847	Birth Place: Fulton, White Side, Illinois
LDS Membership Date: 11 November 1878	LDS Membership Source(s): NFS (ID #: KWJK-4HP)
Death Date: 10 January 1927	Death Place: Los Angeles, California Find A Grave: 82343710 Burial Location: Wasatch Lawn Cemetery, Salt Lake City, Salt Lake, Utah

Notes: [MLM] "CIVIL WAR VETERAN" is carved on his grave marker [FGC]. [NPS] lists an additional "Charles E. Abbott" who served in Company E, 14th Regiment, Illinois Infantry.

ACKROYD, WALTER WILLIAM   (UNION ARMY)   *Baptized after the war.*

Rank: Private	Unit(s): Companies C & E, 18th Regiment, Missouri Infantry Military Service Source(s): MDA, NPS, PI
Birth Date: 7 August 1846	Birth Place: Cormsborough Parish, Yorkshire, England
LDS Membership Date: 1 January 1882	LDS Membership Source(s): MDA, NFS (ID #: K2MH-BYY)
Death Date: 4 February 1924	Death Place: Alberta, Canada Find A Grave: 23417501 Burial Location: Magrath Cemetery, Magrath, Alberta, Canada

424

APPENDIX E

Ackroyd, Walter William (continued)

Notes: He was orphaned in Illinois in 1855 and carried mail on snowshoes in the 1870s. He moved to Bear Lake, Idaho, in 1882 and joined the LDS Church there. He gave lectures on American history in Paris, Idaho. He was ordained an elder in 1884 and became a Sunday School teacher and later served as president of Second Elders Quorum and assistant teacher for Young Men's Theological Class in the Bloomington Sunday School. Regarding the 1890 Manifesto, he wrote, "Certain it is . . . that those Latter-day Saints who are opposed to polygamy are much pleased." He applied for a government invalid pension in 1889. He became a Republican after the Church asked members to join a national party in 1891. Moved to Alberta, Canada, early in the twentieth century [MDA, 2].

ALEXANDER, MORONI WOODRUFF (UNION ARMY) *Baptized before the war.*

Rank: Private	Unit(s): Lot Smith Utah Cavalry Military Service Source(s): ACWS, NPS, Fisher, 1862 MOR
Birth Date: 4 March 1837	Birth Place: Memphis, Shelby, Tennessee
LDS Membership Date: 18 August 1845	LDS Membership Source(s): NFS (ID #: KW8M-TYJ)
Death Date: 8 July 1901	Death Place: Cedar City, Iron, Utah Find A Grave: 17426665 Burial Location: Cedar City Cemetery, Cedar City, Iron, Utah
Notes: [MLM] He sometimes went by the name "Wood Alexander" [Fisher, 72].	

ALLEN, SAMUEL (UNION ARMY) *Baptized before the war.*

Rank: Private	Unit(s): Companies B & D, 3rd Regiment, California Infantry Military Service Source(s): NPS, PI, VBU
Birth Date: 21 August 1834	Birth Place: Arnold, Nottingham, England
LDS Membership Date: 1 April 1849	LDS Membership Source(s): NFS (ID #: KWJ6-XT2)
Death Date: 13 February 1904	Death Place: Salt Lake City, Salt Lake, Utah Find A Grave: — Burial Location: Salt Lake City, Salt Lake, Utah
Notes: The 3rd Regiment, California Infantry, was organized between September 15 and December 3, 1861. Both B and D Companies served at Camp Douglas, Utah Territory [NPS]. [VBU] and [NFS] have slightly differing death dates.	

ALLEN, SAMUEL JACKSON (UNION ARMY) *Baptized during the war.*

Rank: Private	Unit(s): Company D, 18th Regiment, Michigan Infantry Military Service Source(s): 1890 Census, NPS
Birth Date: 8 January 1839	Birth Place: Far West, Caldwell, Missouri
LDS Membership Date: 12 April 1865	LDS Membership Source(s): FGC, NFS (ID #: KWNJ-RGP)
Death Date: 26 September 1907	Death Place: Lewiston, Cache, Utah Find A Grave: 32118361 Burial Location: Lewiston, Cache, Utah
Notes: [MLM] He served in the military for six months and four days beginning on September 1, 1864 [1890 Census]. He managed a cooperative store in Lewiston, Utah, and was the town's first postmaster and first public school teacher [FGC].	

ALLEN, WILLIAM C. (UNION ARMY)   *Baptized before the war.*

Rank: Private	**Unit(s):** Lot Smith Utah Cavalry **Military Service Source(s):** ACWS, VBU, NPS, Fisher, 1862 MOR
Birth Date: 14 February 1843	**Birth Place:** Waitsboro, Calloway, Kentucky
LDS Membership Date: 1 January 1853	**LDS Membership Source(s):** LDSBE, NFS (ID #: KWJ6-3TT)
Death Date: 17 March 1926	**Death Place:** Draper, Salt Lake, Utah **Find A Grave:** 9038027 **Burial Location:** Draper City Cemetery, Draper, Salt Lake, Utah

Notes: "In 1847 he came to Utah, crossing the plains in Abraham O. Smoot's company, and together with his parents, he settled in Draper, Salt Lake County, in 1850. . . . In 1876 he went on a pioneering mission to Arizona. . . . There he presided as bishop for two years, and was subsequently chosen to fill the position of first counselor to Lot Smith, president of the Little Colorado Stake of Zion." After returning to Draper, Utah, in 1884, he served as a bishop there for almost a decade and was "ordained a Patriarch by Pres. Jos. F. Smith" [LDSBE, 1:571]. Differing birth dates are listed in [NFS] and [LDSBE].

AMES, JOHN NELSON   (UNION ARMY)   *Baptized after the war.*

Rank: Musician	**Unit(s):** Company C, 22nd Regiment, Maine Infantry **Military Service Source(s):** NPS
Birth Date: 8 April 1833	**Birth Place:** Bucksport, Hancock, Maine
LDS Membership Date: 17 July 1883	**LDS Membership Source(s):** NFS (ID #: L7NT-M1S)
Death Date: 17 August 1911	**Death Place:** Uncertain **Find A Grave:** — **Burial Location:** Uncertain

Notes: [MLM] The 22nd Regiment, Maine Infantry, was organized at Bangor, Maine, on October 10, 1862, and served for nine months [NPS].

AMOS, JOHN THOMAS   (CONFEDERATE ARMY)   *Baptized after the war.*

Rank: Private	**Unit(s):** Company D, 45th Regiment, North Carolina Infantry **Military Service Source(s):** 1890 Census, NPS
Birth Date: 28 August 1844	**Birth Place:** Roanoke, Virginia
LDS Membership Date: 1 June 1873	**LDS Membership Source(s):** NFS (ID #: KWNL-W1H)
Death Date: 11 May 1928	**Death Place:** Payson, Utah, Utah **Find A Grave:** 36571069 **Burial Location:** Payson City Cemetery, Payson, Utah, Utah

Notes: [MLM] His name was written and then crossed out on the 1890 veteran census form (because he was a Confederate soldier). He served in the Confederate army for two years beginning in 1863 [1890 Census].

ANDERSON, NIELS   (UNION ARMY)   *Baptized before the war.*

Rank: Private	**Unit(s):** Company B, 3rd Regiment, California Infantry **Military Service Source(s):** 1890 Census, Obituary
Birth Date: 8 January 1843	**Birth Place:** Galloe, Denmark
LDS Membership Date: 21 October 1857	**LDS Membership Source(s):** NFS (ID #: KWJD-9NQ)

Anderson, Niels (continued)	
Death Date: 10 June 1908	**Death Place:** Richfield, Sevier, Utah **Find A Grave:** 89699 **Burial Location:** Richfield County Cemetery, Richfield, Sevier, Utah
Notes: He served two years and three months beginning on April 27, 1864. "Rheumatism, weakness of eyes" are listed as service-related disabilities [1890 Census]. His obituary stated: "Mr. Anderson was one of the early settlers of this place (Richfield, Utah) and held the position of postmaster here for a number of years. He was a veteran of the Civil War" (*Deseret News*, June 12, 1908, 3).	

ANDREWS, WILLIAM JEFFERSON (CONFEDERATE ARMY)   *Baptized after the war.*

Rank: Private	**Unit(s):** Company E, 8th Regiment, Georgia Infantry **Military Service Source(s):** 1890 Census, NPS, FGC
Birth Date: 23 September 1835	**Birth Place:** Troup, Georgia
LDS Membership Date: 28 March 1869	**LDS Membership Source(s):** NFS (ID #: KWZ6-N3M)
Death Date: 19 February 1896	**Death Place:** Provo, Utah, Utah **Find A Grave:** 28307627 **Burial Location:** Provo, Utah, Utah
Notes: His name was written and then crossed out on the 1890 veteran census form (because he was a Confederate soldier). He served in the Confederate army for three months. "Shot through leg" is listed as a service-related disability [1890 Census]. "William enlisted in Company E of the 8th Georgia Volunteer Infantry Regiment in May of 1861. He was present at First Manassas, Va.; Gettysburg, Pa., where he was wounded; and Camp Winder Hospital, Richmond, Va., both as a nurse and patient. William J. Andrews mustered in as a private with the 'Miller Rifles,' Company E (Capt. Towers' Company) of the 8th Georgia Infantry, on May 14, 1861. Military records show he was present at First Manassas in July 1861 and at the siege of Yorktown in April and May 1862. He was detailed as a nurse to the General Hospital, Camp Winder (Division 4), Richmond, from May 24, 1862 through Feb. 9, 1863. He participated in the siege of Suffolk, Virginia in April and May 1863 and then was part of the Gettysburg Campaign. William was wounded on July 2, 1863 in the Rose Woods near the wheat field at Gettysburg. He took a mini-ball in the left leg, fracturing the tibia, and was 'captured' by the Union Army on July 5. William stayed at Camp Letterman General Hospital in Gettysburg until October, then transferred to Baltimore, Maryland. He was paroled and sent to City Point, Virginia, and returned to Camp Winder, Richmond, this time as a patient. He was furloughed on Dec. 24, 1863, and did not return to active duty. Although the doctors saved the leg, it caused him pain and trouble the rest of his life" [FGC].	

ARROWSMITH, JOHN (UNION ARMY)   *Baptized before the war.*

Rank: Private	**Unit(s):** Lot Smith Utah Cavalry **Military Service Source(s):** ACWS, NPS, Fisher, 1862 MOR
Birth Date: 25 December 1841	**Birth Place:** Millersburg, Mercer, Illinois
LDS Membership Date: 23 June 1850	**LDS Membership Source(s):** SEB (NFS ID #: KWJ8-TLX)
Death Date: 3 February 1910	**Death Place:** Salt Lake City, Salt Lake, Utah **Find A Grave:** — **Burial Location:** Lewisville, Jefferson, Idaho
Notes: [MLM]	

ASHCRAFT (or ASHCROFT), JAMES ELI

(UNION ARMY [PRESUMED]) *Baptized before the war.*

Rank: Uncertain	**Unit(s):** Uncertain **Military Service Source(s):** Obituary
Birth Date: 15 February 1828	**Birth Place:** Mount Sterling, Montgomery, Kentucky
LDS Membership Date: 2 June 1854	**LDS Membership Source(s):** NFS (ID #: KWJZ-4Z8)
Death Date: 1 March 1906	**Death Place:** Mapleton, Utah, Utah **Find A Grave:** 35999382 **Burial Location:** Evergreen Cemetery, Springville, Utah, Utah

Notes: The 1907 obituary of James's wife, Lavine, stated that she "was the wife of Eli Ashcroft, a veteran of the Civil War, who preceded her in death 16 months" (*Deseret News*, July 26, 1907, 3).

ASHTON, EDWARD (UNION ARMY)

Baptized before the war.

Rank: Corporal	**Unit(s):** Company E, 25th Regiment, Michigan Infantry **Military Service Source(s):** NPS
Birth Date: 22 August 1821	**Birth Place:** Caersws, Montgomery, Wales
LDS Membership Date: 27 June 1849	**LDS Membership Source(s):** PPMU, LDSBE, NFS (ID #: KWJH-TB7)
Death Date: 7 February 1904	**Death Place:** Salt Lake City, Salt Lake, Utah **Find A Grave:** 30341113 **Burial Location:** Salt Lake City Cemetery, Salt Lake City, Salt Lake, Utah

Notes: He "came to Utah, July, 1852, Daniel Jones Company. Seventy; Teacher and Choir Leader" [PPMU, 299]. His son, Edward Treharne Ashton, built many of the first electric power plants in Utah [LDSBE, 1:685].

ATKINSON, JAMES ISAAC (UNION ARMY)

Baptized before the war.

Rank: Private	**Unit(s):** Lot Smith Utah Cavalry **Military Service Source(s):** ACWS, NPS, FGC, Fisher, 1862 MOR
Birth Date: 28 November 1841	**Birth Place:** Sackville, New Brunswick, Canada
LDS Membership Date: May 1854	**LDS Membership Source(s):** PPMU, NFS (ID #: KWZJ-Y2N)
Death Date: 18 December 1933	**Death Place:** South Bountiful, Davis, Utah **Find A Grave:** 38629201 **Burial Location:** Bountiful Memorial Park, Bountiful, Davis, Utah

Notes: "Hauled rock from Granite quarry for building Salt Lake Temple 1860–61. Served as lieutenant in Black Hawk war in Andrew Bigler company from July 1, 1866, to Sept. 1, 1866; Oct 9, 1911, joined the Grand Army of the Republic. . . . High councilor Davis stake. Farmer; cattle raiser" [PPMU, 727]. His death certificate notes that a chronic condition contracted during his army service contributed to his death [FGC].

ATTWOOD, RICHARD H. (UNION ARMY)

Baptized before the war.

Rank: First Sergeant	**Unit(s):** Lot Smith Utah Cavalry **Military Service Source(s):** ACWS, NPS, Fisher, 1862 MOR
Birth Date: 2 August 1825	**Birth Place:** Roxburg, Roxburg, Scotland
LDS Membership Date: 23 January 1850	**LDS Membership Source(s):** NFS (ID #: K27Y-CPZ)

Attwood, Richard H. (continued)		
Death Date: March 1893	**Death Place:** Lamoni, Decatur, Iowa **Burial Location:** Uncertain	**Find A Grave:** —
Notes: [MLM]		

BAIRD, ALEXANDER   (UNION NAVY)   *Baptized before the war.*

Rank: Sailor	**Unit(s):** Uncertain **Military Service Source(s):** 1890 Census	
Birth Date: 10 January 1832	**Birth Place:** Paisley, Renfrew, Scotland	
LDS Membership Date: 18 September 1848	**LDS Membership Source(s):** NFS (ID #: KWNT-7MC)	
Death Date: 31 December 1914	**Death Place:** Mink Creek, Franklin, Idaho **Burial Location:** Brigham City Cemetery, Brigham City, Box Elder, Utah	**Find A Grave:** 36571069
Notes: [MLM] He "came to Utah Oct. 4, 1863, Thomas E. Ricks company. . . . Family home Brigham City, Utah. Sheriff and deputy sheriff for twenty years; watchman" [PPMU, 731]. He served in the Civil War for three months during 1864 [1890 Census].		

BAKER, GEORGE WASHINGTON   (CONFEDERATE ARMY)   *Baptized before the war.*

Rank: Private	**Unit(s):** Company C, 11th Regiment, Tennessee Infantry **Military Service Source(s):** 1890 Census, NPS	
Birth Date: 9 September 1837	**Birth Place:** Promfret, Chautauqua, New York	
LDS Membership Date: 21 August 1857	**LDS Membership Source(s):** NFS (ID #: KWJN-CT9)	
Death Date: 28 October 1924	**Death Place:** Logan, Cache, Utah **Burial Location:** Mendon, Cache, Utah	**Find A Grave:** 37109825
Notes: [MLM] He "came to Utah Oct. 2, 1847, Jedediah M. Grant Company, and Mercy Young. . . . First Mayor of Mendon" [PPMU, 97]. His name was written and then crossed out on the 1890 veteran census form (because he was a Confederate soldier). He served in the Confederate infantry for three years, nine months, and five days beginning on July 4, 1861. The 1890 veteran census schedule lists his rank as Corporal and his unit as Company D, 15th Confederate Infantry" [1890 Census]; [NPS] lists the unit above.		

BALLARD, AUGUSTUS ROSS   (UNION ARMY)   *Baptized after the war.*

Rank: Private	**Unit(s):** Company F, 72nd Regiment, Ohio Infantry **Military Service Source(s):** VBU, NPS	
Birth Date: 3 January 1847	**Birth Place:** Fremont, Ballville, Sandusky, Ohio	
LDS Membership Date: 20 June 1880	**LDS Membership Source(s):** NFS (ID #: KWC5-WTL)	
Death Date: 19 October 1913	**Death Place:** Draper, Salt Lake, Utah **Burial Location:** Draper Cemetery, Draper, Salt Lake County, Utah	**Find A Grave:** 9029953
Notes: The 72nd Regiment, Ohio Infantry, was organized between October 1861 and February 1862. The regiment fought at the battles of Shiloh, Corinth, Vicksburg, and several others [NPS]. His first name is spelled "Agustus" on VBU.		

BALLARD, WINFIELD SCOTT (UNION ARMY) *Baptized after the war.*

Rank: Private	**Unit(s):** Company K, 9th Regiment, Ohio Cavalry **Military Service Source(s):** VBU, NPS, FGC
Birth Date: 26 December 1847	**Birth Place:** Fremont, Ballville, Sandusky, Ohio
LDS Membership Date: 16 December 1882	**LDS Membership Source(s):** NFS (ID #: KWCB-8TG)
Death Date: 23 June 1924	**Death Place:** Salt Lake City, Salt Lake, Utah **Find A Grave:** 9003728 **Burial Location:** Draper Cemetery, Draper, Salt Lake County, Utah
Notes: "PVT 9 OHIO CAVALRY" (Private, 9th Ohio Cavalry) is carved on his grave marker [FGC].	

BALLINGER, JOHN McCLURE (UNION ARMY) *Baptized before the war.*

Rank: Corporal	**Unit(s):** Company C, 15th Regiment, Iowa Infantry **Military Service Source(s):** 1890 Census, NPS
Birth Date: 10 June 1838	**Birth Place:** Brumly Hill, Russell, Kentucky
LDS Membership Date: 5 December 1858	**LDS Membership Source(s):** NFS (ID #: KWNP-9QM)
Death Date: 28 December 1892	**Death Place:** Pleasant Grove, Utah, Utah **Find A Grave:** — **Burial Location:** City Cemetery, Pleasant Grove, Utah
Notes: [MLM] He served in the military one year and three months beginning on October 26, 1861. Notes regarding his military service are found on the 1890 veteran census schedule, but they are illegible [1890 Census].	

BARLOW, JAMES MADISON (UNION ARMY) *Baptized before the war.*

Rank: Quartermaster Sergeant (Second Sergeant)	**Unit(s):** Lot Smith Utah Cavalry **Military Service Source(s):** ACWS, NPS, FGC, Fisher, 1862 MOR
Birth Date: 9 July 1812	**Birth Place:** Georgetown, Scott, Kentucky
LDS Membership Date: 7 August 1850	**LDS Membership Source(s):** NFS (ID #: KWJH-8HQ)
Death Date: 8 February 1893	**Death Place:** Salt Lake City, Salt Lake, Utah **Find A Grave:** 76970181 **Burial Location:** Salt Lake City, Salt Lake, Utah
Notes: "QM SGT UTAH CAVALRY CIVIL WAR" (Quartermaster Sergeant, Utah Cavalry) is carved on his grave marker [FGC].	

BARRETT, WILLIAM RILEY (UNION ARMY [PRESUMED]) *Baptized after the war.*

Rank: Uncertain	**Unit(s):** Uncertain **Military Service Source(s):** Obituary
Birth Date: 11 February 1842	**Birth Place:** Lebanon, Wilson, Tennessee
LDS Membership Date: 1 June 1880	**LDS Membership Source(s):** NFS (ID #: KW68-RMW)
Death Date: 3 May 1914	**Death Place:** Salt Lake City, Salt Lake, Utah **Find A Grave:** — **Burial Location:** Salt Lake Cemetery, Salt Lake City, Salt Lake, Utah
Notes: William's obituary states that he was a "civil war veteran" (*Salt Lake Telegram*, May 5, 1914, 7).	

BARRETT, MAURICE J.   (UNION ARMY)   *Baptized after the war.*

Rank: Private	Unit(s): Company F, 1st Regiment, Maryland Cavalry (Potomac Home Brigade); and/or 18th Regiment, Maryland Infantry Military Service Source(s): 1890 Census, NPS, FGC
Birth Date: 25 December 1846	Birth Place: Galway County, Ireland
LDS Membership Date: 19 October 1879	LDS Membership Source(s): NFS (ID #: K2WM-V7N)
Death Date: 16 September 1895	Death Place: Provo, Utah, Utah Find A Grave: 79373305 Burial Location: Provo, Utah, Utah

Notes: "A soldier of the Union. Co. F. 1st Maryland Cavalry"(Company F, 1st Maryland Cavalry) is carved on his grave marker [FGC]. He served in the military two years, seven months, and twenty days beginning in July 1864 [1890 Census]. [NPS] lists Maryland service; [1890 Census] lists 18th Indiana Infantry service.

BARTON, ISAAC   (UNION ARMY)   *Baptized during the war.*

Rank: Sergeant	Unit(s): Company F, 1st Battalion, Nevada Cavalry Military Service Source(s): LDSBE
Birth Date: 11 December 1842	Birth Place: Saint Helens, Lancashire, England
LDS Membership Date: 17 October 1861	LDS Membership Source(s): PPMU, NFS (ID #: KWJC-CJN)
Death Date: 29 August 1916	Death Place: Salt Lake City, Salt Lake, Utah Find A Grave: — Burial Location: Salt Lake City, Salt Lake, Utah

Notes: He "came to Utah 1861. . . . Bishop of 19th Ward, Salt Lake, 20 years; counselor to president of high priests' quorum. Merchant" [PPMU, 739].

BARTON, WILLIAM HENRY   (UNION ARMY)   *Baptized after the war.*

Rank: Private	Unit(s): Companies A & I, 14th Regiment, Iowa Infantry Military Service Source(s): LDSBE, NPS
Birth Date: 16 June 1843	Birth Place: Henry County, Illinois
LDS Membership Date: 15 August 1866	LDS Membership Source(s): LDSBE, NFS (ID #: KWNJ-DJB)
Death Date: 28 February 1925	Death Place: Woods Cross, Davis, Utah Find A Grave: 33104343 Burial Location: Holladay Memorial Park, Salt Lake City, Salt Lake, Utah

Notes: He served in the military for three years during the Civil War (from August 15, 1862, until June 7, 1865). After being engaged in several battles, his hearing became affected. He was slightly wounded in the battle of Pleasant Hill, Louisiana. After leaving the army, he started for the West and intended to go to Montana, but after arriving in Salt Lake Valley, he liked it so much that he remained among the "Mormon" people and soon became converted, joining the LDS Church late in the fall of 1867. He was a farmer [LDSBE, 2:455].

BATTY, EDWARD   (UNION ARMY)   *Baptized before the war.*

Rank: Private	Unit(s): Company H, 126th Regiment, Illinois Infantry Military Service Source(s): NPS, VBU
Birth Date: 6 August 1826	Birth Place: Monk Bretten, Yorkshire, England

LDS Membership Date: 25 January 1848	LDS Membership Source(s): NFS (ID #: KWJW-R1M)
Death Date: 13 September 1906	Death Place: Salt Lake City, Salt Lake, Utah Find A Grave: — Burial Location: Salt Lake City Cemetery, Salt Lake City, Salt Lake, Utah

Notes: The 126th Regiment, Illinois Infantry, mustered in September 4, 1862, and mustered out July 12, 1865. The unit served from Tennessee to Arkansas and saw action during the Siege of Vicksburg [NPS].

BEASLEY, JOHN FLETCHER   (CONFEDERATE ARMY)   *Baptized before the war.*

Rank: Private	Unit(s): Company H, 2nd Regiment, Georgia Cavalry Military Service Source(s): 1890 Census, NPS, Obituary
Birth Date: 10 December 1842	Birth Place: Monroe, Overton, Tennessee
LDS Membership Date: 1858	LDS Membership Source(s): NFS (ID #: KW68-5YC)
Death Date: 29 March 1917	Death Place: Provo, Utah, Utah Find A Grave: 22081536 Burial Location: Provo City Cemetery, Provo, Utah, Utah

Notes: His obituary stated that he was "a confederate civil war veteran" (*Salt Lake Telegram*, March 30, 1917, 22). He served in the Confederate military four years, eleven months, and three days beginning on May 16, 1861. (His inclusion on the 1890 veteran census form was an error made by his enumerator, as no Confederate soldiers were supposed to be included.) His last name was spelled "Beesley" on the veteran census schedule [1890 Census]. [NPS] also lists 3rd Regiment, Georgia Cavalry, military service for John F. Beasley.

BELL, DANIEL   (UNION ARMY)   *Baptized before the war.*

Rank: Private	Unit(s): Company D, 2nd Regiment, District of Columbia Infantry Military Service Source(s): 1890 Census
Birth Date: 13 September 1803	Birth Place: Knockbrader, Down, Ireland
LDS Membership Date: 11 February 1842	LDS Membership Source(s): NFS (ID #: K271-BS7)
Death Date: 1883	Death Place: Hoytsville, Summit, Utah Find A Grave: 30811622 Burial Location: Hoytsville, Summit, Utah

Notes: [MLM] He served in the military two years and six months beginning in August 1863. If the correct LDS member is identified, the 1890 veteran census schedule (recorded in Box Elder County, Utah) should list his entry as a widow report, as his death date was prior to 1890, but it does not [1890 Census].

BELLAMY, WILLIAM W.   (UNION ARMY)   *Baptized after the war.*

Rank: Private	Unit(s): Company I or J, 27th Regiment, Michigan Infantry Military Service Source(s): 1890 Census, NPS
Birth Date: 16 February 1816	Birth Place: Woodhouse, Yorkshire, England
LDS Membership Date: 9 April 1876	LDS Membership Source(s): NFS (ID #: KWJW-1QQ)
Death Date: 2 December 1893	Death Place: Salt Lake City, Salt Lake, Utah Find A Grave: 53619070 Burial Location: Salt Lake Cemetery, Salt Lake City, Salt Lake, Utah

Notes: [MLM] He served in the military one year and seven months beginning on September 1, 1864 [1890 Census].

BENNION, JOHN R.   (UNION ARMY)   *Baptized before the war.*

Rank: Private	Unit(s): Lot Smith Utah Cavalry Military Service Source(s): ACWS, VBU, NPS, Fisher, 1862 MOR
Birth Date: 1 February 1840	Birth Place: Liverpool, Lancashire, England
LDS Membership Date: 1 January 1850	LDS Membership Source(s): NFS (ID #: KWNC-3B8)
Death Date: 6 May 1899	Death Place: Taylorsville, Salt Lake, Utah Find A Grave: 34306430 Burial Location: Taylorsville Memorial Park Cemetery, Taylorsville, Salt Lake, Utah
Notes: —	

BENNION, SAMUEL ROBERTS   (UNION ARMY)   *Baptized before the war.*

Rank: Private	Unit(s): Lot Smith Utah Cavalry Military Service Source(s): VBU, NPS, Fisher, 1862 MOR
Birth Date: 10 November 1842	Birth Place: Nauvoo, Hancock, Illinois
LDS Membership Date: 9 January 1852	LDS Membership Source(s): LDSBE, PPMU, NFS (ID #: KWJZ-RRX)
Death Date: 16 November 1915	Death Place: Vernal, Uintah, Utah Find A Grave: 33440228 Burial Location: Salt Lake City Cemetery, Salt Lake City, Salt Lake, Utah

Notes: He was "President [of] Uinta (Utah) Stake" [PPMU, 105]. He "came to Utah Oct. 3, 1847, John Taylor Company. Missionary to St. Louis and Illinois 1866–67, and to England 1883–85; president Uinta (Utah) stake 1887–1906 . . . President bank of Vernal; president Vernal Milling and Light Company" [PPMU, 750]. "He came to the [Salt Lake] Valley with his parents in 1847 and settled in North Jordan . . . and was subsequently ordained a Deacon, an Elder and a Seventy successively. Finally, he was chosen as one of the presidents of the 7th quorum of Seventy." [LDSBE, 1:478] lists his baptismal date as January 9, 1851.

BENSON, WILLIAM CARLISLE   (CONFEDERATE ARMY)   *Baptized after the war.*

Rank: Private	Unit(s): Company D or E, 2nd Regiment, Tennessee Infantry Military Service Source(s): 1890 Census
Birth Date: 26 April 1837	Birth Place: Somerville, Morgan, Alabama
LDS Membership Date: 20 July 1884	LDS Membership Source(s): NFS (ID #: KWJ6-C1D)
Death Date: 30 January 1915	Death Place: Provo, Utah, Utah Find A Grave: 70862906 Burial Location: Provo, Utah, Utah

Notes: He served in the military one year and seven months beginning in August 1862. "Lame leg" was listed as a service-related disability [1890 Census]. [NPS] also lists a Confederate soldier named "William Benson" from Tennessee who served in the 7th Regiment, Tennessee Cavalry.

BENZON, ANDREW BECK   (UNION ARMY)   *Baptized before the war.*

Rank: Private	Unit(s): Companies K & M, 3rd Regiment, Missouri Infantry Volunteers Military Service Source(s): NPS, VBU
Birth Date: 16 February 1835	Birth Place: Maribo, Maribo, Denmark
LDS Membership Date: 1 January 1861	LDS Membership Source(s): PPMU, NFS (ID #: KWJC-17L)

Death Date: 14 July 1901	Death Place: Salt Lake City, Salt Lake, Utah Find A Grave: 30259105 Burial Location: Salt Lake City Cemetery, Salt Lake City, Salt Lake, Utah

Notes: He "came to Utah Sept. 26, 1862, James Wareham Company. High Priest; Block Teacher. Salesman" [PPMU, 550]. [NFS] lists middle name as "Bech"; [PPMU] lists "Beck." [PPMU] lists death date as 1895, at Salt Lake City; [NFS] lists 1901.

BESS, WILLIAM   (UNION ARMY)   *Baptized before the war (presumed).*

Rank: Private	Unit(s): Lot Smith Utah Cavalry Military Service Source(s): VBU, ACWS, Fisher, 1862 MOR
Birth Date: 17 January 1841	Birth Place: Greenwood, Steuben, New York
LDS Membership Date: Presumed LDS	LDS Membership Source(s): NFS (ID #: L7BN-LYH)
Death Date: 24 November 1907	Death Place: Salt Lake City, Salt Lake, Utah Find A Grave: — Burial Location: Taylorsville, Salt Lake, Utah

Notes: As a member of the Lot Smith Cavalry Company, he is presumed to be a Latter-day Saint (but his baptismal date and LDS membership could not be confirmed from available sources).

BEVANS, CORYDON HENRY   (UNION ARMY)   *Baptized after the war.*

Rank: Private	Unit(s): Company F, 55th Regiment, Illinois Infantry Military Service Source(s): 1890 Census, NPS
Birth Date: 13 September 1839	Birth Place: Marietta, Fulton, Illinois
LDS Membership Date: 1 January 1877 (confirmation)	LDS Membership Source(s): NFS (ID #: K271-3FT)
Death Date: 4 June 1915	Death Place: Turlock, Stanislaus, California Find A Grave: 55757527 Burial Location: Turlock, Stanislaus, California

Notes: [MLM] He served in the military one year beginning in 1861 [1890 Census]. Served as a probate judge [NFS].

BIGLER, ANDREW   (UNION ARMY)   *Baptized before the war.*

Rank: Corporal	Unit(s): Lot Smith Utah Cavalry Military Service Source(s): VBU, ACWS, Fisher, 1862 MOR
Birth Date: 24 March 1836	Birth Place: Clarksburg, Harrison, West Virginia
LDS Membership Date: 19 March 1854	LDS Membership Source(s): NFS (ID #: KWJ6-38K)
Death Date: 8 January 1892	Death Place: Mendon, Cache, Utah Find A Grave: 36063880 Burial Location: Mendon, Cache, Utah

Notes: —

BIGLOW, ASA ELIJAH   (UNION ARMY)   *Baptized before the war.*

Rank: Surgeon	Unit(s): Field Officer and Staff Company, 3rd Regiment, Illinois Cavalry Military Service Source(s): 1890 Census, NPS
Birth Date: 2 February 1832	Birth Place: Chariton, Clays, Illinois

Biglow, Asa Elijah (continued)	
LDS Membership Date: 1 August 1840	**LDS Membership Source(s):** NFS (ID #: KWJH-XN3)
Death Date: 9 November 1911	**Death Place:** Payson, Utah, Utah **Find A Grave:** — **Burial Location:** Payson, Utah, Utah
Notes: [MLM] He is listed on the [1890 Census] but no service date, rank, or unit affiliation information was recorded for him by the census enumerator.	

BISHOP, FRANCIS MARION   (UNION ARMY)   *Baptized after the war.*

Rank: Enlisted as a Corporal; separated as a Captain	**Unit(s):** Company I, 1st Regiment, Michigan Infantry; and Company H, 2nd U.S. Volunteer Infantry **Military Service Source(s):** VBU, NPS, PPMU
Birth Date: 2 August 1843	**Birth Place:** Pleasant Valley, Essex, New York
LDS Membership Date: 2 July 1894	**LDS Membership Source(s):** NFS (ID #: KWC8-LH2)
Death Date: 22 May 1933	**Death Place:** Salt Lake City, Salt Lake, Utah **Find A Grave:** 24934714, 15151791 **Burial Location:** Salt Lake City Cemetery, Salt Lake City, Salt Lake, Utah
Notes: "Enlisted in Union army July 27, 1861, in 1st Michigan infantry, served five years. Promoted from corporal to sergeant-major, 2nd lieutenant and 1st lieutenant. Transferred V.R.C. [Veteran Reserve Corps], promoted to captain of Company H, 2d U.S. volunteers. Mustered out Nov. 7, 1865, at Fort Leavenworth, Kas. Member Major Powell's exploring expedition in Colorado Canyon 1871–72. Professor natural science in university of Deseret" [PPMU, 758]. Fought in the Second Battle of Bull Run and Antietam; seriously wounded at Fredericksburg. Topographer with Powell on second expedition (1871–72) (Kate B. Carter, ed., *Our Pioneer Heritage* [Salt Lake City: Daughters of Utah Pioneers, 1958–77], 13:202–3). He "came to Utah August, 1870. Started first free school in Utah; prominent in educational and civil matters" [PPMU, 677].	

BLAND, JOSEPH   (UNION ARMY)   *Baptized before the war.*

Rank: Private	**Unit(s):** Company L, 11th Regiment, Kansas Cavalry **Military Service Source(s):** VBU, NPS, PI, FGC, 1890 Census
Birth Date: 7 December 1823	**Birth Place:** Baildon, Yorkshire, England
LDS Membership Date: 18 April 1848	**LDS Membership Source(s):** NFS (ID #: KWV7-5BV)
Death Date: 1 July 1912	**Death Place:** Richfield, Sevier, Utah **Find A Grave:** 31552817 **Burial Location:** Richfield, Sevier, Utah,
Notes: "CIVIL WAR VETERAN COMPANY L ELEVENTH REGIMENT CAVELRY [sic] KANSAS VOLUN-TEER" is carved on his grave marker [FGC]. He served one year and seven months beginning February 1864 [1890 Census].	

BOULDEN, JOSEPH LOUIS   (UNION ARMY)   *Baptized after the war.*

Rank: Quartermaster Sergeant	**Unit(s):** Companies M & I, 1st Regiment, New Mexico Cavalry **Military Service Source(s):** VBU, NPS, PI, FGC
Birth Date: 12 September 1838	**Birth Place:** Piqua, Miami, Ohio
LDS Membership Date: 2 October 1869	**LDS Membership Source(s):** NFS (ID #: KWJZ-8NP)

| Death Date: 28 June 1913 | Death Place: Castle Dale, Emery, Utah   Find A Grave: 46998685 |
| | Burial Location: Castle Dale City Cemetery, Castle Dale, Emery, Utah |

Notes: "1 N.M. CAV" (1st New Mexico Cavalry) is carved on his grave marker [FGC].

BOWRING, CHARLES KINGSFORD (UNION ARMY) *Baptized before the war.*

Rank: Private (Drummer)	Unit(s): Company C, 1st Regiment, Nevada Infantry
	Military Service Source(s): NPS, PI, FGC
Birth Date: 27 February 1849	Birth Place: Warminster, Wiltshire, England
LDS Membership Date: 1 January 1857 (confirmation)	LDS Membership Source(s): NFS (ID #: KP7G-PYB)
Death Date: 19 May 1912	Death Place: Salt Lake City, Salt Lake, Utah Find A Grave: 44529046
	Burial Location: Mount Olivet Cemetery, Salt Lake City, Salt Lake, Utah

Notes: "CO. C 1 NEV. INF." (Company C, 1st Nevada Infantry) is carved on his grave marker [FGC]. There may be an error in either his birth date or confirmation date, as he was not quite eight years old on the date listed.

BOYER, WILLIAM (UNION ARMY) *Baptized during the war.*

Rank: Sergeant	Unit(s): Company H, 4th Regiment, Ohio Cavalry
	Military Service Source(s): 1890 Census, NPS
Birth Date: 5 April 1840	Birth Place: South Shields, Durham, England
LDS Membership Date: 15 November 1863	LDS Membership Source(s): NFS (ID #: KWZM-C1G)
Death Date: 27 June 1913	Death Place: Coalville, Summit, Utah Find A Grave: 74831
	Burial Location: Coalville, Summit, Utah

Notes: [MLM] He served in the military three years beginning in 1861. "Shot in right leg" was recorded as a service-related disability. His unit is listed as Company H, 4th Ohio Cavalry [1890 Census]. There are numerous William Boyers from Ohio who served; none of the soldiers listed on [NPS] served in the 4th Ohio Cavalry.

BOYLE, ALBERT CHARLES (UNION ARMY) *Baptized after the war.*

Rank: Private	Unit(s): Company G, 26th Regiment, Massachusetts Infantry
	Military Service Source(s): 1890 Census, NPS
Birth Date: 18 January 1850	Birth Place: Kirtland, Clinton, Indiana
LDS Membership Date: 7 June 1874	LDS Membership Source(s): NFS (ID #: KWN6-PKV)
Death Date: 23 May 1937	Death Place: Vernal, Uintah, Utah Find A Grave: 80701840
	Burial Location: Elysian Gardens, Salt Lake City, Salt Lake, Utah

Notes: [MLM] Reportedly worked as a carpenter [NFS]. He served in the military one year and six months beginning in 1863 [1890 Census]. There may be an error in his birth date, as he would have been a young recruit.

BRINGHURST, WILLIAM A. (UNION ARMY) *Baptized before the war.*

Rank: Corporal	Unit(s): Lot Smith Utah Cavalry
	Military Service Source(s): VBU, ACWS, NPS, Fisher, 1862 MOR
Birth Date: 26 January 1839	Birth Place: Lionville, Chester, Pennsylvania

Bringhurst, William A. (continued)	
LDS Membership Date: August 1847	**LDS Membership Source(s):** LDSBE, PPMU, NFS (ID #: KWCP-FHY)
Death Date: 8 March 1912	**Death Place:** Toquerville City, Washington, Utah **Find A Grave:** 145679 **Burial Location:** Toquerville City Cemetery, Washington County, Utah
Notes: "He came to the [Salt Lake] Valley in 1847 . . . [and] was ordained a High Priest and Bishop Feb. 15, 1874, by Brigham Young" [LDSBE, 4:678]. He was "Bishop [of] Toquerville (Utah) Ward" [PPMU, 106] and "assessor and collector; sheriff and judge in Kane county (Utah)" [PPMU, 769].	

BROOKBANK, THOMAS WALTON (UNION ARMY)   *Baptized after the war.*

Rank: Private	**Unit(s):** Company C, 209th Regiment, Pennsylvania Infantry **Military Service Source(s):** VBU, NPS, PI, FGC
Birth Date: 23 February 1847	**Birth Place:** Edensburg, Cambridge, Pennsylvania
LDS Membership Date: April 1877	**LDS Membership Source(s):** MDA, NFS (ID #: KW8W-WGR)
Death Date: 2 October 1939	**Death Place:** Salt Lake City, Salt Lake, Utah **Find A Grave:** 170695 **Burial Location:** Mount Olivet Cemetery, Salt Lake City, Salt Lake, Utah
Notes: Studied at the Garrett Biblical Institute in Evanston, Illinois. Active in the Methodist preaching circuit in 1876, he joined the LDS Church after first being antagonistic toward it. He settled in Sunset, Arizona, and joined the United Order in the 1880s. He served two missions to England (1888, 1913), was an editor of the *Millennial Star*. and authored missionary tracts. He also served as a missionary among Indians and in Mexico [MDA, 40].	

BROWN, CAMPBELL McLEOD, SR. (UNION NAVY)   *Baptized after the war.*

Rank: Uncertain	**Unit(s):** West Gulf Blockading Squadron, USS Admiral **Military Service Source(s):** VBU; FGC; Headstones Provided for Deceased Union Civil War Veterans, 1879–1903
Birth Date: 13 April 1847	**Birth Place:** Kingston, St. Vincent, West Indies
LDS Membership Date: 1 October 1871	**LDS Membership Source(s):** NFS (ID #: KJPN-FCV)
Death Date: 16 March 1894	**Death Place:** Salt Lake City, Salt Lake, Utah **Find A Grave:** 36720874 **Burial Location:** Salt Lake City Cemetery, Salt Lake City, Salt Lake, Utah
Notes: "LDS US NAVY CIVIL WAR" is carved on his grave marker [FGC]. The USS Admiral "was renamed (the USS) Fort Morgan on 1 September 1864" (*Dictionary of American Naval Fighting Ships*, Admiral, http://www.history.navy.mil/danfs/a3/admiral-i.htm).	

BROWN, EDWIN (UNION ARMY)   *Baptized before the war.*

Rank: Private	**Unit(s):** Lot Smith Utah Cavalry **Military Service Source(s):** VBU, ACWS, NPS, Fisher, 1862 MOR
Birth Date: 24 June 1841	**Birth Place:** Newbury, Berkshire, England
LDS Membership Date: 11 February 1852	**LDS Membership Source(s):** NFS (ID #: KWZ5-V2H)
Death Date: 17 April 1928	**Death Place:** Murray, Salt Lake, Utah **Find A Grave:** 13421269 **Burial Location:** Murray City Cemetery, Murray, Salt Lake, Utah
Notes: See the Ellsworth-Alford chapter herein for additional information.	

BROWN, JOHN WYLES (UNION ARMY) *Baptized after the war.*

Rank: Private	**Unit(s):** Company A, 84th Regiment, New York Infantry **Military Service Source(s):** VBU, NPS, PI, FGC, Obituary
Birth Date: 23 May 1846	**Birth Place:** New York, New York
LDS Membership Date: 13 August 1871	**LDS Membership Source(s):** NFS (ID #: KWC4-7F7)
Death Date: 25 November 1912	**Death Place:** Provo, Utah, Utah **Find A Grave:** 52749936 **Burial Location:** Provo City Cemetery, Provo, Utah, Utah
Notes: "CO. A 84 REGT. N.Y. VOLUNTEERS" (Company A, 84th Regiment, New York Volunteers) is carved on his grave marker [FGC]. His obituary, entitled "Funeral of Civil War Veteran Tomorrow," states that he was the "state commander of the Grand Army of the Republic" and that "a number of the veterans of the civil war living in Salt Lake City will go to Provo tomorrow to attend the services" (*Salt Lake Telegram*, November 26, 1912, 10).	

BROWN, JOHN WACKLET (UNION ARMY) *Baptized before the war.*

Rank: Private	**Unit(s):** Company A or B, 84th Regiment, New York Infantry **Military Service Source(s):** 1890 Census, NPS
Birth Date: 16 October 1826	**Birth Place:** Frampton, Gloucestershire, England
LDS Membership Date: 1 June 1849	**LDS Membership Source(s):** NFS (ID #: KWVQ-DNJ)
Death Date: 22 July 1896	**Death Place:** Parowan, Iron, Utah **Find A Grave:** 11522440 **Burial Location:** Parowan, Iron, Utah
Notes: [MLM] He served in the military one year beginning on July 15, 1864 [1890 Census].	

BULOW, CHARLES HENRY ENGEL (UNION ARMY) *Baptized during the war.*

Rank: Enlisted as a Sergeant; discharged as a Second Lieutenant	**Unit(s):** Battery K, 1st Regiment, Michigan Light Artillery **Military Service Source(s):** 1890 Census, NPS
Birth Date: 26 January 1835	**Birth Place:** Vordingborg, Copenhagen, Denmark
LDS Membership Date: 26 January 1861	**LDS Membership Source(s):** NFS (ID #: KWV7-T24)
Death Date: 26 March 1891	**Death Place:** Richfield, Sevier, Utah **Find A Grave:** 89912 **Burial Location:** Richfield, Sevier, Utah
Notes: [MLM] He served one year, nine months, and eighteen days beginning September 14, 1864. The census schedule reports that he also used the alias Charles E. Hendrickson [1890 Census].	

BURNHAM, CHARLES C. (UNION ARMY) *Baptized before the war.*

Rank: Private	**Unit(s):** Lot Smith Utah Cavalry **Military Service Source(s):** VBU, ACWS, NPS, Fisher, 1862 MOR
Birth Date: 7 November 1838	**Birth Place:** Nauvoo, Hancock, Illinois
LDS Membership Date: 1 January 1851	**LDS Membership Source(s):** NFS (ID #: KWNB-NKW)
Death Date: 8 May 1926	**Death Place:** Lovel, Big Horn, Wyoming **Find A Grave:** 9542497 **Burial Location:** Draper City Cemetery, Draper, Salt Lake, Utah
Notes: —	

BUTTER, JOHN   (UNION ARMY)   *Baptized before the war.*

Rank: Private	Unit(s): Company K, 134th Regiment, Illinois Volunteers; and H Company, 65th Regiment, Illinois Volunteers Military Service Source(s): 1890 Census, NPS
Birth Date: 5 September 1812	Birth Place: Redbourn, Herefordshire, England
LDS Membership Date: 4 October 1849	LDS Membership Source(s): NFS (ID #: KWC4-RRH)
Death Date: 15 February 1892	Death Place: Spring Lake, Utah, Utah Find A Grave: — Burial Location: Payson, Utah, Utah
Notes: [MLM] Reenlisted with H Company, 65th Illinois Volunteers, and was discharged with his detachment in Greensboro, North Carolina, on June 12, 1865. He served in the military for three months and ten days [1890 Census]. Reportedly worked as "a cordwainer" (a shoemaker or cobbler) [NFS].	

CAHOON, JOHN F.   (UNION ARMY)   *Baptized before the war.*

Rank: Private	Unit(s): Lot Smith Utah Cavalry Military Service Source(s): VBU, ACWS, NPS, 1890 Census, Fisher, 1862 MOR
Birth Date: 19 October 1840	Birth Place: Montrose, Lee, Iowa
LDS Membership Date: 29 January 1851	LDS Membership Source(s): NFS (ID #: 2WXB-CLT)
Death Date: 23 June 1910	Death Place: Salt Lake City, Salt Lake, Utah Find A Grave: 31259868 Burial Location: Salt Lake City Cemetery, Salt Lake City, Salt Lake, Utah
Notes: —	

CALDWELL, THOMAS S.   (UNION ARMY)   *Baptized before the war.*

Rank: Private	Unit(s): Lot Smith Utah Cavalry Military Service Source(s): ACWS, NPS, Fisher, 1862 MOR
Birth Date: 8 February 1842	Birth Place: Barony Finniston, Lanark, Scotland
LDS Membership Date: 17 April 1850	LDS Membership Source(s): NFS (ID #: KWJ6-7ZV)
Death Date: 21 April 1866	Death Place: Brigham City, Box Elder, Utah Find A Grave: — Burial Location: Brigham City, Box Elder, Utah
Notes: [MLM]	

CALKIN, THEODORE J.   (UNION ARMY)   *Baptized before the war.*

Rank: Private	Unit(s): Lot Smith Utah Cavalry Military Service Source(s): ACWS, NPS, Fisher, 1862 MOR
Birth Date: 13 February 1840	Birth Place: Dorr Prairie, Indiana
LDS Membership Date: 1 January 1850 (confirmation)	LDS Membership Source(s): NFS (ID #: L7KQ-5F9)
Death Date: 15 April 1865	Death Place: Uncertain Find A Grave: — Burial Location: Salt Lake City, Salt Lake, Utah
Notes: [MLM]	

CAMPBELL, LEROY (CONFEDERATE ARMY)   *Baptized after the war.*

Rank: Uncertain (Bodyguard)	Unit(s): Capt. Rives' Company, Virginia Light Artillery (Nelson Light Artillery) Military Service Source(s): CSC, NPS
Birth Date: 3 April 1852	Birth Place: Nelson County, Virginia
LDS Membership Date: 1 March 1887	LDS Membership Source(s): NFS (ID #: K2WH-ZN8)
Death Date: 19 February 1933	Death Place: Manassa, Conejos, Colorado Find A Grave: 44104849 Burial Location: Sanford, Conejos, Colorado

Notes: [MLM] There may be an error in his birth date, as he would have been a young recruit.

CANTWELL, FRANCIS R. (UNION ARMY)   *Baptized before the war.*

Rank: Private	Unit(s): Lot Smith Utah Cavalry Military Service Source(s): ACWS, NPS, Fisher, 1862 MOR
Birth Date: 7 April 1841	Birth Place: Manchester, Lancaster, England
LDS Membership Date: 1 February 1850	LDS Membership Source(s): NFS (ID #: KWJK-P1S)
Death Date: 15 November 1898	Death Place: Logan, Cache, Utah Find A Grave: 30738580 Burial Location: Millville City Cemetery, Millville, Cache, Utah

Notes: —

CARDON, THOMAS BARTHELEMY (UNION ARMY)   *Baptized before the war.*

Rank: Bugler	Unit(s): Company G, 10th Regiment, U.S. Infantry Military Service Source(s): NPS, PI, FGC, 1890 Census
Birth Date: 28 August 1842	Birth Place: Prarostino, Torino, Italy
LDS Membership Date: 8 March 1857	LDS Membership Source(s): NFS (ID #: KWZT-645)
Death Date: 15 February 1898	Death Place: Logan, Cache, Utah Find A Grave: 23235188 Burial Location: Logan City Cemetery, Logan, Cache, Utah

Notes: Thomas served four years, six months, and three days with a discharge date of February 3, 1863 [1890 Census]. He immigrated to Salt Lake City from Italy in 1854 and joined the 10th U.S. Infantry as a bugler in September 1858 at age fifteen. He was wounded during the Seven Days Battle. Following the Civil War, he established a photography and jewelry business in Logan (Orson F. Whitney, *History of Utah* [Salt Lake City: George Q. Cannon and Sons, 1892–1904], 4:212–13).

CARNEY, PETER (UNION ARMY)   *Baptized before the war.*

Rank: Private	Unit(s): Lot Smith Utah Cavalry Military Service Source(s): ACWS, NPS, PI, Fisher, 1862 MOR
Birth Date: 4 April 1829	Birth Place: Sorel, Richelieu, Quebec, Canada
LDS Membership Date: 5 September 1852	LDS Membership Source(s): NFS (ID #: KWJ8-TMF)
Death Date: 29 June 1887	Death Place: Woodruff, Rich, Utah Find A Grave: — Burial Location: Woodruff Cemetery, Woodruff, Rich, Utah

Notes: [MLM] [1862 MOR] lists his name as "Peter Carney"; [NFS] lists numerous alternatives for both his first and last names (including "Pierre Corney").

CARPENTER, EZRA DAVIS   (UNION ARMY)   *Baptized after the war.*

Rank: Second Lieutenant	Unit(s): Company B, 18th Regiment, Connecticut Infantry Military Service Source(s): VBU, NPS, PI
Birth Date: 30 July 1833	Birth Place: Thompson, Windham, Connecticut
LDS Membership Date: 25 May 1873	LDS Membership Source(s): NFS (ID #: KWJ4-G44)
Death Date: 23 April 1893	Death Place: Smithfield, Cache, Utah Find A Grave: 63307079 Burial Location: Logan City Cemetery, Logan, Cache, Utah
Notes: The 18th Regiment, Connecticut Infantry, was organized on August 22, 1862, and served mostly in Maryland and West Virginia [NPS].	

CARROLL, JOHN NELSON   (UNION ARMY)   *Baptized after the war.*

Rank: Corporal	Unit(s): Company D, 10th Regiment, U.S. Infantry Military Service Source(s): 1890 Census, NPS
Birth Date: 22 October 1842	Birth Place: Carroll Ridge, New Brunswick, Canada
LDS Membership Date: 22 August 1880	LDS Membership Source(s): NFS (ID #: KWNV-3MF)
Death Date: 4 June 1902	Death Place: Heber City, Wasatch, Utah Find A Grave: 28583856 Burial Location: Heber City, Wasatch, Utah
Notes: [MLM] His 1890 census veteran record is difficult to read but may have listed "Company G" as his unit. His military service began March 13, 1865 [1890 Census].	

CARTER, BENJAMIN   (UNION ARMY)   *Baptized after the war*

Rank: Private	Unit(s): Company G, 58th Regiment, Indiana Infantry Military Service Source(s): VBU, NPS, PI, 1890 Census
Birth Date: 12 June 1843	Birth Place: Petersburg, Pike, Indiana
LDS Membership Date: 18 February 1867	LDS Membership Source(s): NFS (ID #: K2WH-GC9)
Death Date: 3 April 1903	Death Place: Richfield, Sevier, Utah Find A Grave: 89869 Burial Location: Richfield City Cemetery, Richfield, Sevier, Utah
Notes: He served three years beginning on August 26, 1861. Weak eyes and typhoid fever were listed as service-related disabilities [1890 Census].	

CARVER, THOMAS   (CONFEDERATE ARMY)   *Baptized after the war.*

Rank: Private	Unit(s): Company B, 35th Regiment, North Carolina Infantry Military Service Source(s): VBU, NPS
Birth Date: 31 January 1836	Birth Place: North Cove, McDowell, North Carolina
LDS Membership Date: 15 March 1891	LDS Membership Source(s): NFS (ID #: KWJC-614)
Death Date: 23 August 1926	Death Place: Nephi, Juab, Utah Find A Grave: — Burial Location: Vine Bluff Cemetery, Nephi, Juab, Utah
Notes: The 35th Regiment, North Carolina Infantry, was organized by November 1861. Among the battles it participated in were Fredericksburg, Petersburg, and Appomattox [NPS].	

CHAMBERLIN (OR CHAMBERLAIN), JOSEPH

(UNION ARMY)   *Baptized before the war.*

Rank: Private	**Unit(s):** Company B, 14th Regiment, Missouri State Militia Cavalry **Military Service Source(s):** 1890 Census, NPS
Birth Date: 12 May 1812	**Birth Place:** Forked River, Monmouth County, New Jersey
LDS Membership Date: 1 June 1842 (confirmation)	**LDS Membership Source(s):** NFS (ID #: KWVZ-HJ3)
Death Date: 18 April 1879	**Death Place:** Salt Lake City, Salt Lake, Utah **Find A Grave:** 64684705 **Burial Location:** Salt Lake Cemetery, Salt Lake City, Salt Lake, Utah

Notes: [MLM] He enlisted March 15, 1862, at Springfield, Missouri (Company B Muster Roll, 14th Missouri State Militia Volunteer Cavalry, http://www.cwnorthandsouth.com/1862_MR_F.html), and became deaf after an injury [1890 Census]. He served in the military three years. If the correct LDS member is identified, the 1890 veteran census schedule (recorded in Utah County, Utah) should list his entry as a widow report, as his death date was prior to 1890, but it does not [1890 Census].

CHARTER, HENRY WILLARD   (UNION ARMY)   *Baptized after the war.*

Rank: Private	**Unit(s):** Company K, 7th Regiment, Michigan Infantry **Military Service Source(s):** NPS, PI, FGC
Birth Date: 11 April 1843	**Birth Place:** Alabama
LDS Membership Date: 2 April 1896	**LDS Membership Source(s):** NFS (ID #: KWJS-76S)
Death Date: 16 August 1926	**Death Place:** Utah **Find A Grave:** 170492 **Burial Location:** Mount Olivet Cemetery, Salt Lake City, Salt Lake, Utah

Notes: "CO. K 7 MICH. INF." (Company K, 7th Michigan Infantry) is carved on his grave marker [FGC].

CHERRY, JESSE   (UNION ARMY)   *Baptized before the war (presumed).*

Rank: Private	**Unit(s):** Lot Smith Utah Cavalry **Military Service Source(s):** ACWS, Fisher, 1862 MOR
Birth Date: 10 June 1840	**Birth Place:** Adams, Illinois
LDS Membership Date: Before 1864	**LDS Membership Source(s):** SEB, LDSBE (NFS ID #: KWVG-H12)
Death Date: 21 May 1865	**Death Place:** Nottingham, England **Find A Grave:** — **Burial Location:** Uncertain

Notes: He "came to Utah with his parents. . . . On April 22, 1864, he was set apart for a mission to England by Apostle John Taylor and arrived in Liverpool July 1st, following, on the steamship 'Virginia.' . . . He labored faithfully in the land, gaining the confidence of the saints. He was seized by smallpox May 7, 1865. . . . Every effort was made to retard its progress, but without avail." [LDSBE] lists his death date as May 20, 1865 [LDSBE, 3:616–17]. [1862 MOR] lists his name as "Jesse J. Cherry"; [NFS] lists his middle name as "Yelton" and records vicarious baptism information, but he was certainly baptized during his lifetime.

CHLARSON, HANS NADRIAN   (UNION ARMY)   *Baptized before the war.*

Rank: Enlisted as a Private; separated as a Lieutenant	**Unit(s):** 7th New York Regiment, 3rd Brigade, 1st Division **Military Service Source(s):** PI
Birth Date: 17 January 1834	**Birth Place:** Foglabuset, Sodiensvillie, Mimhs, Sweden

Chlarson, Hans Nadrian (continued)	
LDS Membership Date: 2 April 1854	**LDS Membership Source(s):** NFS (ID #: KWJ1-RXV)
Death Date: 10 November 1910	**Death Place:** Thatcher, Graham, Arizona **Find A Grave:** 48003252 **Burial Location:** Thatcher City Cemetery, Thatcher, Graham, Arizona

Notes: Also listed as "Hans Nicholas Chlarson" on his Civil War pension application (http://search.ancestry.com/iexec?htx=View&r=an&dbid=4654&iid=T288_81-0469&fn=&ln=Hans+N.+Chlarson%3b+Hans+Nicholas&st=r&ssrc=&pid=704888). Additional military confirmation sources: http://records.ancestry.com/Hans_Nadrian_Chlarson_records.ashx?pid=11997726 and http://www.fieldinglangford.org/FamilyTree/descendants/fieldingandsarah/jamesharveylangfordsr/jamesharveylangfordjr/chlarson/chlarsonbook.pdf. The death date on his [FGC] grave marker and the information recorded in [NFS] differ by one year. See the Ellsworth-Alford chapter herein for additional information about his life and military service.

CLARK, JOSHUA REUBEN, SR.   (UNION ARMY)   *Baptized after the war.*

Rank: Private	**Unit(s):** Company K, 1st Regiment, Ohio Light Artillery **Military Service Source(s):** NPS; John A. Widtsoe, "A Defender Of The Gospel," *Improvement Era*, August 1951
Birth Date: 11 December 1840	**Birth Place:** Navarre, Stark, Ohio
LDS Membership Date: 14 April 1867	**LDS Membership Source(s):** LDSBE, NFS (ID #: KWZW-LNW)
Death Date: 25 July 1929	**Death Place:** Grantsville, Tooele, Utah **Find A Grave:** 28561560 **Burial Location:** Grantsville City Cemetery, Grantsville, Tooele, Utah

Notes: Father of J. Reuben Clark Jr., a member of the LDS Church First Presidency (John A. Widtsoe, "A Defender Of The Gospel," *Improvement Era*, August 1951). "Patriarch in the Tooele Stake of Zion. . . . In 1865 he passed through Salt Lake City on his way to Montana, but returned to Salt Lake City in the spring of 1867, and [became] converted to 'Mormonism.' . . . He filled a mission to the Northern States and was president of the Mission from January 1, 1895, to June, 1896. . . . He has kept a daily journal for forty years." He was a teacher and a farmer [LDSBE, 3:49–50].

CLARK, THOMAS BENJAMIN   (UNION ARMY)   *Baptized before the war.*

Rank: Private	**Unit(s):** Company I, 17th Regiment, Maine Infantry **Military Service Source(s):** 1890 Census, NPS
Birth Date: 23 November 1820	**Birth Place:** Cambridge, England
LDS Membership Date: 1 August 1852 (confirmation)	**LDS Membership Source(s):** NFS (ID #: KWJZ-C76)
Death Date: 11 October 1910	**Death Place:** Provo, Utah, Utah **Find A Grave:** 25475234 **Burial Location:** Provo, Utah, Utah

Notes: [MLM] Immigrated through New York City during December 1852 [NFS]. He served two years and ten months beginning in April 1861 [1890 Census].

CLARK, WILLIAM H.   (UNION ARMY)   *Baptized before the war.*

Rank: Corporal	**Unit(s):** Company E, 15th Regiment, Iowa Infantry **Military Service Source(s):** VBU, NPS, PI
Birth Date: 10 January 1838	**Birth Place:** Madison, Hancock, Illinois

LDS Membership Date: 1850	LDS Membership Source(s): LDSBE, PPMU, NFS (ID #: 2MR5-JK8)
Death Date: 17 September 1911	Death Place: Richfield, Sevier, Utah Find A Grave: 89303 Burial Location: Richfield, Sevier, Utah

Notes: "He came to Utah with his parents in 1849 and as a pioneer he saw and passed through many trials and hardships; he also participated in several Indian wars." He was ordained an elder, Seventy, and high priest [LDSBE, 2:756–57]. "Deputy sheriff of Weber county (Utah); chief of police of Ogden (Utah); county sheriff and tax assessor and collector of Richfield (Utah) 3 years. Chaplain in Utah legislature in 1893; missionary to Colorado two years; counselor in presidency of Sevier stake 16 years; member of high council Sevier stake (Utah)" [PPMU, 810].

CLEMONS (or CLEMENS), HIRAM B.   (UNION ARMY)   *Baptized before the war.*

Rank: Corporal	Unit(s): Lot Smith Utah Cavalry Military Service Source(s): ACWS, NPS, Fisher, 1862 MOR
Birth Date: 8 September 1816	Birth Place: Concord, Cattaraugus, New York
LDS Membership Date: 23 August 1859	LDS Membership Source(s): NFS (ID #: K81B-CSR)
Death Date: Uncertain	Death Place: Uncertain Find A Grave: — Burial Location: Uncertain

Notes: [MLM] [1862 MOR] lists his name as "Hiram Clemons"; [NFS] lists "Hiram B. Clemens" as the preferred spelling.

COATS, HENRY   (UNION ARMY)   *Baptized during the war.*

Rank: Private	Unit(s): Company C, 3rd Regiment, California Infantry Military Service Source(s): 1890 Census, NPS
Birth Date: 20 February 1841	Birth Place: Chesterfield, Tapton, Darby, England
LDS Membership Date: 21 January 1862	LDS Membership Source(s): NFS (ID #: KWJ4-5CP)
Death Date: 12 March 1922	Death Place: Delta, Millard, Utah Find A Grave: — Burial Location: Mount Pleasant, Sanpete, Utah

Notes: [MLM] He served in the military one year and six months beginning on April 18, 1864. "Loss of left eye" was recorded as a service-related disability [1890 Census].

COLE, THOMAS BENTON   (UNION ARMY)   *Baptized after the war.*

Rank: Private	Unit(s): Company K, 16th Regiment, Indiana Infantry Military Service Source(s): 1890 Census, NPS, Obituary
Birth Date: 27 June 1842	Birth Place: Fountain, Indiana
LDS Membership Date: 19 December 1882	LDS Membership Source(s): NFS (ID #: KWJZ-26S)
Death Date: 4 October 1905	Death Place: Weber County, Utah Find A Grave: — Burial Location: Uncertain

Notes: He served in the military three years beginning on July 15, 1862. "Lung disease" was listed as a service-related disability [1890 Census]. His obituary states that "Benton Cole a veteran of the civil war suicided in Ogden taking a dose of laudanum" (*Emery County Progress*, October 14, 1905, 2).

COLEGROVE, HARLEY (UNION ARMY)   *Baptized after the war.*

Rank: Private	**Unit(s):** Company A, 20th Regiment, Illinois Infantry **Military Service Source(s):** NPS, PI, FGC
Birth Date: 16 November 1837	**Birth Place:** Fairfax, Franklin, Vermont
LDS Membership Date: 28 March 1868	**LDS Membership Source(s):** NFS (ID #: KWJ8-TS1)
Death Date: 12 October 1881	**Death Place:** Fillmore, Millard, Utah **Find A Grave:** 62352119 **Burial Location:** Fillmore Cemetery, Fillmore, Millard, Utah
Notes: A copy of his military discharge papers is available online at [FGC].	

COOK, DANIEL DEAN (UNION ARMY)   *Baptized before the war.*

Rank: Private	**Unit(s):** Company C, Cass Company Home Guard, Missouri Cavalry **Military Service Source(s):** NPS
Birth Date: 13 February 1829	**Birth Place:** Kingsbury, Washington, New York
LDS Membership Date: 1 January 1848 (confirmation)	**LDS Membership Source(s):** NFS (ID #: LCXD-9PD)
Death Date: 18 February 1908	**Death Place:** Provo, Utah, Utah **Find A Grave:** 24132073 **Burial Location:** Provo Cemetery, Provo, Utah, Utah
Notes: [MLM] He served in the military four months and five days beginning on May 25, 1862 [1890 Census]. LDS baptism date listed as 16 February 1935 (posthumous) in the Salt Lake Temple, but his LDS confirmation date is listed as 1 January 1848 [NFS].	

COREY, GEORGE W. (UNION ARMY)   *Baptized before the war.*

Rank: Surgeon	**Unit(s):** 12th Regiment, Missouri Cavalry **Military Service Source(s):** 1890 Census, NPS
Birth Date: 13 December 1839	**Birth Place:** Hancock County, Illinois
LDS Membership Date: 1849	**LDS Membership Source(s):** NFS (ID #: KWVP-2HD)
Death Date: 9 December 1912	**Death Place:** Thornton, Madison, Idaho **Find A Grave:** 23851900 **Burial Location:** Burton Cemetery, Burton, Madison, Idaho
Notes: [MLM] He served two years, two months, and five days beginning February 4, 1864 [1890 Census].	

COTTRELL (or COTTEREL), GEORGE (UNION ARMY)   *Baptized before the war.*

Rank: Private	**Unit(s):** Lot Smith Utah Cavalry **Military Service Source(s):** VBU, ACWS, NPS, PI, Fisher, 1862 MOR
Birth Date: 29 March 1842	**Birth Place:** Little Casterton, Rutland, England
LDS Membership Date: 1 January 1855 (confirmation)	**LDS Membership Source(s):** NFS (ID #: KWCN-JCK)
Death Date: 9 April 1909	**Death Place:** Draper, Salt Lake, Utah **Find A Grave:** 9553552 **Burial Location:** Draper City Cemetery, Draper, Salt Lake, Utah
Notes: [1862 MOR] lists his name as "Geo. Cotterel"; [NFS] lists "George Cottrell" as the preferred spelling.	

COVERT, EVERT (OR EVERET)   (UNION ARMY)   *Baptized before the war (presumed).*

Rank: Private	**Unit(s):** Lot Smith Utah Cavalry **Military Service Source(s):** VBU, FOLD3, FGC, Fisher, 1862 MOR
Birth Date: 8 August 1833	**Birth Place:** Middlesex, Yates, New York
LDS Membership Date: Presumed LDS	**LDS Membership Source(s):** NFS (ID #: 223Y-9ZF)
Death Date: 21 May 1913	**Death Place:** Salt Lake City, Salt Lake, Utah **Find A Grave:** 38259795 **Burial Location:** Big Cottonwood, Salt Lake City, Salt Lake, Utah

Notes: "PVT UTAH TER MIL CIVIL WAR" (Private, Utah Territorial Militia) is carved on his grave marker [FGC]. As a member of the Lot Smith Cavalry Company, he is presumed to be a Latter-day Saint (but his baptismal date or LDS membership could not be confirmed from available sources). His father, William Spencer Covert, was a member of the LDS Church (NFS ID #: KWJC-L25). [1862 MOR] lists his name as "Everet Covert"; [NFS] lists "Evert Covert" as the preferred spelling.

COWLES, WILLIAM H.   (UNION ARMY)   *Baptized after the war.*

Rank: Corporal	**Unit(s):** Company A, 1st Regiment, Pennsylvania Cavalry; and Company M, 50th New York Engineers **Military Service Source(s):** FGC, Obituary
Birth Date: 27 March 1840	**Birth Place:** Lindley, Steuben, New York
LDS Membership Date: 19 August 1876	**LDS Membership Source(s):** NFS (ID #: KWNF-FDQ)
Death Date: 29 June 1912	**Death Place:** Ogden, Weber, Utah **Find A Grave:** 66755503 **Burial Location:** Ogden City Cemetery, Ogden, Weber, Utah

Notes: "CORPL. CO. M. 50 N.Y. ENGRS." (Corporal, Company M, 50th New York Engineers) is carved on his grave marker [FGC]. His obituary, entitled "Veteran of Civil War Answers Call of Taps," states that he was a member of the Grand Army of the Republic and a "survivor of the Wilderness, Cold Harbor and Petersburg" Battles. He was "one of the first to answer President Lincoln's call for volunteers. He served first in Company A of the First Pennsylvania, and second in Company M of the Fiftieth New York engineers. . . . Mr. Cowles was present when General Robert E. Lee surrendered at Appomattox. . . . In 1866, after the war, he settled in Minnesota, later joining the Mormon church and emigrating to Utah in 1876" (*Salt Lake Herald*, July 1, 1912, 6).

COX, JOHN C.   (UNION ARMY)   *Baptized before the war.*

Rank: Private	**Unit(s):** Company A, 1st Regiment, Ohio Infantry **Military Service Source(s):** 1890 Census, NPS
Birth Date: 12 May 1836	**Birth Place:** Wield, Hampshire, England
LDS Membership Date: 18 May 1851	**LDS Membership Source(s):** PPMU, NFS (ID #: KWCC-CV7)
Death Date: 17 November 1915	**Death Place:** Woodruff, Richfield, Utah **Find A Grave:** — **Burial Location:** Woodruff, Richfield, Utah

Notes: [MLM] He "came to Utah July 29, 1847, Mormon Battalion. High Priest; Teacher. Early Settler at Oxford, Idaho" [PPMU, 70, 824]. He served in the military one year beginning in September 1864 [1890 Census].

CRAGUN, JAMES H. (UNION ARMY) *Baptized before the war.*

Rank: Private	Unit(s): Lot Smith Utah Cavalry Military Service Source(s): VBU, ACWS, NPS, Fisher, 1862 MOR
Birth Date: 31 July 1840	Birth Place: Northfield, Boone, Indiana
LDS Membership Date: 15 December 1852	LDS Membership Source(s): NFS (ID #: K271-JF7)
Death Date: 13 February 1919	Death Place: St. George, Washington, Utah Find A Grave: 78628 Burial Location: St. George City Cemetery, St. George, Washington, Utah
Notes: He "crossed the plains, helped his father farm in Mill Creek, and helped build up Washington County (Utah). He farmed at Pine Valley, and lived his later life in St. George" [FGC].	

CRAWFORD, FRANCIS MARION (UNION ARMY) *Baptized after the war.*

Rank: Private	Unit(s): Company A, 6th Regiment, Indiana Cavalry Military Service Source(s): VBU, NPS
Birth Date: 3 August 1835	Birth Place: Williamsport, Warren, Indiana
LDS Membership Date: 15 December 1867	LDS Membership Source(s): NFS (ID #: KWVW-PCB)
Death Date: 13 January 1874	Death Place: Hyrum, Cache, Utah Find A Grave: — Burial Location: Cache Cemetery, Hyrum, Cache, Utah
Notes: The 6th Regiment, Indiana Cavalry, was organized at Indianapolis during 1863 and served from Kentucky to Mississippi [NPS].	

CRAWFORD, JOSEPH HENRY (CONFEDERATE ARMY) *Baptized after the war.*

Rank: Private	Unit(s): 2nd Battalion, Hilliard's Legion, Alabama Volunteers Military Service Source(s): NPS, FGC
Birth Date: 1 April 1836	Birth Place: Pine Flat, Autauga, Alabama
LDS Membership Date: 1 September 1867	LDS Membership Source(s): NFS (ID #: KWVP-752)
Death Date: 24 August 1922	Death Place: Washington, Washington, Utah Find A Grave: 52404 Burial Location: Washington, Washington, Utah
Notes: "PVT. CO. E HILLIARD'S LEGION CONFEDERATE STATES ARMY" (Private, Company E, Hillard's Legion) is carved on his grave marker [FGC].	

CRISMON, CHARLES, JR. (UNION ARMY) *Baptized before the war.*

Rank: Private	Unit(s): Lot Smith Utah Cavalry Military Service Source(s): VBU, NPS, PI, Fisher, 1862 MOR
Birth Date: 14 June 1844	Birth Place: Macedonia, Hancock, Illinois
LDS Membership Date: 1 May 1852	LDS Membership Source(s): LDSBE, PPMU, NFS (ID #: KWVP-QZ5)
Death Date: 16 March 1916	Death Place: Salt Lake City, Salt Lake, Utah Find A Grave: 23688709 Burial Location: Salt Lake City Cemetery, Salt Lake City, Salt Lake, Utah

Notes: He was " a Utah pioneer of 1847 . . . when but two years of age. . . . In 1851 he became one of the pioneer 'Mormon' settlers of San Bernardino, Cal., and was among its leaders in subjugating that part of California to the needs of the people, building mills and aiding in many ways in the development of the resources of the country. When [the] San Bernardino settlement was broken up in 1858, owing to the Johnston Army [Utah War] troubles, the Crismons . . . returned to Utah. . . . At the age of fifteen he brought a drove of sheep from the Missouri river across the plains and mountains to G.S.L. [Great Salt Lake] Valley. . . . In 1862, when Pres. Lincoln called for volunteers from Utah, Bro. Crismon enlisted in Lot Smith's company which went out to protect the mail route from the Indians, leaving Salt Lake City May 1, 1862, destined for Chimney Rock. Later Charles Crismon turned his attention to sheep raising. He went to California and brought a drove of sheep from that State to Utah in 1863. In addition to the sheep he also brought with him a quantity of bees which are said to be the first bees introduced into Utah. . . . Bro. Crismon successfully undertook the business of railroad contracting. . . . [He] is also known as a successful mining man. . . . Bro. Crismon is universally known for his generosity and good will toward his fellowman" [LDSBE, 2:611–12] [PPMU, 828]. He was one of the earliest Lot Smith Utah Cavalry veterans to join the Grand Army of the Republic. For additional information, see the Alford chapter entitled "Mormons and the Grand Army of the Republic" herein.

CULLER, BENJAMIN   (CONFEDERATE ARMY)   *Baptized after the war.*

Rank: Private	**Unit(s):** Company F, 5th Regiment, North Carolina Senior Reserves **Military Service Source(s):** NPS, CSC, MCL
Birth Date: 15 March 1819	**Birth Place:** Forsyth County, North Carolina
LDS Membership Date: 12 June 1869	**LDS Membership Source(s):** NFS (ID #: KWJH-62J)
Death Date: 2 November 1895	**Death Place:** Manassa, Conejos, Colorado **Find A Grave:** 36613136 **Burial Location:** Manassa, Conejos, Colorado

Notes: [MLM] Joseph H. Crute Jr., *Units of the Confederate States Army (Midlothian, VA: Derwent, 1987),* contains no history for his unit [NPS].

DARLING, NED EMANUEL   (UNION ARMY)   *Baptized after the war.*

Rank: Private	**Unit(s):** Companies I & K, 2nd Regiment, California Cavalry **Military Service Source(s):** VBU, NPS, PI
Birth Date: 26 March 1846	**Birth Place:** Cambridge, Guernsey, Ohio
LDS Membership Date: 20 October 1867	**LDS Membership Source(s):** NFS (ID #: KWJH-BWT)
Death Date: 19 March 1934	**Death Place:** Lehi, Utah, Utah **Find A Grave:** 92705 **Burial Location:** Lehi City Cemetery, Lehi, Utah, Utah

Notes: The 2nd Regiment, California Cavalry, was organized at San Francisco during September and October 1861. Company I served in California throughout the war; Company K served in Nevada and Utah Territory; Company K soldiers participated in the Bear River Massacre [NPS]. For additional information, see the Alford chapter entitled "Indian Relations in Utah during the Civil War" and Schindler's "Bear River Massacre" herein.

DAVIS, ALBERT   (UNION ARMY)   *Baptized before the war.*

Rank: Private	**Unit(s):** Lot Smith Utah Cavalry **Military Service Source(s):** ACWS, NPS, PI, Fisher, 1862 MOR
Birth Date: 25 April 1841	**Birth Place:** East Rochester, Columbiana, Ohio

Davis, Albert (continued)	
LDS Membership Date: 29 May 1852	**LDS Membership Source(s):** LDSBE, NFS (ID #: KWCT-X3K)
Death Date: 3 December 1928	**Death Place:** Salt Lake City, Salt Lake, Utah **Find A Grave:** 41262520 **Burial Location:** Salt Lake City Cemetery, Salt Lake City, Salt Lake, Utah

Notes: Brother-in-law to LDS Church President Joseph F. Smith; he and Joseph F. Smith married sisters Melissa J. and Julina L. Lambson, respectively [PPMU, 995]. "Bishop Center Ward. City Councilman" [PPMU, 283]. "His parents joined the Church in 1851 and emigrated with their children to Utah that same year. . . . In the spring of 1862 he went east as a member of the expedition sent out to guard the mail lines under Lot Smith. . . . Again the spring of 1865 he crossed the plains. . . . On their return trip they had an encounter with the Indians about twenty miles west of Fort Laramie, during which several men were wounded and one woman was carried away by the Indians. . . . He left his home [for a mission to the Sandwich Islands, January 1885 to March 1887]. . . . While on this mission he with others witnessed a miraculous healing in the case of a little girl, a daughter of Elder Geo. A. Wilcox, who had accidentally taken a quantity of strychnine. The accident was not discovered until the child was in a dying condition. The Elders administered to her and she was instantly healed. . . . He was ordained a patriarch by Jos. F. Smith" and was a bishop and an ordinance worker in the Salt Lake Temple [LDSBE, 2:410–11].

DAVIS, JOHN BARTON   (UNION ARMY)   *Baptized after the war.*

Rank: Private	**Unit(s):** Company H, 126th Regiment, Illinois Infantry **Military Service Source(s):** NPS, FGC
Birth Date: 27 August 1841	**Birth Place:** Penycae, Denbigh, Wales
LDS Membership Date: 27 May 1884	**LDS Membership Source(s):** NFS (ID #: LHNB-3GH)
Death Date: 14 May 1925	**Death Place:** Salt Lake City, Salt Lake, Utah **Find A Grave:** 159046 **Burial Location:** Mount Olivet Cemetery, Salt Lake City, Salt Lake, Utah

Notes: "CO. H 126 ILL. INF." (Company H, 126th Illinois Infantry) is carved on his grave marker [FGC].

DAVIS, JOHN EUGENE (AKA WILLIAM H. NORMAN)
(GALVANIZED YANKEE)   *Baptized after the war.*

Rank: Private	**Unit(s):** Confederate service: Companies A and E, 1st Regiment, Georgia Infantry; Union service: Company E, 6th Regiment, U.S. Volunteer Infantry **Military Service Source(s):** NPS, Interview, Obituary
Birth Date: 23 April 1845	**Birth Place:** Macon, Bibb, Georgia
LDS Membership Date: 12 May 1877	**LDS Membership Source(s):** NFS (ID #: K2W9-XYN)
Death Date: 18 May 1935	**Death Place:** Annabella, Sevier, Utah **Find A Grave:** 28415090 **Burial Location:** Annabella Cemetery, Annabella, Sevier, Utah

Notes: His Confederate and Union military service was under his birth name, "William H. Norman." Following desertion from the Union Army in 1865, he changed his name to "John Eugene Davis" and lived by that name the remainder of his life (Gerald Davis (grandson of John Eugene Davis), interview with Kenneth L. Alford, October 17, 2011, Provo, Utah). The online *History of the 1st Confederate Regiment Infantry, Bibb County,* "Brown Infantry," states: "Norman, William H.—Private—July 22, 1861. Discharged by expiration of term of service March 18, 1862. Enlisted as a private in Company A, 1st Confederate Regiment Infantry

April 14, 1862. Transferred to 2nd Company E, in 1862. Captured at Nashville, Tennessee December 16, 1864. Mustered into service in Company E, 6th U.S. Infantry March 25, 1865. Deserted therefrom August 3, 1865" (http://www.ranger95.com/civil_war/georgia/infantry/rosters/roster2/1st_confed_inf_regt_rost_1st_c.html). John's obituary, entitled "Funeral Held at Annabella for Civil War Veteran," states that he was affectionately known as "Uncle John" and that he "was born April 23, 1845, in Bibbs [sic] county, Georgia. When he was sixteen years of age he enlisted in the confederate army under General Robert E. Lee. After the Civil War, in 1867, he came to Utah. Later he went to Pioche, Nevada. . . . There he joined the L.D.S. church. . . . Mr. Davis served as an L.D.S. missionary in the southern states in 1887. He was at one time ward chorister, and served as Sunday school superintendent and ward teacher. He was justice of the peace for many years, and was for a number of years postmaster at Annabella" (*Richfield Reaper*, May 23, 1935, 5). For additional information, see the Ellsworth-Alford chapter herein.

DELONG, LEONARD (UNION ARMY) *Baptized after the war.*

Rank: Private	**Unit(s):** Company H, 142nd Regiment, Illinois Infantry **Military Service Source(s):** VBU, NPS, PI
Birth Date: 16 December 1848	**Birth Place:** New York, New York
LDS Membership Date: 25 February 1922	**LDS Membership Source(s):** NFS (ID #: KWJH-ZNY)
Death Date: 18 January 1932	**Death Place:** Ogden, Weber, Utah **Find A Grave:** — **Burial Location:** Salt Lake City Cemetery, Utah
Notes: The 142nd Regiment, Illinois Infantry, was mustered for just one hundred days (beginning June 18, 1864); during that time, thirty soldiers died from disease [NPS].	

DENNIS, WILLIAM TAYLOR (CONFEDERATE ARMY) *Baptized before the war.*

Rank: Private	**Unit(s):** Company F, 14th Regiment, Mississippi Infantry **Military Service Source(s):** NPS
Birth Date: 18 January 1810	**Birth Place:** Nashville, Lincoln, Tennessee
LDS Membership Date: 14 March 1850	**LDS Membership Source(s):** PPMU, NFS (ID #: KWNJ-L71)
Death Date: 22 November 1894	**Death Place:** Marysvale, Piute, Utah **Find A Grave:** 30423104 **Burial Location:** Dennis Cemetery, Piute County, Utah
Notes: [MLM] He "came to Utah in 1855, Gilbert I. Gavin Company" [PPMU, 437].	

DIAL, BURRIS (OR BURRISS) (UNION ARMY) *Baptized after the war.*

Rank: Private	**Unit(s):** Company G, 9th Regiment, Illinois Infantry **Military Service Source(s):** NPS, PI, FGC
Birth Date: 3 April 1843	**Birth Place:** Paradise Prairie, Franklin, Illinois
LDS Membership Date: 1 June 1886	**LDS Membership Source(s):** NFS (ID #: KWC8-H7K)
Death Date: 23 January 1906	**Death Place:** Willard, Box Elder, Utah **Find A Grave:** 28535035 **Burial Location:** Hooper Cemetery, Hooper, Weber, Utah
Notes: "PVT. 9 ILL. INF." (Private, 9th Illinois Infantry) is carved on his grave marker [FGC].	

DOBSON, WILLARD RICHARDS   (UNION ARMY)   *Baptized before the war.*

Rank: Uncertain	**Unit(s):** Uncertain **Military Service Source(s):** Obituary
Birth Date: 25 January 1840	**Birth Place:** Preston, Lancashire, England
LDS Membership Date: 1 January 1848	**LDS Membership Source(s):** NFS (ID #: KWJC-HBJ)
Death Date: 21 September 1913	**Death Place:** Salt Lake City, Salt Lake, Utah **Find A Grave:** — **Burial Location:** Salt Lake City, Salt Lake, Utah

Notes: His obituary, entitled "Civil War Veteran Answers Summons," notes that he was "a war veteran, pensioner of the United States. . . . Early in life he was disappointed in love and he never married but lived alone" (*Box Elder News*, September 25, 1913, 2). There may be an error in either his birth date or baptism date, as he was not quite eight years old on the listed date of his baptism. His unit affiliation cannot be determined, as [NPS] lists numerous William Dobsons who served during the Civil War.

DODDS, GEORGE   (UNION ARMY)   *Baptized after the war.*

Rank: Private	**Unit(s):** Company D, 34th Regiment, New York Infantry **Military Service Source(s):** 1890 Census, NPS
Birth Date: 22 October 1841	**Birth Place:** Kipps, Old Monkland, Lanark, Scotland
LDS Membership Date: 20 March 1887	**LDS Membership Source(s):** NFS (ID #: KWJH-D4L)
Death Date: 13 January 1904	**Death Place:** Panguitch, Garfield, Utah **Find A Grave:** 23380946 **Burial Location:** Panguitch, Garfield, Utah

Notes: [MLM] Diarrhea and jaundice listed as disabilities incurred during his military service [1890 Census].

DOTSON, WILLIAM THOMAS   (CONFEDERATE ARMY)   *Baptized after the war.*

Rank: Private	**Unit(s):** Company C, 5th Regiment, Kentucky Infantry **Military Service Source(s):** NPS, MCL
Birth Date: 10 January 1846	**Birth Place:** Choctaw, Mississippi
LDS Membership Date: 19 September 1879	**LDS Membership Source(s):** NFS (ID #: KWJX-3PF)
Death Date: 19 November 1910	**Death Place:** Manassa, Conejos, Colorado **Find A Grave:** — **Burial Location:** Not available

Notes: [MLM] He began his military service in 1863 [1890 Census]. [NPS] lists an additional William Dotson (no middle name) as having served in Company H, 19th Kentucky Infantry.

DRAPER, PARLEY P.   (UNION ARMY)   *Baptized before the war (presumed).*

Rank: Private	**Unit(s):** Lot Smith Utah Cavalry **Military Service Source(s):** ACWS, Fisher, 1862 MOR
Birth Date: 30 March 1843	**Birth Place:** Pleasantville, Pike, Illinois
LDS Membership Date: Presumed LDS	**LDS Membership Source(s):** (ID #: L4WT-4JS)
Death Date: 28 November 1924	**Death Place:** Moroni, Sanpete, Utah **Find A Grave:** 15829999 **Burial Location:** Moroni, Sanpete, Utah

Notes: The city of Draper, Utah, was named after him [Fisher, 93]. As a member of the Lot Smith Cavalry Company, he is presumed to be a Latter-day Saint, but his baptismal date or LDS membership could not be confirmed from available sources. His father (who is listed as "Bishop William Draper, Jr." on New Family-Search, ID #: LZ4V-FFP) was baptized as a Latter-day Saint March 20, 1833 [NFS].

DUKE, JOHN   (UNION ARMY)   *Baptized before the war.*

Rank: Private	**Unit(s):** Company K, 1st Regiment, U.S. Artillery (Regular Army) **Military Service Source(s):** NPS, PI, FGC
Birth Date: 19 November 1834	**Birth Place:** Albany, Albany, New York
LDS Membership Date: 1 January 1842 (confirmation)	**LDS Membership Source(s):** LDSBE, PPMU, NFS (ID #: KWN2-HLX)
Death Date: 3 November 1919	**Death Place:** Heber City, Wasatch, Utah **Find A Grave:** 158940 **Burial Location:** Heber City, Wasatch, Utah

Notes: "CO. K. 1 U.S. ART." (Company K, 1st Regiment, U.S. Artillery) is carved on his grave marker [FGC]. He was baptized in the Mississippi River. During his lifetime, he was ordained a deacon, elder, Seventy, high priest, and bishop. He was "blessed with a mild and cheerful disposition" [LDSBE, 3:64–65]. He "came to Utah in 1850 [and was a] Black Hawk Indian War Veteran" [PPMU, 201]. There may be a recording error regarding his baptism date, as he was not eight years old by the [NFS] baptismal date.

DUNHAM, LEVI   (UNION ARMY)   *Baptized after the war.*

Rank: Private	**Unit(s):** Company I, 7th Regiment, New Hampshire Infantry **Military Service Source(s):** NPS, PI
Birth Date: 17 April 1847	**Birth Place:** Beekmantown, Clinton, New York
LDS Membership Date: 8 July 1880	**LDS Membership Source(s):** NFS (ID #: KW86-17X)
Death Date: 7 December 1929	**Death Place:** Salt Lake City, Salt Lake, Utah **Find A Grave:** 139963 **Burial Location:** Mount Pleasant, Sanpete, Utah

Notes: The 7th Regiment, New Hampshire Infantry, was organized at Manchester, New Hampshire. The unit mustered in December 13, 1861, and was active until the war's end. The unit served in Florida, South Carolina, and North Carolina [NPS].

DYKES, WILLIAM   (UNION ARMY)   *Baptized after the war.*

Rank: Quartermaster Sergeant	**Unit(s):** Company K, 1st Regiment, Wisconsin Infantry **Military Service Source(s):** 1890 Census
Birth Date: 4 July 1832	**Birth Place:** Culpeper, Culpeper, Virginia
LDS Membership Date: 6 August 1871	**LDS Membership Source(s):** NFS (ID #: K2WZ-W7Q)
Death Date: 3 May 1900	**Death Place:** Batesville/Erda, Tooele, Utah **Find A Grave:** 97089 **Burial Location:** Tooele City Cemetery, Tooele, Tooele, Utah

Notes: [MLM] His name is listed as "'William Dyk" on the 1890 veteran census scheduleform. He served in the military one year and two months beginning in October 1861 [1890 Census].

EARDLEY, JOSIAH   (UNION ARMY)   *Baptized before the war.*

Rank: Musician	**Unit(s):** Lot Smith Utah Cavalry **Military Service Source(s):** ACWS, NPS, PI, Fisher, 1862 MOR
Birth Date: 5 May 1842	**Birth Place:** Blackfordby, Leicestershire, England

Eardley, Josiah (continued)	
LDS Membership Date: 16 May 1854	**LDS Membership Source(s):** NFS (ID #: KWNF-31F)
Death Date: 30 December 1931	**Death Place:** San Diego, San Diego, California **Find A Grave:** — **Burial Location:** San Diego, San Diego, California
Notes: [MLM] He served in the Wyoming State Legislature for five terms (*Salt Lake Telegram*, January 1, 1932).	

EASTMAN, AUBREY (OR ARBURY) CLEVENSELLER

(UNION ARMY [PRESUMED])   *Baptized after the war.*

Rank: Uncertain	**Unit(s):** Uncertain **Military Service Source(s):** MDA
Birth Date: 17 June 1845	**Birth Place:** Rumford, Oxford, Maine
LDS Membership Date: 10 September 1868	**LDS Membership Source(s):** NFS (ID #: KWJ8-TCW)
Death Date: 7 November 1908	**Death Place:** Woodruff, Rich, Utah **Find A Grave:** — **Burial Location:** Rumford, Oxford, Maine
Notes: [MLM] He was a farmer, merchant, rancher, justice of the peace, and postmaster [MDA, 96].	

ECHOLS, LEWIS BARTON   (CONFEDERATE ARMY)   *Baptized after the war.*

Rank: Private	**Unit(s):** Company C, 8th Regiment, Alabama Infantry **Military Service Source(s):** NPS, 1900 Census
Birth Date: 15 May 1834	**Birth Place:** Franklin County, Georgia
LDS Membership Date: 31 August 1881	**LDS Membership Source(s):** NFS (ID #: LC87-BCS)
Death Date: 13 January 1912	**Death Place:** Thatcher, Graham, Arizona **Find A Grave:** — **Burial Location:** Thatcher, Graham, Arizona
Notes: [MLM] The 8th Regiment, Alabama Infantry, was "the first Confederate regiment to be enlisted for the war." Organized at Montgomery, Alabama, in May 1861, it "took an active part in many campaigns from Williamsburg to Cold Harbor, was involved in the Petersburg siege south of the James River, and ended the war at Appomattox" [NPS].	

EDWARDS, MOSES   (UNION ARMY)   *Baptized after the war.*

Rank: Corporal	**Unit(s):** Company L, 3rd Regiment, Kentucky Cavalry **Military Service Source(s):** NPS, FGC
Birth Date: 27 July 1836	**Birth Place:** Kentucky
LDS Membership Date: 17 June 1882	**LDS Membership Source(s):** NFS (ID #: KWJ6-RZX)
Death Date: 30 May 1908	**Death Place:** Manassa, Conejos, Colorado **Find A Grave:** 39957341 **Burial Location:** Manassa, Conejos, Colorado
Notes: "CORP. 3 KY. CAV." (Corporal, 3rd Kentucky Cavalry) is carved on his grave marker [FGC].	

ELLIOTT, JAMES M.   (UNION ARMY)   *Baptized before the war.*

Rank: Private	**Unit(s):** Company A, 105th Regiment, New York Infantry **Military Service Source(s):** 1890 Census, NPS
Birth Date: 17 January 1839	**Birth Place:** Stewarton, Ayr, Scotland

LDS Membership Date: 1 December 1850	LDS Membership Source(s): NFS (ID #: KWJD-T8Z)
Death Date: 3 September 1903	Death Place: Richfield, Sevier, Utah Find A Grave: — Burial Location: Richfield, Sevier, Utah
Notes: [MLM] He served in the military one year, three months, and ten days beginning in 1861 and was "killed in action in 1862." His widow provided his 1890 veteran census schedule listing [1890 Census].	

EMMONS, CHARLES E. (UNION ARMY) *Baptized after the war.*

Rank: Private	Unit(s): Companies I & D, 2nd Regiment, Colorado Infantry Military Service Source(s): VBU, NPS, FGC
Birth Date: 13 November 1835	Birth Place: Brookfield, Madison, New York
LDS Membership Date: September 1867	LDS Membership Source(s): NFS (ID #: K2W7-Q6G)
Death Date: 7 January 1899	Death Place: Provo, Utah, Utah Find A Grave: 30934134 Burial Location: Provo, Utah, Utah
Notes: "PVT CO I 2 COLO CAV CIVIL WAR" (Private, Company I, 2nd Colorado Cavalry) is carved on his grave marker [FGC]. There are birth and death discrepancies between the grave marker and [NFS].	

EMPEY, DAVID ARZA (CONFEDERATE ARMY) *Baptized before the war.*

Rank: Private	Unit(s): Company A, 6th Regiment, Texas Cavalry Military Service Source(s): NPS; "Passing Events," *Improvement Era,* April 1924
Birth Date: 27 March 1840	Birth Place: Osnabruck, Stormont, Ontario, Canada
LDS Membership Date: 1848	LDS Membership Source(s): NFS (ID #: K2WQ-TYJ)
Death Date: 16 January 1924	Death Place: Moab, Grand, Utah Find A Grave: 26830375 Burial Location: Grand Valley Cemetery, Moab, Grand, Utah
Notes: He lived in Nauvoo, Illinois, and Salt Lake City, Utah. His family moved to Texas in 1857. He was one of only seven men to survive from his military unit. Three of his grandsons served in WWI; one was killed in action in the Argonne. He was called "Grandpa" by Moab residents ("Passing Events," *Improvement Era,* April 1924).	

EVANS, CHARLES M. (UNION ARMY) *Baptized before the war.*

Rank: Musician	Unit(s): Lot Smith Utah Cavalry Military Service Source(s): VBU, NPS, PI, Fisher, 1862 MOR
Birth Date: 27 January 1831	Birth Place: Liverpool, Lancashire, England
LDS Membership Date: 1 August 1850	LDS Membership Source(s): PPMU, NFS (ID #: KWVG-KYQ)
Death Date: 20 September 1902	Death Place: Salt Lake City, Salt Lake, Utah Find A Grave: Burial Location: Salt Lake City Cemetery, Salt Lake City, Salt Lake, Utah
Notes: He "came to Utah in 1852 [and was ordained as a] Seventy" [PPMU]. He was a bugler for the Lot Smith Utah Cavalry [Fisher, 63].	

EVANS, DAVID   (UNION ARMY)   *Baptized after the war.*

Rank: Uncertain	Unit(s): Uncertain Military Service Source(s): "A Personal Testimony," *Improvement Era*, June 1910
Birth Date: 17 September 1848	Birth Place: Caernarvon, Wales
LDS Membership Date: 30 April 1904	LDS Membership Source(s): NFS (ID #: KWJX-WMS)
Death Date: 10 January 1929	Death Place: Uncertain Find A Grave: — Burial Location: Uncertain

Notes: He enlisted as a private at age fifteen and fought for the Union and was commander of the John H. Williams Post No. 4, Grand Army of the Republic, Department of Wisconsin ("A Personal Testimony," *Improvement Era*, June 1910).

EVANS, JOHN DAVIS   (UNION ARMY)   *Baptized before the war.*

Rank: Private	Unit(s): Company D, 7th Regiment, Missouri Infantry Military Service Source(s): VBU, NPS, PI, Obituary
Birth Date: 17 March 1841	Birth Place: Penderyn, Breconshire, Wales
LDS Membership Date: 8 March 1850	LDS Membership Source(s): NFS (ID #: KWJ8-76N)
Death Date: 30 July 1908	Death Place: Salt Lake City, Salt Lake, Utah Find A Grave: 83955660 Burial Location: Salt Lake City Cemetery, Salt Lake City, Salt Lake, Utah

Notes: Together with his wife, he started one of the first ice cream companies in Salt Lake City, which they called "Evans Union Ice Cream." The patriotism of the Evans family was evident in the company name and logo. The logo was a red, white, and blue shield which hung on the side of the company wagon that traveled the streets of Salt Lake City (David F. Boone, "The Church and the Civil War," in *Nineteenth-Century Saints at War*, ed. Robert C. Freeman [Provo, Utah: Religious Studies Center, 2006]). His obituary states that "in 1861 he joined a Missouri regiment on the side of the Union and fought three years and three months in the civil war, afterwards returning to Utah" (*Deseret News*, August 1, 1908, 6). It is claimed that "he was the only man from Utah to return to his own state to enlist. This claim is on record at the Utah State Capital [*sic*]. For three months, he drilled in the army with a broom handle because the company didn't have money to buy guns. He was in the Army three years and 13 days. At the battle of Vicksburg, he was wounded in the left leg and was in the hospital for some time. He was honorably discharged in June 1864 and returned to make Utah his home. . . . John Davis [Evans] always said he was born on 4 March 1843. Research has shown this to not be the case. His birth certificate shows his birthdate as 17 March 1841" (http://evansfamilyhistory.org/index.php?option=com_content&view=article&id=79:evans-john-davis&catid=81&Itemid=131). Several birth dates are listed in [NFS]. For additional information, see the Freeman chapter herein.

EVANS, MILTON HAYWOOD   (UNION ARMY)   *Baptized after the war.*

Rank: Captain	Unit(s): 10th Regiment, Kentucky Cavalry Military Service Source(s): NPS, FGC, MCL
Birth Date: 31 March 1839	Birth Place: Marshall County, Alabama
LDS Membership Date: 11 January 1877	LDS Membership Source(s): NFS (ID #: KWNF-F82)
Death Date: 28 March 1909	Death Place: Manassa, Conejos, Colorado Find A Grave: 39764069 Burial Location: Manassa, Conejos, Colorado

Notes: [MLM] "CAPTAIN 10 KY. CAV." (Captain, 10th Kentucky Cavalry) is carved on his grave marker [FGC].

FELT, JOSEPH H.   (UNION ARMY)   *Baptized before the war.*

Rank: Corporal	**Unit(s):** Lot Smith Utah Cavalry **Military Service Source(s):** VBU, NPS, Fisher, 1862 MOR
Birth Date: 9 May 1840	**Birth Place:** Salem, Essex, Massachusetts
LDS Membership Date: 9 May 1848	**LDS Membership Source(s):** NFS (ID #: KWCL-JHM)
Death Date: 15 June 1907	**Death Place:** Salt Lake City, Salt Lake, Utah **Find A Grave:** 19813629 **Burial Location:** Salt Lake City Cemetery, Salt Lake City, Salt Lake, Utah
Notes: —	

FERRIS, JOHN SOLOMON   (UNION ARMY)   *Baptized after the war.*

Rank: Uncertain	**Unit(s):** Uncertain **Military Service Source(s):** Obituary
Birth Date: 5 August 1840	**Birth Place:** Bellville, Richland, Ohio
LDS Membership Date: 12 November 1871	**LDS Membership Source(s):** NFS (ID #: KWV5-ZMH)
Death Date: 26 July 1931	**Death Place:** Beaver, Beaver, Utah **Find A Grave:** 138374 **Burial Location:** Mountain View Cemetery, Beaver, Beaver, Utah
Notes: His obituary, entitled "Utah Mining Man, G.A.R. Veteran Receives Burial," notes that he was a "civil war veteran and Beaver's oldest resident. . . . He had been a staunch Republican since the organization of the party in 1858. He voted for Abraham Lincoln and voted the straight Republican ticket since" (*Paiute County News*, August 7, 1931, 4).	

FISHER, JOSEPH ARMSTRONG   (UNION ARMY)   *Baptized before the war.*

Rank: Private	**Unit(s):** Lot Smith Utah Cavalry **Military Service Source(s):** Fisher, NPS, PI, Fisher, 1862 MOR
Birth Date: 28 July 1841	**Birth Place:** Nauvoo, Hancock, Illinois
LDS Membership Date: 1 January 1852	**LDS Membership Source(s):** PPMU, NFS (ID #: KWCZ-GPK)
Death Date: 5 February 1922	**Death Place:** Salt Lake City, Salt Lake, Utah **Find A Grave:** — **Burial Location:** Salt Lake City, Salt Lake, Utah
Notes: He "came to Utah in 1850, Gilbert & Parish Company" [PPMU, 249]. He was also a "High priest; member stake high council 25 years. Assisted in bringing immigrants to Utah 1863. Road supervisor; city councilman; chief of police. Indian war veteran; served under Capt. Lot Smith 1862. Carpenter and builder" [PPMU, 872]. He is the husband of historian and author Margaret M. Fisher. His wife also served as a Utah officer in the Ladies of the Grand Army of the Republic. For additional information on Mrs. Fisher, see the Alford chapter entitled "Mormons and the Grand Army of the Republic" herein.	

FISHER, JOSEPH R.   (UNION ARMY)   *Baptized before the war (presumed).*

Rank: Private	**Unit(s):** Company D, 1st Regiment, California Cavalry **Military Service Source(s):** SBS; Brig.-Gen. Richard H. Orton, *Records of the California Men in the War of the Rebellion, 1861 to 1867* (Sacramento: State Office of Printing, 1890); Thomas Edwin Farish, *History of Arizona*, vol. 3 (San Francisco: Filmer Brothers Electrotype, 1915)
Birth Date: about 1812	**Birth Place:** Chester County, Pennsylvania

Fisher, Joseph R. (continued)	
LDS Membership Date: Uncertain	**LDS Membership Source(s):** SBS
Death Date: 4 March 1864	**Death Place:** Arizona **Find A Grave:** — **Burial Location:** Uncertain

Notes: He sailed to Yerba Buena (San Francisco), California, with Samuel Brannon and other Latter-day Saints on board the ship *Brooklyn*. Presumed to be LDS [SBS].

FITZGERALD, MILTON HITT   (UNION ARMY)   *Baptized after the war.*

Rank: Private	**Unit(s):** Company G, 5th Regiment, West Virginia Cavalry **Military Service Source(s):** VBU, NPS, PI
Birth Date: 4 July 1847	**Birth Place:** Nelson County, Virginia
LDS Membership Date: 28 August 1889	**LDS Membership Source(s):** NFS (ID #: KWJV-NV1)
Death Date: 3 May 1917	**Death Place:** American Fork, Utah, Utah **Find A Grave:** — **Burial Location:** American Fork City Cemetery, American Fork, Utah, Utah

Notes: The 5th Regiment, West Virginia Cavalry, was organized on January 26, 1864, and served primarily in West Virginia. The unit fought at the Second Battle of Bull Run [NPS].

FORBES, JOSEPH BARLOW   (UNION ARMY)   *Baptized after the war.*

Rank: Enlisted as a Sergeant; discharged as a Second Lieutenant	**Unit(s):** Company H, 2nd Regiment, Maine Volunteers **Military Service Source(s):** CHL, NPS, PI, PPMU
Birth Date: 29 January 1840	**Birth Place:** Bangor, Penobscot, Maine
LDS Membership Date: 29 January 1866	**LDS Membership Source(s):** MDA, NFS (ID #: KWCT-4NF)
Death Date: 5 May 1927	**Death Place:** Goshen, Bingham, Idaho **Find A Grave:** 20609928 **Burial Location:** American Fork Cemetery, American Fork, Utah, Utah

Notes: He was a "2nd Lieutenant of the Civil War and fought in the first battle of Bull Run" [FGC]. He "came to Utah Aug. 1, 1865, Capt. Getchel Company. Married Nancy Cooper Jan 1, 1866, American Fork, Utah. . . . Married Mary Jane Gardner April, 1886, at Salt Lake City. . . . High priest; Sunday school superintendent and teacher; president 1st Y.M.M.I.A. in American Fork; member choir of American Fork. Civil war veteran. School teacher and trustee; city councilman and recorder at American Fork; secretary school board" [PPMU, 616, 874] [MDA, 110]. He is listed as "Joseph Barrow Forbes" and his birth date is listed as January 29, 1847, in [PPMU]. For additional information, see the Ellsworth-Alford chapter herein.

FORBES, JOHN   (UNION MARINES)   *Baptized before the war.*

Rank: Marine	**Unit(s):** Uncertain **Military Service Source(s):** 1890 Census
Birth Date: 10 February 1827	**Birth Place:** Kilbride, Isle of Arran, Bute, Scotland
LDS Membership Date: 4 January 1845	**LDS Membership Source(s):** NFS (ID #: KWJC-2QJ)
Death Date: 28 October 1879	**Death Place:** Layton, Davis, Utah **Find A Grave:** 123415 **Burial Location:** Kaysville, Davis, Utah

Notes: [MLM] He served in the military one year beginning in May 1863. If the correct LDS member is identified, the 1890 veteran census schedule (recorded in Box Elder County, Utah) should list his entry as a widow report, as his death date was prior to 1890, but it does not [1890 Census].

FOX, JOHN SELLMAN   (UNION ARMY)   *Baptized before the war.*

Rank: Private	**Unit(s):** Company A, 11th Regiment, New York Cavalry (Scott's 900) **Military Service Source(s):** 1890 Census, NPS
Birth Date: 12 December 1819	**Birth Place:** Shipston-on-Stow, Worcester, England
LDS Membership Date: 8 November 1846	**LDS Membership Source(s):** NFS (ID #: KWVM-BLG)
Death Date: 18 December 1904	**Death Place:** Murray, Salt Lake, Utah **Find A Grave:** — **Burial Location:** Murray, Salt Lake, Utah
Notes: [MLM] He served in the military three years beginning in April 1861 [1890 Census].	

FRANK, JOHN VALENTINE   (UNION ARMY)   *Baptized after the war.*

Rank: Sergeant	**Unit(s):** Companies C & H, 2nd Regiment, California Cavalry **Military Service Source(s):** 1890 Census
Birth Date: 10 October 1836	**Birth Place:** Odense, Denmark
LDS Membership Date: 16 July 1871	**LDS Membership Source(s):** NFS (ID #: KWJV-RVY)
Death Date: 7 February 1921	**Death Place:** Elsinore, Sevier, Utah **Find A Grave:** — **Burial Location:** Elsinore, Sevier, Utah
Notes: [MLM] He served in the military four years beginning on December 4, 1861. "Chronic rheumatism" is listed as a service-related disability [1890 Census].	

FRYER, JOSEPH   (UNION ARMY)   *Baptized before the war.*

Rank: Private	**Unit(s):** Companies D & C, 3rd Regiment, California Infantry **Military Service Source(s):** NPS, VBU, PI
Birth Date: March 1847	**Birth Place:** Spittlegate, Grantham, Lincolnshire, England
LDS Membership Date: 1 January 1855 (confirmation)	**LDS Membership Source(s):** NFS (ID #: KWVP-9M2)
Death Date: 22 November 1900	**Death Place:** Utah **Find A Grave:** 41002211 **Burial Location:** Deweyville Cemetery, Deweyville, Box Elder, Utah
Notes: There may be an error in either his birth date or his confirmation date, as he was not eight years old on the date listed in [NFS].	

GARDINER, FREDERICK   (CONFEDERATE ARMY)   *Baptized before the war.*

Rank: Private	**Unit(s):** Company A, 5th Regiment, Louisiana Infantry **Military Service Source(s):** NPS, PI, FGC, 1890 Census
Birth Date: 12 November 1832	**Birth Place:** Chalford Hill, Gloucestershire, England
LDS Membership Date: 20 May 1845	**LDS Membership Source(s):** NFS (ID #: KWV7-62Z)
Death Date: 4 July 1903	**Death Place:** Salt Lake City, Salt Lake, Utah **Find A Grave:** 20754798 **Burial Location:** Salt Lake City, Salt Lake, Utah
Notes: "PVT CO A 5 REGT LA INF CIVIL WAR" (Private, Company A, 5th Regiment, Louisiana Infantry) is carved on his grave marker [FGC]. He served in the military from March 11 to August 7, 1865. His census record states he was a hospital steward in Company C, 1st Louisiana Volunteer Infantry [1890 Census].	

GIBBS, GEORGE F (UNION ARMY)   *Baptized before the war.*

Rank: Private	Unit(s): Company I, 33rd Regiment, Massachusetts Infantry Military Service Source(s): NPS, PI
Birth Date: 16 November 1846	Birth Place: Haverfordwest, Pembrokeshire, Wales
LDS Membership Date: 17 November 1854	LDS Membership Source(s): NFS (ID #: KWZT-8QX)
Death Date: 10 March 1924	Death Place: Salt Lake City, Salt Lake, Utah Find A Grave: 32558731 Burial Location: Salt Lake City Cemetery, Salt Lake City, Salt Lake, Utah
Notes: [MLM] The 33rd Regiment, Massachusetts Infantry, was organized August 6, 1862, and participated in numerous battles, including Chancellorsville, Brandy Station, and Gettysburg [NPS].	

GIBSON, JOHN (UNION ARMY)   *Baptized after the war.*

Rank: Private	Unit(s): Lot Smith Utah Cavalry Military Service Source(s): VBU, ACWS, NPS, Fisher, 1862 MOR
Birth Date: 1 March 1849	Birth Place: Paisley, Renfrew, Scotland
LDS Membership Date: 5 December 1883	LDS Membership Source(s): NFS (ID #: KWJ8-1NY)
Death Date: 29 September 1909	Death Place: Utah Find A Grave: 66935273 Burial Location: Salt Lake City, Salt Lake, Utah
Notes: —	

GIBSON, MOSES WASHINGTON (UNION ARMY)   *Baptized before the war.*

Rank: Private	Unit(s): Lot Smith Utah Cavalry Military Service Source(s): ACWS, NPS, PI, Fisher, 1862 MOR
Birth Date: 21 January 1840	Birth Place: Monroe, Union, Mississippi
LDS Membership Date: 1 January 1847	LDS Membership Source(s): NFS (ID #: KWJ9-5KQ)
Death Date: 14 February 1912	Death Place: St. Thomas, Clark, Nevada Find A Grave: 30837969 Burial Location: Logandale Cemetery, Logandale, Clark, Nevada
Notes: [MLM] There may be an error in either his birth date or baptism date, as he was not quite eight years old on the date listed in [NFS].	

GIBSON, SPOTSWOOD NICHOLAS (CONFEDERATE ARMY)   *Baptized after the war.*

Rank: Uncertain	Unit(s): Company C, 27th Regiment, Virginia Infantry Military Service Source(s): CSC, FGC
Birth Date: 1 April 1830	Birth Place: Charlottesville, Albermarle, Virginia
LDS Membership Date: 17 November 1883	LDS Membership Source(s): NFS (ID #: KWJH-58K)
Death Date: 17 October 1894	Death Place: Manassa, Conejos, Colorado Find A Grave: 37509499 Burial Location: Manassa, Conejos, Colorado
Notes: "27TH VA. INF. CO. C C.S.A." (27th Virginia Infantry, Company C, Confederate States of America) is carved on his grave marker [FGC]. He enlisted in Company C, 27th Regiment, Virginia Infantry for one year and was captured on September 25, 1864. He was a wagon maker [FOLD3]. [CSC] spells his middle name as "Spottswood."	

GODDARD, JOSEPH   (UNION ARMY)   *Baptized before the war.*

Rank: Private	Unit(s): Lot Smith Utah Cavalry Military Service Source(s): VBU, ACWS, NPS, PI, Fisher, 1862 MOR
Birth Date: 5 April 1843	Birth Place: Leicester, Leicestershire, England
LDS Membership Date: 1 January 1853 (confirmation)	LDS Membership Source(s): NFS (ID #: KW8L-PT4)
Death Date: 24 July 1911	Death Place: Ogden, Weber, Utah Find A Grave: 36183385 Burial Location: Ogden City Cemetery, Ogden, Weber, Utah
Notes: —	

GOODFELLOW, JOHN SMITH   (UNION ARMY)   *Baptized after the war.*

Rank: Private	Unit(s): Company E, 11th Regiment, New York Infantry Military Service Source(s): 1890 Census, NPS
Birth Date: 24 June 1843	Birth Place: Flowery Field, Hyde, England
LDS Membership Date: 30 May 1883	LDS Membership Source(s): NFS (ID #: KWJ7-4JH)
Death Date: 24 July 1890	Death Place: Salt Lake City, Salt Lake, Utah Find A Grave: 43244926 Burial Location: Salt Lake City Cemetery, Salt Lake City, Salt Lake, Utah

Notes: [MLM] He served in the military for six months and twenty-three days beginning on May 17, 1861. "Wounds in left ankle and forehead" and "crippled in left ankle" are listed as service-related disabilities on his 1890 veteran census schedule [1890 Census].

GORDON, ELI   (CONFEDERATE ARMY)   *Baptized after the war.*

Rank: Private	Unit(s): Company I, 32nd Regiment, Virginia Infantry Military Service Source(s): 1890 Census, NPS
Birth Date: 26 August 1845	Birth Place: Henrico County, Virginia
LDS Membership Date: January 1872	LDS Membership Source(s): NFS (ID #: KWDY-ZCJ)
Death Date: 1 June 1922	Death Place: Lyman, Uinta, Wyoming Find A Grave: — Burial Location: Heber City, Wasatch, Utah

Notes: [MLM] He began his military service in June 1861. "Lame arm" is listed as a disability incurred during his military service [1890 Census].

GRANT, WILLIAM S.   (UNION ARMY)   *Baptized before the war.*

Rank: Private	Unit(s): Lot Smith Utah Cavalry Military Service Source(s): VBU, ACWS, NPS, PI, Fisher, 1862 MOR
Birth Date: 22 August 1842	Birth Place: Nauvoo, Hancock, Illinois
LDS Membership Date: 1 March 1857	LDS Membership Source(s): NFS (ID #: KWJP-7WN)
Death Date: 15 June 1883	Death Place: Woods Cross, Davis, Utah Find A Grave: 77630953 Burial Location: Bountiful City Cemetery, Bountiful, Davis, Utah
Notes: —	

GRAY, WILLIAM A.   (UNION ARMY)   *Baptized before the war.*

Rank: Private	Unit(s): Company B, 194th Regiment, New York Infantry Military Service Source(s): 1890 Census, FOLD3
Birth Date: 1 November 1837	Birth Place: North Hampton, York, New Brunswick, Canada
LDS Membership Date: 1855	LDS Membership Source(s): NFS (ID #: KWCL-9FJ)
Death Date: 28 December 1911	Death Place: Provo, Utah, Utah Find A Grave: 57793623 Burial Location: Provo, Utah, Utah
Notes: [MLM] He served one year and four months beginning April 1864. His military discharge papers were reportedly burned in Chicago [1890 Census]. There is some discrepancy regarding this individual's name: [NFS] lists the primary name as "William Henry Gray," but one of the possible alternate names listed for this individual is "Henry A. Gray." [FOLD3] lists "William A. Gray."	

GREEN, JAMES   (UNION ARMY)   *Baptized before the war (presumed).*

Rank: Private	Unit(s): Lot Smith Utah Cavalry Military Service Source(s): VBU, ACWS, NPS, PI, Fisher, 1862 MOR
Birth Date: 1837	Birth Place: Uncertain
LDS Membership Date: Presumed LDS	LDS Membership Source(s): NFS (ID #: Uncertain)
Death Date: Uncertain	Death Place: Utah Find A Grave: 9033129 Burial Location: Draper, Salt Lake, Utah
Notes: There are dozens of James Greens listed in [NFS] who were born in 1837.	

GRIGG, WILLIAM ALEXANDER   (CONFEDERATE ARMY)   *Baptized after the war.*

Rank: Private	Unit(s): Company I, 21st Regiment, North Carolina Infantry Military Service Source(s): 1890 Census, NPS
Birth Date: 25 February 1835	Birth Place: Tyrell Division Quaker Gap, Surry, North Carolina
LDS Membership Date: 6 August 1868	LDS Membership Source(s): NFS (ID #: KWVH-D5L)
Death Date: 16 April 1901	Death Place: Payson, Utah, Utah Find A Grave: 74129013 Burial Location: Uncertain
Notes: [MLM] He served in the military two years, one month, and ten days beginning June 5, 1861. "Weak lungs" was listed as a service-related disability [1890 Census].	

GUEST, EDWARD F.   (UNION ARMY)   *Baptized before the war.*

Rank: Private	Unit(s): Lot Smith Utah Cavalry Military Service Source(s): ACWS, NPS, PI, Fisher, 1862 MOR
Birth Date: 24 May 1830	Birth Place: Queenstown, Cork, Ireland
LDS Membership Date: 25 April 1848	LDS Membership Source(s): NFS (ID #: KWJZ-TQH)
Death Date: 4 August 1896	Death Place: Salt Lake City, Salt Lake, Utah Find A Grave: 42418765 Burial Location: Salt Lake City Cemetery, Salt Lake City, Salt Lake, Utah
Notes: [MLM]	

HACKETT, GEORGE   (CONFEDERATE ARMY)   *Baptized during the war.*

Rank: Private	**Unit(s):** Company F, 4th Regiment, Missouri Infantry **Military Service Source(s):** 1890 Census, NPS
Birth Date: 24 November 1840	**Birth Place:** Denbighshire, Wales
LDS Membership Date: 4 March 1865	**LDS Membership Source(s):** NFS (ID #: KWJ1-R2X)
Death Date: 26 March 1922	**Death Place:** Salt Lake City, Salt Lake, Utah **Find A Grave:** 13269887 **Burial Location:** Riverton, Salt Lake, Utah

Notes: [MLM] He served in the military three years beginning May 1, 1861. A saber cut on his hand is listed as a service-related disability [1890 Census].

HALE, SOLOMON H.   (UNION ARMY)   *Baptized before the war.*

Rank: Wagoneer	**Unit(s):** Lot Smith Utah Cavalry **Military Service Source(s):** ACWS, NPS, Fisher, 1862 MOR
Birth Date: 30 April 1839	**Birth Place:** Quincy, Adams, Illinois
LDS Membership Date: 1847	**LDS Membership Source(s):** LDSBE, PPMU, NFS (ID #: KWNH-K9L)
Death Date: 11 July 1925	**Death Place:** Boise, Ada, Idaho **Find A Grave:** 38686992 **Burial Location:** Preston, Franklin, Idaho

Notes: He "came to Utah 1848, Heber C. Kimball Company. Councilor in Presidency of Oneida [Idaho] Stake" [PPMU, 154]. His father was a bishop in Nauvoo, Illinois. He was one of the first settlers of Logan, Utah. He "had the reputation of being the best [horse] rider in the country. . . . On May 1, 1862, Mr. Hale enlisted in the government service in Captain Lot Smith's command of Utah Volunteers and was appointed wagon-master and assigned to do duty in protecting the mails on the overland route, all the government troops having been called off the plains, leaving the Indians in almost full control and using their opportunity to murder emigrants, burn stage houses, destroy coaches, kill the guards and generally keep up a state of terror throughout the country. The Utah volunteers were used in restraining the savages and preserving order, putting up wires, protecting stage coaches and keeping up as far as possible communication with the east. They enlisted for ninety days, but were kept in service 115 [days]. . . . In April 1890, he was called by the Church to superintend the erection of the Oneida Stake Academy, at Preston [Idaho], to which town his family moved the following July" [LDSBE, 2:168].

HALL, SAMUEL PARLEY   (UNION ARMY)   *Baptized before the war.*

Rank: Private	**Unit(s):** Company E, 2nd Regiment, California Cavalry **Military Service Source(s):** 1890 Census, NPS
Birth Date: 17 March 1841	**Birth Place:** Liverpool, Lancashire, England
LDS Membership Date: 17 March 1849	**LDS Membership Source(s):** NFS (ID #: KWNF-TQH)
Death Date: 15 October 1918	**Death Place:** Wellsville, Cache, Utah **Find A Grave:** 12636817 **Burial Location:** Wellsville, Cache, Utah

Notes: [MLM] "Farmer" [PPMU, 266]. He served in the military one year, eight months, and twenty-eight days beginning September 5, 1864. "Disabled by fall from horse" is listed as a service-related disability [1890 Census].

HAMBLIN, LEANDER FLOYD (UNION ARMY)   *Baptized after the war.*

Rank: Private	**Unit(s):** Companies A & I, 14th Regiment, Kentucky Cavalry **Military Service Source(s):** NPS, MCL
Birth Date: 2 June 1849	**Birth Place:** Maury, Tennessee
LDS Membership Date: 1 August 1889	**LDS Membership Source(s):** NFS (ID #: LHP7-MFJ)
Death Date: 19 December 1929	**Death Place:** San Luis, Costilla, Colorado **Find A Grave:** — **Burial Location:** Manassa, Conejos, Colorado
Notes: [MLM]	

HANCOCK, GEORGE WASHINGTON (UNION ARMY)   *Baptized before the war.*

Rank: Private	**Unit(s):** Company C, 5th (or 15th) Regiment, Michigan Infantry **Military Service Source(s):** VBU, 1890 Census, NPS
Birth Date: 8 March 1826	**Birth Place:** Columbia, Cuyahoga, Ohio
LDS Membership Date: 14 August 1834	**LDS Membership Source(s):** LDSBE, PPMU, NFS (ID #: KWJ8-RF9)
Death Date: 15 November 1901	**Death Place:** Payson, Utah, Utah **Find A Grave:** 12871311 **Burial Location:** Payson City Cemetery, Payson, Utah, Utah

Notes: He served in the Civil War for ten months beginning in September 1864. "He enlisted in the Mormon Battalion in July, 1846. . . . After being dicharged [*sic*] in 1847, he came to G.S.L. [Great Salt Lake] Valley, arriving there in October, 1847. . . . He assisted in the surveying of a road between California and Utah." Among other things, he started a tannery, a shoe and harness factory, a lumber yard, and a butcher shop. He also built a grist mill and later a creamery and canning establishment. He built the first electric plant in Payson, Utah, and helped build an opera house in that city. In his earlier days, he was ordained a Seventy and acted as a president of his quorum [LDSBE, 2:350–51]. Alias listed as "Charles Edson" [1890 Census]. He "came to Utah in October, 1849" [PPMU, 191]. The [1890 Census] lists unit affiliation as 5th Michigan Infantry; [NPS] lists two George Hancocks who served from Michigan (15th and 18th Regiments, Michigan Infantry).

HARPER, JOHN C. (CONFEDERATE ARMY)   *Baptized after the war.*

Rank: Private	**Unit(s):** Company D, 2nd Regiment, Virginia Cavalry **Military Service Source(s):** NPS; Obituary
Birth Date: 15 April 1846	**Birth Place:** Franklin, Virginia
LDS Membership Date: 2 May 1870	**LDS Membership Source(s):** NFS (ID #: KWJC-N5H)
Death Date: 1 December 1909	**Death Place:** Colonia Juarez, Chihuahua, Mexico **Find A Grave:** 42849810 **Burial Location:** Colonia Juarez, Chihuahua, Mexico

Notes: His obituary noted that he was "a veteran of the Civil War" (*Salt Lake Herald*, December 6, 1909, 23). He "may have been wounded at Meadow Bridge on 12 October 1864. He was present at Appomattox Court House, Virginia, when General Robert E. Lee surrendered to General Ulysses S. Grant of the United States Army. As part of the surrender agreement General Grant allowed the Confederate soldiers to go home as paroled prisoners of war. To ensure their safe travel home each soldier was issued a certificate signed by his commanding officer stating his status as a paroled prisoner of war. . . . John was ordained a Seventy in the LDS church on 16 April 1876, and in 1879 he was elected constable in Payson, Utah, a title he held for several years. John married Fanny Coombs on 23 August 1883 in Salt Lake City and was called to serve a mission in 1887 leaving home on 13 May of that year and arriving at Chattanooga, Tennessee on 19 May 1887. . . .

Many LDS missionaries suffered persecution while in the southern states at this time and John mentioned that tensions were often high. . . . John was made president of the North Carolina Conference on 29 October 1887, having responsibility to direct missionary activities in North Carolina. John, as president of the North Carolina Conference, was also placed in charge of helping the members of the church in the area immigrate to Utah. John also had the opportunity to travel to his home county of Franklin, Virginia, and visit many of his old friends and relatives as well as the grave sites of his mother, sisters, and his first wife, Ruth Anna Hill. John wrote of the reverence he felt at the gravesites of his loved ones and 'how intensified this feeling by the knowledge the gospel brings, by vicorious [sic] work which is a labor of love for us who have the glorious privilege of living in a gospel dispensation.' . . . He was imprisoned in the Utah State Penitentiary by summer 1889 for unlawful cohabitation [polygamy]. While in prison he kept an autograph book which was signed by fellow prisoners. In order to avoid further persecution from the U.S. government for the practice of plural marriage John moved his family to the Mormon town of Colonia Juarez, Chihuahua, Mexico" (*John Claiborne Harper Diary*, vol. 1, 1887–1888, http://lib.byu.edu/digital/mmd/diarists/Harper_John_Claiborne.php).

HARRINGTON, JOHN   (UNION ARMY)   *Baptized after the war.*

Rank: Private	**Unit(s):** Company G, 15th Regiment, New York Engineers **Military Service Source(s):** NPS, PI, FGC
Birth Date: 6 July 1828	**Birth Place:** Oswegotchie, St. Lawrence, New York
LDS Membership Date: 1876	**LDS Membership Source(s):** NFS (ID #: K2WF-5FW)
Death Date: 6 January 1915	**Death Place:** Glenwood, Sevier, Utah **Find A Grave:** 32345531 **Burial Location:** Glenwood, Sevier, Utah

Notes: "NEW YORK PVT 15 ENGINEERS CIVIL WAR" (Private, 15th New York Engineers) is carved on his grave marker [FGC]. While the [NFS] and [FGC] records appear to be for the same individual, there are small date discrepancies between the records.

HARRIS, THOMAS H.   (UNION ARMY)   *Baptized before the war (presumed).*

Rank: Private	**Unit(s):** Lot Smith Utah Cavalry **Military Service Source(s):** ACWS, Obituary, Fisher, 1862 MOR
Birth Date: 7 February 1837	**Birth Place:** Bath, Somerset, England
LDS Membership Date: Presumed LDS	**LDS Membership Source(s):** NFS (ID #: 2Z8S-X4D)
Death Date: 11 July 1912	**Death Place:** Long Beach, Los Angeles, California **Find A Grave:** — **Burial Location:** Uncertain

Notes: [MLM] His obituary states that he was "a Civil war veteran" who "was in the coal business for several years" and moved to Salt Lake in 1890. He died in Long Beach, California (*Salt Lake Herald*, July 12, 1912, 11). The LDS baptism listed for this individual on [NFS] is posthumous. As a member of the Lot Smith Utah Cavalry, he is presumed to be LDS. The veteran record is accurate, but the [MLM] tag is currently warranted.

HARRISON, DANIEL   (CONFEDERATE ARMY)   *Baptized after the war.*

Rank: Private	**Unit(s):** Company B, Walker's Battalion, Thomas Legion, North Carolina **Military Service Source(s):** NPS, 1900 Census
Birth Date: 22 August 1841	**Birth Place:** Rutherford County, North Carolina

Harrison, Daniel (continued)	
LDS Membership Date: 11 July 1880	**LDS Membership Source(s):** NFS (ID #: K2WN-9DN)
Death Date: 24 July 1899	**Death Place:** Nephi, Juab, Utah **Find A Grave:** — **Burial Location:** Nephi, Juab, Utah
Notes: [MLM]	

HASTLER, WILLIAM H.   (UNION ARMY)   *Baptized before the war.*

Rank: Private	**Unit(s):** 3rd Regiment, California Volunteers **Military Service Source(s):** NPS, PI, FGC
Birth Date: 7 September 1828	**Birth Place:** Hunston, Hertfordshire, England
LDS Membership Date: 9 January 1853	**LDS Membership Source(s):** NFS (ID #: KWJQ-KKJ)
Death Date: 14 September 1909	**Death Place:** Salt Lake City, Salt Lake, Utah **Find A Grave:** 172068 **Burial Location:** Mount Olivet Cemetery, Salt Lake City, Salt Lake, Utah
Notes: "CO. C. 3 CAL. INF." (Company C, 3rd California Infantry) is carved on his grave marker [FGC].	

HELM, JOHN   (UNION ARMY)   *Baptized before the war.*

Rank: Farrier	**Unit(s):** Lot Smith Utah Cavalry **Military Service Source(s):** Fisher, NPS, PI, Fisher, 1862 MOR
Birth Date: 16 September 1838	**Birth Place:** Jackson Township, Sandusky, Ohio
LDS Membership Date: 14 November 1855	**LDS Membership Source(s):** NFS (ID #: KWV8-HS7)
Death Date: 8 March 1911	**Death Place:** Utah **Find A Grave:** — **Burial Location:** Uncertain
Notes: [MLM] A farrier is a blacksmith.	

HENDRICKS, SAMUEL ALLEN   (CONFEDERATE ARMY)   *Baptized before the war.*

Rank: Private	**Unit(s):** Captain Nutt's Company (Red River Rangers), Louisiana Cavalry **Military Service Source(s):** NPS
Birth Date: 22 December 1848	**Birth Place:** Red River, Clairborne, Louisiana
LDS Membership Date: 1857	**LDS Membership Source(s):** NFS (ID #: KWJX-VWT)
Death Date: 26 June 1900	**Death Place:** Santiago, Durango, New Mexico **Find A Grave:** — **Burial Location:** Santiago, Durango, New Mexico
Notes: [MLM] He is listed as "Allen Hendricks" in [NPS].	

HIGGINBOTHAM, SIMON SHELBY (CONFEDERATE ARMY)   *Baptized during the war.*

Rank: Private	**Unit(s):** Company K, 18th Regiment, Louisiana Infantry **Military Service Source(s):** NPS, FGC
Birth Date: 20 June 1839	**Birth Place:** Burkes Garden, Tazewell, Virginia
LDS Membership Date: 1 March 1862 (confirmation)	**LDS Membership Source(s):** NFS (ID #: K2WJ-ZN1)

Death Date: 4 January 1889	Death Place: Ogden, Weber, Utah Find A Grave: 34969638 Burial Location: Ogden, Weber, Utah

Notes: The 18th Regiment, Louisiana Infantry, was organized during the summer of 1861 and fought at the Battle of Shiloh [NPS]. Simon's older sister, Nancy, married another LDS Civil War veteran, David Harold Peery, on December 30, 1852 [NFS].

HILL, SAMUEL   (UNION ARMY)   *Baptized before the war.*

Rank: Private	Unit(s): Lot Smith Utah Cavalry Military Service Source(s): ACWS, NPS, PI, Fisher, 1862 MOR
Birth Date: 23 December 1840	Birth Place: Simcoe, Norfolk, Ontario, Canada
LDS Membership Date: 12 March 1849	LDS Membership Source(s): PPMU, NFS (ID #: KWJC-21M)
Death Date: 10 February 1903	Death Place: Salt Lake City, Salt Lake, Utah Find A Grave: 75885719 Burial Location: Salt Lake City Cemetery, Salt Lake City, Salt Lake, Utah

Notes: [MLM] He "came to Utah in 1851. Indian War Veteran" [PPMU, 288]. "High priest. Plasterer" [PPMU, 935].

HINCKLEY, IRA NATHANIEL   (UNION ARMY)   *Baptized before the war.*

Rank: Farrier	Unit(s): Lot Smith Utah Cavalry Military Service Source(s): ACWS, NPS, PI, Fisher, 1862 MOR
Birth Date: 30 October 1828	Birth Place: Bastard, Leeds, Ontario, Canada
LDS Membership Date: 1 July 1843	LDS Membership Source(s): PPMU, LDSBE, NFS (ID #: KWNV-L3N)
Death Date: 10 April 1904	Death Place: Provo, Utah, Utah Find A Grave: 6291111 Burial Location: Provo, Utah, Utah

Notes: A farrier is a blacksmith. He "came to Utah in 1850, David Evans Company" [PPMU, 220]. "He served five years as a policeman in Salt Lake City. in 1856 he superintended the building of a fort for the Y.X. company, 30 miles west of Fort Laramie. In 1862 he was a member of the expedition sent out under Lot Smith to protect the mail route" [LDSBE, 1:528]. "President of Millard (Utah) stake 2 years. Captain of a company to guard U.S. mail from depredations of Indians. Pioneer to Arizona and New Mexico. Called by President Young to build Cove Fort 1867. Policeman at Salt Lake City; mayor of Fillmore (Utah). Blacksmith; farmer and stockman" [PPMU, 936]. Father of Alonzo A. Hinckley (LDS Apostle, 1934–36) and Bryant S. Hinckley (Young Men general board member, president of Northern States Mission); grandfather of Gordon B. Hinckley (President of The Church of Jesus Christ of Latter-day Saints, 1995–2008); great-grandfather of Richard G. Hinckley (LDS First Quorum of the Seventy, 2005–present).

HIXSON (OR HICKSON), JAMES   (UNION ARMY)   *Baptized during the war.*

Rank: Private	Unit(s): Lot Smith Utah Cavalry Military Service Source(s): ACWS, NPS, PI, Fisher, 1862 MOR
Birth Date: 30 March 1833	Birth Place: Indiana
LDS Membership Date: 19 May 1861	LDS Membership Source(s): NFS (ID #: KWC2-1F6)
Death Date: 2 March 1902	Death Place: Wanship, Summit, Utah Find A Grave: 6795684 Burial Location: Wanship Cemetery, Wanship, Summit, Utah

Notes: [MLM] [1862 MOR] lists his name as "James Hickson." [Fisher] lists his name as "James Hixson."

HOAGLAND, JOHN (UNION ARMY)   *Baptized before the war.*

Rank: Corporal	Unit(s): Lot Smith Utah Cavalry Military Service Source(s): VBU, NPS, PI, Fisher, 1862 MOR
Birth Date: 22 May 1833	Birth Place: Royal Oak, Oakland, Michigan
LDS Membership Date: 1 January 1844	LDS Membership Source(s): LDSBE, NFS (ID #: KWJZ-8W1)
Death Date: 6 September 1893	Death Place: Salt Lake City, Salt Lake, Utah Find A Grave: 68271979 Burial Location: Salt Lake City Cemetery, Salt Lake City, Salt Lake, Utah

Notes: "He was with his parents during their exodus from Nauvoo, Ill., and in their temporary sojourn on the frontiers and came to G.S.L. [Great Salt Lake] Valley in 1847, driving an ox team into the Valley, though only 14 years old. While hauling logs for building purposes near Parleys Park, Aug. 17, 1853, together with others, he was attacked by Indians, who killed John Dixon and John Quayle. He himself was wounded in the arm, but he succeeded in unhitcching [*sic*] his horses and riding over the mountains. . . . In 1862 he took an active part in protecting the mail route between Salt Lake City and the East against the Indians, acting as lieutenant in Capt. Lot Smith's company. [Editor's note: [1862 MOR] lists his rank as Corporal.] In 1866–69 he filled a mission to Switzerland" [LDSBE, 2:365].

HOFFMIRE, FRANCIS G. (UNION ARMY)   *Baptized after the war.*

Rank: Private	Unit(s): Company K, 6th Regiment, Ohio Cavalry Military Service Source(s): NPS, PI, FGC
Birth Date: 12 July 1847	Birth Place: Fulton County, Ohio
LDS Membership Date: 3 July 1886	LDS Membership Source(s): NFS (ID #: LHG2-6WV)
Death Date: 7 June 1915	Death Place: Grantsville, Tooele, Utah Find A Grave: 30851999 Burial Location: Grantsville City Cemetery, Grantsville, Tooele, Utah

Notes: Organized in October 1861, the 6th Regiment, Ohio Cavalry, served primarily in Virginia and participated in numerous battles, including Bull Run, Fredericksburg, Brandy Station, the Wilderness, Cold Harbor, and Five Forks. It was present at Lee's surrender on April 9, 1865, at Appomattox Court House, Virginia [NPS].

HOLCOMB, SAMUEL SPENCER (CONFEDERATE ARMY)   *Baptized after the war.*

Rank: Private	Unit(s): Company D, 21st Regiment, Texas Cavalry Military Service Source(s): FOLD3, CSC, 1900 Census
Birth Date: 25 January 1847	Birth Place: Clarkesville, Habersham, Georgia
LDS Membership Date: 15 August 1909	LDS Membership Source(s): NFS (ID #: KWJK-LP4)
Death Date: 20 November 1926	Death Place: Shelly, Bingham, Idaho Find A Grave: 40333449 Burial Location: Manzanola, Otero, Colorado

Notes: [MLM] The 21st Regiment, Texas Cavalry, was popularly known as the 1st Texas Lancers [NPS].

HOLLAND, JAMES M. (UNION ARMY)   *Uncertain when baptized.*

Rank: Served as a First Sergeant and Lieutenant	Unit(s): Company F, 26th Regiment, Kentucky Infantry Military Service Source(s): 1890 Census, NPS, FGC
Birth Date: 1812	Birth Place: Willenhall, Staffordshire, England

LDS Membership Date: NFS lists "Completed"	LDS Membership Source(s): NFS (ID #: 2Z3C-6YV)
Death Date: 6 April 1900	Death Place: Salt Lake City, Salt Lake, Utah Find A Grave: 46141725 Burial Location: Salt Lake Cemetery, Salt Lake City, Salt Lake, Utah

Notes: "1ST LT 26 KY INFANTRY CIVIL WAR" (First Lieutenant, 26th Kentucky Infantry) is carved on his grave marker [FGC]. Baptismal date listed as "Completed" [NFS]. He served two years, one month, and fifteen days beginning on December 16, 1861. He mustered with the "12th U.S. Heavy Artillery Colored; mustered out to accept a commission" as an officer [1890 Census].

HOLMES, WILLIAM H.   (UNION ARMY)   *Baptized before the war.*

Rank: Private	Unit(s): Company B, 1st Regiment, Ohio Infantry Military Service Source(s): 1890 Census, NPS
Birth Date: 15 January 1819	Birth Place: Arnold, Nottingham, England
LDS Membership Date: 8 December 1849	LDS Membership Source(s): NFS (ID #: KWJ3-NJV)
Death Date: 4 October 1876	Death Place: West Weber, Weber, Utah Find A Grave: — Burial Location: West Weber, Weber, Utah

Notes: [MLM] He served in the military one year and six months beginning in 1864. If the correct LDS member is identified, the 1890 veteran census schedule (recorded in Weber County, Utah) should list his entry as a widow report, as his death date was prior to 1890, but it does not. The veteran schedule also lists his first name as "Williams" [1890 Census]. [NPS] includes a "William H. Holmes" who served in the 178th Ohio Infantry; the 1890 Census lists 1st Ohio Infantry.

HOPKINS, RICHARD ROCKWELL   (UNION ARMY)   *Baptized before the war.*

Rank: Captain	Unit(s): Company H, 18th Regiment, Illinois Infantry Military Service Source(s): NPS
Birth Date: 25 December 1821	Birth Place: Edwardsville, Madison, Illinois
LDS Membership Date: July 1850	LDS Membership Source(s): NFS (ID #: K2WV-1HN)
Death Date: 25 December 1882	Death Place: Salt Lake City, Salt Lake, Utah Find A Grave: 74033833 Burial Location: Mount Olivet Cemetery, Salt Lake City, Salt Lake, Utah

Notes: [MLM] He and his wife, Ruth Crandall, came to Utah Territory in the Milo Andrus Pioneer Company (1850) and then traveled on to San Bernardino, California. By 1860, he was back in St. Louis as a part owner and captain of the steamboat Asa Wilgus, which foundered on a snag just a few months after he bought it (Annalies Corbin, *The Material Culture of Steamboat Passengers* [New York: Springer Publishing, 2000]). His obituary stated that he was a miner and a merchant and that "a more deserving man never lived and died in Utah" (*Salt Lake Tribune*, December 27, 1882).

HOWARD, WILLIAM W.   (UNION ARMY)   *Baptized after the war.*

Rank: Private	Unit(s): Company L, 1st Regiment, District of Columbia Cavalry Military Service Source(s): NPS
Birth Date: 15 January 1849	Birth Place: Cooper, Gentry, Missouri
LDS Membership Date: 12 March 1867	LDS Membership Source(s): NFS (ID #: KWCH-12J)

Howard, William W. (continued)	
Death Date: 23 November 1935	**Death Place:** Brigham City, Box Elder, Utah **Find A Grave:** 40726014 **Burial Location:** Brigham City Cemetery, Brigham City, Box Elder, Utah
Notes: The 1st Regiment, District of Columbia Cavalry, was organized between June and December 1863 and was initially "subject only to orders of War Department" until January 1864, after which the unit fought in engagements across Virginia and was present at Lee's surrender at Appomattox Court House on April 9, 1865 [NPS].	

HOWE, RICHARD   (UNION ARMY)   *Baptized before the war.*

Rank: Private	**Unit(s):** Lot Smith Utah Cavalry **Military Service Source(s):** ACWS, NPS, PI, Fisher, 1862 MOR
Birth Date: 30 July 1839	**Birth Place:** Chilvers, Coton, England
LDS Membership Date: 12 April 1855	**LDS Membership Source(s):** NFS (ID #: KWNV-8ZJ)
Death Date: 6 April 1927	**Death Place:** Cottonwood, Salt Lake, Utah **Find A Grave:** 128022 **Burial Location:** Murray City Cemetery, Murray, Salt Lake, Utah
Notes: [MLM]	

HUDDLESTON, HENRY F.   (CONFEDERATE ARMY)   *Baptized after the war.*

Rank: Uncertain	**Unit(s):** 45th Regiment, Tennessee Infantry **Military Service Source(s):** CSC
Birth Date: 13 November 1843	**Birth Place:** Wilson County, Tennessee
LDS Membership Date: 1 January 1884	**LDS Membership Source(s):** NFS (ID #: KVLY-CST)
Death Date: 21 November 1910	**Death Place:** Pueblo County, Colorado **Find A Grave:** — **Burial Location:** Pueblo County, Colorado
Notes: [MLM] Joseph H. Crute Jr., *Units of the Confederate States Army* (Midlothian, VA: Derwent, 1987), contains no history for his unit [NPS].	

HUDSON, LYMAN L.   (UNION ARMY)   *Baptized after the war.*

Rank: Private	**Unit(s):** Company E, 176th Regiment, Ohio Infantry **Military Service Source(s):** VBU, NPS, PI
Birth Date: 16 March 1848	**Birth Place:** Hambden, Geauga, Ohio
LDS Membership Date: 3 July 1872	**LDS Membership Source(s):** NFS (ID #: KW6C-QGR)
Death Date: 11 March 1932	**Death Place:** Salt Lake City, Salt Lake, Utah **Find A Grave:** 68567359 **Burial Location:** Salt Lake City Cemetery, Salt Lake City, Salt Lake, Utah
Notes: The 176th Regiment, Ohio Infantry, was organized during August and September 1864 and served in Tennessee [NPS].	

HUFFAKER, IGNATIUS HENRY   (CONFEDERATE ARMY)   *Baptized after the war.*

Rank: Corporal	**Unit(s):** Company G & A, 36th Regiment, (Broyles) Georgia Infantry **Military Service Source(s):** NPS
Birth Date: 7 April 1840	**Birth Place:** Athens, McMinn, Tennessee

LDS Membership Date: 27 October 1878	LDS Membership Source(s): NFS (ID #: KWNY-XSL)
Death Date: 11 November 1916	Death Place: Monte Vista, Rio Grande, Colorado Find A Grave: — Burial Location: Manassa Cemetery, Manassa, Conejos, Colorado

Notes: [MLM] The 36th Regiment, Georgia Infantry, was "organized at Dalton, Georgia, during the winter of 1861–1862." The unit "was captured at Vicksburg on July 4, 1863"; it was later exchanged, and it fought from Tennessee to Mississippi [NPS].

HUFFAKER, ISAAC ASBURY   (CONFEDERATE ARMY)   *Baptized after the war.*

Rank: Sergeant	Unit(s): Company G, 36th Regiment, Georgia Infantry Military Service Source(s): NPS, FGC
Birth Date: 22 October 1822	Birth Place: Athens, Georgia
LDS Membership Date: 7 July 1890	LDS Membership Source(s): NFS (ID #: KWJC-NPQ)
Death Date: 31 March 1903	Death Place: Manassa, Conejos, Colorado Find A Grave: 37850812 Burial Location: Manassa, Conejos, Colorado

Notes: "CO G 36 GA INF C.S.A." (Company G, 36th Georgia Infantry, Confederate States of America) is carved on his grave marker [FGC].

HUFFAKER, LEWIS ALBERT   (UNION ARMY)   *Baptized before the war.*

Rank: Private	Unit(s): Lot Smith Utah Cavalry Military Service Source(s): VBU, ACWS, NPS, PI, Obituary, Fisher, 1862 MOR
Birth Date: 19 March 1841	Birth Place: Bureau, Bureau, Illinois
LDS Membership Date: 25 September 1851	LDS Membership Source(s): LDSBE, PPMU, NFS (ID #: KWJ4-GP1)
Death Date: 15 June 1918	Death Place: Salt Lake City, Salt Lake, Utah Find A Grave: 60390284 Burial Location: Salt Lake City, Salt Lake, Utah

Notes: "President of the High Priests' quorum of Bingham Stake, Idaho . . . [had a distant recollection] of hearing Joseph Smith the prophet preach. . . . Joined the Utah militia at the age of sixteen and rendered service in the Johnston 'war,' and acted as one of Robert T. Burton's escort to Governor Cummings [sic]. In response to a call of President Lincoln, Bro. Huffaker became one of the 100 troops to go East to restore the Wells-Fargo stage line which had been broken up by the Indians, and was through the greater part of the 'Black Hawk war.' He has done considerable home missionary work and started on a mission to England Oct. 10, 1900, where he spent twenty-seven months in active and useful labor" [LDSBE, 2:54–55]. He "came to Utah in 1847, Jedediah M. Grant company. . . . Member 105th quorum seventies; missionary to England 1900–1902; high priest; home missionary 21 years; acting president high priests of Bingham stake, Idaho, three years; president block teachers. Constable of Summit county [Utah] four years. Took part in Echo Canyon war [Utah War]; Indian war veteran. Farmer and stockraiser" [PPMU, 947]. [PPMU] and [NFS] list birth date as March 19, 1841; [LDSBE] lists March 9, 1841. His obituary, entitled "Veteran of Civil and Indian Wars Dies at Home Here," states that he was a "pioneer of '47 and veteran of the Civil and Indian wars" and "commander of [the] Knowlton post of the G.A.R. . . . A native of Illinois, he crossed the plains with Jedediah M. Grant, the Mormon leader, took part in expeditions against the Indians and was assigned to guarding the United States telegraph, stage and mail line between here and Omaha when he entered the Civil war in 1862." His obituary spells his last name "Huffacker" (*Salt Lake Telegram*, May 15, 1918, 3). For additional information, see the Ellsworth-Alford chapter herein.

HULLINGER, HARVEY COE (UNION ARMY)   *Baptized before the war.*

Rank: Private	**Unit(s):** Lot Smith Utah Cavalry **Military Service Source(s):** VBU, ACWS, NPS, Obituary, Fisher, 1862 MOR
Birth Date: 2 December 1824	**Birth Place:** Mad River, Champaign, Ohio
LDS Membership Date: 14 August 1842	**LDS Membership Source(s):** NFS (ID #: KWJH-X8H)
Death Date: 29 January 1926	**Death Place:** Vernal, Uintah, Utah **Find A Grave:** 15974619 **Burial Location:** Vernal Memorial Park, Vernal, Uintah, Utah

Notes: He "came to Utah Sept. 16, 1859, Edward Stevenson Company. Physician" [PPMU, 490]. "Member 15th quorum seventies of Salt Lake City; missionary to Council Bluffs 1860–61; counselor in 77th quorum seventies of South Cottonwood [Utah]; missionary to Ohio 1902. Called to St. George as a physician 1862–64; first physician of Uintah County [Utah]. County surveyor four years; county commissioners four years; school treasurer. Volunteer surgeon in U.S. army 1862; assisted in bringing immigrants to Utah; member Utah State Medical Association. Recorder at Big Cottonwood [Utah] mining district three years. Worked on Nauvoo temple and all temples in Utah" [PPMU, 948]. At the time of his death (at age 101), he was the oldest practicing physician in the United States, the oldest Civil War veteran in Utah, the second-oldest Civil War Veteran in the nation, and the oldest member of the LDS Church (in terms of continuous membership) (*News Advocate*, February 4, 1926, 3; *Duchesne County Newspaper*, February 5, 1926; and *Vernal Express*, January 29, 1926). He kept a small pocket diary throughout the military service of the Lot Smith Utah Cavalry. He was one of the earliest Lot Smith Utah Cavalry veterans to join the Grand Army of the Republic. For additional information, see the Stuart-Alford chapter entitled "Utah Goes to War" and Alford's "Mormons and the Grand Army of the Republic" herein.

IMLAY, JAMES (UNION ARMY)   *Baptized before the war.*

Rank: Private	**Unit(s):** Lot Smith Utah Cavalry **Military Service Source(s):** ACWS, NPS, Fisher, 1862 MOR
Birth Date: 6 April 1815	**Birth Place:** Imlaystown, Burlington, New Jersey
LDS Membership Date: 1 January 1843	**LDS Membership Source(s):** NFS (ID #: KWNT-9S7)
Death Date: 1 February 1890	**Death Place:** Panguitch, Garfield, Utah **Find A Grave:** 39228819 **Burial Location:** Panguitch City Cemetery, Panguitch, Garfield, Utah

Notes: [MLM]

INMAN, SAMUEL EDWARD (CONFEDERATE ARMY)   *Baptized after the war.*

Rank: First Lieutenant	**Unit(s):** Company G, 23rd Regiment, Tennessee Infantry **Military Service Source(s):** FOLD3, CSC, FGC
Birth Date: 25 September 1818	**Birth Place:** Williamson, Tennessee
LDS Membership Date: 15 October 1881	**LDS Membership Source(s):** NFS (ID #: KWXS-DVY)
Death Date: March 1884	**Death Place:** Richfield, Conejos, Colorado **Find A Grave:** 7145473 **Burial Location:** Sanford Cemetery, Conejos, Colorado

Notes: "CO G 23 TENN INF C.S.A." (Company G, 23rd Tennessee Infantry, Confederate States of America) is carved on his grave marker [FGC].

IREY (OR IREA), CYRUS (UNION ARMY) *Baptized before the war (presumed).*

Rank: Private	**Unit(s):** Company H, 20th Regiment, Pennsylvania Cavalry **Military Service Source(s):** NARA (Microfilm M554 roll 59), FGC
Birth Date: 28 April 1824	**Birth Place:** Philadelphia, Pennsylvania
LDS Membership Date: Presumed LDS	**LDS Membership Source(s):** SBS; The Church of Jesus Christ of Latter-day Saints, Family History Library microfilm 1000133
Death Date: 9 August 1864	**Death Place:** West Virginia **Find A Grave:** 821267 **Burial Location:** Section F, site 1222, Grafton National Cemetery, Grafton, Taylor, West Virginia

Notes: "20 PA. CAV." (20th Pennsylvania Cavalry) is carved on his grave marker [FGC]. "He enlisted with the 20th Pennsylvania Cavalry at Philadelphia in February 1864 as a Private. His unit was assigned to Sigel at Martinsburg, West Virginia in March 1864, where they are attached to the 2nd Brigade, 1st Cavalry Division, Department of West Virginia. It was there that Cyrus Irey died on 9 August 1864. I have checked the battle history of the area and there were no battles fought close to the time of Cyrus' death. The statistics for the 20th Cavalry state that the Regiment lost during service three Officers and twenty-two enlisted men killed and mortally wounded and three Officers and one hundred enlisted men by disease, for a total of one hundred twenty-eight men. It is this author's conclusion that Cyrus fell ill during an encampment near Halltown. His body had apparently been buried in haste and later moved to its present location. His death is recorded as 9 August 1864 and his burial 20 December 1867. The National Cemetery to honor the Civil War dead [at Grafton] was established in 1867 and thousands of known and unknown soldiers were moved from their original burial locations to that cemetery. After his death the word came back to California, and his estate was probated by the San Francisco Superior Court, Index Cyrus Irey record # 4040, Register 6, page 95. The records were lost during the San Francisco fires that occurred after the earthquake of 1906" (Richard Bullock, e-mail to editor, September 19, 2011; see also LDS Family History Library, Salt Lake City, microfilm 1000133). He sailed to Yerba Buena (San Francisco), California, with Samuel Brannon and other Latter-day Saints on board the ship *Brooklyn*. Presumed to be LDS [SBS]. The "Sons of the Utah Pioneers—Utah, Pioneer Companies" database at Ancestry.com lists his last name as "Irea."

ISBELL, ALEXANDER FRANKLIN (CONFEDERATE ARMY) *Baptized after the war.*

Rank: Private	**Unit(s):** Company G, 41st Regiment, Mississippi Infantry **Military Service Source(s):** FGC
Birth Date: 26 November 1841	**Birth Place:** Aberdeen, Monroe, Mississippi
LDS Membership Date: 14 November 1869	**LDS Membership Source(s):** NFS (ID #: KWNJ-GD2)
Death Date: 18 March 1917	**Death Place:** Richfield, Sevier, Utah **Find A Grave:** 111917 **Burial Location:** Richfield City Cemetery, Richfield, Sevier, Utah

Notes: "PVT CO G 41 MISS INFANTRY CSA CIVIL WAR" (Private, Company G, 41st Mississippi Infantry, Confederate States of America) is carved on his grave marker [FGC]. No Confederate service for "Alexander Isbell" is listed in [NPS].

JACK, JAMES HAZLETT (UNION ARMY) *Baptized after the war.*

Rank: Private	**Unit(s):** Uncertain **Military Service Source(s):** SLV, FGC
Birth Date: 24 October 1831	**Birth Place:** Knoxville, Knox, Tennessee
LDS Membership Date: 24 September 1877	**LDS Membership Source(s):** SLV, NFS (ID #: KWNY-XML)

Jack, James Hazlett (continued)	
Death Date: 13 May 1893	**Death Place:** Sanford, Conejos, Colorado **Find A Grave:** 15499957 **Burial Location:** Manassa, Conejos, Colorado
Notes: "CIVIL WAR VETERAN" is carved on his grave marker [FGC]. He had seven brothers who fought for the Confederacy. He reportedly served as a spy, home guard, and scout. His choices to join the Union army and later to join the LDS Church were both difficult for his family to accept. Following the war, he became a high councilor in the San Luis Valley Stake [SLV].	

JACKSON, HENRY WELLS   (UNION ARMY)   *Baptized before the war.*

Rank: Second Lieutenant	**Unit(s):** 1st Regiment, District of Columbia Cavalry (Wissons Mounted Rangers) **Military Service Source(s):** NPS, FGC, http://www.allenbutlerhistory.com/pdf/jackson_henry-wells_history.PDF
Birth Date: 10 March 1827	**Birth Place:** Chemung, New York
LDS Membership Date: 28 January 1844	**LDS Membership Source(s):** NFS (ID #: KWJ8-6XY)
Death Date: 24 May 1864	**Death Place:** Chesapeake Hospital, Hampton, Virginia **Find A Grave:** 85317 **Burial Location:** Hampton National Cemetery, Hampton, Virginia
Notes: "LIEUT." is carved on his grave marker [FGC]. It is possible that he was the first Latter-day Saint soldier to die as a result of injuries sustained in military combat during a U.S. war. For additional information, see the Freeman chapter herein.	

JAGGER, GEORGE   (UNION ARMY)   *Baptized after the war.*

Rank: Private	**Unit(s):** Company F, 17th Regiment, Illinois Cavalry **Military Service Source(s):** NPS, PI, FGC
Birth Date: 27 September 1835	**Birth Place:** Beaghall, Kellington, Yorkshire, England
LDS Membership Date: 17 March 1900	**LDS Membership Source(s):** NFS (ID #: KWCD-HLT)
Death Date: 6 February 1922	**Death Place:** Provo, Utah, Utah **Find A Grave:** 55720759 **Burial Location:** Provo City Cemetery, Provo, Utah, Utah
Notes: "CO. F 17 ILL. CAV." (Company F, 17th Illinois Cavalry) is carved on his grave marker [FGC].	

JARVIES, JOHN J.   (UNION ARMY)   *Baptized after the war.*

Rank: Corporal	**Unit(s):** Company I, 3rd Regiment, Wisconsin Infantry **Military Service Source(s):** NPS
Birth Date: 13 June 1848	**Birth Place:** Amherst County, Virginia
LDS Membership Date: 1 October 1884	**LDS Membership Source(s):** NFS (ID #: KWN5-L62)
Death Date: 31 December 1892	**Death Place:** Manassa, Conejos, Colorado **Find A Grave:** 38459322 **Burial Location:** Manassa, Conejos, Colorado
Notes: [MLM] Mustered in June 19, 1861, the 3rd Regiment, Wisconsin Infantry, served primarily in West Virginia and Virginia and fought in numerous battles, including Bull Run, Antietam, Chancellorsville, Brandy Station, and Gettysburg [NPS].	

JENKINSON, NOAH (UNION ARMY) *Baptized before the war.*

Rank: Private	**Unit(s):** Company F, 33rd Regiment, Massachusetts Volunteers **Military Service Source(s):** NPS, Obituary
Birth Date: 22 October 1825	**Birth Place:** Yorkshire, England
LDS Membership Date: 11 September 1843	**LDS Membership Source(s):** NFS (ID #: KWV3-YKC)
Death Date: 30 April 1903	**Death Place:** Smithfield, Cache, Utah **Find A Grave:** 179400 **Burial Location:** Smithfield, Cache, Utah
Notes: His obituary states that he was "a veteran of the civil war, enlisting in the Thirty-third Massachusetts Volunteers in 1862; was in the battle of Lookout Mountain and was with General Sherman during his march to the sea" (*Deseret News*, May 7, 1903, 7).	

JENSON, LARS (UNION ARMY) *Baptized before the war.*

Rank: Private	**Unit(s):** Lot Smith Utah Cavalry **Military Service Source(s):** VBU, Fisher, 1862 MOR
Birth Date: 14 January 1841	**Birth Place:** Langrup, Denmark
LDS Membership Date: 1 June 1853	**LDS Membership Source(s):** NFS (ID #: KWJZ-TY9)
Death Date: 22 November 1908	**Death Place:** Salt Lake City, Salt Lake, Utah **Find A Grave:** — **Burial Location:** Elysian Gardens, Millcreek, Salt Lake, Utah
Notes: —	

JESSUP, LEVI T. (UNION ARMY) *Baptized after the war.*

Rank: Private	**Unit(s):** Company K, 7th Regiment, California Infantry **Military Service Source(s):** 1890 Census, NPS
Birth Date: 22 March 1846	**Birth Place:** Montrose, Lee, Iowa
LDS Membership Date: 1876	**LDS Membership Source(s):** NFS (ID #: KWJD-DXD)
Death Date: 30 May 1907	**Death Place:** Cedar City, Iron, Utah **Find A Grave:** 17684637 **Burial Location:** Cedar City, Iron, Utah
Notes: [MLM] His military service began in November 1864. Heart disease is listed as a service-related disability [1890 Census].	

JOHNSON, ALFRED (UNION ARMY) *Baptized before the war.*

Rank: Private	**Unit(s):** Company H, 136th Regiment, Indiana Infantry **Military Service Source(s):** NPS, PI, FGC
Birth Date: 6 December 1834	**Birth Place:** Leicester, Leicester, England
LDS Membership Date: 4 May 1852	**LDS Membership Source(s):** NFS (ID #: KWJW-RJJ)
Death Date: 2 October 1905	**Death Place:** Oakley, Summit, Utah **Find A Grave:** 22796936 **Burial Location:** Peoa Cemetery, Peoa, Summit, Utah
Notes: "CO. K. 1?? IND. INF." (Company K, 1[unreadable] Indiana Infantry) is carved on his grave marker [FGC].	

JOHNSON, GEORGE WASHINGTON   (UNION ARMY)   *Baptized before the war.*

Rank: Private	Unit(s): Company D, 81st Regiment, Indiana Infantry Military Service Source(s): 1890 Census, NPS
Birth Date: 19 February 1823	Birth Place: Pomfret, Chautauqua, New York
LDS Membership Date: 9 April 1836	LDS Membership Source(s): LDSBE, PPMU, NFS (ID #: LHVW-K1H)
Death Date: 22 January 1900	Death Place: Moab, Grand, Utah Find A Grave: 9271536 Burial Location: Moab, Grand, Utah

Notes: [MLM] There is a good possibility that the LDS member and Civil War veteran identified may not be the same person. He "came to Utah Sept. 21, 1851, Alfred Cardon Company. Bishop, Physician" [PPMU, 269]. "Helped to build the Nauvoo temple, and in 1848, in connection with David T. LeBaron had charge of it, and was present and saw it while it was burning. Physician; Indian interpreter; compiled the first dictionary of the languages of the Utah Indians. High priest; bishop of Fountain Green [Utah] ward 1860–65. Postmaster for 35 years. Poet. Seedsman and florist" [PPMU, 969]. He served one year beginning August 1, 1862. "Gunshot wound, right thigh ruptured, constitutionally broke down" are listed as service-related disabilities [1890 Census].

JOHNSON, POWELL   (UNION ARMY)   *Baptized before the war.*

Rank: Private	Unit(s): Lot Smith Utah Cavalry Military Service Source(s): VBU, NPS, PI, FGC, Obituary, Fisher, 1862 MOR
Birth Date: 28 March 1839	Birth Place: Ilind, Lulland, Skorringe, Denmark
LDS Membership Date: 1 March 1855	LDS Membership Source(s): NFS (ID #: KWJZ-HZN)
Death Date: 20 November 1927	Death Place: Sevier, Utah Find A Grave: 7735699 Burial Location: Glenwood Cemetery, Glenwood, Sevier, Utah

Notes: His obituary, entitled "Civil War Veteran, Utah Pioneer, Is Laid to Last Rest," states that he "walked every step of the way and drove a team of oxen from the Missouri river to Salt Lake City [in 1854]. . . . He entered the service during the Civil war, April 30, 1862, in Captain Lott Smith's brigade of 100 men, and was a member of the Grand Army of the Republic. He was also a member of the Nauvoo Legion" (*Richfield Reaper*, December 4, 1927, 1). [NFS] also lists several Danish variations of his name.

JOHNSTON, CALVIN C.   (CONFEDERATE ARMY)   *Baptized before the war.*

Rank: Private	Unit(s): Company E, 5th Regiment, North Carolina Infantry Military Service Source(s): 1890 Census, NPS
Birth Date: 25 December 1837	Birth Place: Darlington, Darlington, South Carolina
LDS Membership Date: 14 July 1848	LDS Membership Source(s): NFS (ID #: K2QX-71K)
Death Date: 21 September 1922	Death Place: Salt Lake City, Salt Lake, Utah Find A Grave: 137965 Burial Location: Farmington, Davis, Utah

Notes: [MLM] He served one year and eleven months beginning in 1862. Wounded in left thigh listed as a disability incurred during his military service [1890 Census].

JOHNSTON, FRANCIS   (UNION ARMY)   *Baptized before the war.*

Rank: Sergeant	Unit(s): Company K, 4th Regiment, U.S. Cavalry (Regular Army) Military Service Source(s): 1890 Census, NPS, FGC
Birth Date: 1 November 1836	Birth Place: Glebe, Antrim, Ireland

LDS Membership Date: 1 January 1855	LDS Membership Source(s): NFS (ID #: KWJ4-KX9)	
Death Date: 26 March 1895	Death Place: Midway, Wasatch, Utah	Find A Grave: 31274558
	Burial Location: Midway, Wasatch, Utah	
Notes: "SERGT. CO. K. 4 U.S. CAV." (Sergeant, Company K, 4th U.S. Cavalry) is carved on his grave marker [FGC].		

JOHNSTON, JAMES   (UNION ARMY)   *Baptized before the war.*

Rank: Private	Unit(s): Company H, 48th Regiment, Illinois Infantry	
	Military Service Source(s): VBU, NPS	
Birth Date: 1 November 1836	Birth Place: Orkney Isles, Scotland	
LDS Membership Date: 2 May 1853	LDS Membership Source(s): NFS (ID #: KWJM-RTY)	
Death Date: 25 September 1903	Death Place: Salt Lake City, Salt Lake, Utah	Find A Grave: 36923019
	Burial Location: Salt Lake City Cemetery, Salt Lake City, Salt Lake, Utah	
Notes: He served in the military for five years beginning on May 23, 1860 [1890 Census].		

JONES, HENRY L.   (UNION ARMY)   *Baptized before the war (presumed).*

Rank: Private	Unit(s): Company D, 43rd Regiment, Illinois Infantry	
	Military Service Source(s): 1890 Census	
Birth Date: 25 February 1824	Birth Place: Kidderminster, Worcester, England	
LDS Membership Date: 31 August 1867 (LDS temple ordinances)	LDS Membership Source(s): NFS (ID #: LHVX-2TG)	
Death Date: 3 July 1904	Death Place: Park City, Summit, Utah	Find A Grave: 53605558
	Burial Location: West Jordan, Salt Lake, Utah	
Notes: [MLM] Gunshot wounds and rheumatism listed as service-related disabilities. Alias listed as "H.C. Clay." His first name is spelled "Henery" on the census form. He served in the military two years and eleven months beginning on September 6, 1861 [1890 Census]. LDS initiatory ordinance is listed as August 31, 1867 (clearly indicating that he was baptized into the LDS Church before that time); we presume that he was baptized prior to the beginning of the Civil War [NFS].		

JONES, JOHN L.   (CONFEDERATE ARMY)   *Baptized after the war.*

Rank: Private	Unit(s): Company B, 1st Regiment, South Carolina Artillery	
	Military Service Source(s): VBU, NPS, FGC	
Birth Date: 10 March 1823	Birth Place: Laurens, South Carolina	
LDS Membership Date: 1 January 1866 (confirmation)	LDS Membership Source(s): NFS (ID #: KWVM-639)	
Death Date: 22 February 1883	Death Place: Richfield, Sevier, Utah	Find A Grave: 112544
	Burial Location: Richfield City Cemetery, Richfield, Sevier, Utah	
Notes: "PVT CO B 1 SC ARTILLERY CIVIL WAR" (Private, Company B, 1st South Carolina Artillery) is carved on his grave marker [FGC]. Grave marker lists his birth date as March 10, 1823; [NFS] lists March 10, 1824.		

JONES, ROBERT W.   (UNION ARMY)   *Baptized before the war.*

Rank: Corporal	**Unit(s):** 5th Regiment, Independent Battery, Ohio Light Artillery **Military Service Source(s):** NPS, PI, FGC
Birth Date: 18 June 1838	**Birth Place:** Liverpool, Lancaster, England
LDS Membership Date: 1 January 1850 (confirmation)	**LDS Membership Source(s):** NFS (ID #: KWCJ-YZK)
Death Date: 11 December 1919	**Death Place:** Salt Lake City, Salt Lake, Utah **Find A Grave:** 128723 **Burial Location:** Murray City Cemetery, Murray, Salt Lake, Utah
Notes: "CPL 5 INDPT BTRY OHIO LT ART" (Corporal, 5th Independent Battery, Ohio Light Artillery) is carved on his grave marker [FGC]. [FGC] lists middle name as "Walter" and [NFS] lists both "Wallace" and "Walter."	

JONES, SETH W.   (UNION ARMY)   *Baptized after the war.*

Rank: Private	**Unit(s):** Company B, 113th Regiment, Illinois Infantry **Military Service Source(s):** NPS; FGC; Obituary
Birth Date: 20 August 1845	**Birth Place:** Iroquois, Illinois
LDS Membership Date: 30 July 1885	**LDS Membership Source(s):** NFS (ID #: KW8L-4ZT)
Death Date: 13 April 1939	**Death Place:** Byron, Big Horn, Wyoming **Find A Grave:** 31786499 **Burial Location:** Byron, Big Horn, Wyoming
Notes: "CIVIL WAR VETERAN" is carved on his grave marker [FGC]. His obituary states that he was "a veteran of the Civil war" (*Richfield Reaper*, April 20, 1939, 5).	

JONES, WILLIAM H.   (UNION ARMY)   *Baptized after the war.*

Rank: Private	**Unit(s):** Companies A & F, 40th Regiment, New York Infantry **Military Service Source(s):** 1890 Census, NPS
Birth Date: 9 July 1842	**Birth Place:** Merthyr Tydfil, Glamorganshire, Wales
LDS Membership Date: 6 March 1890	**LDS Membership Source(s):** NFS (ID #: K2M4-JX8)
Death Date: 24 July 1910	**Death Place:** Salt Lake City, Salt Lake, Utah **Find A Grave:** 35008612 **Burial Location:** Wales, Sanpete, Utah
Notes: [MLM] He was a carpenter and did some work on the Manti Temple [FGC]. He served in the military three years, seven months, and twenty-eight days beginning on October 20, 1861 [1890 Census].	

JUDD, JAMES H.   (UNION ARMY)   *Baptized before the war.*

Rank: Steward	**Unit(s):** Field and Staff Company, 45th Regiment, Illinois Infantry **Military Service Source(s):** 1890 Census, NPS
Birth Date: 10 December 1844	**Birth Place:** West End Parish, South Stoneham, Southampton, England
LDS Membership Date: 1 June 1859 (confirmation)	**LDS Membership Source(s):** NFS (ID #: KWNR-73F)
Death Date: 4 May 1901	**Death Place:** Henefer, Summit, Utah **Find A Grave:** 39175362 **Burial Location:** Hoytsville, Summit, Utah
Notes: [MLM] He served in the military two years beginning in January 1862. The 1890 Census lists his rank as "Med. D." [1890 Census]. He died from a fall off a wagon that injured his spine and internal organs [FGC].	

KELLEY, JAMES A. (UNION ARMY)
Baptized before the war.

Rank: Private	**Unit(s):** Company F or G, 6th Regiment, Michigan Cavalry **Military Service Source(s):** 1890 Census, NPS
Birth Date: 25 November 1851	**Birth Place:** Lesmahagow, Lanark, Scotland
LDS Membership Date: 1 January 1859 (confirmation)	**LDS Membership Source(s):** NFS (ID #: LHX5-LXR)
Death Date: 29 October 1933	**Death Place:** Delta, Millard, Utah **Find A Grave:** 61790496 **Burial Location:** Uncertain

Notes: [MLM] He served in the military for four years beginning in April 1861 [1890 Census]. LDS baptism is listed simply as "Completed" on [NFS]. There may be an error in either his birth date or baptism date, as he was not eight years old on the listed date of his confirmation, and his listed birth date would make him a young recruit. [1890 Census] listed Company F; [NPS] listed Company G.

KENDALL, ELI C. (UNION ARMY)
Baptized after the war.

Rank: Private	**Unit(s):** Company B, 6th Regiment, West Virginia Infantry **Military Service Source(s):** VBU, NPS, PI
Birth Date: 10 March 1841	**Birth Place:** Marion, West Virginia
LDS Membership Date: 14 July 1887	**LDS Membership Source(s):** NFS (ID #: KWJH-3YP)
Death Date: 13 September 1924	**Death Place:** Lehi, Utah, Utah **Find A Grave:** 92245 **Burial Location:** Lehi City Cemetery, Lehi, Utah, Utah

Notes: Organized in West Virginia between August and December 1861, the 6th West Virginia Infantry served primarily as a railroad guard unit [NPS].

KENDALL, GEORGE M. (UNION ARMY)
Baptized after the war.

Rank: Private	**Unit(s):** Company A, 61st Regiment, Illinois Infantry **Military Service Source(s):** 1890 Census, NPS
Birth Date: 30 July 1842	**Birth Place:** Dents Run, Marion, Virginia
LDS Membership Date: 14 July 1887	**LDS Membership Source(s):** NFS (ID #: KWJH-3BD)
Death Date: 4 October 1919	**Death Place:** Salt Lake City, Salt Lake, Utah **Find A Grave:** 57044587 **Burial Location:** Salt Lake City Cemetery, Salt Lake City, Salt Lake, Utah

Notes: [MLM] He served in the military one year, six months, and six days beginning on March 8, 1864 [1890 Census].

KENNARD, LEONIDAS HAMLIN (UNION ARMY)
Baptized before the war.

Rank: Private	**Unit(s):** Company B, 18th Regiment, Ohio Infantry **Military Service Source(s):** NPS, PI, PPMU, 1890 Census
Birth Date: 29 January 1842	**Birth Place:** Mount Pleasant, Swan Township, Vinton, Ohio
LDS Membership Date: 13 April 1859	**LDS Membership Source(s):** NFS (ID #: KWCF-QGH)
Death Date: 29 May 1926	**Death Place:** Salt Lake City, Salt Lake, Utah **Find A Grave:** 28921187 **Burial Location:** Farmington City Cemetery, Farmington, Davis, Utah

Kennard, Leonidas Hamlin (continued)

Notes: He "came to Utah Sept. 30, 1867, William Streeper merchandise train. Married Joanna Louisa Gleason Jan. 29, 1869, Farmington, Utah. . . . Family resided Farmington and Riverside, Box Elder Co., Utah. . . . Missionary to Eastern states. School teacher. Clerk Bear River stake; state editor *Deseret News*. President high priests quorum. Civil war veteran Co. B, 18th Ohio Vol. Infantry, and commander Maxwell-McKean G.A.R. Post No. 1, School teacher; superintendent schools in Davis county. Postmaster and merchant at Farmington and Riverside" [PPMU, 984]. He reportedly served at Shiloh, the occupation of Nashville, Stones River, Chickamauga, Browns Ferry, Chattanooga-Ringgold, and Missionary Ridge. He was wounded at Murfreesboro, Tennessee, and captured and paroled. He was mustered out in November 1864 and became a postmaster and storekeeper (Curtis Allen, e-mail to editor, 2011). He served just over three years beginning on September 12, 1861, and was wounded in his left ankle [1890 Census].

KILGROW, JOHN W.   (UNION ARMY)   *Baptized after the war.*

Rank: Private	Unit(s): Company D, 6th Regiment, Tennessee Mounted Infantry Military Service Source(s): NPS, PI
Birth Date: 14 June 1846	Birth Place: Sparta, White, Tennessee
LDS Membership Date: 27 September 1896	LDS Membership Source(s): NFS (ID #: KWNN-Y92)
Death Date: 6 February 1934	Death Place: Salt Lake City, Salt Lake, Utah Find A Grave: 30162810 Burial Location: Bountiful Memorial Park, Bountiful, Davis, Utah

Notes: [MLM] The 6th Regiment, Tennessee Mounted Infantry, mustered in on August 20, 1864, and mustered out on June 30, 1865 [NPS].

KIMBALL, HIRAM   (UNION ARMY)   *Baptized before the war.*

Rank: Private	Unit(s): Lot Smith Utah Cavalry Military Service Source(s): ACWS, NPS, PI, Fisher, 1862 MOR
Birth Date: 22 November 1841	Birth Place: Nauvoo, Hancock, Illinois
LDS Membership Date: 27 March 1857 (LDS temple ordinances)	LDS Membership Source(s): NFS (ID #: L79B-KH5)
Death Date: 8 March 1930	Death Place: Butte, Silver Bow, Montana Find A Grave: 31967356 Burial Location: Salt Lake City Cemetery, Salt Lake City, Salt Lake, Utah

Notes: [MLM]

KIMBROUGH, WILLIAM B.   (CONFEDERATE ARMY)   *Baptized after the war.*

Rank: Private	Unit(s): Company B, 31st Regiment, Mississippi Infantry Military Service Source(s): 1890 Census, NPS
Birth Date: 15 July 1843	Birth Place: Molton, Lawrence, Alabama
LDS Membership Date: 2 February 1890	LDS Membership Source(s): NFS (ID #: KWZS-ZBC)
Death Date: 14 May 1909	Death Place: Salt Lake City, Salt Lake, Utah Find A Grave: 28145067 Burial Location: Salt Lake City, Salt Lake, Utah

Notes: [MLM] His name was written and then crossed out on the 1890 veteran census form (because he was a Confederate soldier). He served in the Confederate army for an undetermined period (that portion of the census form is illegible). "Shot through lung" is listed as a disability incurred during his military service [1890 Census].

KING, FREDERICK AUGUSTUS (UNION ARMY) *Baptized during the war.*

Rank: Private	**Unit(s):** Company D, 20th Regiment, Massachusetts Infantry **Military Service Source(s):** 1890 Census, NPS, NFS
Birth Date: 18 September 1840	**Birth Place:** Greenhill Warley, Halifax, Yorks, England
LDS Membership Date: 3 March 1861	**LDS Membership Source(s):** NFS (ID #: KW8H-NQ7)
Death Date: 18 October 1911	**Death Place:** Ogden, Weber, Utah **Find A Grave:** 27217512 **Burial Location:** Hooper, Weber, Utah
Notes: [MLM] He served in the military two years beginning July 7, 1862. He is listed on the census as "August King" [1890 Census]. Following the Civil War, he served an LDS mission (beginning on March 8, 1873) to Arizona. His occupations included tanner and country doctor [NFS].	

KING, RANSOM B. (UNION ARMY) *Baptized after the war.*

Rank: Private	**Unit(s):** Company E, 125th Regiment, Illinois Infantry **Military Service Source(s):** VBU, NPS, PI, Obituary
Birth Date: 4 March 1830	**Birth Place:** Arcadia, Wayne, New York
LDS Membership Date: 1 December 1885	**LDS Membership Source(s):** NFS (ID #: KW6M-C66)
Death Date: 20 March 1901	**Death Place:** Salt Lake City, Salt Lake, Utah **Find A Grave:** — **Burial Location:** Bountiful City Cemetery, Bountiful, Davis, Utah
Notes: The 125th Regiment, Illinois Infantry, mustered in September 3, 1862, and fought at the Battle of Chickamauga (Georgia) among other battles [NPS]. His obituary states that he "was a veteran of the Civil war and received a pension" and moved to Utah about 1881 (*Deseret News*, March 27, 1901, 2).	

KING, WILEY F. (CONFEDERATE ARMY) *Baptized after the war.*

Rank: Private	**Unit(s):** Companies E & F, 16th Regiment, Georgia Infantry **Military Service Source(s):** NPS
Birth Date: 1 August 1842	**Birth Place:** Longview, Habersham, Georgia
LDS Membership Date: 12 February 1882	**LDS Membership Source(s):** SLV, NFS (ID #: KW6M-FKG)
Death Date: 12 March 1927	**Death Place:** La Jara, Conejos, Colorado **Find A Grave:** — **Burial Location:** Alamosa, Alamosa, Colorado
Notes: [MLM] He was baptized in the Chattahoochee River. His home was burned, his livestock were killed, and his crops were destroyed after his baptism. He served as president of the Mount Blanca (Colorado) Branch [SLV].	

KNAPP, JOHN C. (UNION ARMY) *Baptized before the war.*

Rank: Enlisted as Sergeant, discharged as Second Lieutenant	**Unit(s):** Company I, 97th Regiment, Pennsylvania Infantry **Military Service Source(s):** NPS, FGC
Birth Date: 4 May 1802	**Birth Place:** Chester, Warren, New York
LDS Membership Date: 14 February 1835	**LDS Membership Source(s):** NFS (ID #: LH8P-FMK)
Death Date: 2 December 1870	**Death Place:** Tooele, Tooele, Utah **Find A Grave:** 39305576 **Burial Location:** Toole City Cemetery, Tooele, Tooele, Utah
Notes: "2D LT 97 PA INFANTRY" (Second Lieutenant, 97th Pennsylvania Infantry) is carved on his grave marker [FGC].	

KNIGHT, GEORGE F.   (CONFEDERATE ARMY)   *Baptized after the war.*

Rank: Private	**Unit(s):** Company F, 27th Regiment, Mississippi Infantry **Military Service Source(s):** CSC, FGC
Birth Date: 16 November 1843	**Birth Place:** Jones County, Mississippi
LDS Membership Date: 12 May 1881	**LDS Membership Source(s):** NFS (ID #: KWJC-RY2)
Death Date: 8 March 1926	**Death Place:** Homelake, Monte Vista, Colorado **Find A Grave:** 15669721 **Burial Location:** Sanford Cemetery, Conejos, Colorado
Notes: "CO F 27 MISS INF C.S.A." (Company F, 27th Mississippi Infantry, Confederate States of America) is carved on his grave marker [FGC]. [CSC] entry refers to him as "Franklin Knight."	

KNIGHTON, GEORGE   (UNION ARMY)   *Baptized before the war.*

Rank: Private	**Unit(s):** Company K, 56th Regiment, Massachusetts Infantry **Military Service Source(s):** NPS, PI, FGC, PPMU
Birth Date: 23 April 1845	**Birth Place:** Loscoe, Derby, England
LDS Membership Date: 23 April 1853	**LDS Membership Source(s):** NFS (ID #: KWDM-Y34)
Death Date: 17 May 1897	**Death Place:** Benjamin, Utah, Utah **Find A Grave:** 17235003 **Burial Location:** Benjamin Cemetery, Benjamin, Utah, Utah
Notes: "MASSACHUSETTS PVT CO K 56 REGT MASS INF CIVIL WAR" (Massachusetts Private, Company K, 56th Regiment, Massachusetts Infantry) is carved on his grave marker [FGC]. He "came to Utah 1873, on railroad. Married Eliza Johnson May 15, 1876, Salt Lake City. . . . Elder and ward teacher. Farmer. Served in Civil war 18 months" [PPMU, 992].	

KNOWLTON, J. Q. (JOHN QUINCY)   (UNION ARMY)   *Baptized before the war.*

Rank: Second Lieutenant	**Unit(s):** Lot Smith Utah Cavalry **Military Service Source(s):** ACWS, NPS, PI, FGC, Fisher, 1862 MOR
Birth Date: 9 July 1835	**Birth Place:** Cincinnati, Ohio
LDS Membership Date: 1 April 1844	**LDS Membership Source(s):** NFS (ID #: KWNF-SW4)
Death Date: 13 December 1886	**Death Place:** Tooele, Utah **Find A Grave:** 7737492 **Burial Location:** Salt Lake City Cemetery, Salt Lake City, Salt Lake, Utah
Notes: For additional information, see the Stuart-Alford chapter entitled "The Lot Smith Cavalry Company: Utah Goes to War" and Alford's "Mormons and the Grand Army of the Republic" herein.	

LANGFORD, JOHN W.   (UNION ARMY)   *Baptized after the war.*

Rank: Private (Artificer)	**Unit(s):** Company A, 1st Regiment, Wisconsin Heavy Artillery **Military Service Source(s):** 1890 Census, NPS
Birth Date: 29 January 1841	**Birth Place:** Callerus Mills, Fulton, Illinois
LDS Membership Date: 3 August 1884	**LDS Membership Source(s):** NFS (ID #: KWD2-5YK)

Death Date: 19 April 1916	Death Place: Wardboro, Bear Lake, Idaho Find A Grave: — Burial Location: Wardboro, Bear Lake, Idaho

Notes: [MLM] An artificer is generally a craftsman or skilled mechanic. Langford served in the military one year, ten months, and twenty-two days beginning November 26, 1863. Spinal disease listed as a service-related disability [1890 Census].

LARKINS, JAMES   (UNION ARMY)   *Baptized before the war (presumed).*

Rank: Private	Unit(s): Lot Smith Utah Cavalry Military Service Source(s): ACWS, Fisher, 1862 MOR
Birth Date: 9 October 1842	Birth Place: Beeston, Bedfordshire, England
LDS Membership Date: Presumed LDS	LDS Membership Source(s): NFS (ID #: K2F8-NGF)
Death Date: 24 July 1922	Death Place: Los Angeles, Los Angeles, California Find A Grave: — Burial Location: Kaysville, Davis, Utah

Notes: [MLM] As a member of the Lot Smith Cavalry Company, he is presumed to be a Latter-day Saint (but a nonvicarious baptismal date could not be confirmed from available sources).

LAWSON, JOHN W.   (GALVANIZED YANKEE)   *Baptized after the war.*

Rank: Private	Unit(s): Confederate service: 22nd Regiment, North Carolina Infantry (1863); Union service: 4th Regiment, United States Volunteer Infantry (1864–65) Military Service Source(s): NPS, PI; NARA, microfilm 1290 roll 20 (4th U.S. Volunteers), microfilm 230 roll 23 (22nd North Carolina Infantry)
Birth Date: 20 January 1844	Birth Place: Snow Creek, Stokes, North Carolina
LDS Membership Date: 27 January 1869	LDS Membership Source(s): NFS (ID #: KV5M-G77)
Death Date: 11 April 1926	Death Place: Bountiful, Davis, Utah Find A Grave: 64565460 Burial Location: Bountiful Memorial Park, Bountiful, Davis, Utah

Notes: He was a galvanized Yankee (captured in 1864) who joined the LDS church in Kentucky after being run out of North Carolina as a traitor to the Confederacy [NFS]. "He was described as being light complected with light hair, blue grey eyes, and standing 5 ft. 7 inches tall. In his army application he declared himself to be a farmer" (http://wc.rootsweb.ancestry.com/cgi-bin/igm.cgi?op=GET&db=:2568560&id=I535002395).

LEE, WILLIAM B.   (UNION ARMY)   *Baptized before the war.*

Rank: Private	Unit(s): Company I, 1st Regiment, Tennessee Mounted Infantry Military Service Source(s): 1890 Census, NPS
Birth Date: 17 March 1828	Birth Place: Clayton, Lancashire, England
LDS Membership Date: 17 March 1846	LDS Membership Source(s): NFS (ID #: KWJC-H9V)
Death Date: 11 April 1881	Death Place: Wellsville, Cache, Utah Find A Grave: 43383112 Burial Location: Wellsville, Cache, Utah

Notes: [MLM] He served in the military nine months beginning in November 1864. If the correct LDS member is identified, the 1890 veteran census schedule (recorded in Weber County, Utah) should list his entry as a widow report, as his death date was prior to 1890, but it does not. Liver disease is listed as a disability incurred during his military service [1890 Census].

LEES, JAMES   (UNION ARMY)   *Baptized before the war.*

Rank: Private	Unit(s): Company F, 124th Regiment, New York Infantry Military Service Source(s): 1890 Census, NPS
Birth Date: 23 September 1824	Birth Place: Ashton-Under-Lyn, Lancashire, England
LDS Membership Date: 20 September 1849	LDS Membership Source(s): NFS (ID #: KWJ7-55H)
Death Date: 16 November 1897	Death Place: Springville, Utah, Utah Find A Grave: 82481 Burial Location: Springville, Utah, Utah
Notes: [MLM] He served in the military for four years, two months, and twenty days beginning May 24, 1863. He was injured during his military service, but the nature of the injury is illegible on the census form [1890 Census]. [NPS] lists three James Lees from New York who served, but none of them is associated with the 124th New York Infantry. The unit affiliation is from the [1890 Census].	

LEMMON, LEANDER   (UNION ARMY)   *Baptized before the war.*

Rank: Private	Unit(s): Lot Smith Utah Cavalry Military Service Source(s): VBU, ACWS, NPS, PI, Fisher, 1862 MOR
Birth Date: 10 November 1839	Birth Place: Quincy, Adams, Illinois
LDS Membership Date: 5 April 1853	LDS Membership Source(s): NFS (ID #: KWCN-JV7)
Death Date: 4 October 1907	Death Place: Huntington, Emery, Utah Find A Grave: 28957518 Burial Location: Huntington City Cemetery, Huntington, Emery, Utah
Notes: —	

LEWIS, THEODORE BELDEN   (CONFEDERATE ARMY)   *Baptized after the war.*

Rank: Private	Unit(s): Company K, 1st Regiment, Virginia Artillery Military Service Source(s): NPS
Birth Date: 18 November 1843	Birth Place: St. Louis, St. Louis, Missouri
LDS Membership Date: 29 April 1866	LDS Membership Source(s): LDSBE, NFS (ID #: KWJC-GBZ)
Death Date: 20 July 1899	Death Place: Cambridge, Middlesex, Massachusetts Find A Grave: 20317957 Burial Location: Salt Lake City, Salt Lake, Utah
Notes: [MLM] "He lost both parents when he was quite young. . . . When the Civil War broke out, he joined the Southern army and served under General Price. He was in the battle of Boonville, June 17, 1861, and in a number of engagements later. Being captured in battle Dec. 19, 1861, he was taken to Gratiot Street prison and later to Alton, but was finally paroled in the spring of 1862 and commenced reading law. In 1865 he came to Utah. . . . Becoming a convert to 'Mormonism,' he was baptized in May 1866." Following the war, he served a mission to the Southern states (1868–70) and baptized 108 converts. After his mission, he moved to Provo, Utah, in 1870 and taught at Brigham Young Academy for one year. In 1871, he moved to Payson, Utah, to teach school. In 1872, he moved to Nephi, Utah, where he served as school superintendent and justice of the peace. In 1876, he moved to Salt Lake City and taught school. In 1879, he was elected county superintendent in Salt Lake County. In 1885, he became principal of Ogden High School in Ogden, Utah, where he remained for twelve years. In August 1894, he was appointed as the territorial commissioner of public schools. "He exhibited the characteristics of a fine cultured Southern gentleman of the noblest type of	

his Virginian ancestors" [LDSBE, 3:148–50]. He was "sustained as one of the First Seven Presidents Oct. 8, 1882, at age 38; on Oct. 9, when he was to be set apart, he reported that he was already a high priest, so he was not set apart and did not function" in that position (*2012 Church Almanac* [Salt Lake City: *Deseret News*, 2012], 117–18). The [MLM] tag is warranted because several Confederate soldiers with the name Theodore Lewis are listed on [NPS].

LILL, DANIEL C. (UNION ARMY)

Baptized after the war.

Rank: Private	Unit(s): Lot Smith Utah Cavalry Military Service Source(s): ACWS, NPS, Fisher, 1862 MOR	
Birth Date: 4 October 1830	Birth Place: New Egypt, New Jersey	
LDS Membership Date: 7 January 1878	LDS Membership Source(s): NFS (ID #: K24W-PLY)	
Death Date: Uncertain	Death Place: Uncertain Find A Grave: — Burial Location: Uncertain	
Notes: [MLM] His name is listed as Daniel C. Sill on 1884 U.S. Pension records (NARA).		

LINDSEY, HENRY PORTER (UNION ARMY)

Baptized after the war.

Rank: Private	Unit(s): Company G, 189th Regiment, Ohio Infantry Military Service Source(s): 1890 Census, NPS	
Birth Date: 24 May 1824	Birth Place: Burke County, North Carolina	
LDS Membership Date: 1 December 1874	LDS Membership Source(s): NFS (ID #: KWJC-6VY)	
Death Date: 29 January 1902	Death Place: Salt Lake City, Salt Lake, Utah Find A Grave: — Burial Location: Salt Lake City, Salt Lake, Utah	
Notes: [MLM] All the 1890 census schedule lists is "Sol[dier]"; no service information was recorded by the census enumerator [1890 Census].		

LITZ, JOHN T. (CONFEDERATE ARMY)

Baptized after the war.

Rank: Second Lieutenant	Unit(s): Company F, 22nd Regiment, Virginia Cavalry (Bowen's Virginia Mounted Riflemen) Military Service Source(s): NPS	
Birth Date: 18 April 1834	Birth Place: Burkes Garden, Tazewell, Virginia	
LDS Membership Date: 4 August 1876	LDS Membership Source(s): NFS (ID #: KWVG-526)	
Death Date: 11 February 1901	Death Place: Salt Lake City, Salt Lake, Utah Find A Grave: — Burial Location: Litz Home Place, Healing Springs, Tazewell, Virginia	
Notes: [MLM] The 22nd Regiment, Virginia Cavalry, was organized by October 1863 and "confronted the Federals in Tennessee, western Virginia, and the Shenandoah Valley. During April 1865, it disbanded" [NPS].		

LITZ, PETER GOSE (CONFEDERATE ARMY)

Baptized before the war.

Rank: Colonel	Unit(s): Virginia Home Guard Military Service Source(s): Southern Star, 1:315	
Birth Date: 25 April 1802	Birth Place: Burkes Garden, Tazewell, Virginia	

Litz, Peter Gose (continued)	
LDS Membership Date: Uncertain	**LDS Membership Source(s):** NFS (ID #: LW1Y-7XZ); Andrew Jenson, *Church Chronology* (Salt Lake City: *Deseret News*, 1886), April 2, 1880
Death Date: 3 April 1880	**Death Place:** Burkes Garden, Tazewell, Virginia **Find A Grave:** 16446934 **Burial Location:** Maplewood Cemetery, Tazewell, Tazewell, Virginia
Notes: Listed as an LDS branch president in 1842 (*Southern Star*, 1:315) and 1845 ("*Minutes of a Conference of the Church of Jesus Christ of Latter Day Saints*, Held in Burk's Garden Tazewell County, Virginia . . .," Times and Seasons, 4:63). He was the first member of the LDS Church baptized in Virginia (Andrew Jenson, *Church Chronology* [Salt Lake City: Deseret News, 1886], April 2, 1880).	

LITZ, WILLIAM SAWYERS   (CONFEDERATE ARMY)   *Baptized after the war.*

Rank: Private	**Unit(s):** Company F, 22nd Regiment, Virginia Cavalry (Bowen's Virginia Mounted Riflemen) **Military Service Source(s):** NPS, 1890 Census
Birth Date: 23 April 1837	**Birth Place:** Burkes Garden, Tazewell County, Virginia
LDS Membership Date: 21 March 1879	**LDS Membership Source(s):** NFS (ID #: K2MS-PZC)
Death Date: 10 July 1915	**Death Place:** Lewiston, Cache, Utah **Find A Grave:** 35511185 **Burial Location:** Lewiston City Cemetery, Lewiston, Cache, Utah
Notes: [MLM] He served two years and six months beginning August 15, 1862 [1890 Census].	

LIVINGSTON, ALEXANDER   (UNION ARMY)   *Baptized during the war.*

Rank: Private	**Unit(s):** Companies C & K, 3rd Regiment, California Volunteers **Military Service Source(s):** VBU, NPS, PI
Birth Date: 11 December 1824	**Birth Place:** Kilbarchan, Renfrewshire, Scotland
LDS Membership Date: 1 November 1862 (confirmation)	**LDS Membership Source(s):** NFS (ID #: KWVC-MLX)
Death Date: 11 October 1908	**Death Place:** South Jordan, Salt Lake, Utah **Find A Grave:** 28283243 **Burial Location:** South Jordan Cemetery, South Jordan, Salt Lake, Utah
Notes: The 3rd Regiment, California Infantry, was organized between September 15 and December 3, 1861. Company K participated in the Bear River Massacre on January 29, 1863 [NPS].	

LOFTUS, JOHN   (UNION NAVY)   *Baptized after the war.*

Rank: Fireman	**Unit(s):** USS Sorrel **Military Service Source(s):** 1890 Census, FGC
Birth Date: 8 November 1844	**Birth Place:** Clitheroe, Lancashire, England
LDS Membership Date: 10 September 1874	**LDS Membership Source(s):** NFS (ID #: KWN6-Z44)
Death Date: 6 November 1882	**Death Place:** Salt Lake City, Salt Lake, Utah **Find A Grave:** 32220864 **Burial Location:** Salt Lake City, Salt Lake, Utah

Notes: He served in the U.S. Navy for three years beginning February 3, 1865. His widow, Mary Ann Loftus, reported his military service for the 1890 census [1890 Census]. "John came to the United States in 1863 and served in the Navy for three years" [FGC]. The *USS Sorrel* was "a wooden-hulled steam tug[boat] . . . purchased by the Navy at Philadelphia under the name W. S. Hancock on 1 August 1864. . . . The small steamer apparently served as a general purpose tug at the Philadelphia Navy Yard throughout her naval career" (*Dictionary of American Naval Fighting Ships*, USS Sorrel, http://www.history.navy.mil/danfs/s15/sorrel.htm).

LOGUE, WILLIAM CHARLES TAYLOR

(CONFEDERATE ARMY)												*Baptized before the war.*

Rank: Private	**Unit(s):** Company G, 3rd Regiment, Georgia Infantry **Military Service Source(s):** NPS, MCL
Birth Date: 14 October 1846	**Birth Place:** Glasscock County, Georgia
LDS Membership Date: 14 October 1855	**LDS Membership Source(s):** NFS (ID #: KVPB-HRX)
Death Date: 12 May 1912	**Death Place:** Manassa, Conejos, Colorado **Find A Grave:** 37850932 **Burial Location:** Manassa, Conejos, Colorado

Notes: [MLM] The 3rd Regiment, Georgia Infantry, was organized in April 1861. "It participated in the difficult campaigns of the army from Seven Pines to Cold Harbor, then was involved in the Petersburg siege north and south of the James River and various conflicts around Appomattox" [NPS].

LONGSTROTH, WILLIAM   (UNION ARMY)

Baptized before the war.

Rank: Private	**Unit(s):** Lot Smith Utah Cavalry **Military Service Source(s):** ACWS, NPS, Fisher, 1862 MOR
Birth Date: 15 May 1840	**Birth Place:** Clitheroe, Lancashire, England
LDS Membership Date: 1 January 1851	**LDS Membership Source(s):** NFS (ID #: KWZB-KS1)
Death Date: 19 March 1911	**Death Place:** Mendon, Cache, Utah **Find A Grave:** 54906357 **Burial Location:** Mendon City Cemetery, Mendon, Cache, Utah

Notes: [MLM] His name is listed as "William Langstrough" on [1862 MOR].

LOWE, WILLIAM W.   (UNION ARMY)

Baptized before the war.

Rank: Private	**Unit(s):** Company F, 5th Regiment, Missouri State Militia Cavalry **Military Service Source(s):** 1890 Census, NPS
Birth Date: 16 May 1833	**Birth Place:** Aberdeen, Aberdeen, Scotland
LDS Membership Date: 9 June 1851	**LDS Membership Source(s):** NFS (ID #: KWN2-QJZ)
Death Date: 27 February 1891	**Death Place:** Providence, Cache, Utah **Find A Grave:** — **Burial Location:** Providence City Cemetery, Providence, Cache, Utah

Notes: [MLM] He served in the military for five years and nineteen days beginning December 19, 1861 [1890 Census].

LOWRY, THOMAS ALEXANDER   (CONFEDERATE ARMY)   *Baptized after the war.*

Rank: Private	**Unit(s):** Company C, 11th Regiment, Alabama Infantry **Military Service Source(s):** NPS, Obituary
Birth Date: 2 February 1838	**Birth Place:** Marion County, Alabama
LDS Membership Date: 15 January 1870	**LDS Membership Source(s):** NFS (ID #: K2M4-BMM)
Death Date: 11 December 1911	**Death Place:** Salt Lake City, Salt Lake, Utah **Find A Grave:** 39452311 **Burial Location:** Salt Lake City, Salt Lake, Utah
Notes: His obituary states that he was a "veteran of the civil war in the ranks of the Confederate army and well known carpenter and builder of Salt Lake. . . . With the outbreak of the civil war he enlisted in the Confederate army and fought in many of the important battles. In April, 1870, he emigrated to Utah" (*Salt Lake Herald*, December 11, 1911, 13).	

LUTZ, THOMAS JEFFERSON   (UNION ARMY)   *Baptized before the war.*

Rank: Private	**Unit(s):** Lot Smith Utah Cavalry **Military Service Source(s):** ACWS, NPS, PI, FGC, Fisher, 1862 MOR
Birth Date: 28 February 1837	**Birth Place:** Philadelphia, Pennsylvania
LDS Membership Date: 1 January 1845 (confirmation)	**LDS Membership Source(s):** NFS (ID #: KWNL-JW3)
Death Date: 11 May 1884	**Death Place:** Smithfield, Cache, Utah **Find A Grave:** 181664 **Burial Location:** Smithfield, Cache, Utah
Notes: There may be an error in either his birth date or confirmation date, as he was not eight years old on the listed date of his confirmation.	

LUTZ, WILLIAM W.   (UNION ARMY)   *Baptized before the war (presumed).*

Rank: Private	**Unit(s):** Lot Smith Utah Cavalry **Military Service Source(s):** ACWS, Fisher, 1862 MOR
Birth Date: About 1838	**Birth Place:** York, Pennsylvania
LDS Membership Date: Uncertain	**LDS Membership Source(s):** NFS (ID #: KPS5-NPR)
Death Date: 21 February 1892	**Death Place:** Uncertain **Find A Grave:** — **Burial Location:** Uncertain
Notes: [MLM] His father, Albert Ellis Lutz (NFS ID #: KWJD-1NP), was baptized into the LDS Church on February 12, 1839 [NFS]. As a member of the Lot Smith Cavalry Company, he is presumed to be a Latter-day Saint (but his baptismal date or LDS membership could not be confirmed from available sources).	

LYNCH, WILLIAM   (UNION ARMY)   *Baptized before the war.*

Rank: Private	**Unit(s):** Lot Smith Utah Cavalry **Military Service Source(s):** ACWS, NPS, PI, Fisher, 1862 MOR
Birth Date: 3 November 1831	**Birth Place:** Derrygra, Ardcarn In Boyle, Roscommon, Ireland
LDS Membership Date: 27 January 1847	**LDS Membership Source(s):** NFS (ID #: KWJW-SM5)
Death Date: 25 June 1892	**Death Place:** Salt Lake City, Salt Lake, Utah **Find A Grave:** — **Burial Location:** Salt Lake City, Salt Lake, Utah
Notes: [MLM]	

MANNING, JOSEPH C.   (UNION ARMY)   *Baptized after the war.*

Rank: Private	**Unit(s):** Company E, 16th Regiment, U.S. Infantry **Military Service Source(s):** VBU, NPS
Birth Date: 25 May 1845	**Birth Place:** Springfield, Hampden, Massachusetts
LDS Membership Date: June 1898	**LDS Membership Source(s):** NFS (ID #: KWC4-P1B)
Death Date: 2 December 1950	**Death Place:** Napa, California **Find A Grave:** 29624637 **Burial Location:** Salt Lake City Cemetery, Salt Lake City, Salt Lake, Utah

Notes: His son, Lawrence Eugene Manning, was a casualty in World War I while serving with the Canadian Infantry. Joseph lived to be 105 years old [FGC].

MARSH, GEORGE D.   (UNION ARMY)   *Baptized after the war.*

Rank: Private	**Unit(s):** Companies A & L, 2nd Regiment, California Cavalry **Military Service Source(s):** VBU, NPS, PI
Birth Date: 5 May 1834	**Birth Place:** Steelville, Crawford, Missouri
LDS Membership Date: 5 September 1869	**LDS Membership Source(s):** NFS (ID #: KVP1-5HQ)
Death Date: 15 April 1900	**Death Place:** Grantsville, Tooele, Utah **Find A Grave:** 30739463 **Burial Location:** Grantsville City Cemetery, Grantsville, Tooele, Utah

Notes: The 2nd Regiment, California Cavalry, was organized at San Francisco during September and October 1861. Company A served at Camp Douglas, Utah Territory, until November 1864. Company L served at Fort Churchill, Camp Independence, and Fort Bridger during the Civil War [NPS].

MARSHALL, WILLIAM L.   (CONFEDERATE ARMY)   *Baptized after the war.*

Rank: Uncertain	**Unit(s):** Troop A, 10th Regiment, Kentucky Cavalry **Military Service Source(s):** NPS, FGC, MCL
Birth Date: 14 January 1825	**Birth Place:** Henry County, Virginia
LDS Membership Date: 12 November 1876	**LDS Membership Source(s):** NFS (ID #: KWJB-F57)
Death Date: 2 May 1899	**Death Place:** Manassa, Conejos, Colorado **Find A Grave:** 39956556 **Burial Location:** Manassa, Conejos, Colorado

Notes: "TR. A. 10 KY. CAV" (Troop A, 10th Kentucky Cavalry) is carved on his grave marker [FGC].

MASON, PETER M.   (UNION ARMY)   *Baptized after the war.*

Rank: Private	**Unit(s):** Company E, 9th Regiment, Indiana Volunteers **Military Service Source(s):** 1890 Census
Birth Date: 13 July 1837	**Birth Place:** Binderup, Aalborg, Denmark
LDS Membership Date: 24 March 1874	**LDS Membership Source(s):** NFS (ID #: KWJ9-TYZ)
Death Date: 14 October 1898	**Death Place:** Manti, Sanpete, Utah **Find A Grave:** — **Burial Location:** Manti, Sanpete, Utah

Notes: [MLM] He served in the military for three months beginning in April 1861. "Cut across right hand" is listed as a service-related disability [1890 Census].

MATHEWS, JOHN   (UNION ARMY)   *Baptized before the war.*

Rank: Sergeant	**Unit(s):** Company C, 1st Regiment, Nebraska Cavalry **Military Service Source(s):** VBU, NPS, PI, FGC
Birth Date: 14 January 1842	**Birth Place:** London, Middlesex, England
LDS Membership Date: 15 January 1850	**LDS Membership Source(s):** NFS (ID #: L7JN-575)
Death Date: March 1917	**Death Place:** Midway, Wasatch, Utah **Find A Grave:** 54164 **Burial Location:** Midway Cemetery, Midway, Wasatch, Utah
Notes: "CO. C. 1 NEB. CAV." (Company C, 1st Nebraska Cavalry) is carved on his grave marker [FGC].	

McCUE, AMOS W.   (UNION ARMY)   *Baptized before the war (presumed).*

Rank: Private	**Unit(s):** Company G, 124th Regiment, Pennsylvania Infantry **Military Service Source(s):** NPS, FGC
Birth Date: 1835	**Birth Place:** Pennsylvania
LDS Membership Date: Uncertain	**LDS Membership Source(s):** SBS
Death Date: 20 January 1926	**Death Place:** Pennsylvania **Find A Grave:** 37244864 **Burial Location:** Unionville Cemetery, Unionville, Chester, Pennsylvania
Notes: "CO. G. 124 REGT. PA. VOL" (Company G, 124th Regiment, Pennsylvania Volunteers) is carved on his grave marker. "Amos W. McCue enrolled in Company G, 124th Regiment, Infantry, on July 22, 1862, at West Chester. He mustered into service on August 12, 1862" [FGC]. He sailed to Yerba Buena (San Francisco), California, with Samuel Brannon and other Latter-day Saints on board the ship *Brooklyn*. Presumed to be LDS [SBS].	

McCUE, JAMES P.   (UNION ARMY)   *Baptized before the war (presumed).*

Rank: Saddler	**Unit(s):** Company A, 2nd Regiment, California Cavalry Volunteers **Military Service Source(s):** Brig-Gen. Richard H. Orton, *Records of the California Men in the War of the Rebellion*, 1861 to 1867 (Sacramento, CA: State Office of Printing, 1890); 1890 Census
Birth Date: 1831	**Birth Place:** Uncertain
LDS Membership Date: Uncertain	**LDS Membership Source(s):** SBS
Death Date: 12 October 1900	**Death Place:** Sacramento, California **Find A Grave:** — **Burial Location:** St. Joseph Cemetery, Sacramento, Sacramento, California
Notes: He sailed to Yerba Buena (San Francisco), California, with Samuel Brannon and other Latter-day Saints on board the ship *Brooklyn*. Presumed to be LDS [SBS].	

McENTIRE, ELI   (UNION ARMY)   *Baptized after the war.*

Rank: Private	**Unit(s):** Company G, 5th Regiment, West Virginia Cavalry **Military Service Source(s):** NPS, MCL
Birth Date: 19 March 1846	**Birth Place:** Smith County, Virginia
LDS Membership Date: 16 October 1882	**LDS Membership Source(s):** NFS (ID #: KWJH-BJV)

Death Date: 21 February 1906	Death Place: Manassa, Conejos, Colorado Find A Grave: — Burial Location: Manassa, Conejos, Colorado
Notes: [MLM] The 5th Regiment, West Virginia Cavalry, was organized on January 26, 1864, and served primarily in West Virginia [NPS].	

McNEICE, COLEMAN C.   (CONFEDERATE ARMY)   *Baptized after the war.*

Rank: Private	Unit(s): 1st Regiment, Mississippi Infantry Military Service Source(s): VBU, NPS, FGC
Birth Date: 3 August 1818	Birth Place: Union District, Union, South Carolina
LDS Membership Date: 18 January 1885	LDS Membership Source(s): NFS (ID #: KWJZ-GJW)
Death Date: 6 December 1896	Death Place: Honeyville, Box Elder, Utah Find A Grave: 36194390 Burial Location: Honeyville Cemetery, Honeyville, Box Elder, Utah
Notes: "MISSISSIPPI PVT CO H1 REGT MISS INF CONFEDERATE STATES ARMY" (Mississippi Private, Company H, 1st Regiment, Mississippi Infantry) is carved on his grave marker [FGC].	

McNICOL, DANIEL   (UNION ARMY)   *Baptized before the war (presumed).*

Rank: Private	Unit(s): Lot Smith Utah Cavalry Military Service Source(s): ACWS, Fisher, 1862 MOR
Birth Date: Uncertain	Birth Place: Uncertain
LDS Membership Date: Presumed LDS	LDS Membership Source(s): Presumed
Death Date: July 1862	Death Place: Snake River, Wyoming Find A Grave: — Burial Location: Uncertain
Notes: As a member of the Lot Smith Cavalry Company, he is presumed to be a Latter-day Saint (but his baptismal date or LDS membership could not be confirmed from available sources). McNicol drowned crossing the Snake River as a member of an expedition to return hundreds of horses and mules that had been run off by Indians ("Captain Lot Smith's Company of Volunteers," *Utah Genealogical and Historical Magazine,* January 1911, 138). [1862 MOR] lists his name as "Daniel McNicol"; [Fisher] lists his name as "Daniel McNicol" (p. 29) and "Donald McNicol" (pp. 72, 79).	

MERRILL, EDWIN   (UNION ARMY)   *Baptized before the war.*

Rank: Private	Unit(s): Lot Smith Utah Cavalry Military Service Source(s): ACWS, Fisher, 1862 MOR
Birth Date: 8 January 1836	Birth Place: Byron, Genesee, New York
LDS Membership Date: 1 July 1856 (confirmation)	LDS Membership Source(s): NFS (ID #: L4HK-QZH)
Death Date: 23 September 1912	Death Place: Smithfield, Cache, Utah Find A Grave: — Burial Location: Smithfield City Cemetery, Smithfield, Cache, Utah
Notes: [MLM]	

MILLER, JOHN L.   (CONFEDERATE ARMY)   *Baptized after the war.*

Rank: Private	Unit(s): Company C, 30th Regiment, North Carolina Infantry Military Service Source(s): NPS
Birth Date: 12 October 1836	Birth Place: Salisbury, Rowan, North Carolina
LDS Membership Date: 1 July 1884 (confirmation)	LDS Membership Source(s): NFS (ID #: KWJC-J57)
Death Date: 12 December 1894	Death Place: Midvale, Salt Lake, Utah Find A Grave: 19457863 Burial Location: West Jordan City Cemetery, West Jordan, Salt Lake, Utah

Notes: The 30th Regiment, North Carolina Infantry, was organized in October 1861; it "saw action from Seven Pines to Cold Harbor, marched with [Gen.] Early to the Shenandoah Valley, and was involved in the Appomattox operations" [NPS].

MILLER, REUBEN P.   (UNION ARMY)   *Baptized before the war.*

Rank: Private	Unit(s): Lot Smith Utah Cavalry Military Service Source(s): VBU, ACWS, NPS, PI, Fisher, 1862 MOR
Birth Date: 22 December 1844	Birth Place: Dayton, La Salle, Illinois
LDS Membership Date: 23 March 1861 (LDS temple ordinances)	LDS Membership Source(s): NFS (ID #: KWN2-86Q)
Death Date: 29 March 1901	Death Place: Murray, Salt Lake, Utah Find A Grave: 49915477 Burial Location: Elysian Gardens, Millcreek, Salt Lake, Utah

Notes: For more information, see the Ellsworth-Alford chapter herein.

MITCHELL, JAMES M.   (CONFEDERATE ARMY)   *Baptized after the war.*

Rank: Private	Unit(s): Company D, 1st Regiment, South Carolina Rifles (Orr's Regiment of Rifles) Military Service Source(s): NPS, MCL
Birth Date: 14 February 1841	Birth Place: South Carolina
LDS Membership Date: 21 August 1883	LDS Membership Source(s): NFS (ID #: KWJY-VWM)
Death Date: 17 February 1898	Death Place: Manassa, Conejos, Colorado Find A Grave: 39958724 Burial Location: Manassa, Conejos, Colorado

Notes: [MLM] The 1st Regiment, South Carolina Rifles, was organized July 1861 and fought at Cold Harbor, Petersburg, Gaines's Mill, Second Bull Run, Fredericksburg, the Wilderness, Spotsylvania, and Chancellorsville [NPS].

MITTON, JOHN   (UNION ARMY)   *Baptized before the war.*

Rank: Private	Unit(s): Company D, 5th Regiment, U.S. Reserve Corps, Missouri Infantry Military Service Source(s): VBU, NPS, FGC
Birth Date: 3 July 1834	Birth Place: Soyland, Yorkshire, England
LDS Membership Date: 11 December 1847	LDS Membership Source(s): NFS (ID #: KWJW-54W)

Death Date: 3 April 1889	Death Place: Wellsville, Cache, Utah Find A Grave: 29505952 and 44648567 Burial Location: Wellsville Cemetery, Wellsville, Cache, Utah
Notes: "CO. D. 5 U.S.R.C. MO. INF." (Company D, 5th U.S. Reserve Corps, Missouri Infantry) is carved on his grave marker [FGC].	

MOORE, JOHN L. (UNION ARMY)

Baptized before the war.

Rank: Drummer	Unit(s): Company E, 18th Regiment, Ohio Infantry Military Service Source(s): 1890 Census
Birth Date: 4 May 1847	Birth Place: Alnmouth, Northumberland, England
LDS Membership Date: 18 September 1856	LDS Membership Source(s): NFS (ID #: KWNK-FMZ)
Death Date: 15 December 1904	Death Place: Hooper, Weber, Utah Find A Grave: 28643375 Burial Location: Hooper, Weber, Utah
Notes: [MLM] His name is recorded on the 1890 veteran census schedule, but the enumerator did not record any service information (other than position and unit) [1890 Census].	

MORGAN, JOHN HAMILTON (UNION ARMY)

Baptized after the war.

Rank: Color Sergeant	Unit(s): Company I, 123rd Regiment, Illinois Infantry Military Service Source(s): NPS; LDSBE; *The War of the Rebellion*, series 1, vol. 49, part 1, 395, 454–55; Arthur M. Richardson, *The Life and Ministry of John Morgan* (n.p.: Nicholas G. Morgan Sr., 1965)
Birth Date: 8 August 1842	Birth Place: Greensburg, Decatur, Indiana
LDS Membership Date: 23 November 1867	LDS Membership Source(s): LDSBE, *2012 Church Almanac*, NFS (ID #: KWC4-H6J)
Death Date: 14 August 1894	Death Place: Preston, Franklin, Idaho Find A Grave: 10369966 Burial Location: Salt Lake City Cemetery, Salt Lake City, Salt Lake, Utah

Notes: "During the war of the Rebellion, which broke out when he was eighteen years of age, he joined the Union army, and served with honor and distinction, participating in several of the most important battles. Coming to Utah at the close of the war, he was soon engaged as an instructor in the University, when that institution was conducted in the Council House, Salt Lake City" [LDSBE, 1:204]. He enlisted in the Union army on September 6, 1862, and served until June 28, 1865. His unit fought in numerous battles across Kentucky, Tennessee, Georgia, and Alabama, including Chickamauga, Chattanooga, and Atlanta. From the date of his enlistment until August 15, 1863, his unit pursued and eventually defeated the Confederate General John Hunt Morgan (of Morgan's Raiders fame), who was John Hamilton Morgan's fourth cousin. Several of his Civil War letters have survived. On December 21, 1863, for example, he wrote: "A mother's love is not purchased by either gold or diamonds; in camp, on the march, the bloody field of strife or the chill bivouac—the soldier's veneration for his mother remains the same. Falling on the blood drenched battlefield or stricken down by sickness, his last words are invariably: My mother—My Country! Often I have seen an unbidden tear spring to the eye of the rough soldier who had braved death in a thousand different shapes; whose cheek was unblanched and nerve steady amid the roar of battle; whose voice was as clear and ringing on a charge as the bravest of the brave—I have seen such men moved to tears on receiving a simple short letter from a mother."

He was recognized for bravery during the battle for Selma, Alabama, on April 2, 1865. An account of the battle written by Captain Owen Wiley (the Regiment's commanding officer) reported: "It is unnecessary to make particular mention of either officers or men. All did their duty, so deserve the highest praise. Sergt. John Morgan, Company I is deserving of the highest credit for his credit for his gallantry in action in being

Morgan, John Hamilton (continued)

the first to plant a flag upon the rebel works and for being in the extreme advance until all the rebel forts were captured, planting our colors upon each of them successively." At the end of the war, he was offered an officer's commission if he would reenlist, but he declined the offer. He joined the LDS Church after coming to Utah with a herd of cattle. In 1867, he founded the Morgan Commercial and Normal College—Utah's "first successfully conducted school in Utah for higher education during the period from 1867 to 1875." Students at Morgan College included Heber J. Grant, Brigham H. Roberts, Ira N. Hinckley, Orson F. Whitney, Ruth May Fox, and J. Golden Kimball. He served as president of the Southern States Mission. Beginning in 1878–79, many of his Southern States converts settled in Manassa, Conejos County, Colorado (where Morgan Street was named in his honor). He was ordained by Wilford Woodruff on October 5, 1884, to serve as one of the First Seven Presidents of the Seventy. Arthur M. Richardson, *The Life and Ministry of John Morgan* (n.p.: Nicholas G. Morgan Sr., 1965); *The War of the Rebellion,* series 1, vol. 49, part 1, 454–55; *2012 Church Almanac* (Salt Lake City: *Deseret News,* 2012), 118; "Family home, Salt Lake City" [PPMU, 1044]. See also Leon R. Hartshorn, *Powerful Stories from the Lives of Latter-day Saint Men* (Salt Lake City: Deseret Book, 1974). His baptism date is also listed as November 26, 1867 [LDSBE].

MORRIS, GADDISON   (CONFEDERATE ARMY)   *Baptized after the war.*

Rank: Private	Unit(s): Company C, 40th Regiment, Georgia Infantry Military Service Source(s): NPS
Birth Date: 1830	Birth Place: Franklin County, Georgia
LDS Membership Date: 1 March 1877	LDS Membership Source(s): NFS (ID #: KWNP-TY4)
Death Date: 21 March 1878	Death Place: Winslow, Navajo, Arizona Find A Grave: — Burial Location: Brigham City, Navajo, Arizona
Notes: His name is listed as "Gad Morris" on [NPS].	

MOUSLEY, WILLIAM P.   (UNION ARMY)   *Baptized before the war.*

Rank: Private	Unit(s): Company H, 11th Regiment, Missouri Cavalry Military Service Source(s): 1890 Census, NPS
Birth Date: 22 October 1821	Birth Place: Wilmington, Newcastle, Delaware
LDS Membership Date: 1 January 1841 (confirmation)	LDS Membership Source(s): NFS (ID #: KWJH-GZB)
Death Date: 30 May 1880	Death Place: Moroni, Sanpete, Utah Find A Grave: 62683056 Burial Location: Moroni, Sanpete, Utah
Notes: [MLM] Asthma listed as a disease contracted during his military service. He served during the Civil War two years and two months beginning in 1861. His widow, Margarette, reported his veteran status [1890 Census].	

MURPHY, JAMES D.   (UNION ARMY)   *Baptized before the war.*

Rank: Corporal	Unit(s): Company G, 16th Regiment, New York Infantry Military Service Source(s): 1890 Census, NPS
Birth Date: 4 October 1831	Birth Place: Fayette County, Georgia
LDS Membership Date: 1 August 1858 (confirmation)	LDS Membership Source(s): NFS (ID #: KV5M-ZPQ)

Death Date: 24 February 1893	Death Place: Millcreek, Salt Lake, Utah Find A Grave: — Burial Location: Salt Lake Cemetery, Salt Lake City, Salt Lake, Utah

Notes: [MLM] He served in the military one year and eight months beginning April 28, 1861. "Effected eye" is listed as an injury incurred during his military service. He was discharged from the army for a disability [1890 Census].

MURPHY, JOHN JOSEPH PEDGER   (CONFEDERATE ARMY)   *Baptized after the war.*

Rank: Private	Unit(s): Company C, 48th Regiment, Georgia Infantry Military Service Source(s): NPS
Birth Date: 4 September 1843	Birth Place: Fayette County, Georgia
LDS Membership Date: 6 May 1868	LDS Membership Source(s): NFS (ID #: KWNV-Y79)
Death Date: 3 September 1889	Death Place: Colonia Juarez, Chihuahua, Mexico Find A Grave: 61058946 Burial Location: Colonia Juarez, Chihuahua, Mexico

Notes: [MLM] The 48th Regiment, Georgia Infantry, was organized during the winter of 1861–62. "It served on many battlefields of the Army of Northern Virginia from the Seven Days' Battles to Cold Harbor, then was involved in the long Petersburg siege south of the James River and the Appomattox Campaign." More than 55 percent of the regiment was lost at Gettysburg [NPS]. A copy of his journal is in the possession of Joseph R. Stuart.

MURRAY, GEORGE   (UNION ARMY)   *Baptized before the war.*

Rank: Private	Unit(s): Company F, 12th Regiment, Pennsylvania Reserve Infantry Military Service Source(s): NPS
Birth Date: 3 November 1838	Birth Place: Blackquarie, Glasgow, Lanark, Scotland
LDS Membership Date: 10 October 1850	LDS Membership Source(s): NFS (ID #: KWJ2-2JL)
Death Date: 19 February 1924	Death Place: Alhambra, Los Angeles, California Find A Grave: 40179392 Burial Location: Heber City Cemetery, Heber, Wasatch, Utah

Notes: [MLM] The 12th Regiment, 12th Pennsylvania Reserve Infantry (41st Volunteers), was organized in August 1861 and saw action at Mechanicsville, Malvern Hill, Second Bull Run, Fredericksburg, Gettysburg, the Wilderness, and Spotsylvania, among others [NPS].

MYRICK, NEWTON MOSIAH   (UNION ARMY)   *Baptized before the war (presumed).*

Rank: Corporal	Unit(s): Lot Smith Utah Cavalry Military Service Source(s): ACWS, Fisher, 1862 MOR
Birth Date: February 1836	Birth Place: Apple Prairie, Green, Illinois
LDS Membership Date: Uncertain	LDS Membership Source(s): NFS (ID #: LHRY-P3M)
Death Date: 28 March 1911	Death Place: Union, Oregon Find A Grave: — Burial Location: Uncertain

Notes: [MLM] As a member of the Lot Smith Cavalry Company (and with the Book of Mormon middle name Mosiah), he is presumed to be a Latter-day Saint (but his baptismal date or LDS membership could not be confirmed from available sources).

NANCE, J.Y. (JAMES YOUNG)   (CONFEDERATE ARMY)   *Baptized after the war.*

Rank: Private	Unit(s): Company C, 26th Regiment, North Carolina Infantry Military Service Source(s): VBU, NPS
Birth Date: 12 December 1844	Birth Place: Wilkesburro, Wilkes, North Carolina
LDS Membership Date: 21 September 1887	LDS Membership Source(s): NFS (ID #: KWNR-DKQ)
Death Date: 14 July 1906	Death Place: Kaysville, Davis, Utah Find A Grave: 124458 Burial Location: Kaysville City Cemetery, Kaysville, Davis, Utah

Notes: He was captured at Falling Waters, Maryland, on July 14, 1863. He was a member of a prisoner exchange on March 3, 1864. He deserted on May 25, 1864 (*Deseret News*, August 3, 1906).

NANNEY, RICHARD H.   (UNION ARMY)   *Baptized after the war.*

Rank: Private	Unit(s): Company B, 1st Regiment, Tennessee Light Artillery Military Service Source(s): NPS, PI, FGC, Obituary
Birth Date: 19 September 1845	Birth Place: Williamsburg, Warren, North Carolina
LDS Membership Date: 24 August 1902	LDS Membership Source(s): NFS (ID #: KW81-KT5)
Death Date: 27 July 1924	Death Place: Morgan, Utah Find A Grave: 159018 Burial Location: Mount Olivet Cemetery, Salt Lake City, Salt Lake, Utah

Notes: "CO. B. 1 TENN. L.A." (Company B, 1st Tennessee Light Artillery) is carved on his grave marker [FGC]. His obituary, entitled "Aged Morgan Veteran Dies," states that he was a "veteran of the Civil war. . . . Mr. Nanney was born and raised in the south, but fought with the union forces acting as a scout in the enemy lines most of the time. He was decorated many times for distinguished service. After being discharged he settled in Tennessee. He was a shoemaker by trade and followed this trade until a few months before his death" (*Ogden Standard*, July 28, 1924, 4).

NEFF, BENJAMIN B.   (UNION ARMY)   *Baptized before the war.*

Rank: Private	Unit(s): Lot Smith Utah Cavalry Military Service Source(s): VBU, ACWS, NPS, PI, FGC, Fisher, 1862 MOR
Birth Date: 6 May 1834	Birth Place: Lancaster County, Pennsylvania
LDS Membership Date: 1 January 1848	LDS Membership Source(s): NFS (ID #: KWNL-DKG)
Death Date: 18 February 1883	Death Place: Salt Lake City, Salt Lake, Utah Find A Grave: 9036711 Burial Location: Draper City Cemetery, Draper, Salt Lake, Utah

Notes: "PVT SMITH'S CO UTAH CAV" (Private, [Lot] Smith's Company, Utah Cavalry) is carved on his grave marker [FGC].

NEFF, JOHN   (UNION ARMY)   *Baptized before the war.*

Rank: Corporal	Unit(s): Lot Smith Utah Cavalry Military Service Source(s): VBU, ACWS, NPS, Fisher, 1862 MOR
Birth Date: 28 December 1837	Birth Place: Lancaster County, Pennsylvania
LDS Membership Date: 1 January 1848	LDS Membership Source(s): LDSBE, NFS (ID #: KWJC-GK8)

Death Date: 6 January 1918	Death Place: Salt Lake City, Salt Lake, Utah Find A Grave: 45028249 Burial Location: Wasatch Lawn Memorial Park, Salt Lake City, Salt Lake, Utah

Notes: "The first bishop of East Mill Creek, Salt Lake county, Utah. . . . He came to Utah with his parents in 1847. . . . In 1857 he made a trip to Ft. Bridger in Orrin Porter Rockwell's company, and in 1862 he participated in the expedition sent out under Captain Lot Smith to guard the mail route. In 1872–73 he filled a mission to Great Britain . . . ordained a patriarch Feb. 6, 1912, by President Joseph F. Smith" [LDSBE, 2:787].

NELSON, ALMA FRANKLIN (UNION NAVY)   *Baptized during the war.*

Rank: Boatswain	Unit(s): USS Baltimore Military Service Source(s): 1890 Census
Birth Date: 16 February 1847	Birth Place: Wallsberg, Kalundborg, Denmark
LDS Membership Date: 10 July 1863	LDS Membership Source(s): NFS (ID #: KWJ8-8F3)
Death Date: 13 November 1929	Death Place: Uncertain Find A Grave: 179082 Burial Location: Smithfield, Cache, Utah

Notes: [MLM] He served in the military one year and two months beginning August 1864 [1890 Census]. "During the Civil War, [the *USS*] *Baltimore* served as an ordnance vessel, operating between the Washington Navy Yard and nearby ammunition depots, was used occasionally to ferry Army troops across the Potomac River, and saw some service with the North Atlantic Blockading Squadron as a dispatch and supply vessel. On 9 May 1862, she transported President Abraham Lincoln, and Secretaries Edwin M. Stanton and Salmon P. Chase from Fort Monroe to Norfolk, Va., in an attempt to get a close view of the destroyed Confederate ironclad Virginia" (http://www.history.navy.mil/danfs/b1/baltimore-iii.htm).

NELSON, JOHN L.   (UNION ARMY)   *Baptized after the war.*

Rank: Sergeant	Unit(s): Company A, 1st Battalion, Nevada Cavalry Military Service Source(s): NPS, PI, FGC
Birth Date: 25 August 1840	Birth Place: Kanesville, Pottawattamie, Iowa
LDS Membership Date: 15 September 1867	LDS Membership Source(s): NFS (ID #: KLBW-3MT)
Death Date: 16 May 1897	Death Place: Springville, Utah, Utah Find A Grave: 85100 Burial Location: Springville Cemetery, Springville, Utah, Utah

Notes: "SGT CO A 1 NEV CAVALRY CIVIL WAR" (Sergeant, Company A, 1st Nevada Cavalry) is carved on his grave marker [FGC].

NELSON, WILLIAM (UNION ARMY)   *Baptized before the war.*

Rank: Sergeant	Unit(s): Company E, 14th Regiment, Wisconsin Infantry Military Service Source(s): 1890 Census, NPS
Birth Date: 4 April 1844	Birth Place: Langley Mill, Nottingham, England
LDS Membership Date: 1 January 1852 (confirmation)	LDS Membership Source(s): NFS (ID #: KWJZ-GPR)
Death Date: 4 December 1928	Death Place: St. George, Washington, Utah Find A Grave: 108826 Burial Location: St. George, Washington, Utah

Notes: [MLM] He was a prisoner of war for 19 months [1890 Census]. There appears to be an error with his confirmation date (as he was not eight years old on the date listed for his confirmation). There is another William Nelson, 1839–1913, in [VBU] who served in the Company I, 10th Wisconsin Infantry.

NESLEN, WILLIAM FRANCIS   (UNION ARMY)   *Baptized during the war.*

Rank: Second Sergeant and First Sergeant	Unit(s): Company I, 10th Regiment, Wisconsin Infantry Military Service Source(s): NPS, PI, PPMU, Obituary
Birth Date: 5 January 1841	Birth Place: Lowestoft, Suffolk, England
LDS Membership Date: 1862	LDS Membership Source(s): PPMU, NFS (ID #: KWJC-PFJ)
Death Date: 22 January 1918	Death Place: Salt Lake City, Salt Lake, Utah Find A Grave: 172536 Burial Location: Mount Olivet Cemetery, Salt Lake City, Salt Lake, Utah
Notes: He "came to Utah Sept. 20, 1853. . . . Veteran Civil war 1861–62; and Black Hawk war 1866" [PPMU, 1067]. His obituary states that he was "a Civil war veteran and Utah pioneer" who "fought through a year of the Civil war and was in several stirring engagements" (*Salt Lake Telegram*, January 23, 1918, 12).	

NEWTON, THOMAS D.   (UNION ARMY)   *Baptized before the war.*

Rank: Private	Unit(s): Company A, 62nd Regiment, Illinois Cavalry Military Service Source(s): 1890 Census, NPS
Birth Date: 10 August 1825	Birth Place: Manchester, Lancaster, England
LDS Membership Date: 22 December 1847	LDS Membership Source(s): NFS (ID #: KWJD-M27)
Death Date: 23 April 1916	Death Place: Salt Lake City, Salt Lake, Utah Find A Grave: 12777059 Burial Location: Salt Lake City, Salt Lake, Utah
Notes: [MLM] He served in the military for three years and one month beginning in May 1861. An alias is listed as "Daniel W. Townsend." His left arm was partially paralyzed during his military service [1890 Census]. [NPS] lists a Thomas Newton who served in the 14th Regiment, Illinois Cavalry; the unit affiliation listed is from [1890 Census].	

NOBLE, EDWARD A.   (UNION ARMY)   *Baptized before the war.*

Rank: Private	Unit(s): Lot Smith Utah Cavalry Military Service Source(s): ACWS, Fisher, 1862 MOR
Birth Date: 2 February 1841	Birth Place: Montrose, Lee, Iowa
LDS Membership Date: 16 March 1851	LDS Membership Source(s): LDSBE, NFS (ID #: KW6D-23T)
Death Date: 28 November 1909	Death Place: Saint John's, Apache, Arizona Find A Grave: 33482392 Burial Location: Saint John's Cemetery, Saint John's, Apache, Arizona
Notes: [MLM] "Bishop of Alpine Ward, St. Johns Stake, Arizona from 1880 to 1890. . . . Ordained a High Priest and Bishop by Brigham Young, jun., Sept. 26, 1880." His baptism date is listed as 1850 [LDSBE, 4:597].	

NORMAN, SAUL   (UNION ARMY)   *Baptized during the war.*

Rank: Private	Unit(s): Companies K & L, 2nd Regiment, California Cavalry Military Service Source(s): NPS, PI, 1890 Census
Birth Date: 9 July 1836	Birth Place: Pemilton, Madison, Indiana
LDS Membership Date: January 1865	LDS Membership Source(s): NFS (ID #: KWJZ-Z91)

Death Date: 22 January 1893	Death Place: Mt. Pleasant, Sanpete, Utah Find A Grave: 142757 Burial Location: Mt. Pleasant Cemetery, Mt. Pleasant, Sanpete, Utah
Notes: He served three years, three months, and eight days beginning on August 13, 1862. "Rheumatism and bronchitis" are listed as service-related disabilities [1890 Census]. For additional information, see the Ellsworth-Alford chapter herein.	

NORTH, HIRAM B.   (UNION ARMY)   *Baptized before the war.*

Rank: Private	Unit(s): Lot Smith Utah Cavalry Military Service Source(s): ACWS, NPS, PI, Fisher, 1862 MOR
Birth Date: 16 December 1840	Birth Place: Sugar Creek, Lee, Iowa
LDS Membership Date: 1 January 1849	LDS Membership Source(s): NFS (ID #: KWNT-PY9)
Death Date: 28 May 1915	Death Place: Charleston, Wasatch, Utah Find A Grave: — Burial Location: Midway, Wasatch, Utah
Notes: [MLM]	

OAKASON, HANS   (UNION ARMY)   *Baptized before the war.*

Rank: Private	Unit(s): Company L or M, 2nd Regiment, California Cavalry Military Service Source(s): NPS, PI, PPMU
Birth Date: 12 September 1839	Birth Place: Kyrkheddinge, Malmohus, Sweden
LDS Membership Date: 30 November 1856	LDS Membership Source(s): PPMU, NFS (ID #: KWJF-4CS)
Death Date: 22 January 1924	Death Place: Salt Lake City, Salt Lake, Utah Find A Grave: — Burial Location: Salt Lake City Cemetery, Salt Lake City, Salt Lake, Utah
Notes: He "came to Utah Sept. 21, 1861, Heber C. Kimball company. Married Ingre Stark. Married Marie Olsen, Salt Lake City . . . High priest. Veteran fireman, serving 20 years; veteran of Civil war. California volunteer cavalry, Co. M, 1864–66. Plasterer and builder" [PPMU, 1074].	

OBERLANDER, JOHN   (UNION ARMY)   *Baptized after the war.*

Rank: Secret Service	Unit(s): Uncertain Military Service Source(s): 1890 Census
Birth Date: 9 June 1840	Birth Place: Cincinnati, Hamilton, Ohio
LDS Membership Date: 13 December 1877	LDS Membership Source(s): NFS (ID #: K2HM-J3N)
Death Date: 1 May 1927	Death Place: Salt Lake City, Salt Lake, Utah Find A Grave: 128029 Burial Location: Murray City Cemetery, Salt Lake, Utah
Notes: [MLM] According to the 1890 Census, he served three years and ten months beginning July 15, 1861. There is some question about his service, though, because his military rank is listed on the census form as "Secret Service" [1890 Census]. Two soldiers named "John Oberlander" are listed in [NPS].	

O'BRIEN, JOHN   (UNION ARMY)   *Baptized during the war.*

Rank: Private	Unit(s): Company B, 4th Regiment, New York Cavalry Military Service Source(s): 1890 Census, NPS
Birth Date: 16 May 1839	Birth Place: Baltimore, Maryland

O'Brien, John (continued)	
LDS Membership Date: 1 February 1863 (confirmation)	**LDS Membership Source(s):** NFS (ID #: KWNG-1WV)
Death Date: 29 February 1904	**Death Place:** Layton, Davis, Utah **Find A Grave:** 125446 **Burial Location:** Kaysville, Davis, Utah
Notes: [MLM] He served one year and eight months beginning April 15, 1862 [1890 Census].	

ODOM, DAVID GEORGE WASHINGTON
(CONFEDERATE ARMY)   *Baptized after the war.*

Rank: Sergeant	**Unit(s):** Company F, 51st Regiment, Georgia Infantry **Military Service Source(s):** NPS
Birth Date: 28 May 1847	**Birth Place:** Chattahoochee, Georgia
LDS Membership Date: 15 October 1886	**LDS Membership Source(s):** NFS (ID #: KWD9-JG2)
Death Date: 10 February 1910	**Death Place:** Tyler, Texas **Find A Grave:** — **Burial Location:** Fairview Cemetery, Tyler, Texas
Notes: [MLM] [NPS] also lists Confederate Civil War service for "George Washington Odom" in Company D, 43rd North Carolina Infantry.	

ODOM, PLEASANT   (CONFEDERATE ARMY)   *Baptized after the war.*

Rank: Private	**Unit(s):** Company C, 10th Regiment, Georgia Infantry **Military Service Source(s):** NPS
Birth Date: 5 August 1822	**Birth Place:** Jones County, Georgia
LDS Membership Date: 14 October 1886	**LDS Membership Source(s):** NFS (ID #: KWJC-DF5)
Death Date: 1 October 1915	**Death Place:** Spurger, Tyler, Texas **Find A Grave:** 14721708 **Burial Location:** Antioch Cemetery, Woodville, Tyler, Texas
Notes: "CO C 10 GA INF C.S.A." (Company C, 10th Georgia Infantry, Confederate States of America) is carved on his grave marker [FGC].	

OSBORN, LEWIS D.   (UNION ARMY)   *Baptized before the war (presumed).*

Rank: Private	**Unit(s):** Lot Smith Utah Cavalry **Military Service Source(s):** ACWS, Fisher, 1862 MOR
Birth Date: 19 March 1838	**Birth Place:** Ohio
LDS Membership Date: Uncertain	**LDS Membership Source(s):** NFS (ID #: KLBY-RD7)
Death Date: 3 February 1908	**Death Place:** Bingham Canyon, Salt Lake, Utah **Find A Grave:** — **Burial Location:** Salt Lake City Cemetery, Salt Lake City, Salt Lake, Utah
Notes: [MLM] As a member of the Lot Smith Cavalry Company, he is presumed to be a Latter-day Saint (but a nonvicarious baptismal date or LDS membership could not be confirmed from available sources).	

OSBURN, WILLIAM   (UNION ARMY)   *Baptized after the war.*

Rank: Private	**Unit(s):** Company E, 1st Regiment, Nebraska Cavalry **Military Service Source(s):** VBU, 1890 Census, NPS

Birth Date: 14 July 1848	Birth Place: Dubuque, Dubuque, Iowa
LDS Membership Date: 1869	LDS Membership Source(s): NFS (ID #: KWJH-WB5)
Death Date: 14 May 1931	Death Place: Escalante, Garfield, Utah Find A Grave: — Burial Location: Escalante, Garfield, Utah
Notes: He served in the military two years and four months beginning May 1864. "Partial blindness" is listed as a service-related disability [1890 Census].	

PARK, HUGH D.   (UNION ARMY)   *Baptized before the war.*

Rank: Private	Unit(s): Lot Smith Utah Cavalry Military Service Source(s): ACWS, NPS, PI, Fisher, 1862 MOR
Birth Date: 24 February 1840	Birth Place: Warwick, Kent, Ontario, Canada
LDS Membership Date: 17 February 1847	LDS Membership Source(s): NFS (ID #: KWNV-7KJ)
Death Date: 7 February 1908	Death Place: Millcreek, Salt Lake, Utah Find A Grave: 72449553 Burial Location: Elysian Gardens, Millcreek, Salt Lake, Utah
Notes: There may be an error in either his birth date or baptism date (as he was not eight years old on the listed date of his baptism). A birthdate of 24 February 1839 is also listed in [NFS].	

PARKER, HENRY   (UNION ARMY)   *Baptized after the war.*

Rank: Corporal	Unit(s): Company F, 3rd Regiment, U.S. Infantry Military Service Source(s): 1890 Census
Birth Date: 18 May 1839	Birth Place: Gretton, Gloucestershire, England
LDS Membership Date: 8 January 1871	LDS Membership Source(s): NFS (ID #: KWNP-GXF)
Death Date: 4 June 1902	Death Place: Payson, Utah, Utah Find A Grave: 29897339 Burial Location: Payson, Utah, Utah
Notes: [MLM] He served in the military for four years, two months, and twelve days beginning on May 6, 1861. "Sunstroke in battle" is listed as a service-related disability [1890 Census].	

PEACOCK, ALFRED JAMES   (CONFEDERATE ARMY)   *Baptized before the war.*

Rank: Private	Unit(s): Company H, 3rd Regiment, Florida Infantry Military Service Source(s): 1890 Census, NPS
Birth Date: 4 March 1837	Birth Place: Watford, Hertford, England
LDS Membership Date: 25 November 1852	LDS Membership Source(s): NFS (ID #: KWJH-NWC)
Death Date: 15 January 1891	Death Place: Uncertain Find A Grave: 39039084 Burial Location: Uncertain
Notes: [MLM] He is listed on the [1890 Census], but no service date, rank, or unit affiliation information was recorded for him.	

PEARCE, EDWARD WILLIAM   (UNION ARMY)   *Baptized before the war.*

Rank: Private	Unit(s): Companies A & B, 3rd Regiment, California Infantry (Volunteers) Military Service Source(s): 1890 Census, NPS

Pearce, Edward William (continued)	
LDS Membership Date: 1 January 1849 (confirmation)	**LDS Membership Source(s):** NFS (ID #: 2JT2-MZC)
Death Date: 14 February 1906	**Death Place:** Cannonville, Garfield, Utah **Find A Grave:** — **Burial Location:** Cannonville, Garfield, Utah
Notes: [MLM] He served in the military two years and nine months beginning in 1862 [1890 Census].	

PECK, JOSEPH AUGUSTINE   (UNION ARMY)   *Baptized before the war.*

Rank: Sergeant	**Unit(s):** Company H, 8th Regiment, Vermont Infantry **Military Service Source(s):** NPS, Obituary
Birth Date: 4 April 1830	**Birth Place:** North Danville, Caledonia, Vermont
LDS Membership Date: 8 April 1838	**LDS Membership Source(s):** PPMU, NFS (ID #: K2HQ-74D)
Death Date: 27 March 1916	**Death Place:** Salt Lake City, Salt Lake, Utah **Find A Grave:** 33650190 **Burial Location:** Salt Lake City Cemetery, Salt Lake City, Salt Lake, Utah
Notes: His obituary states that he was "a veteran of the civil war" (*Salt Lake Telegram*, March 27, 1916, 12). He "came to Utah 1848, Brigham Young company. . . . Seventy; high priest; block teacher; missionary to Sandwich Islands. Sealer of weights for Salt Lake county. Blacksmith" [PPMU, 1094].	

PEERY, DAVID HAROLD   (CONFEDERATE ARMY)   *Baptized during the war.*

Rank: Assistant Commissary Officer	**Unit(s):** Confederate Army of Eastern Kentucky **Military Service Source(s):** LDSBE; Orson F. Whitney, *History of Utah* (Salt Lake City: George Q. Cannon and Sons, 1892), 4:270–72; William G. Hartley, "The Confederate Officer and 'That Mormon Girl,'" *Ensign*, April 1982, 53; Robert C. Freeman, *Nineteenth-Century Saints at War* (Religious Studies Center, Brigham Young University, 2006), 130; Edward W. Tullidge, *Tullidge's Histories* (Salt Lake City: Juvenile Instructor Press, 1889), 2:207–13.
Birth Date: 16 May 1824	**Birth Place:** Jeffersonville, Tazewell, Virginia
LDS Membership Date: 13 December 1862	**LDS Membership Source(s):** LDSBE, PPMU, Obituary, NFS (ID #: KWNB-332)
Death Date: 17 September 1901	**Death Place:** Ogden, Weber, Utah **Find A Grave:** 20260609 **Burial Location:** Ogden City Cemetery, Ogden, Weber, Utah

Notes: "President of the Weber Stake of Zion from 1877 to 1882. . . . His early years were spent on his parents' plantation. . . . In 1862 he volunteered and entered the Confederate army of eastern Kentucky. . . . In November 1862, he was baptized by a local Elder, Absolom Young, when the snow was a foot deep and the ice six inches thick. . . . July 18, 1863, while in the army, his residence store and six adjacent houses filled with goods and provisions, property valued at $50,000, were burned to the ground by the Union Army. There was nothing saved and no insurance. After this loss he concluded to go to Utah, and in 1864 he started for the west. . . . The Indians were hostile that year and their train was attacked two or three times, but none of the emigrants were killed. . . . They arrived in Salt Lake City Aug. 31, 1864. . . . June 7, 1882, he was appointed by the Utah Territorial convention as a delegate to Washington, D.C. to labor for the admission of Utah as a State. . . . Mr. Peery was a Virginian of the old school and cherished the courtly traits and traditions of his chivalrous people. His generous hospitality was proverbial throughout the State " [LDSBE, 1:756–58]. "President 76th quorum seventies; missionary to southern states 1875; member Utah legislature 1878–84" [PPMU, 1094]. His obituary called him "one of Utah's most prominent citizens" and noted that he lived an "exemplary life of strictest business integrity, a friendship of truest loyalty for those who deserved it."

His lengthy, front-page obituary further notes that "Mr. Peery was zealous in the execution of his religious duties, and he has been strongly identified with church work in Utah. In 1875 he fulfilled a mission to the Southern States and labored in Texas, Tennessee and Virginia. His ability, sincerity and integrity endeared him to the authorities of his church and he possessed the confidence and esteem of Brigham Young. . . . On May 27, 1877, he was chosen by Brigham Young and sustained by the people as President of Weber Stake and continued in that position until October 19, 1882. . . . Like Lincoln he was a man strong with the common people. He had a cordial Virginia manner and treated the poor man equally as warmly and hospitably as the rich. He recognized merit quickly and was a correct and quick judge of character. His is a household name in every settlement in the county, and frequently remarks that he made years ago are quoted. He was strictly honest; his word was his bond, and he has always held the confidence of the community" (*Ogden Standard*, September 17, 1901, 1). For additional information, see the Ellsworth-Alford and Freeman chapters herein.

PEERY, THOMAS ELBERT   (CONFEDERATE ARMY)   *Baptized after the war.*

Rank: Second Lieutenant	**Unit(s):** Company G, 1st Regiment, Missouri Cavalry **Military Service Source(s):** VBU
Birth Date: 23 April 1846	**Birth Place:** Albany, Gentry, Missouri
LDS Membership Date: 1 August 1908	**LDS Membership Source(s):** NFS (ID #: KWJD-8PQ)
Death Date: 1 April 1935	**Death Place:** Spring Lake, Utah, Utah **Find A Grave:** 31855227 **Burial Location:** Payson, Utah, Utah

Notes: The 1st Regiment, Missouri Cavalry, was formed in summer 1861. "Many of its members had served with the Missouri State Guard." On July 4, 1863, the unit was captured at Vicksburg, Mississippi, but was later exchanged [NPS].

PENFOLD, JOHN   (UNION ARMY)   *Baptized after the war.*

Rank: Private	**Unit(s):** Company A, 91st Regiment, Indiana Infantry **Military Service Source(s):** 1890 Census, NPS
Birth Date: 17 October 1844	**Birth Place:** New Harmony, Posey, Indiana
LDS Membership Date: 7 March 1878	**LDS Membership Source(s):** NFS (ID #: KLGG-FV2)
Death Date: 23 December 1901	**Death Place:** Victor, Teton, Idaho **Find A Grave:** 5346339 **Burial Location:** Victor, Teton, Idaho

Notes: [MLM] His 1890 census enumerator failed to record any service information [1890 Census].

PINCKARD, ROBERT   (CONFEDERATE ARMY)   *Baptized before the war.*

Rank: Private	**Unit(s):** Company C, 10th Regiment, Virginia Cavalry **Military Service Source(s):** NPS
Birth Date: 28 July 1833	**Birth Place:** Rocky Mount, Franklin, Virginia
LDS Membership Date: 28 June 1877	**LDS Membership Source(s):** NFS (ID #: KWJC-NGP)
Death Date: 16 July 1910	**Death Place:** Manassa, Conejos, Colorado **Find A Grave:** 38385112 **Burial Location:** Manassa, Conejos, Colorado

Notes: [MLM] The 10th Regiment, Virginia Cavalry, was earlier known as the 1st Cavalry Regiment, Wise Legion and 8th Battalion. Organized in May 1862, it participated in battles at Sharpsburg, Fredericksburg, Brandy Station, Gettysburg, and Petersburg and in the Appomattox Courthouse operations [NPS].

PLATT, FRANCIS (UNION ARMY)   *Baptized before the war.*

Rank: Saddler	**Unit(s):** Lot Smith Utah Cavalry **Military Service Source(s):** ACWS, NPS, PI, Fisher, 1862 MOR
Birth Date: 14 March 1824	**Birth Place:** Walsall, Staffordshire, England
LDS Membership Date: 20 March 1850	**LDS Membership Source(s):** NFS (ID #: KWJZ-8CV)
Death Date: 14 December 1885	**Death Place:** Salt Lake City, Salt Lake, Utah **Find A Grave:** 19357627 **Burial Location:** Salt Lake City Cemetery, Salt Lake City, Salt Lake, Utah
Notes: A saddler made gear for horses—saddles, harnesses, bridles, and so on.	

POLMANTER, LEWIS L. (UNION ARMY)   *Baptized before the war.*

Rank: Private	**Unit(s):** Lot Smith Utah Cavalry **Military Service Source(s):** ACWS, NPS, PI, FGC, Fisher, 1862 MOR
Birth Date: 30 July 1837	**Birth Place:** Prattsburg, Steuben, New York
LDS Membership Date: 1 March 1860	**LDS Membership Source(s):** NFS (ID #: KNH3-ZHB)
Death Date: 29 July 1929	**Death Place:** Omak, Okanogan, Washington **Find A Grave:** 39279678 **Burial Location:** Riverside Cemetery, Riverside, Okanogan, Washington
Notes: [MLM] His last name is spelled "Polmantur" on [1862 MOR].	

PRIBBLE, JOHN T. (UNION ARMY)   *Baptized after the war.*

Rank: Private	**Unit(s):** Company E, 7th Regiment, Kentucky Cavalry **Military Service Source(s):** NPS, PI, Obituary
Birth Date: 1 December 1843	**Birth Place:** Falmouth, Kentucky
LDS Membership Date: 7 August 1896	**LDS Membership Source(s):** NFS (ID #: KWJV-GKQ)
Death Date: 13 January 1926	**Death Place:** Brigham City, Box Elder, Utah **Find A Grave:** 14012435 **Burial Location:** Brigham City Cemetery, Brigham City, Box Elder, Utah
Notes: His obituary, entitled "Veteran of the Civil War Called," notes that "he was a veteran of the Civil war and a member of the G.A.R. He was also a devoted member of the Mormon church, and had been active in church work for many years" (*Box Elder News*, January 15, 1926, 1).	

PRICE, ELIAS (UNION ARMY)   *Baptized after the war.*

Rank: First Sergeant	**Unit(s):** Company K, 4th Battery, Indiana Light Artillery, 151st Regiment, Indiana Infantry **Military Service Source(s):** NPS, PI, FGC
Birth Date: 3 March 1844	**Birth Place:** Schwabisch, Bavaria
LDS Membership Date: 1 April 1867	**LDS Membership Source(s):** NFS (ID #: KWZ6-XXT)
Death Date: 17 February 1937	**Death Place:** Salt Lake City, Salt Lake, Utah **Find A Grave:** 159221 **Burial Location:** Mount Olivet Cemetery, Salt Lake City, Salt Lake, Utah
Notes: "1 SGT CO. K 1ST IND. INF." (First Sergeant, Company K, 1st Indiana Infantry) is carved on his grave marker [FRC].	

PRICE, MARTIN GOODGE   (CONFEDERATE ARMY)   *Baptized after the war.*

Rank: Private	**Unit(s):** Company I, 56th Regiment, North Carolina Infantry **Military Service Source(s):** NPS
Birth Date: 30 December 1838	**Birth Place:** Rutherford County, North Carolina
LDS Membership Date: 21 May 1886	**LDS Membership Source(s):** NFS (ID #: KWJC-JT5)
Death Date: 17 February 1926	**Death Place:** Morgan-La Jara, Conejos, Colorado **Find A Grave:** 23619929 **Burial Location:** Sanford, Conejos, Colorado
Notes: [MLM] The 56th Regiment, North Carolina Infantry, was organized by July 1862 and served primarily in Virginia [NPS].	

PRINCE, FRANCIS   (UNION ARMY)   *Baptized before the war.*

Rank: Private	**Unit(s):** Lot Smith Utah Cavalry **Military Service Source(s):** ACWS, NPS, PI, Fisher, 1862 MOR
Birth Date: 31 July 1840	**Birth Place:** Sterford, Burwell, Cambridge, England
LDS Membership Date: 1 January 1854 (confirmation)	**LDS Membership Source(s):** NFS (ID #: K2M3-XRJ)
Death Date: 12 August 1929	**Death Place:** New Harmony, Washington, Utah **Find A Grave:** 53427 **Burial Location:** New Harmony Cemetery, New Harmony, Washington, Utah
Notes: [MLM]	

PRINCE, RICHARD   (CONFEDERATE ARMY)   *Baptized before the war.*

Rank: Private	**Unit(s):** 36th Regiment, Georgia Infantry **Military Service Source(s):** VBU, NPS
Birth Date: 26 May 1846	**Birth Place:** Green Point, Humbolt, California
LDS Membership Date: 1 March 1854	**LDS Membership Source(s):** NFS (ID #: KWZ6-35L)
Death Date: 15 August 1927	**Death Place:** Middleton, Washington, Utah **Find A Grave:** 52886 **Burial Location:** Washington City Cemetery, Washington, Washington, Utah
Notes: [MLM] [NFS] lists numerous alternate birth locations. There may be an error in either his birth date or baptism date (as he was not eight years old on the listed date of his baptism). The Richard Prince listed in [VBU] served during the Utah Black Hawk War.	

PUCELL, WILLIAM   (UNION ARMY)   *Baptized before the war.*

Rank: Private	**Unit(s):** Company B, 7th Regiment, Massachusetts Infantry **Military Service Source(s):** NPS, PI
Birth Date: 31 May 1828	**Birth Place:** Winwick, Lancashire, England
LDS Membership Date: 15 November 1850	**LDS Membership Source(s):** NFS (ID #: KWJW-MQ1)

Pucell, William (continued)	
Death Date: 31 January 1912	**Death Place:** Providence, Providence, Rhode Island **Find A Grave:** 43817000 **Burial Location:** Cedar City Cemetery, Cedar City, Iron, Utah
Notes: [MLM] [NPS] also lists a William Pucell who served in Company E, 37th Regiment, Massachusetts Infantry. (There were numerous soldiers named William Purcell who served during the Civil War.)	

QUICK, JACOB SIEGLER (UNION ARMY) *Baptized after the war.*

Rank: Private	**Unit(s):** Company K, 9th Regiment, Iowa Infantry **Military Service Source(s):** NPS
Birth Date: 29 November 1846	**Birth Place:** Logansport, Cass, Indiana
LDS Membership Date: 2 July 1910	**LDS Membership Source(s):** NFS (ID #: KJW8-6PT)
Death Date: 9 September 1921	**Death Place:** Salt Lake City, Salt Lake, Utah **Find A Grave:** 65994846 **Burial Location:** Salt Lake City Cemetery, Salt Lake City, Salt Lake, Utah
Notes: The 9th Regiment, Iowa Infantry, was mustered in September 24, 1861, and served from Arkansas to North Carolina. The unit saw action in several battles, including Pea Ridge, Jackson, Vicksburg, Chattanooga, and Atlanta [NPS].	

RAINBOLT, DAVID (CONFEDERATE ARMY) *Baptized after the war.*

Rank: Private	**Unit(s):** Company G, 23rd Regiment, Tennessee Infantry (Martin's Regiment) **Military Service Source(s):** NPS
Birth Date: 23 June 1837	**Birth Place:** White Oak, McNairy, Tennessee
LDS Membership Date: 22 November 1881	**LDS Membership Source(s):** NFS (ID #: KWJD-FF1)
Death Date: 24 December 1912	**Death Place:** La Jara, Conejos, Colorado **Find A Grave:** 23621136 **Burial Location:** Sanford, Conejos, Colorado
Notes: "CO G 23 TENN. INF. C.S.A." (Company G, 23rd Tennessee Infantry, Confederate States of America) is carved on his grave marker [FGC].	

RAMSEY, GEORGE W. (UNION ARMY) *Baptized after the war.*

Rank: Musician (Fifer)	**Unit(s):** Company I, 130th Regiment, Illinois Infantry **Military Service Source(s):** NPS, PI, Obituary
Birth Date: 12 September 1837	**Birth Place:** Lawrence County, Illinois
LDS Membership Date: 2 November 1884	**LDS Membership Source(s):** NFS (ID #: KWJZ-2XH)
Death Date: 2 February 1908	**Death Place:** Payson, Utah, Utah **Find A Grave:** 31855543 **Burial Location:** Payson City Cemetery, Payson, Utah, Utah
Notes: His obituary, subtitled "Veteran Soldier and Musician Dies From Heart Trouble," noted that "from August 1862, to the end of the Civil war, he served in the Union army, a member of company I, One Hundred and thirtieth Illinois, being a fifer in that organization. He took part in no less than 40 engagements, and became partially deaf as a result of the service he passed through. Mr. Ramsey was a member of the Provo G.A.R." (*Deseret News*, February 3, 1908, 1).	

RAWLINS, JOSEPH SHARP (UNION ARMY) *Baptized before the war.*

Rank: First Lieutenant	**Unit(s):** Lot Smith Utah Cavalry **Military Service Source(s):** VBU, NPS, Fisher, 1862 MOR
Birth Date: 9 April 1823	**Birth Place:** Carlton, Green, Illinois
LDS Membership Date: 4 June 1844	**LDS Membership Source(s):** LDSBE, PPMU, NFS (ID #: KWJ6-QWT)
Death Date: 13 October 1900	**Death Place:** South Cottonwood, Salt Lake, Utah **Find A Grave:** 130379 **Burial Location:** Murray City Cemetery, Murray, Salt Lake, Utah

Notes: "He came to Utah in 1848, and was ordained a High Priest and Bishop June 6, 1872" [LDSBE, 4:445]. He led a pioneer company to Utah that arrived October 1, 1866 [PPMU, 1099]. He was "Bishop South Cottonwood Ward [Salt Lake City, Utah]. Railroad and Canal Constructor. Crossed Plains seven times" [PPMU, 160]. His last name is spelled "Rawlings" on [1862 MOR]. For additional information, see the Stuart-Alford chapter herein.

REDMAN, THOMAS JEFFERSON (UNION ARMY) *Baptized after the war.*

Rank: Private	**Unit(s):** Company B, 5th Regiment, Iowa Cavalry **Military Service Source(s):** 1890 Census, NPS
Birth Date: 4 October 1842	**Birth Place:** Neetsville, Kentucky
LDS Membership Date: 16 February 1882	**LDS Membership Source(s):** NFS (ID #: KWZR-VZW)
Death Date: 5 February 1931	**Death Place:** Yakima, Washington **Find A Grave:** — **Burial Location:** Seattle, King, Washington

Notes: He served in the military three years and eleven months beginning September 12, 1861 [1890 Census]. He was captured at Falling Waters, Maryland, on July 14, 1863, and was a member of a prisoner exchange on March 3, 1864. He deserted on May 25, 1864 (*Deseret News*, August 3, 1906).

REED, JOHN LEVERT (CONFEDERATE ARMY) *Baptized after the war.*

Rank: Private	**Unit(s):** Company D, 13th Regiment, Tennessee Infantry **Military Service Source(s):** NPS, 1900 Census
Birth Date: 20 February 1839	**Birth Place:** Lexington, Henderson, Tennessee
LDS Membership Date: 27 May 1880	**LDS Membership Source(s):** NFS (ID #: KW8W-4TQ)
Death Date: 13 October 1916	**Death Place:** Sanford, Conejos, Colorado **Find A Grave:** 23636954 **Burial Location:** Sanford, Conejos, Colorado

Notes: [MLM] [NPS] also lists another John L. Reed—a Confederate soldier who served in Company F, 27th Tennessee Infantry.

REID, MARQUIS LAFAYETTE (CONFEDERATE ARMY) *Baptized after the war.*

Rank: Private	**Unit(s):** Company K, 8th Regiment, Georgia Infantry **Military Service Source(s):** VBU, NPS
Birth Date: 1 December 1829	**Birth Place:** Oglethorpe, Macon, Georgia
LDS Membership Date: 10 February 1877	**LDS Membership Source(s):** NFS (ID #: KWJC-MWS)

Reid, Marquis Lafayette (continued)	
Death Date: 18 May 1907	**Death Place:** Clinton, Davis, Utah **Find A Grave:** 34164 **Burial Location:** Clinton City Cemetery, Clinton, Davis, Utah
Notes: There were actually three units designated as the "8th Georgia Infantry": (1) 8th Battalion, Georgia Infantry; (2) 8th Regiment, Georgia Infantry; and (3) 8th Regiment, Georgia Infantry (State Guards) [NPS].	

REX, WILLIAM (UNION ARMY) *Baptized before the war.*

Rank: Private	**Unit(s):** Company B, 145th Regiment, Illinois Infantry **Military Service Source(s):** NPS, PI, 1890 Census
Birth Date: 22 November 1844	**Birth Place:** Liverpool, Lancashire, England
LDS Membership Date: 1 January 1854	**LDS Membership Source(s):** NFS (ID #: KWZL-7BY)
Death Date: 6 April 1927	**Death Place:** Randolph, Rich, Utah **Find A Grave:** — **Burial Location:** Randolph, Rich, Utah
Notes: He served four months and two days beginning May 21, 1864 [1890 Census]. For additional information, see the Freeman chapter herein.	

REYNOLDS, PRESTON (CONFEDERATE ARMY) *Baptized after the war.*

Rank: Private	**Unit(s):** Company I, 28th Regiment, Virginia Infantry **Military Service Source(s):** NPS, MCL
Birth Date: 23 November 1842	**Birth Place:** Salem, Roanoke, Virginia
LDS Membership Date: 23 January 1888	**LDS Membership Source(s):** NFS (ID #: KWNW-BS9)
Death Date: 15 June 1908	**Death Place:** Manassa, Conejos, Colorado **Find A Grave:** 39766300 **Burial Location:** Manassa, Conejos, Colorado
Notes: [MLM] [NPS] also lists a Preston Reynolds as having served in the 157th Regiment, Virginia Militia.	

RHODES, WILLIAM H. (UNION ARMY) *Baptized before the war.*

Rank: Private	**Unit(s):** Lot Smith Utah Cavalry **Military Service Source(s):** VBU, ACWS, NPS, FGC, Fisher, 1862 MOR
Birth Date: 17 July 1842	**Birth Place:** Thornley, Lancashire, England
LDS Membership Date: 1 January 1857 (confirmation)	**LDS Membership Source(s):** LDSBE, NFS (ID #: KWJZ-TB2)
Death Date: 3 September 1915	**Death Place:** Salt Lake City, Salt Lake, Utah **Find A Grave:** 66261771 **Burial Location:** Salt Lake City Cemetery, Salt Lake City, Salt Lake, Utah
Notes: He "came to Utah with his father in 1848, crossing the plains in Pres. Brigham Young's company. . . . In 1862 he served under Capt. Lot Smith on the plains, protecting the mail route against the Indians. In 1866 he was called to Sanpete to participate in the Black Hawk war, to protect settlers against the Indians. In fact, he fought the Indians from the beginning and in 1858 at the time of the great move south he stood guard in Salt Lake City; he also hauled provisions to the boys in the canyons during the winter of 1857–1858 [during the Utah War]. He was ordained a Deacon at an early day and became a member of the 61st quorum of Seventy in 1861" [LDSBE, 2:699]. [LDSBE] and [VBU] list his birth date as July 17, 1842; [NFS] lists July 17, 1841. [LDSBE] lists his death date as September 3, 1915; [NFS] lists September 3, 1914. His last name is spelled "Roades" on [1862 MOR].	

RICE, ADELBERT   (UNION ARMY)   *Baptized before the war (presumed).*

Rank: Private	**Unit(s):** Lot Smith Utah Cavalry **Military Service Source(s):** ACWS, Fisher, 1862 MOR
Birth Date: 1839	**Birth Place:** Ypsilanti, Washtenaw, Michigan
LDS Membership Date: Uncertain	**LDS Membership Source(s):** NFS (ID #: KPHM-K3R)
Death Date: 17 November 1879	**Death Place:** Logan, Cache, Utah **Find A Grave:** — **Burial Location:** Uncertain
Notes: [MLM] As a member of the Lot Smith Cavalry Company, he is presumed to be a Latter-day Saint (but his baptismal date or LDS membership could not be confirmed from available sources).	

RICH, LANDON   (UNION ARMY)   *Baptized before the war.*

Rank: Private	**Unit(s):** Lot Smith Utah Cavalry **Military Service Source(s):** ACWS, NPS, Fisher, 1862 MOR
Birth Date: 20 December 1840	**Birth Place:** Fullerton County, Illinois
LDS Membership Date: 17 June 1850	**LDS Membership Source(s):** SEB (ID #: KWJ8-KWQ)
Death Date: 4 May 1908	**Death Place:** Grace, Caribou, Idaho **Find A Grave:** 11761807 **Burial Location:** Grace Cemetery, Grace, Caribou, Idaho
Notes: [MLM]	

RICHARDSON, THOMAS J.   (UNION ARMY)   *Baptized before the war.*

Rank: Private	**Unit(s):** Company K, 54th Regiment, Ohio Infantry **Military Service Source(s):** 1890 Census, NPS
Birth Date: 23 January 1825	**Birth Place:** Plumbley, Cheshire, England
LDS Membership Date: 1 September 1844 (confirmation)	**LDS Membership Source(s):** NFS (ID #: KWJ6-FKF)
Death Date: 25 February 1890	**Death Place:** Smithfield, Cache, Utah **Find A Grave:** 179604 **Burial Location:** Smithfield, Cache, Utah
Notes: [MLM] He served in the military three years beginning in 1862. If the correct LDS member is identified, the 1890 veteran census schedule (recorded in Utah County, Utah) should list his entry as a widow report, as his death date was prior to 1890, but it does not [1890 Census].	

RITER, SAMUEL H. W.   (UNION ARMY)   *Baptized before the war.*

Rank: Sergeant	**Unit(s):** Lot Smith Utah Cavalry **Military Service Source(s):** ACWS, NPS, Fisher, 1862 MOR
Birth Date: 19 September 1835	**Birth Place:** Chester County, Pennsylvania
LDS Membership Date: 1 June 1846	**LDS Membership Source(s):** NFS (ID #: KW83-9F6)
Death Date: 7 February 1908	**Death Place:** Logan, Cache, Utah **Find A Grave:** — **Burial Location:** Logan, Cache, Utah
Notes: [MLM]	

ROBBINS, WILLIAM M. (UNION ARMY)   *Baptized after the war.*

Rank: Private	Unit(s): Companies K and D, 49th Regiment, New York Infantry Military Service Source(s): NPS, PI, Obituary
Birth Date: 14 July 1848	Birth Place: Montreal, Quebec, Canada
LDS Membership Date: 14 August 1876	LDS Membership Source(s): NFS (ID #: KWN5-7KQ)
Death Date: 29 May 1933	Death Place: Snowville, Box Elder, Utah Find A Grave: 39495111 Burial Location: Snowville Cemetery, Snowville, Box Elder, Utah

Notes: His obituary states that he was a "civil war veteran. . . . A native of Canada, Mr. Robbins came to this country when only a few months old, his parents settling in New York state. As a boy of 14 Mr. Robbins joined a New York infantry regiment at the outbreak of the civil war and served throughout the struggle. In 1870 Mr. Robbins came to Utah" (*Salt Lake Telegram*, May 30, 1933, 14). There are several William Robbinses (no middle name) listed in [NPS] who served in New York units—only one, though, served in an infantry unit. The others served in artillery and cavalry units.

ROBERSON, JOHN NEWTON   (CONFEDERATE ARMY)   *Baptized after the war.*

Rank: Private	Unit(s): Company C, 56th Regiment, Georgia Infantry Military Service Source(s): NPS
Birth Date: 17 February 1843	Birth Place: Decatur, DeKalb, Georgia
LDS Membership Date: 19 September 1878	LDS Membership Source(s): NFS (ID #: KWJH-RMZ)
Death Date: 26 July 1915	Death Place: Not Available Find A Grave: — Burial Location: Manassa, Conejos, Colorado

Notes: [MLM] The 56th Regiment, Georgia Infantry (which is sometimes also called the 55th Regiment), was organized in the spring of 1862 and was captured at Vicksburg on July 4, 1863, but was later exchanged [NPS].

ROBERTS, ALBERT F.   (UNION ARMY)   *Baptized before the war.*

Rank: Private	Unit(s): 1st Volunteers, 67th Regiment, Illinois Infantry Military Service Source(s): 1890 Census, NPS
Birth Date: 27 June 1847	Birth Place: Garden Grove, Decatur, Iowa
LDS Membership Date: 18 August 1855	LDS Membership Source(s): NFS (ID #: KWJZ-83P)
Death Date: 7 March 1919	Death Place: Provo, Utah, Utah Find A Grave: — Burial Location: Provo, Utah, Utah

Notes: [MLM] He served in the military eight months and two days beginning June 5, 1863 [1890 Census].

ROGERS, ENOCH MILTON   (CONFEDERATE ARMY)   *Baptized after the war.*

Rank: Private	Unit(s): Company G, 38th Regiment, North Carolina Infantry Military Service Source(s): NPS, CSC, 1900 Census
Birth Date: 23 October 1846	Birth Place: Taylorsville, Alexander, North Carolina
LDS Membership Date: 22 May 1887	LDS Membership Source(s): NFS (ID #: KWZ7-CRF)
Death Date: 7 November 1927	Death Place: Manassa, Conejos, Colorado Find A Grave: 34696108 Burial Location: Manassa, Conejos, Colorado

Notes: [MLM] The 38th Regiment, North Carolina Infantry, was organized in January 1862. "It fought in many conflicts from the Seven Days' Battles to Cold Harbor, then took its place in the Petersburg trenches and saw action in the Appomattox Campaign." It also fought at Second Bull Run, Fredericksburg, Chancellorsville, and Gettysburg [NPS].

ROSE, ALLEY STEPHEN (UNION ARMY)   *Baptized before the war.*

Rank: Private	**Unit(s):** Lot Smith Utah Cavalry **Military Service Source(s):** ACWS, NPS, Fisher, 1862 MOR
Birth Date: 6 March 1841	**Birth Place:** Carthage, Athens, Ohio
LDS Membership Date: 1 December 1850	**LDS Membership Source(s):** PPMU, NFS (ID #: KWJ6-74Z)
Death Date: 5 June 1914	**Death Place:** Ogden, Weber, Utah **Find A Grave:** 137997 **Burial Location:** Farmington City Cemetery, Farmington, Davis, Utah

Notes: "President 56th quorum seventies 34 years; Sunday school superintendent 36 years; missionary to New York 1876; high priest 1905; president Y.M.M.I.A. 4 years. County commissioner 3 years" [PPMU, 1141]. His first name is listed as "Akkey" on [1862 MOR], which appears to be a typing error.

ROSE, WILLIAM WARREN (UNION ARMY)   *Baptized after the war.*

Rank: Sergeant	**Unit(s):** Company H, 15th Regiment, Iowa Infantry **Military Service Source(s):** NPS, FGC, Obituary
Birth Date: 6 May 1832	**Birth Place:** Howard, Steuben, New York
LDS Membership Date: 18 August 1879	**LDS Membership Source(s):** NFS (ID #: KWN2-L8W)
Death Date: 29 November 1899	**Death Place:** Farmington, Davis, Utah **Find A Grave:** 105345 **Burial Location:** Farmington City Cemetery, Farmington, Davis, Utah

Notes: "CO. H. 15 IA. INF." (Company H, 15th Iowa Infantry) is carved on his grave marker [FGC]. His obituary states that he "was a veteran of the civil war" (*Deseret News*, November 30, 1899, 2).

ROSS, ISAAC JAMES (UNION ARMY)   *Baptized after the war.*

Rank: Private	**Unit(s):** Company I, 130th Regiment, Illinois Infantry **Military Service Source(s):** NPS, PI, FGC, Obituary
Birth Date: 29 January 1844	**Birth Place:** Noblesville, Hamilton, Indiana
LDS Membership Date: 15 October 1884	**LDS Membership Source(s):** NFS (ID #: KWNP-G53)
Death Date: 28 May 1920	**Death Place:** Provo, Utah, Utah **Find A Grave:** 31856291 **Burial Location:** Payson City Cemetery, Payson, Utah, Utah

Notes: "CIVIL WAR VETERAN CO I 130 REGIMENT ILLINOIS VOL." (Civil War Veteran, Company I, 130th Regiment, Illinois Volunteers) is carved on his grave marker [FGC]. His obituary, entitled "Veteran Ross is Dead," states that he "was a native of Indiana and a veteran of the civil war" (*Salt Lake Herald*, May 20, 1920, 8).

ROZSA, JOHN (UNION ARMY)   *Baptized before the war.*

Rank: First Sergeant	**Unit(s):** Companies D & E, 10th Regiment, U.S. Infantry **Military Service Source(s):** NPS; 1890 Census; PI; *Recollections of Past Days: The Autobiography of Patience Loader Rozsa Archer* (Logan, Utah: Utah State University Press, 2006)
Birth Date: 7 November 1820	**Birth Place:** St. Anna Comital, Arad, Hungary

Rozsa, John (continued)

LDS Membership Date: 3 December 1858	LDS Membership Source(s): NFS (ID #: KWJX-RMK)	
Death Date: 24 May 1866	Death Place: Fort Kearney, Nebraska Burial Location: Nebraska	Find A Grave: 20126555

Notes: He is listed as "John Rosa" on a widow's report from his wife, Patience R. Archer, on the 1890 veteran census schedule. His rank is listed as "1 Sarg" (First Sergeant) in the 10th U.S. Infantry with five years of military service [1890 Census]. For additional information, see the Ellsworth-Alford and Freeman chapters herein.

SADDLER, SAMUEL   (UNION ARMY)   *Baptized before the war (presumed).*

Rank: Private	Unit(s): Company E, 89th Regiment, Illinois Infantry Military Service Source(s): 1890 Census, Obituary	
Birth Date: 22 August 1835	Birth Place: Carthage, Hancock, Illinois	
LDS Membership Date: "Completed"	LDS Membership Source(s): NFS (ID #: KPCH-84D)	
Death Date: 11 February 1903	Death Place: Salt Lake City, Salt Lake, Utah Burial Location: Salt Lake City, Salt Lake, Utah	Find A Grave: 35519472

Notes: The listed birth, baptism, and death dates match Samuel Smee Sadler [KWJW-TX7]. This Civil War veteran may also be Samuel Saddler (1835–1903, NFS ID #: KPCH-84D) [NFS]. Samuel served two years and eleven months beginning on August 7, 1862. "Shot in left hand" is listed as a disability incurred during his military service. His unit affiliation is listed as 19th Illinois Infantry on the [1890 Census]; his obituary lists the 89th Illinois Infantry. [NPS] lists a Samuel Saddler as having served in both the 19th and 89th Illinois Infantry. The match of his Church and veteran records has been confirmed, but his LDS confirmation is listed as "Completed," which leaves his baptism date indeterminate [NFS]. His obituary states that he "was a veteran of the late civil war" (*Deseret News*, February 12, 1903, 8).

SARGENT, WILLIAM PINKNEY (GALVANIZED YANKEE)   *Baptized after the war.*

Rank: Private	Unit(s): Confederate service: Company B, 43rd (or 45th) Regiment, Georgia Infantry; Union service: Company D, 6th U.S. Infantry Regiment Military Service Source(s): NPS	
Birth Date: 11 November 1845	Birth Place: Canton, Cherokee, Georgia	
LDS Membership Date: 13 September 1866	LDS Membership Source(s): NFS (ID #: KW86-9WH)	
Death Date: 6 December 1907	Death Place: Panguitch, Garfield, Utah Burial Location: Panguitch, Garfield, Utah	Find A Grave: 26007411

Notes: "Served in the 43rd Inf. Reg. Co. B along with several of his brothers during the Civil War. He was captured by the General W.T. Sherman's Yankee forces on Sept. 13, 1864 in Cherokee Co., and imprisoned in the military prison in Louisville, KY. He enrolled in the U.S. Army (Co. D, 6th Infantry Reg.) on March 23, 1865, at Camp Douglas, Illinois, and was sent to Fort Bridger, Utah Territory, where he deserted July 20, 1866. He was aged 19 at the time of his enrollment. . . . William P. Sargent joined the LDS Church and traveled west to Utah after the Civil War, where he married Mariah Lovina Snow and her sister, Julia Maria Snow. He eventually settled in Panguitch where he died in 1907" (http://freepages.genealogy.rootsweb.ancestry.com/~meyer465/pafn26.htm). He served as a member of the Territorial Legislative Assembly Council for Garfield County, Utah, in 1890 and was a Democrat in the Utah Territorial House of Representatives in 1891 (*Ogden Standard*, January 14, 1890, 1). [NPS] lists "William P. Sargent" as having served in Company B, 45th Regiment, Georgia Infantry.

SATTERTHWAITE, JOSHUA WARD   (UNION ARMY)   *Baptized after the war.*

Rank: Private	**Unit(s):** Company H, 79th Regiment, Ohio Infantry **Military Service Source(s):** VBU, NPS, PI
Birth Date: 14 August 1837	**Birth Place:** Waynesville, Warren, Ohio
LDS Membership Date: 27 April 1882	**LDS Membership Source(s):** NFS (ID #: KW68-YZQ)
Death Date: 19 June 1919	**Death Place:** Laketown, Rich, Utah **Find A Grave:** 60995707 **Burial Location:** Laketown Cemetery, Laketown, Rich, Utah
Notes: The 79th Regiment, Ohio Infantry, was organized in August 1862 and served as part of the Army of the Cumberland (from Kentucky to Georgia) [NPS].	

SAXEY, ALFRED   (UNION ARMY)   *Baptized after the war.*

Rank: Sergeant	**Unit(s):** Company F, 10th Regiment, Kansas Infantry **Military Service Source(s):** NPS, PI
Birth Date: 28 February 1840	**Birth Place:** London, London, England
LDS Membership Date: 1 July 1883	**LDS Membership Source(s):** NFS (ID #: KWNK-XVT)
Death Date: 26 March 1913	**Death Place:** Spanish Fork, Utah, Utah **Find A Grave:** 74265679 **Burial Location:** Provo City Cemetery, Provo, Utah, Utah
Notes: [FGC] includes a photo of him in his Grand Army of the Republic uniform.	

SCHREPEL, JOHN FREDERICK   (UNION ARMY)   *Baptized after the war.*

Rank: Sergeant	**Unit(s):** Battery F, 2nd Regiment, Missouri Light Artillery **Military Service Source(s):** NPS, PI
Birth Date: 22 December 1840	**Birth Place:** Cincinnati, Hamilton, Ohio
LDS Membership Date: 1 January 1872	**LDS Membership Source(s):** NFS (ID #: KWJD-85N)
Death Date: 12 December 1914	**Death Place:** Salt Lake City, Salt Lake, Utah **Find A Grave:** — **Burial Location:** Salt Lake City, Salt Lake, Utah
Notes: The Battery F, 2nd Regiment, Missouri Light Artillery, was organized at St. Louis in January 1862 and served in Missouri and Tennessee as well as from Texas to Georgia [NPS].	

SCOTT, ROBERT GRIFFIN   (UNION ARMY)   *Baptized before the war.*

Rank: Private	**Unit(s):** Company G, 4th Regiment, Missouri Infantry **Military Service Source(s):** NPS, VBU, FGC
Birth Date: 17 November 1825	**Birth Place:** Crystal Springs, Copiah, Mississippi
LDS Membership Date: 6 October 1856	**LDS Membership Source(s):** NFS (ID #: KWVC-D64)
Death Date: 28 August 1877	**Death Place:** Ogden, Weber, Utah **Find A Grave:** 83568191 **Burial Location:** Ben Lomond Cemetery, Ogden, Weber, Utah
Notes: "PVT CO G 4 MO INFANTRY CIVIL WAR" (Private, Company G, 4th Missouri Infantry) is carved on his grave marker [FGC].	

SEAMAN, JOHN WHITEHEAD   (UNION NAVY)   *Baptized after the war.*

Rank: Uncertain	**Unit(s):** Uncertain **Military Service Source(s):** VBU, Obituary
Birth Date: 1 September 1842	**Birth Place:** Bollaston, Saratoga, New York
LDS Membership Date: 11 August 1868	**LDS Membership Source(s):** NFS (ID #: K2HD-PFB)
Death Date: 19 February 1930	**Death Place:** Cedar City, Iron, Utah **Find A Grave:** 40038759 **Burial Location:** Cedar City Cemetery, Cedar City, Iron, Utah

Notes: "G.A.R." (Grand Army of the Republic) is carved on his grave marker [FGC]. His obituary, which was entitled "Death Takes Respected Veteran," stated that he was "a noted civil war veteran. He joined the Union navy at the opening of the civil war, at the age of 18 and [served] through the entire struggle with honor." It also claimed that "he was quiet [*sic*] well acquainted with Pres. Lincoln and had the honor of voting for him for president of the United States" (*Iron County Record*, February 19, 1930, 1).

SEGUINE, JOSEPH S.   (UNION ARMY)   *Baptized after the war.*

Rank: Private	**Unit(s):** Company H, 15th Regiment, New Jersey Infantry **Military Service Source(s):** VBU, NPS, PI
Birth Date: 23 August 1847	**Birth Place:** Mansfield Township, Warren, New Jersey
LDS Membership Date: 22 October 1914	**LDS Membership Source(s):** NFS (ID #: K2M4-V5S)
Death Date: 23 January 1917	**Death Place:** Fillmore, Millard, Utah **Find A Grave:** 52311472 **Burial Location:** Fillmore, Millard, Utah

Notes: The 15th Regiment, New Jersey Infantry, mustered in August 25, 1862, and participated in numerous battles— including Fredericksburg, Chancellorsville, Gettysburg, the Wilderness, Spotsylvania, Cold Harbor, and Petersburg—and was present at Lee's surrender on April 9, 1865, at Appomattox Court House [NPS].

SELLERS, DANIEL RICE   (CONFEDERATE ARMY)   *Baptized after the war.*

Rank: Private	**Unit(s):** Company B, 49th Regiment, Alabama Infantry **Military Service Source(s):** NPS, MCL
Birth Date: 31 January 1832	**Birth Place:** Madison County, Alabama
LDS Membership Date: 11 January 1877	**LDS Membership Source(s):** NFS (ID #: KWJD-HV6)
Death Date: 29 December 1913	**Death Place:** Manassa, Conejos, Colorado **Find A Grave:** 39956720 **Burial Location:** Manassa, Conejos, Colorado

Notes: [MLM] The 49th Regiment, Alabama Infantry, was organized at Nashville in February 1862. "It took an active part in the conflicts at Shiloh, Vicksburg, Baton Rouge, and Corinth" [NPS].

SELLERS, SAMUEL SURRATT   (CONFEDERATE ARMY)   *Baptized after the war.*

Rank: Captain	**Unit(s):** Company A, 13th Regiment, Alabama Infantry **Military Service Source(s):** SLV, NPS
Birth Date: 3 June 1845	**Birth Place:** Jackson County, Alabama
LDS Membership Date: 11 January 1877	**LDS Membership Source(s):** NFS (ID #: KWNK-1YM)
Death Date: 7 February 1916	**Death Place:** Chandler, Maricopa, Arizona **Find A Grave:** 53679252 **Burial Location:** Mesa, Maricopa, Arizona

Notes: "He served in Company A, 13th Alabama Infantry of the Confederate States Army. The company was almost completely decimated by the end of 1864. The few men remaining were assimilated into other units, and a few were ultimately present at Appomattox in April 1865" [FGC]. The birth and death years differ slightly between the grave marker and [NFS].

SHARP, GEORGE W. (UNION ARMY) *Baptized before the war.*

Rank: Private	**Unit(s):** Company A, 255th Regiment, Pennsylvania Infantry **Military Service Source(s):** 1890 Census, NPS
Birth Date: 22 July 1836	**Birth Place:** Northampton, Northampton, England
LDS Membership Date: 16 October 1852	**LDS Membership Source(s):** NFS (ID #: KWNK-2PH)
Death Date: 26 March 1923	**Death Place:** East Midvale, Salt Lake, Utah **Find A Grave:** — **Burial Location:** Salt Lake City, Salt Lake, Utah

Notes: [MLM] He served in the military two years, ten months, and five days beginning August 21, 1862. "Gunshot wound in head" is listed as a service-related disability [1890 Census].

SHARP, JAMES (UNION ARMY) *Baptized before the war.*

Rank: Private	**Unit(s):** Lot Smith Utah Cavalry **Military Service Source(s):** VBU, NPS, Fisher, 1862 MOR
Birth Date: 18 November 1843	**Birth Place:** Falkirk, Stirling, Scotland
LDS Membership Date: 1 March 1857	**LDS Membership Source(s):** NFS (ID #: KWJZ-P24)
Death Date: 7 March 1903	**Death Place:** Salt Lake City, Salt Lake, Utah **Find A Grave:** 15788541 **Burial Location:** Salt Lake City Cemetery, Salt Lake City, Salt Lake, Utah

Notes: "Member House Representatives. Mayor Salt Lake City. Regent U. of U. [University of Utah]" [PPMU, 242].

SHINER, GEORGE WILLIAM (UNION ARMY) *Baptized after the war.*

Rank: Private	**Unit(s):** Company G, 14th Regiment, Iowa Infantry **Military Service Source(s):** VBU, NPS, PI, FGC
Birth Date: 11 February 1835	**Birth Place:** Winchester, Frederick, Virginia
LDS Membership Date: 6 April 1876	**LDS Membership Source(s):** NFS (ID #: KWNJ-7XG)
Death Date: 1 October 1918	**Death Place:** Castle Dale, Emery, Utah **Find A Grave:** 47210078 **Burial Location:** Castle Dale, Emery, Utah

Notes: "CO. G. 14 IA. INF." (Company G, 14th Iowa Infantry) is carved on his grave marker. He was enlisted on January 1, 1864, and discharged on August 8, 1865 [FGC]. [NFS] lists October 2, 1918, as his date of death; his grave marker lists October 1, 1918.

SHORT, TEMPLE (UNION ARMY) *Baptized after the war.*

Rank: Private	**Unit(s):** Company C or E, 58th Regiment, Pennsylvania Infantry **Military Service Source(s):** 1890 Census, NPS
Birth Date: 25 July 1841	**Birth Place:** Tioga, Philadelphia, Pennsylvania
LDS Membership Date: 6 August 1887	**LDS Membership Source(s):** NFS (ID #: KWJW-3RF)

Short, Temple (continued)	
Death Date: 29 November 1932	**Death Place:** Ogden, Weber, Utah **Find A Grave:** 76527523 **Burial Location:** North Ogden, Weber, Utah
Notes: He served in the military for three years beginning on October 17, 1861. "Ruptured" is listed as a service-related disability [1890 Census]. [NPS] lists his unit as Company E; [1890 Census] lists Company C.	

SHURTLEFF, EMERSON D.   (UNION ARMY)   *Baptized before the war.*

Rank: Private	**Unit(s):** Lot Smith Utah Cavalry **Military Service Source(s):** VBU, ACWS, NPS, FGC, Fisher, 1862 MOR
Birth Date: 29 July 1839	**Birth Place:** Russell, Hampden, Massachusetts
LDS Membership Date: 1 March 1855	**LDS Membership Source(s):** NFS (ID #: KWVH-CST)
Death Date: 8 August 1868	**Death Place:** Millcreek, Salt Lake, Utah **Find A Grave:** 51396555 **Burial Location:** Salt Lake City Cemetery, Salt Lake City, Salt Lake, Utah
Notes: —	

SIMMON, HARLAN E.   (UNION ARMY)   *Baptized before the war.*

Rank: Private	**Unit(s):** Lot Smith Utah Cavalry **Military Service Source(s):** VBU, NPS, Fisher, 1862 MOR
Birth Date: 28 February 1841	**Birth Place:** Nauvoo, Hancock, Illinois
LDS Membership Date: 12 May 1849	**LDS Membership Source(s):** NFS (ID #: KWZY-FJH)
Death Date: 9 March 1893	**Death Place:** Layton, Davis, Utah **Find A Grave:** 60636485 **Burial Location:** Bountiful Memorial Park, Bountiful, Davis, Utah
Notes: —	

SIMMONS, CHARLES   (CONFEDERATE ARMY)   *Baptized after the war.*

Rank: Private	**Unit(s):** Company D, 30th Regiment, Virginia Infantry **Military Service Source(s):** NPS, FGC
Birth Date: 29 November 1826	**Birth Place:** Vinton, Franklin, Virginia
LDS Membership Date: 1869	**LDS Membership Source(s):** NFS (ID #: KWJC-JWM)
Death Date: 8 July 1901	**Death Place:** Payson, Utah, Utah **Find A Grave:** 13075718 **Burial Location:** Payson City Cemetery, Payson, Utah, Utah
Notes: "PVT CO D 30 REGT VA INF CONFEDERATE STATES ARMY" (Private, Company D, 30th Regiment, Virginia Infantry) is carved on his grave marker [FGC].	

SIZEMORE, WILLIAM MARION   (CONFEDERATE ARMY)   *Baptized after the war.*

Rank: Private	**Unit(s):** Company H, 10th Regiment, Alabama Cavalry **Military Service Source(s):** NPS
Birth Date: 11 August 1836	**Birth Place:** Pikeville, Marion, Alabama
LDS Membership Date: 12 May 1867	**LDS Membership Source(s):** NFS (ID #: KWN5-MV2)

Death Date: 4 November 1903	Death Place: Georgetown, Bear Lake, Idaho Find A Grave: 45046351 Burial Location: Georgetown Cemetery, Georgetown, Bear Lake, Idaho
Notes: [MLM] The 10th Regiment, Alabama Cavalry, "was organized during the winter of 1863–1864. . . . It principally was restricted to outpost duty in the Tennessee Valley and disbanded during the spring of 1865" [NPS].	

SLEATER, ROBERT GIBSON   (UNION ARMY)   *Baptized after the war.*

Rank: First Sergeant	Unit(s): Company H, 6th Regiment, Iowa Infantry Military Service Source(s): NPS, PI, FGC, Obituary
Birth Date: 30 September 1840	Birth Place: Bath, Somerset, England
LDS Membership Date: June 1866	LDS Membership Source(s): NFS (ID #: KWJH-8P3)
Death Date: 26 March 1914	Death Place: Salt Lake City, Salt Lake, Utah Find A Grave: 175716 Burial Location: Mount Olivet Cemetery, Salt Lake City, Salt Lake, Utah
Notes: "1ST SGT CO H 6 IOWA INF CIVIL WAR" (First Sergeant, Company H, Iowa Infantry) is carved on his grave marker [FGC]. His obituary stated that "Mr. Sleator was also prominent as a member of the Grand Army of the Republic, having been among the first to answer President Lincoln's call for volunteers in 1861. He enlisted as a member of company H, sixth Iowa Infantry, when 21 years of age and fought at Vicksburg, Shiloh, Missionary Ridge and twenty-nine other engagements during the entire four years of the civil war. He participated in Sherman's famous march to the sea and was under Grant for several years. He was promoted for bravery at the battle of Shiloh" (*Salt Lake Telegram*, March 6, 1914, 1).	

SMITH, CHARLES WILLIAM EDWARD DILK
(UNION ARMY)   *Baptized after the war.*

Rank: Private	Unit(s): Company H, 148th Regiment, Indiana Infantry Military Service Source(s): 1890 Census, NPS
Birth Date: 9 May 1847	Birth Place: Leicester, Leicester, England
LDS Membership Date: 1 January 1871	LDS Membership Source(s): NFS (ID #: KWJW-2T4)
Death Date: 23 September 1917	Death Place: Salt Lake City, Salt Lake, Utah Find A Grave: 59675241 Burial Location: Salt Lake City, Salt Lake, Utah
Notes: [MLM] He served in the military seven months beginning in February 1865 [1890 Census].	

SMITH, FRANCIS M.   (UNION ARMY)   *Baptized after the war.*

Rank: Private	Unit(s): Company C, 63rd Regiment, Indiana Infantry Military Service Source(s): NPS, PI
Birth Date: 8 January 1839	Birth Place: Alamo, Ripley, Indiana
LDS Membership Date: 1 January 1867	LDS Membership Source(s): NFS (ID #: KWJZ-HR6)
Death Date: 8 February 1899	Death Place: Salem, Utah, Utah Find A Grave: 13218059 Burial Location: Salem City Cemetery, Salem, Utah, Utah
Notes: [MLM] The 63rd Regiment, Indiana Infantry, was organized February 21, 1862. Initially assigned to prison guard duty, the regiment was briefly assigned to defend Washington, DC, and then fought from Kentucky to North Carolina [NFS].	

SMITH, JOHN (UNION ARMY)   *Baptized before the war.*

Rank: Private	**Unit(s):** Company K, 31st Regiment, Indiana Infantry **Military Service Source(s):** 1890 Census, NPS
Birth Date: 25 August 1814	**Birth Place:** Glasgow, Lanark, Scotland
LDS Membership Date: 28 May 1844	**LDS Membership Source(s):** NFS (ID #: LC2J-954)
Death Date: 15 May 1883	**Death Place:** Tooele, Tooele, Utah **Find A Grave:** 99739 **Burial Location:** Tooele, Tooele, Utah
Notes: He served in the military four years and six months beginning September 5, 1861 [1890 Census]. [NPS] lists two soldiers named John Smith who served in the 31st Regiment, Indiana Infantry.	

SMITH, JOSEPH FRANKLIN (UNION ARMY)   *Baptized after the war.*

Rank: Private	**Unit(s):** Companies A and B, 42nd Regiment, Missouri Infantry **Military Service Source(s):** NPS, PI, FGC, Obituary
Birth Date: 26 December 1844	**Birth Place:** Cincinnati, Ohio
LDS Membership Date: 6 February 1876	**LDS Membership Source(s):** NFS (ID #: K2M4-VJJ)
Death Date: 15 June 1932	**Death Place:** Springville, Utah, Utah **Find A Grave:** 85756 **Burial Location:** Springville City Cemetery, Springville, Utah, Utah
Notes: "CO. A. 42 MO. INF." (Company A, 42nd Missouri Infantry) is carved on his grave marker [FGC]. His obituary, entitled "Civil War Veteran Answers Last Call," notes that he was the "last member of the Grand Army of the Republic in this vicinity [Springville, Utah], and also the last charter member of the William T. Sherman post, G.A.R. . . . Mr. Smith enlisted in the civil war at the age of 20 years. He was sent to Tennessee and Alabama with the Forty-second Missouri volunteers' mounted infantry. He took part in skirmishes with Bill Anderson rebel bushwhackers and Quantrill's guerillas. He was honorably discharged at Nashville, Tenn., at the close of the war. Mr. Smith attended the G.A.R. reunion at the battlefield of Gettysburg in 1913 as a representative from this district. He joined the few remaining veterans at the G.A.R. convention in Salt Lake this spring. . . . Mr. Smith was a member of the L.D.S. church and had lived here fifty-four years" (*Salt Lake Telegram*, June 17, 1932, 12).	

SMITH, LOT (UNION ARMY)   *Baptized before the war.*

Rank: Captain	**Unit(s):** Lot Smith Utah Cavalry **Military Service Source(s):** VBU, ACWS, NPS, Fisher, 1862 MOR
Birth Date: 15 May 1830	**Birth Place:** Williamstown, Oswego, New York
LDS Membership Date: 26 January 1851	**LDS Membership Source(s):** LDSBE, NFS (ID #: KWCT-LN6)
Death Date: 21 June 1892	**Death Place:** Tuba City, Coconino, Arizona **Find A Grave:** 23981985 **Burial Location:** Farmington City Cemetery, Farmington, Davis, Utah
Notes: "Lot served his country in the fear of God and with good will to man in the Mormon Battalion. He was, perhaps, the youngest man that bore arms in that military body, being only sixteen years of age. . . . His policy toward the Indians was that of Brigham Young: 'Feed them, not fight them.' . . . His dying words were: 'God bless the wives and children'" [LDSBE, 1:803–6]. "Member of the Deseret Militia; defended settlers at Provo against Indians; major of the Utah militia and in charge at the burning of Johnston's army provision trains on their way to Echo Canyon, Utah" [PPMU, 1169]. He was a pivotal figure during the Utah War (1857–58) and served as the commanding officer of the only active duty military unit to muster and serve	

from Utah Territory during the Civil War. He served as president of the Little Colorado Stake and Sunset United Order in Sunset, Arizona (near present Winslow, Arizona). He was killed by Navajo Indians in Tuba City, Arizona (June 21,1890). He was reinterred in 1902 at Farmington, Utah (http://www.media.utah.edu/UHE/s/SMITH,LOT.html). His name is listed as "Lott Smith" on the [1862 MOR]. For additional information, see the Stuart-Alford chapter herein.

SMITH, LOUIS WILLIAM (UNION ARMY)   *Baptized during the war.*

Rank: Private	Unit(s): Company C or I, 10th Regiment, U.S. Infantry Military Service Source(s): NPS, FGC, Obituary
Birth Date: 30 March 1837	Birth Place: Bennkot, Nassau, Germany
LDS Membership Date: 21 June 1863	LDS Membership Source(s): NFS (ID #: LHP4-BJK)
Death Date: 7 January 1909	Death Place: Salt Lake City, Salt Lake, Utah Find A Grave: 45008423 Burial Location: Kamas Cemetery, Kamas, Summit, Utah

Notes: "CO. C. 10TH U.S. INF." (Company C, 10th U.S. Infantry) is carved on his grave marker [FGC]. His obituary, entitled "War Veteran Dead," noted that he was "a veteran of the civil war and a well known ranch owner" (*Salt Lake Telegram*, January 12, 1909, 5).

SMITH, THOMAS (UNION ARMY)   *Baptized before the war.*

Rank: Captain	Unit(s): Uncertain Military Service Source(s): NPS, Obituary
Birth Date: 10 April 1845	Birth Place: London, Middlesex, England
LDS Membership Date: 27 April 1852	LDS Membership Source(s): NFS (ID #: KWV9-6L4)
Death Date: 9 January 1920	Death Place: Salt Lake City, Salt Lake, Utah Find A Grave: 132953 Burial Location: Midvale City Cemetery, Midvale, Salt Lake, Utah

Notes: [MLM] There may be an error in either his birth date or baptism date (as he was not eight years old on the listed date of his baptism); 10 April 1843 is also listed as a possible birth date on [NFS]. His obituary, entitled "Capt. Thomas Smith," states that he was "a veteran of the civil war and a resident of Salt Lake for fourteen years" (*Salt Lake Herald*, January 10, 1920, 8). There are over 1,500 Union Civil War veterans and over 600 Confederate veterans listed on [NPS] with the name Thomas Smith.

SMITH, WILLIAM B. (UNION ARMY)   *Baptized before the war.*

Rank: Private	Unit(s): Company G, 126th Regiment, Illinois Infantry Military Service Source(s): NPS; Illinois State Archives (Illinois Muster and Descriptive Rolls Database, Record Series 301.020); GAR data (NARA microfilm rolls 1613547 and 1205525)
Birth Date: 13 March 1811	Birth Place: Royalton, Windsor, Vermont
LDS Membership Date: 9 June 1830	LDS Membership Source(s): NFS (ID #: KWJR-TK2)
Death Date: 13 November 1894	Death Place: Osterdock, Clayton, Iowa Find A Grave: — Burial Location: Osterdock, Clayton, Iowa

Smith, William B. (continued)

Notes: William was the sixth child of Joseph Smith Sr. and Lucy Mack Smith and the younger brother of Joseph Smith Jr., founder and first President of The Church of Jesus Christ of Latter-day Saints. Following his 1830 baptism into the LDS Church, William served as both an Apostle and Patriarch of the Church. His apostleship was revoked on October 5, 1845, and he was excommunicated on October 12, 1845. "By May 1846 he was recognized as a Strangite apostle and patriarch" (Susan Easton Black, *Who's Who in the Doctrine and Covenants* [Salt Lake City: Bookcraft, 1997], 300–303). "William Smith, brother of Joseph Smith, Jr., was rebaptized into the LDS Church in 1860 by J.J. Butler. In a letter to Brigham Young, William Smith talked about joining the Saints in Salt Lake. . . . It was not until 9 April 1878 that William Smith was received into fellowship in the RLDS Church. . . . Until his death on 15 November 1893, he was affiliated with that group" (Buddy Youngreen, "Sons of the Martyrs' Nauvoo Reunion—1860," *BYU Studies* 20, no. 4 [Summer 1980: 359n15]). The Illinois Civil War Detail Report database lists the following information regarding his enlistment—residence: Aledo, Clayton County, Iowa; age: 44 (this is clearly in error; whether the clerk recorded it incorrectly or William reported his age incorrectly is unknown); height: 6 feet; hair: dark; eyes: blue; complexion: light; marital status: N/A; occupation: minister; nativity: Royalton, Vermont. The same database reports his military service record information as follows—joined when: February 25, 1864; joined where: Rock Island, Illinois; joined by whom: LTC Birdsell; period (of enlistment): 3 years; muster in: February 25, 1864; muster in where: Springfield, Illinois; muster in by whom: N/A; muster out: July 12, 1865; muster out where: Pine Bluff, Arkansas; muster out by whom: LT Hussey (http://www.cyberdriveillinois.com/departments/archives/datcivil.html). William's pension application is available online at http://www.fold3.com/image/#249|286371. A photograph of his gravesite shows a Grand Army of the Republic veteran marker next to his headstone (http://bycommonconsent.com/2011/02/08/cemetourism-william-b-smith-1811%E2%80%931893). His military service can also be confirmed at the National Archives and Records Administration (NARA), microfilm number M539 roll 84 [NPS].

SNYDER, HENRY T.   (UNION ARMY [PRESUMED])   *Baptized after the war.*

Rank: Uncertain	Unit(s): Uncertain
	Military Service Source(s): Obituary
Birth Date: 2 August 1845	Birth Place: Rogersville, Tuscarawas, Ohio
LDS Membership Date: 18 June 1917	LDS Membership Source(s): NFS (ID #: KWVF-S5G)
Death Date: 12 February 1920	Death Place: Ogden, Davis, Utah Find A Grave: — Burial Location: Uncertain

Notes: His obituary noted that he "was a veteran of the Civil war and took part in the construction of the Union Pacific railroad" (*Salt Lake Telegram*, February 16, 1920, 3). [NPS] lists hundreds of soldiers named Henry Snyder who served in the Union army, and dozens are from Ohio.

SOREN, OLE S.   (UNION ARMY)   *Baptized after the war.*

Rank: Private	Unit(s): Company I, 6th Regiment, Minnesota Infantry
	Military Service Source(s): 1890 Census, NPS
Birth Date: 5 October 1842	Birth Place: Etnedal, Christian, Norway
LDS Membership Date: 3 July 1884	LDS Membership Source(s): NFS (ID #: KW6D-V4Z)
Death Date: 20 February 1902	Death Place: Salem, Utah, Utah Find A Grave: 13217851 Burial Location: Salem, Utah, Utah

Notes: [MLM] He served in the military three years and four days beginning on August 15, 1862 [1890 Census].

SOWARDS, GEORGE WASHINGTON   (UNION ARMY)   *Baptized after the war.*

Rank: Private	**Unit(s):** Company E or H, 39th or 45th Regiment, Kentucky Infantry **Military Service Source(s):** NPS, FGC, 1900 Census
Birth Date: 5 October 1840	**Birth Place:** Pikesville, Pike, Kentucky
LDS Membership Date: 7 June 1879	**LDS Membership Source(s):** NFS (ID #: KWNN-2SD)
Death Date: 14 June 1907	**Death Place:** Manassa, Conejos, Colorado **Find A Grave:** 56861256 **Burial Location:** Manassa, Conejos, Colorado

Notes: "Served in the Civil War on the Union side. Enlisted in Mount Sterling Kentucky and served in Company H, Kentucky 45th Infantry Division [more probably Regiment]" [FGC]. The parents of Jack Dempsey, a world famous prize fighter, stayed in his home [SLV].

SPENCER, HOWARD   (UNION ARMY)   *Baptized before the war.*

Rank: Sergeant	**Unit(s):** Lot Smith Utah Cavalry **Military Service Source(s):** VBU, ACWS, NPS, FGC, Fisher, 1862 MOR
Birth Date: 16 June 1838	**Birth Place:** Middlefield, Berkshire, Massachusetts
LDS Membership Date: 16 June 1846	**LDS Membership Source(s):** NFS (ID #: KWC5-8GR)
Death Date: 4 March 1918	**Death Place:** Orderville, Kane, Utah **Find A Grave:** 5548954 **Burial Location:** Orderville Cemetery, Orderville, Kane, Utah

Notes: "He filled a mission to Europe in 1869–70, and was chosen as first counselor in the Kanab Stake presidency April 18, 1877, being set apart by Orson Pratt" [LDSBE, 4:504]. After a dispute over grazing rights, Spencer was assaulted and had his skull crushed with a rifle butt by First Sergeant Ralph Pike of Camp Floyd's Company I, 10th Infantry, in 1859 at Skull Valley. Spencer recovered and later accosted Pike in Salt Lake City and shot him. Pike died soon after. "Spencer lived in the Fourth LDS Ward in Great Salt Lake City, and in 1862 joined Col. Lot Smith's Utah volunteer battalion to protect the Overland Mail route against Indian depredations. In 1874, Spencer moved to Kanab in southern Utah to live. His was a life of relative obscurity until August 1888 when U.S. Marshals swooped down on Liberty Park in Salt Lake City to round up a number of Mormon men on warrants charging 'unlawful cohabitation,' one of the several legal devices used to nab polygamists. . . . Trial was scheduled for May 6, 1889, before Third District Court Judge J.W. Judd. A 12-member jury, nearly all non-Mormons, was to hear the case. After three days of testimony, the jury brought in a verdict for acquittal. . . . Howard O. Spencer lived to be 80. He died March 4, 1918, after an accidental fall from a bridge in Glendale, Kane County, Utah" ("Is That You, Pike? Feud Between Settlers, Frontier Army Erupts and Simmers for Three Decades," *Salt Lake Tribune*, July 2, 1995; and http://history-togo.utah.gov/salt_lake_tribune/in_another_time/070295.html).

SPRINGER, NATHAN CHATMOND
(UNION NAVY [PRESUMED])   *Baptized after the war.*

Rank: Uncertain	**Unit(s):** Uncertain **Military Service Source(s):** PPMU, PI
Birth Date: 26 June 1843	**Birth Place:** New Bedford, Bristol, Massachusetts
LDS Membership Date: 13 March 1867	**LDS Membership Source(s):** PPMU, NFS (ID #: KWNK-P4Y)
Death Date: 16 November 1888	**Death Place:** Bluefield, Nicaragua **Find A Grave:** — **Burial Location:** Bluefield, Nicaragua

Notes: He "came to Utah 1863, freight train for California. Married Matilda Robey Nov. 2, 1867, Midway, Utah. . . . Elder. Veteran Black Hawk war; civil war veteran. Miner; promoter" [PPMU, 1179].

SPRINGSTEED, HILTON (UNION ARMY)   *Baptized after the war.*

Rank: Corporal	**Unit(s):** Company E, 9th Regiment, Michigan Cavalry **Military Service Source(s):** NPS, PI
Birth Date: 30 June 1835	**Birth Place:** Truxton, Cortland, New York
LDS Membership Date: 6 February 1898	**LDS Membership Source(s):** NFS (ID #: K2HF-Y47)
Death Date: 13 May 1920	**Death Place:** Bountiful, Davis, Utah **Find A Grave:** — **Burial Location:** Uncertain
Notes: The 9th Regiment, Michigan Cavalry, was organized between January and May of 1863 and served from Kentucky to Mississippi [NPS].	

STANDIFIRD, JOHN HENRY (UNION ARMY)   *Baptized before the war.*

Rank: Private	**Unit(s):** Lot Smith Utah Cavalry **Military Service Source(s):** ACWS, NPS, Fisher, 1862 MOR
Birth Date: 21 June 1831	**Birth Place:** Elizabethtown, Hardin, Kentucky
LDS Membership Date: 14 June 1857	**LDS Membership Source(s):** NFS (ID #: KWNK-LPC)
Death Date: 24 November 1924	**Death Place:** Moab, Grand, Utah **Find A Grave:** 45081735 **Burial Location:** Grand Valley Cemetery, Moab, Grand, Utah
Notes: He kept a small pocket diary throughout his military service as a soldier in the Lot Smith Utah Cavalry. See *Life and Journals of John Henry Standifird 1831–1924* (Provo, UT: BYU Press, 1979).	

STEED, JAMES H. (UNION ARMY)   *Baptized before the war.*

Rank: Private	**Unit(s):** Lot Smith Utah Cavalry **Military Service Source(s):** ACWS, NPS, Fisher, 1862 MOR
Birth Date: 31 August 1844	**Birth Place:** Nauvoo, Hancock, Illinois
LDS Membership Date: 1855	**LDS Membership Source(s):** NFS (ID #: KWNK-6YB)
Death Date: 14 September 1885	**Death Place:** Elba, Cassia, Idaho **Find A Grave:** 48417642 **Burial Location:** Elba Cemetery, Elba, Cassia, Idaho
Notes: [MLM]	

STRATTON, JAMES (UNION NAVY)   *Baptized before the war.*

Rank: Uncertain	**Unit(s):** Uncertain **Military Service Source(s):** 1890 Census, NFS
Birth Date: 22 December 1824	**Birth Place:** Hertford, Ware Parish, Hertfordshire, England
LDS Membership Date: 8 August 1840	**LDS Membership Source(s):** FGC, NFS (ID #: KWJC-X7P)
Death Date: 23 March 1907	**Death Place:** Provo, Utah, Utah **Find A Grave:** 32858520 **Burial Location:** Provo City Cemetery, Provo, Utah, Utah
Notes: [MLM] Although he was a British citizen, he served in the American Navy during the Civil War [NFS]. He was baptized as a member of the LDS Church on August 3, 1850. He came in the first Poor Fund	

company to the Salt Lake Valley. While crossing the Atlantic Ocean on the ship Helen Maria, he was married to Frances Clark by LDS Apostle Orson Pratt. In the Salt Lake Valley, he was a soldier and was assigned to picket duty in Echo Canyon to watch for the U.S. Army during the Utah War [FGC]. He is recorded on an 1890 Pleasant Grove and Provo enumeration district sheet for Utah County census sheet, but the enumerator failed to record any information regarding his military service [1890 Census]. At the time of this publication, Civil War sailors are not available on [NPS].

STRONG, WILLIAM H. (UNION ARMY) *Baptized before the war.*

Rank: Private	Unit(s): Company D, 2nd Regiment, Missouri Cavalry Military Service Source(s): VBU, 1890 Census, NPS
Birth Date: 30 October 1827	Birth Place: Strongstown, Indiana, Pennsylvania
LDS Membership Date: 1839	LDS Membership Source(s): FGC, NFS (ID #: KWJC-VWQ)
Death Date: 24 December 1888	Death Place: Salt Lake City, Salt Lake, Utah Find A Grave: 25325936 Burial Location: Salt Lake City Cemetery, Salt Lake City, Salt Lake, Utah

Notes: [MLM] He served as a private in Company E in the Mormon Battalion [NFS]. He was reportedly baptized in the Mississippi River by the Prophet Joseph Smith. After his release from the army during the Mexican War, he helped to build a sawmill in the Santa Cruz Mountains in California [FGC]. He served in the Civil War one year, five months, and ten days beginning October 10, 1863. If the correct LDS member is identified, the 1890 veteran census schedule should list his entry as a widow report, as his death date was prior to 1890, but it does not [1890 Census].

STUART, DAVID CROCKETT (CONFEDERATE ARMY) *Baptized after the war.*

Rank: Uncertain	Unit(s): 4th Regiment, Alabama Cavalry Military Service Source(s): David Crockett Stuart, *A Few Lines From an Old Johnny Reb* (Seattle: Floyd Crockett Stuart, 1950)
Birth Date: 10 December 1842	Birth Place: Florette, Alabama
LDS Membership Date: 21 July 1872	LDS Membership Source(s): David Crockett Stuart, *A Few Lines From an Old Johnny Reb* (Seattle: Floyd Crockett Stuart, 1950); NFS (ID #: KW8L-G66)
Death Date: 22 November 1918	Death Place: Montpelier, Muscatine, Idaho Find A Grave: — Burial Location: Montpelier, Muscatine, Idaho

Notes: He wrote an autobiography describing his wartime service in detail. It is written in the same back-woods style as his namesake, Davy Crockett, would write (David Crockett Stuart, *A Few Lines From an Old Johnny Reb* [Seattle: Floyd Crockett Stuart, 1950]). For additional information, see the Ellsworth-Alford chapter herein.

SULLIVAN, DAVID DOLLEN (UNION ARMY) *Baptized after the war.*

Rank: Private	Unit(s): Company E, 1st Regiment, Missouri State Militia Cavalry Military Service Source(s): NPS, PI, FGC, PPMU
Birth Date: 21 January 1845	Birth Place: Nashville, Brown, Tennessee
LDS Membership Date: 1 December 1865	LDS Membership Source(s): PPMU, NFS (ID #: KWDM-6DG)

Sullivan, David Dollen (continued)	
Death Date: 30 March 1911	**Death Place:** Soda Springs, Bannock, Idaho **Find A Grave:** 11840996 **Burial Location:** Grace Cemetery, Grace, Caribou, Idaho
Notes: "CO. E. 1 MO. S.M. CAV." (Company E, 1st Missouri State Militia Cavalry) is carved on his grave marker [FGC]. He "came to Utah December, 1865, freighting outfit. . . . Civil war veteran. Postmaster at Grace, Idaho, 13 years" [PPMU, 1195].	

SYDDALL, HENRY   (UNION ARMY)   *Baptized before the war.*

Rank: Private	**Unit(s):** Company D, 117th Regiment, Illinois Infantry **Military Service Source(s):** NPS, PI, 1890 Census
Birth Date: 12 June 1835	**Birth Place:** Bolton, Little Lever, Lancashire, England
LDS Membership Date: 22 October 1851	**LDS Membership Source(s):** NFS (ID #: KWJ4-44Q)
Death Date: 3 December 1915	**Death Place:** Monroe, Sevier, Utah **Find A Grave:** — **Burial Location:** Roosevelt, Duchesne, Utah
Notes: He served three years in the military beginning in 1862. "Knee cap hurt and sickness" were listed as service-related disabilities [1890 Census].	

TAYLOR, JOHN JEFFERSON   (CONFEDERATE ARMY)   *Baptized after the war.*

Rank: Sergeant	**Unit(s):** Company E, 53rd Regiment, North Carolina Infantry **Military Service Source(s):** NPS; Hester Bartlett Jackson, *Surry County Soldiers in the Civil War* (Charlotte, North Carolina: Surry County Historical Society, 1992)
Birth Date: 22 June 1843	**Birth Place:** Surry, North Carolina
LDS Membership Date: 27 August 1868	**LDS Membership Source(s):** NFS (ID #: KWZ6-JRZ)
Death Date: 27 June 1923	**Death Place:** Payson, Utah, Utah **Find A Grave:** 31039146 **Burial Location:** Payson, Utah, Utah
Notes: [MLM] He was taken prisoner at Winchester, Virginia, on September 19, 1864, and was placed in a prisoner-of-war camp at Point Lookout, Maryland. He was released from the prison camp on June 30, 1865. He was five feet five inches tall with light complexion, brown hair, and hazel eyes (Hester Bartlett Jackson, *Surry County Soldiers in the Civil War* [Charlotte, North Carolina: Surry County Historical Society, 1992]).	

TAYLOR, JOSEPH J.   (UNION ARMY)   *Baptized before the war.*

Rank: Private	**Unit(s):** Lot Smith Utah Cavalry **Military Service Source(s):** ACWS, NPS, Fisher, 1862 MOR
Birth Date: 8 June 1838	**Birth Place:** Indianapolis, Marion, Indiana
LDS Membership Date: 1847	**LDS Membership Source(s):** NFS (ID #: KW8L-2RY)
Death Date: 31 January 1908	**Death Place:** Magrath, Alberta, Canada **Find A Grave:** 23318947 **Burial Location:** Magrath Cemetery, Magrath, Alberta, Canada
Notes: [MLM] [1890 Census] lists that Joseph served with "Captain Lot Smith's Mounted Utah Volunteers" for three months and fourteen days.	

TERRY, JOSEPH   (UNION ARMY)   *Baptized before the war.*

Rank: Private	Unit(s): Lot Smith Utah Cavalry Military Service Source(s): VBU, ACWS, NPS, Fisher, 1862 MOR
Birth Date: 6 June 1842	Birth Place: Crooked Creek, Bentonsport, Iowa
LDS Membership Date: 8 June 1850	LDS Membership Source(s): LDSBE, PPMU, NFS (ID #: KWJV-B2J)
Death Date: 23 April 1916	Death Place: Draper, Salt Lake, Utah Find A Grave: 9570464 Burial Location: Draper City Cemetery, Draper, Salt Lake, Utah

Notes: When he was "fifteen years old he was ordained a Teacher. . . . He was ordained a Seventy, and later (in the spring of 1901), a High Priest. . . . In 1852 he emigrated to Utah in Capt. Jolley's company, which arrived in Salt Lake City June 6th of that year. He was then only a lad of ten years, but he drove three yoke of cattle across the plains. . . . Elder Terry performed active [service] in the Johnston army campaign in 1857–58, and during the Blackhawk war he served as a messenger and assisted in recruiting and fitting out expeditions. . . . He is recognized as a firm and staunch Church member; . . . and has also been a Sabbath school worker" [LDSBE, 1:572–73]. "Served as ward teacher for over 50 years. Active in settling Draper (Utah)" [PPMU, 1205].

TERRY, WILLIAM R.   (UNION ARMY)   *Baptized before the war.*

Rank: Private	Unit(s): Lot Smith Utah Cavalry Military Service Source(s): ACWS, NPS, Fisher, 1862 MOR
Birth Date: 2 June 1812	Birth Place: Exeter, Washington, Rhode Island
LDS Membership Date: 20 March 1842	LDS Membership Source(s): PPMU, NFS (ID #: KWVM-6S5)
Death Date: 30 May 1868	Death Place: St. George, Washington, Utah Find A Grave: 34142872 Burial Location: St. George City Cemetery, St. George, Washington, Utah

Notes: [MLM] He "came to Utah 1852, at head of own company. . . . Served as first counselor to bishop of Draper, and was the first school teacher in that town" [PPMU, 1205].

THOMPSON, CHARLES   (UNION ARMY)   *Baptized after the war.*

Rank: Private	Unit(s): Company F, 19th Regiment, Massachusetts Infantry Military Service Source(s): NPS, FGC
Birth Date: 9 July 1843	Birth Place: Road, Norway
LDS Membership Date: 25 June 1871	LDS Membership Source(s): NFS (ID #: LHKY-M9X)
Death Date: 28 October 1918	Death Place: Salt Lake City, Salt Lake, Utah Find A Grave: 159093 Burial Location: Mount Olivet Cemetery, Salt Lake City, Salt Lake, Utah

Notes: "CO. F 19 MASS. INF." (Company F, 19th Massachusetts Infantry) is carved on his grave marker [FGC].

THOMPSON, EMANUEL EDWIN   (UNION ARMY)   *Baptized after the war.*

Rank: Private	Unit(s): Company A, 69th Regiment, Ohio Infantry Military Service Source(s): NPS, FGC
Birth Date: 19 October 1843	Birth Place: Mason, Warren, Ohio
LDS Membership Date: 3 December 1884	LDS Membership Source(s): NFS (ID #: KW81-T1B)

Thompson, Emanuel Edwin (continued)	
Death Date: 2 August 1924	**Death Place:** Rich, Bingham, Idaho **Find A Grave:** 40294996 **Burial Location:** Thomas Cemetery, Riverside, Bingham, Idaho
Notes: "CO A 69th OH" (Company A, 69th Ohio Regiment) is carved on his grave marker [FGC].	

THOMPSON, SAMUEL W   (UNION ARMY)   *Baptized before the war.*

Rank: Corporal	**Unit(s):** Company A, 15th Regiment, Ohio Infantry **Military Service Source(s):** VBU, 1890 Census, NPS
Birth Date: 30 March 1813	**Birth Place:** Pomfret, Chautauqua, New York
LDS Membership Date: 1833	**LDS Membership Source(s):** NFS (ID #: KWJD-FVP)
Death Date: 22 April 1892	**Death Place:** Vernal, Uintah, Utah **Find A Grave:** 54209 **Burial Location:** Spanish Fork, Utah, Utah
Notes: [MLM] He served in the military four years and six months beginning in 1861 [1890 Census]. [NPS] lists his rank at separation as corporal; [1890 Census] lists his rank as private. He was reportedly a member of Zion's Camp and also served as a second lieutenant in Company C in the Mormon Battalion [NFS]. His occupations included laborer in Coloma, El Dorado, California (1847–48), carpenter (1860), farmer (1870), millbuilder, and minister [NFS].	

THURSTON, MOSES   (UNION ARMY)   *Baptized before the war.*

Rank: Sergeant	**Unit(s):** Lot Smith Utah Cavalry **Military Service Source(s):** VBU, NPS, Fisher, 1862 MOR
Birth Date: 13 September 1817	**Birth Place:** Belmont, Waldo, Maine
LDS Membership Date: 2 June 1842	**LDS Membership Source(s):** NFS (ID #: K2HR-KBR)
Death Date: 5 August 1873	**Death Place:** Uncertain **Find A Grave:** — **Burial Location:** Salt Lake City, Salt Lake, Utah
Notes: He was captain of a pioneer company that traveled to Utah in 1855 (http://lds.org/churchhistory/library/pioneerdetails/1,15791,4018-1-17252,00.html).	

TILLMAN, JAMES C.   (CONFEDERATE ARMY)   *Baptized after the war.*

Rank: Second Sergeant	**Unit(s):** Company K, 4th Regiment, Georgia Cavalry (Clinch's) **Military Service Source(s):** 1890 Census, NPS
Birth Date: 28 June 1848	**Birth Place:** Bulloch, Georgia
LDS Membership Date: 1 December 1885	**LDS Membership Source(s):** NFS (ID #: KWVL-QRD)
Death Date: 2 June 1902	**Death Place:** Salt Lake City, Salt Lake, Utah **Find A Grave:** — **Burial Location:** Salt Lake City, Salt Lake, Utah
Notes: [MLM] He served in the military eleven months and seven days beginning on June 20, 1864. His 1890 veteran census schedule entry is crossed out with the word "Confederate" written above his name [1890 Census].	

TRAUGOTT, JOHN E.   (UNION ARMY)   *Baptized after the war.*

Rank: Private	**Unit(s):** Company F, 5th Regiment, Missouri State Militia Cavalry **Military Service Source(s):** NPS, PI, Obituary
Birth Date: 7 August 1843	**Birth Place:** Varselles, Morgan, Missouri

LDS Membership Date: 1 November 1877	LDS Membership Source(s): NFS (ID #: 2S4V-F98)	
Death Date: 16 April 1925	Death Place: Clearfield, Davis, Utah	Find A Grave: 123993
	Burial Location: Kaysville, Davis, Utah	

Notes: His obituary, entitled "Union War Veteran Dies," noted that "he was a faithful member of the L.D.S. church. He was a Union soldier in the Civil War, a member of the Missouri Cavalry, Company F" (*Ogden Standard*, April 17, 1925, 16). His obituary in the Davis County newspaper noted his "honorable service in the civil war" (*Davis County Clipper*, April 17, 1925, 1).

TURNBOW, PLEASANT CHILDERS (CONFEDERATE ARMY)   *Baptized after the war.*

Rank: Private	Unit(s): Company G (Covington Sharpshooters), 7th Battalion, Mississippi Infantry	
	Military Service Source(s): VBU, NPS, FGC	
Birth Date: 22 July 1842	Birth Place: Tuscaloosa, Alabama	
LDS Membership Date: 24 October 1882	LDS Membership Source(s): NFS (ID #: KWVH-XJ1)	
Death Date: 16 March 1926	Death Place: Cedar City, Iron, Utah	Find A Grave: 106377
	Burial Location: Mountain View Cemetery, Beaver, Beaver, Utah	

Notes: "PVT CO G 7 BN MISS INF" (Private, Company G, 7th Battalion, Missouri Infantry) is carved on his grave marker [FGC].

TURNER, JOHN EDWARD   (UNION ARMY [PRESUMED])   *Baptized before the war.*

Rank: Private	Unit(s): Uncertain	
	Military Service Source(s): 1890 Census	
Birth Date: 3 May 1821	Birth Place: Tipton, Staffs, England	
LDS Membership Date: November 1849	LDS Membership Source(s): NFS (ID #: KWJD-JKP)	
Death Date: March 1900	Death Place: Wanship, Summit, Utah	Find A Grave: —
	Burial Location: Hoytsville Cemetery, Hoytsville, Summit, Utah	

Notes: [MLM] He served in the military ten months beginning on April 20, 1864. "Old Man, very poor" was included as a comment on his census form. His military unit was recorded but is unintelligible on the [1890 Census].

VANBEEK, GEORGE DAY   (UNION ARMY)   *Baptized before the war.*

Rank: Corporal	Unit(s): Company C, 1st Regiment, Iowa Cavalry	
	Military Service Source(s): NPS	
Birth Date: 9 February 1815	Birth Place: Philadelphia, Pennsylvania	
LDS Membership Date: Before 24 January 1846	LDS Membership Source(s): NFS (ID #: KVVC-TMV)	
Death Date: 21 March 1904	Death Place: Uncertain	Find A Grave: —
	Burial Location: Uncertain	

Notes: [MLM] The 1st Regiment, Iowa Cavalry, was organized in September 1861; unlike most Union units, the soldiers owned their horses and equipment [NPS].

VOGEL, GEORGE WILLIAM   (UNION ARMY)   *Baptized after the war.*

Rank: Private	Unit(s): Company B, 100th Regiment, Ohio Infantry Military Service Source(s): NPS
Birth Date: 21 March 1843	Birth Place: Piqua, Miami, Ohio
LDS Membership Date: May 1894	LDS Membership Source(s): NFS (ID #: KWC4-KYC)
Death Date: 12 January 1941	Death Place: Mesa, Maricopa, Arizona Find A Grave: 84124569 Burial Location: Ogden City Cemetery, Ogden, Weber, Utah
Notes: [MLM] The 100th Regiment, Ohio Infantry, was organized July to September in 1862 and was assigned for duty to the District of Central Kentucky and the Department of North Carolina [NPS].	

WALKER, JOHN H.   (UNION ARMY)   *Baptized before the war.*

Rank: Private	Unit(s): Lot Smith Utah Cavalry Military Service Source(s): VBU, ACWS, NPS, Fisher, 1862 MOR
Birth Date: 6 September 1843	Birth Place: Upper Bullingham, Herefordshire, England
LDS Membership Date: 14 April 1852	LDS Membership Source(s): LDSBE, PPMU, NFS (ID #: KWJ6-DRR)
Death Date: 18 November 1915	Death Place: Union, Salt Lake, Utah Find A Grave: 129134 Burial Location: Murray City Cemetery, Murray, Salt Lake, Utah
Notes: "His parents accepted 'Mormonism' in 1841 and emigrated to America in 1853, crossing the plains to Utah in Claudius V. Spencer's ox company. . . . John H. remained with his father til 1862, when he enlisted in Captain Lot Smith's company, which was engaged in guarding the overland mail, that year. Later he followed freighting by team through California and Montana. . . . He was ordained an Elder in 1869 and later a Seventy, becoming a member of the 93rd quorum. From March, 1895, to May, 1897, he filled a mission to Great Britain. . . . In civil affairs he served one term as justice of the peace and four terms as constable" [LDSBE, 2:109–110]. "President Y.M.M.I.A. . . . superintendent Sunday school; missionary to England 1895–97. Veteran Washakie Indian war, 1862 in Capt. Lot Smith's company. Justice of peace at Union (Utah) 1898; constable 1887–95" [PPMU, 1226].	

WALKER, ROBERT COWIE   (UNION ARMY)   *Baptized before the war.*

Rank: Major	Unit(s): Staff Officer, Pay Department Military Service Source(s): 1890 Census
Birth Date: about 1842	Birth Place: Bonhill, Dumbarton, Scotland
LDS Membership Date: 3 March 1849	LDS Membership Source(s): NFS (ID #: KWDH-2PH)
Death Date: 21 March 1908	Death Place: Coalville, Summit, Utah Find A Grave: 73133 Burial Location: Coalville, Summit, Utah
Notes: [MLM] He began his military service on October 31, 1861. He was listed as a staff officer [1890 Census]. There is some discrepancy regarding the date of his birth.	

WALKER, WILLIAM HENRY   (UNION ARMY)   *Baptized before the war.*

Rank: Private	Unit(s): Companies C & D, 14th Regiment, U.S. Infantry (Regular Army) Military Service Source(s): 1890 Census, NPS
Birth Date: 14 March 1836	Birth Place: Council Bluffs, Pottawattamie, Iowa

LDS Membership Date: 1851	LDS Membership Source(s): NFS (ID #: KWD9-VW9)	
Death Date: 3 May 1916	Death Place: Heber City, Wasatch, Utah Find A Grave: — Burial Location: Heber City, Wasatch, Utah	
Notes: [MLM] He served in the military three years beginning February 28, 1865 [1890 Census].		

WARDELL, MARTIN DOUGLAS   (UNION ARMY)   *Baptized before the war.*

Rank: Private	Unit(s): Company B, New Jersey Light Artillery Military Service Source(s): 1890 Census, NPS
Birth Date: 12 February 1822	Birth Place: Sunderland, Durham, England
LDS Membership Date: 1 May 1852 (confirmation)	LDS Membership Source(s): NFS (ID #: KWJH-P7C)
Death Date: 28 July 1893	Death Place: Millcreek, Salt Lake, Utah Find A Grave: — Burial Location: Elysian Burial Gardens, Salt Lake City, Salt Lake, Utah
Notes: [MLM] [1890 Census] lists his name but provides no service information. On [NFS] his LDS baptism is listed as 8 May 1869, but the date of his LDS confirmation is listed as 1 May 1852 [NFS].	

WATSON, LORENZO DOW   (UNION ARMY)   *Baptized after the war.*

Rank: Private	Unit(s): Company L, 2nd Regiment, Maine Cavalry Military Service Source(s): NPS; PI; Alma Gertrude Watson McGregor and Daniel Clark Watson Jr., *Lorenzo Dow Watson* (Provo, Utah: J. Grant Stevenson, 1970), 1–32.
Birth Date: 17 September 1845	Birth Place: Limerick, York, Maine
LDS Membership Date: 1 January 1868	LDS Membership Source(s): NFS (ID #: KWZ4-5ZM)
Death Date: 1 November 1896	Death Place: Parowan, Iron, Utah Find A Grave: 11703907 Burial Location: Parowan City Cemetery, Parowan, Iron, Utah
Notes: For additional details, see the Ellsworth-Alford chapter herein.	

WEAVER, WILLIAM HENRY   (UNION ARMY)   *Baptized before the war.*

Rank: Private	Unit(s): Company G, 68th Regiment, Indiana Infantry Military Service Source(s): NPS, PI, Obituary
Birth Date: 8 January 1838	Birth Place: New Holland, Lancaster, Pennsylvania
LDS Membership Date: 8 January 1846	LDS Membership Source(s): NFS (ID #: KWCY-QYF)
Death Date: 10 February 1920	Death Place: Coalville, Summit, Utah Find A Grave: 74714 Burial Location: Coalville City Cemetery, Coalville, Summit, Utah
Notes: His obituary, entitled "War Veteran Dies," stated that he was a "veteran of the Civil war, who participated in the battle of Gettysburg and other notable engagements" (*Salt Lake Telegram*, February 11, 1920, 8).	

WEILER, ELIJAH MALIN   (UNION ARMY)   *Baptized before the war.*

Rank: Private	Unit(s): Lot Smith Utah Cavalry Military Service Source(s): VBU, ACWS, NPS, Fisher, 1862 MOR
Birth Date: 18 April 1839	Birth Place: West Nantmeal, Chester, Pennsylvania

Weiler, Elijah Malin (continued)	
LDS Membership Date: 1 January 1849	**LDS Membership Source(s):** LDSBE, NFS (ID #: KWCW-364)
Death Date: 11 November 1921	**Death Place:** Salt Lake City, Salt Lake, Utah **Find A Grave:** 23694042 **Burial Location:** Salt Lake City, Salt Lake, Utah
Notes: "A prominent elder . . . In 1841 he went with his parents to Nauvoo, Ill. Elijah emigrated to the [Salt Lake] Valley in 1847, with his mother, his father having crossed the plains ahead with the original pioneers of 1847. . . . In 1862 he served as a volunteer under Lot Smith and in 1863 he crossed the plains as a night herder under Capt. John M. Woolley. During the Blackhawk war in 1865 he did active military service in Colonel Heber P. Kimball's command. Two years later he was called to settle on the Muddy (now in Nevada) as a missionary settler. . . . Elder Weiler is truly a pioneer, and has done his share of 'killing snakes and building bridges.' He has followed farming and contracting most of his time in life" [LDSBE, 1:603].	

WELDON, FRANCIS MARION   (CONFEDERATE ARMY)   *Baptized after the war.*

Rank: Private	**Unit(s):** Company G, 1st Regiment, Georgia Reserves (Fannin's) **Military Service Source(s):** CSC, NPS
Birth Date: 20 February 1827	**Birth Place:** Harris, Georgia
LDS Membership Date: 10 February 1877	**LDS Membership Source(s):** NFS (ID #: KWZQ-W7B)
Death Date: 25 August 1915	**Death Place:** Manassa, Conejos, Colorado **Find A Grave:** — **Burial Location:** Manassa, Conejos, Colorado
Notes: [MLM] Joseph H. Crute Jr.,*Units of the Confederate States Army* (Midlothian, VA: Derwent, 1987), contains no history for his unit [NPS].	

WELLS, JAMES H.   (UNION ARMY)   *Baptized before the war.*

Rank: Private	**Unit(s):** Lot Smith Utah Cavalry **Military Service Source(s):** ACWS, NPS, Fisher, 1862 MOR
Birth Date: 3 January 1843	**Birth Place:** Sheffield, Yorkshire, England
LDS Membership Date: 1 April 1856	**LDS Membership Source(s):** NFS (ID #: KWNN-G41)
Death Date: 1 April 1905	**Death Place:** Joseph, Sevier, Utah **Find A Grave:** 37363591 **Burial Location:** Joseph Cemetery, Joseph, Sevier, Utah
Notes: [MLM] He also reportedly went by the alias of "Paddy Miles Boy" [Fisher, 72].	

WELSH, JAMES H.   (UNION ARMY)   *Baptized before the war.*

Rank: Private	**Unit(s):** Lot Smith Utah Cavalry **Military Service Source(s):** ACWS, Fisher, 1862 MOR
Birth Date: 21 December 1833	**Birth Place:** Meggars Grant, Halifax, Nova Scotia
LDS Membership Date: 1855	**LDS Membership Source(s):** NFS (ID #: KWVQ-DWZ)
Death Date: 22 October 1917	**Death Place:** American Fork, Utah, Utah **Find A Grave:** — **Burial Location:** Uncertain
Notes: [MLM]	

WESTWOOD, JOSEPH MORONI   (UNION ARMY)   *Baptized after the war.*

Rank: Sergeant	**Unit(s):** Company A, 1st Battalion, Nevada Cavalry **Military Service Source(s):** NPS, PI, FGC
Birth Date: 21 January 1844	**Birth Place:** Marlbrook, Worcester, England
LDS Membership Date: 19 April 1866	**LDS Membership Source(s):** NFS (ID #: KWVW-WZS)
Death Date: 3 March 1929	**Death Place:** Salt Lake City, Salt Lake, Utah **Find A Grave:** 62248 **Burial Location:** Springville City Cemetery, Springville, Utah, Utah

Notes: "SGT CO A 1 BN NEV CAVALRY CIVIL WAR" (Sergeant, Company A, 1st Battalion, Nevada Cavalry) is carved on his grave marker [FGC].

WHITLOCK, EZRA B.   (UNION ARMY)   *Baptized after the war.*

Rank: Private	**Unit(s):** Company C, 15th Regiment, Iowa Infantry **Military Service Source(s):** NPS, FGC
Birth Date: 27 July 1837	**Birth Place:** Russell, Kentucky
LDS Membership Date: 11 September 1872	**LDS Membership Source(s):** NFS (ID #: K2HB-VPP)
Death Date: 23 March 1873	**Death Place:** Springville, Utah, Utah **Find A Grave:** 61529 **Burial Location:** Springville Cemetery, Springville, Utah, Utah

Notes: "PVT CO C 15 REGT IOWA INF CIVIL WAR" (Private, Company A, 15th Regiment, Iowa Infantry) is carved on his grave marker [FGC].

WHITNEY, LEONARD JOTHAM   (UNION ARMY)   *Baptized after the war.*

Rank: First Sergeant	**Unit(s):** 7th Regiment, Volunteer Cavalry **Military Service Source(s):** 1890 Census
Birth Date: 9 July 1842	**Birth Place:** Hinesburgh, Chittenden, Vermont
LDS Membership Date: 19 August 1866	**LDS Membership Source(s):** NFS (ID #: KWNG-4XK)
Death Date: 13 November 1921	**Death Place:** Springville, Utah, Utah **Find A Grave:** 134715 **Burial Location:** Evergreen Cemetery, Springville, Utah, Utah

Notes: His 1890 census enumerator failed to record any service dates. "Frozen feet" is listed as a service-related disability [1890 Census]. In addition to his Civil War military service, he also reportedly fought in the Black Hawk Indian War with the Jesse P. Steele Company. His occupations are listed as carpenter, farmer, miner, sawmill owner and operator, and store and hotel owner and operator. He was reportedly five feet eleven inches tall with blue eyes and auburn hair [NFS]. The [1890 census] lists his military unit as 7th Volunteer Cavalry; [NPS] also lists a Leonard J. Whitney who served with Company F, 1st Battalion Nevada Cavalry.

WILLIAMS, BATEMAN H.   (UNION ARMY)   *Baptized before the war.*

Rank: Private	**Unit(s):** Lot Smith Utah Cavalry **Military Service Source(s):** ACWS, NPS, Fisher, 1862 MOR
Birth Date: Uncertain	**Birth Place:** Nauvoo, Hancock, Illinois
LDS Membership Date: 20 April 1861 (LDS temple ordinances)	**LDS Membership Source(s):** NFS (ID #: MB65-SKQ)

Williams, Bateman H. (continued)	
Death Date: Uncertain	**Death Place:** Uncertain **Find A Grave:** — **Burial Location:** Uncertain
Notes: [MLM]	

WILLIAMS, EPHRAIM H.   (UNION ARMY)   *Baptized before the war.*

Rank: Private	**Unit(s):** Lot Smith Utah Cavalry **Military Service Source(s):** VBU, ACWS, NPS, Fisher, 1862 MOR
Birth Date: 2 May 1842	**Birth Place:** Nauvoo, Hancock, Illinois
LDS Membership Date: 29 April 1854	**LDS Membership Source(s):** NFS (ID #: KWC8-R8T)
Death Date: 21 May 1919	**Death Place:** Mill Creek, Salt Lake, Utah **Find A Grave:** 36546069 **Burial Location:** Wasatch Lawn Cemetery, Salt Lake City, Salt Lake, Utah
Notes: —	

WILLIAMS, GEORGE CALVIN   (UNION ARMY [PRESUMED])   *Baptized after the war.*

Rank: Uncertain	**Unit(s):** Uncertain **Military Service Source(s):** George Calvin Williams, *Reminiscences* (ca. 1915), LDS Church History Library, MS 13382
Birth Date: 27 February 1836	**Birth Place:** Hamilton, Tennessee
LDS Membership Date: October 1881	**LDS Membership Source(s):** NFS (ID #: KWNF-T3Q)
Death Date: 7 November 1916	**Death Place:** Miramonte, Arizona **Find A Grave:** 20813135 **Burial Location:** Miramonte, Benson, Cochise, Arizona
Notes: [MLM] He "was ordained a Bishop Nov. 18, 1883, by Brigham Young, jun." [LDSBE, 4:598]. Thirteen of his relatives were killed in the Mountain Meadows Massacre. He was upset with the Church for not prosecuting the individuals responsible for the massacre and was excommunicated from the LDS Church in 1895 (George Calvin Williams, *Reminiscences* [ca. 1915], Church History Library, MS 13382).	

WILLIAMS, JAMES   (UNION ARMY)   *Baptized after the war.*

Rank: Private	**Unit(s):** Company I, 1st Regiment, Iowa Infantry **Military Service Source(s):** NPS, PI, FGC
Birth Date: 15 April 1831	**Birth Place:** Naugatuck, New Haven, Connecticut
LDS Membership Date: 15 January 1870	**LDS Membership Source(s):** NFS (ID #: KWVW-5Y6)
Death Date: 20 October 1913	**Death Place:** Provo, Utah, Utah **Find A Grave:** 83526 **Burial Location:** Evergreen Cemetery, Springville, Utah, Utah
Notes: "CO. I. 1 IA. INF." (Company I, 1st Iowa Infantry) is carved on his grave marker [FGC].	

WILSON, HAMILTON   (UNION ARMY)   *Baptized after the war.*

Rank: Private	**Unit(s):** Company A, 1st Regiment, Pennsylvania Cavalry (15th Reserves) **Military Service Source(s):** NPS, PI
Birth Date: 17 June 1838	**Birth Place:** Auterim, Cambridge, Ohio

LDS Membership Date: 3 August 1902	LDS Membership Source(s): NFS (ID #: KCK1-6HS)
Death Date: June 1919	Death Place: Uncertain Find A Grave: 77198535 Burial Location: Uncertain

Notes: [MLM] The 1st Regiment, Pennsylvania Cavalry (15th Reserves), was mustered into state service during July and August 1861 and was assigned to the Army of the Potomac [NPS].

WILSON, JOHN PRESLY   (CONFEDERATE ARMY)   *Baptized after the war.*

Rank: Sergeant (Orderly)	Unit(s): Army of Northern Virginia Military Service Source(s): CSC
Birth Date: 20 March 1845	Birth Place: Salem, Oconee, South Carolina
LDS Membership Date: 15 May 1887	LDS Membership Source(s): NFS (ID #: KWZB-NTW)
Death Date: 8 August 1907	Death Place: Manassa, Conejos, Colorado Find A Grave: — Burial Location: Manassa, Conejos, Colorado

Notes: [MLM] The Army of Northern Virginia was commanded by General Robert E. Lee.

WIMER, JOHN P.   (UNION ARMY)   *Baptized before the war.*

Rank: Sergeant	Unit(s): Lot Smith Utah Cavalry Military Service Source(s): ACWS, NPS, Fisher, 1862 MOR
Birth Date: 14 November 1835	Birth Place: Jeffersonville, Clark, Indiana
LDS Membership Date: 7 February 1847	LDS Membership Source(s): NFS (ID #: KWD1-BN3)
Death Date: 28 October 1904	Death Place: Payson, Utah, Utah Find A Grave: 30486354 Burial Location: Payson City Cemetery, Payson, Utah, Utah

Notes: [MLM]

WINNER, GEORGE KING   (UNION ARMY)   *Baptized before the war.*

Rank: Private	Unit(s): Company L, 2nd Regiment, California Cavalry Military Service Source(s): NPS, SBS
Birth Date: 15 August 1807	Birth Place: Toms River, Ocean (Monmouth), New Jersey
LDS Membership Date: 7 July 1847	LDS Membership Source(s): SBS, NFS (ID #: K27M-6RB)
Death Date: 15 September 1877	Death Place: La Honda, San Mateo, California Find A Grave: 12221187 Burial Location: Skylawn Memorial Park, San Mateo, San Mateo, California

Notes: He was a passenger on the ship *Brooklyn* and is recognized as the founder of Yerba Buena, which became San Francisco. He served for a period as the LDS branch president of the San Francisco Branch. He was excommunicated in San Bernardino, California, on Sunday, February 1, 1857. During the Civil War, he served under Colonel Patrick Edward Connor in Salt Lake City. Following the Civil War, he returned to California and joined the Reorganized Church of Jesus Christ of Latter Day Saints. On May 25, 2000, the Office of the First Presidency of The Church of Jesus Christ of Latter-day Saints reinstated him to full fellowship in the Church [SBS].

WOOD, WILLIAM HARRISON (CONFEDERATE ARMY)   *Baptized after the war.*

Rank: Private	**Unit(s):** Company G, 54th Regiment, North Carolina Infantry **Military Service Source(s):** NPS
Birth Date: 18 February 1841	**Birth Place:** Cleveland County, North Carolina
LDS Membership Date: 24 September 1884	**LDS Membership Source(s):** NFS (ID #: KWJH-8K8)
Death Date: 1 June 1913	**Death Place:** Uncertain **Find A Grave:** — **Burial Location:** Uncertain

Notes: [MLM] The 54th Regiment, North Carolina Infantry, was assembled in May 1862. "The 54th was engaged at Fredericksburg and Chancellorsville, then guarded prisoners captured at Winchester during the Pennsylvania Campaign" [NPS].

WOODS, WILLIAM (UNION ARMY)   *Baptized before the war.*

Rank: Private	**Unit(s):** Company D, 9th Regiment, Iowa Infantry **Military Service Source(s):** 1890 Census, NPS
Birth Date: 2 February 1823	**Birth Place:** Hereford, Hertfordshire, England
LDS Membership Date: 23 September 1840	**LDS Membership Source(s):** LDSBE, NFS (ID #: KWJ6-2C2)
Death Date: 18 September 1900	**Death Place:** Minersville, Beaver, Utah **Find A Grave:** — **Burial Location:** Minersville, Beaver, Utah

Notes: LDSBE lists birth date as February 3, 1823. He was "a member of the Mormon Battalion, Company C . . . emigrated to America in 1842, and arrived in Nauvoo May 6, 1843. . . . He finally arrived in the [Salt Lake] 'Valley' in 1848. In 1852 he went to San Bernardino, California, but came back when that settlement was broken up in 1857" [LDSBE, 4:767]. "Says he was in 18 battles" is listed in the remarks section on the veteran census schedule. Unit is listed as Company D, 2nd Division, 3rd Brigade, 9th Iowa Infantry [1890 Census].

WRIGHT, JOHN (UNION ARMY)   *Baptized before the war.*

Rank: Private	**Unit(s):** Company G, 12th Regiment, Illinois Infantry **Military Service Source(s):** 1890 Census
Birth Date: 8 October 1832	**Birth Place:** Thorney, Cambridgeshire, England
LDS Membership Date: 1 August 1854 (confirmation)	**LDS Membership Source(s):** NFS (ID #: KWJH-D3D)
Death Date: 9 May 1893	**Death Place:** Pleasant Grove, Utah, Utah **Find A Grave:** 114134 **Burial Location:** Pleasant Grove City Cemetery, Pleasant Grove, Utah, Utah

Notes: [MLM] He served three years and twelve days beginning August 1, 1861. He noted a problem with his left thigh as a service-related disability [1890 Census].

YATES, JAMES STANLEY (UNION ARMY)   *Baptized after the war.*

Rank: Private	**Unit(s):** Company G, 12th Regiment, Kentucky Cavalry **Military Service Source(s):** NPS
Birth Date: 22 September 1842	**Birth Place:** Big Spring, Hardin, Kentucky
LDS Membership Date: 6 May 1890	**LDS Membership Source(s):** NFS (ID #: KWJ6-BS5)

Death Date: 13 May 1913	Death Place: Bountiful, Davis, Utah Find A Grave: — Burial Location: Bountiful City Cemetery, Bountiful, Davis, Utah
Notes: Organized in Owensboro, Kentucky, on November 17, 1862, the 12th Kentucky Cavalry participated in dozens of campaigns and conflicts between 1862 and 1865 [NPS].	

YOUNG, JOSEPH CHARLES (UNION ARMY) *Baptized after the war.*

Rank: Private	**Unit(s):** Company E, 65th Regiment, Illinois Infantry **Military Service Source(s):** NPS, FGC
Birth Date: 14 December 1823	**Birth Place:** Waynesville, Warren, Ohio
LDS Membership Date: 7 July 1869	**LDS Membership Source(s):** NFS (ID #: KWVS-9HS)
Death Date: 4 August 1880	**Death Place:** Pleasant Grove, Utah, Utah **Find A Grave:** 38118 **Burial Location:** Pleasant Grove City Cemetery, Pleasant Grove, Utah, Utah
Notes: "Joseph fought in the Civil War" [FGC]	

YOUNG, SEYMOUR BICKNELL (UNION ARMY) *Baptized before the war.*

Rank: Private	**Unit(s):** Lot Smith Utah Cavalry **Military Service Source(s):** ACWS, NPS, Fisher, 1862 MOR
Birth Date: 3 October 1837	**Birth Place:** Kirtland, Geauga, Ohio
LDS Membership Date: 1 January 1849	**LDS Membership Source(s):** LDSBE, NFS (ID #: KWCZ-ZTQ)
Death Date: 15 December 1924	**Death Place:** Salt Lake City, Salt Lake, Utah **Find A Grave:** 30549026 **Burial Location:** Salt Lake City, Salt Lake, Utah
Notes: His father was Joseph Young, older brother of Brigham Young. Seymour gained his first experience as a cowboy while being exposed to the raids of hostile Indians and white cattle thieves. His family arrived in Salt Lake City in September 1850. His family was some of the early settlers in Cache Valley, Utah. In 1857, he was called to serve as a missionary in Great Britain and was a member of a missionary group who crossed the plains from west to east using handcarts. Following the Civil War, he became a physician. In October 1884, he was called as one of the first seven presidents of the Seventies and became the senior member in 1893. He was active in the Grand Army of the Republic during the last years of his life [LDSBE, 1:200-202] [MDA, 404]. He "became quarantine and city physician of Salt Lake City, and a little later [after 1874], by invitation of Pres. Brigham Young, became his physician and medical advisor, which position he held until Pres. Young's death, August 29, 1877" [LDSBE, 1:202]. For additional information, see the Alford chapter entitled "Mormons and the Grand Army of the Republic" herein.	

The Battle of Gettysburg was fought in and around the small town of Gettysburg, Pennsylvania, July 1–3, 1863, during which there were approximately 50,000 casualties. This "Plan of the Gettysburg Battle Ground" was drawn by Charles Wellington Reed in 1864. (Library of Congress)

SPECIAL INTEREST CIVIL WAR VETERANS

This appendix lists individuals who are interesting in their own right and who should be recognized but whose Civil War service did not qualify them, for various reasons, for inclusion in appendix E. For example, teamsters and women could not qualify for Appendix E because they were not given Civil War veteran status. Other individuals could not be included because their Latter-day Saint baptismal status is uncertain or because they were not baptized as Latter-day Saints during their lifetime. (Appendix C contains information regarding how this list was researched and created. Appendix D provides explanatory information for each field in the record below as well as an explanation for the various codes and acronyms used.)

ALDER, LYDIA DUNFORD   (CIVIL WAR NURSE)   *Baptized after the war.*

Rank: Nurse	**Unit(s):** N/A **Military Service Source(s):** "Passing Events," *Improvement Era*, April 1923, 584.
Birth Date: 2 July 1846	**Birth Place:** Trowbridge, Wiltshire, England
LDS Membership Date: 13 April 1867	**LDS Membership Source(s):** NFS (ID #: KWJ7-YJT)
Death Date: 1 March 1923	**Death Place:** Salt Lake City, Salt Lake, Utah **Find A Grave:** — **Burial Location:** Salt Lake City Cemetery, Salt Lake, Utah

Notes: "As a young girl she served as a nurse during the Civil War. She was the first president of the National Woman's Suffrage Association in Utah. She visited Palestine and published a volume entitled, 'The Holy Land,' in 1912 on her observations there" (*Improvement Era*, April 1923, 584). A poet and author, she wrote dozens of articles and poems that appeared in the *Improvement Era* between 1900 and 1921 (for example: "Thou Shalt Have No Other Gods Before Me," *Improvement Era*, October 1900, 919–26, and "The First Handcart Company," *Improvement Era,* July 1909, 720–23. "In the North, more than 3,000 women worked as paid army nurses, and 2,000 others worked as volunteers or as affiliates of the Sanitary Commission" (Lesli J. Favor, *Women Doctors and Nurses of the Civil War* [New York: Rosen, 2004], 7). Army nurses "went forth on the perilous path of real service in the war. They were sunshine at the edge of battlefields, voices of solace in hospital sufferings. In ways beyond the power of the chaplains they served the dying, receiving last messages and brightening the last hours of many a boy in blue. The privations and dangers which these noble characters endured called for a fortitude

Alder, Lydia Dunford (continued)

equal in many respects to the valor of the soldier. The army nurse was obliged to respond to duty at all times and in all emergencies. She could not measure her time, sleep, or strength. She was under orders to serve to the fullest. . . . They were willing to dare everything for the sake of union and liberty" (Rev. Edward A. Horton, preface to *Our Army Nurses, by Mary A. Gardner Holland* [Boston: R. Wilkins, 1895], 5–6).

BAGLEY, WILLIAM (UNION ARMY) *Baptized before the war.*

Rank: Teamster	**Unit(s):** Lot Smith Utah Cavalry **Military Service Source(s):** Fisher
Birth Date: 8 October 1841	**Birth Place:** Northampton, St. John River, Carlton, New Brunswick, Canada
LDS Membership Date: 1 January 1855	**LDS Membership Source(s):** NFS (ID #: KWJ4-Z2C)
Death Date: 25 January 1923	**Death Place:** Charleston, Wasatch, Utah **Find A Grave:** 43553612 **Burial Location:** Charleston Cemetery, Charleston, Wasatch, Utah
Notes: [LOT SMITH TEAMSTER] "TEAMSTER UTAH VOLS INDIAN WARS" is carved on his grave marker [FGC]. As they were not eligible for federal military pensions, Lot Smith teamsters were not listed on [1862 MOR].	

BARNARD, LACHONEUS (UNION ARMY) *Baptized before the war.*

Rank: Teamster	**Unit(s):** Lot Smith Utah Cavalry **Military Service Source(s):** Fisher
Birth Date: 27 December 1827	**Birth Place:** Caldwell County, Missouri
LDS Membership Date: 23 October 1851	**LDS Membership Source(s):** NFS (ID #: KWVH-VGB)
Death Date: 9 January 1919	**Death Place:** Roy, Weber, Utah **Find A Grave:** — **Burial Location:** Harper, Box Elder, Utah
Notes: [LOT SMITH TEAMSTER] As they were not eligible for federal military pensions, Lot Smith teamsters were not listed on [1862 MOR].	

BIRD, HENRY (UNION ARMY) *Baptized after the war.*

Rank: Teamster	**Unit(s):** Lot Smith Utah Cavalry **Military Service Source(s):** Fisher
Birth Date: 6 August 1840	**Birth Place:** New Brunswick, Nova Scotia, Canada
LDS Membership Date: 20 April 1874	**LDS Membership Source(s):** NFS (ID #: KWN4-FQZ)
Death Date: 23 October 1907	**Death Place:** Murray, Salt Lake, Utah **Find A Grave:** 129759 **Burial Location:** Murray City Cemetery, Murray, Salt Lake, Utah
Notes: [LOT SMITH TEAMSTER] As they were not eligible for federal military pensions, Lot Smith teamsters were not listed on [1862 MOR].	

CONNOR, PATRICK EDWARD (UNION ARMY) *Not LDS.*

Rank: Brigadier General	**Unit(s):** 3rd Regiment, California Volunteers Infantry **Military Service Source(s):** 1890 Census

Birth Date: 17 March 1820	Birth Place: Kerry, Ireland	
LDS Membership Date: Not LDS	Source(s): NFS (ID #: KJPV-4B9)	
Death Date: 17 December 1891	Death Place: Salt Lake City, Salt Lake, Utah Burial Location: Fort Douglas Cemetery, Salt Lake City, Utah	Find A Grave: 5893995

Notes: An Irishman reportedly born on St. Patrick's Day, he enlisted in the U.S. Army on November 28, 1839, and served in the Seminole War at Fort Leavenworth, Kansas, and in Iowa. After being honorably discharged in November 1844, he enlisted in the Texas Volunteers. Promoted to captain, he fought and was wounded during the Mexican War. Honorably discharged from the army on May 24, 1847, he traveled to California in 1850 and in 1853 was appointed as a lieutenant in the California State Rangers. At the beginning of the Civil War, Connor commanded a unit of the California Militia known as the "Stockton Blues" that was soon redesignated as the Third Regiment California Volunteer Infantry. His regiment was ordered to Utah Territory to protect the Overland Trail from potential Indian and Mormon uprisings. Connor was the senior military officer in Utah throughout most of the Civil War. He commanded the District of Utah, Department of the Pacific, from August 6, 1862, until March 1865, when his district was merged into the District of the Plains (which he was chosen to command). He was often outspoken regarding his distrust of Brigham Young and Mormons. He returned to Utah after the Civil War and was actively involved in mining and politics until his death. See Brigham D. Madsen, *Glory Hunter: A Biography of Patrick Edward Connor* (Salt Lake City: University of Utah Press, 1990); and E. B. Long, *The Saints and the Union: Utah Territory during the Civil War* (Urbana: University of Illinois Press, 1981). He was promoted to colonel (September 29, 1861), brigadier general (March 29, 1863), and brevet major general (April 1, 1866) [1890 Census]. For additional information, see chapters 10 and 18 herein.

DALTON, HENRY (UNION ARMY) *Baptized before the war.*

Rank: Teamster	Unit(s): Lot Smith Utah Cavalry Military Service Source(s): Fisher	
Birth Date: 3 April 1827	Birth Place: Chenango, Broome, New York	
LDS Membership Date: 6 February 1846 (LDS temple ordinances)	LDS Membership Source(s): NFS (ID #: KWJJ-Y8B)	
Death Date: 10 November 1886	Death Place: Centerville, Davis, Utah Burial Location: Centerville, Davis, Utah	Find A Grave: 49826

Notes: [LOT SMITH TEAMSTER] He also served as a private in the Mormon Battalion [FGC]. He is listed as "Henry Dolton" in [Fisher, 30]. As they were not eligible for federal military pensions, Lot Smith teamsters were not listed on [1862 MOR].

DAVIDSON, GEORGE W. (UNION ARMY) *Baptized before the war (presumed).*

Rank: Teamster	Unit(s): Lot Smith Utah Cavalry Military Service Source(s): Fisher	
Birth Date: Uncertain	Birth Place: Uncertain	
LDS Membership Date: Presumed LDS	LDS Membership Source(s): Presumed LDS	
Death Date: Uncertain	Death Place: Uncertain Burial Location: Uncertain	Find A Grave: —

Notes: [MLM] [LOT SMITH TEAMSTER] As they were not eligible for federal military pensions, Lot Smith teamsters were not listed on [1862 MOR].

FULLER, WYLLYS DARWIN   (UNION ARMY)   *Baptized before the war.*

Rank: Teamster	Unit(s): Lot Smith Utah Cavalry **Military Service Source(s):** Fisher; Thomas Edwin Farish, *History of Arizona* (San Francisco: Filmer Brothers Electrotype, 1915), 3:281.
Birth Date: 10 November 1835	**Birth Place:** Windam, Green, New York
LDS Membership Date: 1 January 1845	**LDS Membership Source(s):** LDSBE, NFS (ID #: KWJ3-NBG)
Death Date: 13 June 1920	**Death Place:** Pine, Gila, Arizona **Find A Grave:** — **Burial Location:** Pine Cemetery, Pine, Gila, Arizona

Notes: [MLM] [LOT SMITH TEAMSTER] His name is listed as "Wid Fuller" in [Fisher, 30]. "Bishop of the Leeds Ward, St. George Stake, Utah, from 1875 to 1876 . . . He was ordained a High Priest and Bishop by Geo. A. Smith [on] March 17, 1875" [LDSBE, 4:593]. As they were not eligible for federal military pensions, Lot Smith teamsters were not listed on [1862 MOR].

GRIFFITH, HENRY LIVINGSTON MARSHALL

(UNION ARMY)   *Baptized before the war* (*presumed*).

Rank: Uncertain	Unit(s): E Company, 6th Regiment, California Infantry Volunteers **Military Service Source(s):** Thomas Edwin Farish, *History of Arizona* (San Francisco: Filmer Brothers Electrotype, 1915), 5:284–89.
Birth Date: 20 May 1844	**Birth Place:** Pennsylvania
LDS Membership Date: Presumed LDS	**LDS Membership Source(s):** SBS (LDS membership uncertain)
Death Date: 12 May 1910	**Death Place:** Boulder Creek, Santa Cruz, California **Find A Grave:** — **Burial Location:** Boulder Creek Cemetery, Boulder Creek, Santa Cruz, California

Notes: As a two-year-old child, he sailed to Yerba Buena (San Francisco), California, with Samuel Brannon and other Latter-day Saints on board the ship *Brooklyn* [SBS]. His parents were LDS (Lorin K. Hansen, "Voyage of the *Brooklyn*," *Dialogue: A Journal of Mormon Thought* 21, no. 3 [Autumn 1988]: 47–72).

KANE, THOMAS LEIPER   (UNION ARMY)   *Not LDS.*

Rank: Brevet Major General	Unit(s): K Company, 13th Pennsylvania Reserves Infantry (42nd Pennsylvania Volunteers and 1st Pennsylvania Rifles) **Military Service Source(s):** NPS
Birth Date: 27 January 1822	**Birth Place:** Philadelphia, Pennsylvania
LDS Membership Date: Not LDS	**Source(s):** (NFS ID #: L78R-J8D)
Death Date: 26 December 1883	**Death Place:** Philadelphia, Pennsylvania **Find A Grave:** 5843065 **Burial Location:** Philadelphia, Pennsylvania

Notes: He was a long-time friend of Brigham Young and the LDS Church. Prior to the Civil War, he "developed sympathy for the Mormons, perhaps because of their stand against slavery. He befriended Brigham Young, and in 1858 Kane helped prevent bloodshed by mediating the dispute between the Mormons and the federal government. At the commencement of the Civil War, Kane raised a mounted rifle regiment of western Pennsylvanians that became known as the 'Bucktails' . . . and became its lieutenant colonel on 21 June 1861.

On 22 August 1861, he commanded his men in a skirmish with J. E. B. Stuart at Catlett's Station, Virginia. Later in the year, while leading his men back to their base after a patrol from Dranesville, Virginia, he clashed with Confederates. . . . In the ensuing battle, Kane was wounded. . . . During the spring and summer of 1862, Kane commanded . . . in the Shenandoah Valley. On 6 June 1862 at Harrisburg, Virginia, Kane was captured. After his exchange in the late summer, he was promoted to brigadier general of volunteers and given command of the 2d Brigade, 1st Division, XII Corps of the Army of the Potomac. . . . He commanded a brigade of the same corps at Chancellorsville. Shortly, thereafter he contracted pneumonia and was sent to Baltimore, where he remained in the hospital through June 1863. In the early hours of the battle of Gettysburg, it became apparent that the Confederates had discovered one of the most important Federal ciphers. Someone had to convey this information to the commander of the Army of the Potomac, George Gordon Meade. Kane volunteered, though he had not recovered from pneumonia. Dressed in civilian clothes, he made his way through Confederate territory and even through a portion of Stuart's cavalry to Meade at Gettysburg. On 2 July he resumed command of his brigade, then occupying a position on the extreme right of the Union line—the business end of the 'fishhook.' At 3:30 a.m. on 3 July his position was attacked, and though he was still too weak to sit on a horse, Kane led his men in the repulse of the Confederates through the late morning. The following day Kane's health forced him to relinquish command, and he went to oversee the draft depot at Pittsburg, Pennsylvania. . . . His health never really recovered, though, and he resigned his commission in November 1863. At the end of the war, he received a brevet promotion to major general for gallantry at Gettysburg" (David S. Heidler and Jeanne T. Heidler, eds., *Encyclopedia of the American Civil War: A Political, Social, and Military History* [New York: W. W. Norton, 2000], 1099).

LARSEN, THURSTON (UNION ARMY)   *Baptized before the war.*

Rank: Teamster	**Unit(s):** Lot Smith Utah Cavalry **Military Service Source(s):** Fisher
Birth Date: 23 September 1828	**Birth Place:** Stekka, Strandebarm, Hordaland, Norway
LDS Membership Date: 12 February 1843	**LDS Membership Source(s):** NFS (ID #: KWV9-VFJ)
Death Date: 11 March 1907	**Death Place:** Parker, Fremont, Idaho **Find A Grave:** — **Burial Location:** Parker, Fremont, Idaho

Notes: [MLM] [LOT SMITH TEAMSTER] He "came to Utah with the Mormon Battalion" [PPMU, 115]. "The minimum age to be accepted into the militia was 18, Thurston was only 17, but only three months from his 18th birthday, so he requested to go. In dire need of young men that could take the rigors & hardships of such a campaign, Thurston was permitted to join the army on the 26th of June, 1846. . . . During the Civil War, there was trouble with renegades destroying telegraph wire, railroad tracks, and robbing the mail. Frank Fuller, the acting governor of Utah, called for volunteers from the Nauvoo Legion to patrol the telegraph lines and protect them from destruction. The next day, 24 men under Colonel Robert T. Burton, left for this assignment. Two days later President Abraham Lincoln, through Secretary of War Stanton, authorized Brigham Young to send a group of cavalry to serve ninety days patrolling the same telegraph lines. One hundred & six men responded to the call and Thurston Larson was one of them. The commanding officer was Captain Lot Smith." He also served in Utah's Black Hawk War (http://trees.ancestry.com/tree/20880616 /person/18024378831/media/3?pgnum=1&pg=0&pgpl=pid%7cpgNum). He was "a member of the Mormon Battalion, Company C . . . resided in Nauvoo when the Prophet Joseph Smith was killed. He joined the Battalion and marched to Santa Fe with the sick detachment of the Battalion, and arrived in the Valley July 27, 1847. He took part in the Echo Canyon war and suffered all the trials incident to early days in Utah" [LDSBE 4:750–51]. [Fisher] spells his last name "Larsen"; [LDSBE] spells his last name "Larson." As they were not eligible for federal military pensions, Lot Smith teamsters were not listed on [1862 MOR].

MAXFIELD, ELIJAH H. (UNION ARMY)   *Baptized before the war.*

Rank: Teamster	**Unit(s):** Lot Smith Utah Cavalry **Military Service Source(s):** PPMU, Fisher
Birth Date: 5 November 1832	**Birth Place:** Bedeque, Prince Edward Island
LDS Membership Date: 1 January 1846	**LDS Membership Source(s):** PPMU, NFS (ID #: KWNV-3XB)
Death Date: 7 September 1925	**Death Place:** Salt Lake City, Salt Lake, Utah **Find A Grave:** 18207226 **Burial Location:** Salt Lake City, Salt Lake, Utah

Notes: [LOT SMITH TEAMSTER] "Took part in Civil War. High Priest" [PPMU, 265]. "Assisted in settling 'Dixie' five years. Took part in Civil War. Veteran Indian wars. Brought first library to Utah. . . . High priest; ward clerk . . . Belong[ed] to Y X company [Brigham Young Express and Carrying Company]; rode the pony express and drove fast express" [PPMU, 1028]. [PPMU] also reported that he was a "spy in Johnston's army in the Black Hills," but the actual service referred to is uncertain. Although his teamster service did not qualify him as a pension-eligible Civil War veteran, he is listed on the 1890 veteran census schedule from Piute County, Utah. The [1890 Census] lists "Private" and "Special Company" after his name. He reported three months and fourteen days of military service (from May 8 to August 22, 1862); both dates are about one week later than the period of service of the Lot Smith Utah Cavalry Company. [1890 Census] also lists "3 ribs broken from brass [unintelligible]" as a service-related disability and includes the following explanatory note: "Served in Special Co[mpany] called out by the President of the U.S." As they were not eligible for federal military pensions, Lot Smith teamsters were not listed on [1862 MOR].

McKEE, SAMUEL (UNION ARMY)   *Uncertain if LDS.*

Rank: Captain	**Unit(s):** Mounted Rifle Dragoons Cavalry **Military Service Source(s):** See Notes
Birth Date: About 1835	**Birth Place:** Missouri
LDS Membership Date: Uncertain if LDS	**LDS Membership Source(s):** Uncertain if LDS (NFS ID #: M8HW-XK6)
Death Date: 3 June 1864	**Death Place:** Cold Harbor, Virginia **Find A Grave:** — **Burial Location:** Uncertain

Notes: While there is no indication that he ever joined the LDS Church, he is believed to be first cadet from Utah Territory selected for admission at the United States Military Academy. He graduated from West Point on July 1, 1858 (thirteenth in a class of twenty-seven cadets; Cullum number: 1810). He served in the Mounted Rifle Dragoons Cavalry and was mortally wounded at the battle of Cold Harbor, Virginia, in June 1864 (Paul W. Child, ed., *Register of Graduates and Former Cadets of the United States Military Academy* [West Point, NY: Association of USMA Graduates, 1990]).

MERRILL, MARK (UNION ARMY)   *Baptized before the war.*

Rank: Teamster	**Unit(s):** Lot Smith Utah Cavalry **Military Service Source(s):** Fisher
Birth Date: 6 July 1837	**Birth Place:** Far West, Caldwell, Missouri
LDS Membership Date: 1 August 1850	**LDS Membership Source(s):** NFS (ID #: KWJ6-6BK)
Death Date: 19 December 1862	**Death Place:** Salt Lake City, Salt Lake, Utah **Find A Grave:** 30880801 **Burial Location:** Salt Lake City Cemetery, Salt Lake City, Salt Lake, Utah

Notes: [LOT SMITH TEAMSTER] As they were not eligible for federal military pensions, Lot Smith teamsters were not listed on [1862 MOR].

MURPHY, MARK (UNION ARMY)   *Baptized before the war.*

Rank: Teamster	**Unit(s):** Lot Smith Utah Cavalry **Military Service Source(s):** Fisher
Birth Date: 6 July 1837	**Birth Place:** Far West, Caldwell, Missouri
LDS Membership Date: 1 August 1850	**LDS Membership Source(s):** NFS (ID #: KWJ6-6BK)
Death Date: 29 July 1918	**Death Place:** Salt Lake City, Salt Lake, Utah **Find A Grave:** — **Burial Location:** Salt Lake City, Salt Lake, Utah

Notes: [MLM] [LOT SMITH TEAMSTER] His father, Emanuel Masters Murphy, "came to Utah Aug. 30, 1860, Jesse E. Murphy Company" [PPMU, 501]. As they were not eligible for federal military pensions, Lot Smith teamsters were not listed on [1862 MOR].

RANDALL, ALFRED (UNION ARMY)   *Baptized before the war.*

Rank: Teamster	**Unit(s):** Lot Smith Utah Cavalry **Military Service Source(s):** Fisher
Birth Date: 8 January 1845	**Birth Place:** Nauvoo, Hancock, Illinois
LDS Membership Date: 22 October 1854	**LDS Membership Source(s):** NFS (ID #: KWJC-JNV)
Death Date: 26 September 1907	**Death Place:** Willow Valley, Coconino, Arizona **Find A Grave:** 50749915 **Burial Location:** Pine Cemetery, Pine, Gila, Arizona

Notes: [LOT SMITH TEAMSTER] As they were not eligible for federal military pensions, Lot Smith teamsters were not listed on [1862 MOR].

SIRRINE, GEORGE J. (UNION ARMY)   *Uncertain if LDS.*

Rank: Private	**Unit(s):** I Company, 137th Regiment, New York Volunteers **Military Service Source(s):** SBS
Birth Date: 30 June 1845	**Birth Place:** Phillipstown, Putnam, New York
LDS Membership Date: Uncertain	**LDS Membership Source(s):** SBS (NFS ID #: KCPM-2MZ)
Death Date: 3 July 1863	**Death Place:** Gettysburg, Adams, Pennsylvania **Find A Grave:** 18658228 **Burial Location:** Grove Cemetery, Trumansburg, Tompkins, New York

Notes: He sailed as a small child to Yerba Buena (San Francisco), California, with Samuel Brannon and other Latter-day Saints on board the ship *Brooklyn*. [SBS] His parents were not LDS (Lorin K. Hansen, "Voyage of the *Brooklyn*," *Dialogue: A Journal of Mormon Thought* 21:3 [Autumn 1988], 47–72).

WALTON, WILLIAM H. (UNION ARMY)   *Baptized before the war (presumed).*

Rank: Teamster	**Unit(s):** Lot Smith Utah Cavalry **Military Service Source(s):** Fisher
Birth Date: Uncertain	**Birth Place:** Uncertain
LDS Membership Date: Presumed LDS	**LDS Membership Source(s):** Presumed LDS

Walton, William H. (continued)	
Death Date: Uncertain	**Death Place:** Uncertain **Find A Grave:** — **Burial Location:** Uncertain

Notes: [MLM] [LOT SMITH TEAMSTER] As they were not eligible for federal military pensions, Lot Smith teamsters were not listed on [1862 MOR].

WARNER, HENRY J.   (UNION ARMY)   *Baptism date is uncertain.*

Rank: Private	**Unit(s):** C Company, 3rd California Infantry **Military Service Source(s):** Fred B. Rogers, *Soldiers of the Overland* (San Francisco: Grabhorn Press, 1938), 15–16.
Birth Date: 1843	**Birth Place:** Massachusetts
LDS Membership Date: Uncertain	**LDS Membership Source(s):** SBS (NFS ID #: MMBY-1Y2)
Death Date: 17 June 1862	**Death Place:** near Camp Halleck, Stockton, San Joaquin, California **Find A Grave:** — **Burial Location:** Uncertain

Notes: As a small child, he sailed to Yerba Buena (San Francisco), California, with Samuel Brannon and other Latter-day Saints on board the ship *Brooklyn*. Presumed to be LDS [SBS]. Served under Colonel Patrick Edward Connor (Fred B. Rogers, *Soldiers of the Overland* [San Francisco: Grabhorn Press, 1938], 15–16).

WHITMER, ALEXANDER PETER JEFFERSON   (UNCERTAIN)   *Uncertain if LDS.*

Rank: Uncertain	**Unit(s):** Uncertain **Military Service Source(s):** Andrew Jenson, *Historical Record* (Salt Lake City: 1888), 7:612–13.
Birth Date: 7 February 1842	**Birth Place:** Caldwell County, Missouri
LDS Membership Date: Uncertain if LDS	**LDS Membership Source(s):** Uncertain if LDS (NFS ID #: LHSW-29V)
Death Date: The exact date is uncertain (but he was killed in the Civil War)	**Death Place:** Uncertain **Find A Grave:** — **Burial Location:** Kingston Cemetery, Caldwell, Missouri

Notes: His father, John Whitmer, was one of the Eight Witnesses of the Book of Mormon and served as the first Church Historian (recording much of the Book of Commandments and Revelations, which was used to publish the Book of Commandments in 1833). His father was excommunicated and left the Church in 1838—four years before Alexander was born. "John Whitmer was the father of four children, three sons and one daughter. One of his sons [John Oliver Whitmer] died when about ten years old and another [Alexander Peter Jefferson Whitmer] was killed in the late civil war" (Andrew Jenson, *Historical Record* (Salt Lake City: 1888), 7:612–13). Alexander is not listed in the NPS database. At the time of this publication, it is uncertain if he served in a Union or Confederate unit (as Missouri fielded units for both sides of the conflict).

WIGHT, LEVI LAMONI   (CONFEDERATE ARMY)   *Uncertain if LDS.*

Rank: Private	**Unit(s):** 8th Battalion, Texas Cavalry **Military Service Source(s):** Davis Bitton, ed., *The Reminiscences and Civil War Letters of Levi Lamoni Wight* (Salt Lake City: University of Utah Press, 1970), FGC.

Birth Date: 1 May 1836	Birth Place: Clay County, Missouri
LDS Membership Date: Uncertain if LDS	Source(s): Davis Bitton, ed., *The Reminiscences and Civil War Letters of Levi Lamoni Wight* (Salt Lake City: University of Utah Press, 1970), FGC. (NFS ID #: LHVR-S2Q)
Death Date: 15 May 1918	Death Place: Texas Find A Grave: 15519237 Burial Location: Sweetwater, Nolan, Texas

Notes: He was a son of Lyman Wight (1796–1858) and a member of Zion's Camp who was ordained as an LDS Apostle in 1841; after the death of Joseph Smith Jr., Lyman led a group of Latter-day Saints to Texas. Lyman Wight was disfellowshipped from the LDS Church in 1848 (Davis Bitton, ed., *The Reminiscences and Civil War Letters of Levi Lamoni Wight* [Salt Lake City: University of Utah Press, 1970]). No baptism date was discovered for Levi; he was almost certainly affiliated with the LDS Church before his father was disfellowshipped. Wight's diary states (original spelling preserved), "I entered my name for a Confederate army at Fort Mason, Texas, and endered the ranks of the first Texas Caval, Co C, later Co K same reg. Recd a bounty of $50 and one month's pay, 35 dollars. At the time Confederate money was good but the next year it went down and down till it was worthles and we served out our time with out pay, more than scant clothing, and as for me my wife spun and wove the most part of our clothes and sent them to me with considerable risk of loss." Levi fought at Fredericksburg, Virginia, and in several other battles (Bitton, *Reminiscences*, 23–40). According to the reminiscences of Levi's granddaughter, Ann Wight, after the Civil War, "His income was his quarterly Confederate pension—less than twenty dollars. . . . When his pension came, it burned his pocket until he could spend it on us children. . . . We loved to hear him tell of his Civil War experiences. Robert E. Lee was his idol. He had a large picture of him on the wall of his room. There was also a picture of a reunion of his brigade, and a panel picture of 'Lee and his Generals.' Also hanging on his wall was a Confederate flag" (Bitton, 189–90). There is a GAR veteran marker next to his grave marker [FGC].

WINNER, ISRAEL   (UNION ARMY)   *Baptized before the war (presumed).*

Rank: Private	Unit(s): L Company, 2nd California Cavalry Military Service Source(s): SBS
Birth Date: 1844	Birth Place: Dover, Ocean, New Jersey
LDS Membership Date: Uncertain	LDS Membership Source(s): SBS
Death Date: Uncertain	Death Place: Woodside, San Mateo, California Find A Grave: 11314161 Burial Location: Uncertain

Notes: As a very small child, he sailed to Yerba Buena (San Francisco), California, with Samuel Brannon and other Latter-day Saints on board the ship *Brooklyn*. Presumed to be LDS [SBS].

Much of the famous Salt Lake Tabernacle was constructed during the Civil War. This photograph shows the Tabernacle in 1868. (Library of Congress)

LDS BAPTISM SUMMARY

The following table and lists provide summary information regarding the baptismal dates of the Latter-day Saint Civil War veterans listed in Appendix E.

WHEN BAPTIZED	VETERANS
BEFORE the Civil War	179
BEFORE the Civil War (presumed)	18
DURING the Civil War	16
AFTER the Civil War	170
Baptismal date UNCERTAIN	1
Total	384

Table 1. When LDS Civil War veterans were baptized as members of The Church of Jesus Christ of Latter-day Saints.

BAPTIZED BEFORE THE CIVIL WAR

ALEXANDER, Moroni Woodruff

ALLEN, Samuel

ALLEN, William C.

ANDERSON, Niels

ARROWSMITH, John

ASHCRAFT (or ASHCROFT), James Eli

ASHTON, Edward

ATKINSON, James Isaac

ATTWOOD, Richard H.

BAIRD, Alexander

BAKER, George Washington

BALLINGER, John McClure

BARLOW, James Madison

BATTY, Edward

BEASLEY, John Fletcher

BELL, Daniel

BENNION, John R.

BENNION, Samuel Roberts

BENZON, Andrew Beck

BIGLER, Andrew

BIGLOW, Asa Elijah

BLAND, Joseph

BOWRING, Charles Kingsford

BRINGHURST, William A.

BROWN, Edwin

BROWN, John Wacklet

BURNHAM, Charles C.

BUTTER, John

CAHOON, John F.

CALDWELL, Thomas S.

CALKIN, Theodore J.

CANTWELL, Francis R.

CARDON, Thomas Barthelemy

CARNEY, Peter

CHAMBERLIN (or CHAMBERLAIN), Joseph

CHLARSON, Hans Nadrian

CLARK, Thomas Benjamin

CLARK, William H.

CLEMONS (or CLEMENS), Hiram B.

COOK, Daniel Dean

COREY, George W.

COTTRELL (or COTTEREL), George

COX, John C.

CRAGUN, James H.

CRISMON, Charles, Jr.

DAVIS, Albert

DENNIS, William Taylor

DOBSON, Willard Richards

DUKE, John

EARDLEY, Josiah

ELLIOTT, James M.

EMPEY, David Arza

EVANS, Charles M.

EVANS, John Davis

FELT, Joseph H.

FISHER, Joseph Armstrong

FORBES, John

FOX, John Sellman

FRYER, Joseph

GARDINER, Frederick

GIBBS, George F.

GIBSON, Moses Washington

GODDARD, Joseph

GRANT, William S.

GRAY, William A.

GUEST, Edward F.

HALE, Solomon H.

HALL, Samuel Parley

HANCOCK, George Washington

HASTLER, William H.

HELM, John

HENDRICKS, Samuel Allen

HILL, Samuel

HINCKLEY, Ira Nathaniel

HOAGLAND, John

HOLMES, William H.

HOPKINS, Richard Rockwell

HOWE, Richard

HUFFAKER, Lewis Albert

HULLINGER, Harvey Coe

IMLAY, James

JACKSON, Henry Wells

JENKINSON, Noah

JENSON, Lars

JOHNSON, Alfred

JOHNSON, George Washington

JOHNSON, Powell

JOHNSTON, Calvin C.

JOHNSTON, Francis

JOHNSTON, James

JONES, Robert W.

JUDD, James H.

KELLEY, James A.

KENNARD, Leonidas Hamlin

KIMBALL, Hiram

KNAPP, John C.

KNIGHTON, George

KNOWLTON, J. Q. (John Quincy)

LEE, William B.

LEES, James

LEMMON, Leander

LITZ, Peter Gose

LOGUE, William Charles Taylor

LONGSTROTH, William

LOWE, William W.

LUTZ, Thomas Jefferson

LYNCH, William

MATHEWS, John

MAYNE, William B.

MERRILL, Edwin

MILLER, Reuben P.

MITTON, John

MOORE, John L.

MOUSLEY, William P.

MURPHY, James D.

MURRAY, George

NEFF, Benjamin B.

NEFF, John

NELSON, William

NEWTON, Thomas D.

NOBLE, Edward A.

NORTH, Hiram B.

OAKASON, Hans

PARK, Hugh D.

PEACOCK, Alfred James

PEARCE, Edward William

PECK, Joseph Augustine

PINCKARD, Robert

PLATT, Francis

POLMANTER, Lewis L.

PRINCE, Francis

PRINCE, Richard

PUCELL, William

RAWLINS, Joseph Sharp

REX, William

RHODES, William H.

RICH, Landon

RICHARDSON, Thomas J.

RITER, Samuel H. W.

ROBERTS, Albert F.

ROSE, Alley Stephen

ROZSA, John

SCOTT, Robert Griffin

SHARP, George W.

SHARP, James

SHURTLEFF, Emerson D.

SIMMON, Harlan E.

SMITH, John

SMITH, Lot

SMITH, Thomas

SMITH, William B.

SPENCER, Howard

STANDIFIRD, John Henry

STEED, James H.

STRATTON, James

STRONG, William H.

SYDDALL, Henry

TAYLOR, Joseph J.

TERRY, Joseph

TERRY, William R.

THOMPSON, Samuel W.
THURSTON, Moses
TURNER, John Edward
VANBEEK, George Day
WALKER, John H.
WALKER, Robert Cowie

WALKER, William Henry
WARDELL, Martin Douglas
WEAVER, William Henry
WEILER, Elijah Malin
WELLS, James H.
WELSH, James H.
WILLIAMS, Bateman H.

WILLIAMS, Ephraim H.
WIMER, John P.
WINNER, George King
WOODS, William
WRIGHT, John
YOUNG, Seymour Bicknell

BAPTIZED BEFORE THE CIVIL WAR (PRESUMED)

BESS, William
CHERRY, Jesse Yelton
COVERT, Evert
DRAPER, Parley P.
FISHER, Joseph R.
GREEN, James

HARRIS, Thomas H.
IREY (or IREA), Cyrus
JONES, Henry L.
LARKINS, James
LUTZ, William W.
McCUE, Amos W.

McCUE, James P.
McNICOL, Daniel
MYRICK, Newton Mosiah
OSBORN, Lewis D.
RICE, Adelbert
SADDLER, Samuel

BAPTIZED DURING THE CIVIL WAR

ALLEN, Samuel Jackson
BARTON, Isaac
BOYER, William
BULOW, Charles Henry Engel
COATS, Henry
HACKETT, George

HIGGINBOTHAM, Simon
 Shelby
HIXSON (or HICKSON), James
KING, Frederick Augustus
LIVINGSTON, Alexander
NELSON, Alma Franklin

NESLEN, William Francis
NORMAN, Saul
O'BRIEN, John
PEERY, David Harold
SMITH, Louis William

BAPTIZED AFTER THE CIVIL WAR

ABBOTT, Charles Enoch
ACKROYD, Walter William
AMES, John Nelson
AMOS, John Thomas
ANDREWS, William Jefferson
BALLARD, Augustus Ross
BALLARD, Winfield Scott
BARRETT, William Riley
BARRETT, Maurice J.
BARTON, William Henry
BELLAMY, William W.
BENSON, William Carlisle
BEVANS, Corydon Henry

BISHOP, Francis Marion
BOULDEN, Joseph Louis
BOYLE, Albert Charles
BROOKBANK, Thomas Walton
BROWN, Campbell McLeod, Sr.
BROWN, John Wyles
CAMPBELL, LeRoy
CARPENTER, Ezra Davis
CARROLL, John Nelson
CARTER, Benjamin
CARVER, Thomas
CHARTER, Henry Willard
CLARK, Joshua Reuben, Sr.

COLE, Thomas Benton
COLEGROVE, Harley
COWLES, William H.
CRAWFORD, Francis Marion
CRAWFORD, Joseph Henry
CULLER, Benjamin
DARLING, Ned Emanuel
DAVIS, John Barton
DAVIS, John Eugene
 (aka William H. Norman)
DELONG, Leonard
DIAL, Burris (or Burriss)
DODDS, George

DOTSON, William Thomas
DUNHAM, Levi
DYKES, William
EASTMAN, Aubrey (or Arbury)
    Clevenseller
ECHOLS, Lewis Barton
EDWARDS, Moses
EMMONS, Charles E.
EVANS, David
EVANS, Milton Haywood
FERRIS, John Solomon
FITZGERALD, Milton Hitt
FORBES, Joseph Barlow
FRANK, John Valentine
GIBSON, John
GIBSON, Spotswood Nicholas
GOODFELLOW, John Smith
GORDON, Eli
GRIGG, William Alexander
HAMBLIN, Leander Floyd
HARPER, John C.
HARRINGTON, John
HARRISON, Daniel
HOFFMIRE, Francis G.
HOLCOMB, Samuel Spencer
HOWARD, William W.
HUDDLESTON, Henry F.
HUDSON, Lyman L.
HUFFAKER, Ignatius Henry
HUFFAKER, Isaac Asbury
INMAN, Samuel Edward
ISBELL, Alexander Franklin
JACK, James Hazlett
JAGGER, George
JARVIES, John J.
JESSUP, Levi T.
JONES, John L.
JONES, Seth W.
JONES, William H.
KENDALL, Eli C.
KENDALL, George M.

KILGROW, John W.
KIMBROUGH, William B.
KING, Ransom B.
KING, Wiley F.
KNIGHT, George F.
LANGFORD, John W.
LAWSON, John W.
LEWIS, Theodore Belden
LILL, Daniel C.
LINDSEY, Henry Porter
LITZ, John T.
LITZ, William Sawyers
LOFTUS, John
LOWRY, Thomas Alexander
MANNING, Joseph C.
MARSH, George D.
MARSHALL, William L.
MASON, Peter M.
McENTIRE, Eli
McNEICE, Coleman C.
MILLER, John L.
MITCHELL, James M.
MORGAN, John Hamilton
MORRIS, Gaddison
MURPHY, John Joseph Pedger
NANCE, J. Y. (James Young)
NANNEY, Richard H.
NELSON, John L.
OBERLANDER, John
ODOM, David George
    Washington
ODOM, Pleasant
OSBURN, William
PARKER, Henry
PEERY, Thomas Elbert
PENFOLD, John
PRIBBLE, John T.
PRICE, Elias
PRICE, Martin Goodge
QUICK, Jacob Siegler
RAINBOLT, David

RAMSEY, George W.
REDMAN, Thomas Jefferson
REED, John Levert
REID, Marquis Lafayette
REYNOLDS, Preston
ROBBINS, William M.
ROBERSON, John Newton
ROGERS, Enoch Milton
ROSE, William Warren
ROSS, Isaac James
SARGENT, William Pinkney
SATTERTHWAITE, Joshua Ward
SAXEY, Alfred
SCHREPEL, John Frederick
SEAMAN, John Whitehead
SEGUINE, Joseph S.
SELLERS, Daniel Rice
SELLERS, Samuel Surratt
SHINER, George William
SHORT, Temple
SIMMONS, Charles
SIZEMORE, William Marion
SLEATER, Robert Gibson
SMITH, Charles William
    Edward Dilk
SMITH, Francis M.
SMITH, Joseph Franklin
SNYDER, Henry T.
SOREN, Ole S.
SOWARDS, George Washington
SPRINGER, Nathan Chatmond
SPRINGSTEED, Hilton
STUART, David Crockett
SULLIVAN, David Dollen
TAYLOR, John Jefferson
THOMPSON, Charles
THOMPSON, Emanuel Edwin
TILLMAN, James C.
TRAUGOTT, John E.
TURNBOW, Pleasant Childers
VOGEL, George William

WATSON, Lorenzo Dow

WELDON, Francis Marion

WESTWOOD, Joseph Moroni

WHITLOCK, Ezra B.

WHITNEY, Leonard Jotham

WILLIAMS, George Calvin

WILLIAMS, James

WILSON, Hamilton

WILSON, John Presly

WOOD, William Harrison

YATES, James Stanley

YOUNG, Joseph Charles

BAPTISMAL DATE UNCERTAIN

HOLLAND, James M.

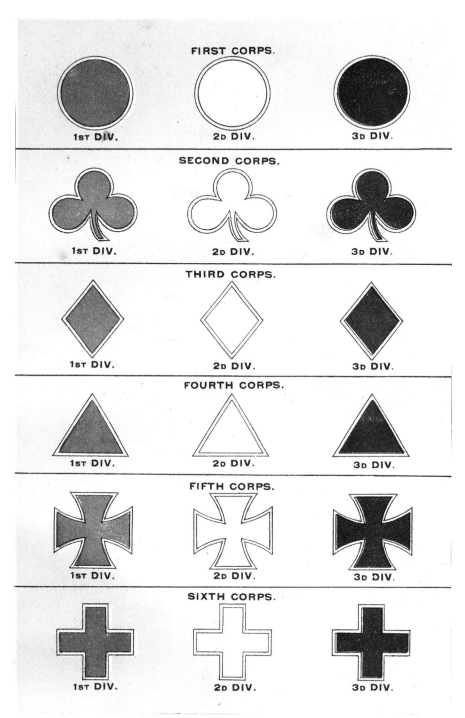

FIRST CORPS.

1ST DIV.   2D DIV.   3D DIV.

SECOND CORPS.

1ST DIV.   2D DIV.   3D DIV.

THIRD CORPS.

1ST DIV.   2D DIV.   3D DIV.

FOURTH CORPS.

1ST DIV.   2D DIV.   3D DIV.

FIFTH CORPS.

1ST DIV.   2D DIV.   3D DIV.

SIXTH CORPS.

1ST DIV.   2D DIV.   3D DIV.

Corps badges such as these were worn during the Civil War on the top of a soldier's forage cap (called a kepi), on the left side of a hat, or on the front of their uniform. The idea is said to have been conceived by Major General Philip Sheridan and was quickly adopted by other units so soldiers could distinguish each other on the battlefield. Badges were colored to distinguish divisions within a corps (first division was red, second division was white, third division was blue). (Beath, History of the GAR)

APPENDIX H

LDS MILITARY
SERVICE SUMMARY

The following tables and lists provide summary information regarding the service affiliation and branches of the Latter-day Saint Civil War veterans listed in Appendix E.

MILITARY AFFILIATION	VETERANS
Union	310
"Galvanized Yankees"[1]	3
Confederate	71
Total	384

Table 1. Military affiliation of LDS Civil War veterans.

SERVICE BRANCH	VETERANS
Union Army	296
Union Army (presumed)	6
Union Navy	6
Union Navy (presumed)	1
Union Marines	1
Union and Confederate Army ("Galvanized Yankees")	3
Confederate Army	71
Total	384

Table 2. Service branches of LDS Civil War veterans.

---

1. See the Ellsworth-Alford chapter herein for an explanation of the term "Galvanized Yankees."

UNION ARMY

ABBOTT, Charles Enoch

ACKROYD, Walter William

ALEXANDER, Moroni Woodruff

ALLEN, Samuel

ALLEN, Samuel Jackson

ALLEN, William C.

AMES, John Nelson

ANDERSON, Niels

ARROWSMITH, John

ASHTON, Edward

ATKINSON, James Isaac

ATTWOOD, Richard H.

BALLARD, Augustus Ross

BALLARD, Winfield Scott

BALLINGER, John McClure

BARLOW, James Madison

BARRETT, Maurice J.

BARTON, Isaac

BARTON, William Henry

BATTY, Edward

BELL, Daniel

BELLAMY, William W.

BENNION, John R.

BENNION, Samuel Roberts

BENZON, Andrew Beck

BESS, William

BEVANS, Corydon Henry

BIGLER, Andrew

BIGLOW, Asa Elijah

BISHOP, Francis Marion

BLAND, Joseph

BOULDEN, Joseph Louis

BOWRING, Charles Kingsford

BOYER, William

BOYLE, Albert Charles

BRINGHURST, William A.

BROOKBANK, Thomas Walton

BROWN, Edwin

BROWN, John Wyles

BROWN, John Wacklet

BULOW, Charles Henry Engel

BURNHAM, Charles C.

BUTTER, John

CAHOON, John F.

CALDWELL, Thomas S.

CALKIN, Theodore J.

CANTWELL, Francis R.

CARDON, Thomas Barthelemy

CARNEY, Peter

CARPENTER, Ezra Davis

CARROLL, John Nelson

CARTER, Benjamin

CHAMBERLIN (or CHAMBER-
   LAIN), Joseph

CHARTER, Henry Willard

CHERRY, Jesse Yelton

CHLARSON, Hans Nadrian

CLARK, Joshua Reuben, Sr.

CLARK, Thomas Benjamin

CLARK, William H.

CLEMONS (or CLEMENS),
   Hiram B.

COATS, Henry

COLE, Thomas Benton

COLEGROVE, Harley

COOK, Daniel Dean

COREY, George W.

COTTRELL (or COTTEREL),
   George

COVERT, Evert

COWLES, William H.

COX, John C.

CRAGUN, James H.

CRAWFORD, Francis Marion

CRISMON, Charles, Jr.

DARLING, Ned Emanuel

DAVIS, Albert

DAVIS, John Barton

DELONG, Leonard

DIAL, Burris (or Burriss)

DOBSON, Willard Richards

DODDS, George

DRAPER, Parley P.

DUKE, John

DUNHAM, Levi

DYKES, William

EARDLEY, Josiah

EDWARDS, Moses

ELLIOTT, James M.

EMMONS, Charles E.

EVANS, Charles M.

EVANS, David

EVANS, John Davis

EVANS, Milton Haywood

FELT, Joseph H.

FERRIS, John Solomon

FISHER, Joseph Armstrong

FISHER, Joseph R.

FITZGERALD, Milton Hitt

FORBES, Joseph Barlow

FOX, John Sellman

FRANK, John Valentine

FRYER, Joseph

GIBBS, George F.

GIBSON, John

GIBSON, Moses Washington

GODDARD, Joseph

GOODFELLOW, John Smith

GRANT, William S.

GRAY, William A.

GREEN, James

GUEST, Edward F.

HALE, Solomon H.

HALL, Samuel Parley

HAMBLIN, Leander Floyd

HANCOCK, George Washington

HARRINGTON, John

HARRIS, Thomas H.

HASTLER, William H.
HELM, John
HILL, Samuel
HINCKLEY, Ira Nathaniel
HIXSON (or HICKSON), James
HOAGLAND, John
HOFFMIRE, Francis G.
HOLLAND, James M.
HOLMES, William H.
HOPKINS, Richard Rockwell
HOWARD, William W.
HOWE, Richard
HUDSON, Lyman L.
HUFFAKER, Lewis Albert
HULLINGER, Harvey Coe
IMLAY, James
IREY (or IREA), Cyrus
JACK, James Hazlett
JACKSON, Henry Wells
JAGGER, George
JARVIES, John J.
JENKINSON, Noah
JENSON, Lars
JESSUP, Levi T.
JOHNSON, Alfred
JOHNSON, George Washington
JOHNSON, Powell
JOHNSTON, Francis
JOHNSTON, James
JONES, Henry L.
JONES, Robert W.
JONES, Seth W.
JONES, William H.
JUDD, James H.
KELLEY, James A.
KENDALL, Eli C.
KENDALL, George M.
KENNARD, Leonidas Hamlin
KILGROW, John W.
KIMBALL, Hiram
KING, Frederick Augustus

KING, Ransom B.
KNAPP, John C.
KNIGHTON, George
KNOWLTON, J. Q. (John Quincy)
LANGFORD, John W.
LARKINS, James
LEE, William B.
LEES, James
LEMMON, Leander
LILL, Daniel C.
LINDSEY, Henry Porter
LIVINGSTON, Alexander
LONGSTROTH, William
LOWE, William W.
LUTZ, Thomas Jefferson
LUTZ, William W.
LYNCH, William
MANNING, Joseph C.
MARSH, George D.
MASON, Peter M.
MATHEWS, John
MAYNE, William B.
McCUE, Amos W.
McCUE, James P.
McENTIRE, Eli
McNICOL, Daniel
MERRILL, Edwin
MILLER, Reuben P.
MITTON, John
MOORE, John L.
MORGAN, John Hamilton
MOUSLEY, William P.
MURPHY, James D.
MURRAY, George
MYRICK, Newton Mosiah
NANNEY, Richard H.
NEFF, Benjamin B.
NEFF, John
NELSON, John L.
NELSON, William

NESLEN, William Francis
NEWTON, Thomas D.
NOBLE, Edward A.
NORMAN, Saul
NORTH, Hiram B.
OAKASON, Hans
OBERLANDER, John
O'BRIEN, John
OSBORN, Lewis D.
OSBURN, William
PARK, Hugh D.
PARKER, Henry
PEARCE, Edward William
PECK, Joseph Augustine
PENFOLD, John
PLATT, Francis
POLMANTER, Lewis L.
PRIBBLE, John T.
PRICE, Elias
PRINCE, Francis
PUCELL, William
QUICK, Jacob Siegler
RAMSEY, George W.
RAWLINS, Joseph Sharp
REDMAN, Thomas Jefferson
REX, William
RHODES, William H.
RICE, Adelbert
RICH, Landon
RICHARDSON, Thomas J.
RITER, Samuel H. W.
ROBBINS, William M.
ROBERTS, Albert F.
ROSE, Alley Stephen
ROSE, William Warren
ROSS, Isaac James
ROZSA, John
SADDLER, Samuel
SATTERTHWAITE, Joshua Ward
SAXEY, Alfred
SCHREPEL, John Frederick

SCOTT, Robert Griffin
SEGUINE, Joseph S.
SHARP, George W.
SHARP, James
SHINER, George William
SHORT, Temple
SHURTLEFF, Emerson D.
SIMMON, Harlan E.
SLEATER, Robert Gibson
SMITH, Charles William
   Edward Dilk
SMITH, Francis M.
SMITH, John
SMITH, Joseph Franklin
SMITH, Lot
SMITH, Louis William
SMITH, Thomas
SMITH, William B.
SOREN, Ole S.
SOWARDS, George Washington

SPENCER, Howard
SPRINGSTEED, Hilton
STANDIFIRD, John Henry
STEED, James H.
STRONG, William H.
SULLIVAN, David Dollen
SYDDALL, Henry
TAYLOR, Joseph J.
TERRY, Joseph
TERRY, William R.
THOMPSON, Charles
THOMPSON, Emanuel Edwin
THOMPSON, Samuel W
THURSTON, Moses
TRAUGOTT, John E.
VANBEEK, George Day
VOGEL, George William
WALKER, John H.
WALKER, Robert Cowie
WALKER, William Henry

WARDELL, Martin Douglas
WATSON, Lorenzo Dow
WEAVER, William Henry
WEILER, Elijah Malin
WELLS, James H.
WELSH, James H.
WESTWOOD, Joseph Moroni
WHITLOCK, Ezra B.
WHITNEY, Leonard Jotham
WILLIAMS, Bateman H.
WILLIAMS, Ephraim H.
WILLIAMS, James
WILSON, Hamilton
WIMER, John P.
WINNER, George King
WOODS, William
WRIGHT, John
YATES, James Stanley
YOUNG, Joseph Charles
YOUNG, Seymour Bicknell

UNION ARMY (PRESUMED)

ASHCRAFT (or ASHCROFT),
   James Eli
BARRETT, William Riley

EASTMAN, Aubrey (or Arbury)
   Clevenseller
SNYDER, Henry T.

TURNER, John Edward
WILLIAMS, George Calvin

UNION NAVY

BAIRD, Alexander
BROWN, Campbell McLeod, Sr.

LOFTUS, John
NELSON, Alma Franklin

SEAMAN, John Whitehead
STRATTON, James

UNION NAVY (PRESUMED)

SPRINGER, Nathan Chatmond

UNION MARINES

FORBES, John

UNION AND CONFEDERATE ARMY
("GALVANIZED YANKEES")

DAVIS, John Eugene
  (aka William H. Norman)

LAWSON, John W.

SARGENT, William Pinkney

CONFEDERATE ARMY

AMOS, John Thomas
ANDREWS, William Jefferson
BAKER, George Washington
BEASLEY, John Fletcher
BENSON, William Carlisle
CAMPBELL, LeRoy
CARVER, Thomas
CRAWFORD, Joseph Henry
CULLER, Benjamin
DENNIS, William Taylor
DOTSON, William Thomas
ECHOLS, Lewis Barton
EMPEY, David Arza
GARDINER, Frederick
GIBSON, Spotswood Nicholas
GORDON, Eli
GRIGG, William Alexander
HACKETT, George
HARPER, John C.
HARRISON, Daniel
HENDRICKS, Samuel Allen
HIGGINBOTHAM, Simon
  Shelby
HOLCOMB, Samuel Spencer

HUDDLESTON, Henry F.
HUFFAKER, Ignatius Henry
HUFFAKER, Isaac Asbury
INMAN, Samuel Edward
ISBELL, Alexander Franklin
JOHNSTON, Calvin C.
JONES, John L.
KIMBROUGH, William B.
KING, Wiley F.
KNIGHT, George F.
LEWIS, Theodore Belden
LITZ, John T.
LITZ, Peter Gose
LITZ, William Sawyers
LOGUE, William Charles Taylor
LOWRY, Thomas Alexander
MARSHALL, William L.
McNEICE, Coleman C.
MILLER, John L.
MITCHELL, James M.
MORRIS, Gaddison
MURPHY, John Joseph Pedger
NANCE, J. Y. (James Young)
ODOM, David George
  Washington

ODOM, Pleasant
PEACOCK, Alfred James
PEERY, David Harold
PEERY, Thomas Elbert
PINCKARD, Robert
PRICE, Martin Goodge
PRINCE, Richard
RAINBOLT, David
REED, John Levert
REID, Marquis Lafayette
REYNOLDS, Preston
ROBERSON, John Newton
ROGERS, Enoch Milton
SELLERS, Daniel Rice
SELLERS, Samuel Surratt
SIMMONS, Charles
SIZEMORE, William Marion
STUART, David Crockett
TAYLOR, John Jefferson
TILLMAN, James C.
TURNBOW, Pleasant Childers
WELDON, Francis Marion
WILSON, John Presly
WOOD, William Harrison

This woodcut, entitled "The Second Fire Zouaves," appeared in Harper's Weekly *on September 7, 1861.*

Entitled "The Campaign in Virginia—'On to Richmond!'", this woodcut was printed in Harper's Weekly *on June 18, 1864.*

ACKNOWLEDGMENTS

The American Civil War has always held an interest and fascination for me. I remember my excitement as a young child during the centennial celebration as I collected stamps, articles, and magazines about the war. I thought it was only fitting that the war's sesquicentennial celebration should include some contribution regarding the way the Civil War affected Latter-day Saints and Utah Territory. This book is the result of that desire, and it is with great pleasure that I am able to acknowledge and thank the many people and organizations who have made this volume possible.

I am deeply grateful to Robert C. Freeman for helping me to better understand how to take an idea such as this from concept to publication and to William P. MacKinnon, who has been both a mentor and friend, providing a steady stream of good ideas and encouragement.

I am thankful for the historians who have spent countless hours researching, writing, and rewriting the chapters in this book. I believe that the final publication presents a more complete and nuanced portrait of both Utah Territory and Latter-day Saints during the Civil War than any one of us alone could have provided. I also wish to express my sincere appreciation for the numerous historians and professors who contributed both their time and expertise to serve as blinded peer reviewers for the chapters and appendices

within this book. Each chapter was improved because of their efforts.

I am pleased that we are able to introduce by name many of the Latter-day Saints who participated in the Civil War—soldiers who served in both the Union and Confederate forces. As is often the case with large research efforts, it is probably good we did not realize how much work creating that list would ultimately require. Preparing that information was far more involved and time-consuming than I initially imagined, but I believe that the results are well worth the effort. The majority of the day-to-day digging, searching, comparing, checking, deciphering, and rechecking was completed by a group of enthusiastic student researchers from Brigham Young University who spent many hundreds of hours in pursuit of this information. I am indebted to Joseph R. Stuart, Mary E. Moberly, Ian S. Lindsay, Nathan Freeman, Phil Abbott, Scott Lovejoy, Trevor Slezak, Elizabeth DeFranco, and Amanda Van Leuven Campos for their positive attitudes, inquisitive natures, attention to detail, and good humor throughout this project. Their help has been invaluable.

Financial assistance received from Brigham Young University's Religious Studies Center made this research possible, and I am grateful to the many donors who made those funds available. We have also been assisted in this research by several individuals who each contributed to the growing list of Latter-day Saint Civil War veterans. Curtis Allen, Ken Nelson, DeBorah Bankston, Robert Hall, LaMar T. Merrill, David Safranski, Robert L. Davis, Gerald Davis, Frank Thomas, Drucilla Smith, and Shirley Williams were especially helpful, and I express my appreciation for their kind assistance.

The patient assistance from knowledgeable and helpful librarians and archivists at the Church History Library and Archives, Brigham Young University's L. Tom Perry Special Collections at the Harold B. Lee Library, the Utah State Historical Society, and the J. Willard Marriott Library at the University of Utah was also most appreciated. Additionally, I wish to thank the editors at *Utah Historical Quarterly* and *Mormon Historical Studies* for allowing us to reprint journal articles that fit so well with the rest of this volume.

The directors, editors, artists, and staff at Brigham Young University's Religious Studies Center made the work associated with preparing this book for publication a pleasure. Devan Jensen, Brent Nordgren, Heidi Sullivan, Jeff Wade, Joany Pinegar, Dana Kendall, Jonathon Owen, Nyssa Sylvester, Art Morrill, Katie Skovran, and Allison Swenson deserve special recognition and thanks for their assistance, good ideas, and professionalism.

I am grateful to my parents, Ken and Dolores Alford, who shared their love of learning and who have always supported me with their love. I am also grateful to my children (Suzanne, Marie, Christine, and Kenneth), their spouses (Kendall, David, Jeff, and Rachel), and my grandchildren; they make life meaningful and fun. My deepest appreciation, though, is reserved for my wife, Sherilee, who is simultaneously my best friend, head cheerleader, therapist, and confidant. Thank you for supporting me on this project and the opportunity costs associated with it. I'm a better person because of you, and I love you with all my heart.

On May 23 and 24, 1865, Washington, DC, hosted the Grand Review of the Armies to mark the ending of the Civil War. On May 23, Major General George Meade led an estimated 80,000 men. Infantry units marched twelve men across; they were followed by divisional and corps artillery units. The cavalry units who participated stretched for over seven miles. The following day, General William Tecumseh Sherman led an additional 65,000 men representing the Army of the Tennessee and the Army of Georgia. (Library of Congress)

Civil War veterans—members of the United Confederate Veterans and Grand Army of the Republic—pose at Gettysburg in 1913. (Library of Congress)

Union and Confederate veterans march together at Gettysburg in 1913 honoring the fiftieth anniversary of the battle. (Library of Congress)

INDEX

P

Pacific Coast, routes to Utah
  Territory from, 388–90
patriotism as motivation for
  enlistment, 185, 186–88. *See
  also* loyalty of Mormons
Pearl of Great Price, 45–46
Peery, David Harold, 188–89,
  256, 288–89
Peery, Elizabeth Letitia Higginbotham, 289
Peery, Nancy Campbell Higginbotham, 288
persecution
  Camp Douglas and, 171
  Civil War as condemnation
    for, 49–51, 84, 86, 94,
    96–100, 108–11
pioneers. *See* emigration
Poland Bill, 311

politics
  Mormon interest in, 112–14
  Mormons' impact on, 62–63
  Utah War and, 14–15
Polk, James K., 85, 86–87
polygamy
  Brigham Young and, 280
  Grand Army of the Republic
    and, 324–29
  legal campaign against,
    118–19
  Lincoln and, 66–67, 73–74
  press coverage on, 276–78
  Reconstruction and, 308–13
Poole, David, 393
popular sovereignty, 87–88, 90
Pratt, Orson
  Civil War prophecy and, 45,
    46–47, 49
  emigration and, 240

press
  Brigham Young in, 278–81
  polygamy in, 276–78
  sources and standards for,
    268–69
  Utah's loyalty questioned in,
    269–74
  Utah's statehood in, 274–76
  Utah Territory in, 267–68,
    281
prison camps, 198
Pritchett, William D., 256
Proclamation 157, xi
Proclamation of Amnesty and
  Reconstruction, 300
prophecy concerning Stephen A.
  Douglas, 63–64, 67–68, 168.
  See also Civil War prophecy
Pugmire, Jonathan, Jr., 148
Pulver, Gilbert H., 343

Q

Quantrill, William Clarke, 12,
  35, 386, 393–96

R

Radical Reconstructionists,
  302–6, 308–10
rage militaire, 185, 186–88
railroad, 72–73, 245, 248, 307
"Rallying Song of the Grand
  Army of the Republic," 324
Ramsey, Amanda Ross, 343
Reconstruction
  goals of, 295–96
  Latter-day Saints and, 306–8,
    312–13
  Lincoln and, 299–302
  polygamy and, 308–12
  Radical Reconstructionists
    and, 305–6

rights of black citizens during,
  302–4
successes and failures of, 312
Reconstruction Acts, 305–6
recruitment, 251–52. *See also*
  enlistment
religion
  Lincoln and, 62
  understanding Civil War
    through, 108
Reno, Jesse Lee, 11
repentance, 100
reservations, Indian, 208–9,
  218–19, 221
Rex, William, 287–88

Reynolds, George, 311
Reynolds, John F., 7
Rich, Charles C., 9
Richards, Franklin D., 147
righteousness, safety through,
  56
road systems, 14
Roberts, B. H., 59n42
Robinson, DeLos, 343–44
Robinson, John Cleveland, 7
Rockwell, Orrin Porter, 6–7
Ross, David J., 144, 148
Rozsa, John, 193–96, 290–92
Russ, Joseph, 230

S

safety through righteousness, 56
Salt Lake Theater, funding for, 18–19n28
salvation, 100–101
San Pete reservation, 209
Schettler, Bernhard, 240
School of the Prophets, 307
Scovil, Lucius, 240
Secession. *See also* loyalty of Mormons
   Brigham Young on, 69–70, 113–14
   Buchanan and, 3
   as cause of Civil War, 24–25
   as process, 27
   of South Carolina, ix
   Utah Territory and, 83–90, 111–12, 269–74
Second Coming, 54, 116–17
"Second Reconstruction," 310–12
self-reliance of Mormons, 307–8
Seven Days Battles, 30
Shaffer, John Wilson, 309
Sheppard, George, 12, 393
Sheridan, Phil, 37
Sherman, William Tecumseh, 36, 37
Shiloh, Battle of, 31–32, 190

Shoshone. *See* Bear River Massacre
slavery
   abolishment of, 33, 36
   Brigham Young on, 100, 123n46
   as cause of Civil War, 24
   Civil War prophecy and, 54–55
   Lincoln and Reconstruction and, 299–302
   as political issue, 112–14
   polygamy and, 67, 276, 278, 324
   in territories, 65
Slidell, John, 245–46, 391–93
Smith, George A., 8
Smith, Gustavus Woodson, 397n18
Smith, Joseph. *See also* Civil War prophecy
   Lincoln and, 64
   martyrdom of, 98
   Mormon exodus and, 84–85
   Stephen A. Douglas and, 63–64, 67–68, 168
   tribute to, 109–10
Smith, Joseph F., 8–9
Smith, Lot, 9–10, 130. *See also* Lot Smith Cavalry Company

Smoot, Reed, 55–56
Snow, Eliza R., 272
Snow, Erastus, 240
Snow, Lorenzo, 8
Snow company, 257
Sons of Veterans of the United States of America, 339n104
sorrow over Civil War, 100–101
South Carolina
   in Civil War prophecy, 46–47, 56
   secession of, ix
Southern States Mission, 310
Spanish Fork reservation, 209
Spanish Fork Treaty, 220
Squires, George B., 334
Stanton, Edwin M., 210–11
Star of the West (ship), viii, x, xii, 268, 269, 405
statehood, Utah, 77, 269–70, 274–76, 308
states' rights, 24–25, 42, 66, 67
Stenhouse, Thomas B. H., 61, 149–50
Stewart, James "Jock," 8
Stuart, David Crockett, 187–88
Swords, Thomas, 388–90
sympathy over Civil War, 100–101

T

Tanner, James, 342, 353
Tariff of Abominations, 42
Taylor, John, 8, 101–2
technological advancements, 24, 29, 32–33, 128
telegraph line
   communication through, 253
   emigration and, 249–50
   impact of, 128
   Indian relations and, 210
   interruptions in, 127, 132
   Lincoln and, 71–72
   press and, 268
Temple Square, 153–54

temple work for Confederate soldiers, 104n29
territorial system, government under, 89
Texas, insurrection in, xi
theology, understanding Civil War through, 108
Thirteenth Amendment, 300
Thomas, George Henry, 385, 386–88
Thomas, Lorenzo, 128–29
Thompson, Franklin, 336n14
Timpanogos War, 205
Tindup, 217

Titus, John, 71
"total" war, 24, 26–27, 29, 30, 37
trade between Mormons and non-Mormons, 307–8
transcontinental railroad, 307
transportation
   railroads, 71–73, 245, 248, 307
   road systems, 14
treaties, Indian, 208, 218–19, 220
trench warfare, 37
Trent Affair, 245–46

U

Uintah reservation, 221,
   225n117
Uintah Valley, 218, 220
Union
   strategy and advantages of,
      26–27, 29–30
   strategy and tactics of, 30–35
Union Pacific, 72–73
United Confederate Veterans,
   336–37n18
Utah Cavalry. *See* Lot Smith
   Cavalry Company
Utah Expedition. *See* Utah War
Utah Territorial Indian Agency,
   207
Utah Territorial Militia. *See*
   Nauvoo Legion
Utah Territory
   during Civil War, 70–76
   Indians and Indian relations
      in, 203–5
   Lincoln and, 64–70

   mourns Lincoln's assassina-
      tion, 298–99
   neutrality of, 99–100,
      111–12, 117–18, 184–85
   Patrick Connor on, 173
   press coverage on, 267–68,
      276–78, 281
   Reconstruction's effects on,
      306–8
   routes from Pacific Coast to,
      388–90
   secession rumors surround-
      ing, 83–90, 269–74
   statehood for, 77, 269–70,
      274–76,
   Utah War's impact on, 14–15
   views on Civil War, 127–28
Utah Valley, 205
Utah War
   camp followers in, 12–13
   cause of, 207
   civilian leaders during, 3–6

   Civil War as condemnation
      for, 111, 112
   Civil War enlistment and,
      183–84
   fatalities in, 2
   generals in, 385–86
   geographical consequences of,
      14–15
   George H. Thomas's strategy
      in, 386–88
   impact of, 2–3
   P. G. T. Beauregard's strategy
      in, 390–93
   Rufus Ingalls' strategy in,
      388–90
   societal forces set in motion
      by, 13–15
   soldiers in, 6–12
   press coverage of, 267–68
   William C. Quantrill and,
      393–96

V

Van Buren, Martin, 97–98, 109
Van Cott, John, 239

Van Der Voort, Paul, 323–26
Vicksburg, Battle of, 35

voluntary enlistment, 27

W

wagon trains, 239, 243–45,
   252–53, 257, 259–61
Waite, Charles B., 75–76
Walker company, 260
war and warfare
   among Indian tribes, 205–6
   Brigham Young on, 108
   in Europe, 254
   evolutions in, 8, 24, 29, 31,
      32–33
   guerrilla, 35–36, 386, 393
   John Taylor on, 101–2
   prophecy on, 52
   reinterpretation of prophecy
      on, 54–56
Washakie, 137
Watie, Stand, xi

Watson, John, 190, 200n33
Watson, Lorenzo Dow "Low,"
   189–90
weaponry
   advancements in, 24, 32–33
   Utah War and, 8
Weber Military District, 154
welfare approach to Indian
   relations, 213–14
Wells, Daniel H.
   Lot Smith Cavalry Company
      and, 130, 131
   Nauvoo Legion and, 146
   press coverage on, 273
   and revival of Nauvoo Legion,
      143
   Utah War and, 8

West, Chauncey W., 154
"When We Were Boys in Blue,"
   335
Whig Party, 38n5, 62, 64
Wilcken, Charles H., 11–12
Williams, Margaret, 290
Willis company, 260
Windemere (ship), 247
Woman's Relief Corps, Auxiliary
   to the Grand Army of the
   Republic, 320–21
Woodruff, Wilford, 8, 112
Wright, George, 166, 175–76,
   214
Wyoming, Nebraska, 256–57

Y

Z